Historical Dictionary of
World War II France

Historical Dictionaries of French History

Historical Dictionary of the French Revolution, 1789–1799
Samuel F. Scott and Barry Rothaus, editors

Historical Dictionary of Napoleonic France, 1799–1815
Owen Connelly, editor

Historical Dictionary of France from the 1815 Restoration to the Second Empire
Edgar Leon Newman, editor

Historical Dictionary of the French Second Empire, 1852–1870
William E. Echard, editor

Historical Dictionary of the Third French Republic, 1870–1940
Patrick H. Hutton, editor-in-chief

Historical Dictionary of the French Fourth and Fifth Republics, 1946–1991
Wayne Northcutt, editor-in-chief

Historical Dictionary of World War II France

The Occupation, Vichy, and the Resistance, 1938–1946

Edited by
BERTRAM M. GORDON

Greenwood Press
Westport, Connecticut

Library of Congress Cataloging-in-Publication Data

Historical dictionary of World War II France : the Occupation, Vichy,
  and the Resistance, 1938–1946 / edited by Bertram M. Gordon.
    p. cm.
  Includes bibliographical references and index.
  ISBN 0–313–29421–6 (alk. paper)
  1. France—History—German occupation, 1940–1945—Dictionaries.
2. World War, 1939–1945—Underground movements—France—
Dictionaries. 3. World War, 1939–1945—France—Colonies—
Dictionaries. I. Gordon, Bertram M., 1943– .
DC397.H58   1998
940.53'44—dc21   97–18190

British Library Cataloguing in Publication Data is available.

Library of Congress Catalog Card Number: 97–18190
ISBN: 0–313–29421–6

First published in 1998

Greenwood Press, 88 Post Road West, Westport, CT 06881
An imprint of Greenwood Publishing Group, Inc.

Printed in the United States of America

The paper used in this book complies with the
Permanent Paper Standard issued by the National
Information Standards Organization (Z39.48–1984).

10 9 8 7 6 5 4 3 2 1

FOR SUZANNE

Contents

Contributors

Alya Aglan, Institut d'Études Politiques, Paris
Éric Amyot, McGill University, Montreal
Claire Andrieu, Institut d'Études Politiques and Université de Paris I
David R. Applebaum, Rowan University, New Jersey
Seth D. Armus, State University of New York at Stony Brook
Philip C. F. Bankwitz, Trinity College, Connecticut
Diane de Bellescize, Université de Droit d'Économie et de Sciences Sociales de Paris—IFP, Paris
Michael L. Berkvam, Indiana University
Jean-Pierre Bertin-Maghit, Université Michel de Montaigne, Bordeaux, France
Konrad Bieber, State University of New York at Stony Brook
Cynthia S. Bisson, Belmont University, Tennessee
Joel Blatt, University of Connecticut at Stamford
Isabel Boussard, Centre d'Étude de la Vie Politique Française, Fondation Nationale des Sciences Politiques, Paris
Nathan Bracher, Texas A&M University
Deborah D. Buffton, University of Wisconsin-La Crosse
Michael Jabara Carley, Aid to Scholarly Publications Programme, Ottawa
Stephen K. Chenault, University of Arkansas
Patrick John Michael Coggins, University of Saskatchewan
Asher Cohen, Strochlitz Institute of Holocaust Studies, University of Haifa, Israel
Oscar L. Cole-Arnal, Waterloo Lutheran Seminary, Waterloo, Ontario
Michèle C. Cone, New York City
Martyn Cornick, University of Birmingham, United Kingdom
Richard F. Crane, Greensboro College, North Carolina
Venita Datta, Wellesley College, Massachusetts
Laurent Ditmann, Spelman College
Nicole Dombrowski, Princeton University
M. Patricia Dougherty, Dominican College of San Rafael, California

Laurent Douzou, Université Lyon II, France
Donna Evleth, Paris
Carole Fink, The Ohio State University
Sarah Fishman, University of Houston
Willard Allen Fletcher, University of Delaware
Hilary Footitt, University of Westminster, London
Wolfgang Freund, University of the Saarland, Germany
Julius W. Friend, George Washington University
James Friguglietti, Montana State University-Billings
Norman J. W. Goda, Ohio University
Milton Goldin, Tarrytown, New York
Richard J. Golsan, Texas A&M University
Bertram M. Gordon, Mills College, California
Claire Gorrara, School of European Studies, University of Wales College of
    Cardiff, United Kingdom
Irene V. Guenther, University of Houston and Houston Community College
Martine Guyot-Bender, Hamilton College, New York
W. Scott Haine, Holy Names College, California
W. D. Halls, University of Oxford
Martha Hanna, University of Colorado
C. James Haug, Mississippi State University
Melanie Hawthorne, Texas A&M University
John Hellman, McGill University, Montreal
Lynn A. Higgins, Dartmouth College
Roland L. Higgins, Keene State College
Stanley Hoffmann, Center for European Studies, Harvard University
William A. Hoisington, Jr., University of Illinois at Chicago
H. Haywood Hunt, Shukutoku University, Mizuhodai Campus, Japan
Paul F. Jankowski, Brandeis University, Massachusetts
Eric T. Jennings, University of Toronto
Nicole T. Jordan, University of Illinois at Chicago
Steven Kale, Washington State University
Bernd Kasten, Schwerin, Germany
Claire Keith, Marist College, New York
Michael Kelly, University of Southampton, United Kingdom
Van Kelly, University of Kansas
William R. Keylor, Boston University
Megan Koreman, Texas Tech University
Kenneth Krauss, College of Saint Rose, Albany, New York
Michel Lacroix, McGill University, Montreal
Christophe Lamiot, Rutgers University
Fred H. Lawson, Mills College, California
Charles Leclerc de Hauteclocque, Mesnil-Guillaume, France
Gérard Le Marec, Meudon-la-Forêt, France

Ronald MacKinnon, State University of New York at Stony Brook
Michael R. Marrus, University of Toronto
Stefan Martens, Deutsches Historisches Institut/Institut Historique Allemand, Paris
Paul Mazgaj, University of North Carolina at Greensboro
Brian A. McKenzie, State University of New York at Stony Brook
Chantal Morelle, Fondation Charles de Gaulle, Paris
Kim Munholland, University of Minnesota
Elizabeth H. Murphrey, Elizabeth City State University, Elizabeth City, North Carolina
Francis J. Murphy, Boston College
Colin W. Nettelbeck, University of Melbourne, Australia
Robert O. Paxton, Columbia University
Suzanne Perkins, Institute for Historical Study, California
Guillaume Piketty, Institut d'Études Politiques, Paris
Alexis Rinckenbach, Centre des Archives d'Outre-mer, Aix-en-Provence, France
Christian Roy, Concordia University, Montreal
Odile Rudelle, (Directeur de recherche au) Centre National de la Recherche Scientifique, Paris
Donna F. Ryan, Gallaudet University, Washington, D.C.
Gisèle Sapiro, Centre National de la Recherche Scientifique, Paris
Samir Saul, Université de Montréal
Andrew W. H. Shennan, Wellesley College, Massachusetts
John C. Simmonds, University of Derby, United Kingdom
Guillaume de Syon, Albright College, Pennsylvania
Anne-Cécile Tizon-Germe, Archives départementales du Loiret, France
Bernard Tricot, Fondation Charles de Gaulle, Paris
Steven Ungar, University of Iowa
Dominique Veillon, Institut d'Histoire du Temps Présent, Paris
Richard C. Vinen, King's College, University of London
Fabrice Virgili, Université de Toulouse Le Mirail
Margaret C. Weitz, Suffolk University, Boston
R. Wesley White, University of South Carolina
Andrew A. Workman, Mills College, California
John Wright, Coventry University, United Kingdom
Robert D. Zaretsky, University of Houston, Texas

Preface

The *Historical Dictionary of World War II France: The Occupation, Vichy, and the Resistance, 1938–1946* is the last in the Greenwood series of historical dictionaries of France from the 1789 Revolution to the Fifth Republic. These historical dictionaries offer comprehensive reference sources for students and scholars, specialists and nonspecialists alike, interested in the rich history of France since the 1789 Revolution. The *Historical Dictionary of World War II France* is designed to be the reference of first recourse for those with questions regarding the Occupation, Vichy, the French Resistance, in short, a broad range of topics related to France and the Second World War. It can also serve as a bibliographic guide for those who would like to know more about the period.

Summarizing the wartime period in any form poses a challenge due to the sheer quantity of relevant published material. More than 50 years after the events covered in this book, the literature is immense. Memoirs have been published about the wartime years, scholars have researched them, symposia have been devoted to them, and collaboration and resistance have been debated on both sides of the Atlantic. The French bibliography series published by the Bibliothèque Nationale (France's national library), which annually lists all the books published in the French language, shows 376 titles for France during World War II in 1992 and 431 in 1993. The *Bibliographie Annuelle de l'Histoire de France*, which lists both books and articles, shows 761 titles in 1994 alone. Although proportionately, the largest number of books on World War II France was published shortly after the liberation and the end of the war, in 1945 and 1946, the late 1980s and 1990s saw an upswing as, with the passing of the wartime generation, the French and others debated those events of half a century earlier.

The trial of former Vichy *milice* (Militia) officer Paul Touvier in 1992 and his subsequent conviction on appeal, in 1994, of crimes against humanity, as well as the June 1993 murder, while awaiting trial on similar charges, of another former Vichy official, the 84-year-old ex-police chief René Bousquet, highlighted the continuing disputes about the period. Increased publicity in 1994 surrounding President François Mitterrand's Vichy activity also intensified debate about the war years in France. Newly elected president in 1995, Jacques Chirac formally acknowledged a moral responsibility of the present French state for the misdeeds of its predecessor during the Occupation, a step Mitterrand had refused to take. In April 1998, Maurice Papon, former Secretary General of the Gironde Prefecture under Vichy and a subsequent high ranking official under the Fifth Republic, was sentenced to a ten year prison term on charges of crimes against humanity for his involvement in the arrest and deportation of more than 1,600 Jews during the Occupation. The year 1997 had seen controversy erupt over the Resistance activities of Lucie and Raymond Aubrac and the postwar accounts of these activities given in memoirs and interviews by Lucie Aubrac. Memories of the war years were also stirred in late summer 1997 by the publication of previously unpublished documents relating to the deportation to their deaths of 16 Jewish children and two adults in the Alpine town of Voiron less than three months before the Allies landed in France. Reports indicated that these children had been refused entry into Switzerland, also in the news because of charges that Swiss banks had failed to seek out survivors and heirs of unclaimed accounts of the war era. Additionally in 1997, the Roman Catholic Church of France, speaking through Archbishop Olivier de Berranger of Saint-Denis, formally apologized for its wartime ''silence'' in the face of French collaboration with anti-Jewish persecution.

Historically, the postwar period will likely be seen as extending through the dissolution of the Soviet bloc in 1989–1991, or, in France, through the last of the war-related trials, most likely that of Papon, and the passing of the wartime generation. For France, the wartime period itself, however, began with the 1938 Munich agreement, which transferred the Sudetenland to the Reich and reestablished the German supremacy in Central Europe, which had been interrupted by its defeat in World War I. Once again Germany became a menace to France.

The wartime period closed in France in 1946, when General Charles de Gaulle resigned as head of the Provisional Government.

The divisions in France that followed the Munich agreement can be seen in the split between ''*bellicistes*'' and ''*pacifistes*,'' opponents and supporters, respectively, of the policy by which Czechoslovakia had been dismembered to meet Hitler's demand that the German-speaking Sudetenland be annexed to the Reich. Often termed ''appeasement,'' the policy of accommodating Mussolini and Hitler in the late 1930s has precedents going back to French concessions to superior force in capitulations to the Burgundians in the Hundred Years War. Divisions over the Munich policy in France were exacerbated in August 1939 by the Nazi–Soviet pact, when the French Communist Party, at least officially following Stalin's line, shifted overnight from an antifascist stance to one of opposition to a war against the Axis powers. This shift exposed the communists not only to charges of sabotage of the French war effort once hostilities began but also to accusations of collaboration with the Germans both before and after the French defeat of May–June 1940. It also split the Communist Party, as not all were willing to follow the new line. Only with the German invasion of the

Soviet Union in June 1941, when the French communists called for all-out war against Germany, was the party again able to align itself with the traditions of French patriotism, but bitterness from the 1939–1941 period remained.

Following the Sudeten and Nazi–Soviet pact crises, the *Historical Dictionary of World War II France* covers the coming of war in September 1939, the "Phoney War" in the West that lasted until the German military breakthrough in May 1940, and the French defeat in June. The account continues through the Occupation, the liberation of 1944, and the subsequent installation of General de Gaulle's Provisional Government. Although the Fourth Republic was not formally established in France until 1947, and the post-liberation purges continued, the immediate wartime period in France can be said to have ended in 1946, with de Gaulle's resignation and the reemergence of the parliamentarian political parties.

Because of the broad ideological, cultural, and social ramifications of the French confrontation with the Axis powers, the *Historical Dictionary of World War II France* takes an encyclopedic approach, covering life in France as broadly as possible during the entire period from Munich through the transition to the Fourth Republic. Both Vichy's National Revolution, on one hand, and the Resistance, on the other, attempted to fashion renewals of French social and cultural life beyond the merely political. Accordingly, in addition to examining military, political, economic, and social developments, entries in the dictionary address the fine arts, literature, music, cinema, dance, theater, fashion, gastronomy, tourism, sports, and daily life, to offer a comprehensive view of France during the war.

The *Historical Dictionary of World War II France* also takes a comprehensive geographical view of France and its empire during the wartime period. Accordingly, it includes a map of European France and a two-page map of the French empire around the world. Emphasis in the *Historical Dictionary*, however, is placed upon developments in the metropole. From the 1940 armistice through November 1942, France was divided into a German-occupied zone in the north and west and an unoccupied, or "free," zone in the south, which was overrun by the Germans on the heels of the Allied invasion of French North Africa. The northern occupied zone, however, was further subdivided in the northeast, with a "reserved" and a "forbidden" zone, the latter including the two northern departments of Nord and Pas-de-Calais, attached to the German military command in Belgium. In addition, Alsace and Lorraine were reannexed in 1940 to Germany. The Italians were given an occupation zone in the southeast, which was extended in November 1942, then taken over by the Germans in August 1943 after the Allied invasion of Italy led to the overthrow of Mussolini. Corsica, occupied by the Italians in November 1942, was liberated in October 1943. France overseas included the African territories that joined the Resistance in 1940, the North African territories before and after the 1942 Allied landings, and Syria, which became a potential staging area for German military use against the British in Iraq in 1941. French Indochina was occupied by the Japanese. Struggles between Vichy and de Gaulle's Free French occurred off the coast of

Canada in the islands of Saint-Pierre and Miquelon, as well as in New Caledonia and French Polynesia.

More than half a century after the war, it is too easy to collapse the period into one undifferentiated block. Although the six-year war and the four-year Occupation were a relatively short period in the history of France, the era witnessed major changes with long-lasting impact. For example, the birthrate, which had declined during the 1930s, began an increase in 1942 that presaged, at least in part, the postwar baby boom, though any relationship between this and Vichy family policy might be debated. In the chronological sequence of the wartime era, the Munich Agreement, so ominous for France, was followed by the war itself with its privations beginning September 1939. Next came the June 1940 defeat, which brought German Occupation and the replacement of the Third Republic by the Vichy government, led by the World War I hero Marshal Philippe Pétain. The French reacted not only to the changing fortunes of the world war but also to shifts in Vichy policies and personnel and the development of an increasingly active Resistance at home and abroad. Both the Vichy government and the Resistance claimed the legacy of "eternal France," and both drew inspiration from the French past, whether in the regionalism and Catholicism of Vichy or the principles of 1789 of the Resistance, which also claimed Catholic values. Anti-Semitism, prominent during the Dreyfus affair of the 1890s, was renewed in the policies of Vichy. With roots in Jacobin, liberal, Catholic, and Marxist traditions of the French past, the Resistance after the war became an establishment with its own orthodoxy and iconography. The prestige acquired by General de Gaulle from his wartime role enabled him to regain power in 1958 during the Algerian crisis and to write a new constitution for France's Fifth Republic.

The *belliciste-pacifiste* division over collaboration with, or resistance to, the Germans and their Italian allies that began with Munich continued into the "Phoney War" of 1939–1940 and foreshadowed the divisions between Vichy and the Resistance. With the June 1940 defeat and Paris occupied by German forces, the French government moved to Bordeaux, where Pétain was invited to form a cabinet with the avowed intention of ending hostilities with the Germans. The new government signed armistices with the Germans and Italians, then settled in the unoccupied spa town of Vichy. There Pétain and his supporters replaced the Third Republic with the more authoritarian État Français (French State), launched under the program of a "National Revolution," whose goals included the restoration of defeated France to a position of influence within the German-dominated "New Order." The National Revolution sought to renew French society by purging its public life of what the new leaders saw as the Republic's amoral materialism and political undesirables, the latter referring to communists, Freemasons, and Jews. Initiated by the Pétain government during the summer of 1940, the National Revolution grew out of French politics and historical sources and was not imposed by the Germans.

Apparently surprised by the scope of their own success in the 1940 campaign, the Germans had neither planned for an armistice with France nor fully considered the various options presented by their victory. Their rush to conclude an armistice—and at Compiègne, the site of the 1918 armistice that marked their defeat in World War I—raises questions about the decision-making process at the highest German levels. Hitler's policy had been simply to neutralize France and thereby force Britain out of the war, freeing him for an attack against Soviet Russia in the east. With his associates, he undoubtedly contemplated replicating the German strategy of 1914: to knock the French out of the war, then move against Russia, though, of course, German plans to invade Britain in 1940 differed considerably from their scenario of 1914. A different perspective, however, was offered by German admiral Erich Raeder, who argued for a Mediterranean strategy that entailed going through Spain into Gibraltar and North Africa, effectively cutting Britain off from most of its empire. Had the Germans moved immediately toward North Africa, it could be argued, General Francisco Franco of Spain might well have had to make an arrangement with them. Circumstances might then have forced Spain to become a full ally, giving the Germans the possibility of flying directly to the Spanish islands in the middle Atlantic. By stopping their offensive when it was in high gear and accepting an armistice with the French, the Germans may have missed a chance to settle things decisively in the west.

Had the French continued to fight from North Africa rather than so quickly requesting an armistice, the Germans might have been forced to rethink their strategy and adopt a more concerted and ultimately successful Mediterranean plan. Conversely, the shortsighted spite of the German leaders may have prevented them from making a more generous peace with the French, which conceivably could have left France a contented continental partner cut off from Britain. That Hitler might well have been incapable of making an amicable and longlasting arrangement with the French, or any of the other powers, only highlights the problems in German decision-making at the time. Either a more generous arrangement with the French or a more thoroughgoing takeover, on the Polish model, might have cut off the British from their overseas empire and freed the Germans for their onslaught in the east. By permitting a semiautonomous and truncated France to exist in the 1940 armistice, the Germans may have cast away the potentialities of their own victory over France by failing to make it permanent.

The possible German blunder in granting an armistice to France in 1940 does not mean that Pétain and his associates foresaw eventual Axis defeat and were acting from a shrewd, prophetic vision to spare France for the present so that it could later victoriously resume hostilities, the "shield-sword" argument (Pétain the shield; de Gaulle the sword) made by Pétain at his 1945 trail and subsequent apologists for Vichy. In June 1940 Axis victory in the war appeared probable, if not inevitable, and many in France believed that political and social reconstruction would have to take place within a Europe dominated by Nazi Germany. The very willingness of the French government to accept the armistice may well have helped blind the Germans to a more consistent strategic conception of their own best interests in the war. Though forced to accept harsh armistice conditions, the Vichy government possessed three major sources of relative independence. First, the Pétain government was left with an unoccupied zone of about two-fifths of the country, where it suffered less interference from the Germans than in the occupied areas. Next, the undefeated French fleet, second in strength only to the British navy in Europe, remained in French hands at Toulon. Lastly, the unoccupied overseas empire was second in size only to that of the British.

The Resistance, meanwhile, had begun with a small group formed around de Gaulle in London in June 1940 during the delay when the Germans failed to exploit their military victory over France. In France, autonomous groups, such as the Musée de l'Homme network in the summer of 1940, also engaged in acts of resistance. Early Resistance activity was marked by symbolic gestures such as a demonstration at the Arc de Triomphe to commemorate the 1918 armistice, on 11 November 1940. Individuals and groups who formed the Resistance within France were often fiercely independent, and it would take de Gaulle years to gain control over the entire movement. Henri Frenay, for example, a cofounder of the Resistance group Combat, did not fall into step with de Gaulle until late 1942. The German invasion of the Soviet Union in June 1941 did not at first substantially change the situation in France, because German victory continued to seem likely, but it changed the character of the Resistance. Mobilized by the invasion of the Soviet Union, the Communist Party, whose structure was well suited for clandestine action, put its full weight into the struggle against the occupation authorities. With increased Resistance activities and attacks against German occupation personnel in France, Vichy began to shift its focus from implementation of the National Revolution to anti-Resistance police action. While the Resistance gained strength, it also suffered new divisions as many of the communists joined some of the earlier noncommunist factions in refusing, although for different reasons, to recognize de Gaulle's authority.

Things shifted dramatically in November 1942. Allied landings in French North Africa were followed quickly by the German occupation of all of metropolitan France. Fearing that its fleet, based at Toulon on the Mediterranean, might fall into the hands of the Germans, Vichy ordered that it be scuttled. With the loss of the unoccupied zone, the fleet, and the overseas empire, Vichy was deprived of its independent leverage. The Allied conquest of the French empire in North Africa brought home to many in metropolitan France the realization that Germany might indeed lose the war. It highlighted the failure of the Germans to develop an effective Mediterranean strategy while fighting in Soviet Russia and provided a base on French territory for General de Gaulle's Resistance organization, which was able to move to Algiers from London. Following their defeat at Stalingrad in early 1943, the Germans turned to a program of "total war." They intensified demands for French industry, agriculture, and labor to support their war machine. Heightened German pressure, together with the increasing subservience of Vichy and intensification of Resistance activity, caused a growing number of the French either to choose sides or to switch previously chosen allegiances. The collapse of Mussolini's Fascist government in Italy during the summer of 1943 brought German occupation forces into the previously Italian-held sections of southeastern France. In October 1943, the liberation of Corsica by Allied and Free French forces set the example for the purges and retributions that would follow the liberation of metropolitan France.

By the end of 1943, Pétain's government had become increasingly a satellite state with collaborationist extremists forced into it by the Germans. Pressured by the Germans, Vichy instituted a labor draft that led many young men to flee to the *maquis*, the scrubland or bush country of southern France, which hid them and became the base of the southern rural underground Resistance. By 1944, the Vichy government had become virtually a fascist state with its paramilitary organizations waging open warfare in collaboration with the Germans against the increasingly well organized Resistance. Vichy forces fought the Resistance and hunted down Jews, communists, and Freemasons in what has been called a "Franco-French" civil war, while Resistance activists assassinated those accused of collaboration with Vichy and the Germans. Passions were embittered by de Gaulle's claim not only to lead the Resistance but to embody French constitutional legality. These Gaullist claims denied all legitimacy to those who had chosen the other side, despite their argument that Pétain had been named premier according to the practice of the Third Republic in June 1940 and had been voted special powers the following month by the legally elected French parliament.

The liberation of metropolitan France in the summer of 1944 ended the Vichy government, though many collaborationists fled to Germany. General de Gaulle was able to command the support of virtually all the Resistance factions, communists included, following an accord with the Soviets. He now led liberated France back into battle against the Nazis. In late 1944 and the spring of 1945, French forces participated in the Italian campaign and the invasion of Germany. With the end of the war, however, the interwar political parties, blamed by both Pétain and de Gaulle for the 1940 defeat, reorganized and began to regain the influence that they had lost during the Occupation. Frustrated in his dealings with the parties and in his attempts to create a stronger executive power than France had prior to 1940, de Gaulle resigned in January 1946. In a referendum on 13 October 1946, a constitutional proposal was approved that established what was to become the Fourth Republic.

Even before the end of the war, a discourse began of differing memories of the Occupation, Vichy, and the Resistance that has continued to the present. The more or less official Resistance argument was offered by de Gaulle, who claimed that, with the exception of a few traitors, the entire French nation had resisted the German occupiers. The summer of 1944 brought both unofficial and official repression of Vichyites and collaborators, the settling of scores, and attempts by those on all sides to tell their versions of the story. Fearful of retribution, many Vichyites and other collaborators went into hiding. Those found in France were either punished by "spontaneous" mob justice or turned over to de Gaulle's Provisional Government authorities for trial. Some of the Vichy officials were reunited in exile in Germany, where a government in exile was established, which finally disappeared with the Nazi Reich in May 1945. The German defeat exposed a new group of collaborators to Gaullist justice.

In retrospect, although the French decision to seek an armistice in June 1940 may be interpreted as an act of collaboration, the language of collaboration had not been used at the time. French armies had been defeated many times in the past, from Crécy and Agincourt through 1815 and 1871, and making peace in 1940 had seemed a reasonable option. It took time for meaningful Franco-German collaboration to emerge and for the Resistance to acquire a political mission beyond simple military opposition to the enemy. De Gaulle's earliest broadcasts from London back to France had not spoken of subservience rather than "collaboration." He had been recognized as head of the Free French on 28 June 1940 and given legal standing by the British on 7 August. Meaningful collaboration emerged only during the summer of 1940 when it became evident that Britain would not be defeated. Collaboration had been officially consecrated by Pétain, following his meeting with Hitler, in October 1940, after the latter's failure to persuade General Franco to enter the war. At this point, France had become the western front line, an immobile and hopeless entanglement for the Germans, not unlike the trenches of World War I's western front. Only then did it begin to appear that the Occupation would be long-term, offering increased hope to the Resistance. Lines were being drawn and there was now a reason to act.

The June 1941 German invasion of Soviet Russia had been a second occasion calling for choice. Pétain had envisioned a mandate from the French people for closer collaboration with Germany, had the Germans suppressed the demarcation line and allowed full authority to his administration in the northern zone. He had authorized French volunteers to fight alongside the Germans in Russia. The autumn 1942 German advance on Cairo had furnished a third chance for the French to choose sides. By then, the Free French had shown their military valor at Bir Hakeim (June 1942), had been renamed "Fighting France," and had become increasingly effective in calling upon the French to choose sides. The 3 November 1942 German defeat at El Alamein, followed within a week by the Allied landings in North Africa, brought the true collaborators to the fore. Failing to see the hopelessness of the German situation in the war, in a *engrenage fasciste*, a declining number of collaborationists after December 1942 had still expected Hitler to guarantee a French empire that was growing ever smaller. By early 1943, at least until the Allied invasion of Sicily, some still envisioned a reconquered French empire, integrated into a continental European New Order. At the same time, came ever more strident warnings from the Free French that assassination and disaster were awaiting those who failed to decide for the Allies. The continuing supporters of Vichy and the collaboration had represented a conservative military mind set that had discounted naval and air power and had seen the war as a land conflict, which would end in a stalemate, favorable to Germany. The Russians would be pushed back, the British left where they were, and the French would maintain their empire under German guarantee. Even at Compiègne in June 1940, Hitler had virtually assured the French that he would preserve their empire against his own allies, Italy and Spain. That vision remained for those who supported the Axis to the end.

The entire wartime experience has been a subject of continuing analyses, explanations, and arguments. Many accepted de Gaulle's depiction of France as a nation of resisters. The liberation of France in 1944 and the purges of Vichyites and collaborators that followed intensified the debate. To some in France, the four-year Occupation was "four years to erase from our history," the title of a book in 1949 by Alfred Mornet, the prosecutor-general in the trial of Marshal Pétain. Neither Mornet, however, who very much favored the Resistance, nor the many others who wrote about the wartime period really wanted to forget it. Controversies over both the Vichy government and the collaboration with, and resistance to, the Germans were fueled by a stream of books and articles, including those of the "Hussard" writers of the late 1940s and 1950s, as well as films such as Marcel Ophuls' *The Sorrow and the Pity*, released in 1971. By the 1980s, the debate had shifted to a more specific focus on French complicity with German extermination policies against the Jews. The extradition from Bolivia to France in 1983 of Klaus Barbie, SS *Obersturmführer* and head of the Lyons Gestapo from 1942 to 1944, and his trial four years later on charges of crimes committed against humanity, followed by the Touvier and Bousquet affairs, together with the controversies surrounding Mitterrand in the early 1990s, intensified debate about the wartime years. The Swiss bank revelations, the Aubrac controversy, the Voiron discoveries, and the Papon trial continued to fuel the debate in 1997.

Summarizing any historical period in a historical dictionary such as this one presents inevitable problems of selection. The method of selection of more than 400 entries to "cover" in some form the wartime years and the postwar perspectives on this period deserves comment. To begin, some 40 books and additional articles published in France, Britain, Germany, and the United States covering a wide range of wartime French activities were scrutinized for both frequencies of mention and depth of discussion of the various relevant subjects. Topics emphasized in these books and articles were used to create a pool of nearly 1,000 possible entries for the *Historical Dictionary of World War II France*. Given the size limitation of the book determined by the Greenwood Publishing Group, the editor decided, for the sake of breadth of coverage, to include a larger number of shorter entries as opposed to longer, more synthetic ones, which were kept to a minimum. A dozen specialists were then consulted to help narrow the pool of entries to a list of some 400 of the most historically significant. In this process, some suggestions for additions were accepted, and many potential entries had to be removed.

Locating the contributors meant drawing upon the resources of many helpful colleagues in several countries. An effort was made to give the *Historical Dictionary of World War II France* an international perspective. Contributors were encouraged to submit their entries in French or German, if they so desired, to facilitate a broader international representation. Consequently, although roughly three-fifths of the contributors are from the United States, an additional one-fifth are from France. Most of the remaining contributors are from Britain and Canada, with representatives also from Australia, Germany, Israel, and Japan. Bibliographical indexes and past programs of professional meetings were scoured for potential contributors. The editor, who served as president/program chairman of the Western Society for French History (1974–1975) and secretary of the Society for French Historical Studies (1983–1989), used the networks of these societies to seek out contributors. Hundreds of letters were sent. Finally, in the case of 15 unassigned entries toward the end of the process, a solicitation was made on H-France, the Internet network of specialists in French culture and history. In most cases, contributors were either personally known to the editor or recommended by scholars in the field. The end result is a historical dictionary of 413 entries, most of which are approximately 300 words, written by 102 contributors in addition to the editor.

Each entry focuses on the chronology of the wartime period. Many relate to events of a longer time span than the wartime years but are centered on that time period. For example, Marshal Pétain's career spanned a half century, and his role as the victor at Verdun in World War I endowed him with the popularity to appear a savior to many in 1940. The entry relating to Pétain, however, centers on his role as head of state at Vichy. Although the political career of François Mitterrand also spanned a half century, the entry devoted to him focuses on his wartime activities and the controversies they later produced. Many of the entry topics in this dictionary may also be found either in its predecessor, Patrick H. Hutton, ed., *Historical Dictionary of the Third French Republic, 1870–1940* (Westport, CT: Greenwood Press, 1986), two volumes, or in its successor, Wayne Northcutt, ed., *Historical Dictionary of the French Fourth and Fifth Republics, 1946–1991* (Westport, CT: Greenwood Press, 1992). Entry topic that appear in the *Historical Dictionary of the Third French Republic* are indicated by an asterisk (*) preceding their bibliographies, and those that appear in the *Historical Dictionary of the French Fourth and Fifth Republics, 1946–1991* are noted with a dagger (†) at the beginning of their bibliographies. Entry topics with both markers appear in both of these dictionaries. In most cases the names of the entries are exactly the same; for the few in which substantively similar entries have different names, the reader is advised to check the index of the dictionary in question. By consulting all three historical dictionaries, the reader interested in, for example, anti-Semitism in France, Simone de Beauvoir, Albert Camus, the economy, Pablo Picasso, the press, Jean-Paul Sartre, or sports can obtain a quick overview of these topics for almost all of the twentieth century. Entries relating to people and events outside France focus directly on the relationship of the subject to France during the wartime period. Each entry starts with a brief introduction identifying the subject, then focuses on its significance in the history of wartime France. A one-volume historical dictionary with space limitations covering so eventful a period as World War II France makes the articles necessarily brief dictionary entries rather than exhaustive encyclopedic surveys. Accordingly, each entry includes a bibliography with references allowing the interested reader to pursue further research. At the end of each entry is the last name of the contributor, preceded by first initial or initials. A list of contributors by full name and affiliation is provided in the introductory material.

Entries include specific persons, such as Marshal Pétain and General de Gaulle, and places that were significant either for political reasons, such as Vichy, or as battle sites, such as Normandy, Allied invasion. Important groups, such as Protestants, Jews, Gypsies, and Freemasons, have their own listings, and there are entries for political parties and movements, such as the Communist Party (Parti Communiste Français). A standard entry, usually on a single, specific person, place, event, or organization, was assigned approximately 300 words. Exceptions were made in a few cases, such as de Gaulle, Jean Moulin, Pétain, Pierre Laval, and Admiral François Darlan, who, because of their historical importance, were assigned 600 words. Topics are occasionally grouped together under larger cluster entries for greater comprehensiveness, and such group entries were often given 600 words. A few larger cluster-type entries, such as "Fine Arts in Occupied France" or "Empire, Overseas," were allotted 1,200 words.

To save space and minimize duplication, newspapers and other periodicals are considered under several entries relating to "Press" or, when relevant, in the entries for the writers or political parties with which they were affiliated. *L'Humanité*, for example, is discussed under "Communist Party." Occasionally, a periodical, such as *Cahiers du Témoignage Chrétien*, was deemed of sufficient historical importance to warrant a separate entry. Books are invariably treated under their authors or other relevant entries; the one exception is *Silence de la Mer*, which has a separate entry. Separate entries were accorded exceptionally prominent films, such as *Les Enfants du Paradis, Casablanca, Night and Fog*, and *The Sorrow and the Pity*, but most are discussed under "Cinema in Occupied France" and "Cinema, Postwar Relating to Occupied France."

Except for Paris, Vichy, and Compiègne, cities do not have separate entries. The reader interested in specific cities is advised to look for the entries to related persons, organizations, or events. Marseilles, for example, is discussed in the entry for Simon Sabiani, who headed the collaborationist Parti Populaire Français there during the Occupation. Readers may consult the index, which, in the case for Marseilles, will direct them to Sabiani. Finally, some entries refer to long-standing historical problems for France, such as "anti-Semitism," that were particularly pronounced during the wartime era and for which readers interested in other periods may consult the relevant historical dictionaries.

The *Historical Dictionary of World War II France* is organized alphabetically. Names beginning with "de" are listed under the letter that begins the substantive part of the name. Examples: de Gaulle is listed under "G"; de La Rocque under "L." For consistency, the particle "de" is always given when part of a surname, even if in French usage one always encounters "de Gaulle" and rarely " 'de' Vlaminck." For ease of use, related entries are cross-referenced by boldface type, and an index is provided with cross-references to help the reader locate desired information. Variations of cross-referenced terms, such as "fascists" under "fascism," "*maquisard*" under "*maquis*," and "symbolic" under "symbols in wartime France," are also in boldface type. "Russia," "Russians," "Soviet," "Soviets," "Soviet Russia," and "Soviet Union" are all cross-referenced to "USSR" and, accordingly, in boldface type. Because of the multiple entries relating to Germany and the large number of cross-references to that country, the latter are not given in boldface type.

There are many people who have played a role in the creation of this *Historical Dictionary*. The editor wishes to thank the National Endowment for the Humanities for a research grant to France and Mills College for several research and travel grants, all of which contributed significantly to the research for this book. In a collective work such as this *Historical Dictionary*, thanks are also due to the 102 contributors from eight countries, without whom this book could not have been compiled. Each brought a unique perspective and style, which have been honored in the editing. Robert O. Paxton's critical readings of early drafts and the preface were especially helpful in defining the scope of the *Historical Dictionary of World War II France* and in arranging the Chronology at the end of the book. Nicole T. Jordan provided invaluable suggestions in the writing of the preface. Sarah Fishman, James Friguglietti, Robert O. Paxton, Robert Soucy, John Sweets, Margaret Collins Weitz, and Eugen Weber helped prune down the original list of entries. Sweets and Claire Andrieu, Odile Rudelle, and John Simmonds were especially helpful in suggestions concerning Resistance entries. Sara Halperyn and Marcel Meslati at the library of the Centre de Documentation Juive Contemporaine in Paris helped in checking some of the more difficult-to-ascertain facts, as did Pierre Mounier-Kuhn in Paris. François Jarraud helped provide suggestions for the maps. Michael Neal, also in Paris, helped the editor keep up with new books published in France concerning the war years while the manuscript was in preparation. The H-France network membership helped provide the website information that is included in the general bibliography at the end of this book.

Lists of potential contributors were furnished by Joel Blatt, Elizabeth Lindquist, and Leah Hewitt. Claire Andrieu, Joel Colton, Richard J. Golsan, John Hellman, Richard Kuisel, and Chantal Morelle all helped recruit additional contributors. Claire Gorrara helped locate British contributors. Wayne Northcutt and Julian Archer shared their experience from previous involvement with the compiling of historical dictionaries. Zahr Said helped with the translation of the many articles written in French. Ellen Rinehart and Natalie Hanson at the Mills College computer center helped educate the editor in the arcana of putting the entries, submitted on what seemed to be every imaginable software program, into one computer format. The maps could not have been drawn without the computer skills of Jean Weishan, also at the Mills computer center. Carol Bardoff and Angie Miller also helped by retyping many of the entries that arrived without computer disks. Jackie Fitzpatrick, Susan Bailey, and Whitney Jensen helped prepare the index and Susan Bailey also helped with proofreading the final draft.

Cynthia Harris and David Palmer, on behalf of Greenwood, worked patiently to see the project through. In a collective work such as a historical dictionary, efforts have been made to assure consistency of style without, however, impinging upon the individual styles and perspectives of the contributors. The editor, however, assumes full responsibility for any errors in translation or otherwise in the text.

Abbreviations

AD	*Archives Départementales* (followed by the name of the department)
AN	*Archives Nationales, Paris*
APP	*Archives de la Préfecture de Police de Paris*
BBC	*British Broadcasting Corporation*
BCRA	*Bureau Central de Renseignements et d'Action*
BN	*Bibliothèque Nationale, Paris*
CDJC	*Centre de Documentation Juive Contemporaine, Paris*
CEVIPOF	*Centre d'étude de la vie politique française*
CFC	*Contemporary French Civilization*
CGQJ	*Commissariat Général aux Questions Juives*
CGT	*Confédération Générale du Travail*
CNR	*Conseil National de la Résistance*
CNRS	*Centre National des Recherches Scientifiques, Paris*
COMAC	*Comité d'Action Militaire*
FFI	*Forces Françaises de l'Intérieure*
FHS	*French Historical Studies*
FNDIRP	*Fédération Nationale des Déportés et Internés Résistants et Patriotes*
FPS	*French Politics and Society*
FTP	*Francs-Tireurs et Partisans Français*
FTP-MOI	*Francs-Tireurs et Partisans-Main d'Œuvre Immigrée*
GP	*Groupes de Protection*
IÉQJ	*Institut d'Étude des Questions Juives*
IHTP	*Institut d'Histoire du Temps Présent, Paris*
JCH	*Journal of Contemporary History*
JMH	*Journal of Modern History*
JOC	*Jeunesse Ouvrière Chrétienne*

LVF	*Légion des Volontaires Français contre le Bolchevisme*
MCF	*Modern and Contemporary France*
MLN	*Mouvement de la Libération Nationale*
MSR	*Mouvement Social Révolutionnaire*
MUR	*Mouvement Unis de la Résistance*
NRF	*Nouvelle Revue Française*
PCF	*Parti Communiste Français* (French Communist Party)
PPF	*Parti Populaire Français*
PSF	*Parti Social Français*
RDHDGM	*Revue d'histoire de la deuxième guerre mondiale*
RNP	*Rassemblement National Populaire*
SOE	*Special Operations Executive*
SOL	*Service d'Ordre Légionnaire*
SS	*Schützstaffel*
STO	*Service du Travail Obligatoire*
UCLA	*University of California at Los Angeles*
UGIF	*Union Générale des Israélites de France*

Maps

METROPOLITAN FRANCE: ZONES OF OCCUPATION, 1940–44

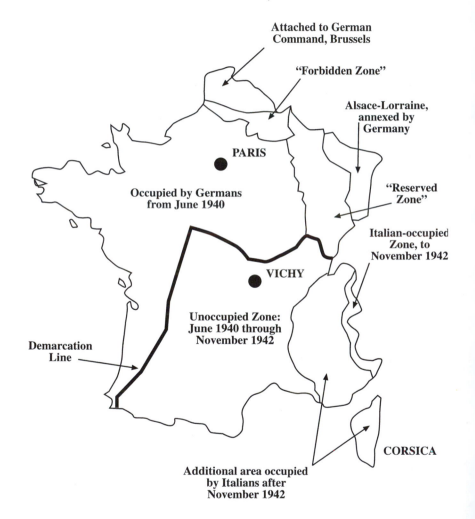

Attached to German
Command, Brussels

"Forbidden Zone"

Alsace-Lorraine,
annexed by
Germany

PARIS

Occupied by Germans
from June 1940

"Reserved
Zone"

Italian-occupied
Zone, to
November 1942

VICHY

Unoccupied Zone:
June 1940 through
November 1942

Demarcation
Line

CORSICA

Additional area occupied
by Italians after
November 1942

FRANCE AND ITS EMPIRE DURING WORLD WAR II

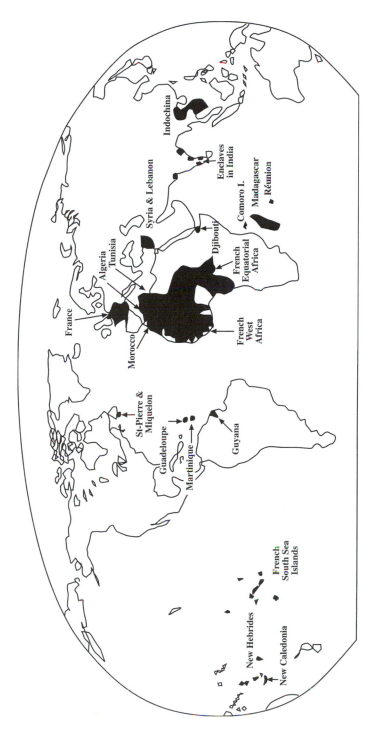

Indochina

Syria & Lebanon

Enclaves in India

Comoro I.

Madagascar

Réunion

Djibouti

Algeria

Tunisia

France

Morocco

French Equatorial Africa

French West Africa

St-Pierre & Miquelon

Guadeloupe

Martinique

Guyana

French South Sea Islands

New Hebrides

New Caledonia

The Dictionary

A

ABELLIO, RAYMOND (GEORGES SOULÈS; 1907–1986), French writer and ranking member of Eugène **Deloncle's Mouvement Social Révolutionnaire (MSR)** after 1941. He helped found the Mouvement Révolutionnaire Français (MRF) in 1943. An engineer by trade, Soulès joined the Jeunesses Socialistes in 1930 and later the **Socialist** Party (SFIO), where he became associated with the Trotskyist wing, the Gauche Révolutionnaire. In 1938 he moved to the Redressement, a pacifist group within the SFIO.

In 1939 he served with the French **army** and was captured and imprisoned in Elsterhorst in Silesia. There he converted to "idealistic" National Socialism and set up a Cercle **Pétain**, a political grouping of **prisoners** supporting **Vichy**. Released in March 1941, he joined Marcel **Déat's Rassemblement National Populaire (RNP)**. Soon he joined the MSR and, with André Mahé, wrote *La Fin du nihilisme*, attempting to define a doctrine for Vichy's **National Revolution**. Rejecting communism, Soulès supported the ascendancy of a new elite to bring France into Europe's **New Order**. In 1943 he broke with Deloncle, formed the MRF, and attempted to work with the **Resistance**. In 1946 Soulès won the Sainte-Beuve prize for *Heureux les pacifiques*, published under his pen name, Raymond Abellio. The following year he fled to **Switzerland**, returning later to live out his life in France.

R. Abellio, *Ma Dernière Mémoire*, 3 vol. (Paris, 1971–1980); M.-T. de Brosses, *Entretiens avec Raymond Abellio* (Paris, 1966); H. Charbonneau, *Les Mémoires de Porthos*, 2 vol. (Paris, 1967–1969); B. M. Gordon, "The Condottieri of the Collaboration: *Mouvement Social Révolutionnaire*," *JCH* 10:2 (April 1975).

D. D. Buffton

ABETZ, OTTO (1903–1958), German ambassador in **Paris** from August 1940 to 1944, a supporter of Franco–German reconciliation, instrumental in attracting prominent French personalities to **collaboration** by means of flattery, sumptuous receptions at the German Embassy, and financial support.

Early in life, Abetz was attracted by French culture. Starting in 1930, he helped organize Franco–German **youth** meetings, where in 1932 he met French journalist Jean **Luchaire**, whose secretary he married. Abetz became a member of the Nazi Party in 1937 and a specialist in French affairs. Suspected of espionage, he was expelled from France in 1939.

Abetz considered all forms of cultural life essential to restore a sense of normalcy in France when he arrived in the summer of 1940. He encouraged the reopening of **theaters**, music halls, and **universities**. He worked closely with Pierre **Laval** and Marcel **Déat** and obtained their release after **Pétain** dismissed Laval and had both men arrested in December 1940. On 5 January 1942, Abetz met with **Hitler** and Ribbentrop to attempt to form a Franco–German military alliance, which, however, failed. After the Allied landings in **North Africa** and the German occupation of the southern **zone**, Abetz was recalled to Berlin in December 1942 and requested to abandon all diplomatic action with France. Following an attempt by Pétain to recall the National Assembly, Abetz returned to **Vichy** in December 1943, the bearer of a letter from Foreign Minister Joachim von Ribbentrop reproaching Pétain for his "**resistance**" to the Germans and demanding the appointment of more dedicated **collaborationists** to the Vichy government. Following the **liberation**, Abetz accompanied the retreating Vichy supporters and collaborators to **Sigmaringen**, where he was finally dismissed as ambassador in December 1944.

Sentenced to 20 years' hard labor by a Paris military court in 1949, Abetz was released 5 years later. He was killed in an automobile crash, which some have viewed as suspicious in origin, in 1958.

O. Abetz, *Das offene Probleme* (Cologne, 1951); O. Abetz, *Pétain et les Allemands* (Paris, 1948); R. Tournoux, *Le Royaume d'Otto* (Paris, 1982).

M. Guyot-Bender

ACTION FRANÇAISE (1899–1944), nationalist and royalist movement of the extreme **Right**, influential in shaping the early phase of **Vichy's National Revolution**. Led by Charles **Maurras** and spearheaded by its daily newspaper, *L'Action Française*, the movement became the avant-garde of the French nationalist Right in the decade before 1914. Mixing violent polemics and street brawling with serious political and literary commentary, the Action Française's influence peaked in the years just after World War I, when its brand of nationalism was widely shared. Between the mid-1920s and the eve of World War II, the movement suffered a long, but gradual, period of decline hastened, first, by the Vatican's condemnation in 1926, resulting in loss of Catholic support, and, second, by the steady defection of younger and more activist recruits to the radical leagues of the 1930s. However, the long-term impact of **Maurrasian** ideas proved to be significant, not only among the many "dissidents" who populated the more radical leagues of the 1930s but also across the spectrum of the nationalist Right.

Though the Action Française had been, from its earliest days, vehemently anti-German, by the late 1930s, it had become a leading force in the neopacifist campaign, culminating with its support of the **Munich agreement.** This paradox can be explained in terms of the alignment of ideological forces, both inside and outside France. Though Maurras had little sympathy for Nazism—which he saw as a variety of despised "Germanism"—he had even less sympathy for those who, he claimed, would benefit from a war against **Hitler**: the **Soviet Union,** French **communists** and their **Popular Front** allies, and **Jews**. Although the Action Française opposed the dreaded "ideological" war to the last day, when it was finally declared, the royalists supported its prosecution.

The defeat of 1940, which brought in its wake the dismantling of the parliamentary **Republic** and the installation of Philippe **Pétain** as head of an authoritarian regime, seemed, at first, to open a new and promising phase in the movement's history. Though the impact of the Action Française on Vichy's National Revolution has sometimes been exaggerated, it was real, specifically because of the number of well-placed Maurrasians close to Pétain and, more generally, because Maurrasian ideas had had a shaping influence on the Catholic and reactionary Right through the years of the Third Republic. The laws, institutions, and moral tone of the **Vichy** government reflected long-standing royalist preferences: from the anti-Semitic laws to the emphasis on the ideals of order, hierarchy, corporation, and authority. Even though the royalist daily, published in Lyons, often criticized the slow pace of the National Revolution and its lax enforcement, it stood unwaveringly behind the figure of Pétain. This benefited the royalists early on, when Pétain's popularity was almost universal; however, as his National Revolution proved increasingly hollow, and his decision to collaborate with the Nazi occupier increasingly disastrous, the Action Française, supporting its surrogate prince to the end, shared in the increasing disfavor directed against his government. Further, the Action Française's habitually vicious attacks on selected groups and individuals—now focused on communists, Gaullists, and Jews—became, in some cases, tantamount to death sentences as officials, both German and French, hunted down their prey. Hence, when the Vichy regime went down in the flames of the Nazi defeat, the Action Française shared its fate.

*F. Ogé, *Le journal l'Action Française et la politique intérieure du gouvernement de Vichy* (Toulouse, 1984); E. R. Tannenbaum, *The Action Française: Die-hard Reactionaries in Twentieth Century France* (New York, 1962); E. Weber, *Action Française: Royalism and Reaction in Twentieth Century France* (Stanford, CA, 1962); M. Winock, *Histoire de l'extrême droite en France* (Paris, 1993).

P. Mazgaj

ALBERTINI, GEORGES (1911–1983) was an interwar **socialist** who became secretary-general of the **collaborationist Rassemblement National Populaire (RNP)** from 1942 through 1944. Born in Châlon-sur-Saône, he was a socialist as a student, and became a teacher and member of the Vigilance Committee of Anti-Fascist Intellectuals. Until the war he supported socialism, pacifism, anti-Bolshevism, and a Franco–German rapprochement.

Following the 1940 **armistice** Albertini renewed contact with Marcel **Déat**, with whom he had been acquainted in his socialist days. Albertini founded a Parti National Populaire in the Aube, where he was a teacher, until being invited to become secretary-general of the RNP in May 1942. There he helped Déat rebuild the RNP, which had been purged of Eugène **Deloncle's** more **right-wing Mouvement Social Révolutionnaire** faction in 1941. Albertini helped the RNP recruit former socialists, **syndicalists**, and others from the interwar non-**communist Left**, giving the party a somewhat ''softer'' image than some of its rivals in the collaborationist camp.

On 17 March 1944, Déat was named minister of labor and national solidarity, and Albertini became his cabinet director. While Déat fled in advance of the **liberation**, Albertini remained in Paris, where he was arrested and sentenced to five years' hard labor, commuted in 1948 by President Vincent Auriol. In prison, Albertini became acquainted with shipowner and banker Hippolyte Worms, for whose bank he worked after his release. Influential in banking and political circles, he also created an archival center with a periodical, *Est-Ouest*, which continued his interwar support of the noncommunist Left against Stalinism.

R. Handourtzel and C. Buffet, *La Collaboration . . . à gauche aussi* (Paris, 1989); L. Lemire, *L'homme de l'ombre, Georges Albertini 1911–1983* (Paris, 1990); Varennes [G. Albertini], *Le destin de Marcel Déat* (Paris, 1948).

G. Le Marec

ALLIANCE was a network of the **British** Intelligence Service, or IS (MI6), founded by Georges **Loustanau-Lacau**, 1 February 1941. Mentioned five times in **army** dispatches during World War I and engaged in **right-wing** conspiracies within the army in the 1930s, Loustanau-Lacau was well acquainted with Marshal **Pétain**. Having come to **Vichy** after his escape on 15 August 1940 from the hospital at Châlons-sur-Marne, where he had been **prisoner of war**, he was named general delegate of the **Légion Française des Combattants**.

At Vichy, using the pseudonym ''Navarre'' and with the help of Marie-Madeleine Méric (later, Fourcade), he reconstituted his interwar army network, the ''Corvignolles,'' which he lodged in the Hotel des Sports in Vichy. As general delegate of the Légion, in October 1940, Loustanau-Lacau recruited a first group of 10 trustworthy men who organized passages into the occupied **zone** and then, in the other direction, into the southern zone. The group became Alliance, part of the non-Gaullist **Resistance**, and worked in close collaboration with the ''**Groupes de protection**'' led by Colonel Georges **Groussard** in Vichy.

Loustanau-Lacau and Léon Faye were arrested 18 July 1941; consequently, leadership of the network returned to Méric, who reconstituted it in the occupied zone beginning in the spring of 1942. The network now specialized in the search for military information in France and **North Africa**. In October 1942, the network liquidated a traitorous infiltrator from within the IS: a certain Blanchet, a member of the British fascist movement of Oswald Mosley, had infiltrated the IS with the help of the Germans.

The real nerve center of the **Giraud** affair, Alliance organized the departure of Giraud for North Africa in November. Throughout the duration of the war, the network Alliance operated independently with the services of the **Bureau Central de Renseignements et d'Action**, with which it made first contact in 1944. In all, Alliance functioned with some 3,000 agents, 100 transmitting stations, and an air liaison with London each month.

M.-M. Fourcade, *Noah's Ark*, trans. K. Morgan (New York, 1974 [original French ed., Paris, 1968]); G. Loustanau-Lacau, *Mémoires d'un français rebelle* (Paris, 1948); unpublished material in *Archives Nationales*, Paris, file 72AJ/35.

A. Aglan

ALLIED EXPEDITIONARY FORCE (SUPREME ALLIED COMMANDER, SAC), SUPREME HEADQUARTERS ALLIED EXPEDITIONARY FORCE (SHAEF) was the armed force (and its commanding officer and organization) set up by the wartime Allies to launch the invasion of **Normandy** (6 June 1944), which would lead to the **liberation** of France and the defeat of Nazi Germany.

At the Casablanca Conference (January 1943), Roosevelt and Churchill agreed to establish an Allied interservice staff to prepare a plan for the invasion of the continent in 1944, Operation Overlord. The **British** 21st Army Group and First **U.S.** Army Group would spearhead the invasion, with General Dwight D. Eisenhower as supreme allied commander (SAC) and Generals Sir Bernard Montgomery and Omar Bradley leading the respective army groups. SHAEF was caught in the middle of Allied arguments about the political future of France: **AMGOT (Allied Military Government of Occupied Territories)** or recognition of local French authority, and there was still confusion on the eve of the landings, with arguments between the Allies and the French on a number of issues.

The Normandy landings, supported by the invasion of southern France (Operation Anvil), in August 1944, not only liberated France but provided an acceptance ''on the ground'' of French authorities, well in advance of the official position of the Allied governments. In August 1944 **Paris** was liberated, with Eisenhower departing from original SHAEF plans, which had been to skirt the city in the drive toward Germany.

When official recognition of the **Provisional Government (GPRF)** came in October 1944, SHAEF had already accepted, on the ground, the establishment of French authorities. With the campaign in Germany, SHAEF was prepared to support the French government to maintain order in the rear of army operations.

F. Donnison, *Civil Affairs and Military Government, North-West Europe, 1944–1946* (London, 1961); H. Footitt and J. Simmonds, *France: 1943–1945* (Leicester, U.K., 1988).

H. Footitt

ALLIED MILITARY GOVERNMENT OF OCCUPIED TERRITORIES (AMGOT) was a system devised for administration of territories that came under military control in the course of liberating Western Europe. The policy was applied in Sicily and parts of mainland **Italy**, but the threat of AMGOT in France led to sharp disagreements between the **United States** and the **Free French**.

The **Americans** established special schools that offered French language, history, and politics courses on college campuses, notably the University of Virginia at Charlottesville. Under AMGOT these civil affairs officers (''90-day wonders'') would administer liberated territory. However, AMGOT was never applied on French territory, despite Roosevelt's insistence that the military commander had the right to establish a military government. In **North Africa** Eisenhower's civil affairs officers provided liaison between the military and French officials but did not govern.

Although AMGOT had been abandoned by the beginning of 1944, the threat of an occupation government for France remained a concern for the Gaullists on the eve of D-Day. Roosevelt authorized American officials to print French currency to be distributed upon landing in **Normandy. De Gaulle** objected that this action usurped French sovereignty, declared the Allied francs to be ''counterfeit,'' and refused to allow French liaison officers to participate in the landings. After bitter negotiations, the occupation currency was abandoned, and Eisenhower urged rapid transfer of administration to officials of the **Provisional Government**. Despite disputes at the highest levels, cooperation between Allied civil affairs officers and French authorities was generally successful, but AMGOT remains a Gaullist memory of American high-handedness.

H. L. Coles and A. K. Weinberg, *Civil Affairs: Soldiers Become Governors* (Washington, DC, 1964); F. S. V. Donnison, *Civil Affairs and Military Government: North-West Europe 1944–1946* (London, 1961); H. Footitt and J. Simmonds, *France 1943–1945* (New York, 1988).

K. Munholland

ALSACE-LORRAINE. With the beginning of the war, on 1 September 1939, 230,000 Lorrainers and 275,000 Alsatians (including all of the residents of Strasbourg) were evacuated to southwestern France. Leaders of the various regional autonomist factions were rounded up and imprisoned at Nancy. The most compromised among them, Karl Roos, an agent of the German Sicherheitsdienst (security service, SD) was convicted of high treason and shot on 7 February 1940.

During the campaign of 1940, the **Maginot Line** forts stood firm, some holding out until the end of June, long after the **armistice**. Five days after the French artillery supporting the line was withdrawn, the German Seventh Army crossed the Rhine: Metz and Strasbourg fell on 17 and 19 June. The entire French bureaucracy in the three *départements* was arrested and expelled immediately. Operating on the lie that a secret clause in the armistice of 25 June had transferred control of Alsace and Lorraine from France to Germany, the Nazis promptly integrated the region into their own pre-1939 frontier districts. The Gauleiters (local leaders) were two party veterans, Joseph Bürckel for Westmark and Robert Wagner (né Backfisch) for Baden-Elsass. Despite a vigorous protest by **Vichy** delegates to the armistice commission at the end of August, the Germans continued their de facto incorporation of Alsace-Lorraine. The proceedings of the commission were secret, and the protest was not known in the region until mid-1941. Meanwhile, the belief that France had deliberately abandoned Alsace-Lorraine to its fate took root.

The first two years of German occupation were spent in applying the Nazi institutions to Alsace-Lorraine. The sharp loss in inhabitants through mass **deportation** (to unoccupied France or, in aggravated cases, "to the East") was partially made up by the return of the evacuees from Périgord. The second period, from mid-1942 to **liberation** at the end of November 1944, was that of rupture between occupier and the indigenous population. The Nazis had promised in 1940 that Alsace-Lorraine would never have to fight in the ongoing war. Suddenly, the conscription of all males between the ages of 16 and 34 was decreed on 25 August 1942. A whole new class was created overnight: the *Malgré-Nous* (Against Our Will). Despite riots and widespread defiance, 105,000 Alsatians and 35,000 Lorrainers went to the eastern front, of whom some 40,000 never returned. [Editor's note: estimates of the numbers of Alsatians and Lorrainers killed vary because of the difficult immediate postwar conditions in France and the reluctance of the **Soviet Union** to supply information after 1945; see **Autonomists**.]

The development and extension of **Resistance** cells and networks in Alsace-Lorraine kept pace with the increasing repression. Many escaped to **Switzerland**, the most notable being General Henri **Giraud** in April 1942. Liberation came when General Philippe **Leclerc**, leading his own French Second Armored Division and three **American** infantry units, cracked the central Vosges defenses on 22 November 1944. The following day, his forces quickly liberated Strasbourg and the territories extending north to the Palatinate and south to the outskirts of Colmar. As General Jean **de Lattre de Tassigny's** First French **Army** entered Mulhouse at the same time, the war seemed over, although a southern feint in the desperate German counterattack in the Ardennes nearly recaptured Strasbourg.

Alsace-Lorraine was quickly **purged** of collaborators: the number of death sentences was the highest in liberated France, but more commutations were also handed down because of the "special circumstances" of German rule in the region. Adjustment to renewed French rule was complicated by popular resentment over the apparent abandonment by the Vichy regime and by the involvement of several adolescent *Malgré-Nous* in the 1944 massacre at **Oradour-sur-Glane**. The nightmare of occupation, however, had underscored the pricelessness of the political freedom for which the French **Republic**, whatever its faults, had always stood.

*P. C. F. Bankwitz, *Alsatian Autonomist Leaders, 1919–1947* (Lawrence, KS, 1977); G.-C. Béné, *L'Alsace dans les griffes nazies*, 6 vol. (Raon l'Étape, 1971–1984); M. Hau, "Les entreprises alsaciennes," in A. Beltran, R. Frank, and H. Rousso, eds., *La vie des* *entreprises sous l'Occupation* (Paris, 1994), 237–49; L. Kettenacker, *Nationalsozialistis-che Volkstumpolitik im Elsass* (Stuttgart, 1973); P. Rigoulot, *L'Alsace-Lorraine pendant la guerre, 1939–1945* (Paris, 1997); P. Rigoulot, *La tragédie des Malgré-Nous* (Paris, 1990).

P. C. F. Bankwitz

ANTI-SEMITISM, an integral component of **Vichy** ideology, was manifest in the systematic persecution of French and foreign-born **Jews.**

Holding Jews to blame for the ''decadence'' of the Third **Republic** and for dragging France into war, Vichy authorities acted independently of the Germans to deprive Jews of their civil liberties and cooperated with the Germans in the confiscation of Jewish property and the internment and **deportation** of Jews from France. The *Statut des Juifs* of 3 October 1940 prohibited Jews from holding positions of authority in the military, the civil service, **education**, and the **press**. Subsequent laws, including a second *Statut des Juifs* in June 1941, extended these prohibitions and restricted Jewish access to higher education and the liberal professions. As of June 1941, Jews could constitute no more than 3 percent of all secondary and postsecondary education students and no more than 2 percent of lawyers (July 1941), doctors, midwives, and pharmacists (August 1941), architects (September 1941), and dentists (June 1942). Administration of these initiatives was the responsibility of the **Commissariat générale des questions juives (CGQJ)**, established in March 1941.

A German ordinance of 18 October 1940 required that all but the smallest Jewish businesses in the occupied **zone** be placed under trusteeship. Vichy responded by creating the Service de contrôle des administrateurs provisoires (SCAP) to guarantee that French trustees assume responsibility for managing, selling, or liquidating Jewish property. A law of 2 July 1941 extended the **Aryanization** of Jewish property to the unoccupied zone. Unemployment and the Aryanization of Jewish property created widespread Jewish impoverishment. Jewish philanthropic organizations attempted to meet the needs of destitute Jews independently but were thwarted by the Germans and Vichy, which in November 1941 created the **Union générale des Israélites de France (UGIF)**. Subsumed under the authority of the **CGQJ** and responsible for the social welfare of Jews resident in France, the UGIF had to register all Jews resident in the occupied zone and supervise the internment of Jews in **concentration camps** throughout France.

As of 4 October 1940 Vichy had the authority to intern foreign-born Jews; three days later it revoked the citizenship of Algerian Jews. Within weeks there were 50,000 Jews interned in concentration camps throughout France and in North Africa. On 2 June 1941 Vichy authorized the internment of any Jew, whether foreign-born or French. After the Wannsee Conference of January 1942 determined how many Jews each region of occupied Europe would have to deport to extermination camps, the German occupation authorities in France demanded that Vichy cooperate in the arrest and **deportation** of 100,000 Jews.

After 29 May 1942, Jews over the age of six residing in the occupied zone had to wear the yellow star; by midsummer they were denied access to most public places, allowed to ride only on the last car on the Métro, and forced to shop only during designated hours. The ordinance requiring Jews to wear the yellow star and the arrest of 12,884 Jews, rounded up in the Vélodrome d'hiver, a bicycle-race stadium, in **Paris** on 16–17 July 1942 provoked civil and religious protests throughout France. Nonetheless, by the end of 1942, 42,500 Jews (including 6,000 children) had been deported. On 11 December 1942 Vichy required all Jews to carry identification papers stamped "Juif." Because Jews in the previously unoccupied zone were not required to wear the yellow star, in 1943, when the Gestapo boarded trains and raided cities in the south of France in search of Jews, the identification papers helped them to find their quarry. Although Pierre **Laval** refused to cooperate when Germany demanded that France revoke the citizenship of Jews naturalized since 1927, Vichy did little else to impede the Final Solution. Of the 75,721 Jews deported from France, two-thirds were foreign-born, who had sought refuge in France; one-third were French citizens. Only 2,500 (3 percent) of the deportees survived.

*†J. Adler, *The Jews of Paris and the Final Solution* (New York, 1987); A. Cohen, *Persécutions et sauvetages: Juifs et Français sous l'Occupation et Vichy* (Paris, 1994); S. Klarsfeld, *Le Mémorial de la déportation des juifs de France* (Paris, 1978); M. R. Marrus and R. O. Paxton, *Vichy France and the Jews* (New York, 1981); S. Zuccotti, *The Holocaust, the French, and the Jews* (New York, 1993.

M. Hanna

ARMISTICE, FRANCO–GERMAN, signed at **Compiègne** on 22 June 1940 and entering into effect on 25 June, ended for a time France's participation in the Second World War after its decisive military defeat by the invading German armies. The armistice was signed at **Hitler's** insistence in the same railway car in which Marshal Ferdinand Foch had signed a previous armistice with Germany on 11 November 1918.

Marshal Philippe **Pétain**, who replaced Paul **Reynaud** as prime minister on 16 June while the French armies retreated in disarray, and the French government was fleeing southward, sued for an armistice less than six weeks after the German offensive against the Low Countries and France. A handful of military officers and political leaders contemplated continuing the war from French North Africa or from the **British** Isles. The vast majority of the demoralized French population, however, who recalled the fate of Warsaw and other Polish cities after the earlier German Blitzkrieg, dreaded the consequences of further **Resistance** and eagerly accepted the armistice. Most French people assumed at the time that Britain would capitulate within weeks and therefore concluded that a fight to the finish was both futile and suicidal. Some on the **Right** feared a repetition of the Franco–Prussian War of 1870–1871, when, in their view, French Resistance to a German invasion had resulted in a revolution in Paris.

Taken by surprise by the unexpectedly swift collapse of the French **army**,

Hitler, apart from ideas about a future French–German border that returned **Alsace-Lorraine** to Germany, had neither planned for an armistice nor for the occupation of France and had to improvise many of the terms that were incorporated in the armistice agreement. The original provisions of the 1940 Franco–German armistice were not terribly harsh. French military forces were disarmed, the northern three-fifths of the country (including the coasts of the Atlantic, the English Channel, and North Sea) was subjected to German military occupation, and the unoccupied **zone** was left entirely under the jurisdiction of the soon-to-be-created **Vichy** regime. France was required to pay occupation costs under Article 18 at the subsequently agreed-upon rate of 400 million francs a day (based on a highly unfavorable exchange rate). The French government was permitted to retain custody of the French fleet interned at the Mediterranean port of Toulon and to exercise sovereignty over France's **empire** overseas. The Germans subsequently obtained much more substantial advantages than those specified in the original armistice agreement through negotiations with the Vichy government representatives on the armistice commission at Wiesbaden. They gained access to French manufactured goods, raw materials, and labor for the German war effort as well as the de facto incorporation of Alsace-Lorraine into the Reich.

The degree to which the armistice and its consequences helped the German war effort has been debated, with some pointing to the avenging of the 1918 defeat, the reduction of French power, the French economic resources obtained by the Germans for their war effort, and the apparent free hand the Germans now had in ultimately arranging the interrelated continental and colonial claims of France, **Italy, Belgium**, and Holland in a potential final settlement. Others have suggested that in signing the armistice that left an unhappy France still a sovereign power with an empire and a navy, the Germans committed themselves to a continuing war in the west when a more generous settlement with the French might have freed German resources for the subsequent campaign against **Soviet Russia**. It has been argued that by signing the armistice, the Germans stopped their own forward drive at a time when **Spain** might have joined them in a successful campaign to take Gibraltar, move into North Africa, and close the Mediterranean while Britain was too weak to react. According to this argument, the halting of the German advance also allowed time to establish the legitimacy of the **Free French** in London. Invasion plans against France had been changed no fewer than 29 times between the defeat of Poland in September 1939 and the actual attack in the west in May 1940. When informed of the armistice arrangements in June, General Franz Halder, the head of the German Army General Staff, complained in his diary of "dilettante interference" in military planning. Only on 30 June was a plan (Felix) developed, to conquer French North Africa. Hitler's own second thoughts regarding the armistice were reflected in his December 1940 signing of the order for Operation Attila, a plan to occupy the zone that the armistice had left unoccupied.

In November 1942 the distinction between the occupied and unoccupied zones as specified in the armistice agreement was erased when the German army did invade the southern zone in response to the Allied military landings in French **North Africa**. After the **liberation**, Pétain's supporters justified the prompt quest for an armistice in June 1940 on the grounds that by ending the fighting the marshal had spared France the wholesale destruction of property and loss of life that they claimed would have resulted from continued resistance within or beyond France's frontiers. His critics who had rallied to the cause of the Free French movement of Charles **de Gaulle** denounced the conditions of the armistice for laying the groundwork for Franco–German **collaboration**.

*J.-P. Azéma, *From Munich to Liberation*, trans. J. Lloyd (Cambridge, U.K., and Paris, 1984 [original French ed. Paris, 1979]); J. Gunsburg, *Divided and Conquered* (Westport, CT, 1979); H. Boehme, *Der deutsch-französische Waffenstillstand im zweiten Weltkrieg* (Stuttgart, 1966); F. Halder, *Kriegstagebuch, I, Vom Polenfeldzug bis zum Ende der Westoffensive (14.8.1939–30.6.1940)* (Stuttgart, 1962); A. Horne, *To Lose a Battle* (Boston, 1969); P. Semonnot, *Le Secret de l'Armistice, 1940* (Paris, 1990).

W. R. Keylor

ARMY, FRENCH, faced the German army in September 1939 with over 100 divisions spread along the **Maginot Line**. The **Battle of France** in the spring 1940 split French forces, with some 110,000 French troops being ferried to **Britain** in the withdrawal from Dunkirk. Many of these troops eventually joined General **de Gaulle's Free French**.

The 1940 **armistice** imposed a limit of 100,000 men on the metropolitan (**Vichy**) force, divided into eight divisions and complemented by an equivalent number in the colonies. This armistice army, poorly equipped, was dissolved in November 1942, when the Germans moved into the southern **zone**. Some of the demobilized men then joined either the internal **Resistance** or **Fighting France** (**FFI**). The latter, structured along the lines of British-type brigades, participated in the campaigns of Ethiopia (1941), Fezzan (1941–1942), Syria (1941), and Libya (1942).

Following the Allied landing in **North Africa**, the Comité français de libération nationale gained control over the French forces stationed overseas, including 217,000 men in Africa. Soon after, several infantry divisions were formed and engaged on the Tunisian front. With the assistance of the **United States**, a new Corps expéditionaire français was constituted (based in part on the previous Armée A). It participated successfully in the Italian campaign between January and June 1944. Meanwhile the Armée B, composed of seven tank divisions, landed in **Provence** in August 1944 (it was renamed First French Army on 7 October). Another group, the second tank division under General **Leclerc**, landed in **Normandy** and participated in the **liberation of Paris**.

After the liberation of the French capital, the Gouvernement provisoire de la République française incorporated the FFI and the colonial troops into a new French army under the Plan du 30 novembre 1944. By May 1945, this army comprised some 400,000 men.

*R. O. Paxton, *Parades and Politics at Vichy: The French Officer Corps under Marshal Pétain* (Princeton, 1966); J. Vernet, "L'armée de terre en 1945–1946," *RDHDGM* 28: 110 (April 1978).

G. de Syon

ARON, RAYMOND (1905–1983), was a noted French philosopher and sociologist who had just been appointed to the Faculty of Letters of Toulouse when World War II broke out. Despite his desire to fight, Sergeant Aron was drafted as a meteorologist. After the fall of France, having just lost his mother and having left his wife and small daughter in Toulouse, Aron, determined to continue to fight Nazism, left on a British boat from St. Jean de Luz.

In London, he joined the small force of the **Free French**, where he served briefly—and frustratingly—as an accountant. One of General **de Gaulle's** aides, André Labarthe (who was to become bitterly anti-Gaullist later on), persuaded him to write for a new monthly, *La France libre*. Throughout the war years, Aron published strategic and political analyses, which were later collected in several volumes, especially *L'homme contre les tyrans* and *De l'armistice à l'insurrection nationale*. The main features of these essays were their unfailing lucidity, their faith in final victory and in France, and their moderation in the analysis of the situation in France.

Aron found the **Vichy** regime's policies more foolish than treasonable and did not hesitate to criticize the abrupt and intensely personal style of General de Gaulle—two factors that alienated him, if not from the general himself, at least from de Gaulle's entourage. As a **Jew**, he felt inhibited from focusing on Vichy's anti-Semitic policies, an attitude he later deplored. His wife and daughter finally reached **Britain** in July 1943. They stayed in London (with a second daughter, born in 1944) until June 1945. Aron himself had returned to liberated Paris in September 1944. He decided not to go back to academe, partly out of bitterness about the exclusion of Jews from higher **education** under Vichy and partly because of his "ambition to take part in national debates" and public service. He chose journalism. With his classmate and friend from the École Normale, Jean-Paul **Sartre**, Aron founded the review *Les temps modernes* in the fall of 1945. In November 1945 he joined the staff (cabinet) of André **Malraux**, minister of information in de Gaulle's government. After de Gaulle's resignation in January 1946, Aron taught in the newly founded École Nationale d'Administration and became a regular columnist for *Le Figaro*.

*R. Aron, *De l'armistice a l'insurrection nationale*, 2d ed. (Paris, 1945); R. Aron, *Chroniques de guerre: La France libre, 1940–1945* (Paris, 1990); R. Aron, *L'homme contre les tyrans* (New York, 1944); R. Aron, *Memoirs: Fifty Years of Political Reflection*, trans. G. Holoch, foreword by H. A. Kissinger (New York, 1989 [original French ed., 1983]); R. Colquhoun, *Raymond Aron*, 2 vols. (London, 1986); S. Hoffmann, "Raymond Aron (1905–1983)," *New York Review of Books*, 8 December 1983; J.-F. Sirinelli, *Deux intellectuels dans le siècle, Sartre et Aron* (Paris, 1995).

S. Hoffmann

ART DEALERS, from **collaborationists**, to opportunists, to dispossessed **refugees**, exemplify the specific repercussions of the Occupation on the art market. Paintings and other artwork were easy to trade and conceal, and their attractiveness as tax-avoiding investments or versatile means of payment raised the stakes in illicit activities and in confiscations.

Anti-Semitic policies led to the dispossession of **Jewish** dealers such as Jacques Seligman, George Wildenstein, and Paul Rosenberg, while other Jewish galleries narrowly survived through an **"Aryanization"** process (the Louise Leiris, formerly Kahnweiler, Gallery). After Nazi confiscation of condemned modern art, accumulated in a back room of the Jeu de Paume museum (see Rose Valland, *Le Front de l'art*), a collaborationist market thrived with the sale of works that had not been appropriated or destroyed by the Germans. Established galleries continued to sell traditional works most in demand, such as those of Courbet, Degas, and **Vlaminck**, while more adventurous young dealers, such as Louis Carré and René Drouin, lent money to avant-garde artists and risked more controversial exhibits. A few art dealers contributed actively to the **Resistance** (René Gimpel, deported and died 1945; Jacques Seligman, executed 1941), while others (Galerie L'Esquisse) provided a front for Resistance activities. Others, such as Marcel Bernheim and Katia Granoff, ceased all activities during the Occupation or, as in the cases of Georges Wildenstein and Paul Rosenberg, joined exiled artists Marc Chagall, Max Ernst, Yves Tanguy, and Piet Mondrian in the **United States**.

Illustrative of unofficial sales and trading channels in occupied **Paris** was the situation of **Picasso**: banned from all public exhibits and under threatening scrutiny by the Nazis, he still had works bought by resister friends, such as Paul Eluard and Georges Hugnet, and contributed drawings for sale to raise money for clandestine causes, while at the same time some of his works, though not owned by the painter, appeared in the private back rooms of galleries of both ends of the political spectrum (Leiris, Vollard).

L. Bertrand Dorléac, *Histoire de l'art: Paris 1940–44, Ordre national, traditions et modernités* (Paris, 1986); J. Cassou, *Le pillage par les Allemands des oeuvres d'art et des bibliothèques appartenant à des Juifs en France* (Paris, 1947); M. C. Cone, *Artists under Vichy, a Case of Prejudice and Persecution* (Princeton, 1992); D. H. Kahnweiler, *Mes galeries et mes peintres* (Paris, 1961); R. Moulin, *Le Marché de la peinture en France* (Paris, 1967); R. Valland, *Le Front de l'art* (Paris, 1961).

C. Keith

ART MARÉCHAL was a term used to describe an abundant production of objects and pictures reflecting the personality cult surrounding Marshal **Pétain**. On one hand, a spontaneous grassroots production emanated from community groups and simple citizens; on the other, an official production was ordered by Pétain in limited editions for the purpose of official gifts inscribed with his name. The first, an expression of the emotional response by the population to the savior figure of the marshal, generated an early profusion of portraits, often commercially distributed, as well as objects adorned with the effigy of the marshal or familiar related **symbols** (the oak leaves or seven stars adorning Pétain's uniform, the *francisque*), to be presented to the marshal as an homage by professional associations or private individuals. The second reflects a concerted propaganda effort but also a concern among officials regarding the possibly detrimental effects of this unchecked and proliferating iconography on the image of the **Vichy** regime. The government sought early to control, through the granting of official stamps of approval, the use of all representations of Pétain's likeness. Through the mobilization of volunteer schoolchildren, postcards of the marshal were distributed to raise money for the Secours National d'Hiver (winter relief), while post offices offered an assortment of portraits for sale. Busts and bronze medals were presented as prizes by the Commissariat général à l'éducation et aux sports, and a bust commissioned from François Cogné was placed in city halls. Traditional folk art, through l'Imagerie du Maréchal à Limoges, contributed a widely distributed coloring book. The Paris Mint, Cristallerie Baccarat, and Porcelaines de Sèvres were enlisted to produce works inscribed with the words "*offert par le Maréchal.*" In April 1944, a new Service Artistique du Maréchal, under the direction of the ceramicist Robert Lallemant, sought to promote an "*art Maréchal*" through exhibits and commissions from artists, a late attempt to establish an ambitious and unified policy to replace what had been a largely improvised and artistically pedestrian effort to engage art in the service of a political cause.

L. Bertrand-Dorléac, *L'Art de la défaite, 1940–1944* (Paris, 1993); C. Faure, *Le projet culturel de Vichy* (Lyons, 1989); L. Gervereau and D. Peschanski, eds., *La propagande sous Vichy, 1940–1944* (Nanterre, 1990).

C. Keith

ARYANIZATION, in the broadest sense, refers to the attempt to eliminate **Jews** from all areas of national life. Not used in France before the defeat of 1940, the term is inseparable from the Nazi doctrine of an "Aryan race" that had been "contaminated" by mingling with other, supposedly "inferior races," particularly the Jews. In occupied France, Aryanization policies derived both from German ordinances and from **Vichy's racial laws**.

Only days after its creation in early July 1940, the Vichy regime began barring Jews from government posts and public employment. Further measures eventually eliminated Jews from the **press, radio**, and **cinema** and severely restricted the number of Jewish doctors, lawyers, and **university** students. Another series of measures aimed to rid the French **economy** of Jewish influence, and in this narrower sense of economic "Aryanization" the term is most often used. By a German ordinance of 18 October 1940, businesses whose owners, directors, associates, or shareholders were Jews were to be sold or liquidated: Jews were forbidden from receiving the proceeds of these sales and from selling their property beforehand. Such expropriations were first, in December 1940, the task of "temporary administrators," Frenchmen chosen and supervised by an overseeing agency connected to the Ministry of **Industrial Production**. They then became the main function of the **Commissariat général des questions juives** after its creation on 29 March 1941. By the end of the occupation, some 9,860 Jewish businesses in France had thus been sold or liquidated. The German "Rosenberg Services" stole thousands of paintings, sculptures, and pieces of furniture and china. In both the narrow and the larger sense, Aryanization was an integral part of the Nazi plan of destroying the European Jews: by striking at the economic vitality of the Jews, the Nazis made it impossible for them to survive social persecution.

J. Billig, *Le Commissariat général aux questions juives,* 3 vols. (Paris, 1955, 1957, 1960); H. Rousso, "L'aryanisation économique—Vichy, l'occupant et la spoliation des Juifs," *Yod* (1982), 41–80.

N. Bracher

ASSOCIATION POUR DÉFENDRE LA MÉMOIRE DU MARÉCHAL PÉTAIN (ADMP), an association, still active, set up to defend and preserve the memory of Marshal **Pétain**.

Following Pétain's death, the ADMP was created in November 1951 to preserve a memory of him as the victor of Verdun and the leader who had protected France from the excesses of Nazi occupation during World War II. Initially, the association was made up mainly of his former colleagues from the Occupation years with an impressive array of former cabinet ministers, prefects, **army** officers, and academics, including General Maxime **Weygand**, honorary president of the ADMP from 1951 to 1965. Today, the ADMP groups together individuals sympathetic to a general **right-wing** agenda, including Jean-Marie Le Pen. Membership numbers are difficult to establish, as the organization has not allowed researchers access to its membership lists. However, current estimates are around 10,000.

The ADMP has three main aims: first of all, to overturn the treason verdict returned at Pétain's postwar trial—between 1950 and 1981, Jacques Isorni, Pétain's defense lawyer, made eight attempts to have the trial verdict reviewed; second, to see Pétain's ashes transferred to Douaumont, near Verdun, to celebrate his reputation as a World War I hero; and third, to rehabilitate Pétain's World War II record and the ideas behind **Vichy's National Revolution**. Although the ADMP has remained on the margins of French politics, its influence has fluctuated with changes in contemporary French life. For example, it held an increased prominence during the Algerian war. With its continuing commemoration of events in Pétain's life, the AMDP, through its publication of the periodical "Le Maréchal" and other activities, highlights the importance of Pétain's memory as a rallying point for a right-wing agenda in modern-day France.

H. Rousso, *The Vichy Syndrome, History and Memory in France since 1944*, trans. A. Goldhammer (Cambridge, MA, 1991).

C. Gorrara

ASTIER DE LA VIGERIE, EMMANUEL d' (1900–1969), was born into a noble and conservative family. Astier enrolled in the Naval Academy in 1918, then left the navy and became a successful poet in the 1920s. He turned subsequently to journalism, attending early Nazi party rallies and was appalled by what he saw. The Spanish civil war turned him further away from **fascism**.

Almost immediately after the 1940 French defeat, he tried unsuccessfully to enlist some of his friends and acquaintances in **Resistance** activities against **Vichy** and the Germans. Astier, however, persevered, meeting leading intellectuals in Clermont-Ferrand and moving with them to Lyons, which was to become the "capital of the Resistance." There he adopted the code name "Bernard." Very tall, his silhouette was well known, and he had to resort to cosmetic and other tricks to disguise his appearance.

Astier became the leader of **Libération-sud** and was summoned to London to meet General **de Gaulle**. Each at once sensed a congenial trait in the other, and a long, trusting, and useful relationship ensued. Astier became a liberal, choosing his adherents from the political center. He included **socialists** but avoided **communists** while meeting some of their representatives to discuss strategy. More difficult were his relations with the staunchly conservative Henri **Frenay**, the leader of **Combat**, the largest Resistance movement at the time. In 1943 Astier was appointed commissioner of the **interior** and, after the **liberation**, minister. During the postwar years he wrote fictional accounts of his experiences, which included having been picked up by **British** submarines to get to London from the continent via Gibraltar.

L. Douzou, *La Désobéissance, Histoire du Mouvement Libération-sud* (Paris, 1995); H. Michel, *The Second World War* (New York and Washington, DC, 1968); H. Michel, *Histoire de la Résistance* (Paris, 1950); J.-P. Tuquoi, *Emmanuel d'Astier—La Plume et l'Épée* (Paris, 1987).

K. Bieber

ATLANTIC WALL, the elaborate defense system constructed along the coast of northern France by German field marshal Erwin Rommel in 1944.

After the defeat of Rommel's forces in **North Africa, Hitler** entrusted him with the task of preparing Germany's defenses against the anticipated Allied invasion of **Normandy**. In light of Allied air superiority after the virtual disappearance of the Luftwaffe from the skies, the renowned German strategist regarded the forward deployment of artillery, machine guns, and armor as the only hope of preventing a successful landing of Allied armies in Europe. Accordingly, he organized the construction of a formidable network of coastal defenses, including gun emplacements and obstacles to landing craft, while planning to repel an amphibious invasion by hurling tank divisions of the Panzer Group West against the Allied forces on the landing beaches. The Allied invasion force succeeded in breaching the Atlantic Wall, which was only partially completed by the time of the invasion in June 1944. The failure of Rommel and his nominal superior, Field Marshal Gerd von **Rundstedt**, to obtain from Hitler direct authority over the armored divisions deployed in Normandy, together with the mistaken belief by the German high command (inspired by a shrewd Allied deception plan) that the main thrust of the invasion would come in the Pas de Calais to the east, prevented the effective use of their armor against the Allied landings on the Normandy beaches. The breaching of the Atlantic Wall in June 1944 led to the opening of the second, or western, front in the European war, the **liberation** of France, and the defeat of Germany.

R. J. Kershaw, *D-Day: Piercing the Atlantic Wall* (Annapolis, 1994); R. Lewin, *Rommel as Military Commander* (Princeton, 1968); T. A. Wilson, ed., *D-Day 1944* (Abilene, KS, 1994).

W. R. Keylor

ATTENTISME is a term referring loosely to a political attitude of wait-and-see in the face of the German occupation. The word was used to denounce the priority given to daily survival by the population, to imply passive **collaboration**, to mean a calculated opportunism, or even a silent hostility to the **Vichy** regime. It appears only after the war in the *Grand Larousse* dictionary, underlining the ad hoc nature of its wartime use as a condemnation of the collective apathy and will to compromise of both the population and the politicians.

Later usage of the term follows the evolution of the historiography of the Vichy period. *Attentisme* was legitimated by Robert Aron in the postwar decade as an honorable response to a difficult situation and reassessed by Robert O. Paxton in the 1970s as "functional collaboration." Subsequent regional case studies by John F. Sweets, among others, generated the term "functional **Resistance**," partially refuting prior usage, and called for a better discrimination between thought and deed, while exposing the difficulty of predicting the full consequences of daily decisions in occupied France. More recent studies of public opinion by Jean-Pierre Rioux and Pierre Laborie have highlighted the fact that vacillation, even more than variety, characterized the response of a citizenry in need of both a refuge and a safe way to avoid collaboration with Vichy and the Germans.

In the last 20 years, *attentisme* and *attentiste* have been used sparingly by historians, reflecting their awareness that the term had acquired too moralistic a tone. A consensus has emerged to use the word for a political, more than an ideological, choice and to define it preferably in opposition to other terms such as *Pétainisme, maréchalisme,* or *collaborationnisme.*

P. Laborie, "L'Évolution de l'opinion publique," in L. Gervereau and D. Peschanski, eds., *La propagande sous Vichy, 1940–1944* (Nanterre, 1990); P. Laborie, *L'Opinion française sous Vichy* (Paris, 1990); J.-P. Rioux, *La Vie culturelle sous Vichy* (Paris, 1990); J. F. Sweets, *Choices in Vichy France* (New York and Oxford, 1986).

C. Keith

AUBRAC, LUCIE, AND RAYMOND AUBRAC (1912– and 1914–, respectively) were French resisters. Lucie Samuel-Aubrac, a former **Communist**

Youth militant, had passed the history examination to teach (*aggrégation*). In November 1940, together with Emmanuel **d'Astier**, Jean Cavaillès, and Georges Zérapha, in Clermont-Ferrand, she founded the Dernière Colonne, which published a tract. By July 1941, she was pregnant and living in Lyons with her husband, Raymond Samuel, an engineer for roads and bridges. They belonged to the small team that created the newspaper *Libération*, around which developed the paramilitary **Resistance** movement of the same name.

By turns a recruiting agent in the Lyon region for *Libération* and editor of the newspaper, Raymond Samuel (pseudonym Aubrac) in 1943 became the head of the paramilitary organization that he had created. In this capacity he was with Jean **Moulin** in the 21 June 1943 Caluire meeting that resulted in Raymond's second arrest, this time by the Gestapo. He owed his survival only to the composure of his wife, who, with *Libération* commandos, staged an operation that led to the freeing of several patriots on 21 October 1943. Until the spring of 1943 the couple had camouflaged their activities under a legal cover, but by the following fall they had to go underground. On 9 February 1944 they were evacuated to London and from there they continued to Algiers.

Named commissioner of the **Republic** for Marseilles (1944–1945), Raymond Aubrac, a **Communist Party** fellow traveler, was active in the peace movement. He established the Bureau d'études et de recherches pour l'industrie moderne (BÉRIM, the Bureau of Study and Research of Modern Industry), which he directed for two years. A technical consultant to Morocco, he later became a high official in the United Nations Food and Agriculture Organization in Rome.

Throughout their lives, Lucie and Raymond Aubrac have never ceased their activities in favor of human rights. In 1997, the publication by Gérard Chauvy of *Aubrac Lyon 1943* called into question some of the details in the Aubracs' accounts of their wartime activities but their Resistance participation has not been seriously challenged.

L. Aubrac, *Outwitting the Gestapo*, trans. K. Bieber (Lincoln, NE, 1993 [original French ed.: *Ils partiront dans l'ivresse*, 1984]); R. Aubrac, *Où la mémoire s'attarde* (Paris, 1997); G. Chauvy, *Aubrac Lyon 1943* (Paris, 1997); L. Douzou, *La Désobéissance: L'Histoire d'un mouvement et d'un journal clandestin: Libération-sud, 1940–1944* (Paris, 1995); C. Gorrara, "Writing and Memory: The Occupation and the Construction of the Self in 1980s French Literature," *MCF* 5:1 (February 1997): 35–45; M. L. Rossiter, *Women in the Resistance* (New York, 1986); M. C. Weitz, *Sisters in the Resistance, the Women's War to Free France* (New York, 1995); web page, http://www.liberation.com/aubrac/index.html.

D. Veillon

AUGIER, MARC ("SAINT-LOUP" AFTER THE LIBERATION; 1908–1991). As a **collaborationist youth** leader, journalist, member of the **Légion des Volontaires Français contre le Bolchevisme** (**LVF**) and French Waffen SS, Augier was thoroughly committed to building a "**New Order**" through **collaboration** with Germany.

Greatly influenced by Jean **Giono** and romantic conceptions of rural life, Augier became an active **youth** leader in the Centre Laïc des Auberges de la Jeunesse, an offshoot of the Catholic youth hostel movement. Although a pacifist throughout the 1930s, during a **youth** conference in 1938, Augier became an ardent anti**communist** and began reassessing his pacifism.

In mid-1940, Augier became the business manager of *La Gerbe*, a pro-German literary magazine created by Otto **Abetz**, then helped create the Jeunesse de l'Europe Nouvelle, a youth organization associated with Alphonse **de Châteaubriant's Groupe Collaboration**. Finding these intellectual collaborators insufficiently anticommunist and activist, Augier joined the LVF, saw combat on the eastern front, and edited the LVF's newspaper, *Le Combattant Européen*. His experiences increased his dedication to two ideologies: racist Pan-Europeanism and the "crusade against Bolshevism." Following the LVF's dissolution, Augier joined the French Waffen SS and became a political officer, serving throughout the rest of the war.

After the **liberation**, Augier fled to **Spain** to avoid prosecution. He worked for dictator Juan Perón in Argentina but eventually returned to France. After adopting the pseudonym "Saint-Loup," he embarked on a prolific career in journalism. Always unrepentant, he supported many extreme **right-wing** movements, including Europe-Action and the racist Comité France-Rhodésie.

J. Algazy, *La Tentation neo-fasciste in France de 1944 à 1965* (Paris, 1984); B. M. Gordon, *Collaborationism in France during the Second World War* (Ithaca, NY, 1980); Saint-Loup, *Les Volontaires* (Paris, 1963).

R. W. White

AUTONOMISTS AND SEPARATISTS, who supported greater decentralization within the French state, or even outright secession from it, were found in several of France's regions during the war. Despite the unifying force of the French Revolution regional differences had subsisted, encouraging a few autonomists and, later, separatists in **Alsace-Lorraine**, Brittany, and French Flanders, sometimes backed by clerics who opposed Third **Republic** secularism. In 1940 Nazi geopoliticians claimed that these provinces belonged to the Germanic or Celtic racial and cultural domain and should be incorporated into Germany or form associated states. With Brittany and Flanders, although separatism was initially encouraged, the Nazis decided formal separation from France should await final victory. While the war with **Britain** continued in these coastal areas, political stability under **Vichy** was vital.

Alsace was different. From 1870 to 1918 it had formed part of the German empire. One and a half million people spoke only German or were bilingual in French also; 200,000 were monoglot French. Thus, in 1940 Alsace and parts of Lorraine were de facto reannexed. Robert Ernst, a native-born Alsatian, returned to head the Elsässischer Hilfsdienst, as the nucleus for an Alsatian Nazi party. Other political parties, such as the Autonomische Landespartei, whose leader, Karl Roos, was executed by the French as a traitor in early 1940, now supported reintegration into Germany. All traces of French rule were removed, **educational** and cultural institutions were Germanized, and conscription into the Wehrmacht was introduced. Some 25,000 Alsatians and Lorrainers died on the eastern front. [Editor's note: estimates of the numbers of Alsatians and Lorrainers killed vary because of the difficult immediate postwar conditions in France and the reluctance of the **Soviet Union** to supply information after 1945; see "Alsace-Lorraine."]

In Brittany 1 million people spoke Breton, but most spoke French as well. Greater regional powers were desired, but few wanted independence. The Parti Autonomiste Breton first sought federalism but then turned toward separatism. In 1939 its leaders, Olier Mordrel and Francis Debauvais, fled to Germany but, returning with the occupation army, installed a Breton National Council at Pontivy. This collapsed when church leaders threatened excommunication, so the Germans withdrew their support. Another party fared better: the Parti National Breton, under Raymond Delaporte, started a regional newspaper, *La Bretagne*, with Yann Fouéré as editor; was tolerated by the Germans; and was viewed benevolently by Vichy, which approved of regionalism. The teaching of Breton in schools, a prime aim, was introduced. Moves to independence were successfully neutralized.

In Flanders a handful of separatists dreamed of a low German (*dietsch* or *thiois*) state embracing the Netherlands and Belgian and French Flanders. As they put it, "Franks, Flemings, and Frisians are first names, German is the family name." In 1940 the *Abbé* Jean-Marie Gantois, who had set up in 1926 a Flemish League of France with initially linguistic and cultural aims, appealed to **Hitler**: "We are Low Germans and we wish to return to the *Reich*." The cry fell on deaf ears, but the movement continued cultural activities until 1943.

*E. Coornaert, *La Flandre française de langue flamande* (Paris, 1970); A. Deniel, *Le Mouvement breton, 1919–1945* (Paris, 1976); E. Schaeffer. *L'Alsace and la Lorraine (1940–1945), Leur occupation en droit et en fait* (Paris, 1970).

W. D. Halls

AYMÉ, MARCEL (1902–1967), a writer of novels, short stories, essays, and plays, whose literary career extended from the mid-1920s to his death 40 years later, was born in Joigny (Yonne) but was raised in and around Dole, in the Jura region. After considering engineering as a career, he was led, following an illness, to take up writing. The success of his novel *La Jumente verte* in 1933 enabled him to devote full time to writing, and he moved to **Paris**.

Aymé continued to publish during the Occupation. His writings, which included the novels *Travelingue* (1941), satirizing the Third **Republic** and the **Popular Front**, and *La Vouivre* (1943), were published in collaborationist periodicals such as Robert **Brasillach's** *Je suis partout* and Alphonse **de Châteaubriant's** *La Gerbe*, but Aymé also openly and at personal risk opposed **anti-Semitism**. Although denounced in newspapers, he was not arrested at the time of the liberation.

Aymé, however, was troubled by what he saw as the breakdown of morality during the Occupation and the severity and hypocrisy of the **purges** that followed. *Le Chemin des écoliers* (1946) focused on the morally corrosive effects of the **black market**, even on **resisters** who were obliged to make use of it to survive. *Uranus* (1948) is the story of a town that had descended into fear, profiteering, **denunciation**, and reprisal, brought on first by the Occupation, then the excesses of the purges. Aymé was one of the leaders in the unsuccessful effort to spare the life of Brasillach, executed in 1945. Seven years later he defended Brasillach's brother, Maurice Bardèche, who incurred legal problems for his claims that the Allies, not only the Axis, had committed war crimes. Aymé's anti-*Résistentialisme* was among the most significant influences on the **Hussards** of the late 1940s and 1950s. *Uranus* was produced as a film by Claude Berri, starring Gérard Depardieu, in 1991.

M. Aymé, *Le Chemin des écoliers* (Paris, 1946), trans. E. Sutton as *The Transient Hour* (New York, 1948); M. Aymé, *Travelingue* (Paris, 1941), trans. E. Sutton as *The Miraculous Barber* (New York, 1950); M. Aymé, *Uranus* (Paris, 1948), trans. N. Denny as *The Barkeep of Blémont* (New York, 1950); N. Hewitt, *Literature and the Right in Postwar France: The Story of the "Hussards"* (Oxford and New York, 1996); N. Hewitt, ''Marcel Aymé and the Dark Night of the Occupation,'' in G. Hirschfeld and P. Marsh, eds., *Collaboration in France: Politics and Culture during the Nazi Occupation, 1940–1944* (Oxford and New York, 1989), 203–26.

B. M. Gordon

B

BARBIE, KLAUS (1913–1991), was SS *Obersturmführer* (First Lieutenant [U.S.]) and chief of Lyons Gestapo from 1942 to 1944. Known as the "Butcher of Lyons," he was responsible for the arrest of Jean **Moulin** and the **deportation** of many **Jews** and **Resistance** members.

The son of an embittered Verdun veteran, Nikolaus (Klaus) Barbie joined the Hitler Youth and the Nazi Party and filled leadership positions in the SS in Holland before being assigned to Lyons in 1942, just as German anti-Resistance activities intensified. He presided over Gestapo raids on the Lyons **Union Générale des Israélites de France** and then signed the report as officer in charge of the 6 April 1943 roundup of Jewish children at their refuge in Izieu. The children all died at Auschwitz. At Caluire on 21 June 1943 he arrested Moulin, who was tortured and died in prison. Barbie is also held responsible for August 1944 massacres at Bron and St. Genis Laval in the Lyons suburbs.

After the war, Barbie worked as an anticommunist agent for the **U.S.** Counter-Intelligence Corps. In 1951, he was helped by a network of sympathizers to get to South America, where, as Klaus Altmann, he became a wealthy shipping magnate and supported **fascist** causes around the globe. France convicted Barbie in absentia and sentenced him to death in 1952 and 1954.

Barbie was finally located in Bolivia and extradited to Lyons in 1983 and tried in 1987. At his trial, defense lawyer Jacques Vergès threatened revelations about **collaboration**, divisions within the Resistance, and French atrocities in Algeria. Resistance veterans and deportees wanted Barbie tried for the murder of Moulin. He was tried, however, for the massacre of the Jewish children of Izieu, considered a crime against humanity, for which France had abolished the statute of limitations in 1964. Sentenced to life in prison, Barbie died there in September 1991. His conviction paved the way for indictments of others, including Frenchmen René **Bousquet** and Paul **Touvier**.

†L. de Hoyos, *Klaus Barbie: The Untold Story* (London, 1985); A. Finkielkraut, *Remembering in Vain: The Klaus Barbie Trial and Crimes against Humanity,* trans. R. Lapidus and S. Godfrey (New York, 1992); S. Lagrange, *Coupable d'être née, Adoles-*

cente à Auschwitz (Paris, 1997); T. Morgan, *The French, the Germans, the Jews, the Klaus Barbie Trial, and the City of Lyon, 1940–45* (New York, 1989); E. Paris, *Unhealed Wounds: France and the Klaus Barbie Affair* (New York, 1985).

L. A. Higgins

BASCH, VICTOR (1863–1944), was president of the Ligue des Droits de l'Homme (League of the Rights of Man) from 1926 until it was dissolved by the **Vichy** government in 1940. He was brought up in France but was of Hungarian origin. From 1906 onward he held various professorial posts at the Sorbonne. In 1898 he had become a member of the league, eventually succeeding Ferdinand Buisson as its president in 1926. The Dreyfus affair had convinced him that intellectuals should ally with the workers in the **socialist** cause. He joined the Socialist Party and remained a lifelong member.

In the interwar years he campaigned for Franco–German rapprochement. A German scholar—his first chair had been in German literature—Basch promoted meetings between French and German young people and until 1933 maintained contact with the German counterpart of the league. From then onward he dissociated himself from his pacifist colleagues and condemned the **fascist** dictatorships. He was active in assisting the Republicans in the Spanish civil war. He opposed the **Munich agreement** and was vociferous in his protests when the **USSR** signed the 1939 pact with Germany.

At the outbreak of war he was too old to take any active part. As a **Jew**, a **Freemason**, and an anticlerical, he was anathema to the Vichy regime, as well as to the Nazis. He refused, however, to hide but moved to Lyons. There he joined the clandestine Comité d'Action Socialiste when it was founded in 1941 and was also in contact with the **Front National**. In January 1944, although aged 81 and unwell, he, together with his wife, Hélène, aged 82, was arrested at the instigation of the Germans and taken away by the *milice*. Their bodies, riddled with bullets, were found by the roadside at Neyron (Ain).

F. Basch, *Victor Basch, De l'Affaire Dreyfus au crime de la Milice* (Paris, 1994); B. Deljarrie and B. Wallon, eds., *La Ligue des Droits de l'Homme, Un Combat dans le siècle* (Paris, 1988); P. Langevin et al., *Victor Basch, 1863–1944* (Paris, n.d. [1945?]).

W. D. Halls

BATTLE OF FRANCE was the final phase of the German military offensive of May–June 1940 that resulted in the German defeat and occupation of France.

Beginning 10 May 1940, the German offensive immediately put French troops on the defensive, starting with the seizure the next day of the Eben-Emael fortress by parachute and glider troops which enabled the German forces to circle the Belgian defenders along the Albert canal and penetrate deeply into Belgium. This disrupted French plans to defeat the Germans in Belgium. Next, skirting the **Maginot Line**, German troops broke through at the Meuse River by 13 May, advancing through the Ardennes forest toward the World War I Verdun and Marne battlefields. On 17 May, in a deteriorating military position, General

Maurice-Gustave **Gamelin**, in charge of the French forces, issued an appeal to his troops and the French population to "Conquer or Die!" The following day, World War I hero Marshal Philippe **Pétain** was named vice-premier. On 19 May, after a week of heavy air bombardment, General Robert-Auguste Touchon of the Sixth **Army** began ordering civilian evacuations of the areas surrounding Reims in the Marne. Although thousands of civilians and officials had already departed, French newspapers reported victory and resolve and encouraged civilians to maintain faith in their fighting forces.

French morale suffered another blow upon reception of the news on 27 May that Belgian king Léopold III had ordered his troops to capitulate. From 28 May through 4 June, the Germans encircled French and **British** troops, forcing an evacuation at Dunkirk. Although the path now lay open for the final blow, the Battle of France, which was launched on 5 June, the German move west, rather than south toward **Spain** and Gibraltar, may have cost them a unique opportunity to close the Mediterranean to the British, thereby gravely impeding, if not destroying, the British war effort.

The actual Battle of France was a disorganized retreat by French troops led by a feeble high command. By 9 June, German troops camped 25 miles north of Paris. In a desperate effort to save the situation, Premier Paul **Reynaud** petitioned Winston Churchill to send British fighter planes. Unwilling to sacrifice his aircraft to what appeared a lost battle, Churchill refused the French request. At the **American** Embassy, Ambassador William Bullitt fruitlessly wired French demands for American aid to President Roosevelt.

On the evening of 9 June, the French cabinet discussed the evacuation of **Paris** and planned its retreat to Tours in the Loire Valley. Reynaud urged General Maxime **Weygand**, who had replaced Gamelin, to create a second line of defense in Brittany to protect France's connection with Britain. Weygand, however, lacked sufficient troops to secure a 125-mile line of defense. On 10 June, **Italy** entered the war. Within days Italian fighter pilots began their assault on the fleeing troops and civilians. French military headquarters relocated to Briare along the Loire River. On 12 June, to avoid the destruction of Paris, Weygand declared it an "open city," meaning that it would not be defended. Of Paris' 2,829,746 population, only some 983,000 remained to greet the uncontested arrival of the German forces on 14 June. Only two civilian officials, Seine prefect Achille Villey and the police prefect, Roger Langeron, remained to receive German general Bogislav von Studnitz at the Hôtel de Ville, the city hall.

Continuing their advance, German forces, using portable pontoon bridges to cross the Loire, pursued and often overtook retreating French troops. Rather than continue to fight in Brittany, the Massif Central, or the Jura mountains, as seems to have been suggested by some, Weygand argued for a cease-fire despite the stiff resistance offered to the invaders by French forces in Tours and the Rhône valley and the continued holding out by the Maginot Line. Having relocated in Bordeaux, the Reynaud cabinet resigned on 16 June in opposition to the forces advocating capitulation led by Pétain, who headed the new government. On 17 June, in a **radio** broadcast speech, Pétain urged the French to "end the fight." Although no official **armistice** was yet in force on the eighteenth, cities of over 20,000 population were declared "open" to avoid destruction, and many French soldiers laid down their weapons, often disbanding so as to avoid capture by German troops. On 21 June, General Charles-Léon **Huntziger** received orders to sign the armistice agreement at a ceremony staged by the Germans at the Rethondes site, near **Compiègne**, of the 1918 armistice. The Battle of France was over.

M. Bloch, *Strange Defeat*, trans. G. Hopkins (New York, 1968 [original French ed., 1946]); A. Geraud, *The Gravediggers of France: Gamelin, Daladier, Reynaud, Pétain, and Laval* (Garden City, NY, 1944); A. Goutard, *The Battle of France, 1940*, trans. A. R. P. Burgess (New York, 1959 [original French ed.: *La Guerre des occasions perdues*, 1956]); H. R. Lottman, *The Fall of Paris: June 1940* (New York, 1992); Militärgeshichtliches Forschungsamt (Research Institute for Military History), Freiburg im Breisgau, Germany, ed., *Germany and the Second World War*, vol. 2: *Germany's Initial Conquests in Europe*, trans. D. S. McMurry and E. Osers (Oxford, 1991).

N. Dombrowski

BAUDOUIN, PAUL (1895–1964), undersecretary of state and secretary of the war cabinet in Paul **Reynaud's** administration (April 1940–May 1940); foreign minister under Marshal **Pétain** (June 1940–January 1941). Baudouin was an influential member of the **Vichy** government in its early days. His diary, *Neuf mois au gouvernement*, published after the war, offers an interesting, though not entirely accurate, account of the last months of the Third **Republic** and the first months of the Vichy regime.

A defeatist, as early as mid-May 1940, he favored signing an **armistice** with Germany. Though appointed to office by Paul Reynaud, Baudouin supported replacing him with Marshal Pétain as premier. Although an Anglophobe and critic of the Third Republic, Baudouin had reservations about the **collaborationist** policies promoted by Pierre **Laval** in the summer of 1940. When the **British** attacked the French fleet at **Mers-el-Kébir** in July 1940, he convinced Pétain not to retaliate militarily but simply to break formal diplomatic relations. As the connection between Laval and Otto **Abetz** in occupied **Paris** grew stronger, however, Baudouin was increasingly marginalized in Vichy. Although he claimed later to have resigned in protest in late October 1940, he actually retained a post as a secretary of state in the cabinet until January 1941, thus through Laval's entire first period in office.

At the end of the war, Baudouin was caught trying to escape to **Spain**. Tried for treason in 1947, he was sentenced to five years of hard labor. He served one year of that term before being released.

P. Baudouin, *Neuf mois au gouvernement* (Paris, 1948); R. O. Paxton, *Vichy France: Old Guard and New Order* (New York, 1972); W. L. Shirer, *The Collapse of the Third Republic* (New York, 1969).

D. D. Buffton

BAUDRILLART, CARDINAL HENRI MARIE ALFRED (1859–1942), rector of the Institut catholique de Paris (Catholic Institute of Paris) since 1907, member of Académie française since 1918, first director of the Dictionnaire d'histoire et de géographie ecclésiastique. He was promoted to bishop in 1921, archbishop in 1928, and cardinal in 1935 because of his contributions to Catholic thought and education. During World War II, Baudrillart was a leading Catholic **collaborationist**.

Baudrillart admired Philippe **Pétain** and wrote a book on him, *La voix du chef* (The Voice of the Leader). Residing in **Paris** under Nazi occupation, Baudrillart approved of the German "Crusade" against the **Soviet Union** because he profoundly feared communism. He was an honorary patron of Alphonse **de Châteaubriant's Groupe Collaboration** and was a member of Comité d'honneur of the Légion des Volontaires Français contre le Bolchevisme (LVF), enhancing the prestige of that organization.

Baudrillart was linked to the Catholic collaborationist weekly in Bordeaux, *Voix française*, through friendship with Paul Lesourd, the director and a former professor at the Institut catholique. He also wrote articles in *La Gerbe* and *Le Nouvelliste*. The French episcopacy did not approve of Baudrillart's collaborationist position.

Of the French hierarchy, Baudrillart was the only one who welcomed the return to power of Pierre **Laval** in April 1942. The following month—at the age of 83—Baudrillart died, and Laval attended his funeral along with a delegation of the LVF.

A. Baudrillart (P. Christophe, ed.), *Les Carnets du cardinal Baudrillart (1914–1918)* (Paris, 1994); J. Duquesne, *Les catholiques français sous l'occupation* (Paris, 1966); A. Guny, "Baudrillart," *Catholicisme: Hier, Aujourd'hui, Demain* (Paris, 1947–1982); W. D. Halls, "Catholicism under Vichy," in R. Kedward and R. Austin, eds., *Vichy France and the Resistance* (Totowa, NJ, 1985); W. D. Halls, *Politics, Society, and Christianity in Vichy France* (Oxford, 1995).

M. P. Dougherty

BAZAINE, JEAN (1904–), French painter who organized with André Lejard the 1941 Vingt Jeunes Peintres de Tradition Française (Twenty Young Painters in the French Tradition) exhibit in **Paris**, the first manifestation in occupied France of an avant-garde, independent art. His articles in several journals, especially the *Nouvelle Revue Française*, along with his works shown in October 1944 within the Salon d'Automne, also called Salon de la Libération, made him one of the most eloquent and sophisticated artists of the period.

Prior to the war, Bazaine had written for Emmanuel **Mounier's** journal *Esprit*. Sent in 1939 to **Lorraine**, Bazaine did not give up drawing, which he had started on a large scale at age 20. The Vingt Jeunes Peintres de Tradition Française exhibit was sponsored by Jeune France, a group influenced by *Esprit*, which continued to publish under Vichy. Bazaine's 1943 paintings *Arbres* and *Les Trois pots au soleil couchant* were both produced in a nonfigurative, or abstract style, as were *Jeanne d'Arc* and *La Messe de l'homme armé*, both of which he painted in 1944. His nonfigurative style in these works opposed the Nazi version of esthetics, which considered the nonfigurative as ''degenerate.''

Although Bazaine's work expressed a certain independence, characteristic of many artists in their refusal to adhere to official Vichy or Nazi norms, he did not formally join the **Resistance**. He continued to enjoy an active and successful career after the war.

J. Bazaine, *Le Temps de la peinture 1938–1989* (Paris, 1990); P. Cabanne et al., *Jean Bazaine* (Geneva and Paris, 1990); M. C. Cone, *Artists under Vichy: A Case of Prejudice and Persecution* (Princeton, NJ, 1992); J.-C. Schneider, *Habiter la lumière: regards sur la peinture de Jean Bazaine* (Paris, 1994).

C. Lamiot

BEAUVOIR, SIMONE DE (1908–1986), was a writer and intellectual. With her companion Jean-Paul **Sartre**, Beauvoir claimed to be part of the **Resistance** during the Occupation, though she has also been accused of quiet **collaborationism** because of her broadcasting work with Radiodiffusion Nationale and because she frequented the Café de Flore, known to be popular with German officers.

At the outbreak of the war, Beauvoir was a teacher in **Paris**. She described the ''**Phoney War**'' in recently rediscovered and published war diaries and letters to Sartre. Beauvoir offers eyewitness accounts of events such as the 1940 **exodus** from Paris but has been faulted for her apparent indifference to the problems of others, such as **Jews**. In October 1940, all French teachers were required to sign an oath that they were neither Jews nor **Freemasons** as a condition of continued employment; Beauvoir signed the declaration, believing that to refuse would not have had any effect. In 1943, however, she was relieved of her teaching duties after the mother of one of her pupils lodged a complaint that Beauvoir was implicated in the corruption of a minor. Sartre used a collaborationist contact to obtain a position for Beauvoir as a writer/producer at Radiodiffusion Nationale, a state-run **radio** station under German control, where she helped select music and text for a one-hour program entitled *Historical Music*.

Beauvoir's first novel, *L'invitée*, which was published during the war (1943), catapulted her into fame, and she incorporated her wartime experiences into works such as her second novel, *Le sang des autres* (1945, translated as *The Blood of Others*, 1948), her only play, *Les bouches inutiles* (1945, translated in 1983 as *Who Shall Die?*), and her memoirs.

*†D. Bair, *Simone de Beauvoir* (New York, 1990); S. de Beauvoir, *Journal de guerre, septembre 1939–janvier 1941* (Paris, 1990); S. de Beauvoir, *Letters to Sartre*, trans. Q. Hoare (New York, 1992 [original French ed., Paris, 1990]); G. Joseph, *Une si douce Occupation* (Paris, 1991).

M. Hawthorne

BELGIUM was occupied by Germany on 10 May 1940, and its economy and government were increasingly aligned with Germany's during the war.

Between May and September 1940 the occupiers followed a policy of relative leniency, wanting Belgians to view German victories as a fait accompli against which resistance would be hopeless. The German occupiers were aided by the Flemish National Party (VNV) and the Rexists, a small **fascist** party created by Léon Degrelle in French-speaking Belgium. The Germans tried to divide Flemish Belgians from the Walloons by exalting Flemish culture and emphasizing its connection to German intellectual life. By late 1940 the Germans began to systematically loot Belgian raw materials and **industrial** products. The Germans realigned Belgium's financial, industrial, and agricultural systems in order to coordinate them with the German war economy. Over 500,000 Belgian workers were deported to Germany to work in war production.

After an initial period of resignation, Belgian resistance to the occupation began to surface. Farmers found ways to hide requisitioned foodstuffs, and local priests refused to say mass at the funerals of collaborators. Teachers of English used the banned speeches of Churchill and Roosevelt as class material. The Université Libre de Bruxelles closed, rather than accept a German director. Belgian refugee politicians organized a government in exile in London. They had managed to remove the gold reserves of the Belgian national bank, and these funds, coupled with revenues from the Congo, allowed it to help finance Resistance activities.

Although Belgian Resistance leaders had developed elaborate plans for a popular uprising to coincide with the arrival of Allied forces, the Allied armies moved into the country so quickly in September 1944 that their services were not needed, and the whole nation was liberated in several days. The main contribution of the Belgian Resistance movement to the **liberation** was in foiling German plans to destroy the port of Antwerp.

*:M.R.D. Foot, *Resistance: European Resistance to Nazism, 1940–1945* (New York, 1977); G. Lovinfosse, "La Resistance belge et les Alliés," in *European Resistance Movements, 1930–45: Proceedings of the Second International Conference of the History of the Resistance Movements, Milan, 1961* (New York, 1964).

C. J. Haug

BELIN, RENÉ (1898–1977), a prominent **syndicalist** leader of the 1930s, was minister of **industrial production** and labor from July 1940 through February 1941 and secretary of state for labor from February 1941 through April 1942.

A member of the **Confédération Générale du Travail** (General Confederation of Labor, **CGT**), Belin became secretary of the postal workers union in Lyons before joining the Paris telephone services. After appointment as postal workers national secretary, he was elected to the federal office of the CGT in 1933, under Léon Jouhaux's mentorship, writing editorials for its daily, *Le Peuple*. In 1936 he launched the anti**communist** *Syndicats*. By 1938 he represented a **right-wing** current within the CGT, favoring strict economic planning and expressing reservations on the 40-hour week.

In May 1940 Belin resigned from the CGT bureau and in July accepted an office under **Vichy** in the belief that within the national renewal promised by the new government the interests of syndicalism could be protected. His cohesive society was not to be. In August 1940 he signed a law dissolving trade unions and in October 1941 contributed to Marshal Petain's corporatist **Labor Charter** setting up a single union body. After 1942 he returned to syndicalist activities. Postwar charges against him were eventually dropped, and he contributed to the independent *Revue Syndicaliste*.

Belin represents an attempt to ensure a pluralism of interests within the Vichy regime, but by 1942 his views were unacceptable to its conformist policy.

R. Belin, *Du secrétariat de la CGT au gouvernement de Vichy* (Paris, 1978); Fondation Nationale des Sciences Politiques, ed. (J. Bourdin and R. Rémond), *Le Gouvernement de Vichy, 1940–42* (Paris, 1972); ''*Syndicalismes sous Vichy*,'' in *Mouvement Social* (Paris, 1992).

J. Wright

BELLICISTES, 1935–1939, was the opprobrious term of the French **Right** applied to politicians, journalists, and other public figures who advocated unstinting military **resistance**, if necessary, to Nazi Germany. Such *bellicistes* also believed in the necessity of a Franco–**Soviet** military alliance to assure French security in Europe.

The *bellicistes* were essentially traditional balance-of-power advocates who saw Nazi Germany, rather than the **USSR**, as the paramount enemy of France. The most important of the *bellicistes* included statesmen Georges **Mandel**, Paul **Reynaud**, Édouard Herriot, Léon **Blum**, Pierre Cot, and journalists Pertinax (André Géraud), Émile Buré, Gabriel Péri, and, later, Henri **de Kérillis**. The formation of the **Popular Front** in 1935 provoked attacks from the right-wing press, which was frightened by the likely electoral success of the Left in 1936 and which saw the *bellicistes* as purveyors of war and communism in France and in Europe. The Rhineland crisis and ratification of the Franco-**Soviet** mutual assistance pact, the outbreak of the Spanish civil war in 1936, *Anschluss* and the **Munich crisis** in 1938, and abortive **Anglo**–Franco–Soviet negotiations in 1939 all marked stages in the violent debate between appeasers and *bellicistes*. ''War party,'' accused the right-wing press, ''Franco-**Russians**, sold out to the Soviets,'' who will lead us to war, ruin, and Bolshevism in Europe. Mandel, a **Jew**, was a special target of the Right, which mixed in **anti-Semitism** with its anti-Bolshevism. In 1938 the **British** ambassador in Paris, Sir Eric Phipps, called Mandel and the other *bellicistes* a ''small but noisy and corrupt war group.'' It was an honorable company, not deluded by the anti-red shibboleths of Nazism. The *bellicistes* represented an alternative to appeasement and the policies that led to the defeat of France in 1940.

C. A. Micaud, *The French Right and Nazi Germany, 1933–1939* (New York, 1964 [original ed., 1943]); J. M. Sherwood, *Georges Mandel and the Third Republic* (Stanford, CA, 1970); R. Young, *France and the Origins of the Second World War* (New York, 1996).

M. J. Carley

BENOIST-MÉCHIN, JACQUES (1901–1983), secretary of state for the Council of Ministers under **Vichy**. Historian and intellectual, Benoist-Méchin joined Jacques **Doriot's Parti Populaire Française (PPF)** in the mid-1930s and showed Nazi sympathies with his work *Éclaircissements sur Mein Kampf d'Adolf Hitler* (Paris, 1939). He also wrote laudatory histories of the German army.

As secretary of state for the Council of Ministers under Vichy, Benoist-Méchin worked with Ambassador Otto **Abetz** for closer Franco–German **collaboration**. Benoist-Méchin hoped that his efforts at collaboration would elevate France's status from subordinate to partner. His plan for closer economic cooperation in February 1941, however, was rejected, as was **Darlan's** *note verbale,* which Benoist-Méchin presented in July 1941, asking the Germans to release Vichy from the **armistice** terms and establish normal relations. In January 1942, he failed again to improve the armistice terms for France because Vichy remained officially neutral in the war. Yet, Benoist-Méchin, with Doriot's assistance, overcame objections from both Germany and Vichy in 1942 to create the Légion Tricolor, which fought against the **Soviets** on the eastern front. Returning to office in April 1942, **Laval** wanted Benoist-Méchin as his foreign minister, but **Pétain** refused. Benoist-Méchin remained secretary of state and later headed the Légion Tricolor. Laval later dismissed Benoist-Méchin on charges of conspiracy to make himself a member of a ruling triumvirate in a new regime.

Condemned to death in 1947, Benoist-Méchin had his sentence commuted to life imprisonment by President Vincent Auriol, who then pardoned him in 1953. After his release, Benoist-Méchin wrote historical works until his death in 1983.

J. Benoist-Méchin, *De la défaite au désastre* (Paris, 1985); B. M. Gordon, *Collaborationism in France during the Second World War* (Ithaca, NY, 1980); R. O. Paxton, *Vichy France: Old Guard and New Order* (New York, 1972).

C. S. Bisson

BENOÎT, FATHER MARIE (Pierre Péteul, 1895–1990), was a Capuchin friar, responsible for the rescue of 30,000 **Jews** in Nice and its environs from transfer to the Nazi death camps in 1942. Father Benoît, whose family name was Pierre Péteul, was born in Bourg d'Iré on 30 March 1895. He entered the Capuchin community in 1913 and was ordained to the priesthood in 1923.

While serving at the Capuchin friary in Marseilles in 1940, Father Benoît first came to know of the plight of Jews and set out to do all he could over the next four years to alleviate their suffering, to facilitate their escape, and eventually, as Nazi and **Vichy anti-Semitism** escalated, to save their lives. The Capuchin friary became the nerve center of a vast rescue network that worked closely with local Jewish organizations. Benoît's most remarkable achievement was his personal intervention with General Guido Lospinoso, the Italian commissioner for Jewish affairs, which resulted in the transfer of the 30,000 Jews in the Nice area to **Italy**, rather than to almost certain death in Germany, in the wake of the German occupation of the southern **zone** of France in November 1942. When his situation in France became untenable, he moved to Rome, where he continued his efforts to save Jews and to provide for those in hiding.

At the end of the war, Father Benoît was hailed by the Jewish communities of Rome and Nice, as well as the governments of Italy, France, and Israel, where he was honored by Yad Vashem with the title of "**Righteous among the Nations**" in 1966. Subsequently, after a long life as a professor of theology, he died on 5 February 1990 in Angers.

F. Leboucher, *The Incredible Mission of Father Benoît* (London, 1970); M. Paldiel, *The Path of the Righteous: Gentile Rescuers of Jews during the Holocaust* (Hoboken, NJ, 1993); S. Zuccotti, *The Holocaust, the French and the Jews* (New York, 1993).

F. J. Murphy

BERGERY, GASTON (1892–1974), **Vichy's** ambassador to the **Soviet Union** and Turkey. Bergery received his law degree in 1912 and volunteered for service in World War I. Wounded and decorated during the war, he served in the secretariat, which did research and performed other bureaucratic tasks for the Paris Peace Conference in 1918. In 1920, he became secretary-general to the War Reparations Commission.

Bergery joined the Radical Socialist Party and became Édouard Herriot's *chef du cabinet* in 1924. Elected deputy from Mantes (Seine-et-Oise) in 1928, Bergery left his party after the 1934 Stavisky riots, eventually creating the anticapitalist and anti**communist** Frontist Party, which never had more than three deputies.

In September 1939, Bergery alone voted against war credits. In early July 1940, he wrote a manifesto that urged the creation of a single mass party and presented it to **Pétain** on 9 July. Containing the signatures of 70 deputies, the manifesto, or Bergery declaration, sought to integrate France into the German **New Order** and create an anticapitalist authoritarian regime.

From March to June 1941 Bergery was Vichy's ambassador to Moscow. Afterward he sat on commissions to study **youth** issues and administrative law reform of the Paris region. In April 1942 he was named ambassador to Turkey. When Turkey welcomed Jacques Tarbé de Saint-Hardouin, the Comité Français pour la libération nationale's representative, in November 1943, Bergery returned to Vichy. Returning to the French Embassy in Ankara in January 1944, Bergery remained there until September 1944, when he turned the facility over to Tarbé de Saint-Hardouin. Only in September 1945 did Bergery return to France. He was tried for his Vichy activity and acquitted in February 1949, when he resumed his work as an international lawyer and contributed occasional columns to *Paris Presse Intransigéant*.

*N. Balsan, *Gaston Bergery* (Nanterre, 1970); P. Burrin, *La dérive fasciste: Doriot, Déat, et Bergery* (Paris, 1986); R. O. Paxton, *Vichy France: Old Guard and New Order, 1940–1944* (New York, 1972).

C. S. Bisson

BERTHELOT, JEAN (1897–1985), engineer and technocrat and minister in the **Vichy** government. Born in Reims, Berthelot was a brilliant student first at the École polytechnique, then at the École supérieure des mines. In September 1938, he was asked by minister of public works Anatole **de Monzie** to serve as his cabinet director. The following year he was named deputy director of the French National Railroads.

On 25 June 1940, Berthelot was named to the **armistice** commission and the following September entered Vichy's Ministry of Communications, quickly advancing to the post of minister. Berthelot was typical of technocrats in Vichy who were able to accommodate themselves to **collaboration** and the special circumstances of the Occupation in order to see their projects for the improvement of France brought to fruition. He seemed to have been most comfortable during **Darlan's** tenure as prime minister and resigned his post in April 1942, when **Laval** returned to power. During his ministry, Berthelot worked to rebuild parts of the French railway system that had been destroyed in 1940, ostensibly to promote French **industrial** growth.

At the **liberation**, Berthelot was arrested and detained for nearly a year at the Fresnes **prison**. While awaiting trial, he wrote a self-justificatory memoir, entitled *Sur les rails du pouvoir* (1968). He failed to mention his willingness to put French technology at the service of the Germans and his wartime assertions that all the problems of France were the fault of **Freemasons, Jews**, and the **Popular Front**. Berthelot was judged sufficiently guilty of active collaboration that the **Haute cour de justice**, in a rare instance of severity for a Vichy administrator, sentenced him to prison, where he spent two years.

J. Berthelot, *Sur les rails du pouvoir* (Paris, 1968); Y. Durand, *Vichy 1940–1944* (Paris, 1972); R. O. Paxton, *Vichy France: Old Guard and New Order, 1940–1944* (New York, 1972); F. Rouquet, *L'Épuration dans l'administration française* (Paris, 1993).

M. L. Berkvam

BIDAULT, GEORGES (1899–1983), president of the **Conseil National de la Résistance (CNR)**, the umbrella organization of **Resistance** movements and anti-**Vichy** political parties and unions. Elected to this post in September 1943, after the arrest and execution of the CNR's founder, Jean **Moulin**, Bidault remained president until September 1944, when he became minister of foreign affairs in General **de Gaulle's Provisional Government**.

Before the war, Bidault had been a history teacher and political activist in the Christian Democratic Parti démocrate populaire. As an editorialist for the

Christian Democratic newspaper *L'Aube*, he had been an outspoken critic of the **Munich agreement** of 1938. In 1940 he saw service as an infantry sergeant and was taken **prisoner** by the Germans. After his release in July 1941 Bidault joined the Resistance movement **Combat**. He became head of the CNR two years later at an important moment of transition. The disappearance of Moulin, who had been de Gaulle's representative as well as CNR president, severed the direct connection between the CNR and the Gaullist organization outside France. With greater distance came a mutual wariness, which at the **liberation** manifested itself in several tense encounters between Bidault and de Gaulle. Bidault's main achievement as head of the CNR was to maintain cohesion among the various groups represented therein and to preside over the formulation of an important reform program, the so-called Resistance Charter of March 1944.

After the liberation, Bidault helped found the Christian Democratic Mouvement républicain populaire, and later served as prime minister and foreign minister before his radical opposition to de Gaulle's Algerian policy forced him into a second episode of clandestine activity in the 1960s.

†G. Bidault, *Resistance* (New York, 1967); Georges Bidault obituary, *Le Monde*, 28 January 1983.

A W. H. Shennan

BIR HAKEIM was a fortified location in the eastern Libyan desert that became the scene of an intense battle between the forces of General Erwin Rommel and Major General Pierre **Koenig's First Free French Brigade**.

At the outset of 1942 Rommel launched an attack against overextended **British** forces in another swing of the seesaw battle in **North Africa**. The British retreated and established a defensive line west of Tobruk that ran from the coast to Bir Hakeim, an important communications junction 35 miles south of Gazala. Composed of forces from the Colonial **Army**, the Foreign Legion, and volunteers of the Pacific Battalion, the Free French Brigade was ordered to hold Bir Hakeim.

Rommel launched an all-out offensive on 26 May 1942. His strategy was to capture Bir Hakeim on the first day and get behind the minefield along the Gazala Line. Although surrounded, the French Brigade refused to surrender and held the fortress for two weeks. When the Gazala Line began to collapse, the British command ordered French forces to withdraw from Bir Hakeim during the night of 10–11 June, and two-thirds of the 3,600 French troops got out. The Germans threatened to execute French **prisoners** captured at Bir Hakeim since they were not part of "a regular army." **De Gaulle** replied that German prisoners previously captured by the Free French would be treated in the same way. No prisoners were executed.

Bir Hakeim had important psychological, political, and military consequences. When informed that the French garrison had escaped, de Gaulle was overcome by "sobs of pride, tears of joy," and he announced that henceforth "Free France" was "**Fighting France**." Bir Hakeim gained Allied respect for the

Free French as a fighting force and contributed to a marked, if brief, improvement in American–Free French relations in the summer of 1942.

E. Bergot, *Bir Hakeim, février-juin 1942* (Paris, 1989); C. de Gaulle, *War Memoirs*, vol. 1: *The Call to Honour*, trans. J. Griffin (London, 1955 [original French ed., Paris, 1954]); P. Koenig, *Bir-Hakeim, 10 juin 1942* (Paris, 1971).

K. Munholland

BLACKS IN FRANCE AND THE EMPIRE contributed, at great cost of life, to France's war effort, endured the rule of **Vichy** in most of Africa and the Antilles, and played a central role in the **liberation** of France. At least 200,000 French blacks fought in World War II. Of the 20,000 to 25,000 who perished, approximately 7,500 died in Nazi camps. Blacks represented roughly 9 percent of total French forces in 1940, as opposed to 3 percent in the First World War.

Vichy's treatment of blacks was relatively "lenient" compared to its persecution of **Jews**. However, despite the absence of antiblack legislation, blacks in Vichy France and its colonies did suffer considerable discrimination. In France, racist placards went up in train stations and at the **Demarcation Line** after the 1940 **armistice**. In the **empire**, the short-lived Vichy colonial era ushered in a reinstitution of forced labor in **Madagascar** and West Africa, the dissolution of all elected local assemblies, and a wave of repression that led to 115 executions in two years in West Africa alone. Recalling segregation in stores and trains in his country, the Senegalese jurist Lamine Guèye saw latent racism under the **Republic** coming to the fore under Vichy. Nevertheless, some blacks cooperated with Vichy, making them collaborators twice over in the eyes of anticolonialists. Henri Lémery, a black Martiniquais and Vichy's first minister of the colonies, called for a return to the soil and for more births in Africa, before being dismissed in September 1940, partly for racial motives.

On the other hand, Félix **Éboué**, black governor of Chad, rallied French Equatorial Africa to General **de Gaulle** in 1940. At **Bir Hakeim** in June 1942, over half of de Gaulle's forces were "colonials." Although the **Brazzaville Conference** of January 1944 paved the way for some decentralization and greater spending in Africa, de Gaulle replaced 20,000 African soldiers of General Jean **de Lattre de Tassigny's** forces with metropolitans in September–October 1944.

M. Echenberg, *Colonial Conscripts. The Tirailleurs Sénégalais in French West Africa, 1857–1960* (Portsmouth, NH, 1991); L. Guèye, *Itinéraire africain* (Paris, 1966); J. Suret-Canale, *L'Afrique noire*, vol. 2 (Paris, 1964).

E. T. Jennings

BLOCH, MARC (1886–1944), French-**Jewish** historian, soldier, and **Resistance** hero. A celebrated medievalist and historian of comparative European civilizations and professor at the **University** of Strasbourg and the Sorbonne, Marc Bloch was cofounder of the influential journal the *Annales d'histoire économique et sociale* (1929). From his earliest youth, Bloch was a patriot who viewed the outcome of the Dreyfus affair and the achievements of the French *poilu* (soldier) in World War I as shining emblems of the liberal Third **Republic**. In 1939, Bloch, the oldest reserve captain in the French **army** and father of six children, returned to service. He witnessed the debacle of 1940 and recorded it in the searing, posthumously published analysis *L'étrange défaite* (Strange Defeat). Foreseeing the danger to his family, Bloch tried and failed to take them to the **United States**. The **Vichy** regime, recognizing his contributions, exempted Bloch from its **racial laws**, allowing him to teach for two years in the unoccupied **zone**. But when the Germans crossed the **Demarcation Line** in late 1942, Bloch decided to take action. Despite his advanced age, he rose rapidly to a leadership post in Lyons in the group **Franc-Tireur**, took part in the **Mouvements Unis de la Résistance**, contributed to the underground **press**, and became a member of the **Comité Général des Études** in **Paris**.

When Bloch was captured in the roundups of March 1944, the Vichy press announced that the Resistance had been decapitated and boasted of the seizure of a ''Jewish-Bolshevik terrorist'' with the bold pseudonym of a southern French city (Narbonne). Interrogated and tortured, Bloch gave only his name. On 16 June 1944, he was shot with 27 young patriots in a field outside Lyons. In 1977 Marc Bloch was reburied, and his wartime testament was read: ''I die now, as I have lived, a good Frenchman.''

*M. Bloch, *Strange Defeat: A Statement of Evidence Written in 1940*, trans. G. Hopkins (New York, 1968 [original French ed., Paris, 1946]); M. Bloch to É. Bloch, *Lettres de la "Drôle de Guerre"* (Paris, 1991); C. Fink, *Marc Bloch: A Life in History* (Cambridge, 1989).

C. Fink

BLONDIN, ANTOINE (1922–), a novelist, was a member of the literary group informally known as the ''**Hussards**'' (Hussars), who critiqued what they saw as a myth of *résistantialisme* in the immediate postwar years. Raised in a bourgeois and literary family in the seventh *arrondissement* (district) of Paris, Blondin studied philosophy.

During the Occupation, he first wrote for the **Vichyite** *Cahiers Français,* then was drafted into the compulsory labor service, the **Service du Travail Obligatoire**, with which he spent the last stages of the war in Germany. After the war, Blondin became involved in the **right-wing** journalism of what was called the ''Opposition Nationale.'' He wrote for the semiclandestine royalist *La Dernière Lanterne*, after which he became a founding editor of *Rivarol*, established in 1951. Plagued by marital and alcoholism problems, Blondin in the 1950s moved increasingly away from politics and became a sportswriter.

Blondin's early novels combined a libertarian critique of existential engagement with a subversion of Résistantialisme. His first novel, and the only one devoted to the war, *L'Europe buissonnière*, published in 1949, was a burlesque series of episodes in which collaboration and resistance were treated with equal degrees of satire. Subsequent novels, including *Les Enfants du Bon Dieu*, which appeared in 1952, and *L'Humeur vagabonde*, in 1955, continued a lighthearted approach aimed at undermining what Blondin saw as the pretentiousness of existentialism and the "myth" of the Resistance. Ever the critic of overweening seriousness, he supported the student revolutionaries in 1968.

A. Blondin, *L'Europe buissonnière* (Paris, 1949); N. Hewitt, *Literature and the Right in Postwar France: The Story of the "Hussards"* (Oxford and New York, 1996).

B. M. Gordon

BLUM, LÉON (1872–1950), lawyer, writer, and politician. During the interwar years, he was the leader of the **Socialist** Party (SFIO) and founder/political editor of *Le Populaire*. First **socialist** and first **Jewish** premier of France, Blum is best known for the **Popular Front** cabinet, 1936–1937. After **Munich**, Blum advocated united resistance to **Hitler** and opposed the pacifist faction of his party, led by Paul **Faure**. In the last session of the Third **Republic's** parliament (July 1940 in **Vichy**), he voted against giving Marshal Philippe **Pétain** full powers.

In September 1940 Blum was arrested by the Vichy government. Charged with weakening and demoralizing France through his social legislation, he was condemned to life imprisonment before his trial. Four months later, he so eloquently defended himself and the Republic that the **Riom trials** were suspended. Blum remained for three years in French **prisons**—mainly at Bourassol—and for two years as a "special prisoner" in Buchenwald (April 1943–1945), where he married his third wife, Jeanne (Janot) Levilliers Humbert. In prison, he supported General **de Gaulle** and wrote an essay on his political experience, *A l'échelle humaine*, published in 1945.

Freed in May 1945, Blum resumed the editorship of *Le Populaire*. He declined participation in de Gaulle's Provisional Government for reasons of age and health. As Socialist Party leader, Blum worked for a fusion of socialism and political democracy. He defended strong parliamentary institutions and opposed de Gaulle's proposal for a strong executive. He actively participated in the establishment of the United Nations Educational, Scientific, and Cultural Organization (UNESCO). After de Gaulle's resignation, Blum served as special ambassador to the United States (1946) to negotiate a postwar loan, and he became premier for a third time, serving from December 1946 through January 1947. Blum died of a heart attack in 1950.

*†J. Colton, *Léon Blum* (New York, 1966); I. Greilsammer, *Blum* (Paris, 1995).

M. P. Dougherty

BOEGNER, MARC (1881–1970), leader of the French Protestant community, was born in Épinal. An early adherent to the Social Christian movement, Boegner joined the ministry in 1905. He quickly rose through the ranks, eventually becoming the president of the Fédération protestante de France (1929–1961) and the Conseil national de l'Église réformée de France (1938–1950).

Boegner attempted to maintain a "*politique de présence*" at **Vichy**, leading him to accept an appointment in 1941 to Vichy's Conseil national. An admirer of Marshal **Pétain**, Boegner was deeply ambivalent toward the marshal's regime. Though critical of the late Third **Republic**, Boegner never surrendered his democratic values. Through early 1941 and the first wave of anti-Semitic laws, Boegner, torn between private outrage and official responsibilities, met repeatedly with Vichy officials to affirm his church's unease. At the same time, he fully supported the work of Cimade and other relief organizations. In March 1941, Boegner sent letters to both the grand rabbi of France, Isaïe Schwartz, and Admiral **Darlan**, voicing the Protestant community's moral outrage over the anti-Semitic legislation. The second letter, though criticized for its focus upon the fate of French **Jews**, was made public by the anti-Semitic paper *Au Pilori* and galvanized public opinion. By mid-1942, Boegner had thrown the weight of the Protestant community behind the **Resistance**. Under his leadership, the Protestant Church hid Jewish refugees, publicly condemned the **Service du Travail Obligatoire**, and provided a spiritual basis for resistance.

M. Boegner, *The Long Road to Unity* (London, 1970); P. Boegner, ed., *Carnets du Pasteur Boegner, 1940–1945* (Paris, 1992); R. Mehl, *Le Pasteur Marc Boegner: Une Humble Grandeur* (Paris, 1987).

R. D. Zaretsky

BONNARD, ABEL (1883–1968), writer and intellectual **collaborationist**, served as minister of **education**, April 1942–August 1944.

Born on 17 December 1883, Bonnard received the Grand Prize for Literature from the Académie française in 1925 and was elected to the Académie française in 1932. Initially sympathetic to the **Action Française**, Bonnard parted company with them during the 1930s because he favored closer ties between France and Nazi Germany.

After the 1940 **armistice**, Bonnard worked to improve intellectual and cultural relations with Germany. He opened the 1940 season of the *Comédie Française,* contributed to the activities of the **Groupe Collaboration**, and, following his appointment to the **Vichy** cabinet, served as honorary president of the Cercles populaires français, which encouraged closer cultural cooperation between France and Germany. The favored candidate of the German authorities, Bonnard entered **Laval's** cabinet as minister of education, even though **Pétain** disliked him. Convinced that only the intellectual elite needed rigorous academic instruction, Bonnard believed that most men and all **women** were imbued with an intuitive wisdom about the world that was corrupted by the bookish curriculum of formal education. As minister of education he created the **Jeunes du Maréchal**, a **youth** organization predicated on social hierarchy and committed to physical training. His campaign against *lycée* instructors unsympathetic to Vichy resulted in the demotion of many prominent scholars, including Jean **Guéhenno** and Maurice Crouzet.

Following the **liberation**, Bonnard fled France and found asylum in **Spain**. Sentenced in absentia to death in July 1945 and stripped of his seat in the Académie française, Bonnard evaded judicial punishment until 1958, when he returned to France. Retried in 1960 and sentenced to exile, he returned to Spain, where he died on 31 May 1968.

N. Atkin, *Church and Schools in Vichy France, 1940–1944* (New York, 1991); J.-M. Barreau, "Vichy, Idéologue de l'école," *Revue d'histoire moderne et contemporaine* 38 (1991); B. M. Gordon, *Collaborationism in France during the Second World War* (Ithaca, NY, 1980); J. Mièvre, "L'Évolution politique d'Abel Bonnard," *RDHDGM* 27 (October 1977).

M. Hanna

BONNET, GEORGES-ÉTIENNE (1889–1973), was foreign minister, 1938–1939, and justice minister, 1939–1940. One of the most prominent and notorious supporters of the **Munich agreement** (*Munichois*), Bonnet played an important role in opposing a policy of firmness toward Nazi Germany.

Bonnet, a member of the Radical Party, was first elected to the Chamber of Deputies in 1924 and was several times a cabinet minister before going to Washington, D.C., as French ambassador to the **United States** (1936–1937) and returning to the cabinet in 1937 as finance minister. The choice of Bonnet as foreign minister in 1938 signaled the government's intention to seek an understanding with Nazi Germany. Bonnet immediately pressured the Czech government to make concessions on the Sudeten question, and when the Munich crisis reached its height in September, he worked surreptitiously to undermine efforts by Georges **Mandel** and Paul **Reynaud** to take an unyielding stand against Nazi aggression. In December 1938 Bonnet signed with Joachim von Ribbentrop, the Nazi foreign minister, a declaration of friendship agreeing to consultation in the event of international difficulties and recognizing the Franco–German frontier. Bonnet allegedly also agreed to a German free hand in the east, which he denied, though he did raise the idea of abrogating French treaty obligations with Poland and the **USSR**.

In 1939 Bonnet continued to pursue a policy of appeasement even as the French government appeared to strengthen its resolve to oppose further Nazi advances. He gave the impression of wanting a tripartite alliance with the USSR, the only important counterweight to Germany in Eastern Europe, while still yielding to **British** policy, which wanted it less. In August 1939, as war loomed, Bonnet flirted with Fascist **Italy** in hopes of convening a conference along Munich lines. Last-minute foot-dragging over an ultimatum to Berlin after the Nazi invasion of Poland on 1 September lent little honor to France. "The man of peace at any price," as J.-B. Duroselle later called him, had to go and was replaced by **Daladier** in mid-September. Typically, Bonnet did not go far, as he was named justice minister and remained in the cabinet until March 1940.

*J.-B. Duroselle, *La décadence, 1932–1939* (Paris, 1979); T. Taylor, *Munich: The Price of Peace* (New York, 1979); R. Young, *France and the Origins of the Second World War* (New York, 1996).

M. J. Carley

BOROTRA, JEAN (1898–1994), a veteran of Verdun, had long been an admirer of Marshal **Pétain** when in 1940 he urged Pétain to leave France for his own safety. Pétain's refusal was seen by Borotra as further evidence that the "Savior of France" was putting the national interest above his own. A part of **Vichy's National Revolution**, with its emphasis on healthy outdoor activities as part of its **youth education** policy, Borotra accepted the post of *Commissaire Général à l'Éducation Physique et aux Sports* in September 1940.

During the interwar years Borotra had become known as "the Bounding Basque" in recognition of his prowess as an international tennis champion. With Henri Cochet, René Lacoste, and Jacques Brugnon he was the foremost member of the "Four Musketeers." An engineer by profession, Borotra was opposed to professionalism in sports, advocating the spirit of disinterest manifest in the original Olympic Games. The same idealism, together with a certain political naïveté, led him to assume political office and to claim that the influence of sports on society under Vichy generated a sense of community and gave the youth a purpose. In 1942, following the German occupation of the southern **zone**, Borotra was arrested while trying to escape to **North Africa** and deported to Itter castle in the Tyrol, together with other prestigious French political figures. However, he was not tried after the **liberation** by the **Haute Cour de Justice**.

After the war, he continued to remain loyal to Pétain, and figured prominently in the **Association pour Défendre la Mémoire du maréchal Pétain**.

J.-L. Gay-Lescot, "La politique sportive de Vichy," in J.-P. Rioux, ed., *La Vie culturelle sous Vichy* (Paris, 1990), 83–115; J.-L. Gay-Lescot, *Sport et Éducation sous Vichy 1940–1944* (Lyons, 1991).

J. Wright

BOULOGNE-BILLANCOURT, ALLIED BOMBING (1942), was a raid on the Renault complex on the southwestern edge of **Paris**, carried out by the Royal Air force (RAF) during the night of 3 March 1942.

From the spring of 1941, virtually the whole of French **industry** was engaged on behalf of the German war effort. Because Renault had responded efficiently to the demands of war production after September 1939, manufacturing tanks, trucks, and aircraft parts, it was inevitable that its factories would become enmeshed in **collaboration**. On 24 June 1940, barely a week after their entry into Paris, the Germans took over. Karl Schippert, formerly a director of Mercedes, was appointed commissioner and converted the Renault complex to German ends. In August 1940 the factories employed 13,834 staff, and by February 1942 this had risen to 20,128, reflecting a steady increase in output.

Churchill's War Cabinet first considered attacking Renault in January 1942, but the Chiefs of Staff had misgivings about attacking French targets because of the likely negative effect on public opinion. On 2 February, however, the decision was taken to proceed with Operation Highball. During the night of 3–4 March three waves of bombers passed over Boulogne-Billancourt, to devastating effect. In the factories the raid left 6 dead and 35 injured, but in the surrounding civilian districts the total killed rose to around 500, with 1,200 wounded. In the days and weeks after, the Paris press conducted a fierce anti-**British** campaign. The RAF countered by dropping thousands of leaflets to explain the military necessity of the raids.

Production was certainly disrupted, but by July 1942 the Renault assembly lines were moving again. On balance, despite the anti-British propaganda, the French population understood—albeit begrudgingly—why the raid had occurred. By the spring of 1942 the repressive nature of the Occupation and the true meaning of collaboration were becoming all too clear.

G. Hatry, "Objectif Renault: le bombardement du 3 mars 1942," *Bulletin de la Section d'Histoire des Usines Renault* 5 (June 1974): 1–23.

M. Cornick

BOUSQUET, RENÉ (1909–1993), **Vichy police** chief (*Secrétaire-général à la police* in the Ministry of the **Interior**), 18 April 1942–30 December 1943.

René Bousquet personified the Vichy bureaucrat. He rose rapidly in the Third **Republic** prefectoral corps through vigor and Radical patronage. Secretary-general of the Marne during the fall of France, he became prefect (France's youngest) in September 1940, regional prefect of the Champagne in August 1941, and chief of police on **Laval's** return in April 1942.

Bousquet applied to police work Vichy's strategy of affirming active French administrative presence in both occupied and unoccupied **zones**. His 1942–1943 accords with the German police leader in France, SS General Carl **Oberg**, gave French police broad autonomy in exchange for assistance against enemies of the Reich.

In response to German preparations for massive **Jewish deportations** from France in May 1942, Bousquet offered up foreign Jews from southern French camps. He personally directed French police in the *Vélodrome d'hiver* roundup of Parisian Jews (July) and in the unoccupied zone (August). Thus, alone in Western Europe, France delivered Jews from areas outside direct German occupation.

In 1949, the **Haute Cour de Justice** found Bousquet guilty of *indignité nationale*. His sentence of five years' *dégradation nationale* (loss of civic rights) was immediately lifted for acts of **resistance**. The court gave limited attention to the Jewish issue, accepting Bousquet's claim of obstruction since the Nazis had ousted him from office in December 1943, and deported him after D-Day to house arrest in Germany.

After the war, Bousquet was an executive of the Banque d'Indochine and of the Radical Toulouse daily, *La Dépêche*, and served on other corporate boards until 1978, when an interview in *L'Express* by Louis **Darquier de Pellepoix** called attention to his central role in deporting Jews. Indicted for crimes against humanity in 1991, on charges brought in 1989 by Serge **Klarsfeld**, Bousquet's prosecution was slowed by powerful friends, including President François **Mitterrand**. He was assassinated 8 June 1993 by an apparent publicity-seeker.

P. Froment, *René Bousquet* (Paris, 1994); R. J. Golsan, ed., *Memory, the Holocaust, and French Justice* (Hanover, NH, 1996); J.-P. Husson, "L'Itinéraire d'un haut fonctionnaire: René Bousquet," in J.-P. Azéma et al., *Vichy et les français* (Paris, 1992), 287–302; B. Kasten, *"Gute Französen": die französische Polizei und die deutsche Besatzsungsmacht im besetzten Frankreich* (Sigmaringen, 1993).

                                                                                                                    R. O. Paxton

BRASILLACH, ROBERT (1909–1945), editor of the **fascist** and anti-Semitic *Je suis partout* and leading figure in the intellectual **collaboration**. In the early 1930s, Brasillach, together with a group of **Maurrasian** intellectuals known as the Jeune Droite with whom he was associated, agonized over "decadence"— French and Western—and sought renewal through the agency of the "new generation." With the rise of the **Popular Front**, Brasillach became more engaged in the politics of the extreme **Right**, assuming editorship of *Je suis partout* in 1937. His fascist-inspired novel, *Les sept couleurs* (1939), and his memoir tracing the stages of his fascist engagement, *Notre avant-guerre* (1941), gave him visibility as a prominent voice for a French fascism.

After his release from a German prison camp in early 1941, Brasillach resumed the editorship of *Je suis partout* in Nazi-occupied **Paris**. Under his editorship, *Je suis partout* became more militantly fascist and anti-Semitic, increasingly critical of the reactionary tenor of the **National Revolution**, and devoted to preparing France to play a role in **Hitler's New Order**. Brasillach also lent his talents to the Nazi attempt to mobilize European intellectuals on behalf of the "struggle for civilization," which hit its stride with the German invasion of the **Soviet Union**.

When, by mid-1943, Nazi defeat seemed certain, Brasillach broke with the majority of the *Je suis partout* staff, which continued to toe the Nazi line on the progress of the war. Brasillach, however, maintained his loyalty to the fascist ideals of his youth and continued to write for other collaborationist publications. After a short trial, he was executed for "intelligence with the enemy" in February 1945.

*M. Laval, *Brasillach* (Paris, 1992); P. Louvrier, *Brasillach* (Paris, 1989); R. Tucker, *The Fascist Ego* (Berkeley, 1979).

                                                                                                                    P. Mazgaj

BRAZZAVILLE CONFERENCE (30 January–8 February 1944) was a meeting of governors of the colonies and delegates of the constituent assembly, in the presence of General **de Gaulle** and presided over by René **Pleven**, commissioner of colonies. Its goals were to define new moral, social, political, and economic relations between France and its colonies and to "choose freely and nobly the path of the new times," in the words of de Gaulle's inaugural speech.

Some 40 people participated, including Governor Félix **Éboué**, who played a key role.

Changes brought on by the war had placed the colonial situation in a new perspective: "an old order must give way to a new equilibrium," as Pleven said. While the **Americans** were proposing a guardianship plan for the colonies, Cordell Hull's "International Trusteeship" program, France insisted that responsibility for the development of the colonies was its alone.

The conference's recommendations excluded any kind of autonomy outside France but called for extensive administrative decentralization, the creation of local assemblies, and parliamentary representation. Specific social and economic measures were also recommended, notably the suppression of the *indigénat* (an administrative system to control indigenous peoples) and forced labor.

A "myth of Brazzaville" held that the conference had been a call for decolonization. In reality, its importance lay in raising the idea of an evolving colonial policy, which monitored the development of France's territories, taking account of their own interests and aspirations while assuring their integration into the French community. The conference foreshadowed the Constitution of the French Union of 1946 and favored the development of a political elite from whom would come the leaders of the future independent states of French Africa.

C.-A. Ageron, *L'Entourage de de Gaulle* (Paris, 1980); *Brazzaville, janvier-février 1944. Aux sources de la décolonisation. Colloque organisé par l'Institut Charles de Gaulle et l'Institut d'Histoire du Temps Présent, les 22 et 23 mai 1987* (Paris, 1987); X. Yacono, *Les Étapes de la décolonisation française* (Paris, 1985 [original ed., 1971]).

A. Rinckenbach

BREKER, ARNO (1900–1991), the most successful sculptor of the Third Reich, was credited with creating a distinctive, Nazi style of sculpture, and was a prime figure in Franco–German artistic **collaboration** during the German occupation of France.

Born in Elberfeld, Germany, Breker studied at the Düsseldorf Academy of Art and lived in Paris from 1927 through 1933. During his years in France, he worked with the sculptors Charles **Despiau** and Aristide **Maillol** and befriended artists Maurice **de Vlaminck** and André Derain, as well as Jacques **Benoist-Méchin**, who later became **Vichy's** secretary of state for the Council of Ministers. Thus, Breker was well placed to play a critical role in fostering collaboration in the art world of occupied **Paris**. In 1936, Breker was awarded silver medals for two sculptures he created for the Berlin Olympic Games. In 1937, Breker became "official state sculptor," receiving a large studio with 43 employees.

On 23 June 1940, **Hitler** flew Breker to Paris so he could give the Führer an artistic tour of the newly occupied city. Within a few months after the French defeat, Benoist-Méchin invited Breker to exhibit in France, with funding provided by both the German and Vichy governments. Breker was well known and admired in France and Germany for the exaggerated virility, flawless proportions, and monumental scale of his heroically posed figurative sculptures. The exhibit was announced as the most important official artistic event of the Occupation. His mammoth retrospective at the Orangerie in Paris, which opened with much fanfare on 15 May 1942, received extensive **press** coverage and was attended by top French artists and Vichy officials. Breker's large earnings during this period helped finance his vast studio at Jäckelsbruch, staffed, in part, with French **prisoners** of war who specialized in foundry work.

After World War II, Breker continued to sculpt (for instance, busts of Jean **Cocteau**, Henry **de Montherlant**, Louis-Ferdinand **Céline**, and Salvador Dali), write, and exhibit. He often encountered criticism for his activities during the Third Reich but claimed never to have mixed art and politics.

A. Breker, *Im Strahlungsfeld der Ereignisse* (Preussisch Oldendorf, 1972); I. Guenther-Bellomy, ''Art and Politics during the German Occupation of France'' (Diss., University of Houston, 1992); B. Noël, *Arno Breker et l'art officiel* (Paris, 1981); J. B. Zavrel, *Arno Breker: His Art and Life* (New York, 1985).

I. V. Guenther

BRINON, FERNAND DE (1885–1947), reached the heights of **collaboration**. Although **Vichy's** representative in **Paris**, he actually was a principal vector for Nazi policy in France.

A journalist, determined that France and Germany should never again go to war, he established contacts with Weimar, then shifted allegiance, without losing a beat, to the Nazis. In November 1935, along with Otto **Abetz**, he founded the **Comité France-Allemagne (CFA)** to convince France's cultural elite to accept Nazi Germany.

Abetz and de Brinon met again in Paris in July 1940, but now France was the junior, not to say servile, partner, as de Brinon recognized. Nevertheless, de Brinon found willing collaborators among those who preferred German to **Soviet** domination of Europe. Abetz received instructions to keep France weak and isolated. De Brinon became his lieutenant, establishing the **Groupe Collaboration** (successor to the CFA) and controlling censorship and German subsidies. In December, he became Vichy's ''ambassador'' in the occupied **zones**.

By year's end the two men had become the chief conduit for German policy (instructions). They held the real power, and most people knew it. De Brinon soon controlled Vichy's propaganda and, in April 1942, was in the cabinet. In March 1943, he became president of the **Légion des Volontaires Français (LVF)**. Although he did sometimes attenuate German policies, he never wavered in his loyalty, ending the war as the head of a French collaborators' shadow government in **Sigmaringen**, Germany.

In 1947, de Brinon went on trial. One of France's most hated men, he was duly found guilty and executed. Ironically, his advocacy of close Franco–German cooperation was eventually to become a reality. He had the right idea, but in the wrong circumstances and at the wrong time.

F. de Brinon, *Mémoires* (Paris, 1949); G. Oltramare, *Les procès de collaboration*

(Paris, 1948); R. Thalmann, *La mise au pas* (Paris, 1991); *Archives Nationales*, Paris, Series F60 and 411 AP.

H. H. Hunt

BRITAIN [ENGLAND, GREAT BRITAIN, UNITED KINGDOM], RELATIONS WITH FRANCE. These relations were those of allies during the two world wars. The relationship, however, weakened badly after 1919, even though the French considered Britain their most important ally. France was "a bad show" to most British Tories during the 1930s, though French politicians returned the compliment. To the British, the French were insensitive and belligerent; to the French, the British casually stood off behind the English Channel, clinging to the hollow comfort of the balance of power in Europe.

As the 1930s progressed, Anglo–French relations worsened. In 1936 Nazi Germany sent troops into the demilitarized Rhineland; France wanted British support to push them out. The British shrugged off the crisis, while French diplomats cried betrayal. Many British Tories thought **Hitler** was not so bad. The **Popular Front** electoral victory disquieted the British government, which thought France was going red. The Spanish civil war seemed to offer the specter of what could happen in France. Franco–**Soviet** relations also made the British uneasy, and they applied heavy pressure to block Franco–Soviet staff talks in 1937. The British treated the French as though they were contemptible and weak and expected them to follow British policy. The French, who lost their nerve after 1934, felt they had little choice.

In the late 1930s the French wanted a British commitment of important ground forces, but the British could send only two divisions at war's outset. The British wanted the French **army** to do the main fighting, while the British contributed air and naval forces. The French High Command objected that France could not fight alone. Some British officials understood and warned that Britain could find itself isolated if Anglo–French relations grew cold. In 1938 the French followed the British line on Anschluss and the **Munich crisis**. In September 1939 British officials became angry because of French delay over a declaration of war. It was an ironic twist that when the British finally resolved to fight, the French were slow to follow.

During the **Phoney War**, relations improved, even if there were disagreements over strategy. When the German army broke through the Ardennes, the new British prime minister, Winston Churchill, offered an Anglo–French union. The French, however, blamed the British for not committing the full power of their air force to battle and for pulling their small army back toward the French coast. Calculating that France had lost the battle, the British decided that they had to preserve their strength for their own defense. The British encouraged the French government to stay in the fight and offered radio time in London to Charles **de Gaulle**, though few heard him. Relations reached their nadir when the British navy attacked the French fleet at **Mers-el-Kébir** to deny it to the enemy.

The British government lent support to the **Free French** and to de Gaulle, but relations were strained between de Gaulle and Churchill, two difficult men who got along with difficulty. Churchill barely forbore, thinking de Gaulle susceptible and aggressive for one possessed of so little military force. De Gaulle was wary of British domination and determined to reclaim France's position as an equal partner in the war. In 1944 before the **Normandy** invasion, de Gaulle and Churchill were barely on speaking terms, but after the **liberation of Paris**, the two leaders walked down the Champs Élysées together to the acclaim of Parisians. Victory made relations better, as did the need to face the overpowering **United States** after the war.

*†M. J. Carley, "Generals, Statesmen, and International Politics in Europe, 1898–1945," *Canadian Journal of History* 30:2 (1995):289–321; M. J. Carley, " 'A Fearful Concatenation of Circumstances': The Anglo–Soviet Rapprochement, 1934–6," *Contemporary European History* 5:1 (1996): 29–69; W. S. Churchill, *The Second World War*, 6 vol. (London, 1948–1953); C. de Gaulle, *The Complete War Memoirs*, 3 vols. trans. J. Griffin and R. Howard (New York, 1964 [original French ed. 1954–1959]; G. E. Maguire, *Anglo-American Policy towards the Free French* (London, 1995).

M. J. Carley

BRITISH BROADCASTING CORPORATION (BBC). General **de Gaulle's Resistance** broadcast on 18 June 1940 created **Free France**. The French Section of the BBC was the political instrument for France's spiritual reconquest. Attached to the Political Warfare Executive (PWE) and Ministry of Information (MoI), Radio-Londres' task was to undermine and destroy enemy morale and support and stimulate the spirit of resistance.

Led by Jacques Duchesne, London responded to **Paris** and **Vichy** with "Les Français parlent aux Français" and Maurice Schumann's "Honneur et Patrie." Its first propaganda victory was "**Radio-Paris** lies, Radio-Paris is German" (*Radio-Paris ment, Radio-Paris est Allemand*) to the air of "La Cucuracha." BBC's forbidden broadcasts, a national pastime throughout the Occupation, reported the execution of hostages, **Darlan's** and **Laval's** economic and military **collaboration**, and German annexation policies. **Symbols** of resistance, such as Joan of Arc, Bastille Day, Danton, Napoleon at Jena, the 1914 Marne miracle, the 1918 armistice, and **Bir Hakeim**, rekindled hope in occupied France. "Black," "unofficial" radio stations ("Radio Gaulle," "Radio Patrie," and "Radio Catholique") worked to rally Pétainists to Resistance. The "V Campaign" was described by Goebbels as "the intellectual invasion of the continent by English radio."

London directed major radio campaigns organizing resistance against labor **deportation** in 1942, supporting the armed struggle of the *maquis* in 1943, and coordinating the national insurrection with the Allied invasion in 1944. Broadcasts on the eve of the **Normandy** invasion signaled the severing of rail and road communications near the Normandy front. On 24 August 1944, BBC announced the arrival of General Philippe **Leclerc's** tanks at the Paris Hôtel de Ville.

J-L. Cremieux-Brilhac, ed., *Les Voix de la Liberté: Ici Londres*, 4 vols. (Paris, 1975); H. Eck, *La guerre des ondes: Histoire des radios de langue française pendant la Deuxième Guerre mondiale* (Paris, 1985).

P. J. M. Coggins

BRITISH EXPEDITIONARY FORCE (BEF), **British** troops dispatched to the continent in September 1939 and evacuated from France in the summer of 1940.

On 22 February 1939, the British government authorized the creation of the BEF, initially of four infantry divisions, to be sent to France in the event of war with Germany. Under the command of Viscount, General John Standish Gort, the first divisions of the BEF took up defensive positions along the Franco–Belgian frontier in October 1939. With the French Seventh **Army** on its left flank and the French First Army on its right, the BEF held the sector immediately to the north of Lille. Reinforced throughout the winter, the BEF had 394,165 men in France, with 237,319 assigned to front-line service by 10 May 1940. Essential equipment was, however, in short supply, and there were few tanks.

In November 1939, the Allied commanders developed "Plan D" to defend **Belgium** and France from invasion. Nine divisions of the BEF and 30 divisions of the French First Army would move north as far as the Dyle River and join forces there with the Belgian army. Executed on 11 May 1940, Plan D exposed the BEF to attack from General Fedor von Bock's Army Group B on 14 May 1940. As Bock's troops pushed the Allied forces back toward the French frontier, General Gerd von **Rundstedt's** Army Group A invaded France through the Ardennes. Bisecting the French line and pushing toward the channel, Rundstedt's offensive cut communications between French and British commands and left the BEF surrounded on three sides. The British authorized Operation Dynamo, the retreat from Dunkirk, on 26 May 1940. By 4 June 1940, 224,320 British troops had been evacuated from Dunkirk. Evacuations from other sites along the channel, Atlantic, and Mediterranean continued through August 1940. British casualties during the **Battle of France** numbered 68,111 killed, wounded, or taken **prisoner**; all British matériel was lost in the evacuations.

L. F. Ellis, *The War in France and Flanders, 1939–1940* (London, 1953); D. Fraser, *And We Shall Shock Them: The British Army in the Second World War* (New York, 1983); E. M. Gates, *End of the Affair: The Collapse of the Anglo–French Alliance, 1939–1940* (Berkeley, 1981).

M. Hanna

BROSSOLETTE, PIERRE (1903–1944), was a member of the **Musée de l'homme** network, then of Colonel **Rémy's** Confraternity of Notre Dame (CND). A leader of the **Bureau Central du Renseignement et d'Action** (BCRA), he carried out three missions in occupied France. Captured by the Germans at the end of the third mission, he committed suicide.

A student in the École Normale Supérieure, Brossolette passed the *agrégation* in history and became a journalist specializing in international affairs. He wrote for *Notre Temps, L'Europe Nouvelle,* and *Le Populaire.* Opposed to **fascism** and Nazism, he denounced the foreign policies of **Hitler** and Mussolini, urged a union of democrats concerned about peace, and passionately opposed the **Munich agreement.** A member of the **Socialist** Party from 1929 on, he headed the Aube department's socialist federation and campaigned with Léon **Blum**, though he failed to win election in the 1934 local and the 1936 national elections.

Brossolette participated in the 1940 campaign as an infantry captain. Following his activity with the Musée de l'Homme and the CND, he made his way to London, where he was assigned in the summer of 1942 to return to France to reorganize the CND and help bring a range of political figures, notably André Philip, Louis Vallon, and Charles Vallin, into **Free France**. Returning to London as head of the BCRA's operations unit, Brossolette helped coordinate **Fighting France's** secret political and military services. On a second mission in France, from January through April 1943, he worked with Colonel **Passy** to coordinate political, **syndicalist**, and religious **Resistance** networks, resulting in the creation of the Comité de Coordination of the northern **zone**.

On 18 September 1943, he left for France once again. His mission was to introduce Émile Bollaërt, the new delegate of the Comité Français de Libération Nationale, to local **Resistance** leaders and to prepare for a renewal of the **press** and the **radio** after the **liberation**. Arrested on 3 February 1944 with Bollaërt and tortured, Brossolette committed suicide on 22 March.

Awarded the Military Cross and the medal of the Resistance, Brossolette was also named a Compagnon de la Libération.

G. Brossolette, *Il s'appelait Pierre Brossolette* (Paris, 1976); G. Piketty, "Pierre Brossolette: Itinéraire intellectual et politique," (Diss., Institut d'Études Politiques de Paris, 1996).

G. Piketty

BUCARD, MARCEL (1895–1946), founder and leader of the Parti franciste, also known as Francisme, the smallest of the main **collaborationist** movements. Established in 1933 in imitation of Italian Fascism, the party was dissolved by the **Popular Front** in 1936, only to be resurrected in 1940 with the authorization of the German military commander and the **Vichy** government.

A highly decorated veteran of World War I and a powerful orator, Bucard entered politics in 1924 under the patronage of André Tardieu and served as director of propaganda for Georges Valois' Faisceau before founding the Parti franciste with financial support from Mussolini. In many respects a successor of the Faisceau, with a similar emphasis on anticommunism, **anti-Semitism**, and **corporatism**, Francisme distinguished itself by its commitment to a **fascist** "revolution" and by the contrast between its marginality and its pretension to build a mass French fascist movement.

Mobilized in 1939, Bucard was detained in **Switzerland** before returning to

France in December 1940. His reconstituted party supported Marshal **Pétain** and provided forces for the **Légion des Volontaires Français contre le Bolchevisme** while remaining critical of the timidity of the **National Revolution**. His effectiveness hampered by the weakness of his movement and persistent health problems resulting from war injuries, Bucard clashed with Vichy over domestic policy and its decision to remain neutral after the Allied invasion of 6 June 1944. As members of the **Waffen-SS** many Francistes fought the **Resistance**, but Bucard was briefly jailed in 1943 for refusing to integrate his small private army into Joseph **Darnand's** *milice*. In August 1944, Bucard retreated with the Germans and joined Pétain in **Sigmaringen**, where his followers organized parachute drops behind Allied lines. Captured in May 1945 by French troops in Merano (Tyrol), Bucard was condemned to death in February 1946 and executed by firing squad on 19 March.

A. Deniel, *Bucard et le Francisme* (Paris, 1979); B. M. Gordon, *Collaborationism in France during the Second World War* (Ithaca, NY, 1980); P.-P. Lambert and G. Le Marec, *Partis et mouvements de la collaboration* (Paris, 1994).

S. Kale

BUREAU CENTRAL DES RENSEIGNEMENTS ET D'ACTION (BCRA), the **Free French** organization that received military intelligence from, and directed supplies to, the interior **Resistance**.

When General **de Gaulle** formed the Free French movement in July 1940, he created a Deuxième [Second] Bureau, commanded by André Dewavrin, known as Colonel **Passy**, assisted by Pierre **Brossolette**. In 1941, the Deuxième Bureau became the Service des Renseignements (Intelligence Service), then reorganized and renamed the Bureau Central des Renseignements et d'Action militaire (BCRAM). It was subdivided into several sections: Renseignements, Military Action, Counter-Espionage, Escape, Study and Coordination, and Documentation and Diffusion. Between July and September 1942, BCRAM was reorganized and became the BCRA.

This intelligence organization contacted domestic Resistance movements and provided them with arms and officers, but the local movements ultimately regarded BCRA actions as outside interference by the London Free French. Despite the disagreement between Jean **Moulin**, on one side, and Brossolette and Passy, on the other, who resisted fusion between the movements and the political parties, even Moulin insisted that the movements turn over their information to the BCRA instead of handing it directly to the **American Office of Strategic Services (OSS)** or the **British Special Operations Executive (SOE)**.

Criticized in London and Washington and accused of torture, the BCRA was hampered by disagreements with the OSS and SOE. Moreover, the French **army** Intelligence Service supported General Henri **Giraud** in 1943 and became BCRA's rival. The result was two intelligence networks for the Free French until an effort was made in April 1944 to create a single network under Jacques **Soustelle**. Despite these difficulties with the interior Resistance and other intelligence services, the BCRA helped direct and carry out sabotage as part of the **Normandy** landings.

R. Hostache, *Le Conseil national de la Résistance* (Paris, 1958); Passy, *Missions secrétes en France* (Paris, 1950); J. F. Sweets, *The Politics of Resistance in France, 1940–1944* (DeKalb, IL, 1976).

C. S. Bisson

C

CAMUS, ALBERT (1913–1960), French writer born in Algeria whose desire to preserve human dignity made him work for the newspaper *Combat* before and after the **liberation** of France, while pursuing a highly successful career in essay, novel, and play writing. Camus is remembered as an intense individual, plagued with recurring bouts of tuberculosis, whose life was built around the pursuit of a renewed, egalitarian "social contract."

In the newspapers *Le soir républicain* in Algiers (September 1939 to January 1940), *Paris-Soir* (March to December 1940), and *Combat* (August 1943 to June 1947), Camus expressed his faith in a solidarity of independent human beings. His editorials from August 1944 to January 1945 strongly professed his sometimes violent views about the postwar reconstruction of France and Europe, while prompting his readers to take more personal responsibility for French and European reconstruction. *L'Étranger* (The Stranger) and *Le mythe de Sisyphe* (The Myth of Sisyphus) in 1942 and *Le malentendu* (The Misunderstanding) and *Caligula* in 1944 testify to his political interests in general, while *Lettres à un ami allemand* (Letters to a German Friend) in 1945, *La peste* (The Plague) in 1947, and *L'État de siège* (State of Siege) in 1948 show how his positions were influenced by the 1940–1944 French situation. In 1957, Camus received the Nobel Prize in literature for the entirety of his work. He was killed in an automobile accident at Petit-Villeblev (Yonne) in 1960.

*†A. Camus, *The Plague*, trans. S. Gilbert (New York, 1948 [original French ed., 1947]); R. Grenier, *Album Camus* (Paris, 1982); J. Lévi-Valensi, and A. Abbou, *Fragments d'un combat 1938–1940: Alger républicain, Le Soir républicain* (Paris, 1978); N. Stokle, *Le Combat d'Albert Camus* (Quebec, 1970).

C. Lamiot

CANADA, FRENCH, was the predominantly French-speaking and Catholic region of North America, where there was notable sympathy for the **Vichy** regime. The province of Quebec both provided substantial war matériel for the **British** empire and harbored supporters of Marshal **Pétain**, eventually engendering a bitter struggle between Vichy sympathizers and supporters of the **Free French**.

After initial shock and dismay at the fall of France, a number of French Canadians welcomed the Pétain regime, which seemed to promise a return to Catholic and prerevolutionary France. Quebec displayed, in the words of historian Marc Ferro, a *"Pétainisme* without the Occupation." Anxious not to offend Quebec nationalists loath to defend the British empire, Mackenzie King's Canadian federal government responded positively to Churchill's suggestion of serving as a diplomatic channel to the new **État Français**.

Despite the odds, Elisabeth de Miribel and other Gaullists from the divided French community of Montreal began promoting the Free French cause. With the unexpected support of influential Cardinal Jean-Marie Rodrigue Villeneuve of Quebec City, as well as the help of federal and provincial authorities, the Gaullists gained a hearing as Vichy and Free French representatives fought a propaganda war for French Canadian opinion.

The 1942 Allied landings in **North Africa** tempted Mackenzie King's government to break with Vichy; however, Ottawa was worried about Quebec's recent vote against military conscription. General Henri **Giraud's** sympathy for the **National Revolution** while resisting the Germans attracted Vichy sympathizers. Giraud's eclipse and the astuteness of Gaullist representative Gabriel Bonneau resulted in the good welcome that **de Gaulle** received on his July 1944 visit to Quebec. Nevertheless, the network of Pétainist and nationalist elites was still able to provide a Canadian safe haven to a number of *milice* war criminals who fled France after the war.

P. Couture, "Politics of Diplomacy: The Crisis of Canada–France Relations" (Diss., York University, 1981); E. de Miribel, *La Liberté souffre violence* (Paris, 1981); P. Prévost, *La France et le Canada, d'un après-guerre à l'autre (1918–1944)* (Saint-Boniface, 1994); D. Thomson, *Vive le Québec Libre* (Toronto, 1989).

É. Amyot (with J. Hellman)

CARREL, ALEXIS (1873–1944), renowned surgeon and physician, Nobel Prize-winner, eugenicist, and regent of **Vichy's** Fondation française pour l'étude des problèmes humaines, better known as the Fondation Carrel.

After taking his medical degree in Lyons in 1890, Carrel faced uncertain career prospects in France. He went to the **United States** in 1906, where he established a laboratory with the help of the Rockefeller Institute of New York. Pioneering work in vascular surgery and tissue cultivation won Carrel the Nobel Prize in medicine in 1912. World War I found him in France, where a Rockefeller-funded laboratory and hospital in **Compiègne** provided the occasion for new surgical innovations related to disinfection that were subsequently adopted universally.

Returning to New York in 1919, Carrel drew international attention for his controversial work with tissue grafts and his Lamarckian eugenicist views, which were publicized in a widely acclaimed best-seller entitled *l'Homme, cet inconnu* (Man the Unknown) (1935). Carrel's **right-wing** sympathies and his concern with racial improvement accorded with Vichy's obsession with France's demographic decline, a coincidence that afforded him the opportunity to establish a publicly funded research institution. The Fondation Carrel was created in January 1942 with the dual mission of developing a "science of man" and studying ways to "improve and develop the French population." The Fondation was concerned with public health and "social hygiene" rather than racial breeding (it recommended the introduction of prenuptial agreements and the *carnet de santé scolaire* [school health report cards for pupils]). Despite important advances made in sociological methodology and in the study of nutrition, habitat, and demography, the work of the foundation was nevertheless discredited by association with the Vichy government. Thanks to Carrel's associates, many of the foundation's researchers went to work for France's Institut national d'études démographiques. Carrel's post was suspended in August 1994. He died of a heart attack in November of that year.

A. Carrel, *Man the Unknown* (New York and London, 1935); Y. Christen, ed., *Alexis Carrel* (Paris, 1986); A. Drouard, *Une inconnue des sciences sociales* (Paris, 1992).

S. Kale

CASABLANCA, a film made in the **United States**, 1942; directed by Michael Curtiz; script: Julius Epstein, Philip G. Epstein, and Howard Koch; sound: Arthur Edeson; editing: George James Hopkins; music: Max Steiner; production: Hal B. Wallis; cast: Humphrey Bogart (Rick), Ingrid Bergman (Ilsa Lund Laszlo), Conrad Veldt (Major Heinrich Strasser), Paul Henreid (Victor Laszlo), Claude Rains (Captain Louis Renault), Peter Lorre (Ugarte); black and white, 102 minutes.

Casablanca, December 1941. The café of Rick Blaine is the meeting place of **refugees** who are desperately seeking to get to Portugal. Side by side one finds illicit merchants, bankers, German and French officers, and **Free France** partisans. One night, Victor Laszlo, one of the heads of the European **Resistance**, and his wife, Ilsa, arrive on the scene. Hunted by the Nazis, they wish to find passage to the United States. Rick, who had an affair with Ilsa in Paris before the war, foils the surveillance attempts of German major Strasser and is helped by Captain Renault, allowing the couple to escape.

A cult film that won three Oscars, *Casablanca* is representative of Hollywood's World War II propagandistic productions. Rick's café is a microcosm of Europe at war. Made just as the United States was renouncing its neutrality— Rick's position is a transposition—Michael Curtiz's film reflects how **Americans** were seeing the European conflict and shows them the only way that they could, and should, become engaged in it. This historical-political approach to understanding *Casablanca* is enriched by the more philosophical perspective of Umberto Eco, who analyzes the film through the prism of the great archetypes of the collective imagination: the myths of purity, sacrifice, unhappy love, impossible love, virile love. Combined, these perspectives elevate the film's narrative from the banal to the sublime.

U. Eco, "Ore 9: Amieto all'assedio di Casablanca," *L'Espresso*, 17 August 1975, 31–33; C. R. Koppes and G. D. Black, *Hollywood Goes to War: How Politics, Profits and Propaganda Shaped World War II Movies* (New York, 1987); C. Shindler, *Hollywood Goes to War: Films and American Society, 1939–1952* (London, 1979).

J.-P. Bertin-Maghit

CASSIN, RENÉ (1887–1976), was a jurist for **Free France** in London in June 1940. President of the *Alliance israélite universelle*, he was the author of the Charter of the Universal Rights of Man of 1948, received the Nobel Peace Prize, and was inducted into France's Pantheon in 1987.

Born in Bayonne, Cassin was wounded in World War I. He was a professor of law, represented France at the League of Nations, and served as president of the veterans' organization, the *Union fédérale des anciens combattants*. At the end of June 1940, Cassin joined the London Free French, for whom he drew up the accord of 7 August 1940 that established a "Force Française constitutée de volontaires" (French force composed of volunteers) signed by Prime Minister Winston Churchill and General **de Gaulle**, head of the Free French. This fighting force was to represent the interests of France, which the **British** undertook to reestablish in its independence and integrity.

Cassin took part in writing all the enactments that (from October 1940, for Brazzaville, to February 1943, for **Madagascar**) would illustrate the fidelity of Free France's struggle to the laws of the **Republic**. In particular, the Declaration of 16 November 1940 denied any legality in the constitutional vote of 10 July 1940 (which created the **État Français** at **Vichy**) and called French to fight behind a provisional power that promised to render accounts on the day of victory. Cassin also helped draft the enactments of the spring of 1943 proclaiming the "reestablishment of Republican legality" in those territories of the **empire** that had joined Free France, where the racist laws of Vichy were declared null and void.

R. Cassin, *Les hommes partis de rien, le réveil de la France abbatue* (Paris, 1975); G. Israél, *René Cassin, 1887–1976: La Guerre hors la loi, avec de Gaulle, les droits de l'homme* (Paris, 1990).

O. Rudelle

CÉLINE, LOUIS-FERDINAND (pseudonym of Dr. Louis-Ferdinand Destouches, 1884–1961), became the most remarkable novelist of the 1930s with his revolutionary and critically acclaimed *Voyage au bout de la Nuit* in 1932. Céline became a notorious anti-Semite as well with his *Bagatelles pour un massacre*, an extended pamphlet published at the end of 1937. A vehement **denunciation** of the **Jews** as conspirators trying to provoke a second world war, it was followed by the like-minded *École des cadavres* (1938) and the vitriolic

Les beaux Draps (1941). They made Céline into the icon of the extremist and racist **Right**.

During the Occupation, Céline worked by day at his dispensary in suburban Bezons (he was a doctor of medicine and a specialist in public health). At night in Montmartre, he wrote the final drafts of *Guignols Band*, a paean to the wartime London of 1915–1916. It was the last of the purely autobiographical novels, begun with *Voyage au bout de la Nuit* and continued with *Mort à Crédit* in 1936. Céline also found time to give interviews for, and write letters to, the **collaborationist press** in **Paris**, all of which were published as lead articles.

Shortly after the publication of the first part of *Guignols Band*, entitled *Le Pont de Londres* and prefaced with a cruelly contemptuous depiction of the mass civilian and military **exodus** of 1940, Céline fled his apartment for the safety of Nazi Germany. His odyssey through the nightmare of wartime Baden-Baden, Berlin, Kränzlin, and, finally, **Sigmaringen**, the post-**liberation** capital of the refugee **Vichy** regime and its collaborationist progeny, became the basis of his last three novels, all of them best-sellers.

After an apocalyptic journey through collapsing Germany in early April 1945, Céline, wanted by the French for breaches of national security, took refuge in Copenhagen. Denounced and gravely ill, he avoided extradition to a liberated France, returning in 1951 only after amnesties had made it safe for him to do so.

*F. Gibault, *Céline*, 3 vols. (Paris, 1977–1985); H. Godard, *Céline scandale* (Paris, 1994); A. Thiher, *Céline: The Novel as Delirium* (New Brunswick, NJ, 1972); F. Vitoux, *Céline, a Biography*, trans. Jesse Browner (New York, 1992).

P. C. F. Bankwitz

CENTRE DE DOCUMENTATION JUIVE CONTEMPORAINE (CDJC), located at the site of the Mémorial du Martyr Juif Inconnu, 17 rue Geoffroy l'Asnier in the fourth *arrondissement* of Paris, is one of the most important sources of information about the **Holocaust** and the persecution of **Jews** in France and Europe.

Begun by Isaac Schneersohn, a French Jew of Russian ancestry, together with a group of Jewish leaders meeting in Grenoble in April 1943, the CDJC was, from its inception, devoted to documenting persecution of the Jews by both **Vichy** and the Germans. In view of holding the perpetrators accountable, it began establishing, as completely and authoritatively as possible, a record of crimes committed against the Jews. Forced to go underground in September 1943, when the Germans swept into the **zone** of southern France formerly occupied by the Italians, the CDJC paid a heavy tribute, eventually losing five of its founding members (René Hirschler, Raymond-Raoul Lambert, Léonce Bernheim, Léo Glaeser, and Nahum Herman) to Nazi repression.

Transferred to Paris after the **liberation**, the center set about the task of bringing a unified, systematic classification to the archives with which it was entrusted: these included the files of the **Commissariat Général aux Questions**

Juives, the *Institut d'Études Juives*, the German Embassy, German Military Administration in France, and the anti-Jewish Gestapo. To these were later added the archives of the International Military Tribunal at Nuremberg, the original lists of deportees on the trains from France, and the court records of war crimes trials having taken place in France and Germany. The CDJC's archival holdings have played a prominent role in the prosecution of war criminals, notably in the trials of Adolf Eichmann and Klaus **Barbie.** The CDJC also houses a library and publishes the journal *Le Monde Juif.*

A. Kaspi, "Le Centre de Documentation Juive Contemporaine," *Revue d'Histoire Moderne et Contemporaine* (April–June 1976): 305–11; M. Mazor, "Centre de Documentation Juive Contemporaine, Paris," in I. Schneersohn, ed., *D'Auschwitz à Israël: Vingt ans après la libération* (Paris, 1968), 458–69; I. Schneersohn, "Avant-Propos," in *D'Auschwitz a Israël* (*Mémoire*, CDJC brochure, 1993), 7–10.

N. Bracher

CENTRE D'INFORMATION INTERPROFESSIONELLE (CII), established on 30 April 1941, was designed to provide information for the **Comités d'organisation** and for the various **Vichy** supply organizations and to serve as liaison between these bodies. Attached to the CII was a consultative committee headed by Gérard Bardet (an **industrialist** and member of the X-crise discussion circle).

The CII epitomized many of the contradictions in Vichy industrial organization. It inherited the funds of the prewar employers' organization, and many employers clearly regarded it as a successor to this body. But the CII was also designed to devise Vichy's new economic order. It produced reports on planning and the control of profits; it established a school of professional organization to preach new attitudes. Some members of the CII, such as Jules Verger, were convinced Vichy supporters, but another member de Tavernost was to become an active opponent of Vichy. Conflict between the CII and the Vichy government eventually led to the dissolution of the CII's consultative committee. A new body, the Conseil Supérieur de l'Économie Industrielle et Commerciale (CSEIC), replaced the consultative committee and inherited most of its personnel. However, there was now a clear distinction between the CSEIC, which participated in the planning of Vichy's economic order, and the CII, which represented employers, often in opposition to Vichy policy.

R. Vinen, *The Politics of French Business 1936–1945* (Cambridge, U.K., 1991).

R. C. Vinen

CEUX DE LA LIBÉRATION (CDLL) was one of the main **Resistance** movements of the northern **zone**, founded in August 1940 in a military milieu, and a member of the **Conseil National de la Résistance (CNR)**. From March 1944 to the **liberation**, it was called Ceux de la Libération-Vengeance (CDLV).

The founder of CDLL was Maurice Ripoche, a manufacturer and veteran fighter pilot of World War I. The CDLL was the most **right-wing** movement represented in the CNR. Its founders were close to interwar **Parti Social Français (PSF)** circles. Although in October 1940 its first manifesto called for a struggle for liberation, it also intended to suppress representative democracy in a future France and to "get rid . . . of the stateless **Jews** and the pitiless international financiers and gangsters." This stance was in obvious contradiction to a fight against a racist dictatorship; it hence became unsustainable and rapidly disappeared.

Early on, the movement recruited its members among reserve officers. It gathered military intelligence, helped allied aviators and resisters escape through **Spain** and **Switzerland**, and aided **Service du Travail Obligatoire** evaders. The Vengeance membership brought to the CDLL expertise in wiretapping into the German communications network. The efficiency of the movement resulted from the competence of its members and its links with the Air Force Intelligence Service in **Vichy**, which was in touch with the **British** Intelligence Service. After the invasion of the southern **zone**, the CDLL joined **Fighting France**. By the end of the war, the movement published an underground paper, *Ceux de la Libération*, which has been called *La France libre* since May 1944.

The CDLL had seven successive leaders. All were arrested except the last, André Mutter, a lawyer and a former member of the PSF, who took the reins in February 1944. A right-wing deputy after the war, Mutter served as minister twice during the Fourth **Republic**.

J. Ballet, "Ceux de la Libération" (Paris, undated); D. Cordier, *Jean Moulin, l'inconnu du Panthéon*, 3 vols. (Paris, 1989–1993); H. Noguères, *Histoire de la Résistance en France*, 5 vols. (Paris, 1967–1981).

C. Andrieu

CEUX DE LA RÉSISTANCE (CDLR) was one of the main **Resistance** movements of the northern **zone**, founded in 1942, a member of the **Conseil National de la Résistance (CNR)**. It was first called the *Organisation nationale de la Résistance*, but in January 1943, in order to avoid confusion with the **CNR**, it was changed to the CDLR.

The CDLR was created by Jacques Lecompte-Boinet, a municipal officer of Paris and graduate of the Institute of Political Studies. He began by gathering the remains of the former "Guédon group," which had been destroyed by the Germans. Focusing on intelligence service, armed struggle, and helping Allied aviators who had landed in occupied France, the CDLR covered northern France from **Normandy** to Franche-Comté. At the insistence of General **de Gaulle's** representatives and in order to be included in the CNR, the CDLR set up a civil service in addition to its military structure. Despite the CNR affiliation, the *Bulletin de Ceux de la Résistance*, started in the spring of 1943, remained an internal CDLR news sheet.

In addition to its participation in the CNR, CDLR was a member of the Comité d'action de la Résistance, as a representative of the noncommunist movements of the northern **zone**. Its delegate, Jean de Vogüé, was an **indus-**

trialist, born of one of the "200 families," supposedly the richest families in France. A partisan of a general uprising against the occupants, de Vogüé was closer to the **communist** Pierre **Villon** than to the leadership of his own movement.

Socially and politically, the CDLR was heterogeneous. Although its founders came from the conservative Paris bourgeoisie, three-quarters of the members lived in the provinces. Léo Hamon, who represented the movement in the Comité Parisien de Libération, called himself a "**left-wing** nationalist." The movement did not survive after the **liberation**.

G. Grandval and A. J. Collin, *Libération de l'Est de la France* (Paris, 1974); M. Granet, *Ceux de la Libération* (Paris, 1964); L. Hamon, *Vivre ses choix* (Paris, 1991); J. Lecompte-Boinet, "Journal 1939–1946" (Archives Nationales, Paris).

C. Andrieu

CHABAN-DELMAS, JACQUES (1915–), politician, sportsman, and Gaullist **Resistance** leader. Born into a middle-class family, Jacques Delmas entered journalism in the 1930s while pursuing both a law degree and courses at the École Libre des Sciences Politiques, receiving degrees in law and from Sciences Po in 1938. Mobilized as a lieutenant, he served along the Italian front in 1939–1940. After the **armistice** he considered joining the **Free French** but was urged to remain in France and establish contacts with emerging Resistance groups. Delmas, who assumed the code name "Chaban," passed examinations for the position of inspector in the Finance Ministry. This position enabled him to travel and extend his Resistance contacts, and he provided Colonel **Passy's Bureau Central de Renseignements et d'Action (BCRA)** in London with intelligence information.

With the formation of the **Conseil National de la Résistance (CNR),** Chaban-Delmas became General **de Gaulle's** national military representative, with the assignment of assuring Gaullist control over the military arm of the Resistance. As the Allies approached **Paris**, the Resistance rose up within the city. Chaban-Delmas feared that a premature uprising would lead to a bloodbath and destruction of the city, as was happening in Warsaw. He left for London, where he tried unsuccessfully to persuade the Allies not to bypass Paris. Upon his return Chaban-Delmas discovered that an uneasy truce had been established. When General **Leclerc's** armored division arrived to accept the surrender of the city from General Dietrich von Choltitz, Chaban-Delmas persuaded Leclerc to have Henri Rol-Tanguy, head of the Parisian FFI, sign for the Resistance, an action that both acknowledged the Resistance and assured Gaullist control of the **Provisional Government**. After the war Chaban-Delmas established a political fiefdom in Bordeaux that became the foundation for a distinguished political career.

†J. Chaban-Delmas, *L'ardeur* (Paris, 1975); J. Chaban-Delmas, *Mémoires pour demain* (Paris, 1997); Patrick Chastenet and Philippe Chastenet, *Chaban* (Paris, 1991); G. Claisse, *Jacques Chaban-Delmas* (Paris, 1974).

K. Munholland

"CHANT DES PARTISANS" (Song of the Partisans), also known as "Le Chant de la Libération" (The Song of the **Liberation**) or "Ami, entends-tu" (Friend, Do You Hear), has become the anthem of the **Resistance**, still sung at commemorative occasions. It is now part of the standard repertoire of French folk songs.

The music, written by Anna Marly, was first heard on the French program of the **BBC**, *Honneur et Patrie*, in May 1943, when the opening notes became the program's signature tune. The words, written by Maurice Druon and Joseph Kessel, were first published in the clandestine journal *Cahiers de la Libération* later in 1943.

The dark tune and brooding words both captured the atmosphere of occupied France and expressed the hopes of resisters for liberation. After the whistled introduction, the words are spoken in the manner of partisans passing information, rather than sung. The 16 short verses call on partisans, workers, and peasants to make the enemy pay for the tears he has brought the country. Asked first if they have seen the enemy's shadow over the land, they are then asked to leave the mines and hills, to bring out their rifles, knives, and dynamite, and to rescue their brothers from prison. The narrator assures his listening friend that, pushed by hatred and by hunger, the French do not dream, as in some countries, but march and kill. In France, one knows that if he falls, another will emerge from the shadows to take his place. The chant ends with the stirring promise that Liberty hears their whistle in the night.

N. Dompnier, *Vichy à travers chants* (Paris, 1996); A. Gillois, *Histoire secrète des Français à Londres, 1940–44* (Paris, 1973); P. Seghers, *La Résistance et ses poètes, France 1940–45* (Paris, 1974).

M. Koreman

CHANTIERS DE LA JEUNESSE (Youth Workshops) was a quasi-military, mass association for young men that embodied the ideological and functional ambitions of Marshal **Pétain's National Revolution**.

Organized under the governmental authority of the *Secrétariat général à la Jeunesse* (SGJ, Secretariat of Youth) the Chantiers, under the supervision of General Joseph **de La Porte du Theil**, served three distinct goals. As an obligatory association of young men aged 20, called up in uniform for eight months, the primary goal of the Chantiers was to form future soldiers in civil service. In the absence of a viable **army**, many viewed the Chantiers as a place to cultivate soldiers who might one day achieve France's revenge. A second goal of the Chantiers was to labor on public works projects, including clearing forests, building infrastructure, and even harvesting crops. The third goal of the Chantiers was to train and discipline young men to serve and support the National Revolution. Gathered in camps in the countryside in Boy Scout style, the young men were indoctrinated in the "return to the soil" ethos of **Vichy**. The SGJ hoped that the Chantiers would help revitalize tradition and morality, training youth in French patrimony and Christianity.

The secretary-general of Youth also supervised various other voluntary youth organizations that competed for the affiliation of French youth, but only the Chantiers de la Jeunesse was obligatory. As a result, it outlasted the voluntary youth organizations. By 1944, of the youth organizations, only the Chantiers endured with their "unconditional obedience" to Marshal Pétain. Suspecting **Resistance** activity among the Chantiers, however, German authorities dissolved the organization in May 1944.

B. Comte, "Les Organisations de Jeunesse," in J.-P. Azéma and F. Bédarida, eds., *Vichy et les Français* (Paris, 1992), 409–21; W. D. Halls, *The Youth of Vichy France* (Oxford, 1988); R. Hervet, *Les Chantiers de la Jeunesse* (Paris, 1962); J. de La Porte du Theil, *Les Chantiers de la Jeunesse ont deux ans* (Paris, 1942).

N. Dombrowski

CHATEAU, RENÉ (1906–1970), philosopher, journalist, and politician who collaborated with Marcel **Déat** during the Occupation. A native of the Charente department, the young Chateau showed a strong aptitude for philosophy, which he studied at the École normale supérieure. After passing his *agrégation* in 1930, Chateau entered the teaching profession. His pacifist sentiments led him to join the Ligue des droits de l'homme (League of the Rights of Man), and he became a member of its central committee. In 1936 Chateau was elected to the Chamber of Deputies as a candidate of the Parti Radical-Socialiste Camille Pelletan. Four years later, after the fall of France, he voted with the majority to invest Marshal **Pétain** with supreme power.

During the Occupation, Chateau worked closely with his fellow philosopher and *normalien* Marcel Déat to form a single political party, the **Rassemblement National Populaire (RNP)**. He also contributed to Déat's *L'Œuvre* and then to *La France Socialiste*, a newspaper devoted to a socialism based on "national community" and pacifist and secular ideals, as well as opposition to the **Vichy** government. By 1943, however, Chateau and Déat quarreled over the formation of party militias and ideology. Expelled from the RNP, Chateau was imprisoned by the Germans but eventually released.

With the **liberation** in 1944, Chateau was arrested and imprisoned again, this time charged with **collaboration**. He managed to escape serious punishment for his wartime activities. Under a pseudonym he published a harrowing account of his second incarceration. He soon returned to teaching and contributed to *Paroles françaises*, which defended victims of the postwar **purges**.

J.-P. Abel [René Chateau], *L'age de Caïn* (Paris, 1947); R. Handourtzel and C. Buffet, *La Collaboration . . . à gauche aussi* (Paris, 1989).

J. Friguglietti

CHÂTEAUBRIANT, ALPHONSE DE (1877–1951), was the founder and director of the **collaborationist Paris** weekly newspaper *La Gerbe*, and founder of the **Groupe Collaboration**, a generally upper-class organization whose aim was to forward cultural collaboration between France and Germany. Condemned to death in absentia in 1948, Châteaubriant died in exile in Austria in 1951, where he had been living under the pseudonym "Dr. Alfred Wolf" since 1945.

A native of Brittany, Châteaubriant launched his literary career with a series of novels celebrating the beauties of his region and the rustic virtues of its inhabitants. Novels such as *Monsieur de Lourdines* (1911), *La Brière* (1923), and *La Réponse du Seigneur* (1933) also champion rigid social hierarchies and an exalted Catholicism tinged with mysticism. These tendencies, combined with strong anti**communist** sentiments expressed in his notebooks of the interwar period, prepared the ground for a conversion to Nazism. Following a lengthy trip to Germany in 1936, Châteaubriant published an uncritical celebration of **Hitler** and Nazi Germany entitled *La Gerbe des forces* (1937), in which, among other absurdities, he argued that Hitler was doing God's work on earth. Although *La Gerbe des forces* earned sharp criticism even from fellow pro-**fascists**, including Robert **Brasillach**, in 1940 it earned the author the German financial and logistical support to launch *La Gerbe*.

From its first issue on 11 July 1940, *La Gerbe* attracted collaborationist luminaries from the worlds of politics as well as the arts, including Fernand **de Brinon**, Pierre **Drieu la Rochelle**, Louis-Ferdinand **Céline**, Henry **de Montherlant**, Jean **Giono**, and many others. Although not known subsequently as fervent collaborationists, other artists, writers, and directors who contributed to the newspaper included Colette, Jean Anouilh, Jean **Cocteau**, Charles Dullin, and Gaston Baty.

*K. Chadwick, "Alphonse de Châteaubriant, Collaborator on Retrial: Un Non-lieu individuel d'une portée nationale," *FHS* 18 (Fall 1994): 1057–82; R. J. Golsan, "Ideology, Cultural Politics, and Literary Collaboration at *La Gerbe*," *Journal of European Studies* 23 (parts 1 and 2): 89 and 90 (March–June 1993): 27–47; B. M. Gordon, *Collaborationism in France during the Second World War* (Ithaca, NY, 1980); L.-A. Maugendre, *Alphonse de Châteaubriant 1877–1951* (Paris, 1977).

R. J. Golsan

CHEVALIER, JACQUES (1882–1962), was a Catholic philosopher who, as minister for **education** under **Vichy**, sought to reintroduce religion into the state school system.

After studying and teaching philosophy in France and **Britain**, Chevalier was mobilized in 1914, serving as an interpreter for the British army and developing a long-lasting friendship with Philippe **Pétain**. Between the wars, as professor and dean at Grenoble **University**, he became an influential exponent of Henri Bergson's philosophy, viewed as an approach to Christianity.

After the June 1940 **armistice** Chevalier became the senior civil servant (general secretary) at the Ministry of Education. In December 1940 the British foreign secretary Lord Halifax, an old friend, persuaded him to broker negotiations with Pétain on a secret **Anglo**-French understanding, which proved inconclusive. Pétain appointed him to the cabinet on the fall of **Laval**, 13 December 1940, as minister for education, health, and the **family**.

As general secretary and minister, Chevalier developed vigorous measures to give state aid to private **Catholic** schools and to reintroduce religious teaching in state schools. He closed teacher training colleges, noted for their attachment to nonreligious education (*laïcité*), and dismissed over 1,000 teachers accused of being **Freemasons**. At the same time he resisted German demands to hand over French teachers in annexed **Alsace** and **Lorraine**.

In February 1941 Admiral **Darlan** transferred the Education Ministry to Jérôme Carcopino, who canceled the more controversial pro-clerical measures. Chevalier lost his remaining cabinet position in a further reshuffle some weeks later and returned to his university post at Grenoble. Arrested at the **liberation**, he was tried at the **Haute Cour de Justice** in March 1946 and sentenced to 20 years' imprisonment with hard labor. He was released in 1947 and devoted his remaining years to writing a scholarly *Histoire de la pensée* (1955–1961).

J. Duquesne, *Les catholiques français sous l'occupation* (Paris, 1966).

M. Kelly

CHEVALIER, MAURICE (1888–1971), French music hall artist, born in the working-class Paris quarter of Menilmontant. Achieved fame in Europe and the **United States** through unfailing public shows of optimism and extraordinary stage presence.

Chevalier was awarded the Croix de guerre for action during World War I and remained a fierce defender of Marshal **Pétain** for the rest of his life. Chevalier's attitude during the Occupation has been judged ambivalent. Although he claimed no political affiliation and did not make pro-German or anti-Semitic declarations, he supported the **Vichy** government throughout the Occupation, never acknowledging Pétain's role in its anti-**Jewish** measures.

According to his most recent biographer, Edward Behr, Chevalier's active participation in the entertainment **industry** was instrumental in the return to normalcy sought after 1940 by the Vichy government and the Nazis. Flattered by his immense success throughout defeated France, Chevalier was able to enjoy a high lifestyle unavailable to most people in occupied France. After 1941, he appeared at the Casino de Paris, where the audience was mostly German and **collaborationist**. Much publicized in the collaborationist press, Chevalier allowed his songs to be broadcast on German-controlled **Radio-Paris**, attended German-organized events, and toured the entire country as well as French **prison** camps in Germany.

In the months preceding the **liberation**, Chevalier was repeatedly denounced as a collaborator by the **Free French** press and sentenced to death in absentia by the Free French Court in Algiers. He was arrested after the liberation in 1944 but was exonerated and enjoyed many more years of glory. Chevalier was pictured as a kind of prototypical collaborator in Marcel Ophuls' film **The Sorrow and the Pity** in 1971.

*E. Behr, *The Good Frenchman* (New York, 1993); D. Bret, *Maurice Chevalier: Up on Top of a Rainbow* (London, 1992); M. Chevalier, *Les Pensées de Momo* (Paris, 1970).
                                                                    M. Guyot-Bender

CINEMA IN OCCUPIED FRANCE. The 220 full-length fiction films made during the Occupation did not present any of the great themes of **Paris press** or **Radio-Paris** propaganda. The single enemy, whether **Jew**, Englishman, **Freemason**, or **communist**, is missing from the scenarios. Anti-Semitic, Anglophobic, **anti-Masonic**, and anti-communist discourse, however, was present in interwar cinema. These unifying themes were to disappear from the screen as soon as they became the components of the political doctrine of **Vichy** and of antinationalist (**collaborationist**) groups. The tone of the Occupation-era film production made little reference to extremist ideology.

Films avoided the reality of the era because the public wanted to escape it. Directors turned out comedies and period films with lavish costumes and reproduced the **American** styles popular during the interwar years (musical comedies and grade B police thrillers). In all, only 10 films made explicit reference to the war and Occupation. Does this mean that the productions ignored reality? Hardly—behind the laughter and the escapism the reality of contemporary life is evident. Despite the many filmmakers (some 50 producers and 65 directors), the films are homogeneous in form and content, evoking a solidly conservative France. The atmosphere of Vichy shows through, but the world represented under Vichy was present already in films before 1940. Even if some of the values of Vichy were present in interwar films, however, the advent of the regime brought a wave of some 1,300 new films. Beginning in June 1940, Vichy values were the only ones shown. However, choices were made, and the most odious of them—**anti-Semitic** and anti-Masonic, for example—disappeared.

Analyses of film narratives reveal recurring itineraries or paths. The search by the protagonist (a couple, group, or family) expresses a certain logic, emphasizing the dominant values without which the established order cannot be perpetuated: community, struggle, and success. From these values emerges a message that nothing is won in advance and that one must earn one's good fortune. Yet within what kind of society? A society in which the bourgeoisie is ubiquitous—in the countryside as in Paris. The film narratives feature a social critique when they represent the Third **Republic's** ruling elite, symbolized in the defense of Maître Loursat (Raimu) in Henri Decoin's *Les Inconnus dans la maison*. It is a social critique that protects the existing order and institutions when the situation calls for creating a new world. This perspective reflects the aspirations of a France that sees its future in the continuity of economic and political power after having purged itself of certain pre-1940 moral values. Essentially, the couple, generally between ages 20 and 30, and the bourgeois family are the foundations of this society in formation, where big business is seldom shown, replaced instead by technocrats and the liberal professions as town notables. This cinematic narrative form also features a Catholic bourgeoisie, subject to authority personified by the father or the leader (*chef*), who thinks for the others and who upholds a sense of tradition. When this authority figure speaks, he exalts union in Jacques Daniel-Norman's *La Loi du printemps*, the redemptive earth in Émile Couzinet's *Andorra*, victory over oneself in Louis Daquin's *Premier de cordée*, the leader in Léo Joannon's *Carrefour des enfants perdus*, family honor in Jean Dréville's *Les Roquillard*, love for others in André Hugon's *Le Chant de l'exilé*, nationalism in the Christian-Jaque film *La Symphonie fantastique*, and solidarity in Louis Daquin's *Nous les gosses*.

The evolution of this society is through the child, who is the bearer of the future, even if, at given moments, as depicted in certain narratives, he is also the source of frustrating problems, as in *Monsieur des Lourdines* by Pierre de Hérain, or if he defies his parents, as in *Mariage de chiffon* by Claude Autant-Lara.

The woman is confined within a well-defined role. As ever, there is a vamp; three heroines play the roles of beauties, Ginette Leclerc in Henri-Georges Clouzot's *Le Corbeau* and Jacques Houssin's *Le Mistral*; Mireille Balin in Jacques Becker's *Dernier Atout*; and Viviane Romance in Abel Gance's *La Vénus aveugle*. **Women** of the demimonde in fashionable society are themes in Jacques de Baroncelli's *La Duchesse de Langeais* and Maurice Tourneur's *Mam'zelle Bonaparte*. However, the woman is more generally synonymous with duty and sacrifice, as in Jean Stelli's *Le Voile bleu*. Above all, she represents mother.

Nevertheless, beginning in 1941, a new image of the family began to crystallize, in which sincere and fecund love dominate, and so much the worse if it resulted in a deviation from habitual norms. Films portray the recognition of the "illegitimate child" and the rehabilitation of the unmarried mother. The latter, temporarily marginalized by society, ends up by reintegrating into society and marrying, as in Marcel Pagnol's *La Fille du puisatier* and Émile Couzinet's *Andorra*. The family is an indispensable unit, without which the child cannot receive a complete **education**. The films, however, never preach in favor of large families. If, in a given narrative, the father or mother is left alone with the children, as in *Les Ailes Blanches* by Robert Péguy, the situation turns out to be temporary.

This society is not disturbed by class struggle. Before 1940, the worker was portrayed as practically mute, solitary, and certainly not a union member. Beginning in 1941, he might protest strongly against his working conditions, as in André Cayatte's *Au Bonheur des dames*, but after a period of agitation, everything returns to order and perfect harmony based on the **Labor Charter**. If the boss behaves in a despotic manner with respect to his workers—showing the working world is, however, the exception; worker–boss relations are replaced by those of servant–master—the boss' attitude is generally criticized by the internal logic of the film. Mean-spirited employers will have no place in the new society depicted at the end of the story, as in Jacques Becker's *Goupi Mains Rouges*.

The homogeneity of the Occupation cinema can be fully explained neither by state censorship directives nor by self-censure on the part of the filmmakers. It was produced, instead, by consensus. With the **liberation**, directors agreed unanimously that the Occupation years had been a golden age for French cinema. They cited the benefits of legislation that did away with the anarchy of the 1930s in the profession and that, by banning **Anglo-American** films, suppressed competition. At the same time, they were not responsible for the persecutions and purges of 1940, due essentially to external forces. Doesn't this view recognize, however, that the film world accommodated itself quite well to the political circumstances of the Occupation?

*†J.-P. Maghit, *Le Cinéma français sous l'Occupation* (Paris, 1994); J.-P. Bertin-Maghit, *Le Cinéma sous l'Occupation* (Paris, 1989); P. Darman, *Le Monde du Cinéma sous l'Occupation* (Paris, 1997); F. Garçon, *De Blum à Pétain* (Paris, 1984); P. Léglise, *Histoire de la politique du cinéma français entre deux Républiques, 1940–1946* (Paris, 1977).

J.-P. Bertin-Maghit

CINEMA, POSTWAR, RELATING TO OCCUPIED FRANCE. Since 1945, some 250 French films have dealt with the war and the Occupation. In studying these films, vectors of memory, the historian can create a map of representations and reconstruct the memory of one of the cruelest of the contemporary Franco-French wars. Five distinct periods emerge.

From 1944 through 1946, a myth was formed. All the films, whether made by the Service Cinématographique aux Armées (SCA) (**Army** Film Service) or by the Comité de Libération du Cinéma Français (CLCF) (**liberation** Committee for French Film) and its production cooperative or whether or not made commercially, offer the same image: a France that is entirely resistant. *La Bataille du rail* by René Clément in 1945 is symbolic of this heroic behavior. In this imagery, popular desire and the will of the political authorities seem to converge; the specificity of **Vichy** is not addressed, thereby combining the two Gaullist concepts of ''**Republican** continuity'' and ''the Thirty Years' War,'' seeing World War II as an extension of the 1914 conflict. The focus on the *soldats de l'ombre* (soldiers of the shadows; sometimes called soldiers of the night), the **Resistance** fighters, shows a movement linked to London but willfully ignores the internecine struggles of Gaullists and **communists**. The entire country is seen at war, mobilized against the German, the hereditary enemy, except for a few collaborating traitors—and the genocide is hidden. If offers an essentially patriotic view, taking up the challenge of reconstruction and allowing an avoidance of questions of national identity.

From 1947 through 1957, the facade of myth cracks. Through their fictional portrayals, Sacha **Guitry**, Claude Autant-Lara, and Henri-Georges Clouzot, themselves victims of the postwar **purges**, express their bitterness regarding the excesses of the purges or legitimate the attitude of those who, unreflectingly, had figured out how to profit from the Occupation. This cinema shows a wait-

and-see France anxious about daily life and skeptical, as in *Nous sommes tous les assassins* by André Cayatte, 1951, and, as in Autant-Lara's *La Traversée de Paris*, 1956, recalling the less glorious aspects of the Occupation, such as the **black market**. Black legend comes to replace heroic legend. The specificity of racial **deportation** is still obscured. The films do not establish any distinction between a **concentration camp** and an extermination camp. *Nuit et Brouillard* (**Night and Fog**) by Alain Resnais in 1956 shares the characteristics of this period.

From 1958 through 1969, a Gaullist myth grew. While a minority antiheroic cinema continued to explore the dark regions of the past to illuminate the new confrontations of the Algerian war, as in Jean Dewever's *Les Honneurs de la guerre*, 1961, the dominant cinema projected an "ecumenical Gaullism," evoking the new politics of memory that the general embodied after his return to power in 1958. This perspective glorified the "*armée de l'ombre*," extolled in André **Malraux's** speech on the occasion of the transfer of Jean **Moulin's** ashes to the Panthéon in 1964. The cinema of these years—for example, *Babette s'en va-t-en guerre* by Christian-Jaque in 1959 and *Paris brûle-t-il?* by René Clément in 1967, focusing on the Resistance hero and on the general—deals more with celebrations than with analyses. *L'Armée des Ombres*, by Jean-Pierre Melville in 1969, concludes this period and marks a turning point. Admittedly, the author pays personal homage to several historical figures, but the film places more emphasis on the internal contradictions of the characters, Philippe Gerbier, Mathilde, and Luc Jardie, who in the end are victims of their primordial and sentimental drives. As to the evocation of the genocide, it appears together with the increasingly awakening **Jewish** memory that occurs throughout the 1960s. *L'Enclos*, by Armand Gatti (1961), is the first French work of **fiction** to address the topic.

From 1969 through 1974 the myth takes a beating. The arrival of a new political class, less closely linked to the Resistance, the film *Le Chagrin et la Pitié* (The **Sorrow and the Pity**) by Marcel Ophuls (1969), and Anglophone historical research that proposes a new reading of Vichy and the Occupation with *Vichy France* by Robert O. Paxton in 1973 provoke a true revolution, rejecting the then-current conformism in historical perspective and removing the taboos that had sustained the mythology of Gaullism. Ophuls' film expresses a real reversal of perspective. He depicts a Vichy resulting from the defeat and the Occupation and equally from the political and ideological history of France. He brings to light a specifically French **anti-Semitism** and raises questions relating to choice and engagement, a problem central to the 1974 film of Louis Malle, *Lacombe Lucien*. The way is open for a cinema that contradicts accepted ideas. *Souvenirs d'en France* by André Téchiné in 1975 denounces a Gaullism that had permitted the artificial maintenance of a form of capitalism, entirely illusory and ill adapted to international competition. *L'affiche rouge* by Franck Cassenti in 1976 retraces the history of the Manouchian group, composed, in large part, of immigrant Resistance members. Through their story, the film poses the fundamental question of representation in history. *Les Guichets du Louvre* by Michel Mitrani in 1974 and *Un sac de billes* by Jacques Doillon in 1975 evoke the persecution of the Jews.

Since the 1980s, despite the emotion aroused by the Klaus **Barbie**, René **Bousquet**, and Paul **Touvier** affairs, one sees a trivialization in the evocation of history, a virtual absence of analysis—with the exception of Jean Chérasse's *La Prise du pouvoir de Philippe Pétain* of 1979—along with humanistic personal memoirs and expiatory images of the national bad conscience, as in *Shoa* by Claude Lanzmann in 1985 and *Au revoir les enfants* by Malle in 1987; iconoclastic parody or anarchist pamphleteering that delegitimates all the actors in the conflict, as in *Papy fait la résistance* by Jean-Marie Poiré in 1982 and *Uranus* by Claude Berri in 1991; a more consensual viewpoint in *Le Dernier Métro* by François Truffaut in 1980; and, finally, a return to conformity in the evocation of the Resistance in *Boulevard des Hirondelles* by Josée Yanne in 1992.

The cinematic representations of the dark years of the Occupation have carefully avoided tackling the question of Vichy ideology and of the role of Marshal **Pétain**. Two films in close succession, however, defied the stereotype: *L'Œil de Vichy* by Claude Chabrol and *Pétain* by Jean Marbeuf. With *L'Œil de Vichy*, Chabrol wanted to unmask the lies told by the daily newspapers of a regime that extolled the unity of all the French around the marshal and the **National Revolution**. *Pétain*, a piece of fiction adapted from Marc Ferro's book, intertwines a history seen from on high, from the experience of statesmen, with another history, this one seen from below, which shows the anonymous French. Independently of the genres, of the positions taken, of the successes or failures, for the first time, with these films, cinema came to address the role of Vichy based on historical analysis rather than political pamphlet.

J.-P. Bertin-Maghit, J.-M. Andrault, and G. Vincent, "Le Cinéma Français et la Seconde Guerre mondiale," *La Revue du cinéma, Image et son* 378 (December 1983): 70–111; H. Rousso, *The Vichy Syndrome, History and Memory in France since 1944*, trans. A. Goldhammer (Cambridge, MA, 1991 [original French ed. 1987]); A. Wieviorka, *Déportation et génocide* (Paris, 1992).

J.-P. Bertin-Maghit

CLAUDE, GEORGES (1870–1960), scientist, member of the Académie des sciences and Alphonse **de Châteaubriant's Groupe Collaboration**, and advocate of close Franco–German ties.

Claude was born in Paris and studied at the École de physique et de chimie. He conducted research during World War I on liquid chlorine and was awarded the Legion of Honor in 1915. In 1926 he was elected to the Académie des sciences. Claude did research on natural thermal energy and invented liquid air.

After World War I Claude ran unsuccessfully for the National Assembly. He joined **Action Française** and turned his political efforts to a justification of **fascist** expansionism, especially opposing sanctions against **Italy** after the invasion of Ethiopia. In 1940, Claude became a vocal supporter of Franco-German **collaboration** and spoke frequently on **Radio-Paris**. He often delivered three lectures and personally paid for their publication: *"De l'hostilité a la collaboration"* (From Hostility to Collaboration), *"De l'Europe nouvelle"* (On the New Europe), and *"Français, il faut comprendre"* (French, You Must Understand).

Claude was arrested on 17 August 1944 and tried the following year. He was convicted of collaboration with the enemy and treason but was acquitted of the accusation that he had turned over secrets to the Germans, enabling them to build the V1 "buzz bomb" rocket. He was condemned to life imprisonment and national disgrace and removed from the rolls of the Legion of Honor. A petition in his favor was signed by members of the Académie des sciences, and he was released from prison on 30 December 1949. He spent the remainder of his life doing research on thermal energy and on the cultivation of wheat.

M. Dank, *The French against the French: Collaboration and Resistance* (Philadelphia, 1974); Y. Durand, *La France dans la deuxième guerre mondiale, 1939–1945* (Paris, 1989); P. Kingston, "The Ideologists," in G. Hirschfeld and P. Marsh, eds., *Collaboration in France* (Oxford, 1989), 47–71; G. Ragache and J.-R. Ragache, *La vie quotidienne des écrivains et des artistes sous l'occupation, 1940–1944* (Paris, 1988).

M. L. Berkvam

CLAUDEL, PAUL (1868–1955), playwright, poet, essayist. Considered the major Catholic dramatist of his time, Claudel developed a poetic, deeply spiritual **theater** that focuses on the struggle between God and humanity.

Born in Villeneuve-sur-Fèure, he attended the Lycée Louis-le-Grand in Paris. Profoundly influenced by the symbolist poets, he studied for the diplomatic service while torn by spiritual conflict. A mystical experience at Notre Dame in 1886 precipitated his conversion to Catholicism in 1890, which influenced his career as diplomat (1893–1935) and writer. After considering monastic life, Claudel directed his energies into playwriting. His plays, complex and long, often panoramic in scope, were produced only many years after publication.

During the Occupation, Jean-Louis Barrault approached Claudel for permission to perform *Le Soulier de Satin* (written 1929). Claudel reluctantly agreed to work with Barrault on cutting the mammoth script. Its premiere at the *Comédie Française* in 1943 became the period's major theatrical event. In spite of shortages of electricity and material for props, the innovative production proved extremely popular. German authorities, who had combed the script but found nothing objectionable, were suspicious of the enthusiasm that the production generated and eventually closed it. The Occupation saw revivals of Claudel's *L'Annonce Fait à Marie* in **Paris** (1941–1942) and, thanks to Louis Jouvet's touring company, throughout Latin America (1941–1945) and also of the opera *Jeanne au bûcher*, for which Claudel wrote the libretto for Arthur Honegger's music.

Although Claudel's conservative sympathies prompted him to write "Ode au

Maréchal,'' celebrating Philippe **Pétain**, his work, especially as staged by Barrault, inspired admiration across the political spectrum. His postwar career, which peaked with Barrault's premiere of *Partage du Midi* (written 1905; performed 1948), enhanced Claudel's reputation as a brilliant—and eminently performable—dramatist.

*L. Chaigne, *Paul Claudel, The Man and the Mystic* (Westport, CT, 1978); B. Knapp, *Paul Claudel* (New York, 1982); P.-A. Le Sort, *Paul Claudel par lui-même* (Paris, 1963); M. Ryan, *Introduction to Paul Claudel* (Cork, 1951).

K. Krauss

COCTEAU, JEAN (1889–1963), artist, playwright, poet, filmmaker. Despite his notoriety as both a homosexual and drug user, which set French **fascists** against him, Cocteau survived the Occupation thanks to his many connections.

Born in Maisons-Lafitte, Cocteau moved with his family to Paris in 1899, where he attended the Lycée Condorcet. He volunteered as an ambulance driver during the First World War and fraternized in Montparnasse with painters, composers, and poets, including Guillaume Apollinaire, whose passion for surrealism he shared. After the war, Cocteau wrote the themes for two innovative ballets. His affair with novelist Raymond Radiguet and Radiguet's early death in 1923 led him back to opium, to which he had previously been addicted. Along with writing poetry, the memoir *Opium* (1929), and fiction, notably *Thomas l'imposteur* (1922) and *Les enfants terribles* (1929), Cocteau worked prolifically as a playwright, completing *Orphée* (1926), *La Machine Infernale* (1934), and *Les Parents Terribles* (1938), and directed the film *Le Sang d'un Poète* (1931). His relationship with actor Jean Marais, which lasted until Cocteau's death, began in 1937.

As France neared defeat in 1940, Cocteau fled to Perpignan, returning with a new script, *La Machine à écrire*. Its debut (1941) caused a riot, due more to Cocteau's reputation than the play, and it and *Les Parents Terribles* were banned. His *Renaud et Armide* (1943), written for the *Comédie Française*, was safer and thus praised, as was his screenplay for the film *L'Éternel Retour* (1943), which starred Marais. Cocteau walked a precarious tightrope, maintaining relations with the occupiers as well as with his avant-garde friends. He was photographed attending Arno **Breker's** opening at l'Orangerie but petitioned Otto **Abetz** to save **Jewish** poet Max Jacob from Drancy. One of Cocteau's major discoveries during the Occupation was the writer Jean Genet.

After the **liberation**, Cocteau was attacked in print but cleared of **collaboration**. His literary, artistic, and theatrical activities continued while his career in **cinema** made him world-famous.

D. Chaperon, *Jean Cocteau: La Chute des Anges* (Lille, 1990); J. Cocteau, *Journal 1942–1945* (Paris, 1989); B. Knapp, *Jean Cocteau* (Boston, 1986); F. Steegmuller, *Cocteau: A Biography* (Boston, 1986).

K. Krauss

COLLABORATION and, by extension, its explicitly articulated ideology—collaborationism—in virtually all Western languages are terms with both positive connotations of cooperation and negative ones of treason, the latter from World War II usage, especially in France. Evaluations of collaboration can change over time. In France, for example, the writer Paul **Morand**, an ambassador under **Vichy**, was silenced after 1945, yet his work regained popularity several years later. Discussions of collaboration often focus on the more public cases: writers such as Robert **Brasillach**, shot in 1945, or the **women "horizontal collaborators,"** who had sexual relations with German soldiers and at the **liberation** were paraded with their heads shorn and otherwise humiliated. High-level administrators, such as those involved in the surrender to the Germans of the French-owned Bor copper mines in Yugoslavia, often went unpunished.

The positions taken by collaborators after the 1940 defeat had historic roots in France. In September 1936, Roger Martin du Gard wrote that he preferred even **fascism** in France and **Hitler** to a war that might mean the triumph of communism, words nearly reechoed by Pierre **Laval** in 1943, when he publicly supported a German victory. The German victory of 1940, which appeared definitive to so many, drew collaborators from throughout the French political spectrum, including ex-**socialist** Marcel **Déat**, ex-**syndicalists** Hubert **Lagardelle** and René **Belin**, libertarian, literary, nonconformist author Louis-Ferdinand **Céline**, and witty gastronomes Robert Courtine and Pierre Andrieu. Even the **communists** thought they could work with the Germans. Some outside the pre-1940 French power structure now had an opportunity to settle private scores. The June 1941 attack on the **Soviet Union** brought fervent anticommunists, many of whom were in ex-communist Jacques **Doriot's Parti Populaire Français (PPF)**, into collaboration or intensified their dispositions toward it. Philippe **Henriot**, who became a powerful voice on Vichy radio in 1944, was strongly anticommunist. A turning point was the Allied landing in **North Africa** in November 1942, which signaled to many that the war was lost for the Germans, but collaboration extended through the end of the Occupation and beyond in the phantom **Sigmaringen** government and in apologetic postwar positions.

There are, broadly, six ways the collaboration has been seen, involving not always parallel arguments about consequences and intentions. The worst-case scenarios hold that France had many collaborators with base motives taking advantage of the situation as in *Chantons sous l'occupation* (Singing under the Occupation), as the title of Alphonse Halimi's 1976 film satirically put it. Collaboration's consequences neither saved the Jews nor helped France; they aided **Hitler**. Marshal **Pétain's** "sinister rendezvous" with Hitler at **Montoire**, in the words of historian Marc Ferro, led to the **deportation** of **Jews**—negotiated by Vichy police chief René **Bousquet**—the fervent wishes for German victory, and the *milice*, created in 1943 to fight against the **Resistance**. Collaborators could be Jews trying to save themselves. Usually advanced by historians and sometimes by the French **press**, though never by collaborators themselves, this is generally the argument of the **Left**, holding that without French collaboration, the Germans could not have done the damage that they did.

A second, middle group of arguments sees collaboration as hard to prove. Motivations were often unclear, and the consequences mixed; for example, the French could not decide how to respond to Operation Torch in North Africa, so their actions had little consequence in the unfolding of events. Most historians argue that, in the long run, collaboration mattered little: the Allies won the war, and France reemerged to create a Fourth **Republic** barely different from the Third.

A third range of scenarios suggests that collaboration was rare because what may have appeared as such was really resistance. Collaboration was really a disaster for Germany. Expressed in the title of a 1966 memoir, *Pétain contre Hitler* (Pétain against Hitler) by Gabriel Jeantet, a former member of Vichy's **Groupes de protection**, this postwar interpretation of collaboration has been termed "Pétaino-Gaullist" by historian Fred Kupferman. In an odd way, it was Hermann **Göring's** argument—that the French were deceiving the Germans at every opportunity, trying to strengthen themselves to actively reenter the war against them. Some former collaborators have suggested, in a fourth view, although without evidence, that General **de Gaulle's** 1940 resistance, independent of his motivations, worked to get more out of the Germans for Pétain.

In a fifth view of collaboration, whatever its intentions, it fended off a "polonization" of France, or reduction of France to the status of German-administered Poland, where losses were much higher. In this view, Vichy may have inadvertently helped save its own enemies: Jews, **Freemasons**, and communists. That the existence of Vichy saved the French from a worse fate and halted the German advance in the west is argued by Pétainists, who claim that this was the goal of collaboration, and by historians who suggest that this was a consequence but that it had nothing to do with the intentions of the collaborators. Seen this way, this sixth view holds the very nature of Germany's French enterprise to have been a mistake. By permitting Vichy to exist in 1940, the Germans failed to realize the potentialities of their own victory. In the euphoria of their 1940 victory, the Germans halted their advance toward **Spain**, Gibraltar, and North Africa when they might have disrupted the **British** empire. Continued French Resistance from North Africa might have forced the Germans into a more thorough and successful Mediterranean strategy.

Conversely, by failing to make peace with the French, the Germans committed themselves to a two-front war after 1941, when they desperately needed their military resources for use in **Russia**. A contented and neutral France, like Sweden, might have provided the Germans goods they needed and broken the French-British alliance, possibly in return for only Wallonia, a suggestion made during the Occupation by one of the collaborationists, Pierre Clémenti. Laval told the Germans that they could not win in the east without a settlement in the west. In this view, the Germans, despite their spoliation of occupied France to the extent of hundreds of millions of francs, got the worst of all combinations by neither pressing their 1940 victory nor making peace with France.

The mere existence of Vichy and the very enthusiasm of French collaboration sufficiently beguiled the Germans—perhaps against their own better judgment—into accepting a halfway solution that might well have lost them the war. In June 1940, no one in France could have imagined that the Germans would not follow up their victory with a forward southern strategy, nor could they foresee the invasion of Russia. Had there been a real collaborationist conspiracy or **double game**, the Germans would have learned of it. Essentially without reserves after the 1943 Battle of Kursk, the Germans had to commit large numbers of troops to the defense of France. Liberated France in 1944 had suffered fewer casualties and less destruction than any of the other major belligerents.

Many collaboration apologists and subsequent historians combine the various arguments about intentions and consequences in their work, making it hard to separate them. At present, with memories still at fever pitch because of the recent trials in France and many documents still to assess in French archives, it is unclear how history will choose among the options or in what combination.

B. M. Gordon, *Collaborationism in France during the Second World War* (Ithaca, NY, 1980); B. M. Gordon, "The Morphology of the Collaborator: The French Case," *Journal of European Studies* 23 (parts 1 and 2): 89 and 90 (March–June 1993): 1–25; R. Handourtzel and C. Buffet, *La collaboration . . . à gauche aussi* (Paris, 1989); G. Hirschfeld and P. Marsh, eds., *Collaboration in France, Politics and Culture during the Nazi Occupation, 1940–1944* (Oxford, 1989); H. Rousso, *La collaboration, Les noms, les thèmes, les lieux* (Paris, 1987).

B. M. Gordon

COMBAT (GROUP: 1940–1943 AND NEWSPAPER: 1941–1947), **Resistance** organization founded by Henri **Frenay** in the unoccupied **zone** and Robert Guédon in the occupied zone, under the name **Mouvement de Libération Nationale**, which merged with François **de Menthon's** Liberté in November 1941, resulting in the publication of the newspaper *Combat*.

The most militarily and socially important **Resistance** movement from within metropolitan France, at least in terms of numbers (75 to 80 percent of the recruits for the Armée Secrète come from its ranks), Combat is remembered for its strong geographic organization and the range of its activities. In July 1943, when it merged with Libération and **Franc-Tireur**, it gave its structure to the ensuing Mouvements Unis de Résistance. Its Service Social (devoted to helping imprisoned resisters and their families), its systematic preparation of paramilitary groups, and its Écoles de Cadres (Cadres' Schools) for the organization of the various **maquis** testify to its scope.

Edited in Lyons, then **Paris**, and published in Lyons, the newspaper *Combat* increased its publication from 40,000 copies in 1943 to 300,000 in January 1944. Its first issue, in December 1941, exhorted the French to fight against the Germans and their collaborators. Starting with its 35th issue in October 1942, the

Gaullist Croix de Lorraine (Cross of **Lorraine**) appeared on its front page. After the **liberation of Paris** and under Albert **Camus'** editorial leadership, *Combat* became one of the formative French newspapers, attracting such prestigious contributors as André **Malraux**, André **Gide**, Jean-Paul **Sartre**, André Breton, and Brice Parain.

Y.-M. Ajchenbaum, *A la vie, à la mort* (Paris, 1995); D. Cordier, *Jean Moulin, l'inconnu du panthéon*, 3 vols. (Paris, 1989–1993); M. Granet and H. Michel, *Combat* (Paris, 1957); N. Stokle, *Le Combat d'Albert Camus* (Quebec, 1970).

C. Lamiot

COMET LINE was probably the best-known escape network of the Second World War. It was founded in Brussels in 1940 by Andrée de Jongh, nicknamed Petit Cyclone, alias Dédée, and her father, Frédéric, alias Paul, a primary school headmaster. The line concentrated on returning fighting men, particularly shot-down airmen, to **Britain**. Dédée established a route from Brussels to the British consulate in Madrid, via France, the Pyrenees, and Bilbao. Among the line's many helpers were Elvire de Greef, alias Tante Go, and her husband, Fernand, alias l'Oncle. Others included Albert "B" Johnson, Charlie and Elvire Morelle, Jean Ingels, and the Basque guide Florentino.

Following the penetration of the line in 1942, Paul fled to **Paris** and was replaced by Baron Jean Greindl, alias Nemo, director of the Cantine Suèdoise in Brussels. In 1943 Dédée was betrayed and arrested, as was Nemo, among others. She was imprisoned in **concentration camps** and after her release resumed her nursing career. Jean-François Nothomb, alias Franco, replaced her. Nemo died in prison in an Allied bombing raid. Paul was arrested and executed. He was replaced by Count Jacques Legrelle, alias Jérôme, while Nemo was replaced by Count Antoine d'Ursel, alias Jacques Cartier. Tante Go was also arrested but released. Florentino was badly wounded.

There was a heavy toll on the line's helpers, with more than 100 perishing, yet it succeeded in returning some 800 Allied troops to Britain. Dédée, its principal architect, generated loyalty and dedication among the line's helpers, who shared her conviction and sense of Christian duty. She served as a **symbol** of courage and defiance, to become one of the legends of the **Resistance**.

A. Neave, *Little Cyclone* (London, 1954); S. Wittek, *Comète, histoire d'une ligne d'évasion* (Brussels, 1948).

J. Wright

COMITÉ D'ACTION MILITAIRE (COMAC; 1944), the military commission of the **Conseil Nationale de la Résistance (CNR)** that claimed to control all interior **Resistance** military activity. Known originally as the Comité d'information et d'action (COMIDAC) from March to May 1944, COMAC was a commission within the **CNR** that sought to control the interior Resistance's military activity. It organized a general staff of the Forces Françaises d'Intérieure

(FFI) and hoped that the interior Resistance would form a new **army** to liberate France.

COMAC's claims led to difficulty with the exterior Resistance because the concept of a centralized military command endangered the interior Resistance and because the **Bureau Central des Renseignements et d'Action (BCRA)** perceived a large **communist** presence in the CNR and COMAC. A compromise centralized COMAC's organization and decentralized its command. COMAC's control over the FFI would last until the **liberation** began. At that point, the FFI would be under General Pierre **Koenig**.

When the liberation began, COMAC refused to renounce its original role as the command unit of the FFI. On 17 August 1944 the CNR confirmed COMAC's original claim of supreme command of the FFI but said it would assist in the Allied effort by working with General Koenig.

COMAC participated in the **Paris** insurrection in August 1944. Though limited to the Paris region, COMAC insisted on remaining a command unit, and **de Gaulle** would not recognize its members. Finally, on 28 August 1944 the **Provisional Government** dissolved the general staff of the FFI and all other command organizations in Paris and the liberated areas, absorbing the FFI into the French **army**. COMAC became a consultative unit in the Ministry of War.

R. Hostache, *Le Conseil national de la Résistance* (Paris, 1958); H. Noguères, *Histoire de la Résistance en France*, vol. 5: *Au grand soleil de la libération* (Paris, 1981); J. F. Sweets, *The Politics of Resistance in France, 1940–1944* (De Kalb, IL, 1976).

C. S. Bisson

COMITÉ FRANCE-ALLEMAGNE was a French organization, founded in November 1935, to promote Franco–German partnership and reconciliation through cultural understanding.

Under the patronage of Jules Romains, its founding members included the journalist Fernand **de Brinon**, the first French interviewer of **Hitler**, and Deputies Georges Scapini, Jean Goy, and Henri Pichot, the latter two presidents of war veterans associations. Its journal was the *Cahiers franco-allemands*, whose contributors included Alphonse **de Châteaubriant** and Pierre **Drieu la Rochelle**. Among the members of its sister organization in Germany, the Deutsch-Französische Gesellschaft, were the prominent academics Achim von Arnim and Friedrich Grimm.

The Comité was envisioned during the 1930 Sohlberg **youth** congress, which brought together the German Francophile teacher Otto **Abetz**, future ambassador to occupied France, and the journalist Jean **Luchaire**, editor of *Notre Temps*, and resulted in the forming of the Comité d'entente de la Jeunesse pour la rapprochement allemand. These organizations continued the desire for peace and understanding expressed by a previous Comité franco-allemand that had existed in the 1920s.

A network of contacts was established, notably including the Ribbentrop-

Dienststelle (Ribbentrop Office), the diplomatic section of the Nazi Party and instrument of Hitler's propaganda in France. Through **de Brinon**, Abetz and Ribbentrop were introduced to French political circles. While the *Comité* received German government financial support, the *Cahiers* were subsidized by the Nazi party Dienststelle. Cooperation was fostered through visits to Nazi Germany by young people, war veterans, and writers. Exploited by Ribbentrop, the Comité came to be seen in France as a **fifth column**. Instead of acting as a pressure group for rapprochement, it was suspected of Nazi sympathy and the neutralization of anti-Nazi groups. It was dissolved in 1939.

In helping to form the personnel and articulate the language of French rapprochement with Nazi Germany, the interwar Comité helped set the stage for the **collaboration** that followed the French defeat of 1940. De Brinon and Luchaire, both of whom became collaborationist leaders during the Occupation, were executed after the war.

O. Abetz, *Histoire d'une politique franco-allemande* (Paris, 1953); F. de Brinon, *Mémoires* (Paris, 1949); J. Defrasne, *Histoire de la Collaboration* (Paris, 1989).

J. Wright

COMITÉ GÉNÉRAL D'ÉTUDES (CGÉ, July 1942–August 1944) was a clandestine organ of the **Resistance** government, created officially by Jean **Moulin** to plan the political and administrative structures of post-**liberation** France.

Parachuted into France during the night of 31 December 1941, Moulin, delegate of the national committee in London, was commissioned to achieve unity of action with all those resisting the enemy. Henri **Frenay**, the founder of **Combat**, introduced him to François **de Menthon**, professor of political economy in the Lyons Law Faculty, who suggested the creation of a committee of policy experts. With the agreement of London, the committee was set up in July 1942. At first it comprised Menthon, the **syndicalist** Robert Lacoste, former cabinet minister Paul Bastid, and the State Council (Conseil d'État) member Alexander **Parodi**. In the autumn they were joined by law professor Pierre-Henri **Teitgen**; economist René Courtin; in 1943, when the CGÉ had moved from Lyons to **Paris**, by Jacques Charpentier, the head of the bar; Michel **Debré**, another member of the State Council; and Pierre Lefaucheux, an **industrialist**.

A true State Council, the clandestine CGÉ studied questions of justice, in particular a future **purge**; the **press**, notably the future banning of the **collaborationist** press; and administration, with attention to the nomination of new prefects and commissioners of the **Republic**. The economic and constitutional future of France also came under study. The CGÉ published a clandestine review, the *Cahiers politiques*, where a project similar to the future Fifth Republic was sketched out by Debré. By the time Parodi had succeeded Moulin, the CGÉ had become a quasi-governmental organ, arousing the ire of the Resistance movements, jealous of their own independence. However, the CGÉ contributed to the success of the peaceful transition from the État Français to the Republic.

D. de Bellescize, *Les Neuf Sages de la Résistance, Le Comité Général d'Études dans la clandestinité* (Paris, 1979).

O. Rudelle

COMITÉS DÉPARTEMENTAUX DE LIBÉRATION (CDLs) were the departmental committees of **liberation** that organized civil power on the local level at the liberation.

Francis Closon began organizing the CDLs in 1943 under the authority of the **Conseil National de la Résistance**. Because the committees reflected all strands of patriotic opinion in an area, members represented **Resistance** organizations, political parties, and syndicates, including **women's** associations. Original plans had given the CDLs an administrative role after the liberation, but they became actively involved in organizing and fighting for the liberation of their departments. Once their areas had been liberated, the CDLs tackled such significant problems as establishing and maintaining **Republican** order, reestablishing communications, providing food, and reopening the schools.

Distrusting the CDLs as possible **Soviets**, General **de Gaulle** insisted that they play an exclusively consultative role. He preferred to put all executive authority in the provinces into the hands of the prefects and the *Commissaires de la République*, 18 ''superprefects'' given full powers in their regions until the reestablishment of the central government's authority throughout the country. The *Commissaires* themselves lost their offices in early 1946, thus ending the possibility for the decentralization of political power represented by the CDLs at the liberation.

The activity and influence of the CDLs varied by department according to local personalities and local Resistance history. In some areas resisters mimicked the CDLs on the cantonal and municipal levels with *comités locaux de libération*. After the elections of new *conseils généraux* in September 1945 made them redundant, the CDLs faded away.

C.-L. Foulon, *Le Pouvoir en province à la libération* (Paris, 1975); J. F. Sweets, *The Politics of Resistance in France, 1940–1944* (De Kalb, IL, 1976).

M. Koreman

COMITÉS D'ORGANISATION (CO) were established by a law of 16 August 1940. The law was hastily drawn up by labor minister René **Belin** and a small group of civil servants with little opportunity for business interests to influence its drafting. The COs were designed as a response to immediate pressures: the starved **economy**, the need to counteract German economic organization in the northern **zone**, and the need to rapidly find men with **industrial** expertise. The law proposed the establishment of a committee to deal with each sector of the economy. These committees were to draw up plans for production and to coordinate measures taken by various companies.

Suggestions that the COs anticipated the more etatist and organized economy of post-1945 France—and, indeed, they survived, under a slightly different name, until 1946—place too much emphasis on the coherence and purpose of Vichy industrial organization. There was great variation in the importance of the various COs, specifically differences between those run by men with strong ideas about the ways to change their industries (as François **Lehideux** had about the automobile industry) and those run by men who wished to represent their industries as had the prewar employers' syndicates. Many plans for long-term industrial change were undermined by the scarcity of raw materials, which sometimes made the Organisation Centrale de Répartition des Produits Industriels, established on 27 September 1940, more important than the COs. Finally, industrial organization at Vichy was always a chaotic matter. Roger Martin, who became an official with a CO, suggested that "individuals, employers, and the nation itself were tied up in a bitter battle for survival and the total absence of information made all preparation for the future impossible. The real interest of these institutions was to offer a welcoming structure to uprooted men and to offer them some means of subsistence."

A. Jones, "Illusions of Sovereignty: Business and the Organization of Committees in Vichy France," *Social History* 2 (1986): 1–33; R. Kuisel, *Capitalism and the State in Modern France: Renovation and Economic Management in the Twentieth Century* (Cambridge, U.K., 1981); H. Rousso, "L'organisation industrielle de Vichy," *RDHDGM* 116 (1979): 27–44; R. Vinen, *The Politics of French Business 1936–1945* (Cambridge, U.K., 1991).

R. C. Vinen

COMMISSARIAT GÉNÉRAL AUX QUESTIONS JUIVES (Office for Jewish Affairs; CGQJ), government agency established by the **Vichy** government in March 1941 to coordinate anti-**Jewish** policy and prepare and administer legislation in this field. Established at the prodding of the occupation authorities, but with its jurisdiction extending to both the occupied and unoccupied **zones**, the CGQJ was first headed by Xavier **Vallat**, a strong **anti-Semite** but also an anti-German nationalist.

Under Vallat the CGQJ attempted to unify anti-Jewish policy throughout both zones and to do so energetically and efficiently. Implicit in Vallat's approach was the hope that the Germans would gradually withdraw from this field, leaving the task to the French alone. After issuing a comprehensive anti-Jewish law on 2 June 1941 redefining the Jews, the CGQJ sponsored a flurry of decrees in one field after another, drastically limiting the number of Jews in commerce and the professions and announcing a detailed census of Jews in the unoccupied zone, a grave step that profoundly shocked Jewish opinion and that was to have fatal consequences later when Jews were rounded up and deported. Also, by a law of 22 July 1941 the CGQJ launched a vast process of "**Aryanization**," the confiscation of Jewish property in the unoccupied **zone**.

Eager to ensure that Jewish property did not find its way to the Reich, the French government designated the CGQJ as the agency taking charge of confiscating Jewish property throughout France. The goal was to liquidate or sell all Jewish holdings for the benefit of France. This vast project, which eventually involved more than 42,000 Jewish enterprises, drained the legislative and administrative energies of the CGQJ. Corruption and inefficiency followed, despite Vallat's efforts to combat both.

Under Vallat's successor, Louis **Darquier de Pellepoix**, venality became widespread. The agency spawned a para**police** organization, the Sections d'enquête et de contrôle (Investigation and Control Sections). Darquier and his lieutenants were not adverse to working with the Nazis and did so notably when roundups and **deportations** spread throughout France in the summer of 1942. When possible, Vichy kept the CGQJ at arm's length, but the anti-Jewish machinery continued to function and even to accelerate the rate of persecution.

In late 1943, the Germans pressured Vichy to drop Darquier, recognizing that he was unable to bring the Vichy government fully into line with Nazi policy. His successor was Charles Mercier du Paty de Clam, an undistinguished civil servant descended from the famous officer who arrested Alfred Dreyfus in 1894. With the end in sight, du Paty de Clam left his office in May. Pierre **Laval**, to the end concerned to maintain control and government continuity in this sphere as in others, named Joseph Antignac, one of its top officials, to head the commissariat. Remarkably, "business as usual" remained the policy of the CGQJ even after the Allies went ashore in **Normandy**. Yet finally, along with the rest of the Vichy administration, the agency melted away with the **liberation** of France.

J. Billig, *Le Commissariat général aux question juives (1941–1944)*, 3 vols. (Paris, 1955–1960); Centre de Documentation juive contemporaine, *La France et la question juive 1940/1944: la politique de Vichy, l'attitude des Églises et des mouvements de Résistance* (Paris, 1981); S. Klarsfeld, *Vichy-Auschwitz: Le rôle de Vichy dans la solution finale de la question juive en France,* 2 vols. (Paris, 1983, 1985); M. R. Marrus and R. O. Paxton, *Vichy France and the Jews* (New York, 1981).

M. R. Marrus

COMMUNIST PARTY (Parti Communiste Français, PCF). Outlawed in 1939 and opposing the war, after **Hitler's** invasion of the **Soviet Union** the PCF became the most vigorous single force in the **Resistance**.

Belligerently anti-Hitler as war approached in 1939, the PCF approved the Molotov–Ribbentrop pact but said the enemy remained Hitlerian **fascism**. Almost immediately, the parliament banned the party press. However, on 2 September PCF deputies, with Moscow's approval, voted war credits. In late September parliament dissolved the PCF and affiliated organizations. By 7 September Stalin had decided to term the war "imperialist." Ordered to desert, PCF leader Maurice **Thorez** complied on 4 October and arrived in Moscow in November. In October, the French government suspended numerous communist municipal councils. Arrests continued until May 1940.

The now disorganized party argued that the workers had no interest in an imperialist war begun by the French and **British** bourgeoisie. After the 1940

armistice the party condemned the bourgeoisie for having led the country to defeat and continued to denounce the British. Clandestine leader Jacques **Duclos**, in radio contact with Moscow, tried unsuccessfully to get German permission for the party daily *Humanité* to reappear legally.

From November 1940, a clandestine *Humanité* began an anti-**Vichy**, anti-German line, still attacking British imperialism. In May 1941 *Humanité* urged the working class to profit from the crisis to move toward an international revolutionary movement. The Nazi attack on the **USSR** rallied the PCF to a war now characterized as an antifascist **liberation** struggle.

In October 1941 the PCF Organisation Spéciale ordered sabotage and actions against German personnel. The following February, the party called for armed struggle, organizing underground partisans and **franc-tireurs (FTP)**. Guerrilla war was not possible in most of France, and sabotage actions were conducted by small groups until mid-1943, when the first *maquis* was formed.

In March 1943 **de Gaulle's** envoy Jean **Moulin** won PCF agreement to participate in a **Conseil National de la Résistance**. Meanwhile, the USSR supported the new Comité Française de libération nationale (CFLN), established in Algiers under de Gaulle and, briefly, General Henri **Giraud**. The **Soviets** granted the CFLN a higher degree of recognition as a **Provisional Government** than did the British or the **Americans**, and in rallying to it and de Gaulle, the PCF gained full reintegration into the national community from which it had been excluded in 1939.

The PCF succeeded in controlling the armed forces of the Resistance, the **Forces Françaises de l'Intérieur (FFI)**, while its own FTP kept its autonomous organization. However, immediately after the liberation of Paris, in which the communists played a major role, de Gaulle moved quickly to deprive the PCF of any autonomous military power. The general staff of the FFI was dissolved, and the organization itself amalgamated to the **army** of Africa and **Italy**. De Gaulle also dissolved the paramilitary communist *gardes civiques*.

De Gaulle amnestied **Thorez** and permitted him to return to France in November 1944. In December, Thorez issued a call for surrender of the arms stockpiled by PCF organizations. Under instructions from the Soviets, the party had chosen peaceful means to gain power—or to await a time when Soviet power would be greater. Thorez became deputy prime minister, and in the 1945 elections the PCF became the strongest party.

*† J.-P. Azéma, A. Prost, and J. P. Rioux, eds., *Les Communistes français de Munich à Châteaubriant, 1938–1941* (Paris, 1987); P. Buton, *Les lendemains qui déchantent* (Paris, 1993); P. Buton, "Le parti, la guerre, et la révolution, 1939–1940," *Communisme* 32–34 (1993); S. Courtois, *Le PCF dans la guerre* (Paris, 1980); A. Kriegel and S. Courtois, *Eugen Fried, le grand secret du PCF* (Paris, 1997); M. Narinski, "Le Komintern et le Parti Communiste français, 1939–1942," *Communisme* 32–34 (1993).

J. W. Friend

COMMUNISTS TURNED COLLABORATORS in organized movements were scattered in different groups, notably the **Parti Populaire Français, (PPF)**, headed by Jacques **Doriot**, a former **communist (Parti Communiste Français PCF)**. However, during the Occupation, a small group of prominent **communists** who had rejected the August 1939 Nazi–**Soviet** pact and who also distrusted Doriot and the PPF formed a new faction, the Parti Ouvrier et Paysan Français (POPF).

Leaders were Marcel Gitton (Giroux), a former member of the communist political bureau dating from 1932 and deputy from the Seine district since 1936; Marcel Capron, mayor of Alfortville; Senator Jean-Marie Clamamus; and several other deputies, including Marcel Bront, Armand Pillot, Léon Piginnier, and Fernand Valat, all of whom had resigned from the PCF in 1939. With the German attack on the Soviet Union, however, the communists, now in armed resistance, were able to hunt those they considered traitors. Gitton was assassinated on 4 September 1941.

Capron called for a "social, national, and popular" revolution, and Charles Bourneton, a former **syndicalist** placed in charge of the southern **zone** POPF, spoke of elevating the "national" while not forgetting the "social." The party platform, which differed little from the other **collaborationist** parties based in **Paris**, was expounded in two "open letters" to communist workers: on 5 September 1941, the day after Gitton's assassination, and again in May 1942. Despite its well-known leaders, the group attracted very few followers.

* B. M. Gordon, *Collaborationism in France during the Second World War* (Ithaca, NY, 1980); P.-P. Lambert and G. Le Marec, *Partis et Mouvements de la Collaboration, Paris 1940–1944* (Paris, 1993).

G. Le Marec

COMPAGNONS DE FRANCE was the official **Vichy youth** movement for teens, promoting patriotic service, scouting virtues, and physical rejuvenation. Inspired by the *"compagnonnage,"* or solidarity, of medieval artisanal journeymen, Scout leader Henri Dhavernas invited 46 young leaders from the various French youth organizations to camp out in Randan forest, near Vichy, from 1 through 4 August 1940, where, after a visit from Marshal **Pétain**, they pledged to follow the *compagnons'* example in reconstructing France.

"Chef [head] *compagnon"* Dhavernas commanded, in medieval ascending order in size, *"compagnies," "cités," "provinces,"* and *"pays,"* with strict discipline, hierarchy, and rituals. They sported blue berets, dark blue shirts with the *"coq gaulois,"* shorts, and a Nazi-like salute. *Compagnies* of 50 cleared land, repaired roads, harvested grapes, built **sports** fields, and aided **refugees**. They did six hours of daily work, got indoctrinated, and launched myriad publications—directly inspired by the **Uriage** school—that were communitarian, anticapitalist, antiliberal-democracy, and contemptuous of the bourgeoisie. Pétain's "vanguard of the **National Revolution**," although given generous subsidies, never attained the anticipated enrollment. Officially sanctioned and directed, they were closely watched as possible harbingers of a single totalitarian state youth movement.

The Randan camp-school produced 12 successive cohorts until, in February 1941, leading 30,000 *compagnons*, Dhavernas lost favor. Young commandant Guillaume de Tournemire, who had served under Marshal Hubert Lyautey and General Henri **Giraud**, took over as *chef compagnon*, directing 200 *compagnies*, 600 work sites, and 13 camp-schools where 3,000 cadres had graduated at a rate of 500 a month. The July 1942 anniversary drew 7,000 young enthusiasts to renew their vows in Randan forest, but the occupation of the southern **zone** soon decimated membership. Tournemire went into hiding in October 1943 as the *compagnons* split in their attitudes toward Pétain and the Germans. They were dissolved on 21 January 1944.

P. Giolitto, *Histoire de la jeunesse* (Paris, 1991); W. D. Halls, *The Youth of Vichy France* (Oxford, 1981); J. Hellman, *The Knight-Monks of Vichy France, Uriage, 1940–45* (Montreal and Kingston, 1993); R. Hervet, *Les Compagnons de France* (Paris, 1965).

J. Hellman

COMPAGNONS DE LA LIBÉRATION, those individuals who were made fellows of the Ordre de la Libération for their exceptional contribution to the **liberation** of France and its colonies.

The Ordre de la Libération was created by General **de Gaulle** at Brazzaville on 16 November 1940 and was awarded until 23 January 1946 (although Winston Churchill was made a *compagnon* in 1958, as was George VI posthumously in 1960). A medal was awarded in the form of a bronze shield with a double-edged sword overlaid with a cross of **Lorraine**. It carried the Latin motto *Patriam servando victoriam tulit*. De Gaulle was the grand master who presided over the award ceremony, which attributed only one rank of award, the Compagnon de la Libération.

Altogether, 1,059 Compagnons de la Libération were created, of which 238 were posthumous. The youngest *compagnon* was Mathurin Henrio, known as Barrioz, who died under torture at the age of 14 in 1944. Only six of the *compagnons* were **women**: Bertie Albrecht, Laure Diebold, Émilienne Evrard, Marie Hackin, Marcelle Henry, and Simone Michel Lévy. Famous *compagnons* include General Philippe **Leclerc**, Jacques **Chaban-Delmas**, René **Pleven**, Maurice Schumann, André **Malraux**, Romain Gary, Jean **Moulin**, and Pierre **Brossolette**. Some 300 *compagnons* were still alive in January 1990.

The award was seen after the war as proof of an individual's **Resistance** credentials. However, it was criticized by some, including Claude Bourdet, for **symbolizing** a particularly Gaullist and unrepresentative view of Resistance activities in occupied France.

C. Bourdet, *L'Aventure incertaine* (Paris, 1975); D. Frémy and M. Frémy, *Quid 1991* (Paris, 1990).

C. Gorrara

COMPIÈGNE is the town where German propaganda minister Joseph Goebbels orchestrated the June 1940 **armistice**-signing ceremony with defeated

France. It has been argued that the armistice itself was Goebbels' idea. It was signed in the same railway car, at the Rethondes clearing near Compiègne in northern France, in which Marshal Ferdinand Foch had dictated armistice terms to German representatives in November 1918. Foch's railway car had been moved back to Rethondes for the 1927 anniversary of the 11 November armistice.

Replete with **Hitler's** gloating and vengeful expressions, the story of the armistice signing and the terms dictated to the French was broken by the **American** correspondent William L. Shirer, who managed to listen in on the negotiations. Carefully staged by the Germans, the ceremony was later described as "Goebbels' big show." A monument at Rethondes to the return of **Alsace** and **Lorraine** to France in 1918 was destroyed at Hitler's order, but he allowed a statue of Foch to remain there. The Germans let the clearing become overgrown. Following the signing of the 1940 armistice, Goebbels had the car moved to Berlin, where it was shown to German crowds for several weeks near the Brandenburg Gate. It was then garaged and in 1944 moved to Ohrdruf in Thuringia. Upon the arrival of the Americans the railway car was destroyed by SS units.

Following the **liberation**, on 11 November 1944, the site was ceremonially **purged** by fire and rededicated in the presence of General Pierre **Koenig**, head of the **Forces Françaises de l'Intérieur,** French and American soldiers, and veterans of World War I. A replacement car, similar to the one destroyed, was found in Romania and refitted exactly as the original. The 1918 armistice continues to be celebrated at the Compiègne site annually, often in the presence of the president of the **Republic**. Although the 1940 armistice is rarely mentioned, Compiègne is a reminder of the flaws of German decision making during a brief moment of opportunity, when the Germans might have engaged Spain as an ally and moved south to Gibraltar and North Africa or, conversely, granted the French a more generous settlement that might have allowed Germany to disengage in the west and focus its resources on Central and Eastern Europe.

S. Barcellini and A. Wieviorka, *Passant, souviens-toi! Les lieux du souvenir de la Seconde Guerre mondiale en France* (Paris, 1995); M. Codevelle, ed., *Armistice 1918 Sa Signature, la Clairière Compiègne* (Compiègne, 1950); "Compiègne," *Der deutsche Wegleiter* 30 (16–31 October 1941): 17–20; R. Manvell and H. Fraenkel, *Dr. Goebbels, His Life and Death* (New York, 1961 [1960]); W. L. Shirer, *Berlin Diary, the Journal of a Foreign Correspondent, 1934–1941* (New York, 1941).

B. M. Gordon

CONCENTRATION CAMPS IN FRANCE were used by both the Third **Republic** and **Vichy** to detain immigrants and **refugees** considered "undesirable aliens." Such internments were first authorized in November 1938 in response to the streams of largely Jewish refugees fleeing Nazism and to the influx of refugees from the Spanish civil war. In February 1939, the first French concentration camp was opened at Rieucros. Some 330,000 Spanish civil war **refugees** were temporarily detained there and at other camps in southwestern France.

Following France's declaration of war with Germany, in a second wave of detention, some 18,000 to 20,000 refugees from Germany and Austria, now viewed as "enemy nationals," were, along with certain members of the banned **Communist** Party, sent to the camps in the fall of 1939. While most of these detainees were released a few weeks later, the German invasion in May 1940 provoked a third series of internments, as Premier Paul **Reynaud** ordered that enemy nationals once again be detained in camps. Inheriting the camps from the Third Republic, Vichy targeted Jews by authorizing departmental prefects to intern them at will. By the end of 1940, some 40,000 detainees, including 28,000 Jews, were being held in French concentration camps in the southern, unoccupied **zone**.

Although not intended for the purpose, the French concentration camps facilitated the Nazi Final Solution in France, since it was primarily from these camps that Jews were taken to be deported. The largest camp in the occupied zone, Drancy, served as the point of departure for the great majority of trains to Auschwitz, including the first, which left on 27 March 1942. French camps were never killing centers, but conditions varied from poor to severely harsh: some 3,000 internees died in French custody. A number of Jewish, **Protestant**, and **Catholic** relief organizations, coordinated by the umbrella group called "Le comité de Nîmes," tried to alleviate suffering, providing supplemental food, shelter, and medical care and alerting world opinion to the problem.

A. Grynberg, *Les camps de la honte: Les internés Juifs des camps français, 1939–1944* (Paris, 1991); S. Klarsfeld, *Vichy-Auschwitz: Le rôle de Vichy dans la solution finale de la question juive en France,* 2 vols. (Paris, 1983, 1985); D. Tartière, *A House near Paris* (Paris, 1946); J. Weill, *Contribution à l'histoire des camps d'internement dans l'Anti-France* (Paris, 1946); S. Zucotti, *The Holocaust, the French, and the Jews* (New York, 1993).

N. Bracher

CONFÉDÉRATION GÉNÉRALE DU TRAVAIL (CGT) was France's largest prewar labor organization. Dissolved by the **Vichy** government in 1940, it reemerged triumphant after the **liberation**.

In 1939 the CGT was a declining organization whose membership had fallen from 5.3 million in 1937 to about 1 million. The **Communist** Party (PCF) was influential within the CGT but fell into disarray following the Nazi–**Soviet** pact of 23 August 1939. The PCF and CGT were further disoriented when Soviet troops crossed the Polish border on 17 September. **Right-wing** factions, led by René **Belin**, became ascendant within the CGT. When the Édouard **Daladier** government expelled communist deputies from parliament, the right-wing leadership of the CGT followed suit and expelled communists from its ranks in September 1939. The transformation was complete when Belin accepted the post of minister of production and labor in the **Pétain** government. The CGT offered to collaborate with the Vichy regime, but its concessions were not enough. On 9 November Belin signed a decree dissolving the CGT and all other unions.

In 1940 the Pétain government issued its **Labor Charter** (*Charte du travail*), which replaced the CGT with a system of corporatist groupings that united workers and employers in similar **industries**. The CGT did not disappear completely. It retained an underground presence, and its members cooperated with the **Resistance**. On 27 July 1944 the **Provisional Government** in Algeria issued a decree abolishing the *Charte du travail* and restoring the CGT and other unions to their prewar positions. Hundreds of right-wing militants who had cooperated with Belin were banned from further union activity. By 1946 communists controlled nearly all federations involved in mass production and four-fifths of the departmental unions.

*† G. Lefranc, *Les expériences syndicales en France de 1939 à 1950* (Paris, 1951); G. Ross, *Workers and Communists in France from Popular Front to Eurocommunism* (Berkeley, 1982).

C. J. Haug

CONSEIL NATIONAL DE LA JEUNESSE (National Council for **Youth**) was created during Pierre-Étienne **Flandin's** brief tenure as foreign minister by the law of 22 January 1941, which established a representative assembly based upon the "living forces of the nation." This conservative, consultative body set up several commissions, one of which concerned the nation's youth. The first commission, led by Georges Lamirand, head of the Secretaire Général de la Jeunesse (SGJ), included directors of the major youth movements—such as the Scouts and the Association Catholique de la Jeunesse Française (ACJF)—as well as Henri Dorgères of Jeunesses Paysannes and Pierre **Dunoyer de Segonzac**, leader of the École Nationale des Cadres d'**Uriage**. Minister of the **interior** Pierre **Pucheu**, minister of **education** Jérôme Carcopino, and writer Henri Massis were also influential.

These youth commissions reflected the same tension that beset virtually all **Vichy** youth organizations: whether to permit a plurality of youth groups with the Catholic Church playing a dominant role, or to move toward a single, state-controlled movement, as in Nazi Germany. Throughout the existence of the National Council, the Catholics were able to block the attempts of Pucheu and other **collaborators** to emulate the Hitler Youth, and these commissions therefore failed to develop a coherent youth policy.

P. Giolitto, *Histoire de la jeunesse sous Vichy* (Paris, 1991); J. Hellman, *The Knight-Monks of Vichy France: Uriage, 1940–1945* (Montreal, 1993); W. D. Halls, *The Youth of Vichy France* (Oxford, 1981); M. Cointet, *Le Conseil national de Vichy: Vie politique et réforme de l'état en régime autoritaire (1940–1944)* (Paris, 1989).

W. S. Haine

CONSEIL NATIONAL DE LA RÉSISTANCE (CNR), the National Council of the **Resistance**, which represented the interior Resistance in 1943–1944.

Representatives of eight Resistance movements, six political parties, and two trade unions first met as the CNR in **Paris** on 27 May 1943 under the presidency of Jean **Moulin**. The CNR declared **Vichy's** actions void and voted Charles **de Gaulle** full confidence as representative of the nation's interests, an endorsement that considerably helped the general in his negotiations with the Allies. For his part, de Gaulle promised to restore France's democratic rights as soon as possible. The resisters, who distrusted the politicians from the Third **Republic's** parties, refused to give the CNR executive authority over their movements. But the CNR did appoint a steering committee of five, which met regularly and oversaw the work of several commissions designed to prepare for the **liberation** and the transfer of power, the most important of which was the **Comité d'action militaire (COMAC)**, which coordinated the Resistance army and the **maquis**. Georges **Bidault** became president of the steering committee after the arrest of Moulin in June 1943.

At the liberation, de Gaulle refused the CNR any role in the state as the representative of the Resistance. Some of its members, however, did join his government. Although kept away from power or the appearance of it at the liberation, the CNR exercised a lasting influence through its Charter of 15 March 1944.

The CNR Charter represented the social and economic reforms that many rank-and-file resisters thought they had been fighting for, and enactment of its provisions were continually demanded by the local **press** and local organizations. Its great popularity influenced those who drafted the constitutions of the Fourth and Fifth Republics. The charter proclaimed that resisters would remain unified after the liberation in order to accomplish the five following goals: (1) establish the Republic under de Gaulle; (2) punish traitors and **purge** collaborators from the administration and professions; (3) confiscate the profits of war profiteers and **black marketeers**; (4) reestablish universal suffrage and civil liberties, including the absolute equality of all citizens before the law and respect for individual human rights; and (5) promote reforms to create true economic and social democracy, including nationalization of the greatest **industrial** and financial companies, creation of the means of worker participation in management, subordination of the **economy** to a plan, establishment of the right to work and to rest, guarantee of an adequate wage level, reestablishment of independent trade unions, implementation of a comprehensive social security plan, extension of political, social, and economic rights to colonial citizens, and establishment of **educational** equality in order to create an elite of merit rather than of birth.

The Constituent Assembly made attempts to fulfill some of these provisions in 1945–1946. They nationalized the coal fields, the gas and electric companies, the Banque de France and four other banks, the Renault factories, and the aircraft industry. They also reorganized the social security system and created committees meant to give workers access to management in large companies. Nevertheless, some on the **Left** consider the CNR Charter to have been a missed opportunity.

C. Andrieu, *Le Programme commun de la Résistance* (Paris, 1984); R. Hostache, *Le*

Conseil national de la Résistance (Paris, 1958); A. Shennan, *Rethinking France: Plans for Renewal, 1940–1946* (Oxford, 1989); J. F. Sweets, *The Politics of Resistance in France, 1940–1944* (De Kalb, IL, 1976).

M. Koreman

CORPORATION PAYSANNE was the sole agricultural professional organization under **Vichy**. It was envisioned by the law of 2 December 1940. Although discussed thereafter, such a "corporation" did not really exist, and Pierre Caziot, the minister of agriculture, has been seen erroneously as its "father." A specialist on land-related questions, Caziot was no corporatist and was barely interested in **syndicalism**. He intervened only from fear of being short-circuited by Marshal **Pétain's** entourage and from anxiety about the ambitions of the corporatists. Obligatory membership, an immediate end to the Chambres d'Agriculture (bodies elected by the **peasants** to represent their interests before the government), and all-powerful government commissioners at all levels were rejected, and the proportion of members designated by the state trustees was reduced—all moves counter to the demands of the corporatists.

All the members of the peasant corporate national organizing committee, a provisional body, and its president, Hervé Budes de Guébriant, were named by the minister (Caziot), as were all the regional delegates, also provisional. On the other hand, in a case unique under Vichy, the permanent trustees, including the national trustee, Adolphe Pointier, and the adjunct national trustee, Camille Laurens (who was to become minister of agriculture in 1951), were elected by their peers, the minister only ratifying their selections. The corporations were created virtually everywhere according to the principle of unity for all the professional organizations, which required many mergers and did not always pass without problems. The national corporative council was established by a law of 16 December 1942.

With the **liberation**, the **purge** was quite limited. Many of these men had already been leaders in their profession before the war, especially in the Union nationale des syndicats agricoles. They suffered an "eclipse" in 1944–1945, but 1946 would see the "return of the evicted," in the words of Pierre Barral.

I. Boussard, *Vichy et la Corporation paysanne* (Paris, 1980); M. C. Cleary, *Peasants, Politicians and Producers, The Organisation of Agriculture in France since 1918* (Cambridge, U.K., 1989); J. Hourcade, *L'Organisation corporative de l'agriculture française* (Bordeaux, 1943); L. Salleron, et al., *Un Régime corporatif pour l'agriculture* (Paris, 1937, 1943); M. Tissot, *L'Organisation corporative de l'agriculture* (Paris, 1942).

I. Boussard

CORPORATISM was a doctrine in many European countries in the early twentieth century. In France, its founder was René de La Tour du Pin and his *Vers un ordre social chrétien, Jalons de route 1882–1907* (Toward a Christian Social Order, Blazing the Trail), which appeared in 1907. The best historical analysis of French corporatism is that of Matthew H. Elbow.

Corporatism was characterized by four traits. First of all, it did not seek to return to the corporations of the Old Regime (prior to the French Revolution), which were said to need replacement by the new. Accordingly, the term "neo-corporatism" is often used for the twentieth-century varieties. Second, corporatists did not deny the reality of the Marxist class struggle but claimed to want to go beyond, or transcend, it. From this desire came the need for mixed *syndicats* (trade associations) grouping together bosses and workers, employers and employees. Third, corporatism was not opposed to **syndicalism**; instead, it sought to transform or perfect it. "The corporation is the profession having reached a higher form of organization," Eugène Duthoit argued in 1942. The fourth characteristic of corporatism was to give, not total political power, but a regulatory and representational authority to the professions. Corporatists were not always in agreement nor very clear as to whether this power was to be given to a remodeled senate comprising representatives of the professions or whether a special body, separate from political institutions, was needed.

The coming of the **Vichy** government brought corporatism to the forefront of political consideration. Corporatists were numerous in the entourage of **Pétain**, who was persuaded that corporatism was a good third way between liberalism and Marxism. In the *Revue des deux mondes*, 15 September 1940, for example, Pétain wrote of the "need to organize professions on a corporative basis where all the elements of a business could meet, face each other, and settle things; the need to have in the heart of an organized profession, a representative of the state fully empowered to arbitrate otherwise irreconcilable differences; the need to have above and beyond the corporations or business communities a state organism empowered to guide national production, according to the possibilities of the domestic and foreign markets, thereby avoiding waste in labor and wealth."

Corporatist tracts proliferated under Vichy as writers such as Maurice Bouvier-Ajam, Firmin Baconnier, M. H. Lenormand, and Louis Baudin attempted to bring the older doctrine into harmony with the France of the early 1940s. Duthoit, one such writer, argued that "precorporative" institutions had existed before the war but that true corporatist institutions had been created only after June 1940. Governmental attempts to put corporatist ideas into practice included provisional organizing committees for **industrial** production (law of 16 August 1940), a central office for distribution of industrial products (law of 10 September 1940), a corporative organization for agriculture (law of 2 December 1940), the **Labor Charter** (law of 4 October 1941 on the social organization of professions), and laws organizing specific professions, such as physicians (law of 7 October 1940) and architects (law of 31 December 1940).

The problem was that nearly all the French corporatists favored associational non-*étatiste* versions as opposed to one in which the state was all-powerful. Accordingly, they rejected German, Italian, Spanish, and even Portuguese models of corporatism, though the last more closely approximated their ideas. Associational corporatism, however, has never been put into practice. The circumstances of the Occupation in France made things even more difficult. All of the institutions created, even the **Peasant Corporation (Corporation pay-sanne)**, the best among them, were controlled by the state.

L. Baudin, *Le Corporatisme* (Paris, 1942); M. Bouvier-Ajam, *La Doctrine corporative* (Paris, 1937, 1941, 1943); E. Duthoit, *Rénovation française* (Paris, 1942); M. H. Elbow, *French Corporative Theory* (New York, 1953); J.-P. Le Crom, *Syndicats nous voilà! Vichy et le corporatisme* (Paris, 1995).

I. Boussard

CORSICA, an island lying off the southern coast of France, became the first department in France to be liberated by the Allies in 1943. Despite its proximity to **Italy** and its Italian heritage, Corsica remained loyal to the French cause throughout World War II.

After France's defeat in 1940, Corsica came under **Vichy's** administration. Italian claims on the island were denied because of **Hilter's** desire to retain Vichy France as an ally. **Resistance** began in early 1942 but failed to gain wide appeal until the Italians occupied Corsica on 11 November 1942 in response to Allied landings in **North Africa.**

The collapse of Mussolini's government on 8 September 1943 created an opportunity for the Corsican partisans. The local **Front National** rose against the Italian and German occupation forces. Unprepared for this move, the Allies and the **Free French** could only rush a hastily assembled small force to the island. This attack, dubbed Operation Firebrand, began on 11 September 1943 and was led by the French general Alphonse Juin. Eventually, the Free French contingents numbered 6,500 and were assisted by the Office of Strategic Services (OSS) and 400 **American** Marines. Their forces were complemented by roughly 10,000 members of the Resistance. They were opposed by 40,000 Germans who maintained control of Bastia and the island's eastern plains. A guerrilla war ensued.

Toward the end of September, with the evacuation of Sardinia complete, the Germans decided to withdraw from Corsica, and by 4 October, as General **de Gaulle** noted, ''the first French department was liberated.'' Corsica remained in Allied hands for the duration of the war and served as an important staging point for the invasion of southern France in August 1944.

†F. Gambiez, *Libération de la Corse* (Paris, 1973); R. Ramsey, *The Corsican Time Bomb* (Manchester, U.K., 1983).

S. K. Chenault

COULAUDON, ÉMILE (1907–1977), called ''Colt'' or ''Colonel Gaspard,'' headed the **Mouvements Unis de la Résistance** in the department of Puy-de-Dôme during the Occupation. A man of extraordinary abilities, Coulaudon led the military **Resistance** in the Auvergne.

Taken **prisoner** of war during the 1940 campaign, Coulaudon escaped in the summer and returned to Clermont-Ferrand in the Puy-de-Dôme. There he founded a Resistance network and led operations of sabotage, retaliation, and liberation of prisoners. Threatened with imminent arrest in 1943, he took to the *maquis* and established a Resistance headquarters in the Mont Mouchet forest. By the end of March 1944, intensified German repression forced him to order all the Auvergne Resistance functionaries into hiding in the Mont Mouchet region. Coulaudon met with **British** major Maurice Southgate of the **Service Operations Executive** at Montluçon on 15 April and agreed to put into action Plan Caïman, whose goal was to tie down local German military forces on D-Day. On 20 May Coulaudon ordered the general mobilization of all Auvergne Resistance fighters. Three thousand seven hundred Resistance soldiers gathered in three areas around Mont Mouchet, from whence they disrupted local German operations but waited in vain for an expected Allied airlift of supplies. The Germans, meanwhile, brought in 3,000 men of their Ost Legion, who terrorized the local civilian population and attacked Coulaudon's troops on 10 and 11 June. Compelled to retreat to the banks of the La Truyère river, Coulaudon's forces withstood a second German attack on 20 June. Coulaudon then ordered the dispersal of his Resistance units.

After the war he became president of the Fédération nationale des maquis de France.

H. R. Kedward, *In Search of the Maquis: Rural Resistance in Southern France, 1942–1944* (Oxford, 1993); G. Lévy and F. Cordet, *A nous, Auvergne!* ([Paris], 1990); F. Maury-Fernandez, "Lieu de mémoire et de commémoration: Le Mont Mouchet 1944–1989," in A. Gueslin, ed., *De Vichy au Mont-Mouchet: L'Auvergne dans la guerre (1939–1945)* (Clermont-Ferrand, 1991), 147–72.

W. Freund

COUVE DE MURVILLE, JACQUES MAURICE (1907–), was a high-ranking official in the **Vichy** Ministry of Finance who rallied to General Henri **Giraud** in **North Africa** in 1943 and served as Commissaire aux finances in the Comité français de libération nationale (CFLN) between June and November 1943. He was then appointed by General **de Gaulle** to the Commission des affaires italiennes, the first step in a lengthy and distinguished diplomatic career, which culminated in a 10-year stint as the Fifth Republic's first minister of foreign affairs.

Couve de Murville, an *inspecteur des finances* during the 1930s, was a rising star in the Treasury. In 1940, Marshal **Pétain's** minister of finance, Yves Bouthillier, put him in charge of a new office of foreign finances, which was responsible, among other tasks, for controlling the transfer of shares in French companies to German authorities. Couve de Murville was one of the principal members of the French delegation to the **armistice** commission at Wiesbaden and, in that capacity, conducted frequent negotiations with the Germans over a period of more than two years, remaining in office even after Bouthillier had been replaced as minister.

As with a number of other prominent Vichy officials, Couve de Murville found Giraudism a convenient transition between the *État Français* and the emerging Gaullist state. He was nominated to the CFLN by Giraud but soon realized the latter's political shortcomings and switched allegiance to de Gaulle. De Gaulle, in turn, appreciated the technical expertise of this quintessential mandarin, *"très au courant et très assuré"* (very much up to date and confident), as de Gaulle noted approvingly in his *War Memoirs*.

†F. Bloch-Lainé, *Hauts fonctionnaires sous l'Occupation* (Paris, 1996); Y. Bouthillier, *Le drame de Vichy,* 2 vols. (Paris, 1950–1951); M. Margairaz, *L'État, les finances et l'économie,* 2 vols. (Paris, 1991).

A. W. H. Shennan

D

DAKAR, a city in French West Africa (now in Senegal), site of an **Anglo–**Gaullist attack (23–25 September 1940) against the French naval base there. In an effort to pry away as much of the French **empire** as possible from **Vichy**, a force of **British** and **Free French** ships appeared off Dakar on 23 September. The hope was to persuade the Vichy garrison there to rally to the **Anglo–**Gaullist side without a shot's being fired. **De Gaulle** himself was on board the Allied fleet and sent a small party ashore to negotiate. Dakar's defenses, however, had been reinforced only nine days earlier by ships from Toulon, and the Vichy commander, General Pierre Boisson, was in no mood to parley. The Gaullist envoys were chased off. Dakar's shore batteries and the guns of the aircraft carrier *Richelieu* opened fire.

Even so, de Gaulle still thought he detected some hesitancy in the Vichy response and attempted a landing at the nearby fishing port of Rufisque. Vichy troops and aircraft, however, left no doubt that the Free French were unwelcome, and they were forced to withdraw. On the twenty-fourth the British changed tactics with an ultimatum to Dakar to surrender or face the full force of the Allied fleet. Boisson refused, and two days passed in heavy exchanges of fire, yet without clear result. Finally, on the twenty-fifth the Allied fleet withdrew.

Dakar was an Allied defeat for which de Gaulle had to accept much of the blame. French West Africa had not rallied to Free France by Gaullist persuasion or Allied force. For Vichy, Dakar was a victory. It proved to Germany that Frenchmen would fight against Frenchmen, which led to reduced German controls on Vichy's navy and colonial armies.

A. Marder, *Operation "Menace": The Dakar Expedition and the Dudley North Affair* (London, 1976); R. O. Paxton, *Parades and Politics at Vichy: The French Officer Corps under Marshal Pétain* (Princeton, 1966).

W. A. Hoisington, Jr.

DALADIER, ÉDOUARD (1884–1970), was premier, 1938–1940, and war minister, 1936–1940. In France many hoped that Daladier could be the Georges

Clemenceau or Raymond Poincaré to lead the nation against Nazi Germany. Daladier, known to many as "Dala" or the "Bull of the Vaucluse," the electoral district that he represented, was reputed to be a man of action who could unite the French against the Nazi menace. "A bull, with snail's horns," commented Neville Chamberlain, who himself was hardly a paragon of firmness against Nazi Germany. Daladier's reputation exceeded his talents; often full of fight at first, then equivocating and capitulating.

During the war of 1914–1918, Daladier received a field commission and was cited for valor. In the 1920s he rose to prominence in the Radical Party, leaning **left** with Radical young Turks and willing to work with the **socialists**. In 1936 he was one of the main leaders of the **Popular Front**. He succeeded **Blum** as premier in April 1938 and went to **Munich** in September 1938 to condone the dismemberment of Czechoslovakia. Some say Daladier had no choice; others say that he failed to support the *bellicistes* in his cabinet. He turned against the **Communist** Party and broke up the Popular Front in November 1938, crushing a general strike against government take-backs of gains made in 1936. Daladier opposed strengthening the Franco–Soviet mutual assistance pact (1935); opposed Franco–Soviet military staff talks (1936–1938); and did not pursue with sufficient energy an **Anglo**–Franco–Soviet alliance in 1939, instructing his chief delegate to staff talks in Moscow (August 1939) not to agree to Red Army passage across Poland to fight the enemy.

After September 1939 Daladier quarreled with Paul **Reynaud** and stubbornly defended General Maurice-Gustave **Gamelin** against charges of failing to pursue the war with sufficient vigor. Daladier resigned as premier in March 1940, as his reputation and political power crumbled. After the French collapse in June 1940, he was arrested and imprisoned until the end of the war.

*M. Alexander, *The Republic in Danger* (Cambridge, U.K., 1992); J. Jackson, *The Popular Front in France Defending Democracy, 1934–38* (Cambridge, U.K., 1988); E. du Réau, *Édouard Daladier, 1884–1970* (Paris, 1993); R. Young, *France and the Origins of the Second World War* (New York, 1996).

M. J. Carley

DANNECKER, THEODOR (1913–1945), from 1940 through 1942 headed the Gestapo **Jewish** office in France (Judenreferat). Having joined the Nazi Party and SS in 1932 and the Sicherheitsdienst (security service) in 1934, Dannecker began to work for Reinhard Heydrich in 1937. Adolf Eichmann's protégé, Dannecker arrived in **Paris** in August 1940, where he initiated a vigorous **anti-Semitic** program. He was instrumental in the creation of the **Commissariat Général aux Questions Juives**, the **Union générale des Israélites de France,** and the propaganda unit **Institut d'études des questions juives**, organizations central to the Final Solution in France. He was an author of the **Madagascar** Plan to deport all European Jews to the African island.

In 1941 Dannecker personally directed the arrest of Jews in the 11th *arondissement* of Paris. He consistently exaggerated the Jewish population of France in order to demand more Jews to deport or hold as hostages. Young, ambitious, and zealous, Dannecker performed his assignments well enough to be promoted to *Hauptsturmführer* (captain) in early 1942. That March, he accompanied the first French convoy to Auschwitz. He implemented the wearing of the yellow star of David badge in the occupied **zone**. Dannecker was absent from Paris for the **Vélodrome d'hiver** roundups because he had gone to the camps of the unoccupied zone to search for ''deportable'' Jews.

In late July 1942 Heinz Röthke replaced Dannecker. This was probably the result of a disagreement between Dannecker and his superior, Helmut **Knochen**. Dannecker later served the SS in Bulgaria, Hungary, and **Italy**. In December 1945, he hanged himself while under arrest at the **American** prison at Bad-Tölz.

J. Adler, *The Jews of Paris and the Final Solution* (New York, 1987); S. Klarsfeld, *Vichy-Auschwitz: le rôle de Vichy dans la solution finale de la question juive en France*, 2 vols. (Paris, 1983, 1985); M. R. Marrus and R. O. Paxton, *Vichy France and the Jews* (New York, 1981).

                                                                                          D. F. Ryan

DARLAN, JEAN-FRANÇOIS (1881–1942), head of the French navy from 1937 to 1942, was one of the most powerful men in the **Vichy** regime, ranking alongside Pierre **Laval**.

Born into a family with political and naval connections, he became a fixture in the corridors of power from the mid-1920s. Promoted to admiral in 1929, he served as France's naval expert at various international conferences. He also helped draw up a plan, approved in 1932, for the refurbishment of the navy. In 1937 he became naval commander. The principal naval theater for France, he concluded, would be in the Mediterranean against the Italians (and possibly the Spanish).

By 1939, Darlan was ready for war and saw his job as ensuring French access to the men and materials of its **empire**. The defeat of the **army** in 1940 enhanced this logic, for the ''undefeated'' navy and the French empire became doubly important, as the only bargaining chips a defeated France held. They also made the man responsible for them very important. On 16 June 1940 he became Marshal **Pétain's** naval minister. From the start of the **armistice** period, Darlan gave standing orders to his crews to scuttle their ships, rather than surrender to anyone.

After Laval was fired on 13 December, Pétain needed someone to whom the Germans would talk. Darlan saw **Hitler** for a Christmas visit and, on 3 February 1941, visited Otto **Abetz**, the German ambassador in **Paris**. On 9 February, Pétain named him his heir apparent (replacing Laval), and he became the vice president of the Council of Ministers, minister of foreign affairs, and minister of information and, of course, continued as navy minister. Darlan argued for a policy of military neutrality, but economic cooperation with Germany. In search of a formal peace, he visited Hitler in May 1941, then, on 28–29 May, drew up the Protocols of Paris as a basis for normalized relations. They, however, never bore fruit.

After June 1941, all opposition was seen as **communist**-inspired and thus subject to the harshest repression. At the same time, Germany placed increasingly heavy demands on the French and their **economy**. To meet them, a new wave of regulations and laws was issued, all designed to ensure good order and governmental authority. Darlan had, however, failed to win major German concessions and was replaced by Laval on 17 April 1942.

Darlan, who commanded all Vichy forces after August 1941, had also been talking with the Allies. On 5 November he came to **North Africa** to visit his son, who had contracted polio. On 8 November the Allies, under cover of Operation Torch, also paid a visit. Darlan ordered resistance against the Allies. On 10 November he was taken **prisoner** but refused to order a cease-fire until the next day, when the Germans invaded the unoccupied rump of France. On 14 November Darlan joined the Allies, "inviting" the French fleet to sail to North Africa, but, instead, it was scuttled on 27 November. Without his fleet, Darlan's value quickly dropped. On 24 December 1942 he was assassinated. Not many people mourned his passing.

While Darlan's organizational skill was beyond doubt, his precise political leanings were anything but clear. It is perhaps easiest to understand him as a technocrat and a pragmatist: he looked for what "worked" and went with the prevailing political current, laying the foundation for a postwar France that would place great faith in the ability of a technical elite to solve its national problems.

*H. Coutau-Bégarie and C. Huan, *Darlan* (Paris, 1989); H. Michel, *François Darlan* (Paris, 1993); R. O. Paxton, "Darlan, un amiral entre deux blocs," *Vingtième Siècle* 36 (October–December 1992): 3–19.

H. H. Hunt

DARNAND, JOSEPH (1897–1945), head of **Vichy's** militia (**Milice Française**). Named to head the Vichy **police** in December 1943, he helped fight the **Resistance** during the last year of the Vichy government. A man of action and physical courage, Darnand possessed neither extensive intellectual nor oratorical skills.

Cited for bravery in World War I, Darnand was called by President Raymond Poincaré an "artisan of victory," an accolade he shared only with Marshal Ferdinand Foch and Premier Georges Clemenceau. During the 1920s, Darnand supported the royalist **Action Française** while he operated a trucking company from his home in Nice. By the mid-1930s, tired of the inaction of Action Française, Darnand joined more activist **right-wing** organizations.

He volunteered for military duty when war broke out again in 1939, and his picture appeared on the cover of the 21 March 1940 issue of the magazine *Match* for bravery in fighting along the **Maginot Line**. Taken **prisoner** in June 1940, Darnand escaped to Nice, where he subsequently headed the Pétainist

Service d'Ordre Légionnaire, which in 1943 evolved into the Milice Française. Intensified **Resistance** activity and German pressure led to his being named to head the police in December 1943. During the spring of 1944, Darnand's forces helped the Germans fight the Resistance, as on the **Glières** plain in southern France. Darnand, who joined the **Waffen-SS**, also created secret courts-martial to try and often execute resisters. Following the **liberation**, he fled to Germany. With the German defeat, he fought against **communist** partisans in northern **Italy**. Returned to France, he was tried and executed in 1945.

J. Delperrie de Bayac, *Histoire de la Milice* (Paris, 1969); B. M. Gordon, *Collaborationism in France during the Second World War* (Ithaca, NY, 1980); B. M. Gordon, "Un soldat du fascisme," *RDHDGM* 27:108 (October 1977) 43–70; B. Kasten, *"Gute Französen": die französische Polizei und die deutsche Besatzungsmacht im besetzten Frankreich* (Sigmaringen, 1993).

B. M. Gordon

DARQUIER DE PELLEPOIX, LOUIS, pseudonym of Louis Darquier (1897–1980), French **anti-Semite**, coordinator of **Vichy's** anti-**Jewish** program 1942–1944. A failed businessman, onetime municipal politician, **right-wing** agitator, and notorious anti-Semitic rabble-rouser, Darquier was chosen to head the Vichy government's General Office for Jewish Affairs or **Commissariat Général aux Questions Juives** in May 1942, succeeding Xavier **Vallat**, whom the SS in France found too moderate. At this point, the Nazis were about to begin the massive **deportation** of Jews from France to Auschwitz. Spending most of his time in **Paris**, Darquier helped coordinate these deportations and worked closely with the German authorities. Quite apart from its hitherto de-emphasized biological racism, Darquier's administration was characterized by corruption, cruelty, and incompetence. The Germans finally requested his removal, and he left office in February 1944. Darquier fled to **Spain**, where he lived until his death in 1980. In 1978 he achieved special notoriety by giving an interview to the weekly *L'Express*, in which the ailing exile claimed that the **Holocaust** was "pure and simple invention—Jewish invention, of course."

*S. Klarsfeld, *Vichy-Auschwitz: Le rôle de Vichy dans la solution finale de la question juive en France*, 2 vols. (Paris, 1983, 1985); J. Laloum, *La France antisémite de Darquier de Pellepoix* (Paris, 1979); M. R. Marrus and R. O. Paxton, *Vichy France and the Jews* (New York, 1981).

M. R. Marrus

DAS REICH DIVISION, Second Waffen-SS *Panzerdivision* (tank division), stationed in southern France from February through June 1944, responsible for massacres in Tulle and **Oradour-sur-Glane**.

After suffering heavy losses on the eastern front, the division, under the command of Major General Heinz Lammerding in February 1944, was stationed in the Montauban vicinity, to be reoutfitted and restocked with new recruits to make it again combat-ready. By May 1944, as a result of the weakness of

German forces in the region, the division was ordered to participate in the fight against the **Resistance**. Influenced by the intense National Socialist ideology of their Waffen-SS training and their experiences fighting in the east, the soldiers proceeded most brutally against the civilian population.

When, after learning of the invasion of 6 June 1944, the Resistance movements attacked the small occupation garrisons in the towns of Guéret and Tulle, the *Das Reich* division was ordered to take a detour from its march northward toward the **Normandy** front and fight the *maquis*. The story that the Resistance delayed a prompt arrival of the *Panzerdivision* at the Normandy front is not borne out by the facts. Instead, the German High Command held the group, together with other elite forces, in reserve in the expectation of a second landing in the days after the invasion.

In revenge for the French attack on the German garrison in Tulle, 120 men were hanged in the town on 9 June. On the same day, other units of the division murdered 67 inhabitants of the village Argenton in the Indre department. On 10 June, soldiers of the First Battalion of the ''Der Führer'' regiment, under Major Otto Dickmann, killed nearly the entire population of the village **Oradour-sur-Glane,** more than 600 men, **women**, and children. The division was nearly wiped out during the battles that followed on the Normandy front. After the war, several of those responsible for the massacres were brought to trial in France. Lammerding, however, died in the Federal Republic of Germany in 1971, before proceedings could be instituted against him.

J. Delarue, *Trafics et crimes sous l'occupation* (Paris, 1993); M. Hastings, *Das Reich* (London, 1981); E. Jäckel, *Frankreich in Hitlers Europa: Die deutsche Frankreich politik im zweiten Weltkrieg* (Stuttgart, 1966).

B. Kasten

DÉAT, MARCEL (1894–1955), was a French political figure whose politics evolved from socialism in the early 1930s to **collaborationism** during the Occupation. The chief political columnist for the newspaper *L'Œuvre*, he also headed the **Rassemblement National Populaire (RNP)**.

Born in Guérigny in the Nièvre, Déat studied at the École Normale Supérieure, then in World War I received five citations for valor and rose from private to captain. Elected a deputy on the **socialist** ticket, he supported ''order, authority, nation,'' at the 1933 party congress, creating a split with Léon **Blum**. Déat, with Barthelémy Montagnon, Adrien **Marquet**, and 24 like-minded deputies, was expelled from the Socialist Party and in 1934 established the Parti Socialiste de France, better known as the ''Neo-Socialists.'' Déat called for state economic planning to fight the depression and a rapprochement with Germany. On 4 May 1939, as war threatened, *L'Œuvre* published his article ''Faut-il mourir pour Dantzig?'' (Must One Die for Danzig?), which asked why the French should be asked to save Danzig for Poland.

With the defeat of 1940, Déat tried to create a single mass party to support the new government of Marshal **Pétain** and Pierre **Laval** at **Vichy**. Failing, he returned in September to **Paris**, where he continued to write for *L'Œuvre* and, in February 1941, became, with Eugène **Deloncle**, a founding leader of the RNP. After surviving an assassination attempt in August of that year, for which he blamed Deloncle, Déat organized a purge of the RNP and became its uncontested leader for the duration of the war. Constantly chiding Vichy for being insufficiently "revolutionary" and too *"attentiste,"* he also quarreled with other collaborationist rivals, notably Jacques **Doriot**. Under German pressure, Déat was finally named minister of labor and national solidarity in March 1944, although his effectiveness was circumscribed by Laval and cut by the evolving war situation. With the **liberation**, Déat fled to **Sigmaringen**. At the end of the war, he and his wife found refuge in a Catholic convent in Turin, where he died 10 years later.

*P. Burrin, *La Dérive fasciste, Doriot, Déat, Bergery, 1933–1945* (Paris, 1986); M. Déat, *Mémoires politiques* (Paris, 1989); E. H. Goodman, "The Socialism of Marcel Déat" (Diss., Stanford University, 1973); B. M. Gordon, *Collaborationism in France during the Second World War* (Ithaca, NY, 1980).

G. Le Marec

DEBRÉ, MICHEL (1912–1996), was a statesman from the **Resistance** governmental structure organized by Jean **Moulin.** Debré later wrote the 1958 constitution and was prime minister from 1959 through 1962.

Auditor for the Conseil d'État (State Council) in 1934, Debré joined Paul **Reynaud's** cabinet after the **Munich agreement**. With the coming of the war he was drafted, then taken **prisoner**, but escaped in the fall of 1940. After failing to renew contact with his old Saumur colleagues, he traveled to Morocco in 1941, where Emmanuel Monick, the resident general, put him in charge of liaison with the **Americans** in anticipation of an eventual Allied invasion. Convinced of the need for a Resistance headed by General **de Gaulle**, however, Debré returned to France and met Alexandre **Parodi** (Moulin's successor as general delegate of the government in 1944) and Pierre-Henri **Teitgen** of **Témoignage Chrétien**. A member of the Comité Général d'Études, Debré planned for the post-**liberation** political and administrative structures. With Émile Laffon, who was sent by de Gaulle, Debré created the commission to designate future prefects and commissioners of the **Republic**, who at the time of the liberation were to assume full power against any pretensions to the contrary by **Vichy** or an **Allied Military Government of Occupied Territories**. At the town of **Laval** on 22 August 1944, as commissioner of the Republic for the Angers region, Debré received General de Gaulle, president of the **Provisional Government**, who was en route from Cherbourg to **Paris**, where General **Leclerc** had just gone, ahead of the Allied troops.

Debré entered de Gaulle's cabinet in April 1945, where he planned and had signed on 9 October the directive creating the École Nationale d'Administration. From 1948 through 1958 he was a senator. Elected a deputy in 1963, he served from 1966 through 1973 as economics, foreign affairs, and defense minister.

†M. Debré, *Trois Républiques pour une France, Mémoires*, 5 vols. (Paris, 1984–1994).

O. Rudelle

DECOUX, JEAN (1884–1963), French naval officer and governor-general of Indochina during **Vichy**. In June 1940 the **Japanese** government demanded that the governor-general of Indochina, General Georges Catroux, permit a Japanese military mission in Tonkin to assure closure of the Haiphong-Yunnan railway supplying the Chinese Nationalist forces. Catroux wished to continue the war under General **de Gaulle's** leadership but believed he had to yield to Japanese demands to gain time. Vichy then replaced him with Admiral Decoux, who initially favored **Resistance** but obeyed Vichy's order to negotiate a settlement when the Japanese increased their demands in September. A Japanese attack against the French stronghold at Langson along the Chinese frontier resulted in a French defeat, demonstrating the futility of resistance. While the Japanese recognized French sovereignty in Indochina, they obtained the right to station troops in Tonkin. In July 1941, 35,000 Japanese troops landed in Saigon and occupied Cambodia, assuring military domination of the entire colony.

Seeking protection from Gaullist and **British** ''designs'' upon the French **empire**, Decoux turned to **collaboration**. Japan stripped the colony's resources, and rice shortages in 1945 led to an estimated 2 million deaths from starvation. Decoux repressed the Vietnamese nationalist movement severely, which went underground in resistance to both the Japanese and the French, although he tried to win the loyalty of Vietnamese elites through concessions.

When the war turned against the Axis, Decoux contacted representatives of de Gaulle's **Provisional Government**. Suspicious, the Japanese arrested him on 9 March 1945. Fighting between French forces and the Japanese army led to the deaths of 1,700 French soldiers and brought complete Japanese military and political control of Indochina. Admiral Decoux's collaboration illustrates the dilemmas of many French colonial administrators during World War II.

J. Decoux, *À la barre de l'Indochine* (Paris, 1949); J. Dreifort, *Myopic Grandeur: The Ambivalence of French Foreign Policy toward the Far East, 1919–1945* (Kent, Oh, 1991); E. Hammer, *The Struggle for Indochina 1940–1955: Vietnam and the French Experience* (Stanford, CA, 1966); P. L. Lamant, ''La Révolution Nationale dans l'Indochine de l'Amiral Decoux,'' *RDHDGM* 138 (1985).

K. Munholland

DÉFENSE DE LA FRANCE (DF) was begun by a student–faculty group, led by Philippe Viannay, his wife-to-be, Hélène, and Robert Salmon. They began publishing a newspaper from the cellars of the Sorbonne in July 1941, with financial aid from the **industrialist** Marcel Lebon. The traditional Catholic backgrounds of the early DF leaders allowed a wide range of conservative opinions in their journal from Gaullism to unrefined patriotism, but they generally avoided party affiliations. The journal had 47 numbers, with a print run of 5,000 at the beginning, rising to 250,000 in late 1943 and 450,000 at the **liberation**.

From the distribution networks of the newspaper, DF established intelligence and escape networks, a false papers service, and eventually a *"corps franc militaire."* Pierre **Brossolette** and Colonel **Passy** (from the French National Committee in London and **Bureau central de renseignements et de l'action**) met DF in March 1943, after which they joined the **Conseil National de la Résistance** and, in January 1944, were founding members of the non **communist** Mouvement de la libération national (MLN). This marked their move toward Gaullism, but they maintained a traditionally conservative view of a future "Fourth **Republic**." By early 1944 they had a large military (mainly *maquis*) as well as **press** organization, and both Claude Monod and Viannay became military leaders in the MLN. *Defense de la France* played an important part in the liberation of the provinces and of **Paris**.

M. Granet, *Défense de la France* (Paris, 1960); witness accounts by Hélène Viannay, Philippe Viannay, and Robert Salmon in the *Institut d'Histoire du Temps Présent* (Paris).

J. C. Simmonds

DELESTRAINT, CHARLES (1879–1945), was a French soldier and resister whose advocacy of armored divisions before 1940 and **Resistance** activity thereafter involved him closely with Charles **de Gaulle**.

A disciple of armored warfare advocate General Jean-Baptiste Estienne, Delestraint lobbied for the creation of large-scale armored units in the 1930s and, in this capacity, formed a friendship with de Gaulle, who was briefly his subordinate. Their shared vision of a modernized French **army** failed to reach fruition, and both officers were accordingly disillusioned by what they saw as the vindication of their ideas in the May–June 1940 debacle. Unlike de Gaulle, Delestraint remained in France, where from retirement in Bourgy-en-Bresse, he soon became an open critic of **Vichy's collaboration**.

In August 1942, after making a clandestine voyage to London, Delestraint accepted de Gaulle's invitation to lead the paramilitary activities of the Resistance groups united in the Gaullist Secret Army (*Armée secrète*). Delestraint took the code name "Vidal." Initially organizing in the unoccupied **zone**, by February 1943 the Secret Army's activities encompassed all France, coinciding with Jean **Moulin's** countrywide political direction of the **Conseil National de la Résistance** from January 1943.

The year 1943 saw a stepped-up Nazi/Vichy offensive against the Resistance. SD (German security service) agents posing as resisters captured Delestraint on 9 June 1943 at a rendezvous at the **Paris** *métro* station of La Muette. Moulin fell into the hands of Lyons SS chief Klaus **Barbie** 12 days later. While Moulin died under torture, Delestraint was deported to the Reich. He was shot by his SS captors at Dachau shortly before the **liberation** of the camp.

J. Lacouture, *De Gaulle*, 2 vols., vol. 1: *The Rebel, 1890–1944*, trans. P. O'Brian (New York, 1991); J.-F. Perrette, *Charles Delestraint: Officier de chars, commandant de l'Armée secrète* (Paris, 1972).

R. F. Crane

DELONCLE, EUGÈNE (1890–1944), extreme **right-wing** political leader of the interwar Cagoule and wartime **Mouvement Social Révolutionnaire**. A *Polytechnicien*, after distinguished service in World War I, Deloncle achieved success in naval engineering and business. In the mid-1930s, he broke with the **Action Française**, which he saw as too timid, and established, with Jean Filiol and others, a clandestine political organization nicknamed the Cagoule (the hooded ones), whose goal was a coup d'état that would initiate a right-wing dictatorship. Between mid-1936 and 1937, they resorted to bombings and murders, including those of Carlo Rosselli, a prominent Italian antifascist, and his brother Nello, in Normandy. Deloncle's anti-government plot failed, however, and he was arrested in November 1937. Freed at the outbreak of World War II, he reentered the navy.

In September 1940, Deloncle established the **collaborationist Mouvement Social Révolutionnaire** (MSR) in **Paris**. In early 1941, he and Marcel **Déat** created the **Rassemblement National Populaire (RNP)**. After the German invasion of the **Soviet Union** on 22 June 1941, Deloncle helped found the **Légion des Volontaires Français (LVF)**. His role in the assassination on 25 July 1941 of Marx Dormoy, minister of the **interior** at the time of his arrest in 1937, remains moot. Suspicion also arose that Deloncle helped arm Paul Colette, who wounded Pierre **Laval** and Déat in an assassination attempt in August 1941. On 2–3 October 1941, Deloncle and the MSR blew up synagogues in Paris with SS support; they also confiscated property of **Jews**. In the fall 1941, Déat evicted Deloncle from the RNP. Then in May 1942, Deloncle was forced out of the MSR. Foreseeing German defeat, he developed contacts with Admiral **Darlan**, probably also with the German *Abwehr* of Admiral Wilhelm Canaris, and with the **British**. After a brief detention by the Germans in 1942, he was killed on 7 January 1944 in a shootout at his home with Gestapo agents who had come to arrest him.

P. Bourdrel, *La Cagoule* (Paris, 1992 [first ed., 1970]); B. M. Gordon, *Collaborationism in France during the Second World War* (Ithaca, NY, 1980); B. M. Gordon, "The Condottieri of the Collaboration: *Mouvement Social Révolutionnaire*," *JCH* 10:2 (April 1975): 261–82.

J. Blatt

DEMARCATION LINE, the irregular boundary established by Article 3 of the 1940 **armistice**. It ran from the Swiss border west to the Loire River and south to the Pyrenees, separating the unoccupied **zone** from the occupied zone. Passage across the line was limited, with **Vichy** offices at Moulins, Chalons, and Langon. Mail traffic was limited to 300 letters per day. Additional rail checkpoints existed at Sauveterre-de-Béarn, Orthez, Mont-de-Marsan, Montpont, Fleuré, Jardres, Vierzon, Paray-le-Monial, and Mouchard.

The line separated families and inhibited communications as well as travel. Because of the line's negative effects on public opinion, its relaxation was among Pierre **Laval's** chief concerns in his negotiations with Germany at the end of 1940. Laval's successes, however, were limited, and the permeability of the line remained under the control of the German authorities. To show his disapproval of Laval's dismissal on 13 December 1940, the German ambassador to France, Otto **Abetz**, limited passage across the line to high-ranking officials. Later, Admiral **Darlan** achieved limited relaxation of the Demarcation Line in exchange for substantial concessions to Germany in the Protocols of Paris, 28 May 1941. The minor concessions that Laval and Darlan achieved received maximum publicity from the **Vichy press**.

The Demarcation Line remained a point of contention until its existence was rendered immaterial by the complete occupation of France on 11 November 1942. It was not officially suppressed, however, until February 1943.

La Délégation français auprès de la commission allemande d'armistice, vol. 1 (Paris, 1947); R. O. Paxton, *Vichy France: Old Guard and New Order, 1940–1944* (New York, 1972); Rémy (G. Renault), *La Ligne de Démarcation* (Paris, 1964).

B. A. McKenzie

DENATURALIZATION, the **Vichy** government policy to correct what it considered the excessive liberality of the Third **Republic's** naturalization laws. Vichy felt the law of 6 August 1927 had let in too many "undesirable" foreigners, notably **Jews**. On 22 July 1940, it passed a retroactive law providing for systematic review of all naturalizations after 1927 and cancellation of some of them.

A naturalization review commission was created for this purpose within the **Justice Ministry**. Headed by a councillor of state, its 10 members included judges and representatives of the Ministries of Foreign Affairs, Defense, **Youth** and **Family**, and, eventually, Colonies. The commission was not required to give reasons for its decisions. Reviews of naturalizations began in the fall of 1940 and continued through May 1944. Those whose naturalizations were canceled were listed in the *Journal Officiel* of the French State. Over 15,000 people were stripped of their French nationality and often were left stateless. Among them were children born in France who, under the 1927 law, were French citizens by right of being born on French soil. Original nationality seems to have been the most important factor in determining who was denaturalized. Italians and Poles accounted for half the total. The vast majority of the Poles were doubtless Jews, although the exact number cannot be known, since the *Journal Officiel* did not mention race or religion. The total number of Jews among all those denaturalized has been estimated at about 40 percent.

In May 1944, the French **Provisional Government** canceled the Vichy denaturalization law.

K. Labernède, *Les retraits de nationalité française sous Vichy 1940–1944* (Aix-en-Provence, 1990); B. Laguerre, "Les dénaturalisés de Vichy 1940–1944," *Vingtième Siècle* 20 (October 1988).

D. Evleth

DENUNCIATIONS (*délations*) most often took the form of letters sent to the **Vichy** or occupying authorities to inform on **Jews**, political dissidents, or rivals.

These letters are difficult to quantify because they were often either dispersed or destroyed. André Halimi has advanced the figure of 3 million to 5 million denunciations. Contemporary evidence reveals the pervasiveness of informing. A **Radio-Paris** show, *Répétez-le* was devoted to denunciation letters. According to Jean **Guéhenno**, even the smallest hamlets had a "village snitch," often the local head of the **Légion Française des Combattants.**

Délation affected all levels of society. Vichy encouraged it as a social cleansing act, making it an acceptable civic duty. This explains the standard form of many letters, beginning: "I have the honor" and signed "a veteran" or "a patriot." Motives for whistle-blowing included ideology but also personal rewards, revenge, and jealousy. The most famous wartime denunciation was the turning in of Jean **Moulin**, coordinator of the **Resistance** in 1943.

Rather than being a German import, the practice of denunciation was indigenous to France. The French language counts no fewer than 36 colloquial terms for snitching. Informing had been widespread during the Revolution of 1789 and after the Commune of 1871. Wartime denunciations created an atmosphere of fear, which muted dissent under Vichy. As a personal manifestation of **collaboration**, they also facilitated the work of the occupier. They illustrate how latent hatreds and private rivalries under the **Republic** could become deadly and arbitrary tools of public repression under an authoritarian regime. With the **liberation** in 1944–1945 came counterdenunciations.

J. Guéhenno, *Journal des années noires* (Paris, 1947); A. Halimi, *La Délation sous l'occupation* (Paris, 1983); J. Papp, *La Collaboration dans l'Eure* (Montreuil, 1993); *Practices of Denunciation in Modern European History*, special issue, *Journal of Modern History* 68:4 (December 1996); J. F. Sweets, *Choices in Vichy France* (Oxford, 1986).

E. T. Jennings

DÉON, MICHEL (1919–), a writer, member of the informal **right-wing** literary group the "**Hussards**" (Hussars), was raised in a royalist family and studied law in Paris. As a *lycéen* (secondary school student) in the 1930s, Déon opposed Léon **Blum**, joined the **Action Française** student affiliate, and subsequently worked as a literary journalist for the movement.

In Lyons during the Occupation, Déon worked as an editorial assistant for Charles **Maurras**, the head of Action Française. Criticizing what he saw as **Resistance** irresponsibility for provoking German reprisals, Déon was also appalled by what he considered the excesses committed at the time of the **liberation**. Like his fellow Hussard Roger **Nimier**, Déon was scandalized by the execution of the collaborationist writer Robert **Brasillach**. He was also angered by the sentence of life imprisonment handed down to Maurras, whom he subsequently visited in prison.

Following the war, Déon continued his journalism in right-wing circles. Although he later wrote that the Hussards' activity was oriented toward the reintroduction into literature of the pleasures of the melancholy of life, implying a separation from politics, his writing reflected the anti-*Résistantialisme* of his fellow Hussards, Roger **Nimier**, Antoine **Blondin**, and Jacques **Laurent**. The winner of literary prizes in the 1970s for *Les Poneys sauvages* and *Un Taxi mauve*, works that chronicled the previous 40 years, Déon was named to the Académie Française in 1978, the same year in which his autobiographical *Mes arches de Noé* appeared.

M. Déon, *Mes arches de Noé* (Paris, 1978); N. Hewitt, *Literature and the Right in Postwar France: The Story of the "Hussards"* (Oxford and New York, 1996); P. Vandromme, *Déon, ou le nomade sédentaire* (Paris, 1991).

B. M. Gordon

DEPORTATION, a term that commonly designates the forcible removal from France by the Germans of approximately 139,000 people as part of the repressive policies of occupation. **Jews** constituted 54 percent of this total, some 75,721 men, **women**, and children. The remainder—63,085, according to a conservative estimate—included those deemed by the Nazis to be **Resistance** activists or political enemies, hostages, people caught in roundups, or ordinary criminals. Of the Jews, almost all of whom were sent to killing centers in Poland, only 2,500, or 3 percent, survived the ordeal; of the others, sent to **concentration camps** in the Reich, 95 percent returned to France after the war.

The Germans deported French men and women to concentration camps beginning in 1940; systematic deportations of Jews to Poland began in the summer of 1942. From 1943, however, the term "deportation" came to be used in a quite different sense as well, referring to the forcible transfer of French workers to work in Germany, beginning with the conscription of individuals in September 1942 and proceeding through drafts of entire age groups with the **Service du Travail Obligatoire**, set up in February of the following year. These "deportees," eventually numbering over 600,000, were often termed "*déportés*" or "*déportés de travail*." Important because of their strategic and political significance, this category of persons sent to Germany attracted much more attention—notably by the BBC, which referred to them as "deportees" in broadcasts by the French Resistance—than those sent eastward as part of a repressive occupation policy. In consequence, particularly in the postwar period, there was some confusion over the meaning of the term and bitter animosity between associations of "*déportés-résistants*" and "*déportés de travail.*"

M. R. Marrus and R. O. Paxton, *Vichy France and the Jews* (New York, 1981); A. Wieviorka, *Déportation et génocide: entre la mémoire et l'oubli* (Paris, 1992).

M. R. Marrus

DESPIAU, CHARLES (1874–1946), French painter and sculptor famous for his neoclassical style. Considered avant-garde before World War I, Despiau saw his popularity drop off gradually but it was revived in the 1930s and 1940s.

In 1937 he participated in the Berlin Exhibit of French artists, and in 1941 he toured Germany with 12 other French artists on a trip paid for by the German Ministry of Propaganda. In interviews during the war he indicated his high regard for German cultural practices. Although he claimed that art was a refuge from world events, not a reflection of them, his work was, nonetheless, admired by Nazis in Germany and their supporters in France for its idealized portraiture.

During the war Despiau exhibited frequently at Galerie Charpentier, along with **Hitler's** official sculptor, Arno **Breker**. He served on a committee that organized a mammoth retrospective of Breker's work at the Orangerie in **Paris** in May and June 1942. As a result of his wartime activities, a **purge** committee headed by the painter André Fougeron forbade Despiau to exhibit and sell for two years beginning 1 September 1944. Despiau died in Paris in 1946.

L. Bertrand Dorléac, *L'art de la défaite 1940–1944* (Paris, 1993); M. C. Cone, *Artists under Vichy: A Case of Prejudice and Persecution* (Princeton, 1992); M. Gauthier, *Charles Despiau* (Paris, n.d). B. Hinz, *Art in the Third Reich* (Oxford, 1980).

D. D. Buffton

DIEPPE RAID (19 August 1942), the largest Allied raid on occupied Europe to date, demonstrated the difficulties of launching a successful cross-channel invasion.

When planning for the Dieppe raid began in the spring of 1942, Churchill wanted to prove that the Allies could launch an assault on the continent. Stalin wanted his western allies to open a second front. Recognizing that a full-scale assault on France was impracticable in 1942, the **British** chiefs of staff authorized Lord Louis Mountbatten to assume responsibility for the strategic planning of cross-channel raids. Mountbatten assigned the Dieppe raid to the Canadian army, whose commanding officers had requested a more active role for their troops in the European war.

Launched on the night of 18 August 1942, Operation Jubilee deployed 6,100 troops in a three-pronged, amphibious assault on the coast of Dieppe. Intended to destroy the German defenses that secured the coast, the raid failed completely. Going ashore without the support of tanks (which arrived 20 minutes later) and facing gun emplacements that had not been fully demobilized by British fighter aircraft, thousands of troops landed at dawn on 19 August 1942 to face intense German artillery fire. Of the 4,963 Canadian troops who had embarked, 2,211 returned to Britain, 1,944 were taken **prisoner**, and 906 were killed in action. German losses were 121 dead and 206 wounded.

The Dieppe raid offered **Vichy** an opportunity to seek military concessions from Germany. **Pétain** asked that France now be allowed to contribute troops to its own defense. **Hitler** refused this request but agreed to the establishment of a French armored unit in **North Africa**. To reward the town for not rallying in support of the Allied raid, Hitler authorized the liberation of 750 citizens of Dieppe held as prisoners of war in Germany.

B. Loring Villa, *Unauthorized Action: Mountbatten and the Dieppe Raid* (New York, 1989); R. O. Paxton, *Vichy France: Old Guard and New Order, 1940–1944* (New York, 1972); C. P. Stacey, *The Canadian Army, 1939–1945* (Ottawa, 1948).

M. Hanna

DORIOT, JACQUES (1898–1945), leader of the **Parti Populaire Français (PPF)**. Until his death, Doriot competed with other major **collaborationists** in attempting to establish his party as the dominant force in government. A talented orator who was exceptionally tenacious, Doriot epitomized the **fascist** leader.

During World War I, Doriot served in combat and won the Croix de Guerre. After the war, he became a **communist** of international repute, serving jail sentences and being elected mayor of Saint-Denis. In 1934, Doriot broke with the communists and, two years later, founded the PPF, which became increasingly fascist. Joined by other former communists, he made his new party a formidable force.

During the Occupation, Doriot welcomed the opportunity to collaborate and attempted to influence **Vichy** policy. Frustrated by Vichy's lack of enthusiasm for his brand of collaboration, he moved his operations to **Paris**, only to be thwarted by the official German policy of limited partnerships with the French pro-fascists. Until June 1941, Doriot even had to suppress his staunch anticommunism. With the attack on the **USSR**, however, he increased efforts to cooperate with Germany, launching verbal assaults from his party's newspaper, *Cri du peuple*, and helping to establish the **Légion des Volontaires Français contre le Bolchevisme**. Doriot eventually joined this French unit in German uniforms fighting the **Soviets**. This endeavor, however, detracted from his PPF work. The party's influence waned after 1942 despite the prestige his efforts brought in collaborationist circles. Doriot's most significant contribution to German efforts in France was an instrument to pry concessions out of Vichy by threatening to allow the PPF to rule France. During exile in Germany, Doriot was killed in an Allied strafing attack in February 1945.

*J. Brunet, *Jacques Doriot. Du communisme au fascisme* (Paris, 1986); P. Burrin, *La Dérive fasciste: Doriot, Déat, Bergery, 1933–1945* (Paris, 1986); D. Wolf, *Die Doriot-Bewegung* (Stuttgart, 1967).

R. W. White

"DOUBLE GAME" (*DOUBLE JEU*), an idea propagated by **Vichy** apologists after the war, purporting that Marshal **Pétain** and his aides had foreseen an Allied victory and had pursued an official policy of acquiescing to a minimum of German demands in order to stave off destruction of the country, while simultaneously maintaining secret contacts with the **British**.

Another variation of the "double game" theory pits Pétain as the national savior against Pierre **Laval**, the active collaborator. After the war, Pétain defined his actions as passive defense, declaring, "If I could not be your sword, I tried to be your shield." The double game never existed officially. Vichy pursued negotiations with Britain late in 1940 and in early 1941 concerning the British blockade of French ports and its support of General Charles **de Gaulle**, but increasingly, Vichy's position was one-sided, favoring the Germans. Indeed, Vichy, with the full knowledge of Pétain, eventually sought active **collaboration** with the Germans in the hope of securing a better place for France in a new German world order.

In practical terms, the "sword and shield" theory is indefensible. France did not "avoid the worst" by giving in to German demands. Indeed, among the occupied countries it supplied more war materials and foodstuffs to the Germans than even Poland. If Vichy saved most French **Jews** from the death camps, it did so at the expense of foreign Jews who had sought refuge in France. At any rate, without the active assistance of the French **police**, the Germans would have been unable to round up these individuals. In the final analysis, Vichy's sovereignty was a liability rather than an asset.

R. Frank, "Vichy et les Britanniques 1940–1941: Double jeu ou double langage?" in J.-P. Azéma and F. Bédarida, eds, *Vichy et les Français* (Paris, 1992); R. O. Paxton, "La collaboration d'État," in J.-P. Azéma and F. Bédarida, eds., *La France des années noires*, vol. 1 (Paris, 1993); R. O. Paxton, *Vichy France: Old Guard and New Order, 1940–1944* (New York, 1982 [original ed., 1972]).

V. Datta

DRIEU LA ROCHELLE, PIERRE (1893–1945), editor of the *Nouvelle Revue Française* (*NRF*) in Nazi-occupied **Paris** and a leading voice of the intellectual **collaboration**. Haunted by what he perceived as the decadence of bourgeois France, Drieu, beginning in the mid-1930s, began to see redemption in **fascism**, idiosyncratically defined, yet inspired by what he took to be the energy, youth, and virile force of the Nazi regime. With dissidents from the **Left** and **Right**, he participated in attempts to forge a "*rassemblement national*" (national assembly), culminating with the formation of the **Parti Populaire Français** in 1936, where he remained until the eve of the war.

Though he supported the war effort, Drieu quickly became, in the wake of the defeat in June 1940, an advocate of a Nazi-style revolution that would allow France to play a role in **Hitler's** Europe. Disdainful of the **Vichy** regime, he pressed Otto **Abetz**, an old friend and now German ambassador in Paris, to facilitate the creation of a *parti unique* (single party) as a first step toward a French National Socialism. Inasmuch as Berlin stood behind the Vichy government, Abetz, envisioning a "cultural," rather than a political, role for Drieu, convinced him to take over editorship of the *NRF* instead. In spite of Drieu's hope to maintain the review's prestigious reputation, its increasingly obvious collaborationist line alienated much of the talent that he hoped to recruit and led to its rapid decline. The realization of his failure, combined with a growing recognition that the Germans had lost the war, threw Drieu into a state of increasing despair. Though he continued to write publicly for collaborationist publications, his private disenchantment led to three suicide attempts, of which the last, in March 1945, was successful.

*P. Andreu and F. J. Grover, *Drieu la Rochelle* (Paris, 1979); R. Soucy, *Fascist Intellectual: Drieu la Rochelle* (Berkeley, 1979).

P. Mazgaj

DUCLOS, JACQUES (1896–1975), French **communist** leader from the **Popular Front** until his death, edited his party's clandestine newspaper during the German occupation. A baker by trade, by 1926 Duclos had become a member of the French Communist Party's (**PCF**) central committee. He remained one of France's most prominent communists until his death in 1975. During the interwar period he was a deputy in the Chamber of Deputies and after the war was elected to the National Assembly. From 1959 until his death he was a member of the French Senate.

Duclos rose to national prominence with the Popular Front, for which he was a leading spokesperson. After the Nazi–**Soviet** Pact of 1939 the French parliament outlawed the Communist Party. With Benoît Frachon, Duclos led the clandestine PCF from 1939 until Maurice **Thorez** returned from Moscow in November 1944. He edited the clandestine *Humanité*, the party's major newspaper. No one doubts the significant role played by the communists in both the armed (**Franc-Tireurs et Partisans**) and propaganda (**Front National**) wings of the **Resistance** after **Hitler's** invasion of the Soviet Union in June 1941. Some accuse Duclos and the party, however, of collaborating with the Germans between the Nazi–Soviet Pact and Hitler's offensive against the **USSR**; others insist that the communists resisted both the occupying Germans and **Vichy** from the fall of France. Evidence seems to be in favor of the latter position. PCF regional newspapers and small groups of armed communists were quick to join the anti-German and anti-Vichy struggle. Above all, the early months of the Occupation witnessed confusion among the previously outlawed communists.

Duclos remains a paradigm of French communism from 1920 until his death. His blend of Marxism–Leninism with the democratic and Jacobin values of the French Revolution defined his party as well during the war years.

*†J. Duclos, *Memoires*, vols. 1–6 (Paris, 1968–1972); H. R. Kedward, *Resistance in Vichy France* (Oxford, 1978); H. Noguères, *Histoire de la Résistance en France*, vols. 1–4 (Paris, 1967–1976); R. Tiersky, *French Communism 1920–1972* (New York, 1974).

O. L. Cole-Arnal

DUNOYER DE SEGONZAC, PIERRE (1906–1968), a loyal Pétainist, was *chef* (head) of the École Nationale Superieure des Cadres d'**Uriage**, the **Vichy** regime's flagship national leadership school, from the summer of 1940 until it was dissolved by Pierre **Laval** in late 1942.

Dashing, handsome, and charismatic, the cavalry officer Segonzac was first charged with training leaders for the Chantiers de la Jeunesse but soon pretended to orient the whole **National Revolution**. A provincial, rooted traditionalist, **Maurrasian** Catholic, contemptuous of money but proud to have 10 children, Segonzac represented the virtues of a hard, elitist, "total" **education**. Like General **de Gaulle**, he was interested in innovative, mechanized warfare and the innovative social thinking of the Dominicans.

While Vichy called his castle-school at Uriage the *"École Normale des chefs supérieures de la Jeunesse,"* the *"Vieux Chef"* (old leader) planned for the total reshaping of French **youth**. Although close to Henri **Frenay** of **Combat**, he was awarded Vichy's *francisque* and maintained direct access to **Pétain**, in whom he maintained total confidence until the occupation of the southern **zone** in November 1942. In early 1943, when his school was replaced, Segonzac kept a hard-core alumni network intact in an order bound by vows. He worked with anti-German, but also anti-**communist**, resisters such as the groups around Frenay, François **Mitterrand**, and General Henri **Giraud**, but a 1944 approach to de Gaulle was rebuffed.

With the June 1944 landings, Segonzac was leading his Uriage-style *"corps franc Bayard"* within the **Forces Françaises de l'Intérieur**; in October they became the 12th dragoons in General Jean **de Lattre de Tassigny's** first **army**, fighting with distinction in the Haute-Saône, the Vosges, **Alsace**, and the Black Forest. Promoted to brigadier general during the Algerian war, where he tried Uriage techniques as "Directeur du Service de formation des jeunes," Segonzac remained proud and unrepentant. At his death in 1968 he left a remarkably loyal—and influential—contingent of comrades and disciples.

B. Comte, *Une Utopie combattante, L'École des cadres d'Uriage, 1940–1942* (Paris, 1991); A. Delestre, *Uriage, une communauté et une école dans la tourmente, 1939–1945* (Nancy, 1989); P. Dunoyer de Segonzac, *Le Vieux Chef, Mémoires et pages choisies* (Paris, 1971); J. Hellman, *The Knight-Monks of Vichy France, Uriage, 1940–45* (Montreal and Kingston, 1993).

J. Hellman

DURAS, MARGUERITE (1914–1996), prolific writer and filmmaker, author of filmscript for Alain Resnais' *Hiroshima mon amour* and of *La Douleur* (The War: A Memoir).

Born Marguerite Donnadieu to French schoolteachers in colonial Indochina, Duras worked during the Occupation in the Cercle de la Librairie, overseeing paper **rationing**. In 1943, she became active in the **Resistance**, where she met François **Mitterrand**. Her husband, writer and political activist Robert Antelme, was deported. In 1944, Duras joined the **Communist** Party. Following the **liberation**, Mitterrand, now undersecretary in charge of **refugees, prisoners**, and deportees, located Antelme in Dachau, and Duras nursed him to health from near starvation.

Duras protested the Communist Party's stand on intellectuals but, although expelled in 1950, remained a committed communist. In 1959 she wrote the screenplay for *Hiroshima mon amour*, a collage of stories: a French actress in **Japan** has a brief love affair with a Japanese atomic bomb survivor, with whom she remembers her love for a German soldier during the Occupation. The film helped launch the New Wave. *La Douleur* (1985) was a collection of semiautobiographical pieces Duras claimed to have written during the Occupation and rediscovered years later. Included were the story of Antelme's release, an account of her attempts to free him by consorting with a French **Gestapo** agent, and a vignette of Resistance members torturing a **collaborator** during the post-

liberation purge. Revelations in this last piece provoked lawyer Jacques Vergès to subpoena Duras for the Klaus **Barbie** defense, but she declined, saying she had no evidence to give.

A writer above all, Duras was more emotionally, than ideologically, motivated. Resistance was central to her vision, as was identification with the dispossessed, especially **Jews**, who had a mythical significance in her writing.

M. Duras, *La Douleur* (Paris, 1985); M. Duras, *Hiroshima mon amour* (Paris, 1960), in English as *Hiroshima Mon Amour*, screenplay, trans. R. Seaver (New York, 1961); M. Duras and F. Mitterrand, ''Entretien,'' *L'Autre Journal* 1 (February–March 1986): 32–40; L. Higgins, *New Novel, New Wave, New Politics* (Lincoln, NE, 1996).

L. A. Higgins

E

ÉBOUÉ, FÉLIX (1884–1944), was governor-general of French Equatorial Africa (AEF) during the war and led the first French colony to switch from **Vichy** to **Free France**, 26 August 1940.

A black man from Guyana, Éboué was educated at the colonial school. He gained fame in Oubangui-Chari (present Central African Republic), where he had a 23-year administrative career, and was in charge of road construction, the introduction of cotton cultivation, and the creation of schools. Interested in native customs, he wrote several ethnological studies. Secretary-general of Martinique in 1932 and of French Sudan in 1934, he became governor of Guadeloupe from 1936 through 1938, one of the first **blacks** to hold positions of such importance.

Governor of Chad in 1939, Éboué prepared the territory for war, recruiting and training native troops and maintaining strategic roads. The rallying of Chad to the **Free French** forces opened the way to Libya through the Sahara to General **Leclerc's** troops. Rich in gold, lumber, and rubber, AEF constituted an economic and military arsenal for the Allied effort. Named *Compagnon de la Libération*, Éboué mobilized the entire war effort of the territory, which he modernized at the same time.

In favor of the assimilation of the natives of the colonies, Éboué attempted to put his ideas into practice: his administrative directive "*Une Nouvelle politique indigène*" in 1941 formed the basis of the 1944 **Brazzaville Conference**, which became the colonial policy of the Comité Français de la Libération Nationale.

Exhausted by his five years of life overseas and work as governor-general of an AEF at war, Éboué died while on a visit to Cairo to rest. He is the only black to have the honor of burial at the Panthéon in Paris.

A. Maurice, "Félix-Adolphe-Sylvestre Éboué," *Hommes et destins* 1 (1972): 212–15; U. Sophie, *Le gouverneur Félix Éboué* (Paris, 1949); B. Weinstein, *Éboué* (New York, 1972); unpublished material, file EE (II) 4094 (1), in *Archives Nationales, Centre des Archives d'Outre-Mer*, Aix-en-Provence, France.

A.-C. Tizon-Germe

ECONOMY UNDER VICHY was an important dimension to the history of World War II France because (1) hardship and forced labor alienated ordinary people and drove some to active **resistance**, (2) state intervention increased, and (3) postwar inflation originated during the Occupation.

France's economy from 1940 to 1944 was shaped by a combination of two factors. First, defeat and occupation truncated, disorganized, and impoverished the country. France was a vanquished nation, and its resources lay within reach of the victors. Second, **Vichy** tried to remodel the economy and respond to wartime circumstances of zonal division, restrictions on international trade, and transport difficulties.

As of 1940, Germany held directly the richest areas of France. Two-thirds of the population was under its rule. The occupied **zones** grew 72 percent of the country's wheat, 78 percent of the barley, 80 percent of the oats; they produced 87 percent of the butter and 100 percent of the sugar; they raised 65 percent of the cattle. In the north were mined 76 percent of the coal and all the iron. **Industry** was concentrated there—95 percent of steel production, most of the mechanical engineering, and the manufacture of all textile goods. The unoccupied zone produced nearly all the wine, oil, soap, and bauxite. About 1.5 million French **prisoners** of war were in Germany; the labor force shrank, and with it overall production. The **British** blockade cut irreplaceable supplies. Petroleum, cotton, and wool were previously imported. So was one-third of the coal. Colonial commodities such as rice, coffee, and rubber stopped arriving.

German demands strained the French economy. Alongside outright plunder, several mechanisms siphoned the country's wealth. The 1940 **armistice** stipulated that the costs of the army of occupation would be borne by France. On 18 August 1940, Germany unilaterally fixed the daily amount at 400 million francs, a huge levy, sufficient for the upkeep of 18 million men. The rate was lowered to 300 million (May 1941), then raised to 500 million (January 1943) and 700 million (June 1944). From June 1940 to August 1944, France paid 632 billion francs, plus 48 billion for lodging German troops and officials, in all, 10 times real occupation expenses and 46 percent of state expenditures. Over the five years, 11 percent, 19 percent, 21 percent, 37 percent, and 28 percent of national revenue went to Germany. The basic German device for pumping France's resources was to buy them with money collected as tribute.

Purchasers were aided by the overvaluation of the mark at 20 francs, 8 more than was warranted. The "compensation accord" of 14 November 1940 regulated bilateral trade. In fact, Germany imported but did not export. The French clearinghouse paid French exporters with francs it did not possess, there being no payments to it by importers of German goods. The French treasury covered a deficit of 165 billion francs.

To gain a foothold in French companies, Germany used "**Aryanization**" as a lever. It also purchased shares. For instance, Mundus took a 47.6 percent interest in the Havas news and advertising agency in March 1941. I. G. Farben controlled the dye industry through Francolor, a company in which 49 percent of the equity was in French hands. Germany acquired French-owned mines in Yugoslavia and Poland and French holdings in Romanian oil and banks.

Vichy authorities had to ensure economic survival in the face of daunting challenges. Gross production dropped regularly. Manufacturing and agricultural indexes fell to 44 and 69, respectively, in 1944 (1938 = 100). Germany also drained an increasing volume of commodities. Shortages compressed national consumption and led to **rationing**, a price and wage freeze, and the growth of a **black market**. In reality, official prices of manufactured goods doubled; those of agricultural products tripled. Prices on the parallel market were from 2 to 30 times higher. Inflationary tensions mounted as the disparity between supply and demand widened. The authorities absorbed unusable purchasing power by issuing public loans. In any case, these loans were needed to bridge the gap between state revenues and expenditures.

The ills of the economy and the hemorrhaging provoked by transfers to Germany elicited responses aimed at staving off collapse and initiating long-range changes. The law of 16 August 1940 created the **Comités d'organisation** to assist business in taking stock of assets, programming production, and regulating activity sector by sector. In 1944, 234 committees were operational. On 10 September 1940, a law established an Office central de répartition des produits industriels (Central Office of Industrial Product Allocation) to allocate scarce resources. A ministère de la production industrielle came into being on 27 September 1940, followed by a Délégation générale de l'équipement national on 23 February 1941. The latter elaborated the Plan d'équipement national (February 1942) and the Tranche de démarrage (Bloc of Initiatives) (May 1944). For the first time, a state agency worked with large companies to draw up investment programs. But no firm targets were set, and no order of priorities determined. In the end, the plans were not implemented.

Notwithstanding officially sanctioned traditionalism and honors heaped on farmers and craftsmen, necessity led Vichy to give scope to modernizing technocrats such as Yves Bouthillier, René **Belin**, Jean Bichelonne, and François **Lehideux**. Economic policy was an odd mix of quasi *dirigisme* (quasi directivism) and near **corporatism**. Neither a type of state management of the economy nor one of corporatist self-management by all strata of a profession, the *Comités* fell under the control of big business. Small firms were marginalized, and employees excluded. A form of corporatism materialized in the **Corporation paysanne** created on 2 December 1940, but not in the Charte du travail enacted on 26 October 1941. Employee participation was confined to social services; economic matters remained in the hands of the employer-dominated *Comités*.

In June 1940, the cabinet group headed by **Pétain** had sued for an armistice, indeed for peace, on the assumption that the war was over. Peace and the advent of a European **New Order** seemed imminent. When these forecasts proved wrong, provisional **armistice** terms became open-ended, extortionate arrangements. Hoping to restrain the occupiers, maintain the appearance of authority, and continue revamping French society, Vichy proposed **collaboration** in October 1940. It was a fateful step that set the course until 1944. Vichy settled into the role of willing partner, putting itself in the forefront, making German policy its own, even anticipating it. Far from hindering economic exploitation, Vichy facilitated it.

Blitzkrieg and expectations of rapid peace were scuttled by German defeats. The ensuing war economy required the mobilization of all of Europe's resources. Relentlessly, Germany requisitioned the French labor force. Despite low wages at home, only 150,000 French workers volunteered to go to Germany from 1940 to 1942, and half of them returned. In May 1942, the **Relève** attracted one-fifth of the 250,000 men requested. On 4 September 1942, the **Service du Travail Obligatoire** instituted forced departures to Germany. Vichy assisted Germany throughout; prefects selected workers, and **police** rounded up runaways. State bodies intended to protect and reform the French economy became instruments for harnessing it to the German war machine. The *Comités* carried out German instructions transmitted by Vichy. French companies worked largely to fill orders for the Wehrmacht or as subcontractors for German companies. In 1944—until the **liberation**—Germany took all aircraft built, 80 percent of public works, 78 percent of ships, 77 percent of automobiles, and 65 percent of rubber items and paint produced.

From 1940 to 1944, France provided Germany with one-third of the supplies and 42 percent of the financial revenues it drew from occupied Europe, a proportion unequaled by any other country.

*†A. Beltran et al., *La vie des entreprises sous l'Occupation* (Paris, 1994); I. Boussard, *Vichy et la corporation paysanne* (Paris, 1980); J.-C. Hazera, *Les patrons sous l'occupation* (Paris, 1995); R. F. Kuisel, *Capitalism and the State in Modern France* (Cambridge, 1981); M. Margairaz, *L'État, les finances et l'économie, Histoire d'une conversion, 1932–1952* (Paris, 1991); M. Margairaz and H. Rousso, "Vichy, la guerre et les entreprises," *Histoire, économie et société* 11:2 (Fall 1992); A. S. Milward, *The New Order and the French Economy* (Oxford, 1970); R. Vinen, *The Politics of French Business, 1936–1945* (Cambridge, 1991).

S. Saul

ÉDITIONS DE MINUIT (1941–1944) was a clandestine **press** that published 43 unsigned or pseudonymous texts by authors including Louis Aragon, Paul Eluard, André **Gide**, Jean **Guéhenno**, François **Mauriac**, Edith Thomas, and Elsa Triolet. It also printed a translation of John Steinbeck's *The Moon Is Down*.

Minuit's goal was to print and distribute uncensored essays, **fiction**, and poetry by French authors writing in occupied France. Founded by Jean Bruller (pen name Vercors) and Pierre de Lescure, the venture formed around Jean **Paulhan**, who became unofficial leader of the literary **Resistance** in **Paris** after resigning in September 1940 as editor in chief of the *Nouvelle Revue Française*.

By day, Paulhan frequented Francophile Germans; by night, he worked with the **communist** militant Jacques Decour to establish the underground newspaper *La Pensée libre* and its successor, the ***Lettres Françaises***.

In February 1942, Minuit printed Bruller-Vercors' 40-page short novel, the ***Silence de la Mer***, about an idealistic German officer billeted in the home of a Frenchman and his niece shortly after the fall of France. The novel's sympathetic portrait of the German soon made it an object of controversy and debate. By 1944, the novel had been reprinted by the **Free French** forces exiled in London, where Cyril Connolly's English translation brought it worldwide attention. Other Minuit titles appeared in editions of up to 2,000 copies before the press went aboveground after the **liberation** with three volumes of *Chroniques* as well as the anthologies *La Patrie se fait tous les jours* and *L'heure du choix*. A decade later and under new ownership, Minuit was **publishing** avant-garde novelists such as Samuel Beckett, Alain Robbe-Grillet, Marguerite **Duras**, and Michel Butor.

P. Fouché, *L'Édition française sous l'occupation, 1940–1944* (Paris, 1987); A. Simonin, *Les Éditions de Minuit, 1942–1955, Le Devoir d'insoumission* (Paris, 1994); Vercors (J. Bruler), *The Battle of Silence* (New York, 1968).

S. Ungar

EDUCATION UNDER VICHY was characterized by a **Vichy** position that laid much of the blame for France's defeat in 1940 on its "secular" and "bookish" educational system. Marshal **Pétain** and his followers placed particular blame on the Third **Republic's** free and universal primary schools, its teachers (*instituteurs*), and their labor union (Syndicat National des Instituteurs). Pétain's aide René Benjamin had asserted that unionized *instituteurs*, along with café owners, were, essentially, secular and **left-wing** demagogues. Long concerned with educational reform, Pétain himself discoursed on the problem in a 1941 essay collection. Schools, he argued, must educate students to fit within the **family**, society, and nation, with both the Catholic Church and the **army** playing vital roles in this task. In short, he believed that France must develop a "national education" rather than "public instruction" and must strive also "to develop physical strength, temper the heart, and forge the will." These sentiments became distilled in a program of "general education" that was to include not only a renewed emphasis on Catholicism but also a new stress on artistic activities and physical training.

A succession of ministers of education (an unprecedented six in four years) tried simultaneously to dismantle the Republican system and implement a "national" one. All the ministers were conservative, but their ideology was no antidote to the crosscurrents bedeviling the regime. The first, Sorbonne professor Albert Rivaud, appointed on 17 June 1940, was dismissed after less than a month for his outspoken opposition to the Nazis. Émile Mireaux, a senator and codirector of the newspaper *Le Temps*, held the post only slightly longer—seven weeks—because Pétain distrusted parliamentarians. Next came Georges Ripert, dean of the Paris law faculty, who established the foundations for national education. He abolished the primary teaching colleges (*écoles normales*), their consulting bodies, and the teachers' union, replacing these bodies with Instituts de Formation Professionnelle and state-controlled professional associations. Despite Ripert's professed allegiance, Pétain suspected him of being loyal to **Laval**, and when the latter fell from power on 13 December 1940, Ripert also was dismissed. Ripert's successor, Jacques **Chevalier**, represented Catholic influence at its crest. This general's son, trained as a philosopher, had founded during the 1930s a **right-wing** schoolteachers' association and now reintroduced religious education in state primary schools and granted subsidies to Catholic schools. These moves caused such a storm of protest among the teachers, with consequent unease among the Nazis, that Pétain had to remove Chevalier after less than two months in office.

In February 1941 Pétain appointed the minister who proved to have the most dramatic impact on education: Jérôme Carcopino, a professor of ancient Roman history at the Sorbonne. Skillfully navigating between the Catholics and the collaborators on the question of Catholicism in education, Carcopino moderated, against Pétain's wishes, the zeal of his predecessors. He rescinded the right to teach Catholic dogma or display its **symbols** in public schools and ended state subsidies to Catholic schools. These positions, satisfying neither Catholics nor secularists, did not end the turmoil produced by Chevalier's reforms. Carcopino stood steadfast against the efforts of collaborators to destroy the autonomy of French education. For example, he did not **purge** the College de France of **communists** and **Freemasons**, as many collaborators wished, nor did he promote the persecution of these groups or their removal from the rest of the educational system.

Carcopino's most important reforms, known as the "*réforme Carcopino*," involved the transformation of the secondary system. Again he strove for the middle ground among the warring factions. On one hand, his law of 15 August 1941 restored the elitism and classicism of the *lycées* by reimposing tuition and restoring the mandatory teaching of Greek and Latin. On the other hand, some of his reforms moved in the direction supported by the **Popular Front** education minister Jean Zay and the post-1945 reforms, mitigating the elitism of the *lycées* by creating the *diplôme des études primaires préparatoires* (DÉPP), which permitted bright students from the mass primary schools to obtain scholarships to the *lycée*. The law of 15 August 1941 upgraded the secondary education of the upper primary schools (*écoles primaires superieurs*) by turning them into *collèges* that concentrated on modern languages and technical education.

With the return of Laval to power and the growing interference of the Nazis in Vichy affairs, Carcopino was ousted and replaced by Abel **Bonnard**, salonist and writer, in April 1942. Bonnard, who had been involved in the Maurresian educational group Cercle Fustel de Coulanges, would hold this post until August 1944, making him both the last and longest-serving Vichy education minister.

Long on rhetoric, Bonnard articulated Vichy axioms, such as bringing education closer to life through increased emphasis on technical education, but he was short on action. True to his **collaborationist** inclinations, he was the first minister of education to speak openly of politicizing the profession and devoted much of his effort to helping the German war effort. (Laval is rumored to have quipped that Bonnard was more German than the Germans.) To this end he authorized, first, the spying on, and subsequent rounding up of, communists; second, the wearing of the *"francisque,"* a Vichy honor **symbol**, in schools; and, third, the renewed purging of "unacceptable teachers." In general, this crackdown affected primary teachers more than secondary teachers.

In general, Vichy's grandiose aims for education were stillborn. Teachers, to say nothing of students, turned a cold shoulder to Vichy's moral and religious call to arms. In addition, the church never regained its pre-1789 influence. At the **liberation**, Carcopino's reforms were swept out, but his *collèges* proved to be a prototype of the *"école moyenne"*—serving as the transition between primary and secondary education—realized by the Christian Fouchet and René Haby reforms after 1945.

*†B. Comte, *Une utopie combattante. L'école des cadres d'Uriage (1940–1942)* (Paris, 1991); P. Giolitto, *Histoire de la jeunesse sous Vichy* (Paris, 1991); W. D. Halls, *The Youth of Vichy France* (Oxford, 1981).

W. S. Haine

EMERGENCY (AMERICAN) RESCUE COMMITTEE (ERC, 1940–1942) was a privately funded **American** organization founded in New York three days after the German defeat of France. Its objectives were to raise money and to secure the safety of well-known European artists, intellectuals, and politicians. With the assistance of the Museum of Modern Art's Alfred Barr, Jr., his wife, Margaret Barr, Albert Einstein, Thomas Mann, Frank Kingdon, and several other prestigious advisers, a list was compiled of those persons with the most immediate need to escape from France due to the "surrender on demand" clause in Article 19 of the Franco–German **armistice**.

Varian Fry (1907–1967), a former Harvard classics scholar and editor, volunteered to direct the Marseilles-based ERC operations. He arrived there on 15 August 1940 with a list of 200 names and $3,000. Needing a legal cover for this illegal rescue operation, the Centre Américain de Secours (CAS) was established to aid needy **refugees** with food, money, and lodging. Despite dwindling funds, tightening of border regulations, increasing harassment from Gestapo and **Vichy** officials, and a lack of cooperation from American officials, Fry, with a small staff, was able to procure forged exit visas, identification cards, financial assistance, and underground escape routes to help many of the threatened cultural luminaries flee the Vichy and Nazi governments.

Between the fall of 1940 and August 1941, the ERC organized the escape of approximately 1,500 people, including Heinrich Mann, Franz Werfel, Marc Chagall, Jacques Lipchitz, Marcel Duchamp, André Masson, André Breton, Hannah

Arendt, and Lion Feuchtwanger. On 29 August 1941, Fry was arrested by agents of the Sûreté Nationale for protecting **Jews** and anti-Nazis as well as for assisting the political enemies of France. A few days later, he was escorted to the border and expelled from France with the approval of both the American and French governments. The committee's activities, however, did not end with Fry's departure. Daniel Bénédite, Fry's chief aid, managed to keep the ERC and CAS going. He successfully procured overseas passage for some 300 additional people, including Jean Malaquais, Wanda Landowska, Mané Katz, Moise Kisling, and Marcel Duchamp, who sailed out of Marseilles in May 1942, the last client of the ERC.

Altogether the ERC provided various forms of assistance to more than 4,000 people, as well as smuggling some 300 **British** servicemen out of France, all without the help of Vichy or the American State Department. Both, according to Fry, greatly hindered the ERC's operations. On 12 April 1967, Fry was awarded the Croix du Chevalier of the French Legion of Honor for his efforts in rescuing the cultural figures of Europe during World War II.

D. Bénédite, *La Filière Marseillaise* (Paris, 1984); L. Fittko, *Escape through the Pyrenees* (Evanston, IL, 1991); V. Fry, *Surrender on Demand* (New York, 1965); V. Fry archives, Columbia University, New York.

I. V. Guenther

EMPIRE, OVERSEAS, became a major object of contention between **Vichy** France and **Free France** during the war. At the outset of the conflict the empire was expected to play a major role in supplying troops and resources to sustain a long-term French war effort. With the collapse of the northeastern front in May–June 1940, Premier Paul **Reynaud** entertained the possibility of continued resistance from overseas, and 26 deputies and a senator left Bordeaux for Morocco aboard the SS *Massilia*. Several colonial governors and military leaders, such as General Auguste **Noguès** in Morocco, Governor-General Georges Le Beau in Algeria, and High Commissioner Gabriel Puaux and General Eugène Mittelhauser in Syria, initially considered continuing the war but rejected the idea when Marshal **Pétain**, who had replaced Reynaud, signed an armistice and insisted on obedience. Only General Georges Catroux in Indochina decided to continue but resigned without rallying the colony to the cause of General **de Gaulle**.

Subsequently, parts of the empire rallied to the Free French, beginning with Governor Henri Sautot in the New Hebrides and continuing with rallies in Equatorial Africa led by Governor Félix **Éboué** in Chad. With the addition of Gabon in November all of French Equatorial Africa had joined the Free French. Pondicherry and the other French enclaves in India rallied quickly to the Free French, and Tahiti joined them in September 1940. The Americans subsequently set up a base on Bora Bora in French Polynesia. In the French West Indies the black population favored the Free French, but Admiral Georges Robert, the high commissioner, repressed any signs of dissidence. There would be no further rallies until a British–**Free French** force ousted the Vichy regime from Syria and Lebanon in July 1941, and a Free French expedition liberated St. Pierre and Miquelon in December that year.

The empire was one of the main bargaining counters that Vichy held in negotiating with Germany, and Vichy officials played this chip at every opportunity but obtained few advantages. Although the empire was to be neutral according to the **armistice**, Admiral **Darlan** granted Germany landing rights in Syria and allowed supplies to reach General Erwin Rommel by way of Tunisia. Vichy drew up plans to reconquer the African colonies that had rallied to de Gaulle, requesting that the German armistice commission allow reinforcement of French troops for the purpose. Admiral Jean **Decoux** proposed that **Japanese** forces assist in the recovery of the Free French colonies in the Pacific.

Vichy policy toward the empire was one of preservation in the face of defeat. Loyalty and obedience were expected, and measures were introduced to assert Vichy's **New Order** in the empire. Anti-Semitic legislation reached North Africa, where revocation of the Crémieux decrees abrogated **Jewish** citizenship, and institutions of the **National Revolution**, such as the **Légion Française des Combattants**, also appeared in the empire. In West Africa forced labor was reintroduced. In Indochina **Decoux** offered Vietnamese elites a wider role in the administration and created a Vietnamese advisory board, but these were limited gains designed to counter Japanese propaganda and to undermine Vietnamese nationalism.

Some Vichy reformers considered investment in the empire a source for the renewal of France, but lack of resources foreclosed plans for an imperial ''**industrialization**.'' Trade with the empire declined to two-thirds of its prewar level as a result of the British blockade. Imperial goods that reached metropolitan France increasingly served German requirements. Vichy's version of an imperial mission for France remained largely propaganda rhetoric for metropolitan consumption, expressed through ''colonial weeks,'' films, and **radio** broadcasts that were laced with **denunciations** of perfidious Albion and Yankee imperialists. With the Allied invasion of **North Africa** in November 1942, Vichy lost its imperial card and any claim to imperial glory, although Vichy officials continued to propose imperial reforms throughout 1943. From Vichy's perspective both defeat at the hands of the Axis and the successful **Anglo-American** invasion of North Africa undermined French imperial prestige.

The ''dissident'' empire provided de Gaulle with a territorial basis for his claim that France remained in the war despite the armistice. Yet the empire proved a cause of contention between the Allies. The Free French, no less than Vichy, considered British and American actions threats to French imperial sovereignty. The Anglo–Free French operation in Syria ended in recrimination when the British commander negotiated a settlement with Vichy authorities that excluded the Gaullists, and a British force liberated **Madagascar** without consulting de Gaulle in advance. Although the British turned over control of Syria and Madagascar to the Free French, suspicion of British intentions remained.

The **United States'** entry into the war raised further alarms over the status of the French empire. De Gaulle hoped that Free French control of strategic territories would gain American recognition of them as trustees of French sovereignty. After Pearl Harbor, de Gaulle agreed to allow American bases to be established on Free French territory in Africa and in the Pacific. In turn the Americans extended Lend-Lease to the Free French, recognized Free French authority in the administration of territories that joined de Gaulle, and promised a postwar restoration of French sovereignty over all areas held in 1939.

Despite such promises, Roosevelt became convinced that the era of empire was ending and that France, particularly Gaullist France, should not be allowed to regain full control of its prewar empire. He proposed that strategic parts of the empire, including **Dakar**, Bizerte, New Caledonia, and Indochina, be placed under a trustee arrangement. At the Casablanca Conference, Roosevelt expressed support for an independent Morocco to the sultan. At Teheran Roosevelt and Stalin agreed that France should not be allowed to retain Indochina, and Roosevelt indicated that parts of France's colonial empire should become part of an internationalized system after the war. By the end of the war, Roosevelt's anticolonialism yielded to American recognition that loss of empire would weaken France as an ally, but the Gaullists' wartime fears of American policies persisted.

De Gaulle recognized that the empire's contribution to France's recovery and **liberation** required a revision of the prewar imperial structure. Troops from the empire made up the bulk of General **Leclerc's** forces, of French combatants in the Tunisian campaign, of General Alphonse Juin's Expeditionary Force in **Italy**, and of General Jean **de Lattre de Tassigny's army** in **Provence**. The parts of the empire that had joined de Gaulle had been taxed to defray the costs of rearmament and to support the Free French administration. The empire had been instrumental in the restoration of French prestige, and de Gaulle recognized the imperial contribution in several wartime speeches in which he promised a large measure of autonomy for the colonies. In the **Brazzaville Conference** of January–February 1944 he proposed the formation of a less centralized French Union.

Brazzaville implied a more liberal imperial rule, but the promise fell short of expectations, reflected in a series of challenges that de Gaulle's Provisional Government faced at the war's end. On the day that the German surrender was signed in Europe, nationalist demonstrations in Algeria brought swift repression, and the sudden end of the war in the Pacific produced a power vacuum in Indochina that **Ho Chi Minh** filled by proclaiming an autonomous Vietnam, another expectation denied when the Provisional Government reasserted French authority. The empire provided **Free France** with the means of redemption, but liberation of metropolitan France was not liberation for the empire. Retention of the empire became necessary for a postwar French assertion of power and grandeur amid the gathering storm of the cold war.

*C.-R. Ageron, "La deuxième guerre mondiale et ses conséquences pour l'empire," in J. Thobie, et al., *Histoire de la France coloniale 1914–1990* (Paris, 1990); J.-B.

Duroselle, *L'Abîme* (Paris, 1982); P.-M. de la Gorce, *L'Empire Écartelé 1936–1946* (Paris, 1988); J. Marseille, "L'empire," in J.-P. Azéma and F. Bédarida, eds., *La France des années noires*, vol. 1 (Paris, 1993); M. Shipway, *The Road to War: France and Vietnam, 1944–1947* (Providence and London, 1996).

K. Munholland

LES ENFANTS DU PARADIS (Children of Paradise), probably the most famous and certainly one of the greatest of all French films, is a fine example of the continuities and of the divisions of French public life in the "dark years" of 1940–1944.

The team of Marcel Carné, the director, and Jacques Prévert, the screenplay's author, had, before the war, produced a series of remarkable and successful movies that blended social realism and romanticism, such as *Le jour se léve* in 1939. Arletty, who acted in many of them, was the star of the movies they made under **Vichy**. But the **cinema** of the Occupation, with very few exceptions, left current realities aside and focused on the filming of nineteenth-century novels and on escape into fantasy. The best example of the latter was the Carné-Prévert *Visiteurs du soir* (1942).

Les enfants du paradis is a complex and deeply romantic story of love and frustration—four men gravitating around Garance (Arletty)—that takes place in the world of **theater** and pantomime, Boulevard du Temple, in the 1820s and 1830s; three of the men—the mime Baptiste Deburau (Jean-Louis Barrault), the actor Frédéric Lemaître (Pierre Brasseur), and the dandy assassin P. F. Lacenaire (Marcel Herrand)—had been "real characters." The movie's filming began in August 1943 and took place mainly in Nice. It was interrupted when the Germans occupied Nice in September 1943 and did not resume until February 1944. It ended just before D-Day, but Carné did not want to release the film before the complete **liberation** of France, and it had its premiere on 9 March 1945.

Despite its length (3 ½ hours), it became a huge success and a **symbol** of the vitality of French art. But this spectacular and costly historical romance had been affected by the vicissitudes of the "Franco-French war." On one hand, as in the case of *Les Visiteurs du soir*, two of the **Jewish** collaborators of Prévert and Carné, the composer Joseph Kosma and the set designer Alexandre Trauner, had to work for the film clandestinely. On the other hand, the **collaborationist** actor Robert Le Vigan fled to Germany before completing his part and had to be replaced (by Pierre Renoir); as for Arletty, she was charged with having had a long affair with a Luftwaffe officer, was **purged** after the liberation, and was in jail when the movie came out. It was the next-to-last of the Carné-Prévert films and the last of their triumphs. Their return to poetic realism in *Les portes de la nuit* (1946)—which deals with the Occupation and its effects—was a flop.

M. Carné, *La Vie à belles dents: souvenirs* (Paris, 1975 [subsequent eds., Paris, 1979, 1989]; M. Carné and J. Prévert, *Les Enfants du paradis* (Paris, 1974); J. Prévert, *Children of Paradise, a Film by Marcel Carné*, trans. D. Brooke (New York, 1968); J. Prévert, *Les Enfants du Paradis* (Paris, 1967); G. Sellier, *Les Enfants du Paradis: Marcel Carne et Jacques Prevert, Étude critique* (Paris, 1992); E. B. Turk, *Child of Paradise: Marcel Carné and the Golden Age of French Cinema* (Cambridge, MA, 1989); N. Warfield, *Notes on Les Enfants du Paradis* (New York, 1967, 1973).

S. Hoffmann

ESPRIT was a review that originated and promoted the communitarian personalism common to the **National Revolution** discourse of the **Vichy** regime.

The young Catholic intellectual elite that had founded *Esprit* in 1932 divided over Vichy. Founder Emmanuel **Mounier**, Jean Lacroix, and Hubert Beuve-Méry (all lecturing at the **Uriage** school) prevailed, however, and, from November 1940, *Esprit* promoted Vichy projects, some of them of Jacques **Chevalier** (**education** minister, former mentor of Mounier and Lacroix). *Esprit* wanted to become "one of the main creative centers of a true France and of a true revolution," with its "Program for the French **Youth** Movement" attacking vulgar money-mindedness, defending "the simple life," "authority and collective discipline," the communitarian commitment, and the way in which "the German revolution" assimilated **socialist** aspirations and promoted "the sense of working for the German people." French young people were to transcend the outdated categories of **Left** and **Right**, become healthy and hardworking, and enjoy "festivals, liturgies, and games." *Esprit* particularly backed the "Jeune France" movement's cultural renovation projects and the flagship Uriage school, where *Esprit's* personalism became the unofficial doctrine. In 1941 *Esprit* prospered, having almost doubled its circulation, but **Action Française** jealousy helped silence it in late summer 1941. Undaunted, Beuve-Méry, Lacroix, et al. continued to promote *Esprit*'s ideas at Uriage and in the youth movements.

In October 1944 the secret Uriage network helped *Esprit* rush to publication in liberated **Paris**, as Beuve-Méry was founding *Le Monde*. Mounier adroitly situated *Esprit* as left-wing, having a cleverly camouflaged **Resistance** message in 1940–1941. Along with *Le Monde* and the **publishing** firm Les Éditions du Seuil it drew progressive Catholics and other antimaterialist communitarians, as it promoted anti-individualism, anti-Americanism, *tiers-mondisme* (Third Worldism), and openness to the **communist** movement.

J. Hellman, *Emmanuel Mounier and the New Catholic Left, 1930–1950* (Toronto, 1981); D. Lindenberg, *Les Années souterraines, 1937–1947* (Paris, 1990); P. de Senarclens, *Le Mouvement "Esprit," 1932–1941* (Lausanne, 1974); M. Winock, *Histoire politique de la revue "Esprit"* (Paris, 1975).

J. Hellman

ESTEVA, JEAN-PIERRE (1880–1951), was admiral of the fleet. Born to a champagne merchant, Esteva rose to become commander in chief of the Mediterranean fleet in 1939. He served as first officer of the watch on the *Waldeck-Rousseau* in 1912 and was wounded in the First World War. By 1932 he was responsible for developing the aeronautical branch of the navy and in 1937 was promoted to Admiral "South," taking command of an antitorpedo squadron to protect French interests in the western Mediterranean during the Spanish civil war.

After the **armistice** of June 1940, Esteva replaced Marcel **Peyrouton** as resident-general of Tunisia (1940–1942). During the first part of his tenure in the protectorate Esteva did his best to maintain the "neutrality" of the **Vichy** government against the combined threats of Axis and Allied forces in this most sensitive strategic area, holding sway too against increasing nationalist pressures in Tunisia. While Esteva might have been an officer of the "old school," displaying a clear devotion to following orders, politically he was untried and ill suited to his role. At the time of the **Anglo-American** landings (Operation Torch) in November 1942, although there was some confusion about whose authority he should obey, Esteva followed orders from the Vichy government and was forced to allow German and Italian reinforcements, aircraft, and equipment to land at Tunis and Bizerta. The Germans also captured French warships stationed at Bizerta. One major consequence of these developments was the rapid decline of French authority in Tunisia.

Admiral Esteva was the first French military commander to be tried after the **liberation**. Condemned to life imprisonment by the High Court (**Haut Cour de Justice**), he was released in 1950, suffering from ill health, and died in his hometown of Reims in 1951.

H. Couteau-Bégarie and C. Huan, *Darlan* (Paris 1989); Haute Cour de Justice, *Procès de l'amiral Esteva* (Paris, 1948); R. O. Paxton, *Parades and Politics at Vichy: The French Officer Corps under Marshal Pétain* (Princeton, 1966).

M. Cornick

ÉTAT FRANÇAIS (FRENCH STATE), the regime based in Vichy, which ruled those areas of southern France left unoccupied by Germany according to the June 1940 **armistice**. In theory, the regime's authority extended also to the northern, occupied **zone**, but its actions there were always subject to the German authorities in **Paris**. The État·Français continued to claim the status of a legal government throughout the Occupation, even though the Germans occupied Vichy's "free" zone in November 1942.

Though born of military defeat, the Vichy regime was not a puppet government; it was constituted by a vote in the National Assembly (10 July 1940) suspending the **Republican** constitution and vesting full powers in the new head of state, Marshal **Pétain**, to draw up a constitution. In adopting the term "French State," the Vichy government sought to distinguish itself from the French Republic, a distinction that it reinforced by replacing the Republican triad *Liberté, Égalité, Fraternité* (liberty, equality, fraternity) with the new motto of *Travail, Famille, Patrie* (work, **family**, fatherland).

The État Français began with a level of legitimacy and popular acceptance that it was never to attain again. It retained control over the fleet and most parts of the **empire** and received broad diplomatic recognition. Inside France **Pétain** was revered as a national savior, and his political program, termed the "**Na-**

tional Revolution,'' capitalized on widespread revulsion at the previous regime. With only **Britain** standing between **Hitler** and total victory, the war appeared definitively lost, and the Vichy government's policy of accepting the inevitable seemed the only realistic one.

These favorable indications for Vichy did not last long. Though Pétain's personal prestige remained high well beyond 1940, popular enthusiasm for his regime eroded considerably within a year. The unanticipated continuation of the war undermined the fundamental assumptions of the regime. The National Revolution, which began with pretensions to a moral and patriotic renewal, revealed itself to be mostly concerned with settling political scores with the Republic, the **Popular Front**, and the traditional *bêtes noires* of the **Right** (labor unions, **communists, Freemasons**, immigrants, and **Jews**). Though a range of ideological viewpoints, including **left-wing** and technocratic as well as traditionalist, vied for control in Vichy, the regime's inclinations were fundamentally reactionary and divisive. Nothing illustrated this better than the anti-Jewish legislation enacted in the fall of 1940 without pressure from Germany.

Still more damaging to the État Français was its protracted effort to exploit the naval and strategic assets that it—alone among German-occupied nations— retained in order to negotiate a favorable accommodation with Hitler. The mirage of a mutually beneficial **"collaboration"** drew Vichy governments (notably those led by Pierre **Laval** and Admiral **Darlan**) into compromising, unpopular, and essentially fruitless negotiations with the Nazis.

After Laval returned to power in April 1942, the État Français moved toward closer cooperation with Germany, initiating the **deportation** of foreign Jews from France, adopting increasingly draconian measures against the **Resistance**, and sending French civilians to work in Germany. In the last year of its existence, the regime waded ever deeper into repression, and extremist collaborators such as Joseph **Darnand**, Philippe **Henriot**, and Marcel **Déat** entered the government. At the **liberation**, the members of the government, including Pétain, were transported to the German castle of **Sigmaringen**. It was a pathetic end to a regime that had been launched amid unfounded hopes of making the best of a disaster but ended up exacerbating French divisions and discrediting the French State even further.

J.-P. Azéma and F. Bédarida, eds., *Le régime de Vichy et les français* (Paris, 1992); F. Bloch-Lainé, *Hauts fonctionnaires sous l'Occupation* (Paris, 1996); J.-B. Duroselle, *L'abîme* (Paris, 1982); R. O. Paxton, *Vichy France: Old Guard and New Order, 1940– 1944* (New York, 1972).

A. W. H. Shennan

EXODUS [EXODE] OF 1940 was the flight of French civilians south before advancing German armies during the German western offensive of May–June 1940. Despite French promises to resist the German advance, official orders to remain in place, and optimistic news reports in May 1940, much of the civilian population of northern France, seeing a flood of fleeing Belgian **refugees**, packed suitcases, loaded wagons, wheelbarrows, cars, even horse-drawn carts, and departed on the road south.

The exodus swelled as Parisians, witness to aerial bombardments, and their retreating countrymen joined the march. Between 28 May and 10 June many families, often headed by **women** chaperoning children, filled the train stations, hoping to find a place on "the last train out." The fortunate few found places on trains departing to France's southwest, while most walked, often overtaking soldiers from the disbanding French **army** and the advancing German troops. By 10 June **Paris** appeared emptied.

While the government fled to Bordeaux, civilians pushing south were met with several deadly air assaults from Italian bombers. Although total civilian casualties during the exodus are still unknown, the prefect of the Corrèze, a department offering relief to **refugees**, reported 300 casualties. The procession continued well after Marshal **Pétain's** 17 June request for an **armistice**. Former minister of health and **education** Louis Pommery demanded a halt to the human flight, which he declared "undignified."

The refugee population registered approximately 8 million. Nearly 1 million returned to their homes before the closing of the **Demarcation Line** after the armistice took effect. During July and August, **Vichy** officials negotiated the return of the French and Belgian refugees with a reluctant German armistice commission. By September 1940 most civilians had returned to the occupied **zone**, but at least 250,000 **Alsatians, Lorrainers, Jews**, and foreigners remained in the unoccupied zone.

N. Dombrowski, "Beyond the Battlefield: The French Civilian Exodus of May–June 1940"(Diss. New York University, 1995); J. Vidalenc, *L'Exode de mai-juin 1940* (Paris, 1957); L. Werth, *33 Jours* (Paris, 1992).

N. Dombrowski

EXPOSITIONS, PRO-VICHY, ANTI-MASONIC, ANTI-SEMITIC. Anti-**Jewish** and anti-Masonic propaganda proliferated during the Occupation through pamphlets and expositions presenting **Freemasons** and Jews as the ills and enemies of mankind, belonging to a vast financial and political plot against France.

Long before the war, the journalism of Édouard Drumont and Henry Coston had depicted Freemasonry as an occult and anticlerical power, bent on subverting French **family** life and virtue. After the outlawing of Freemasonry on 13 August 1940, the first anti-Masonic exposition was opened at the Petit Palais in **Paris** in October 1940. Highly graphic and supposed to represent scientific observation, its front door poster announced, "You will find inside neither lies nor insults, only facts and evidence." The exposition showed the interiors of lodges, initiation rites, triangles, skulls, liturgical ornaments and vestments, and related accessories. An accompanying brochure contained lists of Freemasons, who were said to be strangling France.

A similar anti-Semitic exposition was organized by the **Institut d'Études des Questions Juives** at the Paris Palais Berlitz in September 1941 in order to sensitize **youth** to the mythical Jewish power. With free admission for school groups and the unemployed, the exposition was arranged in a pedagogical way that featured visual aids stressing the so-called disastrous impact of Jews in all French public domains, including literature, entertainment, the **economy**, and politics. It included life-size pictures of French Jewish personalities, a gigantic fresco stereotyping Hebrew history, and excerpts from the Talmud supposedly illustrating Jewish supremacy, as well as enlarged photographs of extracts of the 14 June 1941 discriminatory legislation against the Jews.

The exposition was accompanied by a booklet signed by Jean Marquès Rivière and prefaced by the secretary of the institute, Captain Paul Sézille, that implied a complete and objective presentation of the Jews. This booklet traced the history of the Jews, focusing on supposedly racial and religious characteristics. It denounced the mythical Jewish "type," suggesting that "Jewishness" would always prevail over national citizenship, thereby rendering the assimilation of Jews impossible. Failures of the **Popular Front** government and the 1940 defeat were attributed to Jews, including former premier Léon **Blum**. The conclusion implied that "dominating" and "megalomaniac" Jews were holding France hostage.

Similar expositions were organized all over France. These included the *Unité européenne du Reich* (European Unity of the Reich), promoting the idea of the necessity of peaceful European **collaboration** and *Le Bolchévisme contre l'Europe* (Bolshevism against Europe), both in 1943. Expositions such as these intensified the climate of suspicion and betrayal during the Occupation.

P. Chevallier, *Histoire de la Franc-Maçonnerie française* (Paris, 1974); *Exposition le Juif et la France au Palais Berlitz sous l'Égide de l'Institut d'Études des Questions Juives* (Paris, 1941); J. Katz, *Jews and Freemasons in Europe, 1723–1939* (Cambridge, MA, 1970); J. Lalloum, *La France antisémite de Darquier à Pellepoix* (Paris, 1979); D. Pryce Jones, *Paris in the Third Reich* (New York, 1981).

M. Guyot-Bender

F

FABIEN, COLONEL (Pierre Georges; 1919–1944), **communist Resistance** hero. Son of a Paris baker, Fabien was raised from earliest youth in an environment marked by the French Communist Party (**PCF**). Volunteering at age 17 to fight in the Spanish civil war, he was badly wounded in 1938 and evacuated to France. At the outbreak of war in 1939 he was made head of five **Paris** regions of Communist youth and was arrested and interned, escaping after the German invasion.

Fabien entered history when, on 21 August 1941, in the first high-visibility Resistance action against German personnel he shot and killed a German naval officer in the Paris subway. Escaping, Fabien worked first in the Paris area, then in the Franche-Comté, specializing in blowing up trains. He was wounded but escaped, was again arrested, tortured, and handed over to the Germans. He escaped again in June 1943.

By this time Fabien was recognized as a leader. He organized among those refusing to obey the **Service du Travail Obligatoire** in the Centre, then in the Nord. Sent to Brittany, he kidnapped PCF founding member Marcel Cachin, a highly symbolic figure, from house arrest and brought him to safety. Fabien was in Paris in July 1944 to help organize the insurrection. By this time he was signing orders as Colonel Fabien. Subsequently, a unit commanded by Fabien was melded into the regular French forces, ultimately as the 151st Infantry Regiment. Fabien was killed in **Alsace** on 27 December 1944 when his command post near Mulhouse blew up.

Glorified as early as 1945 in a hagiographic PCF pamphlet, Fabien's name was given to the square in Paris where the Communist Party headquarters now stands.

S. Courtois, *Le PCF dans la guerre* (Paris, 1980); A. Ouzoulias, *Les bataillons de la jeunesse* (Paris, 1967); P. Robrieux, *Histoire intérieure du parti Communiste*, vol. 4 (Paris, 1984).

J. W. Friend

FAMILY POLICY, VICHY, reinforced traditional concerns for family and **youth** that emphasized the domestic role of **women** as housewives and mothers, and preservers of the family unit. On 20 June 1940, Marshal **Pétain** declared that the war had been lost because there had been "too few children, too few arms, too few Allies." The belief that the women of France had "neglected" their duty to the state by not producing enough children was central to **Vichy** family policy. Proponents of the **National Revolution** often equated childbirth with military service. Government publications referred to the mother as the "privileged worker" who would rebuild the nation. Childbearing offered women an opportunity to redeem themselves and ensure the future of France. The problems posed by the fact that almost 2 million Frenchmen were captive in Germany were largely ignored.

The Vichy press embarked upon a campaign to help carry out government efforts to strengthen and increase the family. Sensitive to possible comparisons with Germany, Vichy claimed its natalist policy was moral and conservative, in contrast to the former's racial and secular approach. To compensate for the heavy casualties of World War I, a law had been passed in 1920 banning contraception; another, in 1923, condemned abortion. Vichy strengthened this already severe legislation. Abortion was classified as a crime against the state, hence subject to the death penalty. At least one woman abortionist (a mother) was guillotined. To protect the dignity of the home, Vichy passed a law in 1942 dealing specifically with adultery involving the wife of a **prisoner** of war, considered a more serious offense than "ordinary" adultery. Divorce became more difficult to obtain.

Vichy extended financial benefits of the 1939 Family Code that favored families with three or more children. Mothers of large families received supplementary rations and preferential treatment—in food queues, for example—along with medals and their pictures in local papers. Fathers of large families were to receive job preference, while bachelors were penalized. The **Catholic** Church hierarchy applauded the imposition of measures intended to bolster the family.

A General Commission on the Family (Commissariat Général à la Famille) to coordinate family policies was set up, but it was severely handicapped by German demands. Early in October 1940, Vichy instituted laws prohibiting a married woman from government work if her husband's salary was deemed adequate (a term never fully defined). However, the increasing manpower shortage soon forced Vichy to reverse its policies and urge women to work outside the home, even ordering a census of all unmarried women aged 18 to 45 deemed capable of undertaking work judged "useful to the higher interest of the nation." Adverse circumstances, including the absence of hundreds of thousands of male heads of families as prisoners of war in Germany, obliged Pétain to change some provisions of the paternalistic Napoleonic Code in women's favor. Women's legal incapacity was ended, although the husband remained lawful head of the household.

Early on Pétain had proclaimed that the family, as the central social structure, was the essential foundation of the nation. If it gave way, he maintained, all was lost. Yet as the Occupation progressed, French families were increasingly separated, not strengthened; his government's policies proved largely inadequate to meet its own proclaimed goals.

A. Coutrot, "La Politique familiale de Vichy," in Fondation Nationale des Sciences Politiques, J. Bourdin and R. Rémond, ed., *Le Gouvernement de Vichy, 1940–42* (Paris, 1972), 245–63; S. Fishman, *We Will Wait: Wives of French Prisoners of War, 1940–1945* (New Haven, CT, 1991); F. Muel-Dreyfus, *Vichy et l'éternel féminin* (Paris, 1996); M. C. Weitz, *Sisters in the Resistance: How Women Fought to Free France* (New York, 1995).

M. C. Weitz

FASCISM, a term derived from an ancient Roman political **symbol**, the fasces or bundles wrapped together to signify strength in unity, was the name selected by Benito Mussolini's Italian movement, which came to power in 1922. The term has since come to refer to political movements extolling nation or race, with a centralized authoritarian government headed by a dictator regimenting society and suppressing opposition.

Historians are divided over the degree to which the term is generic, referring to a variety of movements in different countries from the end of World War I through the end of World War II, and whether it can also apply to political movements in the post-1945 world, or whether it should be limited in use only to those movements that applied the term to themselves, notably the Italian Fascists. Because of the popular association of "fascism" with responsibility for World War II and the **Holocaust**, the term has become a political epithet, used often to slander one's opponents.

Historians also disagree as to what extent France produced fascist movements and whether or not the **Vichy État Français** was fascist. René Rémond has argued that French political traditions of royalism, Bonapartism, and counter-revolution were not fascist and that whatever fascism France did produce, for example, Georges Valois' mid-1920s Faisceau and the **Parti Populaire Français (PPF)** of 1936–1945, was the result of imported influences. Zeev Sternhell, on the contrary, argued that a late-nineteenth-century synthesis of socialism and nationalism in the ideas of Georges Sorel and others produced in France the ideas that helped give rise to interwar fascism.

Historians have also quarreled over the fascist credentials of the **Vichy** government, with Roger Bourderon suggesting that there was a logic of fascism inherent in Vichy, which was fully manifest in the **police** state of 1944. Most, however, have argued that, because it lacked a single mass party similar to the Italian Fascists and the German Nazis, Vichy was more conservative or counterrevolutionary than fascist. The more extreme **collaborationist** movements, such as the **Rassemblement National Populaire (RNP)**, the PPF, and the **Milice Française**, generally eschewed the term "fascism." RNP leader Marcel **Déat**, for example, referred to his movement more as "national socialism" than as "fascist."

R. Bourderon, "Le régime de Vichy était-il fasciste? Essai d'approche de la question," *RDHDGM* 23 (July 1973): 23–45; P. Burrin, "Le fascisme," in J.-F. Sirinelli, ed., *Histoire des Droites en France, vol. 1* (Paris, 1992), 603–52; M. Cointet-Labrousse, *Vichy et le fascisme* (Brussels, 1987); W. Laqueur, *Fascism Past Present Future* (New York, 1996); P. Milza, *Fascisme français passé et présent* (Paris, 1987); R. Rémond, *The Right Wing in France from 1815 to de Gaulle*, trans. J. M. Laux (Philadelphia, 1969 [from the French ed. of 1962; originally published as *La Droite française de 1815 à nos jours*, Paris, 1954]); Z. Sternhell, *Neither Right nor Left: Fascist Ideology in France*, trans. D. Maisel (Berkeley and Los Angeles, 1986 [original French ed., 1983]).

B. M. Gordon

FASHION (COUTURE) in **Paris** witnessed profound changes beginning in September 1939. Prestigious houses, such as those of Gabrielle Chanel and Madeleine Vionnet, closed. The influence of military dress was felt in the 1939–1940 winter collections, while a fashion of practicality made its appearance: severe cuts, "Alert" pajamas (to be worn in comfort and style in air raid shelters), and neutral colors.

The realities of the Occupation followed soon after the defeat. In the summer of 1940, the Reich proclaimed its intention to integrate French haute couture into a German structure with headquarters in Berlin or Vienna. The head of the haute couture syndical organization, Lucien Lelong, aware of a patrimony to safeguard and a savoir faire to protect, managed to prevent this transfer. However, the number of "authorized" houses of couture diminished consistently, from 85 in June 1941 to some 50 in 1943, as did the dresses presented in the collections (75 in 1942, 60 in 1944). Through the Comité d'organisation, **Vichy** imposed a measurement on each haute couture design, while the length of the hems and the making of the garments themselves were debated. Some 20,000 **women** benefited from a special couture designer card that gave them the right to procure clothing at the grand couturiers.

Fashion adapted to the context of penury: the bicycle, returned to honor due to the lack of other transport, necessitated suitable outfits (divided skirts). To replace stockings in the summer, women colored their legs with a lotion. With the scarcity of leather, boot makers used wooden soles while staple fiber and rayon replaced linen and cotton. Milliners rivaled the elegance of the **theater** and **cinema** in imagination with turbans, cavaliers' hats, felt brims with flowers or fruits, birds, tiny *bibis* (from styles of the 1830s); all was possible. With the **liberation**, haute couture did not disappear. New names appeared, among them Jacques Fath and Christian Dior.

*H. Le Boterf, *La vie parisienne sous l'Occupation*, 2 vols. (Paris, 1974–1975); L. Taylor, "The Work and Function of the Paris Couture Industry during the German Occupation of 1940–44," Dress, 22 (1995): 34–44; D. Veillon, "La mode comme pratique culturelle," in J.-P. Rioux, ed., *La vie culturelle sous Vichy* (Paris, 1990), 351–76; D. Veillon, *La mode sous l'Occupation: Débrouillardise et coquetterie dans la France en guerre (1939–1945)* (Paris, 1990).

D. Veillon

FAUCHER, LOUIS EUGÉNE (1874–1964), soldier and *résistant*. On 23 September 1938, Faucher, chief of the French Military Mission in Prague, resigned in protest against appeasement and the French High Command's unwillingness to contemplate an offensive in support of Czechoslovakia. He then volunteered to fight alongside the Czechoslovak soldiers he had helped train and command since 1919. A week later, Czechoslovakia's acceptance of the **Munich agreement**, yielding the Sudetenland, forestalled a German invasion but terminated the Franco–Czechoslovak alliance and made the remnant of Czecho-Slovakia a Nazi satellite.

Faucher subsequently opposed appeasement in France, accusing *Je suis partout* and other **right-wing** papers of knowingly or unknowingly assisting Nazi/ **fascist** propaganda efforts. After the outbreak of war the French government recalled him from retirement to help form a Czechoslovak army in France, which saw action in the May–June 1940 campaign. In the chaos of defeat, Faucher disobeyed the new **Pétain** government's order to disband his mission and instead facilitated the Czechoslovaks' escape via the southern port of Sète, saving them from a Nazi firing squad.

During the Occupation, Faucher took a leading role in the **Resistance** in his native Deux-Sèvres, commanding the Secret **Army** in southwest France (Region B) and working closely with Libération nord, the **Alliance** network, and the **Organisation Civile et Militaire**. The Gestapo arrested him on 29 January 1944 and deported him first to Bad Godesberg and then to Plansee in the Tyrol. **American** troops freed the 70-year-old Faucher on 7 May 1945. After repatriation he spent the rest of his life working toward Franco–Czechoslovak friendship and the advocacy of human rights in communist-controlled Czechoslovakia.

A Protestant general of peasant origins and **Republican** convictions, Louis Eugène Faucher personifies the **resistance** to appeasement in 1938 that anticipated resistance to capitulation and **collaboration** after 1940.

M. Chaumet and J.-M. Pouplain, *La Résistance en Deux-Sèvres. 1940–1944* (Parthenay, 1994); R. F. Crane, *A French Conscience in Prague: Louis-Eugène Faucher and the Abandonment of Czechoslovakia* (Boulder, CO, 1996); E. V. Faucher, ''Un protestant face au nazisme et à la Révolution Nationale: Le général Faucher,'' in Société de l'Histoire du Protestantisme Français, ed., *Les Protestants français pendant la seconde guerre mondiale* (Paris, 1994).

                                                                                    R. F. Crane

FAURE, PAUL (1878–1960) was the secretary-general of the French **Socialist** Party (SFIO) in the years before the war. His dogmatic pacifism split the party and rendered it impotent after the **Munich crisis**.

Faure, an uncompromising Guesdist (follower of the turn-of-the-century leader Jules Guesde), hated everything connected with war, from **communists** to munitions manufacturers. Short of accepting an outright invasion of France, he was prepared to consider any concession. This brought him into open conflict with Léon **Blum** who, in the face of the Nazi threat, had moved from the party's traditional pacifism to a willingness to confront the danger.

Faure was not at **Vichy** in July 1940, when the deputies and senators of the Third **Republic** handed their powers to Marshal **Pétain**, but his legacy was, as his supporters voted almost unanimously in favor of Pierre **Laval's** proposals to realign France with the **New Order**. During the Vichy period, Faure played a low-key role. He met with numerous top Vichy and German officials, often pleading for clemency for socialist militants selected for **deportation** or execution. His only overt act of support was joining Vichy's ephemeral National Council.

In August 1945, he was expelled from the SFIO but was still influential enough to take about 10 percent of the party's officials with him into his Parti Socialiste Démocratique. He never recanted his views and continued to pass off his self-righteous narrow-mindedness (he refused to testify for Blum at his 1942 trial in **Riom**) as noble principle. His actions contributed to undermining French morale, and thus he was probably a more effective **fifth columnist** than any of **Hitler's** friends in the *Comité France-Allemagne* of Fernand **de Brinon**.

*M. Dreyfus, "Pacifistes Socialistes et humanistes dans les années trente," *Revue d'histoire moderne et contemporaine* 35 (July–September 1988): 452–90; P. Faure, *De Munich à la Cinquième [sic] République* (Paris, [1948]); M. Sadoun, *Les Socialistes sous l'Occupation* (Paris, 1982).

H. H. Hunt

FAUX-MAQUISARDS, or "false partisans," was the label given to individuals who committed thefts or assaults ostensibly in the name of the **Resistance** but actually for their own gain.

In 1943 and 1944 *maquis* units stole from **Vichy** offices or requisitioned from the local populace the food and supplies they needed to survive in the French countryside and fight the battle for **liberation**. Some units were able to pay for requisitioned goods with cash; others used notes or coupons guaranteeing payment to the bearer after the liberation. Not all units felt obligated to offer payment to collaborators for goods taken from them. Shows of force during these requisitions, doubts about the validity of the notes, the lack of a common system for the notes, and general anxieties over the current situation and the future led to controversy over the requisitions. Some people called them theft.

Unscrupulous individuals took advantage of this controversy and the erosion of governmental authority in the spring and summer of 1944 to engage in simple banditry. Claiming to be *maquisards*, they terrorized and stole from the **peasantry** for their own benefit. Authentic *maquisards*, whose own reputations were badly sullied by such activities, took action against these *"faux-maquisards,"* condemning some by court-martial and executing them for banditry. After the liberation, police continued to investigate complaints against "*faux-maquisards*" and to bring them to trial. The problem continued, however, into 1945, as individuals used the vigilantism in areas such as Savoie to cover their own criminal activities by claiming to be vigilantes.

Institut d'Histoire des Conflits Contemporains, *Colloque sur les maquis* (Paris, 1986);

H. R. Kedward, *In Search of the Maquis: Rural Resistance in Southern France, 1942–44* (Oxford, 1993).

M. Koreman

FAŸ, BERNARD (1893–1978), was a royalist historian who studied in the **United States**, obtained a master's degree at Harvard, and during the interwar years wrote extensively about **American** history, including a biography of Benjamin Franklin. He became director of the Bibliothèque Nationale in the summer of 1940 after the resignation of his **Jewish** predecessor, Julien Caïn. Faÿ also established the Centre de Documentation Contemporaine, which was given the task of collecting documents from Masonic lodges dissolved by law of 13 August 1940. An obsessive opponent of Masonic influence, Faÿ soon claimed to have accumulated 120 tons of archives on the subject. In October 1941 he published the first number of *Documents Maçoniques*.

How much influence Faÿ had either with the Germans in **Paris**, where he chose to stay, or with **Vichy** is open to doubt. Anti-Masonic activity was never pursued with as much enthusiasm as **anti-Semitism** or anticommunism, and the Vichy government itself included former Masons, such as Marcel **Peyrouton**. Furthermore, Faÿ's extremism distanced him even from other members of the Catholic **Right**, for example, General Augustin Laure protested when Faÿ claimed that the bishop of Orléans was under Masonic influence.

For all his ideological fervor, Faÿ engaged largely in standard bureaucratic work during the Vichy period. He arranged to send 3 million books to French **prisoners** of war in Germany and endured the sniping of the *Revue Historique*, which believed that Masonic documents ought to have been deposited in the Archives Nationales. His attempts to centralize the administration of French libraries fit in with longer-term strategies of senior administrators: his 1943 report on the subject quoted extensively from the report written by Julien Caïn in 1940 and was itself eventually published by Caïn after the latter's return to the Bibliothèque Nationale in 1945. Faÿ was arrested at the **liberation**, but he survived to write numerous books and articles, including one that called for the rioting students of 1968 to be treated with sympathy.

B. Faÿ, *La franc-maçonnerie et la révolution intellectuelle du XVIIIe siècle* (Paris, 1942); D. Rossignol, *Vichy et les franc-maçons: la liquidation des sociétés secrètes 1940–1944* (Paris, 1981).

R. C. Vinen

FÉDÉRATION DES SOCIÉTÉS JUIVES (FEDERATION OF JEWISH ORGANIZATIONS, or FÉDÉRATION), was an umbrella organization (of 80 to 200 organizations by countries of origin: *landsmannschaften*) established by immigrant **Jews** in 1913. It sponsored a variety of social, cultural, and educational activities, inspired by Jewish traditions brought from Eastern Europe. In the late 1930s, when some 20,000 families were direct or indirect members, it was chaired by the **socialist** Zionist leader, Marc Jarblum. Its very existence reflected the complex and problematic relationship between immigrant and native-born French Jews (*israélites*).

With the Occupation in 1940, large numbers of Jews and all the major Jewish organizations left **Paris**. Only a few unofficial organizations of the immigrant Jews continued their social assistance work. Preeminent among these was the newly created Committee of the "rue Amelot," which included the Fédération and most of Paris Jewish immigrant political parties, except for the **communists**. In November 1941, under German pressure, the French government instituted the Union général des israélites en France (UGIF), a single umbrella organization to which all **Jews** were required to belong. Jarblum and other Fédération leaders refused to take part, although some cooperation between the underground Fédération and the official and state-controlled UGIF did exist.

The Fédération in the southern **zone** and "rue Amelot" in Paris both worked most importantly to help the impoverished Jews, many living clandestinely and lacking their pre-1940 sources of income. This financial help permitted many trapped immigrant families to survive. The Fédération also helped finance **youth** movement rescue activities, and some local branches helped falsify identity papers. Sources of income came mainly either legally from the UGIF or illegally from the **American** Joint Distribution Committee, the Zionist Organization, and the World Jewish Congress in **Switzerland**. Many Fédération activists were caught in their underground work, deported, and killed.

A. Cohen, *Persécutions et sauvetages, Juifs et Français sous l'Occupation et sous Vichy* (Paris, 1993); L. Lazare, *Rescue as Resistance: How Jewish Organizations Fought the Holocaust in France*, trans. J. M. Green (New York, 1996); D. H. Weinberg, *A Community on Trial* (Chicago, 1977).

A. Cohen

FÉDÉRATION NATIONALE DES DÉPORTÉS ET INTERNÉS RÉSISTANTS ET PATRIOTES (FNDIRP [NATIONAL FEDERATION OF RESISTER AND PATRIOTIC DEPORTEES AND INTERNEES], 1945–), is a benevolent and watchdog organization that emerged in France after World War II to defend and help those who were deported and imprisoned during the war.

With hospitals and rehabilitation centers FNDIRP cared for those who were injured and who suffered from diseases such as tuberculosis contracted in the camps. FNDIRP continues to aid survivors of the camps and the widows and orphans of camp inmates. A key part of FNDIRP's mission is to keep the memory of the wartime **concentration camps** alive, and it does so by **publishing** related books and other materials. Under its name, it sells a number of works on the **Resistance** and the **deportation**. It also defends the causes of the deportees by taking legal action when books and films do not seem to give what it considers the true story.

The founder and first president of FNDIRP was Marcel Paul, who was deported to Auschwitz and Buchenwald. FNDIRP is located at 10, rue Leroux, 75116 Paris.

S. Maurel, *Aux origines de la Fédération Nationale des Déportés et Internés Résistants et Patriotes (FNDIRP) 1944–1946* (Paris, 1993); H. Rousso, *The Vichy Syndrome, History and Memory in France since 1944*, trans. A. Goldhammer (Cambridge, MA, 1991).

E. H. Murphrey

FICTION IN LITERATURE RELATED TO OCCUPIED FRANCE. World War II and the Nazi Occupation have been the subjects of considerable French literary fiction in the second half of the twentieth century. This literature reflects the perspectives of successive ideologies as they look back to the wartime period.

Few texts dealing with the Occupation were published before the **liberation**, the most important of which remains the *Silence de la Mer* by Vercors (1942), which recounts the power of silence as a means of opposition to the German presence in the occupied **zone**. Postwar literary currents were mainly autobiographical and testimonial, with texts bearing witness to the Nazi presence in France, such as *Les Années noires* (1947), Jean **Guéhenno's** diary during the German presence in **Paris**; Jean-Louis Bory's *Mon Village à l'heure allemande* (1945), an account of French passivity in the face of the German invasion; and *Le Premier accroc coûte deux cents francs* by Elsa Triolet (1947), inspired by **Resistance** activities.

Most immediate postwar fiction was inspired by a search for truth and a desire to set records straight. Some distanced themselves from factual information and personal memory to consider broader issues raised during the Occupation. Among these were Albert **Camus'** *La Peste* (1947), one of the only allegories of the period, and Simone **de Beauvoir's** *Le Sang des autres* (1944), a didactic novel focusing on the ethics of militancy. Jean-Paul **Sartre's** writings, *L'Huis-clos* (1944), *La Putain respectueuse* (1946), and *Les Mains sales* (1948), also inspired by the trauma of the Occupation, reflected political commitment to freedom, although the wartime experience was not directly treated. Often with irony or cynicism, other fiction examined passive **collaboration** and the **black market** during the Occupation. *Au bon beurre* (1952) by Jean Dutourd and Marcel Aymé's *Le Chemin des écoliers* (1946) and *Uranus* (1948) denounced self-interest in times of restrictions. *La Bâtarde* by Violette Leduc (1964) addressed issues of indifference and survival by any means.

New Wave novelists, who were either children during the Occupation or born after 1945, have more recently turned to the ambiguities of the Occupation years and the stories of their parents involved in the politics of the period. Among them are Jean-Michel Bloch with *Daniel et Noémie* (1971), Pascal Jardin, whose narratives *La Guerre à neuf ans* (1971) and *Le Nain jaune* (1978) rely on personal childhood memories, and Joseph Joffo with *Un Sac de billes* (1978). Most important, Patrick Modiano's novels, such as *La Place de l'Étoile* (1968) and *Voyage de noces* (1991) and, less so, *Villa triste* (1972), evoke both collaboration and the problems of coherence in memory.

These more recent novels, sometimes called "retro," acknowledge the weight of narrative technique in the account of "lived" experience, ignored by earlier accounts and by historical texts. They also attack the good conscience typical of the Gaullist era, evoking the interconnection of persons and events during the Occupation, as did also Serge Doubrovsky's *La Dispersion* (1969), which denounced French hypocrisy and complicity in the **Aryanization** process.

During the last 50 years in France, the Occupation and, more generally the Nazi experience have been used as a background to discuss human relationships to problems of war, power, and social, racial, and religious ethics, as well as connections between individual and collective histories.

M. Attack, *Literature and French Resistance: Cultural Politics and Narrative Forms* (Manchester and New York, 1989); J.-F. Fourny and R. J. Golsan, eds., *The Occupation in French Literature and Film, 1940–1992*, special issue of *L'Esprit Créateur* 33:1 (Spring 1993).

M. Guyot-Bender

FIFTH COLUMN, a term used mostly during the "**Phoney War**" to describe a fear of unnamed traitors and spies who were supposed to have infiltrated France and who were working for the Third Reich. The term originated during the Spanish civil war (1936–1939), when, as General Franco's forces laid siege to Madrid, commanding officer General Emilio Mola referred to a "fifth column" that would sabotage the city's defenses and help his forces, marching in four columns, take the city.

Many of those who lived through the Occupation recall a general fear of spies or traitors who were supposed to be working for the Third Reich and sabotaging the war effort in the early days of the war. Historians such as Jean-Pierre Azéma believe there is little proof of a widespread presence of Nazi spies in France during the Phoney War, but he does point to the negative effect French Nazis had on general morale, for example, Paul Ferdonnet on Radio-Stuttgart, who repeated Goebbels' words that "the English would fight to the last Frenchman." Few future collaborators sided with such attacks on the war effort. Most spoke more openly for Germany only after the defeat.

Left-wing groups, particularly the **communists**, used the term "fifth column" for political purposes in late 1939; for example, in the clandestine October 1939 copy of *l'Humanité*, the writers made up a list of so-called French **fascists**, including Édouard **Daladier** and Léon **Blum**. It named the **Comité France-Allemagne** as "the Fifth Column of capitalism and fascism." After the 1940 defeat and **armistice**, some came to blame the fifth column for the fall of France, while others believed that it was invented to cover up more complex causes of defeat. The term was still in use at the **liberation**, referring to unknown individuals who wished to sabotage peace.

J.-P. Azéma, *From Munich to the Liberation*, trans. J. Lloyd (Cambridge, U.K., and Paris, 1984 [original ed., 1979]); M. Gallo, *La Cinquième colonne . . . et ce fut la défaite de 40* (Brussels, 1984 [original ed., Paris, 1970]); H. R. Kedward, *Resistance in Vichy France* (Oxford, 1978).

C. Gorrara

FINE ARTS, EXPATRIATES FROM FRANCE, generally hesitated in leaving their homeland immediately after the French defeat in June 1940. However, once **Vichy** embarked on a policy of **collaboration** with the Nazis and began implementing its **National Revolution**, large numbers of French avant-garde artists emigrated.

French artists were not persecuted specifically because of their modernist aesthetics, as in Nazi Germany, although much modern art, such as cubism and surrealism, was officially disallowed. French artists who were **Jewish** were in jeopardy due to Vichy's **anti-Semitic** policies. Others were in danger because of Vichy's agreement to ''surrender on demand'' any person wanted by the Third Reich, as stipulated in Article 19 of the 1940 Franco–German **armistice**. Also in danger were recently naturalized French citizens.

Marshal **Pétain's** announcement that architecture, sculpture, and painting should now serve the needs of the new French State and that artists should save the nation from social decomposition by employing a moralizing aesthetic echoed Nazi cultural policies. Numerous French avant-gardists, horrified by such statements, feared that France, historically a land of political asylum and the cradle of modern art, would now initiate repressive measures against them because of their art.

Among the thousands of **refugees** trapped in France's unoccupied area after the French defeat were the prominent French artists André Masson, whose wife was **Jewish**, André Breton, Marcel Duchamp, and recently naturalized French citizens Marc Chagall and Jacques Lipchitz. Rather than choosing to stay in France, all of these artists managed to emigrate. By 1944, over 2,000 scholars, artists, musicians, and actors had come to the **United States**, including virtually all of the French surrealists, an enormous influx of cultural expatriates that profoundly influenced the evolution of the arts in America, helping to transform New York into the postwar international art capital.

S. Barron, *Exiles and Emigrés: The Flight of European Artists under Hitler* (New York, 1997); Centre de la Vieille Charité, *La Planète affolée: Surréalisme, dispersion et influence, 1938–1947* (Paris, 1986); M. C. Cone, *Artists under Vichy: A Case of Prejudice and Persecution* (Princeton, 1992); I. Guenther-Bellomy, ''Art and Politics during the German Occupation of France'' (Diss., University of Houston, 1992); S. Janis, ''School of Paris Comes to U.S.,'' *Decision* (November–December 1941): 85–95.

I. V. Guenther

FINE ARTS, EXPATRIATES IN FRANCE, included Europe's leading artists, some of whom had been prominent in the French art world for many years and others who fled to France beginning in 1933, when **Hitler** came to power.

Initially viewing France as a safe haven from antimodernist, antiforeigner, and **anti-Semitic** Nazi policies, expatriate artists formed several organizations in **Paris**. Both the Kollektiv deutscher Künstler (1936) and the Freier Künstlerbund (1938) held exhibits, published accounts of the dangers of Nazi ideology and policy, and agitated for individual freedom in the arts. Members included the artists Otto **Freundlich**, Gert Wollheim, and Max Ernst, as well as art historians Paul Westheim, Carl Einstein, and Walter Benjamin, all Germans, along with many French sympathizers.

With the French defeat and **Vichy's** decision to collaborate with Germany, hundreds of expatriate artists were subjected to internment and persecution, their French citizenship often revoked. Others hid, joined **Resistance** efforts, fled overseas, were deported to extermination camps, or died in France as a result of Vichy's legislation. Artists such as Hans Reichel, Gert Wollheim, Wols (Wolfgang Schulze), Hans Belmer, and Victor Brauner, a Romanian **Jew**, hid in the countryside throughout the Occupation, suffering extreme deprivation. Recently widowed Sonia Delauney remained in Grâsse with a few artists until the **liberation**. Many, however, such as Chaim Soutine and Sylvain Itkine, did not survive the Occupation years. Otto Freundlich, Charlotte Salomon, Rudolf Lévy, Jacques Gotko, and approximately 80 other Jewish artists died in the **Holocaust**, most having first been sent to internment and **deportation** camps in France. The **Alsatian** Hans Arp escaped to **Switzerland**, and Joan Miró returned to **Spain**, while Max Ernst, Richard Lindner, Wilfredo Lam, and hundreds of other cultural luminaries eventually made their way to North America, Central America, or Cuba.

Labeled Judeo-Marxist decadents, Wassily Kandinsky (a French citizen since 1939) and the Spaniard Pablo **Picasso** were not allowed to exhibit but were never interned and continued to paint throughout the war years. Marc Chagall, a French citizen since 1937 of Russian-Jewish background, was released within hours from an internment camp once prison officials realized who he was. Neither Kandinsky nor Chagall had his French citizenship revoked. Undoubtedly, these artists' international stature provided them with some degree of protection from the hardships faced by other expatriate artists in France.

Although France was initially one of the most important havens for cultural figures fleeing the Third Reich, it proved to be most inhospitable to expatriates after 1939. By the end of 1940, not a Jew or anti-Nazi refugee was left among **art dealers**, exhibiting artists, collectors, and critics in the official French art world.

S. Barron, *Exiles and Emigrés: The Flight of European Artists under Hitler* (New York, 1997); R. Fabian and C. Coulmas, *Die deutsche Emigration in Frankreich nach 1933* (Munich, 1978); D. Schiller and K. Pech, *Exil in Frankreich* (Frankfurt am Main, 1981); K. Silver and R. Golan, *The Circle of Montparnasse: Jewish Artists in Paris, 1905–1945* (New York, 1985); H. Strauss and W. Roder, eds., *International Biographical Dictionary of Central European Emigrés, 1933–1945*, vols. 1, 2: *The Arts, Sciences, and Literature* (Munich, 1983).

I. V. Guenther

FINE ARTS IN OCCUPIED FRANCE were summarized shortly after the **liberation of Paris** by **American** correspondents who told surprising stories. John Groth, in *The Art Digest* of 1 December 1944, noted: "In Paris, I found the studios and galleries full of new and exciting works . . . I was astounded at the great number of art publications of the last four years. Books of color reproductions of the paintings of the old masters . . . and of the modern masters—Van Gogh, Degas, **Picasso**." John Pudney, writing in the *New Statesman and Nation*, 16 September 1944, found Picasso's studio "packed with [the] four years' work" and Picasso himself safe and voluble. France, an uncontested center of fine arts creation and display before World War II, had changed. It took more than a visit to the art galleries or an interview with Picasso, however, to recap the impact on the fine arts of four years of occupation.

"Freedom" in the fine arts had been only skin-deep during the Occupation years. The art world had been under close surveillance by Nazi censors, or "*referats*." Germans attended openings, controlled the printing and distribution of posters that announced exhibitions, and could, at their discretion, close a show and have works removed or even destroyed by slashing. A number of galleries that belonged to **Jews** were "**Aryanized**"; no art by the expressionist Jewish painter Chaim Soutine could be shown in a gallery or museum, and any gallery showing art by Jewish artists risked being closed, and the owner arrested. At least 80 Jewish artists disappeared in the **Holocaust**, including Otto **Freundlich**, Moishe Kogan, and Max Jacob, the last better known for his free verse and discovery of Picasso than for his paintings. Soutine is said to have died of fright. Picasso had been forbidden to exhibit his work and had not been spared occasional visits from the Gestapo.

France's artistic patrimony—the contents of its national museums and leading private collections, particularly those owned by Jews—had been jeopardized by **Hitler's** and **Göring's** desires for masterpieces for the mammoth museums they were planning to create in the large German-centered Europe of the future. Prior to the 1940 debacle, major works from Paris museums and other sources had been transferred southward, but the **armistice** lines had forced a second move and left a number of key works at the mercy of the occupying forces. French museum collections escaped major depradations thanks to the guile of curators, such as Rose Valland, but important private collections belonging to Jews disappeared as did their owners. Furthermore, a succession of officially ordered purges emptied many public squares of statues in bronze, allegedly melted down for military use. Not until the Allied troops defeated Germany did the extent of the looting become known.

Of course, the Occupation years had not been damaging to all; academic and classical sculptors avid for commissions had a hard time resisting offers from the Nazi and **Vichy** authorities. The veteran *fauve* painters, André Derain and Maurice **de Vlaminck** in particular, found themselves and their works in the limelight once again. Indeed, their participation with 11 of their peers in a propaganda trip to Germany in 1941 would bring accusations against them after the war. Henri **Matisse**, who lived in southern France, which was occupied by the Germans only in November 1942, went on working and exhibiting, as did Pierre Bonnard and Francis Picabia, who lived nearby. Matisse's wife and daughter were arrested for **Resistance** activity. Picabia's first wife, Gabrielle, also belonged to a Resistance network. All three survived.

The wartime departure for the Americas of a handful of international modernist painters left a vacuum in the Paris art world that was soon filled by French painters who, in the 1930s, had worked in their shadow. Gathered in Paris by Jean **Bazaine**, a leader of the pro-Vichy Jeune France organization, some 21 painters, whose styles ranged from hyperclassical to nearly abstract, held a first exhibition at the Braun Gallery in 1941 under the name Jeunes Peintres de Tradition Française (Young Painters in the French Tradition). Then the group split. Several, calling themselves the "*bleu-blanc-rouge subjectives*" (blue, white, red subjectives), coalesced around a shared definition of French tradition harking back to medieval church muralists. They incorporated the formal and color innovations of early twentieth-century French art, but excluded the more international sources, expressionism and surrealism. The leading artists in this group were Bazaine, Maurice Estève, Alfred Manessier, Gustave Singier, Édouard Pignon, and André Fougeron. It was their paintings that the liberators of Paris first saw in the summer of 1944.

Art history has not been kind to the Bazaine group; they have not gained the international recognition that Jean Dubuffet and Jean Fautrier, partisans of a radical break with tradition and contemporaries of the former, have achieved. Fautrier, whom the **anti-Semitic** critic Lucien **Rebatet** had placed at the top of his list of degenerate artists, was one of the rare, younger painters to express sympathy for the oppressed with a series of works called *Hostages*, thick, pasty surfaces in pink and purple tones suggesting the crushed heads and bodies of victims of torture.

Overall and with very few exceptions, the suffering endured by France during four years of Occupation was not reflected by its painters and sculptors. The painters and sculptors who were allowed to show their art tended to avoid controversy by censoring themselves, and the unusual economic situation of occupied France served some of them well.

*†M. C. Cone, " 'Abstract' Art as a Veil: Tricolor Painting in Vichy France," *The Art Bulletin* 74:2 (June 1992): 191–204; M. C. Cone, *Artists under Vichy. A Case of Prejudice and Persecution* (Princeton, 1992); H. Feliciano, *The Lost Museum* (New York, 1997 [original ed.: *Le Musée Disparu*, Paris, 1995]); R. Golan, *Modernity and Nostalgia: Art and Politics in France between the Wars* (New Haven, CT, 1995); L. Nicholas, *The Rape of Europa: The Fate of Europe's Treasures in the Third Reich and the Second World War* (New York, 1994).

                                                                                    M. C. Cone

FLANDIN, PIERRE-ÉTIENNE (1889–1958), premier in 1934–1935 and leader of the interwar **right**-of-center Alliance Démocratique, was at the forefront of the antiwar and pro-appeasement forces during the **Munich crisis**. When the crisis ended, Flandin sent an obsequious and very public telegram of congratulations to the führer. He also sent similar telegrams to Mussolini, Chamberlain, and **Daladier**. After the declaration of war in September 1939, Flandin and Pierre **Laval** quickly became the parliamentary focus of those opposed to the conflict, though Flandin played no part in the overthrow of the Paul **Reynaud** cabinet on 16 June 1940. Indeed, he tried to outmaneuver Laval at **Vichy**, giving the most eloquent tributes of the entire conclave to the vanquished **Republic**, when Marshal **Pétain's** dictatorship was established.

Flandin was appointed foreign minister at Vichy when Laval fell from power on 13 December 1940. As Pétain's most important official, Flandin pursued a cautiously **collaborationist** policy toward the Reich until Vichy intrigues and German pressure forced the marshal to dismiss him after eight weeks in office. Flandin spent the next 20 months preparing for his move to **North Africa**, which took place shortly before the Allied landings in November 1942. A year later, he was arrested by General **de Gaulle's** government at Algiers, accused of violating, as Pétain's minister, Article 75 of the Penal Code, which deals with national security.

Flandin was at length acquitted by the **Haute Cour de Justice** in 1946, condemned to only 12 hours of national indignity. However, a vote by the chamber later that year prohibited former ministers of Pétain from running for national political office. Flandin's fate was similar to that suffered by much of the pre-1944 Right, compromised by a pacifism and a collaboration that were anathema to a liberated France.

*J.-B. Duroselle, *Politique étrangère de la France, 1871–1969*, 2 vols., vol. 1: *La décadence, 1932–1939*, vol. 2: *L'Abime, 1939–1945* (Paris, 1979–1982); P.-E. Flandin, *Politique française, 1919–1940* (Paris, 1947); "Fonds Flandin," unpublished material in the Bibliothèque nationale, Paris; France, Ministère de la Justice, *Le Procès de Flandin, Pierre-Étienne, 1943–1946* (in Archives Nationales, Paris).

P. C. F. Bankwitz

FONTENOY, JEAN (1899–1945), was a journalist, one of the lesser-known and more adventurous figures in the **collaboration**, called by Robert **Brasillach**"the strangest character I have ever met." He studied at the École des Langues orientales (School of Oriental Languages), then became a correspondent for the news agency Havas in Moscow, 1924–1926, and in China. Fontenoy joined the **Communist** Party, then followed Jacques **Doriot** into the **Parti Populaire Français**. He acquired some notoriety as the author of four books, never republished: *L'École du renégat* in 1936; *Cloud ou le Communiste à la page* in 1937; *Shanghaï secret*, a Prix Marianne winner in 1938; and *Le Songe du voyageur* in 1939. He married Madeleine Charnaux, a well-known sculptor and aviatrix, the holder of six international flight records, in 1938.

In 1939 Fontenoy fought against **Soviet** forces in Finland, where he was gravely wounded. Returning to France, he became an intermediary between his friend Otto **Abetz** and Pierre **Laval** in the days immediately after the defeat of France. With Eugène **Deloncle**, Fontenoy helped create the collaborationist

Mouvement Social Révolutionnaire in late 1940, and in early 1941 the two men participated in the founding of the **Rassemblement National Populaire**.

Fontenoy wrote for several **Paris** collaborationist newspapers, including *Révolution nationale*, where there appeared periodic rumors of his suicide or assassination, it being known that he had been a drug user since his China days. He joined the **Légion des Volontaires Français** briefly as a war correspondent in late 1941 before returning to France. At the end of 1943 Laval appointed him adjunct director of the Office Français d'Information, created in 1940 by **Vichy** to replace Havas. In 1943, Madeleine Charnaux died of cancer, and, in August 1944, Fontenoy fled France with the departing Germans. All that is known of his subsequent fate comes from a press dispatch of October 1945 reporting that he had committed suicide in May 1945 in Berlin to avoid falling into the hands of the **Russians**.

B. M. Gordon, "The Condottieri of the Collaboration: *Mouvement Social Révolutionnaire*," *JCH* 10: 2 (April 1975): 261–82; B. M. Gordon, *Collaborationism in France during the Second World War* (Ithaca, NY, 1980).

G. Le Marec

FRANC-TIREUR, one of the southern **zone's** three major **Resistance** movements, along with **Combat** and Libération, was born in Lyons. An outgrowth of France-Liberté, it included members of Jeune République (Antoine Avinin), political figures from Lyons (Auguste Pinton and Noël Clavier), and former **communists** (Elie Péju and Jean-Jacques Soudeille). These men had in common **Republicanism**, maturity, and a solid political education. They mobilized against **Vichy** and the Germans. The arrival of Jean-Pierre **Lévy** enabled them to publish a clandestine newspaper, *Le Franc-Tireur*, with a run of 5,000 in December 1941. Thanks to Lévy's friendship, family, and professional networks, the movement created around the newspaper spread throughout the southern **zone**. In addition to Lyons and its neighboring departments, it had important antennae in the Mediterranean area, the Auvergne, and the Limousin. The journalist Georges Altman took over partial charge of publishing the newspaper when Eugène Claudius-Petit joined the group in 1942. Subsequently, noted persons, including political writer Albert Bayet and historian Marc **Bloch**, also joined Franc-Tireur.

The year 1942 witnessed the first contacts with **Combat** and Libération. Following a decisive meeting with an emissary of General **de Gaulle** in March 1942, Franc-Tireur solidly supported Jean **Moulin** in his struggles with **Combat** and *Libération*. Despite discussion within the group, it recognized General de Gaulle as head of the Resistance and accepted the formation of a single secret **army** as well as the amalgamation of the three south zone movements. On the eve of the **liberation**, its newspaper was printed in both zones, in runs of 150,000. Sociologically, Franc-Tireur recruited in the middle classes, among shopkeepers, schoolteachers, and professors. Politically, it was on the **Left**, calling for the return of the Republic, the nationalization of business, and the disappearance of capitalism. It was characterized by an opposition spirit taken from Jacobinism's defense of the Republic and democracy.

L. Douzou and D. Veillon, "La Résistance des mouvements: ses débuts dans la région lyonnaise (1940–1942)," in *Mémoire et Histoire: La Résistance* (Toulouse, 1995), 149–59; Cl. Lévy and D. Veillon, "Aspects généraux de la presse clandestine," in *La Presse clandestine, 1940–1944, Actes du colloque d'Avignon 20–27 juin 1985* (Avignon, 1987), 17–37; D. Veillon, *Le Franc-Tireur: un journal clandestin, un mouvement de Résistance, 1940–1944* (Paris, 1977); D. Veillon and O. Wieviorka, "La Résistance," in J.-P. Azéma and F. Bédarida, eds., *La France des années noires*, vol. 2: *De l'Occupation à la Libération* (Paris, 1993), 65–91.

D. Veillon

FRANCS-TIREURS ET PARTISANS FRANÇAIS (FTP), dominated by **communists**, was the largest of the military organizations of the **Resistance**. Not to be confused with the **socialist Franc-Tireur**, its name recalls the French irregulars of the Franco–Prussian War and **Soviet** partisan forces.

Following the German invasion of **Soviet Russia** in 1941, the Communist Party encouraged the beginning of armed struggle against the occupying army, sponsoring groups that included the Organisation secrète, Bataillons de la jeunesse (**Youth** Battalions), and Main d'œuvre immigré (Immigrant Labor). In February 1942, these three groups were substantially merged into a new structure under the title Francs-Tireurs et partisans français. Initially composed of communists, it rapidly opened its ranks to resisters of all persuasions. During 1942, the FTP became the military wing of the political movement **Front National**. It also published a newspaper, *France d'abord* (France First).

Stronger in the northern **zone**, the FTP also operated in the south, based mainly in the larger towns and cooperating closely with clandestine trade union movements. It was organized in a pyramid, based on "triangles" of three members reporting upward to a member of the next triangle in seniority. This proved a flexible and relatively secure structure, particularly in the early stages, when most members combined clandestine activities with a "normal" life. From 1943, members increasingly became full-time underground fighters, with more attacks on German forces and against **industrial** and infrastructure targets, including railways, electricity cables, and telephone lines.

The FTP was vigorously led by Charles **Tillon**. Its leadership included Marcel Prenant, Eugène Henaff, André Ouzoulias, and Georges Vallet. The FTP's most dashing figure, Pierre Georges, known as *le colonel* **Fabien**, was both the first to kill a German officer, in August 1941, and a leader of the insurrection that led to the **liberation of Paris** three years later.

Regarded with suspicion by Gaullists and the Allied leadership because of their communist complexion, the FTP also rejected the tactics urged on the Resistance from London, especially the *"attentiste"* approach of deferring military activity in France until the Allies had launched their offensive. FTP leaders argued that their armed actions could pave the way for the offensive and open the "second front" urged by the beleaguered Soviet Union. They also rejected attempts to shape the Resistance into a classical **army**, arguing that the guerrilla warfare of small, highly mobile units was more effective in tying down the German army and less prone to heavy losses.

Consequently, the FTP were rarely the recipients of materiel dropped into France from **Britain** and depended on weapons and ammunition seized in increasingly audacious raids on the German army, the *milice*, the **police**, and remnants of the **Vichy** armed forces. As D-Day approached, too slowly for the FTP's taste, the organization joined with the Armée secrète of the noncommunist **Mouvements Unis de la Résistance** to form the **Forces françaises de l'Intérieur**. Coordinating their activities with the Allied campaign in the spring of 1944, the FTP won the grudging respect of the Allies and was responsible for liberating large areas outside the main Allied advance, especially in Brittany and the southwest.

Though some FTP members harbored plans to lead a revolutionary uprising on the Bolshevik model, the Communist Party, following Stalin's directives, rejected these aspirations. FTP fighters had to choose between enrolling in the regular French army, as many did, or returning to civilian life in liberated France.

J.-P. Azéma, *From Munich to the Liberation, 1938–1944*, trans. J. Lloyd (Cambridge, U.K., and Paris, 1984 [original French ed., 1979]); H. R. Kedward, *Occupied France: Collaboration and Resistance* (London, 1985); H. Noguères, *Histoire de la Résistance en France,* 5 vols. (Paris, 1967–1981).

M. Kelly

FRANCS TIREURS ET PARTISANS—MAIN D'OEUVRE IMMIGRÉE (FTP-MOI) was the immigrant organization within the French **communist** armed **Resistance** movement Les Francs tireurs et partisans (français) (FTP[F]), notable for its direct action against German occupiers and **collaborators**. The dissolution of the French Communist Party (**PCF**) in September 1939 thrust the existing **communist** immigrant organization (Section de la Main d'Œuvre immigrée [MOI]) into clandestinity, where it was persecuted by the **Vichy** regime. Louis Gronowski, Jacques Kaminiski, and Arthur London reorganized the movement in liaison with the clandestine PCF. Its members, led by Francis Boczor, were in the original armed resistance of the PCF, the Organization spéciale, beginning in August 1940. In April 1942, when this became the FTP(F), individual groups were encouraged to become independent, and the large MOI groups became FTP-MOI. By the autumn of 1942 there were five fighting units of the FTP-MOI in **Paris** with units being established in Lyons, Toulouse, Marseilles, Grenoble, Nord-Pas-de-Calais, and Nice. In late 1942, the Paris FTP-MOI suffered a round of arrests by the French **police**; however, by August 1943, it had 65 members, centered in two units and a special assassination squad, including the Manouchian Group. Arrested in November 1943, they were made famous by a German "red poster" denouncing the French Resistance as the "*armée du crime*" (army of crime). The composition of the FTP-MOI was almost entirely immigrant, mainly political **refugees, Jews**, and veterans of the Spanish civil war. The intensity of their resistance can be seen in the 261 verified and over 100 unsubstantiated actions of the FTP-MOI Carmagnole in Lyons and the 820 actions of FTP-MOI 35th Brigade in the Toulouse region.

S. Courtois, et al., *Le sang de l'étranger* (Paris, 1989); M. Manouchian, *Manouchian* (Paris, 1974); S. Rayski, *Nos illusions perdues* (Paris, 1985).

J. C. Simmonds

FREE FRANCE, FREE FRENCH, FIGHTING FRANCE, FIGHTING FRENCH (France Libre, France Combattante, Forces Françaises de l'interieur, FFI; Forces Françaises Libres, FFL), was established on 18 June 1940, when General **de Gaulle** appealed to all French men and **women** to continue **resistance** to Nazi Germany. At first de Gaulle expected prominent political and military leaders to rally to the cause. When none did, he assumed responsibility for leading the Free French.

Despite differences, Winston Churchill supported de Gaulle throughout the war. He provided access to the **BBC** and on 7 August 1940 agreed to support the Free French financially. At the time only 7,000 Free French were in the U.K., and de Gaulle controlled no French territory, although a series of rallies in the latter half of 1940 produced Free French control over portions of the **empire** from the Pacific to Equatorial Africa. An attempt to rally French West Africa failed when fighting broke out between **Vichy** naval forces and an **Anglo-**French expedition sent to **Dakar** in late September. Stung by Vichy accusations that the Free French were tools of **British** imperialism, de Gaulle decided to give the movement a political legitimacy. Following the Dakar setback de Gaulle reached Brazzaville, where he formed a Council for the Defense of the Empire to administer the rallied territories, and in November he declared that Vichy was not free to defend French interests as a result of the **armistice** and that it was an illegal regime.

Free French claims to legitimacy clashed with both Vichy and the attitudes and actions of Britain and the **United States**. De Gaulle shared Vichy's fear that "Anglo-Saxon" powers intended to exploit French weakness to deny restoration of French control over imperial territory. After a bitter clash over Syria and Lebanon, Churchill tried to limit de Gaulle's power within the Free French movement by encouraging the formation of a committee to oversee his actions, whereupon de Gaulle converted the French National Committee, formed in September 1941, into a nucleus for a Free French **Provisional Government**, supplanting the Council for Defense of the Empire as the political arm of the Free French.

American diplomatic ties with Vichy complicated Free French relations with the United States, although the United States acknowledged Free French authority in those colonies that had rallied. De Gaulle objected that this policy encouraged disunity. The issue became acute when the Allies landed in **North**

Africa on 8 November 1942, and General Eisenhower accepted Admiral **Darlan** as high commissioner for North Africa in exchange for Darlan's ordering a cease-fire. After Darlan's assassination, Roosevelt promoted the royalist General Henri **Giraud** to head French forces and share power with de Gaulle. After protracted negotiations with his rival, de Gaulle reached Algiers on 30 May 1943 and agreed to cochair the French Committee of National Liberation with Giraud. In the next few weeks, de Gaulle outmaneuvered Giraud to gain sole political and military leadership of the Free French, called "Fighting French" after **Bir Hakeim**.

By this time all elements of the Resistance acknowledged de Gaulle as leader of Free France. De Gaulle purged Vichy elements from the colonial administration, and he established a Consultative Assembly in Algiers with representation from all political parties resisting **fascism**. Fearing American intentions to establish a military government (**AMGOT**) upon landing in **Normandy**, de Gaulle announced, on the eve of D-Day, the creation of political commissioners to exercise authority in the name of the Provisional Government. Although excluded from the planning for Normandy, de Gaulle's representatives became the administrators of the liberated territory. The **liberation of Paris** assured Free French control as the Provisional Government of France, which was formally recognized by the Allies in October 1944.

J.-P. Cointet, *La France libre: textes choisis* (Paris, 1975); J.-L. Crémieux-Brilhac, *La France Libre: De l'appel du 18 juin à la libération* (Paris, 1996); J.-L. Crémieux-Brilhac, "La France libre," in J.-P. Azéma and F. Bédarida, eds., *La France des Années Noires,* vol. 1 (Paris, 1993); G. E. Maguire, *Anglo-American Policy towards the Free French* (London, 1995); H. Michel, *Histoire de la France libre* (Paris, 1980).

K. Munholland

FREEMASONS (Grand Orient de France), along with **Jews**, schoolteachers, foreigners, and **communists**, were **Vichy** scapegoats for the evils of democracy, individualism, rationalism, and secularism. The Grand Orient lodge was deemed especially culpable because of its involvement in **education** and, according to the 1943 propaganda film *Forces Occultes*, for helping to start the war in 1939.

To eradicate Freemasonry, Vichy promulgated a law on 13 August 1940 dissolving secret societies. All French lodges were banned: the Grande Orient, Grande Loge, and the Droit humain. Freemasons had to declare publicly their membership and civil servants had to swear that they were not Masons. Few sanctions were taken against those who renounced their membership. In May 1941 fresh declarations were required, and those who had held Masonic office were forced to resign. The *Journal Officiel* in August 1941 published the names of 14,600 French officials allegedly remaining Masons. A secret society service, under the control of Bernard **Faÿ**, head of the Bibliothèque nationale and a scholar of Masonry's alleged influence on the French Revolution, was set up to centralize propaganda and repression. Faÿ's department also created a museum and library devoted to Masonic "perfidy." The results of his investigation were published in *Les Documents Maçonniques* from October 1941 to 1942.

By 1943 Marshal **Pétain** realized that the purge of Freemasons had been futile. While one of his first ministers of education, Émile Mireaux, in office just a few weeks in the summer of 1940, initiated sanctions against teachers who were Masons, his successor, Jérôme Carcopino, who lasted from February 1941 to April 1942, effectively ended this hunt. By the end of the Vichy regime 1,328 teachers had been dismissed as being Masons, but many remained because of the wartime shortage of qualified teachers and the uneasiness of the Nazis with the religious zeal behind the purge.

Aside from the government publications listed earlier, the only history to focus specifically on the Masons during the Vichy era is Dominique Rossignol, *Vichy et les Francs-Maçons. La liquidation des sociétés, 1940–1944*, published in 1981.

*D. Rossignol, *Vichy et les Francs-Maçons. La liquidation des sociétés secrètes, 1940–1944* (Paris, 1981).

W. S. Haine

FRENAY, HENRI (1905–1988), an ex-**army** officer who cofounded the **Resistance** group **Combat** and was instrumental in the fusion of three southern Resistance movements to form the Mouvements de résistance unis (MUR).

A career officer, Frenay broke with his bourgeois family background when he became involved in the Resistance. After escaping from a prisoner of war camp in 1940, he spent some time as a garrison officer in Marseilles. Yet he was increasingly attracted to the notion of creating a secret army and intelligence networks. By early 1941, he had created a Resistance group, the **Mouvement de Libération Nationale**, producing the *Bulletin d'information et de propagande*. This clandestine publication was superseded by *Les petites ailes* (Little Wings) and *Vérités* (Truths), which, in November 1941, combined with François **de Menthon's** Liberté to create the journal and Resistance movement *Combat*.

Starting from an anti-German but pro-**Vichy** position, Frenay moved toward a more open critique of Vichy in early 1942, partly influenced by his companion and fellow resister, Bertie Albrecht. His prewar army career had given him links with Vichy, which he severed after a series of controversial meetings with Vichy interior minister Pierre **Pucheu** in February 1942.

An anti**communist**, Frenay was generally mistrustful of all prewar political parties. His image of the Resistance as a new force for the future led him to question the political control of London over the internal Resistance. However, after a series of meetings with General **de Gaulle** in the autumn of 1942, in January 1943 he became one of the leaders of the MUR.

Frenay was closely involved in the preparations for the **liberation** as a member of the **Provisional Government** and was subsequently appointed minister for deportees, **prisoners** of war, and **refugees**.

H. Frenay, *La Nuit finera* (Paris, 1973); H. R. Kedward, *Resistance in Vichy France* (Oxford, 1978).

C. Gorrara

FREUNDLICH, OTTO (1878–1943), pioneer German abstract artist living in **Paris** during the interwar years. His 1912 sculpture, *Der Neue Mensch*, was chosen as the 1937 catalog cover of Adolf **Hitler's** traveling exhibition, *Entartete Kunst* (Degenerate Art). Freundlich painted and sculpted in both Germany and France and associated with many great artists of the twentieth century—for example, Pablo **Picasso**, Hans Arp, and Wassily Kandinsky—and wrote for art magazines, including *Die Aktion, Der Ventilator*, and *A bis Z*.

For the last 19 years of his life, Freundlich barely eked out a living in France (in Paris until the war broke out). In 1929, he met artist Jeanne Kosnick-Kloss (1892–1966), who became his lifelong companion. He participated in the abstract art movements: Cercle et Carré, Abstraction-Création, and Réalités Nouvelles.

After the outbreak of World War II, Freundlich was arrested as an enemy alien. Interned at Francillon, Cépoy, and Bassens, he was freed, imprisoned, then freed again in May 1940. He took refuge in Saint Paul de Fenouillet, where he continued to draw, paint, and write until he was arrested because of his **Jewish** ancestry and deported to Poland, where he died in the Maidenek **concentration camp**.

His surviving paintings with the characteristic elements of bright colors and two-dimensional, irregular patterns have been widely exhibited.

M. C. Cone, *Artists under Vichy: A Case of Prejudice and Persecution* (Princeton, 1992); *Otto Freundlich et ses amis* (Pontoise, 1993); E. Roditi, "The Art of Otto Freundlich," *Arts* 32 (April 1958).

M. P. Dougherty

FRONT NATIONAL was the largest of the **Resistance** political movements and the only one operating in both main **zones**. Dominated by the **communists**, it is not to be confused with its later **right-wing** homonym.

After **Hitler's** invasion of the **USSR**, the French Communist Party (**PCF**) abandoned its "**Popular Front**" strategy in favor of a "National front for the independence of France," already adumbrated in its clandestine newspaper *L'Humanité* in May 1941. The party immediately launched an organization based on its prewar, broad "Front" structures. Based on working-class and communist activists, it was also designed to attract **Left**-leaning intellectuals and the liberal professions, among whom Resistance activity had already begun to emerge. It rapidly broadened its scope to attract Gaullists and Catholics, with the aspiration of encompassing the entire Resistance movement, and from September 1942, it assumed political supervision of the Francs Tireurs et Partisans Français (FTP) military movement. Its activities north and south were brought under one national executive committee, led by Pierre **Villon**, director of the northern **zone** after the arrest of Georges Politzer, and included the psychologist Henri Wallon, the physicist Frédéric Joliot-Curie, and the Carmelite Father Philippe.

In the spring of 1943 Jean **Moulin** persuaded the movement to join his National Resistance Council (**CNR**), whose charter Villon played a key role in drafting. Strongly supported by the PCF, Front National (FN) members were prominent in local and departmental Resistance committees throughout France. Though it was formally incorporated into General **de Gaulle's Fighting France**, proposals for merger between the FN and other Resistance movements, notably the **Mouvement de Libération Nationale**, foundered on mutual fears of the postwar political consequences.

Among its many activities, the FN organized intellectual Resistance, especially through the clandestine National Writers Council (CNÉ), grouped around its clandestine literary review, the *Lettres Françaises*, directed by Louis Aragon and supported by François **Mauriac** and Jean **Paulhan**, among others.

S. Courtois, "Le Front national," in J.-P. Azéma and F. Bédarida, eds., *La France des années noires,* 2 vols. (Paris, 1993).

M. Kelly

FRONT NATIONAL DES ARTS (National Front of the Arts) grouped together art world personalities intent on resisting **collaboration** in the visual arts. Their most tangible achievement was the publication of a clandestine newsletter, *L'Art Français*, and, in early 1944, an album of subversive lithographs, *Vaincre*.

Its membership drawn mostly from the 1930s **left-wing** Association des peintres, sculpteurs, dessinateurs, graveurs de la Maison de la culture (Association of Painters, Sculptors, Designers, Engravers of the House of Culture), the front included **communists** such as Jean Lurçat, Édouard Pignon, André Fougeron, and Boris Taslitzky and the noncommunist Francis Gruber. The symbolist painter Maurice Denis (born 1870), who although an ardent Catholic and a **right-winger**, refused to be co-opted by either **Vichy** or the Nazis, was named honorary chairman. He died in November 1943.

L'Art Français, mimeographed clandestinely at Fougeron's studio, exhorted readers to vigilance and action and reported news unavailable anywhere else. Its second issue, October 1942, reported, "Thousands of **Jewish** children, most of them born in France, have been separated from their mothers [and] deported to Germany in cattle cars." Some images in the album *Vaincre*, published anonymously in early 1944, depicted Nazi atrocities in an expressionist style, while others caricatured Marshal **Pétain** and Pierre **Laval**. Shortly after the **liberation**, Fougeron ran the **purge** committee created to sanction artist collaborators. Pablo **Picasso** was named chairman of the committee.

M. C. Cone, *Artists under Vichy: A Case of Prejudice and Persecution* (Princeton, 1992); J. Debu-Bridel, *La Résistance intellectuelle, Textes et Témoignages* (Paris, 1970); M. Denis, *Journal III: 1921–1943* (Paris, 1959).

M. C. Cone

G

GALTIER-BOISSIÈRE, JEAN (1891–1966), journalist and **publisher** who recorded conditions in **Paris** during the Occupation. A native Parisian, Galtier-Boissière served courageously during World War I but lost all illusions about military glory and became a pacifist.

In 1915 Galtier-Boissière founded *Le Crapouillot,* a newspaper that depicted the grim realities of trench warfare. After demobilization, he transformed it, first into an avant-garde literary and artistic review, then in 1930 into a "nonconformist" monthly that exposed the barbarities of war and inequities of modern society. On the eve of World War II, he suspended publication of *Le Crapouillot* before the **Daladier** government could suppress it because of its pacifist views.

Galtier-Boissière remained in the capital throughout the German Occupation. From his apartment, located on the Place de la Sorbonne, he carefully observed and faithfully recorded in his personal diary scenes of everyday life: the cruelties perpetrated by the occupiers, shortages of food and fuel, spiraling prices, and black marketeering, as well as the remarkable vitality of the city's cultural life. While not an active *résistant*, Galtier-Boissière ardently hoped for an end to oppressive German rule. He closely followed the progress of the war, eagerly awaited the Allied invasion, and joyfully welcomed the **liberation of Paris** in August 1944.

Soon afterward he reopened his publishing business, printing his wartime diary and issuing a brochure denouncing Marshal **Pétain's** treason. He also resurrected *Le Crapouillot*, which printed a detailed history of the conflict that he had vainly sought to avert.

J. Galtier-Boissière, *Mon journal pendant l'Occupation* (Paris, 1944); *Histoire de la guerre, 1939–1945* (Paris, 1948–1949); *Mémoires d'un Parisien*, 3 vols. (Paris, 1960–1963); *Tradition de trahison chez les maréchaux* (Paris, 1945).

J. Friguglietti

GAMELIN, MAURICE (1872–1958), as chief of staff (1931–1935) and then head of the French **army** (January 1935–19 May 1940), pursued a strategy of fighting the enemy elsewhere than on French soil, which rapidly brought defeat in 1940.

Born to a military family, Gamelin received almost perfect marks as a young soldier. An aide to General Joseph Joffre in 1914, he is said to have devised the plan for the "Miracle at the Marne." Experience of that critical battle, however, left him with a lifelong fear of not being able to hold the Germans again. He rose quickly in the interwar army, aided by political contacts, especially ties with two politicians of the **Right**, André Tardieu and Pierre **Laval**. Unabrasive, he reassured his political mentors by telling them what he sensed they wanted to hear.

Gamelin inherited from the **Pétain**-dominated General Staff of the 1920s the doctrine of a continuous front composed of fortifications and France's Belgian ally, which he adapted in an attempt to modernize the lessons of the last war. His own strategy relied on allies to transport the conflict away from French soil. From January 1933, he saw as given an imminent German reoccupation of the Rhineland, to presage **Hitler's** movement to the east. By 1935 he made plain to his government his preference for a war in the east in which **Italy** would serve as a bridge for a French expeditionary force to a Central European front. With the Rhineland reoccupation in March 1936, he insisted on the need to solder the French and Belgian frontiers, so that the French army could move into **Belgium** in the event of German aggression in Central Europe. By late 1936, he redefined his strategic reserve: from an uncommitted force to be called to any front as needed, it became a specialized, mobile force to be committed to the neutral Low Countries from the first hours of a conflict. The continuous front doctrine was thus extended into Holland in a maneuver later called the Breda Variant.

Mussolini's defection to Hitler's camp after 1936 and the onslaught of international crises in 1938–1939, which brought German ascendancy over Austria and Czechoslovakia and finally over Poland, reduced Gamelin's strategic options from the unencumbered eastern terrain to the narrow confines of Belgium. After Poland's fall in September 1939, he convinced the **British** to accept his plan for a mechanized advance far into the Low Countries, to Breda in southern Holland. On 10–15 May 1940, as German tanks broke through the Ardennes in the south into France, he squandered his strategic reserve in a futile dash to Breda (10–12 May).

On 16 May, Gamelin, who had disdained radio contact with the front, conceded defeat to the French and British prime ministers. He insisted that the battle was lost because he had no further reserves. Paul **Reynaud** grasped that once the French front was broken, there could be no repetition of the Marne miracle. The collapse in 1940 stemmed not, as Gamelin later alleged, from inferior French troops but from the doctrine of continuous fronts, which precluded regrouping for in-depth defense on French soil with an adequate strategic reserve. By Gamelin's dismissal on 19 May, the bulk of France's military accepted that defeat had been sealed: "Henceforth, all decisions were taken in an atmosphere of pre-**armistice**'' (F. Delpla). Demanded not by Gamelin, but by his successor—although there was no change in strategic response with Maxime **Weygand's** 11th-hour reappearance—the timing of the armistice served the purposes for which Gamelin's strategy had been devised. The armistice ensured that there would be no prolonged conflict on French soil and no repetition of the national bloodletting of 1914–1918. By continually attempting to fight the war elsewhere, Gamelin in effect made it impossible to fight at all.

*M. Bloch, *Strange Defeat: A Statement of Evidence Written in 1940*, trans. G. Hopkins (London and New York, 1949 [original French ed., 1946]); N. Jordan, *The Popular Front and Central Europe* (Cambridge, U.K., 1992); N. Jordan, ''Strategy and Scapegoatism: Reflections on the French National Catastrophe, 1940,'' *Historical Reflections* (Winter 1996): 10–32; P. Le Goyet, *Le mystère Gamelin* (Paris, 1976).

N. T. Jordan

GAULLE, CHARLES DE (1890–1970), leader of the **Free French** during World War II, founder and president of the Fifth Republic, 1959–1969. May–June 1940: **Hitler's** armies defeated the French and **British**, invaded France, and took **Paris**. The elderly Marshal Philippe **Pétain** asked for an **armistice**. On 18 June, speaking on London radio, de Gaulle appealed to the French to join him and continue the fight. Nothing, he said, was lost. France still had an **empire**, it was still allied to Britain, and it could count on the vast industrial potential of the **United States**.

Born 22 November 1890, a graduate of the Saint-Cyr military academy and subsequently becoming an officer, de Gaulle was wounded, gassed, and taken prisoner during the First World War. Four times he tried to escape. Repatriated in 1918, he became a military instructor, wrote *La discorde chez l'ennemi*, and criticized the military command's influence on the civilian authorities. After two years' service in the Middle East, he entered the Defense Ministry. His books, *Le fil de l'épée* (1932) and *Vers l'armée de métier* (1934), recommended a professional **army** of armored divisions with full offensive capabilities. France's military command and, with the exception of Paul **Reynaud**, its political leaders rejected his suggestions.

On 10 May 1940 armored German forces invaded France. Commanding a tank division, de Gaulle was named to the Reynaud government. Discouraged by the deteriorating military situation, however, Reynaud gave way to Pétain, who was surrounded by politicians, such as **Laval**, who favored accommodation with Hitler. Despite harsh terms, an armistice was signed on 22 June.

Having participated in Franco–British talks aimed at continuing the war, de Gaulle arrived in London, where, with Churchill's agreement, he broadcast over the **BBC**, telling the French to continue the struggle against Germany. In **Vichy**, Pétain ordered him to return, but de Gaulle refused. De Gaulle faced many obstacles: Vichy sentenced him to death, he tried unsuccessfully to rally the French outpost at **Dakar**, Franco–British rivalry hampered him in the Middle East, and Roosevelt mistrusted this self-assured officer and created many problems for him. However, several colonies, at first in Equatorial Africa and the Pacific, rallied to him. From Chad, General Philippe **Leclerc** was able to attack Italian Libya. After 1942 Morocco, Algeria, and Tunisia supplied forces that eventually fought in **Italy**. In 1944 the Leclerc Division liberated Paris and General Jean de Lattre de Tassigny's army, having landed in **Provence**, reached **Alsace**.

De Gaulle struggled tenaciously for the liberation, unity, and independence of France. Free France announced that it would reestablish **Republican** laws and overturn the racial edicts of Vichy, which it later did. Thanks to Jean **Moulin**, the home **Resistance's** networks and *maquis* recognized General de Gaulle's authority. With the liberation, the French gave an enthusiastic welcome to de Gaulle, first in the provinces, then, despite several unsuccessful sabotage attempts, in the 26 August 1944 parade down the Champs Élysées in Paris.

The war, however, was not yet over. German counteroffensives in late 1944 were repulsed by the Allies, led by General Dwight Eisenhower. De Lattre de Tassigny advanced toward the Rhine at Strasbourg, and Leclerc toward the Danube. With the German surrender in May 1945, what had been announced on 18 June 1940 had been achieved. Unable to get the political parties to adopt his view of an efficient Republican government, however, de Gaulle withdrew from the government in January 1946. Twelve years later, the Algerian war recalled him to power. He then established the Fifth Republic, which he led until 1969. General de Gaulle died in retirement in his home at Columbey-les-deux-Eglises on 9 November 1970.

*†C. de Gaulle, *Discours et Messages*, 5 vols. (Paris, 1970); C. de Gaulle, *The Army of the Future* (Philadelphia, 1941); C. de Gaulle, *The War Memoirs, 1940–46* (New York, 1964); J. Lacouture, *De Gaulle*, 2 vols., vol. 1: *The Rebel, 1890–1944,* trans. P. O'Brian, vol. 2: *The Ruler, 1944–1970*, trans. A. Sheridan (New York, 1991–1992); R. Rémond, "De Gaulle," in J.-P. Azéma and F. Bédarida, eds., *1938–1948 Les Années de tourmente, de Munich à Prague, Dictionnaire Critique* (Paris, 1995), 561–67.

                                                                                    B. Tricot

GAZOGÈNE, a combustion engine using wood, charcoal, or coal as fuel instead of gasoline. When France, totally dependent on foreign oil, was cut off from its supplies during the Occupation, there was a massive conversion to *gazogène* engines for powering vehicles. From 7,200 in 1939, their number had risen to 50,000 by mid-1941. The *gazogène* engine had a large, tanklike generator where the fuel was burned to produce gas. The gas was then cooled, filtered, and mixed with air before going to the motor. *Gazogène* engines were mounted on the roofs of buses, behind the cabs of trucks, and in the trunks or on the running boards of cars.

Gazogène engines had many drawbacks. They were bulky, cumbersome, and hard to start. They required extensive maintenance, much of it on a daily basis. Ashes had to be removed from the generator, filters had to be cleaned, and the frequent leaks at joints in the machinery had to be watched for and immediately repaired. Because of these maintenance difficulties *gazogène* engines were more practical for trucks, buses, boats, and industrial tractors handled by professional drivers and mechanics than for private automobiles. When the war ended, and gasoline again became available, *gazogènes* disappeared from circulation.

D. Baldensperger, "Le renouveau du *gazogène*," *Le Journal de la France* 121 (1971); L. Bourcier, *Automobiles à gazogène* (Paris, 1941); *Guide du gazogène et des énergies de remplacement* (Paris, 1943); D. Veillon, "Une politique d'adaptation spécifique: les ersatz," in D. Veillon and J.-M. Flonneau, eds., *Le temps des restrictions en France (1939–1949)* (Paris, 1996), 59–74.

D. Evleth

GEORGES, ALPHONSE-JOSEPH (1875–1951), is best known for the influential role he played as a member of the interwar Conseil supérieur de la Guerre and for serving as operational commander in the ill-fated 1940 battle.

Georges entered the military college at Saint-Cyr in 1895 and the École supérieur de Guerre in 1905. His talents merited important postings subsequently at the War Ministry and in Morocco. He was seriously wounded in the opening clashes of World War I in September 1914, keeping him from the front for the remainder of the conflict.

In 1925 Georges served as Philippe **Pétain's** chief of staff in the campaign against the rebellious Rif tribes of Morocco. A 1929–1931 stint as war minister André Maginot's chief military adviser put Georges in the heart of political and military decision making, but in October 1934 he was gravely wounded in the Marseilles assassination of Yugoslav king Alexander that also took the life of foreign minister Louis Barthou. In January 1935, Georges was passed over for promotion to the top post in the French **army**, despite outgoing Inspector General Maxime **Weygand's** support. Georges resented his successful rival, the politically adept Maurice-Gustave **Gamelin**.

Frosty relations between Gamelin and Georges did not prevent the latter from receiving the command of the northeast front in 1939–1940, but the lack of harmony between the two generals did nothing to help the French army recover its balance after being shattered by the May 1940 German Blitzkrieg. Georges retired soon after the fall of France, playing no part in **Vichy**. He did reappear briefly, in June 1943, in an Allied scheme to buttress General Henri **Giraud's** power in Algiers against General **de Gaulle**, but when de Gaulle emerged triumphant by November, Georges' career was finally over.

*C. de Gaulle, *War Memoirs*, 3 vols., vol 2: *Unity, 1942–1944*, trans. R. Howard (New York, 1959); "Georges, Alphonse," in M. Prevost, R. D'Amat, and H. Tribout de Morembert, eds., *Dictionnaire de Biographie Française*, vol. 15 (Paris, 1982).

R. F. Crane

GERLIER, CARDINAL PIERRE-MARIE (1880–1965), primate of the Gauls and cardinal-archbishop of Lyons from 1937 to his death. In November 1940, he proclaimed, **"Pétain** is France, and France today is Pétain." By 1942 he was among the handful of bishops who publicly opposed the **deportation** of the **Jews.**

Trained in law, a good orator, and former president (1907–1913) of the Association catholique de la jeunesse française (Catholic Association for French **Youth**), Gerlier became a priest in 1921 and bishop of Tarbes in 1929. After the 1940 defeat, this sole cardinal in the unoccupied zone was a frequent visitor to **Vichy**; he advocated state support for Catholic schools as opposed to the separation of church and state enacted in 1905.

Gerlier supported traditional Catholic teaching, which preached obedience to established authorities. The Vichy laws recruiting labor for the Third Reich prodded him and others to moderate this position. At first through official channels and then later in public pronouncements, Gerlier objected to Vichy's treatment of the Jews. In December 1940, he protested the inhuman conditions at the Gurs camp. Along with the Protestant pastor Marc **Boegner**, he became the honorary president of Amitié chrétienne. He asked religious orders to hide Jewish children. On 6 September 1942, his statement against **deportations** was read in all churches of his diocese. Consequently, the **collaborationist press** attacked him—calling him a traitor, a "new Cauchon," in reference to Pierre Cauchon, bishop of Beauvais, who had presided over the ecclesiastical trial in which Joan of Arc was declared a heretic and subsequently burned as a witch, thereby serving the interests of the English invaders of France during the Hundred Years' War.

Because of his reticence to oppose Pétain and his participation in a memorial service for the assassinated collaborationist Philippe **Henriot** in 1944, Gerlier may have been on Charles **de Gaulle's** list of "undesirable" bishops. Nonetheless, Gerlier participated in **liberation** ceremonies and remained in office until his death.

J. Duquesne, *Les catholiques français sous l'occupation* (Paris, 1966); X. de Montclos et al., eds., *Églises et chrétiens dans la IIe guerre mondiale* (Lyons, 1978).

M. P. Dougherty

GERMANY, EMBASSY IN OCCUPIED PARIS, one of several official German government delegations and representations in occupied **Paris** from June 1940 to August 1944. The German Embassy on the rue de Lille reopened in June 1940 after being closed following declaration of war in September 1939. The German Foreign Ministry named Otto **Abetz** as its representative in Paris. His mission was to coordinate liaison with the German military occupation authorities at the Hotel Majestic.

Abetz had resided earlier in France and had been expelled for espionage by the **Daladier** government. His French wife, Suzanne, had been introduced to him by his friend Jean **Luchaire**. His staff included staunch Nazis such as first secretary Rudolf Schleier and political section chief Ernst Achenbach. Karl Epting was named head of the Deutsches Institut, the cultural affairs branch of the embassy.

After his official appointment as ambassador in late 1940, Abetz set about coordinating the various French collaborators and **collaborationist** groups in Paris and the official collaboration of **Vichy** with Germany. The German Embassy played a central role in orchestrating Pierre **Laval's** return to power in 1942. Embassy personnel constantly found themselves in precarious positions between French collaborationist factions and rival German offices in Paris, notably the military command, the propaganda offices that reported back to Goebbels, and the SS under Carl **Oberg** after 1942.

The German Embassy was the center of Parisian social life, with receptions given by the ambassador and his wife. Louis-Ferdinand **Céline** described the artistic and cultural world there as "Otto's kingdom." As Allied forces advanced on Paris in August 1944, The German Embassy retreated, with a number of French collaborators and Vichy officials, to **Sigmaringen** castle in Germany, where Abetz was nominally replaced as ambassador by Otto Reinebeck.

Y. Durand, *La France dans la deuxième guerre mondiale, 1939–1945* (Paris, 1989); B. M. Gordon, *Collaborationism in France during the Second World War* (Ithaca, NY, 1980); D. Pryce-Jones, *Paris in the Third Reich: A History of the German Occupation, 1940–1944* (New York, 1981).

M. L. Berkvam

GERMANY, MILITARY AUTHORITIES IN OCCUPIED FRANCE, according to stipulations of the 1940 **armistice**, were charged with supervision of the French administration.

In the beginning, the German military commander (Militärbefehlshaber) in France was General Otto von Stülpnagel, who was dismissed, however, in February 1942 because of his protest against the shootings of hostages ordered by **Hitler**. His successor, General Karl-Heinrich von Stülpnagel, a cousin, was arrested and executed after his participation in the 20 July 1944 plot against Hitler.

In addition to the administrative and command staffs in **Paris**, field commanders supervised the French prefects. The military command also included several security regiments, which were no longer combat-ready and, in fact, were far too weak to engage the **Resistance** in southern France in 1944. Combat-ready troops, stationed mainly along the coasts under the western command (Oberbefehlshaber West), were normally not available for duties related to the occupation. Oversight of the unoccupied **zone** until 1942 was entrusted to the German armistice commission in Wiesbaden, which maintained several control commissions for this purpose in southern France.

In addition to responsibility for the preservation of internal security, which was turned over in 1942 to the Supreme SS and Police Command (Höhere SS- und Polizeiführer), the most important task of the military authority was the exploitation of French resources for the German war economy. Since France provided considerable resources, the German military authorities advocated a moderate line and tried to follow a correct **collaboration** with the French offices.

H. Böhme, *Der deutsch-französische Waffenstillstand im Zweiten Weltkrieg* (Stuttgart, 1966); H. Umbreit, *Der Militärbefehlshaber in Frankreich 1940–1944* (Boppard, 1968).

B. Kasten

GERMANY, POLICE IN OCCUPIED FRANCE, the German occupation forces of order, drawn from the military Geheime Feldpolizei (GFP, Secret Field Police) and Feldgendarmerie (Field Police), as well as the Sicherheitspolizei (Security Police) from the SS.

From 1940 to 1942 the regional command of the GFP, responsible for the security of the German troops, was under the authority of the Military Command. The Sicherheitspolizei, often erroneously called the "Gestapo," was led by SS-Obersturmbannführer Helmut **Knochen** and represented only a small force. There was no threat to internal security in France until the summer of 1941. However, following attacks against German soldiers in the fall of 1941, **Hitler** ordered, on 9 March 1942, the creation of a Höhere SS-und Polizeiführer (higher SS and police leader) and the transfer of the GFP into the Sicherheitspolizei.

Due to insufficiencies in numerical strength (2,200 men in December 1943), lack of training in police work, and no familiarity with the country, language, and population, the Sicherheitspolizei was totally overwhelmed by its task and absolutely dependent on the French **police** for the preservation of order. The activities of most of the commanding officers, consequently, were limited by practical considerations. Undoubtedly, suspects were tortured in all the bureaus and deported to **concentration camps**. Both Sicherheitspolizei and military command, however, rejected mass reprisals against the local population. This changed, however, in 1943, above all in southern France and Brittany, with the increasing activity of the **Resistance** movement and the increased posting in France of commanding officers with experience fighting partisans in the east. In these regions the Sicherheitspolizei took a bloody revenge.

J. Delarue, *Geschichte der Gestapo* (Düsseldorf, 1964), English ed., *The Gestapo: A History of Terror*. Trans. M. Savill (New York, 1964, 1987), original French ed., *Histoire de la Gestapo* (Paris, 1962); B. Kasten, *"Gute Franzosen: die französische Polize: und die deutsche Besatzungsmacht im besetzten Frankreich"* (Sigmaringen, 1993).

B. Kasten

GERMANY, POLICY TOWARD FRANCE (1938–1945); following the **Munich agreement** of 29 September 1938, Adolf **Hitler's** Germany prepared for war with France and **Britain**. The elimination of Franco–British power was seen as a prerequisite to the racial reordering of the East, and Hitler preferred to fight the Western democracies while Germany still held an advantage in arms and conscripts. The joint German–French declaration of 6 December 1938, which recognized mutual frontiers, was a German ploy to lull France into slower rearmament efforts. Yet Poland's refusal to submit to German tutelage by joining the Anti-Comintern Pact meant that Germany would attack Poland in 1939 and

France and Britain thereafter. Hitler hoped the Western democracies would abandon Poland or at least delay any response. The Nazi–**Soviet** nonaggression pact (23 August 1939) and Germany's proclamation of its peaceful intentions toward Britain and France were designed to create such a pause, but if the Western democracies were to honor their treaty commitments to Poland, then Germany would fight them too. After attacking Poland on 1 September 1939, Hitler ignored the Anglo–French ultimatum that called for withdrawal; thus, he triggered British and French declarations of war on 3 September.

Following Poland's swift destruction, Germany sent peace feelers to London and Paris, hoping to delay a war in the West until conditions were more opportune. Germany argued that the object of the ultimatum—Poland—now ceased to exist. Since the governments of Neville Chamberlain and Édouard **Daladier** refused to consider peace until the Germans had evacuated Austria, Czechoslovakia, and Poland, the Germans simultaneously prepared a western offensive. Hitler's hope to attack in November 1939 was delayed by logistics, but following the occupation of Denmark and Norway in April 1940, German ground forces attacked the Low Countries and France in May. The offensive through the Ardennes and drive toward the Atlantic divided, disoriented, and demoralized the French forces, while the British evacuated the continent at the end of the month. Convinced that France had lost the war and that national renewal under strong leadership was necessary, Marshal **Pétain's** government asked for **armistice** terms on 17 June.

Due to Hitler's hope for a French government able to maintain stability and end **resistance** in the metropole and in the **empire**, the Germans infused a certain restraint into the German–French **Armistice** Treaty, signed 22 June 1940. Three-fifths of France would be occupied for the continuation of the war against Britain; the French would bear all occupation costs; French armed forces would demobilize to prescribed limits; **prisoners** would remain in captivity for the war's duration; and air, sea, and **radio** traffic would need prior German approval. Yet France's still-intact fleet would remain under French command, and no territorial changes or occupation of imperial possessions was mentioned. Germany pressed the Italian government—which had declared war on 10 June in expectation of territorial rewards—into similar restraint in its own armistice with France (24 June 1940). In the final peace settlement, French military power would vanish, and Germany and **Italy** would take parts of France and its empire.

After British raids at **Mers-el-Kébir** (3 July 1940) and **Dakar** (23–25 September 1940) and General **de Gaulle's** coup in French Equatorial Africa (26–30 August 1940), the French government attempted to collaborate actively in Germany's war effort in return for a relaxation of armistice terms and assurances regarding France's future. Meetings between Hitler, Pétain, and Vice Premier Pierre **Laval** at **Montoire** (22 and 24 October 1940) brought a French pledge to fight the British and Gaullists in French Africa, and Germany allowed the French to delay colonial disarmament while approving the deployment of modest colonial forces for this purpose (July–December 1940). Yet to Hitler, **col-**

laboration meant accelerated German exploitation of France. Germany demanded air bases in Casablanca (15 July 1940), hinting at a forward Mediterranean strategy that they never consistently pursued (See **Spain**). They also carried out mass expulsions from **Alsace-Lorraine** (November–December 1940), insisted that French **industries** produce for the German war effort (2 September 1940), remained silent when the **Japanese** occupied Indochina (22 September 1940), and assumed control of French mineral interests in Yugoslavia (November 1940). The Germans also avoided promises concerning the French government's return to **Paris**, the relaxation of the **Demarcation Line**, which separated France's occupied and unoccupied **zones**, the reduction of exorbitant occupation costs, the future status of the departments Nord and Pas-de-Calais, and France's imperial future. To Hitler, Germany had been generous enough when it allowed the reinterment of the duke of Reichstadt (Napoleon's son) in the Invalides (15 December 1940).

Pétain's 13 December 1940 dismissal of Laval, whom Hitler had viewed as the motor behind French collaboration, brought angry reaction. France, Hitler felt, had reverted to its traditional hatred of Germany. Any possibility of meaningful German concessions thus vanished amid steeper demands, even after Laval's return as premier in April 1942. French food delivery quotas for Germany were sharply increased in June 1942, and the conscription of French labor for work in Germany began in September. Germany, meanwhile, rejected French requests to augment their **North African** forces and to have a defense sector on the French Atlantic coast to repulse Allied attacks. The Allied invasion of North Africa (8 November 1942) brought swift reaction by German forces instead, which landed in Tunisia (9 November) and swept into France's unoccupied zone (11 November). **Vichy's** policy of firing on Allied troops but not German ones brought no reward from Berlin, which viewed the armistice between Admiral **Darlan** and the **Americans** (11 November) and the scuttling of the French fleet at Toulon (28 November) as confirmation of French treachery. Hitler ordered the 100,000-man French **army** allowed under the **armistice** dissolved on 27 November.

Germany also expected French cooperation in the elimination of Europe's **Jews**. Despite Vichy's desire to end Jewish influence in French national life, the Germans were irritated at what they perceived as official obstruction to their policy of mass murder. In the occupied zone, German authorities began using the French bureaucracy in September 1940 for the registration of Jews, **"Aryanization"** of Jewish property, and **deportation** to Auschwitz, which began in March 1942. German deportation quotas, which included the unoccupied zone, began in June 1942. Laval's attempt to surrender only foreign Jews in return for political concessions brought only complaints of French circumvention, and Germany's takeover of the unoccupied zone in November 1942 and of **Italy's** small occupation zone in July 1943 brought all Jews in France directly under German control anyway. Of the 330,000 Jews in France in 1940, 76,000 were deported to Poland, and 30 percent of these were French citizens. The remainder of France's Jews were saved not by Vichy but by the Allied **liberation**.

Despite the steady erosion of whatever sovereignty the Vichy regime had once possessed, Germany depended on Pétain's prestige until the end of the Occupation. Concerns in August 1943 regarding an Allied invasion attempt brought German demands that the Pétain government maintain order in France should a landing materialize. The Allied attack of June 1944, the liberation of France, and the stream of Frenchmen joining a vengeful Resistance showed that the Germans, through their policies, had eroded Pétain's prestige beyond repair. As a final gesture of futility, the Germans in August 1944 attempted to create a "government-in-exile" under Pétain, whom they removed to the Hohenzollern castle of **Sigmaringen** in southwestern Germany.

*†H. Böhme, *Der deutsch-französische Waffenstillstand im Zweiten Weltkrieg* (Stuttgart, 1966); E. Jäckel, *Frankreich in Hitlers Europa: Die deutsche Frankreichpolitik im zweiten Weltkrieg* (Stuttgart, 1966); K.-V. Neugebauer, *Die deutsche Militärkontrolle im unbesetzten Frankreich und in Französisch-Nordafrika 1940–1942* (Boppard am Rhein, 1980); R. O. Paxton, *Vichy France: Old Guard and New Order 1940–1944* (New York, 1972); G. L. Weinberg, *The Foreign Policy of Hitler's Germany*, vol. 2: *Starting World War II 1937–1939* (Chicago, 1980).

N. J. W. Goda

GERMANY, PROPAGANDA IN FRANCE, was an important instrument for securing French assent to the German occupation.

The main responsibility was taken by the Propaganda Abteilung (Propaganda Department), set up by the German army in **Paris** and linked to Joseph Goebbels' Propaganda Ministry. Its four regional Propaganda Staffeln covered the occupied **zone**, and five national groups controlled the **press**, literature, **radio**, culture, and "active propaganda." Its officials were in liaison, but not without occasional friction, with German ambassador Otto **Abetz**, who from 1942 secured responsibility for cultural exchanges.

Control often extended to ownership, and the Pressegruppe, which allocated all newsprint, also took over several publications, including *Paris-soir*. The German-owned Continental was the most prolific French film production company of the period, and the main northern French radio network, Radio-Paris, grouped the stations under German control.

The more conspicuous examples of direct German propaganda had mixed fortunes. Ubiquitous flags, banners, and signs in German were generally resented; the military bands that appeared early in the Occupation were discreetly mocked, and the **anti-Semitic** film *Jew Süss* aroused widespread indignation. Films, radio, even television programs, and an active press were produced for German occupying forces. Some of this was translated for French consumption, including the glossy magazine *Signal*. Wall posters, regularly issued, called for cooperation or condemned national or racial enemies but were vulnerable to defacement. Successful cultural initiatives included the Arno **Breker** sculpture

exhibition of 1942 and the lectures and published *Cahiers* of the Institut allemand, which also organized well attended German-language classes.

While high-profile cultural events attracted the Parisian elite, probably the
most powerful propaganda was indirect, through detailed censorship, control of
news and information, and the willing services of **collaborationist** French writers and broadcasters, all carefully managed and monitored by the Abteilung.

J.-P. Azéma, *1940, l'année terrible* (Paris, 1990); P. Ory, *Les collaborateurs* (Pans,
1976); R. Thalmann, *La Mis au Pas: Idéologie et stratégie sécuritaire dans la France
occupée* (Paris, 1991).

M. Kelly

"GESTAPO, FRENCH," auxiliary **police** unit of French civilian recruits connected to the German Geheime Staats Polizei, called the Gestapo.

The "French Gestapo," also called Gestapo de la rue Lauriston for its location on that street near Étoile in **Paris**, mirrored its German parent organization.
Its leader, Henri Chamberlin, a prewar petty criminal with numerous arrests and
convictions, was recruited by the German counterintelligence Abwehr during
the early days of the Occupation. He changed his name to Lafont and was
allowed by the Germans to pick his staff among criminals in the Fresnes **prison**.
Chamberlin-Lafont and his men became "purchasing agents" for the Bureau
Otto and quickly demonstrated their abilities to the Germans, who suggested
they expand their activities to include tracking and arresting individuals and
infiltrating **Resistance** groups. In 1941, now under direct Gestapo control and
thus immune from his enemies in the French police, Chamberlin-Lafont moved
to 93 rue Lauriston, an address that became synonymous with arbitrary detention
and torture and struck terror into the hearts of people throughout France. Chamberlin-Lafont enjoyed watching the torture of suspects and often participated in
beatings himself, especially if the suspect was **Jewish**. A large number of **Resistance** groups was infiltrated by these Gestapists.

Chamberlin-Lafont was well known in Parisian high society and, after being
introduced to Pierre **Laval** by Jean **Luchaire**, boasted of a close personal friendship with the head of government. In the final days of the German occupation,
the French Gestapo went on a killing rampage and organized the **deportation**
of more than 400 Jews and Resistance members. Arrested after the **liberation**,
Chamberlin-Lafont was tried and executed on 26 December 1944. Many French
Gestapists joined the regular French **army** and were thus able to hide their
bloody past after the war. An excellent literary depiction of French Gestapists
and their activities can be found in the characters of Merkel and Philippe Lar-
réguy in Jean-Louis Curtis's novel *Les Forêts de la nuit*.

M. Dank, *The French against the French: Collaboration and Resistance* (Philadelphia,
1974); M. Hasquenoph, *La Gestapo en France* (Paris, 1975).

M. L. Berkvam

GIDE, ANDRÉ (1869–1951), was an essayist, novelist, dramatist, and critic
who received a Nobel Prize in literature in 1947. In 1940, Gide was in **Vichy**.

He continued to live in the unoccupied **zone** until 1942, when he moved to French North Africa, where he remained for the rest of the Occupation.

Gide had flirted with communism and had spoken out against Nazi Germany in the 1930s, but he was slow to denounce the Vichy government. His hesitations have been described as *attentisme*, or waiting to see who would win, and he was accused of defeatism in 1944. Pierre de Boisdeffre, who called him a *"résistant malgré lui"* (resister in spite of himself), and others who defend him cite his use of literary criticism to make veiled attacks on the Vichy regime and his covert encouragement of **resistance**.

Gide continued to publish in the *Nouvelle Revue Française*, directed by the **collaborationist** Pierre **Drieu la Rochelle** through 1940, but resigned from the editorial board on 21 May 1941, prompted by fellow contributor Jacques Chardonne's collaborationist book *Chronique privé de l'an 1940*. In 1944, Gide participated in the founding of *L'Arche* with, among others, Albert **Camus**.

*K. Bieber, "André Gide and the German Occupation," *Modern Language Quarterly* 15 (1954): 246–51; P. de Boisdeffre, "André Gide, homme d'action," *Cahiers André Gide* 3 (1972): 163–78; A. Gide, *Journal, 1939–1949* (Paris, 1954); H. Lottman, *The Left Bank* (Boston, 1982).

M. Hawthorne

GIONO, JEAN (1895–1970), was a novelist, essayist, and playwright, blacklisted by the National Committee of Writers after the **liberation** in 1944 and imprisoned between September 1944 and January 1945 for wartime **collaboration**.

During the 1930s Giono became an increasingly outspoken advocate of peace at any price and of conscientious objection. In the Occupation years, he became a regular contributor to collaborationist reviews, newspapers, and magazines, including Alphonse **de Châteaubriant's** *La Gerbe*, Pierre **Drieu la Rochelle's** *Nouvelle Revue Française*, and *Cœmédia*. In March 1942, in an interview in *La Gerbe*, Giono praised **Vichy** and its call for a return to a "patriarchal, peasant civilization."

Unlike collaborators such as Robert **Brasillach**, Drieu la Rochelle, and Henry **de Montherlant**, Giono's collaborationism did not spring from pro-Nazi sentiments but from a deep-seated pacifism gleaned from combat experiences during World War I. His relations with the Germans were cordial to friendly. To Alfred Fabre-Luce, he described **Hitler** as a "poet in action." In January 1943, the Nazi magazine *Signal* devoted a photo-essay to Giono in his native Provence, which resulted in a bomb's being exploded in front of his home. The German Library promoted his works, putting a photo of Giono on the cover of its catalog. He also apparently accepted an invitation to attend a Nazi cultural congress in Weimar, but he never, in fact, attended.

After the liberation, Giono abandoned politics and devoted himself to writing novels and plays relating to his native Provence.

P. Citron, *Giono* (Paris, 1990); J. Giono, *Récits et essais* (Paris, 1989); J. Giono, *Jean*

Giono, journal Poèmes, essais (Paris, 1995); J. Guéhenno, *Journal des années noires* (Paris, 1947); P. Hebey *La "Nouvelle Revue Française des années sombres 1940–1941* (Paris, 1992).

R. J. Golsan

GIRAUD, HENRI (1878–1949), was a French general who, supported by the **American** government in 1942–1943, challenged General **de Gaulle** as head of pro-Allied French forces. After merging his organization with de Gaulle's to form the Comité français de libération nationale (CFLN) in mid-1943, Giraud was quickly marginalized by de Gaulle, his more politically adept copresident.

Before World War II, Giraud had built a successful military career on the basis of a dashing appearance and daring style. He commanded the Seventh **Army** in 1940 and was taken **prisoner**. After escaping from Königstein prison in 1942, Giraud found that his brand of politically conservative, anti-Axis patriotism appealed to those in France who had initially supported the Vichy regime and remained sympathetic to Marshal **Pétain** but were becoming uneasy about the extent of **collaboration** with Germany and aware that the military tide had turned in favor of the Allies. The Americans, meanwhile, hoped to capitalize on Giraud's influence in French **North Africa** to ease their invasion there (November 1942). In fact, Giraud arrived from France too late to be of much help during the invasion, and the American commanders turned instead to the ex-Vichy prime minister Admiral **Darlan**. However, when Darlan was assassinated in December 1942, Giraud became civil and military commander in chief. This was the high point of his power. Over the next six months, in spite of American backing, he was forced to give ground repeatedly in his negotiations with the Gaullists. Soon after the formation of the CFLN he was elbowed aside by General de Gaulle. In November 1943 Giraud lost his seat on the CFLN, and the following April he retired from the army. He had proved a talented, if hardly brilliant, soldier and an inept politician.

G. de Charbonnières, *Le Duel Giraud-de Gaulle* (Paris, 1984); J.-B. Duroselle, *L'abîme* (Paris, 1982); A. Funk, *The Politics of TORCH* (Lawrence, KS, 1974); H. Giraud, *Un seul but: la victoire* (Paris, 1949).

A. W. H. Shennan

GIRAUDOUX, JEAN (1882–1944), playwright and diplomat. After serving as information minister for the Third **Republic**, he became director of historical landmarks under **Vichy**, retiring in 1941 to write. Although stagings of his plays during the Occupation scored limited successes, postwar productions enhanced his international reputation.

Born in the Limousin, Giraudoux attended the École Normale Supérieure and entered the foreign service in 1910, holding various embassy, then other government, posts. Simultaneously, he wrote novels and essays. With director and friend Louis Jouvet, he composed his first play, *Siegfried* (1928). Major prewar plays include *Amphitryon 38* (1929), *Judith* (1931), *Intermezzo* (1933), *La*

Guerre de Troie n'aura pas lieu (1935), *Électre* (1937), and *Ondine* (1939), all directed by Jouvet. Remarks against foreigners in his book *Pleins Pouvoirs* (1939), written while he was **Daladier's** information minister, have prompted speculation about his **anti-Semitism**.

During the Occupation, Giraudoux's theatrical career was hampered by Jouvet's absence. He sent his one-act *L'Apollon de Marsac* to Jouvet in Rio de Janeiro, where it premiered (1942), and found another director for his full-length *Sodome et Gomorrhe* (1943). He completed two filmscripts—*La Duchesse de Langeais* (1942) and *Les Anges du péché* (1943)—and *Électre* was revived (1943). Giraudoux's son, Jean-Pierre, joined **de Gaulle** in London; the playwright's own position, though somewhat ambiguous during the Occupation (because he remained, and his works continued to be performed, in France), was nonetheless viewed positively after the **liberation**, when *La Folle de Chaillot* (1945) became his greatest success. He died of food poisoning (1944), convinced the Germans would soon leave **Paris**.

Posthumous works include memoirs, *Visitations* (1947) and *Souvenir de Deux Existences* (1975), letters (1975), and the play *Pour Lucrèce* (1953). Since the 1960s, when his plays were still frequently performed around the world, his popularity abroad declined.

J. Body, *Giraudoux et l'Allemagne* (Paris, 1976); J. Body, *Jean Giraudoux: The Legend and the Secret* (Rutherford, NJ, 1991); P. Duay, *Jean Giraudoux: Biographie* (Paris, 1993); K. Krauss, "The Play Intended: Giraudoux's *L'Apollon*," *Journal of Dramatic Theory and Criticism* 8:2 (Spring 1994).

K. Krauss

GLIÈRES BATTLE took place in March 1944 on the wooded Glières plateau, near Annecy in Haute-Savoie at an altitude of 1,500 meters, between the *maquis* and German forces supported by Joseph **Darnand's** *milice*. It constituted the largest single battle between **Resistance** forces and the *milice*.

Under the charismatic leadership of Théodose Morel, alias Tom, the Bataillon des Glières, comprising some 450 men, formed a bastion of resistance, rather than the guerrilla force desired by Tom's superiors. Its objective was to clear a drop zone for Allied supplies prior to Allied landings. The force represented all sections of the **Resistance** and included 56 Spanish Republicans, plus Poles and Italian antifascists.

In mid-February and early March the **British** dropped arms and ammunition, with 90 tons being dropped in a single night. German troops pro-Nazi GMR (Groupes Mobiles de Réserve) pinpointed the drop and surrounded the plateau. Morel (Tom) and two key aides were killed in an attempt to rescue a captured medic. General Carl **Oberg** assembled some 12,000 German troops, including a crack Alpine division, and units of the *milice* for an all-out assault on the plateau. In the ensuing pitched battle between 23 and 25 March 1944, the *maquis*, despite a stout defense, was defeated by the manifestly superior enemy

force, with 155 *maquis* killed, including their new leader, Captain Maurice An-
jot. This amounted to the annihilation of the Glières *maquis*.

The battle came to **symbolize** Resistance courage in the face of overwhelming
odds and, with the battle of the **Vercors** plateau in July 1944, took its place in
Resistance legend. Yet, opinions vary as to whether the battle was an epic, but
tragic, struggle and example of outstanding heroism or a misguided and tacti-
cally unsound attempt at military resistance.

L. Jourdan-Joubert, *Glières, première bataille de la Résistance* (Annecy, 1978); F.
Musard, *Les Glières* (Paris, 1965); D. Schoenbrun, *Soldiers of the Night: The Story of
the French Resistance* (New York, 1980); J. Truffy, *Les mémoires du curé des maquis
des Glières* (Annecy, 1979).

J. Wright

GÖRING, HERMANN WILHELM (1893–1946), was *Reichsmarschall*, Prussian prime minister, and commander of the Luftwaffe. Heading the German four-
year economic plans from 1936 on, he systematically exploited occupied France
for the German war machine. A quick learner and a good speaker, jovial, ostentatious, unscrupulous, and self-seeking, Göring lacked perseverance and was
particularly obsequious to **Hitler**.

A fighter pilot in World War I, Göring joined Hitler in 1922. He was elected
president of the Reichstag after the 1932 elections and in 1933 was one of three
National Socialist ministers in the new Hitler government. Göring supported
close ties between the Reich and **Italy**, Poland, and Southeast Europe. After the
Anschluss with Austria in March 1938, he lobbied for an "economic appeasement" of **Britain**. Because of overlapping interests in eastern and Southeastern
Europe, he was uninterested in an accord with "arch enemy" France. Hitler,
who saw in Göring an architect of the **Munich conference** and attendant peace
policy, withdrew his confidence from Göring, and peace initiatives that the latter
sponsored through the beginning of 1940 went nowhere.

Defeat in the air battle of Britain accelerated Göring's downfall. Still head of
the four-year plans, he lost influence to Fritz Todt and, after 1942, Albert Speer.
Meetings with Marshal **Pétain** (1 December 1941) and Pierre **Laval** (9 November 1940 and 15 March and 19 December 1942) failed because Göring saw
France only as a source of raw materials, armaments, and manpower, never as
a potential partner of the Reich.

After Stalingrad and the beginning of Allied air attacks on German cities,
Göring avoided Hitler, took stimulants, and sought distraction in travel, hunting,
and his collections of stolen art. Removed from his posts by Hitler shortly before
the latter's suicide, Göring surrendered to the **Americans** on 7 May 1945. He
tried unsuccessfully to play down National Socialism during the Nuremberg
trials but was sentenced to death. On 15 October 1946, prior to his scheduled
execution, Göring committed suicide.

J. C. Fest, *The Face of the Third Reich* (London, 1972); A. Kube, *Pour le mérite und
Hakenkreuz. Hermann Göring im Dritten Reich* (Munich, 1986); S. Martens, *Hermann*

Göring, "Erster Paladin des Führers und 'zweiter Mann im "Reich" (Paderborn, 1985);
R. J. Overy, *Göring, the Iron Man* (London, 1984).

S. Martens

GROUPE COLLABORATION was a club of "cultivated intellectuals and
bourgeois" under the patronage of **Vichy's** "ambassador" to the occupied **zone**,
Fernand **de Brinon**, interested in developing ties between France and Germany
during the Occupation.

Successor to the interwar **Comité France-Allemagne**, the Groupe was established in September 1940 by the writer Alphonse **de Châteaubriant**, known for
his 1937 apologia for Nazism, *La Gerbe des forces*. Honorary patrons included
the physicist Georges **Claude**, Cardinal Alfred **Baudrillart**, and the literati Abel
Bonnard and Abel Hermant, the last three of whom were members of the Académie Française. Routine administration was handled by Jean Weiland. The
Groupe published the *Cahiers Franco-allemands* and sponsored lectures by
prominent Frenchmen, including Claude, and touring German dignitaries, such
as Professor Friedrich Grimm, a lawyer who before the war had written on
Franco–German relations. Audiences could reach 1,500, as one did at Tours in
March 1944. With a network throughout France, the Groupe also broadcast a
weekly program on **Radio-Paris**.

The Groupe was not a political party and maintained friendly ties with the
various **collaborationist** movements. Its activities, however, had a clear political
message, which was friendship with Nazi Germany. The organization also received German funds. In addition, the Groupe supported affiliated organizations,
such as the more militant Jeunesse de l'Europe Nouvelle. As the war turned
against the Axis, many of the older, better-established members of the Groupe
tried to distance themselves quietly from the movement, while some of the more
strident younger members joined more militant collaborationist formations, such
as the *milice*. **Resistance** infiltrators also were able to use the cover of the
Groupe to spread false information to Vichy.

P. Burrin, *Living with Defeat: France under the German Occupation, 1940–1944*,
trans. J. Lloyd (New York, 1997) [original ed.: *La France à l'heure allemande, 1940–
1944* (Paris, 1995)]; B. M. Gordon, *Collaborationism in France during the Second World
War* (Ithaca, NY, 1980).

G. Le Marec

**GROUPEMENT DES INDUSTRIES MÉTALLURGIQUES MÉCA-
NIQUES ET CONNEXES DE LA RÉGION PARISIENNE** (GIMMCP) was
founded in 1917 to represent the metallurgical industries that sprang up in the
industrial suburbs of Paris. Firms attached to the GIMMCP employed a total of
around 200,000 workers, and the body was important enough to be represented
in the Hotel Matignon negotiations between employers and trade unions orchestrated by the government in 1936.

Unlike the more prominent employers' associations such as the Confederation

Générale du Patronat Français, the GIMMCP was not dissolved in 1940. Consequently, the minutes of its central committee meetings provide a rare glimpse of business sentiment under the **Vichy** regime. The GIMMCP's small business section was particularly active during this period. It expressed the discontent of small-scale **industrialists** who believed that larger enterprises were better equipped than they to extract benefits from the German war economy. However, the criticisms of small-business men in the GIMMCP were always more restrained than those of their colleagues in other organizations. This was partly because the GIMMCP itself contained some very large enterprises (notably Renault). It was also because the very high demand for metallurgical goods during wartime and the tradition of subcontracting that existed in the sector meant that small entrepreneurs tended to be exploited rather than eliminated.

R. C. Vinen, *The Politics of French Business 1936–1945* (Cambridge, U.K., 1991).

R. C. Vinen

GROUPES DE PROTECTION, VICHY (GP, 1940), was a shadowy and short-lived paramilitary **police** force set up in **Vichy** during the late summer of 1940. The principal aim was, as the name suggests, to protect Marshal **Pétain's** political "revolution."

During August 1940, a number of former *cagoulards* in Vichy, including the "mysterious" Doctor Henri Martin, François Méténier, Gabriel Jeantet, and Colonel Georges **Groussard**, one of a number of prominent **army** officers who had moved in Cagoule circles during the 1930s, held secret discussions with another leading *cagoulard*, Eugène **Deloncle**. The latter, now in favor of maneuvering into a politics of **collaboration** with the occupiers, first had the idea of the *"groupes de protection."* Groussard was persuaded to present the idea as his own.

Between August and November 1940, four *cagoulard*-related organizations were created to monitor the population and to help further the **National Revolution**: these were Deloncle's Mouvement Social Révolutionnaire in the occupied **zone** and the Centre d'informations et d'études (CIÉ), the **Légion Française des Combattants**, and the Amicale de France, all in the unoccupied **zone**. The major grouping, set up by Groussard at Vichy, was the CIÉ; one branch fulfilled a civilian intelligence role, while the GP were uniformed paramilitaries. This amounted essentially to a continuation of cagoulard activities, since Groussard appointed Commander Robert Labat (head of the military Cagoule in Marseilles) as his adjutant, Martin as chief organizer and recruitment officer, and Méténier as head of operations. However, after the removal of **Laval** from power in the so-called plot of 13 December, in which the GP were directly implicated, Groussard was forced to disband the GP because Otto **Abetz, Hitler's** ambassador in **Paris**, strongly disapproved of the arrest of Laval. The intelligence branch of the CIÉ, discreetly making contact with anti-German elements that would serve Groussard's patriotic ends later, continued operating until February 1941.

G. Groussard, *Service secret 1940–1945* (Paris, 1964); H. du Moulin de Labarthète, *Le Temps des illusions. Souvenirs, juillet 1940–avril 1942* (Geneva, 1946); P. Péan, *Le mystérieux Docteur Martin, 1895–1969* (Paris, 1993).

M. Cornick

GROUSSARD, GEORGES ANDRÉ (1891–1980), an **army** officer, significant at **Vichy**, and a **Resistance** leader. A graduate of the military academy at Saint-Cyr, Groussard served with distinction during World War I. His interwar career included intelligence activity in the Balkans and colonial and Parisian posts. At the behest of Marshal Louis Franchet d'Esperey he also developed contacts with the Cagoule, though he denied ever joining that group. In 1938 and 1939 Colonel Groussard commanded Saint-Cyr. During the **Battle of France**, he headed general staffs in the **Alsace** and **Paris** military regions.

In Vichy, Groussard left the army and became inspector general of the Sûreté Nationale. He also established the Centre d'Information et d'Études (CIÉ), a supplemental **police** service. For the newly created **Groupes de Protection (GP), Pétain's** praetorian guard, Groussard chose ex-*Cagoulard* François Méténier, who recruited his men from the prewar "national parties." On 13 December 1940, Groussard participated in the palace coup against Pierre **Laval**; subsequently, he lost his post, and the CIÉ and GP were dissolved. Supported by General Charles-Léon **Huntziger**, Vichy's minister of war, Groussard met in London in June 1941 with **British** leaders, including Churchill, the **American** ambassador, and representatives of General **de Gaulle**. Groussard sought links between Vichy and Britain and, he later asserted, with the **Free French**. Admiral **Darlan**, however, arrested him on 15 July. Imprisoned, then placed under house arrest, Groussard escaped to **Switzerland** when the Germans occupied southern France in November 1942. There he organized and directed the "Gilbert" intelligence network in France.

After the war, Groussard wrote a number of books and protested against the loss of the French **empire**. He portrayed his work at Vichy as cover for intelligence and organizational activity against Germany in pursuit of French recovery.

P. Bourdrel, *La Cagoule* (Paris, 1992 [original ed., 1970]); M.Digne, "Groussard, Georges," in M. Prevost et al., *Dictionnaire de biographie française*, vol. 16 (Paris, 1985), 1358–60; G. A. Groussard, *Service secret, 1940–1945* (Paris, 1964), originally *Chemins secrets* (Mulhouse, 1948).

J. Blatt

GUÉHENNO, JEAN (1890–1978), educator, coeditor of *Europe* (1928–1936) and *Vendredi* (1935–1938), was a leading pacifist writer in the 1930s. His *Journal des années noires, 1940–44* depicts occupied France and typifies intellectual **resistance**.

Guéhenno studied at the École normale supérieure (class of 1911) and fought in World War I. He joined Romain Rolland's pacifist entourage in the 1920s and coauthored the initial "oath" of the Front populaire (14 July 1935). During the Spanish civil war and the **Munich agreement**, he shifted away from integral pacifism. Guéhenno was professor of advanced classes in **Paris** *lycées* (Lakanal, 1929–1941 and Louis-le-Grand, 1941–1943). In 1943, he was demoted for antifascist sympathies.

The *Journal des années noires* was animated by Guéhenno's ideal of an intellectual enclave of resistance, *"une France qu'on n'envahit pas"* (an unassailable France). Living conditions during the Occupation, **deportations**, executions, students' ideologies, the *maquis*, and literary figures (**Drieu la Rochelle**, André **Gide**, Jean **Paulhan**, François **Mauriac**, and others) are discussed. Portions of the journal appeared clandestinely at **Éditions de minuit**. In 1941 Guéhenno helped found the Comité national d'écrivains. After the **liberation**, he pursued his career as writer and educator. He joined the French Academy in 1962.

J.-P. Azéma, *From Munich to the Liberation 1938–1944*. Trans. J. Lloyd (Cambridge, U.K. and Paris, 1984 [original French ed. 1979]); J. Guéhenno, *Journal des années noires* (Paris, 1947, reprinted 1973); G. Leroy and A. Roche, *Les écrivains et le Front populaire* (Paris, 1986); J.-F. Sirinelli, *Génération intellectuelle: Khâgneux et Normaliens dans l'entre-deux-guerres* (Paris, 1988).

V. Kelly

GUILBAUD, GEORGES (1915–), played a key role in establishing a single unified administration of the Tunis French community behind the **Vichy** government during the 1942–1943 military campaign in **North Africa**.

Born in Cuzion (Indre), Guilbaud became an accountant and in 1933 joined the **Communist** Party, which he quit after a visit to the **Soviet Union** five years later. A supporter of Marshal **Pétain** after the 1940 defeat, Guilbaud took a post with the Secrétariat Général à l'Information, whose head, Paul **Marion**, had also been a communist. His work there took him to Algeria.

Following the Allied landings in North Africa in November 1942, Pierre **Laval** sent Guilbaud to represent Vichy's Information Services in Tunis, where he had to deal with French and German civilian and military authorities, as well as Italians and Arabs, and the threat of Allied attack. To mobilize the French population there, on 10 December, Guilbaud launched a daily, the *Tunis-Journal*, and the following 5 January created the Comité d'unité d'action révolutionnaire (CUAR), to unify the pro-**Vichy** groups there. The CUAR included representatives of the **Légion Française des Combattants**, the **Service d'Ordre Légionnaire**, the **Parti Populaire Français**, the **Compagnons de France**, and adjunct members Jean Scherb and Lucien Estève.

Even more than Vichy's resident-general, Admiral Jean-Pierre **Esteva**, the CUAR governed Tunisia. The committee was supported by the German ambassador in Tunis, Rudolf Rahn, who also facilitated their return to France via Rome on 25 April 1943, just before the Allies swept into Tunisia. The brief CUAR administration was an exceptional case of a single party governing any part of the French **empire** during the Vichy years.

Returning to **Paris**, Guilbaud created a Lavalist newspaper, *l'Echo de la France*. With the end of the war he fled to **Spain**, then, in 1947 to South America, returning to France in 1971.

B. M. Gordon, *Collaborationism in France during the Second World War* (Ithaca, NY, 1980); R. Pellegrin, *La Phalange Africaine, la L.V.F. en Tunisie 1942–1943* (Paris, 1973); R. Rahn, *Ruheloses Leben, Aufzeichnungen und Erinnerungen* (Düsseldorf, 1949).

G. Le Marec

GUITRY, SACHA (1885–1957), was a dramatist, director, and actor, the author of five theatrical works written during the Occupation (*Pasteur, Louis XI, Ceux de chez nous, Le Bien Aimé*, and *Vive l'Empereur*) and three films (*Le Destin fabuleux de Désirée Clary, Donne-moi tes yeux*, and *La Malibran*). He also published an anthology of the French publications *De Jeanne d'Arc à Philippe Pétain*, dedicated to the marshal. Without doubt, he was the artist who evoked the greatest controversy during the three years of his post-**liberation** trial. Charged with collusion with the enemy, he was arrested 23 August 1944, but his case was dropped by two different courts in 1945 and 1947.

Guitry's position was symbolic of the social **collaboration** in occupied **Paris**. Above all, his position as *persona grata* (favored person) of the Paris intelligentsia was later denounced, as well as his attendance at cocktail parties at the German Embassy, his relations with Fernand **de Brinon**, and his presence at the ceremony of the transfer of the ashes of the king of Rome (Napoleon's son) to the Invalides in December 1940. Undeniably, he refused to allow his own plays to be performed in Berlin during the entire Occupation period. He quarreled with the German censors, who banned two of his plays, *Mon auguste grand-père* for its criticism of racism and *Le Dernier Troubadour* for its anti-German allusions. He contributed to the repatriation of 11 **prisoners** and helped prevent 14 **deportations**, including those of Tristan Bernard and his wife. Nevertheless, his privileged position gave him far from insignificant advantages: the cancellation of a requisition of his Ternay property, recourse against the subordinate officials in the German censorship office, and the obtaining of a travel pass. The failure to proceed with the charges against him after the liberation left public opinion with the feeling of a failed **purge**.

S. Added, *Le Théâtre dans les années Vichy, 1940–1944* (Paris, 1992); P. Assouline, *L'Épuration des intellectuels* (Paris, 1985); J.-P. Bertin-Maghit, *Le Cinéma sous l'Occupation* (Paris, 1989); G. Ragache and J.-R. Ragache, *La Vie quotidienne des écrivains et des artistes sous l'Occupation, 1940–1944* (Paris, 1988).

J.-P. Bertin-Maghit

GYPSIES, common name for Roma, an ethnic group interned in French camps between 1940 and 1946. Because they were often nomadic, Roma were considered wartime security risks, subject to incarceration in France as early as April

1940. Roma were among the groups the Nazis deemed genetically inferior and targeted for **deportation** to the labor and death camps of Eastern Europe. In December 1940, the Germans expelled all Roma from **Alsace-Lorraine** and sent them elsewhere in France, where **Vichy** authorities interned them.

With German endorsement, most of the French camps created for Roma were in the occupied **zone**. The most famous of these were Montreuil-Bellay (Maine et Loire) and Coudrecieux (Sarthe). In 1942 Vichy opened a camp for Roma at Saliers (Bouches-du-Rhône), adjacent to the Roma traditional gathering place at Saintes-Maries-de-la-Mer in the Camargue. Romany families confined to these centers occupied their own wagons or makeshift buildings, where chronic shortages of food, clothing, heat, and clean water led to health problems and occasional epidemics. Specific death tolls for Roma in the camps are difficult to discern, as many vagrants, often in poor health before their incarceration, were probably among the fatalities. It is also hard to ascertain global figures for Roma interned in France during the war. Estimates vary from 3,000 to 30,000, though the actual number is probably closer to the smaller figure.

Although Nazi racial policies targeted Roma for extermination, only one convoy went east from **Belgium**, in January 1944, including 351 Roma, most of whom had been arrested in France. Only 12 people from that convoy survived the war.

D. Peschanski, *Les Tsiganes en France 1939–1946* (Paris, 1994); J. Sigot, *Un camp pour les tsiganes . . . et les autres: Montreuil-Bellay 1940–1945* (Bordeaux, 1983).

D. F. Ryan

H

HARDY, RENÉ (1911–1987), a former official of the French national railroads, code-named "Didot," was a member of the **Resistance** group **Combat** and in charge of railroad sabotage operations. Many of his former Resistance colleagues believe Hardy to have been a Gestapo informer whose betrayal led directly to the arrest and subsequent death of Resistance hero Jean **Moulin**. After the **liberation**, he was tried for collaboration, once in 1947 and again in 1950 but was acquitted both times.

On the night of 7–8 June 1943, Hardy was en route to a meeting with General Charles **Delestraint**, head of the Secret **Army**, when he was arrested by Klaus **Barbie**, Gestapo chief of Lyons. Released shortly thereafter, he was again arrested on 21 June 1943, along with Jean Moulin and other colleagues, while attending an important meeting of Resistance leaders at Caluire, a suburb of Lyons. Alone among them, he escaped, taking a bullet in one arm. Subsequently recaptured, Hardy claimed to have escaped once again.

Accusations against Hardy are based on the improbability of his two escapes and the fact that at Caluire, he, unlike his peers, was not handcuffed. More important, Hardy admitted to lying about his first arrest by Barbie, declaring that he feared being blamed for Delestraint's capture. Finally, Barbie long maintained that Hardy had been his informant. Documents in French and German archives seem to confirm the thesis of Hardy's guilt, although this is impossible to determine with complete certainty.

After the war, Hardy wrote a number of novels, two of which won literary prizes. In his autobiography, he continued to deny having betrayed Moulin, commenting bitterly that he was a "vanquished victor."

J.-P. Azéma and D. Veillon, "Le point sur Caluire," *Jean Moulin et la Résistance en 1943* (Paris: Cahiers de l'IHTP, June 1994); R. Hardy, *Derniers Mots* (Paris, 1984); J.-M. Théolleyre, "Les amertumes d'un naufrage," *Le Monde*, 13–14 May 1984; "René Hardy est mort," *Le Monde*, 15 April 1987.

V. Datta

HAUTECŒUR, LOUIS (1884–1973), was secretary-general of Beaux-Arts under **Vichy** from 1940 through 1944. A student at the Lycée Henri IV in Paris, then at the École Normale Supérieure and the French School in Rome, he attained the *doctorat d'État* in history and geography. He began his career as a professor at the **University** of Caen, became adjunct conservator at the Louvre, then conservator at the Museum of **Luxemburg**, director-general of Beaux-Arts in Cairo, and professor at the École nationale supérieure des Beaux-Arts in **Paris**.

He became secretary-general of Beaux-Arts, near ministerial rank, and a *conseiller d'État* (state councillor) beginning July 1940 and lasting until March 1944. In his postwar memoir, *Les Beaux-Arts en France*, Hautecœur described his wartime duties as having no political role, rather being solely to protect monuments and other works of art and reopen **theaters** and schools. A traditionalist in his artistic tastes, Hautecœur has been generally considered a moderate among the Vichy officials who believed that the state should play a directing role in the art world and also tried to funnel funds to the artists he supported. He also helped defend French art collections against the desires of the Occupation authorities.

Hautecœur's work for Vichy did not harm his subsequent career. By a decree of 19 April 1946 he was restored to his post, but he preferred to retire. He was elected to the Académie des Beaux-Arts, one of five academies of the Institut de France, in 1952. His works in the history of classical architecture are still considered authoritative in France.

L. Bertrand Dorléac, *Histoire de l'art, Paris, 1940–1944* (Paris, 1986); M. C. Cone, *Artists under Vichy, a Case of Prejudice and Persecution* (Princeton, 1992); P. Dehaye, "Discours prononcé à la séance publique tenue par l'Académie des Beaux-Arts pour la réception de Pierre Dehaye, section des members libres, en remplacement de Louis Hautecœur" (Paris, 1975); L. Hautecœur, *Les Beaux-Arts en France, Passé et Avenir* (Paris, 1948).

I. Boussard

HAUTE COUR DE JUSTICE (1944–1949) was established on 18 November 1944 to discharge the promise in Article 2 of the **Conseil National de la Résistance** charter to punish traitors and those leaders actively associated with **Vichy**. It tried cases covering the period from 17 June 1940 through the **liberation**. Competence was limited to the head of state, head of government, ministers, *commissaires généraux* and *secrétaires généraux*, residents, governors-general, and high commissioners. Criminal procedures were followed loosely. There were three magistrates and 24 jurors selected from a pool of 50. The jury pool came from among those deputies who had refused to support Marshal **Pétain** in 1940 and from the justice and **purge** commission.

Admiral Jean-Pierre Esteva, resident-general in Tunisia, was tried first, convicted for having allowed the 1942 German landing in Tunisia. His death sentence was commuted to life imprisonment. General Alphonse Juin, who transmitted—with some element of choice in this action—**Esteva's** orders was never charged and became chief of staff. Pétain's death sentence was commuted by General **de Gaulle** to life imprisonment. **Laval's** trial was a shouting match, followed by his death sentence, attempted suicide, and execution. Pétain's defense, used by others, was that he was really playing a **double game** of **Resistance**. Some denials of complicity with the Germans and autonomous choice by French leaders were rejected.

The trials were intended to produce consensus on the meaning of the Vichy experience and shape clear definitions of guilt and responsibility. Instead, these show trials, whose initial scenes were broadcast to the nation on radio and reported in a sensationalist press, generated court as spectacle with inconsistent procedures followed by arbitrary decisions.

L. Noguères, *La Haute Cour de la Libération, 1944–1949* (Paris, 1965); P. Novick, *The Resistance versus Vichy, the Purge of Collaborators in Liberated France* (New York, 1968).

D. R. Applebaum

HENRIOT, PHILIPPE (1889–1944), the "French Goebbels," was appointed minister of information and propaganda for Vichy in January 1944. A supporter of General Édouard de Curières de Castlenau's interwar *National Catholic Federation*, elected as Bordeaux deputy in 1932, Henriot denounced Premiers Camille Chautemps' and Édouard **Daladier's** complicity in the 1934 Stavisky affair. He opposed the League of Nations, **British** intervention in the Ethiopian crisis, and the Franco–**Soviet** alliance of 1935. Anticommunist, Henriot opposed the **Popular Front** in France while supporting Franco's Nationalists in **Spain** and defending appeasement of the Axis powers.

The defeat of 1940 confirmed Henriot's anti-**Republican** prejudice, and he became one of the great orators for **Pétain's National Revolution**. His initial diffidence toward **collaboration** was overcome with the British attacks at **Mers-el-Kébir** and **Dakar** in 1940 and **Madagascar** and Syria in 1941. The German invasion of the **Soviet Union** tipped the balance: Henriot regarded the Russo-German war as a Christian crusade. The **American** invasion of **North Africa** and the German invasion of the **Vichy** rump state in November 1942 decided Henriot's collaborationism. Joining Joseph **Darnand's Milice Française** after the Battle of Stalingrad, Henriot, conforming to Nazi propaganda, attempted to discredit the Resistance as **communists**.

His appointment as minister of information and propaganda in January 1944 coincided with the installation of *milice* leader Joseph Darnand as head of the Vichy police. German technical assistance permitted Henriot to broadcast from the **Glières** battle against the *maquis*. Fears that Henriot's defeatism threatened to undermine resistance inspired the popular Henriot **radio** debates with the **BBC's** Pierre Dac. Assassinated by "Morlot's" **Comité d'Action militaire (COMAC)** group on 28 June, Henriot was accorded a state funeral at Notre Dame. The *milice* murdered Georges **Mandel** in revenge.

*A. Brissaud, *La Dernière année de Vichy (1943–1944)* (Paris, 1965); H. R. Kedward, "The Vichy of the Other Philippe," in G. Hirschfeld and P. Marsh, eds., *Collaboration in France: Politics in France during the Nazi Occupation, 1940–1944* (Oxford, 1989), 32–46.

P. J. M. Coggins

HÉROLD-PAQUIS, JEAN (1912–1945), **Radio-Paris** broadcaster, whose signature slogan was "England, like Carthage, will be destroyed." A member of **Action Française**, Hérold-Paquis enlisted in the Bandera française of the Spanish Foreign Legion in 1937. Propagandist for Franco's Radio-Saragossa, Hérold-Paquis was intoxicated by "the atmosphere of radio combat." His propensity for risk, adventure, and violence attracted him to **fascism**.

Appointed to **Vichy's** propaganda services in 1940, Hérold-Paquis, however, left Vichy for the more pro-Axis Radio-Paris, becoming its military chronicler in January 1942. Joining both Jacques **Doriot's Parti Populaire Français** and the Waffen SS, Hérold-Paquis broadcast "red specter" messages linking French communism to the war against the **Soviet Union** and predicting a class war in France in the event of Soviet victory. Roosevelt was caricatured as gang lord of racist America. Allied demands for unconditional surrender and "terror bombing," he proclaimed, would fail to curtail Germany's war effort. The second front, according to Hérold-Paquis, was an illusion; the Katyn massacre offered a concrete example of Soviet intentions in Europe. The German field-gray uniform defended Europe: "[T]he LVF offers its blood; the **Jews** of London offer their saliva." His broadcast of 8 January 1944, "Vive la mort" (Long live death) exalted violence and bloodshed. In return, Pierre Dac's "Hérold-Paquisades" broadcast by **BBC** reminded Hérold-Paquis that "Germany, like Carthage, will be destroyed." At his trial in 1945 Hérold-Paquis claimed to be only a man of words whose violence was a mark of his sincerity. He was executed in 1945.

S. Douay, "La Voix de l'Occupation," *Historama* 24 (1986): 23–29; J. Goueffon, "La Guerre des Ondes: Le Cas de Jean Hérold-Paquis," *RDHDGM* 108 (October 1977); J. Hérold-Paquis, *Des illusions . . . désillusions* (Paris, 1984); P. Ory, *Les Collaborateurs, 1940–1945* (Paris, 1976).

P. J. M. Coggins

HERSANT, ROBERT (1920–1996), was a media baron and politician in post-war France. The owner of the leading French press group, which now holds an interest in many French newspapers and magazines, including *Le Figaro* and *France Soir*, Hersant was also majority shareholder in the television channel Le Cinq. His political activities since the 1950s were linked to Jacques Chirac.

Hersant's career was marked by controversy, not only because of his later career but also because of his political actions during the 1930s and 1940s. He first came to public attention as a teenager during the late 1930s, when he joined several pro-**fascist** groups. In 1940 Hersant formed a pro-fascist group called

Jeune Front (Young Front). The next year he served as director of a Marshal **Pétain Youth** Center in Brevannes and started a newspaper called *Jeunes Forces* (Young Forces). He also published articles in the **collaborationist press** and was later accused of taking property from Parisian **Jews** and operating a black market ring.

Hersant spent a month in prison in 1947 for collaborationist acts, and his civil rights were taken away for 10 years. They were restored under the terms of a general amnesty in 1952. Elected deputy from the Oise in 1956, he was denied his seat because of his wartime activities. This was a ploy by his political enemies, who really cared little about his wartime activities. However, his constituency refused to turn him out, and he was returned to his seat in a subsequent election. Hersant is an example of how youthful activities can haunt a subsequent career, especially for someone who becomes an important public figure.

†N. Brimo, *Le Dossier Hersant* (Paris, 1977); H. Rousso, *The Vichy Syndrome, History and Memory in France since 1944*, trans. A. Goldhammer (Cambridge, MA, 1991).

E. H. Murphrey

HITLER, ADOLF (1889–1945), was German Führer and Chancellor whose mistrust for "arch enemy" France remained unchanged throughout his lifetime. In *Mein Kampf*, Hitler formulated his goal of conquering "living space in the east." Bolshevik **Russia** was the primary opponent, for geographical and ideological reasons. France, as traditional rival for primacy in Europe and a potential ally of **Russia**, was the greatest obstacle to the development of Hitler's vision.

Once in power, Hitler demonstratively renounced claims to **Alsace** and **Lorraine** but also demanded international equality for the Reich. He lost all respect for the French when they failed to respond to his occupation of the Rhineland in March 1936; his contempt was confirmed by the **Munich conference**, the "**Phoney War**," and the French military collapse of 1940. Pierre **Laval**, Joachim von Ribbentrop, and Otto **Abetz** sought vainly to persuade him of the utility of **collaboration**, but Hitler saw the 1940 **armistice** and his 24 October 1940 **Montoire** meeting with Marshal **Pétain** solely in strategic terms. Although his granting of the 1940 armistice may have doomed him in a two-front war, for Hitler, **Vichy's** willingness to collaborate appeared to free up troops for the coming war in the east. French colonies and the fleet were removed from **British** clutches after 1940; French manpower and material resources were available for German arms production. When, after the Allied landings in **North Africa**, the rear and flank for the war against the **USSR** were no longer protected, Hitler on 11 November 1942 ordered the occupation of the southern **zone** and forced the construction of the "**Atlantic Wall**." France would become the decisive theater where a repulsed Allied landing would shatter the alliance of Roosevelt, Churchill, and Stalin.

Hitler never wavered from his mistrust for France. Shortly before his suicide on 30 April 1945, he commented characteristically that French SS units newly arrived to help defend Berlin were "worthless."

A. Bullock, *Hitler and Stalin, Parallel Lives* (London, 1990); C. Carlier and S. Martens, eds., *La France et l'Allemagne en guerre, septembre 1939–novembre 1942* (Paris, 1990); E. Jäckel, *Frankreich in Hitlers Europa: Die deutsche Frankreichpolitik in Zweiten Weltkrieg* (Stuttgart, 1966); E. Jäckel, *Hitler's Weltanschauung: A Blueprint for Power* (Middletown, CT, 1972); N. Rich, *Hitler's War Aims*, 2 vols. (New York, 1973–1974).

S. Martens

HO CHI MINH (1890–1969), **communist** leader of the Vietnamese independence movement. When, after France's 1940 defeat, **Japanese** forces displaced the French in Indochina, Ho saw an opportunity. He declared his nation's independence shortly after the Japanese surrendered, but his dream was delayed by years of negotiations and war, first with France, then with the **United States**.

Son of a patriotic Confucian teacher, Ho was born as Nguyen Sinh Cung in north-central Vietnam. The young Ho worked his way by ship to London and Paris, where, as Ai Quoc (the Patriot), he wrote anticolonial articles for **socialist** papers and helped found the French **Communist** Party. A true internationalist activist, after a period of training in Moscow, he traveled to Canton and struggled for both the Chinese and Vietnamese revolutions. His writings, knowledge, and perseverance gained him many devoted followers among his compatriots, and under the name Ho Chi Minh he founded the Vietnamese Revolutionary Youth League in 1925, which became the Indochinese Communist Party (ICP) in 1930. After arrests, imprisonments, and a 30-year exile, Ho returned to Vietnam in 1941, where he founded the Vietminh (League for the Independence of Vietnam) to resist both **Vichy** and Japan. In this he gained some support from the Western allies.

When Japan surrendered, Ho established a **Provisional Government** and declared independence for the Democratic Republic of Vietnam, hoping in vain that the Allies would honor the change. Instead, **British** and Chinese troops arrived and restored the country to France. Believing that France's new leaders, including some of his old friends, would be conciliatory, Ho tried negotiation, to little avail. Independence would be gained only after a 30-year military struggle, first with France, then with the United States.

*W. Duiker, *Sacred War: Nationalism and Revolution in a Divided Vietnam* (New York, 1995); J. Lacouture, *Ho Chi Minh: A Political Biography* (New York, 1968); M. Shipway, *The Road to War: France and Vietnam, 1944–1947* (Providence and Oxford, 1996).

R. L. Higgins

HOLOCAUST, the term designating the wartime persecution, roundup, and **deportation** of **Jews**, eventually leading in France to the deaths of some 80,000 men, **women**, and children, the great majority of whom died in Auschwitz, between the summer of 1942 and the summer of 1944.

In the summer of 1940, there were about 330,000 Jews in France, half of whom were foreigners. Persecution began almost immediately, both in the German-occupied **zone** and in what was left under French control. Regular deportations of Jews, however, began only in the summer of 1942. In all, over 75,000 were dispatched to killing centers in Poland, most of whom were murdered in gas chambers. In addition, over 3,000 died in French camps or were shot in France during the course of the war. Of all these, close to one-third were French citizens.

The unusual context of the Holocaust in France is the considerable degree of autonomy accorded the French during the Nazi occupation. In this respect France differed substantially from fully occupied countries like **Belgium**, Holland, and Denmark or puppet states like Norway. After the war defenders of **Vichy** claimed that the work of this government limited the damage, preventing even higher numbers of Jewish deportations from France. However, close examination of the German documentation and research on the role of Vichy and its agencies underscore the importance of the help accorded by the **collaborationist** regime.

The deportations of 1942–1944 were, in fact, the culmination of two years of aggressive legislation and persecution, including laws that defined the Jews, isolated them in French society, took away their livelihood, interned many, and registered them with the **police**. Beginning in 1940, the Vichy government moved against the Jews on its own and in March 1941 established a central agency to coordinate anti-Jewish legislation and activity, the General Office for Jewish Affairs (**Comissariat Général aux Questions Juives**, or **GGQJ**).

The government considered it extremely important that its **anti-Semitic** laws apply throughout the entire country, in the occupied as well as the unoccupied zones. Vichy's leadership assumed that the Germans would be grateful to the French for pursuing their own anti-Jewish policy and would respond by yielding greater control over this and other spheres of national policy. In addition, the French were most anxious to see that the property confiscated from the Jews would not fall into the hands of the Germans. Vichy inaugurated an extensive program of "**Aryanization**" in July 1941, with the important objective of maintaining formerly Jewish property in France. Thereby, the occupation authorities relieved themselves of much of the trouble of persecution while drawing the French into areas where even some Vichyites showed signs of discomfort.

In January 1942 the Nazis began to prepare for deportations of Jews from France and other Western European countries. Through negotiations the Nazis did their best to ensure the cooperation of the French government and administration. The spring and summer of 1942 were the turning point. In May, Pierre **Laval** replaced the legalistic and anti-German Xavier **Vallat** at the head of the CGQJ with the racist collaborator Louis **Darquier de Pellepoix**. Simultaneously, the Wehrmacht yielded authority over repressive activity in France to the SS. The French police under René **Bousquet** worked out an arrangement with the SS by which the former were given an important degree of autonomy, in exchange for agreeing to work against the enemies of the Reich. In their own zone the Germans cleared the way for deportations by imposing the wearing of a yellow star on all Jews (7 June), rounding up large numbers, and controlling the movements of the rest.

Pierre Laval and the French cabinet agreed to help with the first round of deportations. Throughout the summer and autumn, roundups of Jews occurred in both the occupied and unoccupied zones, with most of the work done by the French police. In all, 42,500 Jews were sent eastward in 1942, about one-third of them from the unoccupied zone. The deportations of the summer and autumn of 1942 stirred the first opposition to Vichy in certain segments of French opinion. A split developed in the Catholic Church, hitherto solidly behind **Pétain** and the **"National Revolution"**. Difficulties arose as the deportations gradually included French Jews as well as outsiders. As early as February 1943, when massive deportations from both zones resumed, the Germans reported that the French police were no longer as reliable as they once had been in assembling and dispatching the Jews. Even Laval dragged his feet, refusing in August 1943 to agree to strip French Jews of their citizenship so as to facilitate their deportation. Despite occasional protests and difficulties, however, the deportations continued, the last convoys leaving France in the summer of 1944. To the end, Vichy enforced the extensive apparatus of anti-Jewish laws that legitimated the deportations in the eyes of some and certainly facilitated the process of deportation.

It is true that the final toll—about one-fourth of the Jews killed—seems less, proportionately, than in many other countries. But there is no evidence that Vichy authorities attempted in a concerted way to limit deportations. Popular opposition grew during the course of deportations, but by then the powerful anti-Jewish machinery had been in place and had been functioning for some time. Recent research rejects the theory of a consciously plotted strategy to save as many Jews as possible.

Centre de Documentation juive contemporaine, *La France et la question juive 1940/ 1944: la politique de Vichy, l'attitude des Églises et des mouvements de Résistance* (Paris, 1981); A. Cohen, *Persécutions et sauvetages: Juifs et Français sous l'Occupation et Vichy* (Paris, 1994); S. Klarsfeld, *Vichy-Auschwitz: Le rôle de Vichy dans la solution finale de la question juive en France,* 2 vols. (Paris, 1983, 1985); M. R. Marrus and R. O. Paxton, *Vichy France and the Jews* (New York, 1981); R. Poznanski, *Être Juif en France pendant la Seconde Guerre mondiale* (Paris, 1994).

M. R. Marrus

"HORIZONTAL COLLABORATORS" and "sentimental collaborators" are terms that have been used since the Occupation to accuse French **women** who had sexual relations with members of the German army.

Behind this colorful expression different degrees of fraternization with the occupation troops may be discerned. Prostitutes were pardoned most readily, as they were said to have only followed their "profession." For women who had relations with only one German, encountered by chance, love was invoked as an excuse. More serious in the scale of condemnation were the cases of those who in groups had socialized with the Germans or had publicly consorted with them or whose relations with them had been of a professional or commercial nature. Worst were the women collaborators whose relations with the Germans had been only the extension of pro-Nazi sentiments.

In reality, horizontal **collaboration** had little effect on the course of the war. With the **liberation**, however, the **purge** of horizontal collaborators assumed considerable importance. Those who had "slept with the *Boches*" (a term of insult for Germans) were suspected of having given away secrets during their lovemaking. They were reproached for having lived in high style while the majority of the population had suffered from restrictions of all kinds. Special condemnation was reserved for those seen as oversexed, such as **prisoners of war wives** who had committed adultery with Germans, an act regarded as treason against the nation as well as against their husbands. Horizontal collaborators were thereby targeted for special punishment, the shaving of their heads. This ostentatious violence against them was intended to exclude these women from the community by marking their bodies but at the same time to reappropriate these bodies "defiled by the enemy" in an attempt to erase the memory of the humiliation of the Occupation. Practiced virtually throughout France, head shaving, turned horizontal collaboration into a pronounced **symbol** of the period. Like the GIs (**American** soldiers) and the FFIs (French Forces of the Interior, the military **Resistance**), the "*tondue*" (shaven woman) has become one of the enduring images of the liberation.

A. Brossat, *Les tondues un carnaval moche* (Paris, 1992); L. Capdevilla, "La collaboration sentimentale: antipatriotisme ou sexualité hors-norme?" in F. Rouquet and D. Voldman, eds., *Identités féminines et violences politiques (1936–1946), Cahier de l'IHTP* 31 (October 1995), 67–82; F. Rouquet, "Épuration, Résistance et représentations: quelques éléments pour une analyse sexuée," in *La Résistance et les Français, Enjeux stratégiques et environnement social* (Rennes, 1995); F. Virgili, "Les tondues à la Libération: le corps des femmes enjeu d'une réappropriation," *CLIO, Histoire, Femmes et Sociétés* 1 (1995): 111–27; F. Virgili, "Les tontes de la Libération en France," in F. Rouquet and D. Voldman, eds., *Identités féminines et violences politiques (1936–1946), Cahier de l'IHTP* 31 (October 1995), 53–66.

F. Virgili

HUNTZIGER, CHARLES-LÉON (1880–1941), commander of Second **Army**; head of the French delegation to the German **armistice** commission at Wiesbaden, June–September 1940; minister of war, 6 September 1940–12 November 1941. Half **Alsatian**, half Breton, Huntziger was graduated from the St. Cyr military academy in the class of 1901. He saw colonial service before and after World War I and received the Croix de Guerre in 1916. France's youngest general in 1939, Huntziger was considered the most brilliant man in the Senior Command, likely to succeed Maurice-Gustave **Gamelin** as supreme commander. Huntziger's Second Army suffered a decisive blow at Sedan in mid-May 1940. He parceled his armored divisions into small "packets," which rendered his tanks incapable of withstanding Germany's attack or mounting a counteroffensive. Still, **de Gaulle** pressed Premier Paul **Reynaud** in early June to replace General Maxime **Weygand** with Huntziger as supreme commander.

Huntziger considered the Armistice Army, reduced to 100,000, an **educational** and propaganda tool. His foreign policy inconsistencies reflected violent anti-German feeling, mistrust of **Britain**, and pro-**Pétain** sentiments. After **Mers-el-Kébir**, Huntziger implied that France was ready to join the war against Britain, saying to German General Gerd von **Rundstedt**, that "the English must be expelled." He tried to negotiate broad Franco-German **collaboration** but by late 1940 retreated from joint operations with Germany against British Africa. After **Laval's** dismissal, 13 December 1940, Huntziger, Pierre-Étienne **Flandin**, and Admiral Jean-François **Darlan** ruled France as a triumvirate. In June–July 1941, Huntziger secretly supported General Georges **Groussard's** last attempt at rapprochement with Britain, even as fighting over Syria erupted. Huntziger died in an airplane accident in the Cévennes after touring North Africa, on 12 November 1941.

A. Horne, *To Lose a Battle* (Boston, 1969); R. O. Paxton, *Parades and Politics in Vichy France* (Princeton, 1966); E. Ruby, "Un Grand français: le général Huntziger," *Écrits de Paris* (August 1955).

S. Fishman

"HUSSARDS" (HUSSARS) is a term applied to a group of French writers who, in the decade after the **liberation**, expressed antiestablishment views that criticized the predominant modes of **Sartrian** existentialism in literature and the retrospective *résistantialiste* view of a France united against a handful of malevolent **collaborators** during the Occupation. Against what they saw as the overbearing heaviness of existential aesthetics and the hypocrisy of a *résistantialisme* that failed to credit "sincere" collaborators with high-minded intentions, the Hussards argued for a more lighthearted, ironic, libertine, sometimes insolent, aesthetics and a relativity of moral judgment that equated wartime collaboration and resistance.

Because the Hussards did not form a closed movement, various names are occasionally mentioned as members, but the major figures were Roger **Nimier**, Antoine **Blondin**, Michel **Déon**, and Jacques **Laurent**, all young writers, alienated in late 1944 by the political atmosphere of liberated France, who clustered together with the *Cahiers de la Table ronde*. As a name, "Hussard" appears to have come from the title of Nimier's 1950 novel, *Le Hussard bleu*, but it also reflected the elegance and bravado of hussars, the light cavalry. The young Hussards were influenced by a cluster of older writers sympathetic to the **Right**, including André Fraigneau, Jacques Chardonne, Paul **Morand**, Marcel **Aymé**,

Pierre **Drieu la Rochelle**, and Robert **Brasillach**, the last two paying with their lives for collaboration with Nazi Germany.

The significance of the Hussards lies in their having been a link in the history of the French Right, from the "nonconformists" of the 1930s, through the defenders of French Algeria in the late 1950s and early 1960s, down to the National Front of Jean-Marie Le Pen in the 1980s and 1990s. Their attempts to subvert what they perceived as *résistantialiste* hypocrisy linked them to *mode rétro* films of the 1970s, notably Marcel Ophuls' *Sorrow and the Pity* and Louis Malle's *Lacombe Lucien*.

N. Hewitt, *Literature and the Right in Postwar France: The Story of the "Hussards"* (Oxford and New York, 1996); R. Nimier, *The Blue Hussar*, trans. J. Russell and A. Rhodes (London, 1952) [original French ed.: *Le Hussard bleu* (Paris, 1950); P. Van-dromme, *La Droite buissonnière* (Paris, 1960).

B. M. Gordon

I

INDUSTRIALISTS often welcomed the **Vichy** regime as an opportunity to reimpose their authority over economic affairs after the supposedly pernicious influence of the **Popular Front** government of 1936–1937. Their attitude of "business as usual" in the face of German occupation was based on the premise that safeguarding France's economic structure justified collaborating with the Germans, an outlook followed unswervingly by Jean Bichelonne (1904–1945), the brilliant *ex-Polytechnicien* who was appointed secretary-general for commerce and industry (July 1940–April 1942) and minister for **industrial production** from November 1942 onward. By the end of 1941, 7,000 French businesses were fulfilling orders for the Germans, and by 1944 this figure had doubled, meaning that the great majority of large-scale French businesses worked directly or indirectly for the German war effort.

Large-scale industrialists found their interests most effectively promoted by the **Comités d'organisation (CO)**, founded by a number of technocratic administrators who, with Bichelonne, remained active in government circles: Jacques Barnaud, François **Lehideux**, Pierre **Pucheu**, and Gabriel Leroy-Ladurie. Designed to coordinate production under war conditions, allocate scarce resources, and protect their own sectoral interests, the CO were largely *dirigiste*, limiting some companies' room for maneuver because committee chairmen were chosen from the biggest concern in a given branch. Lehideux, director of Renault, headed the Automobile Committee, while Auguste Detoeuf, a director of Alsthom, led the Electrical Energy Committee. Initially, the CO appeared to fulfill the corporatist ambitions of the **National Revolution**, yet even in **Pétain's** entourage their development toward domination by the "trusts" drew sharp criticism, and some saw a "synarchist" conspiracy aimed at controlling the French **economy**.

For all this, French industrialists became ever more enmeshed in German-imposed demands, particularly after the beginning of the Relève in 1942. Whereas most industrialists reluctantly accepted German orders to compensate for the contraction of business due to limited export markets, all the while keeping an eye on the possibility of a future German victory, a minority of others entered more enthusiastically into negotiations with their German counterparts. Louis Renault decided to maximize production, producing tanks directly for the German war effort during 1943 despite his factories' being the target of Royal Air Force (RAF) bombers. Others entered into partnerships with German companies. The great **Paris** stores (Printemps, Samaritaine, and les Nouvelles Galeries) struck deals with their German opposite numbers (Karstadt, Erwege, and Hertie). With varying degrees of success French chemical firms negotiated with the German giant IG Farben. Whereas René Duchemin, director of Kuhlmann, came under pressure from Pucheu to accede to German demands, Rhône-Poulenc, located in the unoccupied **zone**, was in a better position to resist. Raoul de Vitry, too, head of Pechiney, the French aluminum manufacturer, objected to delivering to the occupiers an increasing proportion of its production when the French market could absorb it. Eventually, however, under **Vichy** pressure, Pechiney was forced to comply.

As the war went on, the French economy was increasingly exploited by the Germans, and those industrialists who shared Pierre **Laval's** desire to find a place in the Nazi **New Order** followed the **collaborationist** logic. Bichelonne, the architect of so much Vichy policy, embodied in the Speer-Bichelonne, Accords of September 1943, remained a convinced proponent of Franco–German collaboration until his death in Germany in 1945.

*A. Beltran, R. Frank, and H. Rousso, eds., *La vie des entreprises sous l'Occupation* (Paris, 1994); H. W. Ehrmann, *Organized Business in France* (Princeton, 1957); J.-C. Hazera, *Les patrons sous l'occupation* (Paris, 1995); M. Margairaz, *L'État, la Direction des finances et de l'Économie en France (1932–1952)*, vol. 1 (Paris, 1991); A. Milward, *The New Order and the French Economy* (Oxford, 1970); R. de Rochebrune and J.-C. Haura, *Les Patrons sous l'occupation* (Paris, 1995); R. Vinen, "The French Coal Industry during the Occupation," *The Historical Journal* 33: 1 (1990): 105–30.

M. Cornick

INDUSTRIAL PRODUCTION, MINISTRY OF, was a body fashioned out of the ineffectual interwar Ministry of Commerce and Industry in the summer of 1940, endowed with powers of intervention in the **economy** unknown under the Third **Republic**. In the face of falling production and the severe terms imposed by the Germans, the ministry undertook to allocate resources and regulate production and prices, as well as to safeguard French producers against inroads by German business. Its main instruments for these purposes were the Office Central de Repartition des Produits Industriels (OCRPI) and the **Comités d'organisation (CO)**, organized on a sectoral basis following legislation of 16 August 1940.

Amid the general backlash against **collaborationism** and *étatisme* at the time of the **liberation**, the **Provisional Government** was at first able to maintain this component of **Vichy's** administration as a weapon against the continuing problems of shortages and inflation. In 1946, however, the CO (renamed Offices

Professionnels) and OCRPI were abolished. The ministry was thus reduced to more modest functions and was renamed the Ministry of Industry and Commerce in 1947.

Though constrained in their actions by the circumstances of war and occupation, the leading figures of this ministry left an enduring legacy for subsequent regimes in the domain of policy attitudes. With their keen interest in rationalization, concentration, and modernization, such ministers as Pierre **Pucheu**, François **Lehideux**, and Jean Bichelonne helped make the Ministry of Industrial Production one of the foremost exemplars of the technocratic and modernizing aspects of the État Français, which marked a shift in governmental attitudes in favor of growth and expansion and away from the interwar emphasis on protectionism.

G. Brun, *Technocrates et Technocratie en France 1918–1945* (Paris, 1985); R. Kuisel, "Technocrats and Public Economic Policy: From the Third to the Fourth Republic," *Journal of European Economic History* 4 (1973): 53–99; R. Vinen, *The Politics of French Business, 1936–1945* (Cambridge, U.K., 1991).

R. MacKinnon

INDUSTRY AND REQUISITIONS were part of German exploitation of French resources, including workers, for their war effort, divided into two periods in both the occupied and unoccupied **zones**: from the Franco–German **armistice** (June 1940) to the **Anglo–American** invasion of **North Africa** (November 1942) and from that invasion to the expulsion from France of the German occupation forces, by December 1944.

Industry and population were concentrated in the occupied northern zone of France; food production, in the southern zone. Both zones in both periods witnessed a merciless Nazi exploitation of France. France, far more than occupied **Russia**, served Germany as a resource for economic exploitation. Within weeks of the armistice, Caudron-Renault requested permission from the Ministry of Aviation to manufacture airplanes to serve as Luftwaffe trainers. After talks in Wiesbaden and **Paris** (November 1940–November 1941), French dye manufacturers relinquished 51 percent control over their industry to I. G. Farben. By the end of 1941, some 59,000 French had volunteered to work in German factories. Parisian shopkeepers welcomed German soldiers. An exchange rate fixed in Berlin at 20 francs to the mark enabled soldiers to buy out stocks, providing the Reich with floods of consumer goods. Vichy protested that an occupation levy decreed in the armistice terms could maintain 18 million troops, but the Germans refused to compromise. Capital thus acquired funded German **industrialists** who bought French plants in France and French assets in the Balkans.

German losses at Stalingrad in late 1942 and early 1943 and in Tunisia by May 1943 mandated a total war effort. The Reich now demanded economic *Gleichschaltung* (coordination) in France. By autumn 1943, virtually 50 percent of French production was earmarked for Germany. The critical issue in Franco–German relations was now French workers in Germany's service. In France, the

Reich's plenipotentiary for the deployment of labor, Fritz **Sauckel**, offered to release any French prisoner of war (POW) who agreed to work in a German factory. He also offered to release one POW for every three French civilians laboring in the Reich. Sauckel argued that while Germany fought to save Europe from Bolshevism, the least Vichy could supply was laborers. Pierre **Laval** reluctantly agreed to impose death sentences on French officials who blocked recruitment.

Recruitment, however, did not reach desired levels, and Laval instituted a forced labor program, the **Service du Travail Obligatoire**, which drove many of the young French into the *maquis*. Trying another approach, Reich minister of war production Albert Speer struck a deal with Vichy's minister of **Industrial Production** Jean Bichelonne, whereby French workers could remain in France if employed in designated plants, known as S-Betriebe, that were working for the German war effort. Speer would later claim victory over Sauckel, but neither side prevailed entirely. During the course of the occupation, some 798,000 French worked for Germany in France, and 875,952 French worked for Germany in Germany.

One estimate of the occupation cost for France was in excess of 154 billion francs (1938), including payments for services. The degree to which French **industrialists** cooperated in this colossal robbery remains to be precisely assessed. More than a half century after World War II, Paris has yet to open key files.

E. Jäckel, *Frankreich in Hitlers Europa, Die Deutsche Frankreichpolitik im zweiten Weltkrieg* (Stuttgart, 1966); A. S. Milward, *The New Order and the French Economy* (Oxford, 1970); R. O. Paxton, *Vichy France, Old Guard and New Order, 1940–1944* (New York, 1972).

M. Goldin

INSTITUT D'ÉTUDE DES QUESTIONS JUIVES (IÉQJ, INSTITUTE FOR THE STUDY OF JEWISH QUESTIONS), **anti-Semitic** propaganda group in **Paris** sponsored and funded by the Nazis. The IÉQJ was created in May 1941 by Theodor **Dannecker**, German SS officer in charge of **Jewish** questions in France. Its members were French anti-Semites. Its secretary-general, Captain Paul Sézille, had been active in Louis **Darquier de Pellepoix's** prewar "Rassemblement antijuif" (Anti-Jewish Assembly). The group's aims were to propagate racism and give the Germans information. It was independent of the **Vichy** government's **Commissariat Général aux Questions Juives (CGQJ)**.

The IÉQJ published two periodicals, *Cahier jaune*, for the general public, and *La Question Juive en France*, with scientific pretensions. A special service of the IÉQJ ferreted out and reported hidden Jews, and the organization participated in the economic **Aryanization** of Jewish property. The IÉQJ was best known for organizing an anti-Semitic **exposition**, *Le Juif et la France*, in 1941–1942. Although it gave a French cover to this exposition, funding came from the Germans. Captain Sézille, corrupt and incompetent, proved incapable of doing the desired propaganda job. When Darquier de Pellepoix became head of the CGQJ in May 1942, the IÉQJ was incorporated into it, and Sézille was phased out. The IÉQJ was reorganized in 1943 as the Institut d'Étude des Questions Juives et Ethnoraciales, with anti-Semitic ethnologist George **Montandon** as its head.

J. Billig, *Le Commissariat général aux questions juives* (Paris, 1955–1960); M. R. Marrus and R. O. Paxton, *Vichy France and the Jews* (New York, 1981); L. Poliakov, "Le procès de l'Institut d'étude des questions juives," *Le Monde Juif* 25 (November 1949).

D. Evleth

INSTITUT D'HISTOIRE DU TEMPS PRÉSENT (IHTP), is a specialized library and research center in Paris. The IHTP operates under the auspices of the Conseil National de la Recherche Scientifique (CNRS) and serves two major functions. First, it carries on the work of its predecessor institution, the Comité d'Histoire de la Deuxième Guerre Mondiale. Second, it has, since 1981, simultaneously placed major emphasis on the history of Europe in the period since World War II. During the years 1978–1990, under the direction of François Bédarida, the IHTP developed into one of the major European centers for the study of the period since the 1930s. Its current director is Henry Rousso.

The library of the IHTP contains more than 20,000 volumes, as well as extensive archives, periodicals, maps, microfilms, and audiotapes. Its collections concerning the **Resistance** and **deportation** are especially noteworthy. Since its inception, the IHTP has aimed to acquire every work concerning World War II published in France as well as principal foreign works on the subject.

The research mission of the IHTP is carried out by a team of 20 specialists, who work collaboratively on pertinent projects. In addition, they publish the *Bulletin de l'IHTP*, organize conferences, conduct interviews, and work in cooperation with major French **universities** in fostering a deeper, scholarly understanding of World War II and contemporary Europe.

M.-T. Chabord, "Le Comité d'histoire de la Deuxième guerre mondiale et ses archives," *La Gazette des archives* 116 (1982): 5–19; K. Reader, *A Guide to Library and Archive Resources in France* (Kingston-upon-Thames, U.K., 1990).

F. J. Murphy

INTERIOR MINISTRY was the bureaucracy in charge of law enforcement and internal security under the Third **Republic**. It survived the collapse of that regime to become a cornerstone of **Vichy** authoritarianism and **collaboration**. The network of prefects and subprefects on which the ministry was based was left intact even in the occupied **zone**, which was crucial to the Vichy regime's aspirations to exercise power there. As the **État Français** broke with Republican practices in the case of other institutions, moreover, prefects enjoyed a relative rise in power during the Occupation, having been freed from the scrutiny of parliamentarians and local bodies. The climate of suspicion and intolerance at

Vichy rendered the Interior Ministry and its prefectoral structure all the more valuable to the new regime—surveillance was greatly heightened, paid informants were used more frequently, and internment on the basis of mere suspicion was not uncommon.

Through 1942, interior ministers and their subordinates sought to exercise greater **police** authority in the occupied zone and looked to secure the assent of the occupiers by visibly and vigorously pursuing suspected assassins and "terrorists." These and other such repressive measures meant to win favor with the German authorities, such as the creation of special police units to deal with **Jewish** affairs, succeeded mainly in drawing the French law enforcement apparatus into closer collaboration with Nazi violence and repression. By 1943, with all of France occupied, the Germans were encouraging the creation of separate organizations, such as the *milice*, as more suited to their purposes than the existing French police administration. All the same, **purges** of prefectoral and police institutions after the **liberation** were the most extensive of any public administration.

C.-L. Foulon, *Le pouvoir en province à la libération: Les Commissaires de la République* (Paris, 1975); B. Kasten, *"Gute Französen:" die Französische Polizei und die deutsche Besatzungsmacht im besetzten Frankreich* (Sigmaringen, 1993); B. Lecornu, *Un préfet sous l'occupation allemande: Châteaubriant, Saint-Nazaire, Tulle* (Paris, 1984); M. Rajsfus, *La police de Vichy: Les Forces de l'ordre françaises au service de la Gestapo 1940–1944* (Paris, 1995).

R. MacKinnon

ITALY, RELATIONS WITH FRANCE had been ambivalent before the war. Under Foreign Minister Pierre **Laval**, the French pressed for rapprochement with Italy, resulting in the Stresa Accord of April 1935. This agreement among **Britain**, France, and Italy purported to present a common front against **Hitler's** expansionist ambitions. However, France objected to the Italian invasion of Ethiopia in the autumn of 1935 and supported the League of Nations' imposition of sanctions against Italy, resulting in Mussolini's rapprochement with Hitler and giving rise to a period of tension that lasted until the French collapse in June 1940.

Italy did not oppose German annexation of Austria in March 1938 and supported Hitler's position during the **Munich Conference**; clearly, Mussolini had now chosen to ally with Germany. Italy made known its territorial claims on Tunisia, Djibouti, **Corsica**, and Nice and the Savoy, all of which directly affected France. The conclusion of the Pact of Steel (22 May 1939) sealed the alliance between Italy and Germany. With the outbreak of war, Mussolini declared that Italy would be a "nonbelligerent" state, but on 10 June 1940, as the French were being crushed by the Blitzkrieg (lightning war), the Italian dictator declared war on Britain and France. Italy's military operations against France were confined to air attacks on Corsica and Marseilles, an unsuccessful attempt at a landing near Menton, and a failed sortie into France through the Alps.

During the war Franco–Italian relations were entirely subordinated to Mussolini's relationship, as junior partner, with Hitler, and to the latter's designs on France. On 18–19 June 1940, Mussolini and his foreign minister Galeazzo Ciano met Hitler in Munich to decide on **armistice** terms for France. Mussolini proposed the severest conditions, including occupation of the whole country and confiscation of the French fleet. Hitler, however, wishing to avoid the possibility of a French decampment to **North Africa** to pursue the war from there with Britain still fighting, insisted on a milder approach. He had no objections to Italy's occupation of southeastern France or to its claims on Corsica, Tunisia, and Djibouti. The Italians went along with Hitler's wishes.

On 24 June 1940, at the Villa Incisa near Rome, Marshal Pietro Badoglio and General Charles-Léon **Huntziger** met to sign the Italo–French armistice. This entitled the Italians to occupy the territory held by their army at the moment the armistice came into effect, thus confining their occupation to the frontier area around Menton. A demilitarized **zone** of 50 kilometers was also included, with zones 200 kilometers wide in Algeria and in territories bordering on Libya, plus an area in southern Tunisia and the coast of Somaliland. Italy also gained Djibouti and the Djibouti-Addis Ababa railroad, but the armistice contained no economic or financial clauses. The Italian zone was nonetheless considerably enlarged in November 1942, when the Germans extended their own occupation: departments in Italian hands comprised Basses-Alpes, Alpes-Maritimes, Var, Hautes-Alpes, Savoie, Haute-Savoie, and the Drôme, in addition to **Corsica** and parts of the Rhône valley.

The differences between Italian and German styles of occupation were highlighted in the summer of 1943 after the collapse of Mussolini's regime: many **Jews** and others who had been given refuge in the Italian zone were imprisoned and deported by **Vichy** and German authorities.

*P. Badoglio, *L'Italia nella seconda guerra mondiale* (Milan, 1946); P. Baudouin, *Neuf mois au gouvernement: avril–décembre 1940* (Paris, 1948); Royal Institute for International Affairs, *Documents on International Affairs 1939–1946*, vol. 2: *Hitler's Europe* (London and New York, 1954); A. and V. Toynbee, eds., *Survey of International Affairs 1939–1946, the Initial Triumph of the Axis* (London and New York, 1958); M. Weygand, *Rappelé au service, Mémoires*, vol. 3 (Paris, 1950).

M. Cornick

J

JADE-FITZROY was an Intelligence Service (IS) network, created in December 1940 by Claude Lamirault, age 22, the son of a lawyer in Maisons-Laffitte and a fervent Catholic.

Lamirault was an **Action Française** militant and a member of its shock troops, the Camelots du roi. In October 1940, he left for London via Gibraltar. Parachuted into France for the first time, in January 1941, with money and a **radio** transmitter, he created a group initially connected to the Jade-Amicol network. The other person of note in the network was Pierre Hentic, known as Maho, a **communist youth** militant, who became the head of air and sea operations in 1943. After a first year of organizing and recruiting, the network engaged in the search for military information for the MI6 in London. Eventually, it comprised some ten subnetworks, specializing in both geography and technology throughout France.

The network collected its most extensive intelligence concerning the location of the German army, aeronautic production, port activity, transmissions both by telephone and telegraph, and the sites of coastal defenses and of the launch pads of the V1 and V2 rockets. Documents collected were photographed and developed in miniature format to be conveyed to London by plane.

In 1942, a split between Jade-Amicol and Jade-Fitzroy, in addition to a series of arrests, weakened the network. A second misfortune struck the group in December 1943, when Lamirault was arrested in **Paris**. His wife took over the direction of the group until her own arrest in April 1944. Reconstituted locally in July 1944 under the name Panta Group, it was linked to the **Bureau Central de Renseignements et d'Action** and participated in the **liberation of Paris** by facilitating the entry of the Allied troops into the capital. For the total period of the Occupation, the group numbered 708 members, principally in the **Paris** region.

A. Aglan, *Mémoires résistantes, le réseau Jade-Fitzroy (1940–44)* (Paris, 1994).

A. Aglan

JAPAN, RELATIONS WITH FRANCE. Japan exploited France's 1940 defeat to pressure the **Vichy** government into relinquishing Indochina. Faced with a Vietnamese declaration of independence after Japan's surrender, France tried, but failed, to regain Indochina militarily.

Between the wars, France's Far Eastern policy consisted of defending the colonial status quo from the challenges of rising Asian nationalism and Japanese militaristic expansionism. Japan's growing naval power and encroachments on Chinese territory encountered Western disapproval. When the Japanese invaded Manchuria in 1931, France concurred in the League of Nation's censure of Japan. This ended Franco–Japanese amity stemming from a 1907 agreement respecting each other's Asian spheres of interest. Western suspicions of Japan were exacerbated in 1936, when Japan's military-dominated government signed an Anti-Comintern Pact with Germany. Japan's war with China in July 1937 and Japanese prime minister Fumimaro Konoe's articulation of a **New Order** for East Asia, a "Co-Prosperity Sphere" under Japanese dominance, led the **United States** to condemn Japan and ship supplies to Chiang Kai-shek's Chinese nationalists.

Germany's defeat of France and the Netherlands encouraged Japan's pro-Axis foreign minister Yosuke Matsuoka to obtain a neutrality pact with the **Soviet Union** to prepare an "advance" southward to "liberate" European-held Southeast Asian colonies. To Japan's security analysts, the attraction of French Indochina was its strategic resources (tin, rubber) and vulnerability under Vichy rule. Due to **American** retaliatory reduction of exports, especially oil and scrap iron, Japan required new sources of supply to achieve its Great Power aspirations.

Under German auspices Japan opened an embassy in Vichy, seeking to extract concessions in Indochina. To stem the flow of supplies via the Hanoi-Nanning Railway to Chiang Kai-shek's forces in western China, Japan pressured Vichy's governor of Indochina, Admiral Jean **Decoux**, to station its troops in north Vietnam (September 1940). Although French administrators continued to govern, this **collaboration** with Japan was the first step in France's loss of colonial control. In July 1941, more negotiations with Vichy led to Japanese military occupation of southern Vietnam as well.

The basis for Franco–Japanese cooperation ended once the Vichy regime was replaced by General **de Gaulle's**, and the latter declared war on Japan. In a surprise *coup de force* on 9 March 1945, the Japanese military arrested their French collaborators, imprisoned them, and seized direct control of Indochina. The coup, however, stimulated the Indochinese Communist Party, under **Ho Chi Minh** and the revolutionary Vietminh Front, to prepare for a general insurrection, a move made more urgent by de Gaulle's stated intention to restore the colonial system in Indochina.

The insurrection began as soon as word of Japan's surrender arrived (13 August). Within two weeks, the Vietminh controlled most of Vietnam, including major cities. This "August Revolution" precipitated the abdication of puppet

emperor Bao Dai (30 August) and Ho Chi Minh's formal declaration of Vietnamese independence (2 September). Cambodia and Laos followed with similar
proclamations. These actions were soon blocked by Chinese Nationalist forces
occupying northern Vietnam and **British** troops entering the south, accompanied
by a token **Free French** force attempting to reoccupy the colony. Several
months of military operations and negotiations failed to produce a workable
compromise between recolonization and independence for Vietnam. In fall 1946,
the long road to eventual French defeat at Dien Bien Phu began.

Coming after the 1940 defeat, the French military's inability to restore national honor and prestige through successful reoccupation of Indochina after
Japan's surrender was an additional blow to its morale. This setback contributed
to the deterioration of French control in Algeria as well.

J. E. Dreifort, *Myopic Grandeur: The Ambivalence of French Foreign Policy toward
the Far East, 1919–1945* (Kent, OH, 1991); T. Hodgkin, *Vietnam: The Revolutionary
Path* (New York, 1981); J. W. Morley, ed., *The Fateful Choice: Japan's Advance into
Southeast Asia, 1939–1941* (New York, 1980); M. Shipway, *The Road to War: France
and Vietnam, 1944–1947* (Providence and Oxford, 1996).

R. L. Higgins

JARDIN, JEAN (1904–1976), Pierre **Laval's** cabinet chief from April 1942 to
October 1943 who maintained extensive contacts with the **Resistance** while
remaining loyal to **Vichy**. Moved by concern for the continuity of the French
state and by personal loyalty to Laval, Jardin sought with Laval's consent to
ease the transition from one regime to the next.

A founding member of the **Ordre Nouveau** movement in 1930, Jardin later
made a brilliant career in the new state railways, until he was called to work in
Yves Bouthillier's Finance Ministry in January 1941. Following a brief spell as
cabinet chief to Robert Gibrat, Laval's secretary of communications, Jardin was
called to Laval's own secretariat and soon became his right-hand man, entrusted
with delicate missions. All the while, Jardin's office and home were notoriously
open to **Jews** and resisters, many of whom he helped to leave the country, along
with civil servants on their way to Algeria to join the Resistance. The enmity
thus incurred by Jardin forced Laval to send him away to Bern as acting head
of the French embassy, there to serve as go-between with Allen Dulles and the
Office of Strategic Services (OSS) as well as French Resistance circles in **Switzerland**. While covering his activities and preparing a smooth transfer of the
French administration, starting with his own embassy, Jardin also helped compromised Vichy figures find refuge in Switzerland, including his friend the writer
Paul **Morand**, whose appointment as Vichy's last ambassador in Bern he arranged. Despite his many services to the Resistance, Jardin's refusal to disavow
Vichy held him back from returning to France, but he later came to play an
important role behind the scenes in French politics.

P. Assouline, *Jean Jardin 1904–1976. Une éminence grise* (Paris, 1986); C. Roy,
Alexandre Marc et la Jeune Europe 1904–1934 (Montreal, 1993).

C. Roy

JEANSON, HENRI (1900–1970), journalist and screenwriter who opposed the Occupation and **Vichy** regimes. A native Parisian, he sought early on a career in the theater. His keen wit and wry humor soon led him first into journalism, and then into screenwriting. During World War I Jeanson posed as a military commentator, using the pseudonym "General N." During the 1920s and 1930s he contributed to such newspapers as *La Flèche* and *L'Intransigeant* but gained celebrity for the biting articles he published in the satirical weekly *Le Canard enchaîné*. He also produced screenplays for a number of successful films.

His irreverent journalism frequently brought him into court on charges of "apologies for crime" and "anarchistic propaganda." In 1939 Jeanson was imprisoned for praising the **Jewish** refugee Herschel Grynszpan, who had assassinated the German Embassy secretary Ernst vom Rath. At the outbreak of World War II, he displayed his pacifist feelings by signing the tract "Immediate Peace."

The war and Occupation proved difficult times for him. Mobilized in 1939, he was soon convicted for having published an article entitled "No, My **Daladier**, We Will Not Fight Your War" in a **left-wing** newspaper. Freed in May 1940, he resumed his career as a journalist. In September he founded *Aujourd'hui*, a daily that maintained its editorial independence as it launched sharp barbs against the Vichy government. Personal attacks against Jeanson from the **collaborationist press** led the German occupiers to remove him as editor and imprison him in November. Released, rearrested, and again released, Jeanson found himself barred from writing for both press and **cinema**. In 1942 he escaped further persecution by taking refuge with Parisian friends until the capital was liberated. He then returned to journalism, displaying his wit with fresh enthusiasm. Jeanson completed his irreverent memoirs shortly before his death.

Le Crapouillot n.s. 9 (1950): 108–9; H. Jeanson, *Soixante-dix ans d'adolescence* (Paris, 1971); J. Quéval, *Première page, cinquième colonne* (Paris, 1945).

J. Friguglietti

JEUNES DU MARÉCHAL (November 1940–May 1943) was a **youth** movement started at the Lycée Voltaire in **Paris** by a **right-wing** teacher, Jacques Bousquet, later active in the **collaboration**. Gathering pupils from the upper sections preparing for the "*grandes écoles*," the self-named Jeunes du Maréchal claimed that it would purge schools of political dissent, restore discipline and a sense of honor, and enforce the politics of morality of schools initiated by the state. The movement quickly spread to nearby schools, with some 300 militants by July 1941. With the very tight organization characteristic of most Pétainist groups, members of the Jeunes du Maréchal wore a khaki shirt and blue beret, adopted military style salutes toward their professors, and practiced unarmed military drills, exhibiting early on a **fascist** orientation, which met with alarm from some school authorities. Approved by **Pétain** in September 1941 and by the rector of **Paris** in 1942, the movement was allowed to recruit in schools, youth centers, and establishments of higher **education**, but its blatant collaborationist rhetoric and noisy public displays failed to generate massive support. Internal rivalries and a public call by some leaders to serve in the Wehrmacht further eroded the movement's credibility and led to its dissolution in May 1943. The Jeunes du Maréchal can be distinguished from other collaborationist youth movements committed to a Nazi-style ideology by the personal patronage of Pétain and the authorized access it had to schools for recruiting.

B. Comte, "Encadrer la jeunesse," in L. Gervereau and D. Peschanski, eds., *La propagande sous Vichy, 1940–1944* (Nanterre, 1990); P. Giolitto, *Histoire de la jeunesse sous Vichy* (Paris, 1991); W. D. Halls, *The Youth of Vichy France* (Oxford, 1981).

C. Keith

JEUNESSE OUVRIÈRE CHRÉTIENNE (JOC), Catholic action movement for and by young workers that aims at transforming society by re-Christianizing the working class. Founded in 1927 by Father Georges Guérin (1891–1972) and modeled after the Belgian JOC of Father Joseph Cardijn, the JOC grew rapidly in the 1930s to 45,000 members in 1939. It maintained its autonomy within the Association catholique de la jeunesse française (Catholic Association for French **Youth**), the umbrella organization for five specialized youth groups.

During the war, JOC was officially banned but unofficially tolerated in the occupied **zone**; it remained largely independent in the southern zone. Jocists Émile Mithaut and Jeanne Aubert (founder of the feminine branch, JOCF, in 1928) worked in the Ministry of Youth Affairs during the early years of the **Vichy** regime.

JOC was critical of Vichy's 1941 **Labor Charter** and of the 1942 **Service du Travail Obligatoire** (STO). Nevertheless, many Jocists supported sending volunteers to Germany to minister to French youth laboring there. "I go as a missionary," announced Marcel Callo, martyred at Mauthausen and beatified in 1987. To avoid the STO, other Jocists joined the *maquis* and the **Resistance** group Jeunes chrétiens combattants (Fighting Young Christians). In reprisal for resistance to the STO, the Gestapo closed the JOC in **Paris** and arrested Guérin in 1943. In the same year, two Jocist chaplains (Henri Godin and Yvan Daniel) published *France pays de mission? (France, Country of Missions?)*, which questioned the ability of parishes to reach the de-Christianized working class. This booklet became one basis for the worker–priest experiment in the postwar years.

After the war, the JOC experienced a crisis over its exclusive identification with the working class and over its relationship to the Catholic hierarchy. Currently, JOC publishes *Équipe ouvrière* and *Jeunesse ouvrière*. Its **publishing** house is Éditions Ouvrières.

H. Bourdais, *La J.O.C. sous l'occupation allemande* (Paris, 1995); G. Cholvy and Y.-M. Hilaire, *Histoire réligieuse de la France contemporaine* (Toulouse, 1985); A. Dansette, *Destin du catholicisme français* (Paris, 1957); P. Pierrard et al., *La J.O.C.* (Paris, 1984).

M. P. Dougherty

JEWISH YOUTH ORGANIZATIONS in interwar France included, above all, the Scout Éclaireurs Israélites de France, established in 1923 by Robert Gamzon, then 16 years old. By 1940 it had 2,500–3,000 members. Less significant were several Zionist **youth** movements of diverse political tendencies and the Jewish **communist youth**, all composed essentially of immigrants.

During the first two years of the Occupation the Scouts concentrated on Jewish **education** and established children's homes and agricultural centers in the unoccupied **zone**. In May 1942, a unified Zionist youth movement, Mouvement de Jeunesse Sioniste (MJS), was founded. When the extensive roundup of foreign **Jews** started (in **Paris** in July 1942, followed in the southern zone in August), the fate of the children (whom Pierre **Laval** asked to deport) was still undecided. Hundreds were collected by the youth movements and by the communist Jewish organization (Solidarité). A large underground organization (the clandestine Oeuvre de Secours à l'Enfance [OSE]) began to function by hiding children.

Widening rescue programs by 1942 included the Jewish Resistance group (Armée Juive, or AJ), manned mainly by Scouts, led by Gamzon, and the MJS. These groups also produced false identities to safeguard entire families. By the end of 1943, they possessed sophisticated tools to concoct a great diversity of papers in their own "laboratories." These ever-expanding activities were conducted in close **collaboration** with non-Jews, such as Catholic and **Protestant** clergymen and organizations, including monasteries, the Quakers, and the Protestant youth organization the Comité inter-mouvements auprès des évacués (CI-MADE). By 1944, the AJ (later called Organisation Juive de Combat) participated, as a Jewish military unit, in the **liberation** of France.

By 1944, many of the tens of thousands of Jews living clandestinely were supported by the secret Jewish youth organizations. Some 8,000 to 10,000 (including some 1,500 smuggled to **Switzerland**) were rescued, mainly with the cooperation of Jewish and non-Jewish underground youth movements.

A. Cohen, *Persécutions et sauvetages, Juifs et Français sous l'Occupation et sous Vichy* (Paris, 1993); A. Latour, *The Jewish Resistance in France* (New York, 1981).

A. Cohen

JEWS IN OCCUPIED FRANCE numbered some 330,000, including 195,000 French citizens and 135,000 noncitizens in 1940. As many as 150,000 had come since the end of World War I, first to fill a need for workers in the context of liberal French immigration and naturalization policies of the 1920s and then to flee ever-increasing Nazi oppression in the 1930s.

As in World War I, many French Jews served in the 1939–1940 campaign, while 30,000 foreign Jews, eager to defend France against the Nazis, also joined the French armed forces. In the wake of the May–June debacle, however, Jews became scapegoats and were subjected to a series of anti-Jewish laws. **Vichy** eliminated Jews from government and public employment, severely restricted and expropriated Jewish businesses, placed strict limits on Jewish access to higher **education** as well as to medical and legal professions, revoked the citizenship not only of many recently arrived Jewish immigrants but also of 115,000 Algerian Jews, and gave free reign to **anti-Semitic** propaganda. Vichy's first Statut des Juifs, 3 October 1940, specified who was a Jew in terms more severe than those of the Germans. A special government agency, the **Commissariat Général aux Questions Juives**, was created in March 1941. Headed first by Xavier **Vallat** and then, from 6 May 1942, by Louis **Darquier de Pellepoix**, it supervised expropriations, enforced **racial laws**, and tracked down Jews hunted by Vichy and the Germans. While daily existence became more and more problematic for Jews due to ever-increasing restrictions on their movements and activities, thousands of them were summarily removed from public life entirely and detained in camps. Many others were arrested and held in camps for various infractions or in reprisal for **Resistance** activity. From these camps Jews were shipped to German death camps, usually to Auschwitz.

The Germans, in the context of their Final Solution, initiated these **deportations** and demanded that Vichy supply Jews to fill trains to the east, but French **police** and administrative personnel organized and carried out numerous roundups of Jews in **Paris**, Marseilles, and other cities. However, the deportation of foreign Jews from the so-called free **zone** was actually first suggested by René **Bousquet**, as was the inclusion of children under 16 among those to be deported. The conditions of detainment and transportation imposed by French authorities on Jews in their custody were just as severe as those imposed by the Germans. By the end of the occupation in August 1944, 75,721 Jews had been deported to the east. Only some 2,800 of these survived. In addition, about 3,000 Jews succumbed to the harsh conditions in French camps, and 1,100 had been executed. The 77,021 victims represent more than 24 percent of the Jewish community present in France at the outset of the Occupation. At the same time, more than three-fourths, or about 250,000, survived, most often disguising their identities or living clandestinely and benefiting from the assistance of those sympathetic to their plight. This widespread complicity of the French people, coupled with the proximity of **Spain** and **Switzerland** and large expanses of mountainous or sparsely inhabited terrain, contributed to making the survival rate for Jews in occupied France greater than that of any other country under German control. Vichy, however, was the only government in Western Europe to deliver Jews from *unoccupied* territory to the Nazis.

*R. Badinter, *Un Antisémitisme Ordinaire: Vichy et les avocats juifs (1940–1944)* (Paris, 1997); A. Cohen, *Persécutions et sauvetages, Juifs et Français sous l'Occupation et sous Vichy* (Paris, 1993); A. Kaspi, *Les Juifs pendant l'Occupation* (Paris, 1991); M. R. Marrus and R. O. Paxton, *Vichy France and the Jews* (New York, 1981); R. Poznanski, *Être Juif en France pendant la Seconde Guerre mondiale* (Paris, 1994); D. F. Ryan, *The Holocaust and the Jews of Marseille: The Enforcement of Anti-Semitic Policies in Vichy France* (Champaign, IL, 1996); S. Zucotti, *The Holocaust, the French, and the Jews* (New York, 1993).

N. Bracher

JEWS IN RESISTANCE includes **resistance** by Jewish groups and by **Jews** in non-Jewish organizations against the Nazis and their **collaborators**. Any history of Jews in the Resistance must take into account both the conditions under which the general Resistance operated and the specificity of the situation of Jews, who were singled out for persecution by the Nazis. In studying the resistance of Jews in France, one must further distinguish between French **Jews** and **Jews** of foreign origin.

On the eve of World War II, there were 330,000 Jews in France, two-thirds of whom were of foreign origin. The majority of these foreign Jews had emigrated from Eastern Europe and Germany, especially during the 1930s. Most Jews in France lived in **Paris**, but many fled to the southern **zone** after the German occupation of the city.

The most important difference between French and foreign Jews was in their attitudes toward Judaism and toward the state. French Jews, long used to a strong tradition of acculturation, were more trustful of the state and attempted to find legal means of dealing with the **Vichy** government's anti-Jewish measures. They were much less likely to participate in Jewish Resistance movements, especially during the first years of the war. Foreign Jews were more likely to view the state as a hostile force and were therefore more willing to go underground. French Jews were more likely to join non-Jewish Resistance groups, their integration facilitated by the fact that the general Resistance in France opposed **anti-Semitism**, although some members of certain groups expressed anti-Semitic sentiments. Foreign **Jews**, on the other hand, tended to join Jewish organizations.

There were also important legal differences in their situations. The first victims of Vichy's anti-Jewish measures were foreign Jews who were interned and were the first to be deported. Militant foreign Jews, either **communist** or Zionist, were among the first Jews to join the Resistance. Furthermore, Jews already associated with a communist organization preceded their non-Jewish colleagues in adopting ideas favorable to resistance. Clandestine branches of the official Jewish institutions developed much later, after the roundups of the summer of 1942 and especially after the German occupation of the southern zone in November of that year.

As with the general Resistance movement, Jewish Resistance groups were diverse and carried out a variety of activities. While the Jewish Resistance was largely nonviolent, sabotage and other violent attacks were the special domain of Jewish communists, indeed, of the communist Resistance in general. Other armed Jewish Resistance groups included the Armée Juive (it became the Organisation Juive de Combat, or the OJC, in 1944), which served as the military arm of other Jewish groups specializing in rescue missions, and the noncommunist Jewish *maquis*, attached to the Gaullist Secret **Army**.

Other forms of Resistance included polemics. Most of the underground Jewish **press** in France was the work of Jewish communists. The bulk of Jewish Resistance activities, however, consisted of defensive resistance. Such rescue operations included the placement of Jewish children in non-Jewish homes, the supplying of false identity papers, and the transportation of Jews across the border into **Spain** and **Switzerland**. In France, these networks worked under the cover of official Jewish organizations, operating both aboveground and underground. Organizations specializing in the rescue of children include the Oeuvre de Secours à l'Enfance (OSE), the Sixième (the Sixth), a branch of the Israelite Scouts of France (ÉIF), and the Young Zionist Movement (MJS). Tens of thousands of Jews were saved through the efforts of these organizations.

R. Cohen, *The Burden of Conscience: French Jewish Leadership during the Holocaust* (Bloomington, IN, 1987); H. J. Kieval, "Legality and Resistance in Vichy France: The Rescue of Jewish Children," and R. Poznanski, "A Methodological Approach to the Study of Jewish Resistance in France," in M. R. Marrus, *The Nazi Holocaust: Jewish Resistance to the Holocaust*, vol. 7 (Westport, CT, 1989), 482–509 and 443–81, respectively; L. Lazare, *Rescue as Resistance: How Jewish Organizations Fought the Holocaust in France*, trans. J. M. Green (New York, 1996); M. R. Marrus, "Jewish Resistance to the Holocaust," *JCH* 30 (1995): 83–110.

V. Datta

JÜNGER, ERNST (1895–1998), German novelist and essayist, stationed as a military officer in occupied France. His book *In Stahlgewittern* (1920), translated into English as *Storm of Steel* in 1929, is the journal of the leader of an assault group in World War I. Jünger's nationalistic leanings led him to various semimilitary adventures in the early days of the Weimar Republic. He also became a lifelong enthusiast for entomology and wrote prolifically about insects. Attracted to extreme **right-wing** movements, Jünger, however, soon developed strong private doubts about the Nazi regime. He published a novel, *Auf den Marmorklippen* (On the Marble Cliffs) in 1939, a thinly veiled allegory of totalitarianism.

Reactivated as an officer during World War II, Jünger followed the German troops into France and spent extended periods posted there, where he kept a journal, published in 1949 as *Strahlungen*. Although a strong German nationalist, Jünger was also a humanist, open to the understanding of cultures other than his own. In occupied France, he seized every opportunity offered him as a well-known writer to meet French authors, artists, and other thinkers, mostly **collaborationists** with Nazi Germany. Fluent in French, he also had a keen sense of how deeply average Frenchmen hated uniformed Germans.

Jünger, who foresaw German defeat in the war, also became close to Colonel (later, General) Hans Speidel and had advance knowledge of the attempt on **Hitler's** life in July 1944. Although he escaped the purge that followed, Jünger was discharged from the army for "unsatisfactory military conduct" in October of that year. His subsequent publications confirm his move from nationalism to a more humanistic position. On the occasion of his 100th birthday in 1995, Jünger was congratulated by German chancellor Helmut Kohl and French president François **Mitterand**.

H. L. Arnold, *Ernst Jünger* [in German] (Muhlacker, 1966); E. Jünger, *Journal de guerre et d'occupation 1939–1948*, trans. H. Plard (Paris, 1965); G. Loose, *Ernst Jünger* [in German] (Frankfurt, 1957), [in English] (Boston, 1974); K. Paetel, *Ernst Jünger* [in German] (New York, 1946).

K. Bieber

JUSTICE MINISTRY, VICHY, was led by Raphaël Alibert (12 July 1940–27 January 1941), Joseph Barthélemy (27 January 1941–26 March 1943), and Maurice Gabolde (after 27 March 1943). There was unprecedented political intervention in criminal justice. Special courts and commissions were created with magistrates chosen on the basis of "loyalty and firmness." **Republican** leaders were brought before the Supreme Court in **Riom**, and martial law courts functioned in some locations, while other jurisdictions had **Special Sections** in criminal cases attached to appeals courts.

Most magistrates retained office after 1940. *Ius sanguinis* (nationality and blood) replaced *ius civilis* (citizenship and Republican culture) in defining access to justice. Some 500,000 immigration cases, dating to 1927, were reviewed; 15,154 were denaturalized, including 6,307 **Jews**. Those arbitrarily excluded by bloodlines faced persecution. Émigrés from 10 May 1940 to 30 June 1940 lost their citizenship. Separation of powers was rejected as authority emanated from the head of state, Marshal **Pétain**.

Ministerial control included the use of photographs and scrutiny of family status. Married **women's** employment outside the home was restricted, but inside the home wives secured increased property rights. Abortion was shifted from criminal courts with jury trials to correctional courts with three-judge panels. Reduced penalties were intended to increase conviction rates. Adoption and legitimation became easier; divorce, more difficult. The **prison** population grew from 18,000 to over 50,000 in about two years. Wartime shortages added to deterioration in prison conditions. There were prison uprisings in **Paris** and Eysses.

Professions regulated by the ministry, such as lawyers and notaries, were reformed. Lawyers needed certificates of aptitude and obtained a monopoly on representation in court actions, and notaries were reorganized into departmental and regional groups to facilitate the regulation of professional practice. Few of those involved in the Vichy Justice Ministry were purged after 1944.

J. Barthélemy, *Ministre de la Justice, Vichy 1941–1943* (Paris, 1989); J.-C. Farcy and H. Rousso, *Justice, répression et persécution en France, fin des années 1930—début des années 1950* (Paris, 1993); R. H. Weisberg, *Vichy Law and the Holocaust in France* (New York, 1996).

D. R. Applebaum

K

KÉRILLIS, HENRI DE (1889–1958), was an interwar journalist, elected as a deputy in 1936, who tried to form a broad-based conservative movement. Opposed to Nazi Germany, he was the only **right-wing** deputy who, joining one **socialist** and 75 **communists**, voted against the 1938 **Munich agreement**.

Rejecting the 1940 **armistice** and hunted by the Gestapo, Kérillis fled to the **United States**, where he initially supported General **de Gaulle** but believed that the general should limit himself to military activity on behalf of the Allies while staying out of politics, a view shared by about a third of the French exiles in the United States. With other such ''dissident'' journalists, including Geneviève Tabouis and Pertinax (André Géraud), Kérillis founded a newspaper, *Pour la Victoire*, in January 1942. In a 1945 book entitled *De Gaulle dictateur*, he later expanded his view of the general as a political usurper. Following the Allied landings in **North Africa**, November 1942, Kérillis supported the State Department's attempts to marginalize de Gaulle by dealing with first Admiral **Darlan**, then General Henri **Giraud**. Kérillis' violent articles against de Gaulle in *Pour la Victoire* were opposed by the **American** Gaullist organization France Forever. Kérillis greeted the creation of the Comité Français de Libération Nationale in 1943 with a passionate campaign, in which he wrote that, actually hampering the **liberation** of France, ''de Gaulle had installed in Algiers the most dictatorial constitution that France had ever known.'' Following the liberation, Kérillis, preferring direct American military rule to de Gaulle, argued that France no longer had a legal government.

Kérillis and his colleagues, including Alexis Léger, in large measure agreed with Roosevelt, fearing the dictatorial power of de Gaulle, whom they saw as a military man, nationalistic, ambitious, and antidemocratic, with no popular investiture. In addition, however, Kérillis had a son, who had joined **Free France**, was parachuted into France, then was caught and tortured to death by Gestapo agents. Kérillis accused de Gaulle's secret services of having denounced his son. This episode helped justify and sharpened Kérillis' already virulent anti-Gaullism. Kérillis never returned to France and died in New York in 1958.

H. de Kérillis, *De Gaulle dictateur: une grande mystification de l'histoire* (Montreal, 1945); C. W. Nettelbeck, *Forever French: Exile in the United States 1939–1945* (Oxford and New York, 1991).

Ch. Morelle

KLARSFELD, SERGE (1935–). Lawyer, historian, and indefatigable Nazi hunter, Klarsfeld, along with his wife, Beate, is responsible for bringing a number of important Nazi officials and their French collaborators to justice.

Himself a victim of the **Holocaust**, Klarsfeld is president of the Association of the Sons and Daughters of Jews Deported from France. His father was arrested by the Gestapo in Nice in 1943 and deported to Auschwitz, where he died. The Klarsfelds have dedicated themselves to preparing dossiers on, and confronting, unpunished Nazi war criminals. They were instrumental in bringing to justice Kurt Lischka and Klaus **Barbie**, former Gestapo chiefs of **Paris** and Lyons, respectively.

The Klarsfelds have pursued Nazi war criminals by any means—preferably legal—but extralegally if necessary. Both Klarsfelds were charged with the 1971 attempted kidnapping of Lischka. Serge Klarsfeld has also admitted to involvement in an assassination plot against Barbie, which was canceled when the Bolivian government agreed to extradite him. In France, the Klarsfelds compiled evidence against René **Bousquet** and Jean Leguay, the French **police** officials responsible for the roundup of **Jews** at the **Vélodrome d'hiver**. Leguay was indicted in 1979 but died in 1989 before standing trial. Bousquet, assassinated by a deranged gunman, also died before being brought to trial. The Klarsfelds' son, Arno, was the legal representative of the seven victims of former **Milicien** Paul **Touvier**, who became the first Frenchman to be tried for crimes against humanity.

Serge Klarsfeld is the author of numerous works, including *Le mémorial de la déportation des Juifs en France* (1978), *Vichy*-Auschwitz (1983), and *Les enfants d'Izieu* (1984).

É. Conan and H. Rousso, *Un passé qui ne passe pas* (Paris, 1994); P. Hellmann, "Nazi-Hunting Is Their Life," *New York Times*, 4 November 1979; A. Klarsfeld, *Touvier, un crime français* (Paris, 1994).

V. Datta

KNOCHEN, HELMUT, SS-Obersturmbannführer (Colonel) (1910–), commander of the Sicherheitsdienst (SD) and Security Police in occupied France from 1940 to 1944. From Knochen's arrival in France until his recall to Berlin in August 1944, he proved himself a meticulously efficient Nazi administrator.

During the 1930s, Knochen became identified with a clique of young, exceptionally educated National Socialists whose intelligence and dedication provided a conduit for the commission of the era's worst crimes. He received a doctorate in 1935. In 1937, the Sturmabteilung (SA) veteran joined the SD to investigate the refugee press.

After Knochen arrived in France in the summer of 1940, he began planning the destruction of French **Jewry**. Although he encountered hostility from the German military administration and the **Vichy** government as well as intrigues among his subordinates, Knochen carried out roundups and the **deportation** of large numbers of Jews. He worked closely with René **Bousquet** and other Vichy officials to denaturalize Jews, facilitating their deportation. He was also able to use the French **police** to arrest Jews. Knochen used these two strategies during the Grande Rafle, the roundup of Jews in July 1942 at the **Paris** Vélodrome d'hiver. Despite his efficient pursuit of Jews, Knochen was careful not to elicit unfavorable reactions from Vichy or the French public. To attain this balance, he often restrained his more fanatical subordinates.

After a **British** trial in 1946 for his participation in shooting downed airmen, French authorities sentenced Knochen to death in 1954. The term was soon reduced to 20 years' penal servitude. Despite his active role in the Final Solution, Knochen received a full pardon in 1962. Interviewed in the 1990s, Knochen took the position that his ''debt'' had been paid.

M. Marrus and R. O. Paxton, *Vichy France and the Jews* (New York, 1981); S. Zuccotti, *The Holocaust, the French, and the Jews* (New York, 1993).

R. W. White

KOENIG, PIERRE (1898–1970), led the **Free French** forces in Africa and the Middle East. He was also commander of the French Forces of the Interior (FFI) in 1944.

At the age of 18 Koenig joined the infantry for the duration of the First World War. He left with the rank of cadet and a military medal. During the 1920s he served with the French forces in Silesia and with the occupation troops in the Ruhr. In 1930 he went to Morocco, where he began an African career that lasted until 1944. He was promoted to captain in 1940. After successful service in Norway, he was in **Britain** when General **de Gaulle** called Frenchmen to join him in bringing about a Free France. Koenig responded without hesitation.

In 1940 and 1941 Koenig fought **Vichy** forces in Africa and the Middle East. He was promoted to general in the autumn of 1941. He then led Free French forces in the Battle of Bir-Hakeim, a battle that made him famous and marked the renaissance, in 1942, of the French **army** which had been defeated in 1940. In July 1943, after further campaigns in Africa, Koenig quit his command to go to Algiers, where he became deputy chief of staff for the army. At the beginning of 1944 he was named commander of the French forces in Britain. Then he was named commander in chief of the FFI, in time for the campaign of June 1944.

His African career over, Koenig became military governor of **Paris** in August 1944 and commander in chief of the French zone of occupation in Germany from 1945 through 1949. He retired from active duty in 1951, when he was elected deputy from the Bas-Rhin and served as president of the defense commission and in 1954 as minister of defense. He resigned this last position because of disagreements with the government's Moroccan policy. In 1984 Koenig was posthumously given the title of marshal.

M. R. D. Foot, *SOE in France, an Account of the Work of the British Special Operations Executive in France, 1940–1944* (London, 1966); P. Koenig, *Bir-Hakeim, 10 juin 1942* (Paris, 1971).

E. H. Murphrey

L

LABOR CHARTER (CHARTE DU TRAVAIL) was promulgated by the **Vichy** government in October 1941 to replace prewar employer and trade union confederations with an obligatory corporatist structure of social and professional groups. Elaborated by a seven-member consultative Comité d'organisation professionnelle, the charter gave expression to Vichy's rejection of class conflict and represented a compromise between the traditional corporatist preference for mixed groupings of workers and employers and the desire of large employers, labor leaders, and the government to guarantee social peace through regulated arbitration.

Local committees composed of employers and employees, called *comités sociaux*, were established by the charter to regulate various **industries**, but the government's ability to dissolve or suspend any *comité social* canceled their autonomy. Unions lost the power to negotiate collective contracts, but the authority of employers within individual enterprises was preserved. Although the charter outlawed strikes and lockouts, it mandated a minimum wage and arbitration procedures for resolving conflicts between competing interests.

Originally conceived as a step toward the evolution of an Iberian-style corporatist regime, the charter was applied under officials (Hubert **Lagardelle** and Marcel **Déat**) who were hostile to its initial formulation and under circumstances that rendered it moribund. The German invasion of the unoccupied **zone** in November 1942 and the institution of the **Service du Travail Obligatoire** in February 1943 made it irrelevant. By the time of the Allied invasion in June 1944, a reconstituted *Confédération Général du Travail* (the prewar labor movement) had joined the **Resistance**, and only 1 of the 24 commissions set up under the charter to organize the professions had completed its work. Many of the charter's local units existed only on paper, had become covers for Resistance activities, or represented only employers.

*†J. Julliard, "La Charte du travail," in Fondation Nationale des Sciences Politiques, ed. (J. Bourdin and R. Rémond), *Le Gouvernement de Vichy, 1940–1942* (Paris, 1972);

J.-P. Le Crom, ''Le Syndicalisme ouvrier et la Charte du Travail,'' in J.-P. Azéma and F. Bédarida, eds., *Vichy et les français* (Paris, 1992).

S. Kale

LACOMBE LUCIEN was a film set during the Occupation, made in France, 1974; director: Louis Malle; script: Louis Malle and Patrick Modiano; sound: Tonino Delli Colli; editing: Henri Vergnes; music: Django Reinhardt and songs of the era; production: Claude Nedjar for Nef and UPF (Paris), Vides Film (Rome), and Halleluyah Film (Munich); cast: Pierre Blaise (Lucien), Aurore Clément (France), Holger Lowenadler (Albert Horn); color, 135 minutes.

The setting is June 1944 in a little village in southwestern France. Following a sequence of chance events, the young Lucien Lacombe joins the French auxiliary of the German police, the *gestapistes*. He meets a **Jewish** tailor, Albert Horn, who has fled **Paris** and is in hiding, helped by the French *gestapistes*. Lucien falls in love with Horn's daughter, France.

In the end, the film arouses intense emotion and provokes violent and polemical reactions because the theme of political engagement, handled clumsily earlier in *Le Chagrin et la Pitie* (The **Sorrow and the Pity**), is presented as governed by chance, by psychological contingencies far removed from any ideological or moral conviction. Lucien, who comes from a troubled family (his father is a **prisoner**, and his mother is seeing a man who rejects Lucien), finds the recognition he craves among the *gestapistes*, who accept him as one of their own. He gains some power and in Albert Horn finds the father he no longer has. The Jews themselves are equally not spared as France, the tailor's daughter, falls in love with the young militiaman.

Behind the simple question of political engagement, Louis Malle offers his point of view on social behavior: compromises are possible only for a while, after which society reasserts its claims; all people are condemned who reject the rules of their social milieu and who have gained in social status by profiting from a specific situation.

J.-P. Bertin-Maghit, J.-M. Andrault, and G. Vincent, ''Le Cinéma français et la Seconde Guerre mondiale,'' *La Revue du cinéma, image et son* 378 (December 1982): 70–111.

J.-P. Bertin-Maghit

LAGARDELLE, JEAN-BAPTISTE HUBERT (1874–1958), labor leader and theoretician, member of the **Vichy** government.

Born in Haute-Garonne, Lagardelle was an early **socialist** follower of Jules Guesde's Parti ouvrier français. In 1899 he founded the journal *Mouvement Socialiste* and joined the Socialist Party in 1905. Lagardelle looked to the revolutionary tradition of Marx and Engels and became increasingly estranged from the legalism of Jean Jaurès. He published such works as *L'évolution des syndicats ouvriers en France de l'interdiction à l'obligation* (1901), *La grève générale et le socialisme* (1905), and *Le socialisme ouvrier* (1911).

Lagardelle met Mussolini at international socialist gatherings, and they became friends. Named to the French diplomatic mission in Rome in 1933, Lagardelle remained there until 1940. In 1935 he was instrumental in inviting then prime minister Pierre **Laval** to visit Rome and meet Mussolini. Upon his return to France, Lagardelle became a partisan of the Vichy government and the **National Revolution**. Along with another **syndicalist**, René **Belin**, Lagardelle shaped Vichy's labor policies first as undersecretary and then as minister of labor. He also developed a theoretical approach to labor questions at the Institut d'études corporatives et sociales and the Centre français de synthèse. He was brought to trial in 1946 and spent a brief time in prison. Upon his release, he retired from active life and published articles on labor and syndicalism.

B. M. Gordon, *Collaborationism in France during the Second World War* (Ithaca, NY, 1980); R. O. Paxton, *Vichy France: Old Guard and New Order, 1940–1944* (New York, 1972).

M. L. Berkvam

LA PORTE DU THEIL, JOSEPH DE (1884–1976), was the head of **Vichy's Chantiers de la Jeunesse**, an organization created by Vichy for the demobilized young men from the **army** in the southern **zone**.

Born in Mende (Lozère), La Porte du Theil was the son of a water and forestry official. After an outstanding military career in artillery and the military scouts, in which he rose to general, he headed the Seventh Army Corps during the 1940 campaign. Following the defeat, he organized what became the Chantiers de la Jeunesse from the ranks of the demobilized men, many of whom were unemployed. La Porte du Theil organized his men into forestry service groups that helped in given areas with agricultural tasks. By October 1940, the Chantiers had come to be considered an obligatory eight-month national service. La Porte du Theil emphasized the moral virtues of order and the rugged, country, outdoor life. The organization promoted loyalty to Marshal **Pétain** and the **National Revolution** but was not pro-**collaborationist**. Although its agenda was the maintenance of social order rather than **resistance**, it spawned many *résistants* and **maquisards** and, in North Africa, the cadres for a reconstituted French Africa **army**. Altogether, some 329,100 men wore the forest-green uniform of the Chantiers.

Suspicious of the Chantiers, the Germans progressively disbanded it after November 1942, when they occupied the southern zone. One hundred thousand of the men were sent to work in Germany; many never returned. On 4 January 1944, La Porte du Theil was arrested and deported to Germany, where he remained until freed, 4 May 1945. The **Haute Cour de Justice** dropped all charges against him on 18 November 1947.

The Chantiers, officially dissolved by a law of 10 June 1944, were considered by General **de Gaulle**, among others, as the most noteworthy institution of the **État Français**. When General de La Porte du Theil died in 1976, he left behind an extensive documentary collection relating to the Chantiers.

W. D. Halls, *The Youth of Vichy France* (Oxford, 1981); R. Hervet, *Les Chantiers de la Jeunesse* (Paris, 1962); J. de La Porte du Theil, *Les Chantiers de la Jeunesse ont deux ans* (Paris, 1942).

G. Le Marec

LA ROCQUE, FRANÇOIS DE (1885–1946), military officer and nationalist who opposed the German Occupation. The son of a general and descendant of an old noble family, he was educated at the St. Cyr military academy. La Rocque served as an officer, first in North Africa, then during World War I on the western front, where he was wounded and decorated.

After retiring from the **army** in 1928, he joined the Croix de Feu, a veterans organization. La Rocque soon assumed leadership and considerably expanded its membership. Nationalistic, anticommunist, and antiparliamentary, the Croix de Feu participated in the riots of 6 February 1934 that threatened the Third **Republic**. In 1936, when the **Popular Front** government dissolved all paramilitary organizations, La Rocque transformed his group into the **Parti Social Français**, employing legal means to advance its conservative program.

La Rocque was not elated when the Republic collapsed in 1940, for he detested the German occupier. He employed his newspaper, the *Petit Journal*, to reorganize his party, renamed the *Progrès Social Français*. Appointed to Marshal **Pétain's** Conseil national in 1941, he publicly supported the **National Revolution**. Secretly, however, La Rocque passed information to the **Resistance** forces in London through a network called the Klan. After Germany invaded the unoccupied **zone** in November 1942, he was placed under surveillance, then, in March 1943, arrested and deported. La Rocque spent more than two years in harsh captivity.

Freed by **American** forces, he was flown to France, where the **liberation** government immediately arrested and imprisoned him. La Rocque died before he could be tried as a collaborator. Fifteen years later, President Charles **de Gaulle** wrote to his widow and recognized his wartime services.

*W. D. Irvine, "Fascism in France and the Strange Case of the Croix de Feu," *JMH* 63:2 (June 1991); J. Nobecourt, *Le Colonel de La Rocque: Biographie d'un personnage clé de la IIIème République, à la croisée de la droite conservatrice et du fascisme* (Paris, 1996); P. Rudaux, *Les Croix de feu et le P.S.F.* (Paris, 1967).

J. Friguglietti

LATTRE DE TASSIGNY, JEAN DE (1889–1952), charismatic general who served both **Vichy** and General **de Gaulle**. In 1940 General de Lattre led the 14th Division with distinction against General Heinz Guderian's panzers during the **Battle of France**. Following the **armistice**, he became commander of the 13th military district (Puy-de-Dôme) and established his residence in a medieval chateau in the village of Opme, where he set up a training center to prepare leaders for the regeneration of France, much in the spirit of **Uriage**. In September 1941 General Maxime **Weygand** summoned him to strengthen French defenses in Tunisia. German pressure brought de Lattre's recall in February 1942, whereupon he became commander of the 16th military district at Montpellier.

When German forces crossed the **Demarcation Line** at the time of the Allied landings in **North Africa**, de Lattre resisted, but Vichy authorities arrested him and sentenced him to 10 years' imprisonment. He escaped and made his way to London and Algiers, where de Gaulle appointed him commander of **Army** Group B, designated to land in **Provence** (Operation Dragoon) alongside General Alexander M. Patch, Jr.'s Seventh **American** Army. The rapid success of the Riviera landings enabled de Lattre's army to liberate Toulon and Marseilles ahead of schedule. He and Patch raced north, and in September their armies linked with Allied forces pressing eastward from **Normandy**.

De Lattre incorporated approximately 135,000 **Resistance** fighters into what became the First French Army (Rhin et Danube). Under General Jacob Devers' Sixth Army group, de Lattre's troops participated in the **liberation** of **Alsace**. De Lattre refused to evacuate Strasbourg at the time of the German winter counteroffensive, defying Eisenhower's orders. The First French Army then resumed the offensive, cleared the Colmar pocket, crossed the Rhine, occupied Stuttgart, and advanced into western Austria. De Lattre represented France at the German surrender ceremony ending hostilities in Europe. He was made marshal of France posthumously in 1952.

J.-L. Barre, *De Lattre et la 1ère Armée* (Paris, 1989); A. Clayton, *Three Marshals of France: Leadership after Trauma* (London, 1992): J. de Lattre, *Histoire de la première armée française: Rhin et Danube* (Paris, 1949); G. Salisbury-Jones, *So Full of Glory: A Biography of Marshal de Lattre de Tassigny* (London, 1954).

K. Munholland

LAUBREAUX, ALAIN (also known as Alin Laubreaux and Michel Daxiat; 1898–1968), journalist and **theater** critic for *Je suis partout* and other newspapers. His Occupation writings, expressing clearly his sympathy for the Germans and identification with French **fascists**, were responsible for the death sentence imposed on him (in absentia) by the Cour de Justice de la Seine in 1947.

Born and raised in New Caledonia, son of a commerce representative, Laubreaux went to France in 1921 and over the next 15 years worked for a number of publications, including *L'Œuvre, Paris Matinal*, and *Candide*, and wrote several books. Beginning in 1936, he wrote for *Je suis partout* (founded by Robert **Brasillach**) as theater critic, a position he held until the weekly ceased in 1944. After a brief incarceration, along with his colleague Charles Lesca, in June 1940 Laubreaux returned to journalism, working on *Le cri du peuple*, reviewing drama for *Le Petit Parisien*, and, when *Je suis partout* resumed publication in February 1941, he resumed his theater column while contributing political articles and writing the novel *Capitaine* (1943), and the memoir *Écrit pendant la guerre* (1943). Acerbic, fanatically fascist, xenophobic, and **anti-Semitic**, his work often employs humor and satire.

His only stage play, an especially anti-Semitic retelling of a financial scandal, entitled *Les Pirates de Paris (L'Affaire Stavisky)*, was written under the alias Michel Daxiat (a name given the villainous critic in *Le Dernier métro*). The melodrama (the script for which has disappeared) played a few weeks at the Ambigu in Paris in March and April 1942, receiving negative reviews except from Laubreaux himself, who in *Je suis partout* extolled Daxiat's efforts. Shortly before the **liberation of Paris**, Laubreaux fled, first to Germany, then to **Spain**, where he remained an exile until his death in 1968.

P.-M. Diodonnat, *Je Suis Partout 1930–1944* (Paris, 1987); P.-M. Diodonnat, *Les 700 Rédacteurs de "Je Suis Partout," 1930–1944* (Paris, 1993); Alain Laubreaux, *Écrit pendant la guerre* (Paris, 1944).

K. Krauss

LAURENT, JACQUES (1919–), a prolific writer, member of the postwar **right-wing** group informally known as the "**Hussards**" (Hussars), and opponent of the dominant creeds of **résistantialisme** and **Sartrian** existentialism in the late 1940s and 1950s.

The son of a lawyer, raised in the middle-class ninth *arrondissement* (district) of Paris, Laurent was also the nephew of Eugène **Deloncle**, leader of the 1930s right-wing Cagoule and the wartime collaborationist **Mouvement Social Révolutionnaire**. Drafted in 1940, Laurent experienced the French defeat while still in training. He was then attached to the **Armistice Army**, where he was assigned duties policing the **Demarcation Line**, which separated the occupied from the unoccupied zones of France. He subsequently served in **Vichy's** Information Ministry. As France was being liberated, Laurent was assigned to arrange an escape of Marshal **Pétain** to the **Resistance** but failed to prevent the Germans from spiriting Pétain off to **Sigmaringen**. Joining the Resistance, Laurent served briefly in General **de Lattre's army,** then was detained briefly by French authorities before being allowed to go free.

A highly successful novelist who wrote many of his books under the name "Cécil Saint-Laurent," after the war, Laurent suggested that there was little difference in the motivations of **collaborators** and resisters. Antoine, the major protagonist in his 1954 novel, *Le Petit Canard*, joins the anti-Bolshevik **Légion des Volontaires Français** out of pique at having been jilted by a woman in favor of a Polish officer, implying that under different circumstances he might as easily have joined the Resistance. This theme was reiterated in the film *Lacombe Lucien* 20 years later.

To Laurent, Vichy had concealed an anti-German Pétainist resistance that had been subverted by General **de Gaulle**. De Gaulle's return to power in 1958 brought out the full force of Laurent's opposition, in *Mauriac sous de Gaulle* (1964) and *Année 40* (1965), to what he considered the Gaullist myth of *résistantialisme*. In the late 1960s Laurent defended the cause of South Vietnam, and he continued to write fiction and nonfiction into the 1990s. In 1986 he was elected to the Académie Française.

J. Laurent, *Mauriac sous de Gaulle* (Paris, 1964); J. Laurent, *Le Petit Canard* (Paris, 1954); J. Laurent and G. Jeantet, *Année 40: Londres, De Gaulle, Vichy* (Paris, 1965); N. Hewitt, *Literature and the Right in Postwar France: The Story of the "Hussards"* (Oxford and New York, 1996).

B. M. Gordon

LAVAL, PIERRE (1883–1945), was five times foreign minister and four times premier before 1939. Twice he was head of the **Vichy** government after the fall of France. He opposed war in 1939 and sought to ease the fate of a defeated France after June 1940. For Laval, the war was like any other, not the crusade against **fascism** that Winston Churchill was determined to wage. Laval justified cooperation with Nazi Germany to save France and Europe from the spread of Bolshevism and to spare it the worst consequences of Nazi occupation. To protect the greater number, he would sacrifice foreign **Jews** and anti-Nazi **refugees, communists**, and **maquisards**.

Laval began his political career as a **socialist** (Section Française de l'Internationale Ouvrière SFIO) and pacifist deputy on the eve of the First World War, and he was on a list of **pacifists** and potentially seditious persons to be jailed in the event of war. In November 1917 Georges Clemenceau offered him a position in his new cabinet. Laval declined out of respect for party discipline, but he soon drifted away from the SFIO. His politics veered to the **Right**, and in 1931, a strong anticommunist, he became premier and foreign minister. Again foreign minister in 1935, Laval signed the Franco–**Soviet** pact of mutual assistance, after gutting it of substance. Fearful of the spread of communism, Laval signed the pact because an intransigent **Hitler** left him little choice. Having promised Soviet leader Joseph Stalin speedy ratification, Laval delayed it until his fall from power in January 1936. During the last years before the outbreak of war, Laval remained out of power, nursing grudges against the socialists and Radicals who had overthrown his government. He had a reputation for being a slippery politician with no firm principles; however, there were two consistent courses in Laval's politics: anti-Bolshevism and a desire for settlement with Nazi Germany.

When France fell in June 1940, Laval opposed further **resistance**. In early July, he used his considerable parliamentary skills to engineer the National Assembly vote that gave constituent powers to Marshal **Pétain**, thereby helping create the **État Français** in Vichy, where Laval emerged as head of the government. In this role, Laval met Hitler at **Montoire** (October 1940) to talk conciliation and cooperation. It was inconceivable to Laval that Germany would fail to win the war. He wanted to make the best of it; repatriate French prisoners of war (POWs) and obtain the signature of a peace treaty with Germany. Laval was toppled in December 1940 in a palace intrigue led by Marshal Pétain's entourage. The German Embassy in **Paris** threw its protection over Laval, and he survived to return to power.

In June 1941 the German army invaded the **USSR**, and in April 1942 German pressure helped return Laval to power. For Laval, the war was a crusade against Bolshevism. "I hope for the victory of Germany," he said, "because without it, communism would soon be established everywhere in Europe" (June 1942). Laval held to this line even when German victory seemed less certain. To collaborate, he was willing to support the sending of French workers to Germany in exchange for French POWs. He approved the roundup of foreign Jews and other undesirables. When the Nazis did not keep to their bargains, Laval continued to negotiate for negligible concessions. "Laval, the Nazi puppet!" he was called by the **Free French** on the **BBC**.

By early 1944 Laval supported an all-out campaign against the anti-Nazi **Resistance**. In June 1944 he urged the French to stay neutral and not to assist Allied forces, though at the end of 1943 he had advocated all-out war against French communists and "terrorists." For his efforts, the retreating German army arrested Laval and Pétain and took them off to Germany as hostages. It hardly acquitted Laval of his role in the Vichy government, and he was turned over to French authorities in August 1945. In October, Laval was condemned to death in a drumhead trial, before jurors who taunted him and a judge and prosecutor who had served the Vichy government. He attempted suicide on the morning of his execution but was revived to be dragged, staggering and vomiting, to his firing squad.

*Y.-F. Jaffré, *Il y a 50 ans Pierre Laval* (Paris, 1995); F. Kupferman, *Laval, 1883–1945* (Paris, 1988); G. Warner, *Pierre Laval and the Eclipse of France* (London, 1965).

M. J. Carley

LEBRUN, ALBERT (1871–1950), last president of the Third French **Republic**, one of the least impressive of all French presidents.

Educated at the *École Polytechnique* as a mining engineer, Lebrun was elected a deputy for the moderate Union républicaine from his native Meurthe-et-Moselle in 1900, becoming a senator in 1920. He was minister for colonies in the Caillaux, Poincaré, and Doumergue governments from 1911 through 1914 and Georges Clemenceau's minister for the blockade in 1917 and for the liberated regions in 1918–1919.

Lebrun was elected president of the Senate in 1921. He was elected president of the Republic after the assassination of Paul Doumer in 1932 and with Édouard **Daladier's** urging was reelected in April 1939, becoming only the second president of the Third Republic to achieve this honor. He interpreted his office as requiring complete passivity. Noting that of 8,267 state documents covering the years from 1932 through 1939, Lebrun's name appears in only 7, historian Jean-Baptiste Duroselle wrote that, "No greater void appears in the history of the French Republics."

When Paul **Reynaud** resigned as prime minister in the collapse of June 1940, Lebrun rejected advice to rename him and instead chose Marshal **Pétain**. When the parliament voted on 10 July 1940 to give full powers to Pétain, and the marshal promulgated his first *Acte constitutionnel* the next day, naming himself "chief of the **État français**," Lebrun's function ended. He withdrew to a property near Grenoble, was arrested by the Germans in 1943, and was briefly deported to the Tyrol. Lebrun played no further role in public life after the **liberation**. Lebrun was the perfect type of French president whose job, in the sardonic words of **de Gaulle**, was to "*inaugurer les chrysanthèmes*" (inaugurate flower shows).

*J.-P. Azéma, *From Munich to the Liberation*. Trans. J. Lloyd (Cambridge, U.K. and Paris, 1984 [original French ed. Paris, 1979]); A. Dansette, *Histoire des présidents de la République* (Paris, 1960); J.-B. Duroselle, *La décadence* (Paris, 1979).

J. W. Friend

LE CHAMBON-SUR-LIGNON, in the mountainous Cevennes region of southern France, in which a small Protestant community hid and furthered the escape of thousands of **Jewish refugees** fleeing the genocidal policies of **Hitler's New Order** in Europe. The nonviolent **resistance** of the Chambonnais entailed great personal risk, defying the authority of the **Vichy** regime and the power of an SS division stationed in the area.

The humanitarian mission of the Le Chambon community was inspired and directed by the pastor and his wife, André and Magda Trocmé. These socially conscious activists had met in America, and his Franco–German parentage, together with her Italian–Russian roots, brought a cosmopolitan sensitivity to the otherwise isolated and insular parish. With remarkable openness and compassion, the Trocmés led their fellow villagers in responding to the flight of hunted persons, many from Germany and Eastern Europe. The work of rescue also received indirect aid from the purposeful inattentiveness of the German garrison commander in nearby Le Puy, Major Julius Schmähling, a devout Catholic and former schoolteacher.

Still, the **resistance** of Le Chambon to the Final Solution faced the threatening scrutiny of both the **milice** and the SS. On 29 June 1943, the Gestapo achieved its only success against the long-suspected activity of the Chambonnais, capturing 19 mostly Jewish refugees and their teacher, Daniel Trocmé, André's cousin. Daniel died at the Maidanek camp the following April.

Despite this tragic episode, the resistance of the Chambonnais achieved overwhelming success. Unlike other resisters, these villagers eschewed violence and followed no ideological or even patriotic call. In 1972 the government of Israel posthumously awarded André Trocmé the Medal of **Righteousness**.

P. Bolle, ed., *Le Plateau Vivarais-Lignon: Accueil et Résistance 1939–1944: Actes du Colloque du Chambon-sur-Lignon* (Le Chambon-sur-Lignon, 1992); P. Hallie, *Lest Innocent Blood Be Shed* (New York, 1979); C. Rittner and S. Meyers, eds., *The Courage to Care: Rescuers of Jews in the Holocaust* (New York, 1986).

R. F. Crane

LECLERC, PHILIPPE [PHILIPPE LECLERC DE HAUTECLOCQUE] (1902–1947), later marshal of France, was an early supporter of General **de**

Gaulle, and in August 1944, at the head of the Second Armored Division, **liberated Paris.** He received the surrender of General Dietrich von Choltitz and the German garrison on 25 August 1944.

Philippe de Hauteclocque entered the Saint-Cyr military academy in 1922 and was subsequently posted to Morocco. Wounded and taken **prisoner** in the 1940 campaign in France, he escaped, joined General de Gaulle in July 1940, and assumed the name Leclerc. Given the mission of rallying Cameroun to the **Free French**, General Leclerc was named military commander of French Equatorial Africa. On 2 March 1941, he captured Koufra and vowed "to stop only when the French flag again flies over Metz and Strasbourg."

After successful campaigns in Tripoli and Tunisia, Leclerc formed the Second Armored Division in Morocco. Transferred in April 1944 to **Britain**, this division crossed the channel on 1 August 1944, joining General Wade Hampton Haislip and his 15th Corps, part of General George S. Patton's army. Leclerc's division liberated Alençon on 12 August and Paris on the twenty-fifth, and on 23 November, the general fulfilled his Koufra oath by entering Strasbourg. His forces crossed the Rhine and helped capture **Hitler's** "Eagle's Nest" in Berchtesgaden, 4 May 1945. Named commander in chief of the French forces in the Far East, Leclerc signed, in France's name, the **Japanese** act of surrender on board the battleship *Missouri* on 6 September.

In October, General Leclerc arrived in Saigon, where he took charge of the French expeditionary forces, which, under Vice Admiral Thierry d'Argenlieu, were attempting to arrange with **Ho** Chi Minh and Chinese forces in the north a peaceful reentry of French troops north of the 16th parallel. A preliminary accord was reached in March 1946 with Ho, whom Leclerc met in Hanoi on the eighteenth, but differences in political approaches between Leclerc and d'Argenlieu caused the former to request to be relieved of his command. In July, Leclerc left Saigon and took up a post in North Africa. The situation worsened in Indochina, however, and Leclerc undertook another mission, in December 1946, to help arrange a political settlement there. Although asked in February 1947 to return to Indochina as high commissioner, Leclerc felt too isolated politically to be effective. On 27 November 1947, on a mission at Colomb-Béchar, he was killed in a plane crash.

J.-P. Azéma, "Leclerc," in J.-P. Azéma and F. Bédarida, eds., *1938–1948 Les Années de tourmente, de Munich à Prague, Dictionnaire Critique* (Paris, 1995), 725–31; A. Clayton, *Three Marshals of France: Leadership after Trauma* (London, 1992); M. Cordier and R. Fouquer, *Le général Leclerc, ou, Se commander à soi-même* (Paris, 1990); R. Dronne, *Le Serment de Koufra* (Paris, 1965); H. Maule, *Out of the Sand, the Epic Story of General Leclerc and the Fighting Free French* (London, 1966).

C. Leclerc de Hauteclocque

LÉGION DES VOLONTAIRES FRANÇAIS CONTRE LE BOLCHEVISME (LÉGION DES VOLONTAIRES FRANÇAIS, LVF) was an organization formed in **Paris** by political rivals Jacques **Doriot**, Eugène **Deloncle**, and Marcel **Déat** that fielded a French military force to fight the **Soviets**.

After Operation Barbarossa in June 1941, Doriot and Déat secured permission from the German foreign office and **Vichy** government to form the LVF. By October, the organization had attracted a regiment of volunteers that was soon incorporated into a German infantry division. The French advanced on Moscow in late November, but Soviet counterattacks routed the insufficiently trained, inadequately led soldiers before they reached their objective. Political power struggles also contributed to the unit's poor performance. In early 1942, the LVF underwent a major reorganization to eradicate its glaring deficiencies. Three battalions spent the remainder of 1942 and 1943 on antipartisan operations behind German lines. The LVF was more suited to its new duties and performed well in several engagements in White **Russia**. After a significant antipartisan operation in early 1944, the Soviet summer offensive inflicted heavy casualties on the LVF, forcing its retreat and dissolution by August. The remaining men either returned to France or joined the growing French Waffen SS.

Despite its lack of major contributions to the German war effort, the LVF's home front apparatus claimed the support of many well-known individuals in French society and government, including Alphonse **de Châteaubriant**, Robert **Brasillach**, Pierre **Laval**, and Philippe **Pétain**. The LVF even received Vichy's official sanction after August 1942. Activities of the considerable LVF bureaucracy in France included distributing propaganda, organizing rallies, recruiting replacements, and aiding wounded legionnaires and their families. Many LVF members were executed or imprisoned after the war.

J. Delarue, *Trafics et crimes sous l'occupation* (Paris, 1968); B. M. Gordon, *Collaborationism in France during the Second World War* (Ithaca, NY, 1980).

R. W. White

LÉGION FRANÇAISE DES COMBATTANTS was established on 29 August 1940 to unite all veterans in patriotic loyalty to Marshal **Pétain**. It did not succeed. Many veterans' associations objected to their forced dissolution and to the transfer of their funds to the legion. The legion appealed more to former members of conservative veterans' associations such as the Union National des Combattants than to **left-wing** veterans; war cripples, whose dependence on the state had influenced their politics, were particularly dubious about the legion.

The head of the legion, François Valentin, was a former member of Colonel François **de la Rocque's Parti Social Français**. The average age of legionnaires was around 50, and it appealed more to veterans of the 1914–1918 war than to those of the 1940 war. Finally, the legion appealed more to those in the countryside more than those in the city: in the Loire 60 percent of the legionnaires were **peasants**, and only 4.5 percent of them were urban workers. In France as a whole the legion and some of its associated bodies claimed around 1.5 million members at the movement's peak in 1941.

As time went on, the legion began to experience problems. The movement's leaders sometimes set themselves up as the main pillar of the **National Revolution** and began to interfere in matters, such as the establishment of a corporatist state, that, having little to do with them, brought them into conflict with other authorities. The legion also became increasingly, if reluctantly, associated with **collaboration**. In May 1943 the mayor of a small town in the Loire suggested, perhaps in a bid to embarrass the legion, that its members might undertake the collection of radios that had been ordered by the Germans. In the Loire membership dropped from 10,000 in 1941 to 4,500 in 1944. In the Auvergne, even the peasantry, at whom the legion had directed so much of its propaganda, began to display hostility toward the organization.

J.-P. Cointet, "Anciens Combattants. La Légion Française des Combattants," in Fondation Nationale des Sciences Politiques, ed. (J. Bourdin and R. Rémond), *Le Gouvernement de Vichy, 1940–1942* (Paris, 1972), 123–43; J.-P. Cointet, *La Légion Française des Combattants* (Paris, 1995); J. Delperrié de Bayac, *Le Royaume du Maréchal* (Paris, 1975).

R. C. Vinen

LEHIDEUX, FRANÇOIS (1904–), was minister of **industrial production** in the early **Vichy** government. In 1929 Lehideux married Françoise Renault, niece of the engineer and automobile builder Louis Renault. This began a lifelong career of interest in heavy **industry** and technocracy. During the 1930s Lehideux was administrator for a number of industrial organizations and in 1938 for Renault aviation motors.

In July 1941 Lehideux was appointed minister of industrial production in the Vichy government of Admiral **Darlan**. With others in the government, he worked for a planned **economy**. Especially concerned with the industrial challenge presented by the **United States**, he was responsible for a 10-year plan that was to enable the Vichy government to close inefficient plants and raise industrial productivity. He left the government with the return of Pierre **Laval** to power in April 1942. It has been said that Lehideux, a technocrat above all, could have written the first chapter of *The American Challenge*, a 1960s bestseller in France.

After the war, Lehideux was active, serving as chairman of the board of directors in the **Association to Defend the Memory of Marshal Pétain**. In 1970 he participated in a colloquium organized by René Rémond and Janine Bourdin on the early years of the Vichy government. In it Lehideux defended his role in, and the policies of, the early Vichy government.

Fondation Nationale des Sciences Politiques, ed. (J. Bourdin and R. Rémond), *Le Gouvernement de Vichy 1940–1942* (Paris, 1972); J.-C. Hazera, *Les patrons sous l'occupation* (Paris, 1995); R. O. Paxton, *Vichy France, Old Guard and New Order, 1940–1944* (New York, 1972; H. Rousso, *The Vichy Syndrome, History and Memory in France since 1944*, trans. A. Goldhammer (Cambridge, MA, 1991).

E. H. Murphrey

LETTRES FRANÇAISES (LF, 1942–1972) was a clandestine literary journal, the organ of the Comité national des écrivains (National Writers' Committee,

CNÉ). Founded by Jacques Decour and Jean **Paulhan**, *Les Lettres Françaises,* one of the principal tribunes of the literary **Resistance**, effectuated an alliance of **communist (PCF)** and noncommunist writers.

In the context of the unified line adopted in mid-May 1941 by the clandestine PCF, and the subsequent project to set up a national front of intellectuals, Decour was commissioned to gather writers from all sides to launch a journal. In the fall of 1941, with Paulhan, he founded the first Front National des écrivains, the future CNÉ, enlisting Jean Blanzat, Jacques Debû-Bridel, Jean **Guéhenno**, François **Mauriac**, Father Jean Maydieu, and Charles Vildrac. A meeting to put together *LF*'s first issue occurred in December 1941, but the project was still-born. The arrest and execution of Decour in the spring of 1942 deferred publication of the journal, confided now to Claude Morgan, soon to be assisted by Georges Adam.

Dated September 1942, the first published issue was due to Morgan's efforts alone. It contained Decour's manifesto, which raised the question of a writers' struggle against the oppressor. Only with the fifth issue, January–February 1943, thanks to Edith Thomas, who reestablished contact with the CNÉ, did *LF* become a true literary journal. Henceforth, events, such as the Châteaubriant hostage massacre, and Resistance stories appeared together with poems, critiques, echoes of literary life, portraits exposing **collaborationist** writers, warnings addressed to the **Nouvelle Revue Française** and the Académie Goncourt (sympathetic to Vichy), and advertisements for clandestine works published by Éditions de Minuit. Mimeographed at first, the journal was printed beginning October 1943, going up to a run of 12,000. It was regularized as a monthly in 1944. In addition to those already cited, contributors included Louis Aragon, Albert **Camus**, Paul Eluard, André Frénaud, Jean Lescure, Michel Leiris, Loys Masson, Louis Parrot, Claude Roy, Raymond Queneau, André Rousseaux, Jean-Paul **Sartre**, Pierre Seghers, Jean Tardieu, and Elsa Triolet. Beginning with issue 14, March 1944, *LF* took under its wing *L'écran français* (French Screen) and *La scène française* (French Stage), organs of the Front National du cinéma and the Front National du théâtre, directed by René Blech.

Having become a weekly at the time of the **liberation,** *LF* published a "black list," drawn up by the CNÉ, of "undesirable" writers. *LF* remained the organ of the CNÉ through 1946, before being taken over by the PCF in 1947.

V. Conley, *Lire les Lettres françaises 1942–1972* (Madison, WI, 1973); J. Debû-Bridel, *La résistance intellectuelle* (Paris, 1945); C. Morgan, *Les Don Quichotte et les autres* (Paris, 1979); G. Sapiro, "La raison littéraire. Le champ littéraire français sous L'Occupation (1940–1944)," *Actes de la recherche en sciences sociales* 111–12 (March 1996): 3–35; A. Simonin, *Les Éditions de minuit 1942–1955: le devoir d'insoumission* (Paris, 1994).

G. Sapiro

LÉVY, JEAN-PIERRE (1911–1996), a resister, was head of the movement **Franc-Tireur**. From a **Jewish Alsatian** family and on the commercial staff of a jute weaving firm, he was drafted as a lieutenant in artillery in September 1939 and took refuge in Lyons, where he took up his trade again at the end of 1940. Anti-Nazi and wishing to fight against **Vichy**, he contacted Antoine Avinin and through him joined the France-Liberté group, which included Auguste Pinton, Noël Clavier, Elie Péju, and Jean-Jacques Soudeille. Lévy was the first to propose creating a clandestine newspaper, the *Franc-Tireur*, which appeared in December 1941. Around this paper there soon formed a movement with the same name. Young, with no political past, but profoundly **Republican**, democratic, and anti-Vichy, Lévy took over the leadership, thanks to his organizational skills and his profession, which allowed him to travel. In 1942 he met Henri **Frenay** and Emmanuel **d'Astier**, the leaders of **Combat** and Libération, respectively, and then General **de Gaulle's** emissary, Jean **Moulin**, who was impressed by Lévy's moderation. In favor of recognizing General **de Gaulle** as leader of the **Resistance**, he played the role of conciliator with the leaders of Combat and Libération, accepting the formation of the Secret **Army**, and then the establishment of the Mouvements Unis de Résistance. Interrogated three times in Lyons by the French **police** in 1941 and 1942, Lévy went into hiding.

Shortly after returning from a trip to London, in September 1943, Lévy was installed in **Paris** as representative of Franc-Tireur to the **Conseil National de la Résistance**. Arrested in October 1943, he was imprisoned in the Santé, from which a Franc-Tireur commando was able to free him in June 1944. Named a Compagnon de la Libération in the spring of 1943, Lévy refused to enter politics after the war and became instead a high state functionary.

L. Douzou and D. Veillon, "La Résistance des mouvements: ses débuts dans la région lyonnaise (1940–1942)," in *Mémoire et Histoire: La Résistance* (Toulouse, 1995), 149–159; D. Veillon, *Le Franc-Tireur: un journal clandestin, un mouvement de Résistance, 1940–1944* (Paris, 1977).

D. Veillon

LIBÉRATION refers to the removal of German and **Vichy** authority from France in favor of the **Provisional Government** of Charles **de Gaulle** and the **Resistance**. Since the war, the liberation has entered the realm of myth with interpretations on opposite ends of the political spectrum.

The military liberation of France began with the **Normandy** landings on 6 June 1944 and ended with the surrender of the last German troops from the Atlantic pockets on 8 May 1945. Most of the country, however, was liberated between July and October 1944 through the efforts of the Allied armies and the Resistance. France has no common date of liberation.

The "liberation," however, stands for more than the military struggle. It often refers to the few days during which the Germans withdrew from an area, and the local Resistance assumed control. These were highly emotional days, filled with **symbolic** gestures such as **maquisard** parades and public head-shavings of **women** accused as "**horizontal collaborators**." The "liberation" also refers to the entire troubled period encompassing the restoration of **Republican** government in **Paris**, the resumption of electoral democracy, the **purge** of collaborators, and the deterioration of food supplies. This period might be dated from 6 June 1944 to the time of the return of the political deportees and **prisoners** of war from German captivity in April and May 1945, to de Gaulle's resignation as president on 20 January 1946, or to the acceptance of a new constitution in November 1946. All of these indicate the provisional nature of the liberation as a transitional period between war and peace.

A. Bendjebbar, *Libérations rêvées, Libérations vécues* (Paris, 1994); A. Brossat, *Libération, fête folle* (Paris, 1994); M. Koreman, "A Hero's Homecoming: The Return of the Deportees to France, 1945," *JCH* 32:1 (January 1997): 9–22; T. Todorov, *A French Tragedy: Scenes of Civil War, Summer 1944*, trans. M. B. Kelly (Hanover, NH, 1996 [original French ed., 1994]).

M. Koreman

LIBÉRATION-NORD was one of the largest **Resistance** movements in the northern **zone**, created by Christian **Pineau** in November 1941 and active until the **liberation of Paris** in August 1944. The movement was built around a group that signed, on 15 November 1940, the "Manifesto of the Twelve," consisting of **syndicalists** who had formed a committee of economic and syndicalist studies. Among the signers of this manifesto are to be found nine **Confédération Générale du Travail** (GCT) members: Oreste Capocci, François Chevalme, Albert Gazier, Eugène Jaccoud, Robert Lacoste, Pierre Neumeyer, Christian **Pineau**, Louis Saillant, and Victor Vandeputte; and three Christian syndicalists: Maurice Bouladoux, Gaston Tessier, and Jules Zirnheld. The work of this committee was published regularly in a legalized bulletin that served as a cover for the clandestine newspaper *Libération-nord*, whose first issue appeared 1 December 1940. The first issues of the newspaper were edited and produced by Pineau, who used the **BBC** as his main source of information.

The Liberation-nord movement, whose official birth was announced in its newspaper of 30 November 1941, expressed the syndicalist viewpoint of the noncommunist elements of the clandestine GCT, the Confédération française des travailleurs chrétiens, and the **socialists** in the Resistance. Syndicalist organization, with vertical and horizontal structures, permitted a quick and extensive recruitment of fighters. Following Pineau's return from his first trip to London in the spring of 1942, the Liberation-nord movement was largely under socialist influence. At its head was Henri Ribière; its newspaper was turned over to Jean Texcier. By the start of 1943, the movement began to organize armed groups under the impetus of Jean Cavaillès and under the direction of Colonel Georges Zarapoff. *Liberation-nord* was represented in the **Conseil National de la Résistance (CNR)** but in December 1943 refused to participate in the **Mouvement Unis de la Résistance (MUR)**.

M. Granet, "Liberation-Nord"; C. Pineau, *La simple vérité* (Paris, 1983).

A. Aglan

LIBÉRATION-SUD was a **Resistance** movement born of the desire "to do something" in the fall of 1940 in Clermont-Ferrand. Included were the journalist Emmanuel **d'Astier** de la Vigerie, the philosopher Jean Cavaillès, the history teacher Lucie **Aubrac**, and the banker Georges Zérapha.

After having just scraped by in the winter of 1940–1941, this small core, whose activity consisted at first of plastering walls with inscriptions and leaflets, then spreading tracts, in July 1941 began publishing a newspaper with the title *Libération*. Marked by its radical opposition to the **Vichy** government, the group grew, thanks to the support of Léon Jouhaux for the **Confédération Générale du Travail (CGT)** and Daniel **Mayer** for the clandestine **Socialist** Party. By the summer of 1941, Libération-sud was in contact with Libération-Nationale, headed by Henri **Frenay**, and Liberté, led by Pierre-Henri **Teitgen** and François **de Menthon**. A merger, which had been discussed beginning in 1941, was achieved at the beginning of 1943 when **Combat** (itself a product of the fusion of Libération-Nationale and Liberté at the end of 1941), **Franc-Tireur**, and Libération-sud formed the **Mouvements Unis de la Résistance (MUR)**.

Beginning in the spring of 1943, Libération-sud was suspected of harboring clandestine **communist** agents. Some historians have seen Libération-sud as the **Communist** Party's Trojan horse in the leadership of the unified **Resistance** in 1943 and 1944. Archival material presently accessible does not support this assertion, which reflects less the historical reality than the ideological struggles played out during the past 50 years concerning the history of the French Resistance.

L. Douzou, *La désobéissance. Histoire du mouvement Libération-sud* (Paris, 1995); H. Noguères, M. Degliame-Fouché, and J.-L. Vigier, *Histoire de la Résistance en France de 1940 à 1945*, 5 vols. (Paris, 1967–1981); unpublished material, Archives Nationales, Paris, file 72 AJ 60.

L. Douzou

LIÉNART, CARDINAL ACHILLE (1884–1973), French prelate of progressive reputation who sought neutrality during the Occupation yet felt compelled to resist the Germans in specific instances. When war was declared against Germany in 1939, Achille Liénart had been the bishop of Lille for over a decade and a cardinal for nine years. Described by Catholic critics as the "red cardinal" because of his support of the organized textile workers of his diocese, Liénart was also critical of **Action Française** and the **right-wing** Fédération Nationale Catholique. Enmeshed in the anti-Bolshevism characteristic of the interwar French church, he rejected **communist** overtures to the Catholics.

A patriot, Liénart chose in 1940 to remain at his post as pastor and urged the defeated French neither to side with the victor nor to resist. Nonetheless, he was caught up in the episcopate's collective support and veneration of **Pétain**. Like his colleagues, Liénart was happy to see a pro-Catholic state replace the Third **Republic**, even though **Vichy** was authoritarian.

In spite of this he remained circumspect, and his lack of enthusiasm for Nazi

Germany made him suspect in the eyes of the occupiers. He was also critical of Vichy's Labor Charter, which abolished free trade unions. Liénart also joined other church leaders in protesting the roundup of **Jews** at the **Vélodrome d'hiver** in **Paris** (July 1942). Liénart's main **resistance** activity was his vigorous protest against the labor requisition program, the **Service du Travail Obligatoire**.

Achille Liénart's career as a prince of the church was fraught with ambivalence. His anticommunism and suspicion of the Republic inclined him favorably toward Pétain. His progressive and pro-worker instincts, however, led him toward resistance and led him to play a creative role in moving his church in radical directions after the **liberation**.

J. Duquesne, *Les Catholiques français sous l'occupation* (Paris, 1966); J. Vinatier, *Le cardinal Liénart et la Mission de France* (Paris, 1978); J. Vinatier, *Les Prêtres ouvriers, le cardinal Liénart et Rome* (Paris, 1985).

O. L. Cole-Arnal

LIGUE FRANÇAISE was a Parisian **collaborationist** movement, founded on 15 September 1940 by Dominique Félix Pascal, better known as Pierre Costantini. Born in 1889 in Sartène, **Corsica**, Costantini became a pilot who flew missions in World War I. He was secretary-general of the **Comité France-Allemagne** in Berlin in 1936. During the 1940 campaign, he served as a commander in the reserves.

Angered by the 3 July 1940 **British** attack on the French fleet at **Mers-el-Kébir**, Costantini created the Ligue Française d'épuration, d'entraide sociale et de collaboration européene (French League for Purification, Mutual Social Aid, and European Collaboration), better known by the first two words of its name. In January 1941, the Ligue Française was granted official German sanction by Julius von Westrick, a consular official acquainted with Costantini from his Berlin days. Beginning 6 March 1941, Costantini published a newspaper, *L'Appel* (The Call) and the following summer joined the steering committee of the newly created anti-Bolshevik **Légion des Voluntaires Français**. Costantini's erratic behavior meant he was taken less seriously than other collaborationist leaders, and his party was unable to develop the strength of some of its rivals. He therefore allied with the larger **Parti Populaire Français**, 2 September 1941.

On 14 and 15 November, the Ligue Française held a party congress but could attract at most 2,000 or 3,000 from all France, of whom 150 to 200 came from **Paris**. By June 1944, the movement had clearly failed, and Costantini went to the **Russian** front. He returned at the end of July to participate in the evacuation of his men. After fleeing to Germany, he was arrested and returned to France. In 1952 he was judged not responsible for his actions. He quietly lived out the rest of his days in Corsica, dying as a near centenarian in 1986.

B. M. Gordon, *Collaborationism in France during the Second World War* (Ithaca, NY,

1980); P.-P. Lambert and G. Le Marec, *Partis et Mouvements de la Collaboration, Paris 1940–1944* (Paris, 1993).

G. Le Marec

LOUSTAUNAU-LACAU, GEORGES (1894–1955) was an **army** officer, **right-wing** politician, and **Resistance** figure. A Saint-Cyr graduate, Loustaunau-Lacau saw heroic service in World War I. Blaming the **Left** and the army's leadership for failures to modernize the army, he established the Corvignolles in 1936, an unofficial organization of army officers, ostensibly to combat **communists** in the military but possibly to prepare a military coup on the model of General Franco's in **Spain**. He established contact with Eugène **Deloncle** but denied ever having joined Deloncle's Cagoule. Cashiered in 1938 for his political activity by defense minister Édouard **Daladier**, Loustaunau-Lacau created a political movement espousing anticommunism, **anti-Semitism**, and patriotism but failed to achieve a large following. With the outbreak of World War II, Loustaunau-Lacau rejoined the army, was wounded, and was taken **prisoner**. He escaped on 15 August 1940 and made his way to **Vichy**.

With his return to France, Loustaunau-Lacau rebuilt his prewar group, which in 1941 he turned over to his most trusted political colleague, Marie-Madeleine Méric (after World War II, Marie-Madeleine Fourcade), who helped develop the group into the **Alliance Resistance** network. Fourcade, who twice escaped from Nazi arrest, won later renown for her leadership role in the Resistance. Loustaunau-Lacau himself maintained contacts with Vichy, **Paris**, and London. In Algiers in May 1941, he discussed a revolt of French North Africa against Germany but was arrested by French authorities there. Released, he returned to metropolitan France but was arrested again in July. Sentenced by Vichy to two years' imprisonment for "dissidence," Loustaunau-Lacau was sent in 1943 by the Germans to the Mauthausen **concentration camp**, from which he emerged barely alive at the end of the war.

Loustaunau-Lacau testified on behalf of **Pétain** in 1945, wrote books, and in 1951 was elected a deputy from the Basses-Pyrénées. He was promoted to reserve brigadier general by Premier Pierre Mendès-France but died soon after of a heart attack, on 11 February 1955.

M.-M. Fourcade, *Noah's Ark*, trans. K. Morgan (New York, 1974); G. Loustaunau-Lacau, *Mémoires d'un français rebelle 1914–1948* (Geneva, 1972 [original ed., Paris, 1948]).

J. Blatt

LUCHAIRE, JEAN (1901–1946), French journalist and president of the Corporation de la presse française and longtime friend of the German ambassador in **Paris**, Otto **Abetz**, with whom he promoted Franco–German **youth** congresses from 1930 to 1932. Commissioned to organize the first **Abetz–Laval** meeting as soon as the **armistice** was signed, Luchaire was valued both by the German forces and, at the beginning of the Occupation, by the **Vichy** government for his support of a Franco–German reconciliation. He received financial support from both sides.

Luchaire was in charge of giving directives to the **press**. During the Occupation, he became the editor in chief of *Le Matin*, then restarted *Notre Temps,* a newspaper he had founded in 1927, under the new name *Les Temps Nouveaux.* With its weekly magazine, *Toute la Vie, Les Temps Nouveaux* appeared until August 1944 and was strongly pro-**collaborationist**. Luchaire became coeditor of *L'Oeuvre* with Marcel **Déat** and joined the Comité d'honneur of the anti-Bolshevik Legion (LVF) in 1941. Instrumental in Laval's return to the political scene in 1942, Luchaire sought an alliance with Germany, where even **Pétain** and Laval hesitated. In 1943, he signed an anti-Vichy government "Plan de redressement national français," denouncing Vichy for being insufficiently **fascist** and too reticent in collaboration with Germany.

Following the **liberation** in 1944, he fled Paris and was nominated Commissaire à l'Information of the **Sigmaringen** government, where, with German help, he broadcast a **radio** program, *Ici la France*, and published a daily newspaper, *La France*, supporting continued collaboration with Germany. With the German defeat, Luchaire fled to **Italy** before being turned over to the French authorities. He was sentenced and executed in December 1946.

Les Procès de Collaboration (Paris, 1948); C. Luchaire, *Ma drôle de vie* (Paris, 1948).

M. Guyot-Bender

LUXEMBURG was neutral after the London Treaty of 1867. The Grand Duchy was occupied by Germany from 1914 through 1918 and from May 1940 through September 1944 and was partly overrun during the December 1944 Ardennes offensive. Luxemburg was strictly neutral during the **Phoney War**, but popular sympathy there strongly favored the Allied cause.

Alerted to the predawn invasion of 10 May 1940, the grand ducal government fled to France and eventually to **Britain**. A German military government was replaced in August 1940 by a civil administration under *Gauleiter* Gustav Simon, whose objective was the incorporation of Luxemburg into Germany. Laws and regulations attempted to obliterate French cultural influences and initiated a comprehensive National Socialist *Gleichschaltung* (coordination). Parliamentary government and political parties were abolished. A German-sponsored political party, the Volksdeutsche Bewegung (VdB), closely supervised by Simon and his Nazi cohorts, failed to win popular support for union with Germany. Active and passive opposition precipitated German retaliation, arrests, executions, or resettlement in eastern Germany. The **Jewish** community was an early target for **deportation** and eventual annihilation.

Simon's program culminated in August 1942 in the introduction of military conscription for the classes of 1920 through 1924, the final step in a de facto annexation. Over 3,000 *Enrôlés de force* (forced enrollees) perished, but others evaded military service, aided by Luxemburg **Resistance** groups working with networks of the Armée blanche, a Belgian Resistance movement in the Ardennes area, and the **Forces françaises de l'intérieur (FFI)**. The government-in-exile's decision to abandon neutrality permitted an active, if modest, role in the **liberation** by U.S. forces in September 1944.

P. Dostert, *Luxembourg zwischen Selbstbehauptung und nationaler Selbstaufgabe: die deutsche Besatzungspolitik und die Volksdeutsche Bewegung, 1940–1945* (Luxemburg, 1985); W. A. Fletcher, "*Plan und Wirklichkeit*: German Military Government in Luxemburg, 1940," in G. O. Kent, ed., *Historians and Archivists* (Fairfax, VA, 1991), 145–72; E. Haag and E. Krier, *La Grande-Duchesse et son gouvernement pendant la deuxième guerre mondiale: 1940, l'année du dilemme* (Luxemburg, 1987).

W. A. Fletcher

M

MADAGASCAR RESETTLEMENT PLAN was an idea, never implemented, that involved the transport of European **Jews** to the French colony of Madagascar during the Second World War. Although serious attempts to carry out the plan were never made, it was well known and publicized throughout the Reich, even to the extent that **prisoners** at Treblinka often believed themselves to be on the verge of transfer to Madagascar.

The interwar idea of moving Jews to Madagascar seems to have had both Zionist and **anti-Semitic** origins. The French **socialist** deputy Marius Moulet had written of the possibility of sending Jewish immigrants to settle in this sparsely populated Indian Ocean island, and the idea appears to have been discussed in the 1938 meeting between German and French foreign ministers Joachim von Ribbentrop and Georges **Bonnet**.

The wartime plan, first formulated by Nazi governor-general of Poland Hans Frank, apparently had the support of **Hitler**, who occasionally mentioned it, although he avoided details. After the defeat of France, Madagascar was to be ceded to the Reich, which would then establish a ''colony'' of European Jews there who could be supervised by the SS. The transfer, which would be funded by the sale of seized Jewish property, was to provide for a ''solution'' to the ''Jewish Question,'' although it is unlikely that it was ever conceived of as the Final Solution. Reinhard Heydrich, in particular, liked the plan, and it was used primarily for propaganda purposes, convincing both Jewish prisoners and concerned Germans that the **deportation** of Jews was part of a benevolent plan. Evidence for this is suggested by the fact that Hitler continued to speak of the plan as late as October 1942, by which time at least 2 million Jews had already been murdered. Madagascar, in any event, soon after passed into **British** and then Gaullist hands.

R. Hilberg, *The Destruction of the European Jews* (New York, 1985 [original ed., 1961]); M. R. Marrus and R. O. Paxton, *Vichy France and the Jews* (New York, 1981).

S. D. Armus

MAGINOT LINE was the construction during the 1930s of a fortified barrier in northeast France to protect against German invasion. Based on funding voted upon in the Chamber of Deputies in 1929, these fortifications aptly carried the name of war minister André Maginot, a wounded veteran of World War I. The building of the Maginot Line reflected a civilian and military consensus in the 1920s reflecting a shared appreciation of the demographic and economic losses of World War I. With military service requirements reduced from three years to one under popular pressure during this decade, the High Command formulated the military doctrine of total defense of French soil.

Originally, the Maginot Line was to provide security against a German attack, but it also underlined France's unwillingness to undertake offensive military planning after the four-power 1925 Locarno agreement that was to guarantee the Franco–German border. The Maginot Line also enhanced the lengthy mobilization plans and wait for Allies that had come to characterize French war planning. Finally, a "Maginot mentality" produced an unwillingness or inability to fulfill eastern alliance obligations, an all-or-nothing approach to mobilization that precluded graduated deterrence, and a reluctance among generals and politicians to consider military innovation or psychologically prepare the French nation for war.

The still-controversial decision not to extend the line from the Ardennes to the North Sea helped ensure that a German attack would occur in **Belgium** rather than in France, but a Belgian shift to neutrality after German remilitarization of the Rhineland in 1936 further confused French planning. When the German Blitzkrieg finally hit on 10 May 1940, the Maginot Line played a very minor role in an ensuing battle characterized by a panzer drive through the Ardennes as the bulk of the French **army** misguidedly moved into beleaguered Belgium. The Maginot Line came to **symbolize** a futile and wasteful mismanagement by a shortsighted military elite. Still the property of the French army, Maginot Line fortifications may be visited today.

*H. Dutailly, *Les Problèmes de l'armée de terre française* (Vincennes, 1980); P. Gamelin, *La Ligne Maginot, Images d'hier et d'aujourd'hui* (Paris, 1979); J. Hughes, *To the Maginot Line: The Politics of French Military Preparedness in the 1920s* (Cambridge, MA, 1970); V. Rowe, *The Great Wall of France, the Triumph of the Maginot Line* (London, 1959).

R. F. Crane

MAILLOL, ARISTIDE (1861–1944), French sculptor, painter, and woodcut artist noted for his massive female nudes and neo-classical style. He was greatly admired by the Germans, including the "Reich sculptor in chief," Arno **Breker**.

Maillol is considered one of the most important figures in the transition from the style of Rodin to modernist sculpture. Celebrated in France during the early twentieth century, his popularity began to decline in the 1930s. The rise of Nazism boosted his career because the Nazis greatly admired his art, seeing in it the manifestation of their ideals of heroism and nostalgia for a simple agrarian life. Invited to tour Germany in 1942 with other French sculptors, he declined because of his advanced age.

Maillol's relationship to the Nazis was not entirely clear. He did not object to Nazi control over art, and throughout the war he exhibited in shows that they promoted. Furthermore, his son was a member of the **Milice Française**. However, Maillol's **Jewish** model, Dina Vierny, ran a small **Resistance** network of which he was aware. Moreover, he allowed his studio in Puyg del Mas to be used as a hiding place for **refugees** and resisters escaping to **Spain**. When Vierny was arrested by the Germans, Maillol's friend Arno Breker got her released. Nazi approval of Maillol's work led to recriminations after the **liberation**. He died as a result of a car accident shortly after the liberation, in September 1944.

L. Bertrand Dorléac, *L'art de la défaite 1940–1944* (Paris, 1993); M. C. Cone, *Artists under Vichy: A Case of Prejudice and Persecution* (Princeton, 1992); J. Fenton, "The Secrets of Maillol," *New York Review of Books* 43:8 (9 May 1996): 47–55; D. Pryce-Jones, *Paris in the Third Reich* (New York, 1981).

D. D. Buffton

MALRAUX, ANDRÉ (1901–1976), **left-wing** novelist who joined the **Resistance** in 1944 and became a disciple of **de Gaulle**.

With the publication in 1933 of *La Condition humaine,* Malraux established himself as a writer sympathetic to revolutionary causes. In the same year he and André **Gide** traveled to Germany, seeking the release of prominent communists charged with the Reichstag fire. Copresident of the World Committee against **Fascism**, he fought against Franco in the Spanish civil war.

Following the Spanish Republican defeat in 1939, Malraux returned to France. Disillusioned by the Nazi–**Soviet** nonaggression pact, he volunteered for military service in September 1939. Assigned to a tank division situated far from the front lines, he was taken **prisoner** in the retreat of June 1940. He escaped in September 1940 and sought refuge in the unoccupied **zone**, where for two years he led an apolitical life. When Germany occupied the southern zone in November 1942, Malraux moved inland from the Mediterranean to Périgord, where his brother was a **maquisard**. Adopting the code name Colonel Berger, Malraux joined the Resistance in 1944, coordinating the *maquis* units in his region. Working with **British** agents, he supervised a massive arms drop in July 1944 that enabled the maquisards to obstruct the German army as it moved north. Captured days later, imprisoned, and interrogated by the Gestapo, he was freed on 18 August 1944 by the German retreat from Toulouse. Appointed commander of the **Alsace-Lorraine** Brigade, he and his unit fought vigorously during the fall of 1944 to liberate Alsace. He broke with the **communists** in January 1945, joined the Movement de libération national, and in 1946 served briefly as minister of information. Henceforth a devoted Gaullist, Malraux returned to politics in 1959 as de Gaulle's minister of cultural affairs, a position he held until 1969.

In 1996, 20 years after his death, in a high honor to his memory, Malraux's remains were transferred to the Panthéon of France.

*†J. Lacouture, *André Malraux* (New York, 1975); H. Lebovics, "André Malraux: A Hero for France's Unheroic Age," *FPS* 15:1 (Winter 1997): 58–69; A. Madsen, *Malraux: A Biography* (New York, 1976); A. Malraux, *Anti-Memoirs* (New York, 1968); J. Wilkinson, *The Intellectual Resistance in Europe* (Cambridge, MA, 1981).

M. Hanna

MANDEL, GEORGES (1885–1944), was a French statesman and patriot, one of the most important of the *bellicistes*, who opposed appeasement of Nazi Germany and strongly favored a Franco–**Soviet** alliance. He refused to accept defeat in 1940, was jailed by the **Vichy** government, and was murdered by the **Milice Française** in July 1944.

Mandel, of **Jewish** ancestry, was a journalist in Paris at the turn of the century. He later worked for Georges Clemenceau, **interior** minister and premier (1906–1909). During Clemenceau's second tenure as premier (1917–1920), Mandel became his right-hand man on the home front in the repression and prosecution of defeatists and control of the **press** and the labor movement. His role as Clemenceau's hatchet man won him both hatred and respect.

Mandel entered the government for the first time in 1934 as postal minister. In 1936 he advocated the formation of a National Union government, and he pressed for a Franco–Soviet military alliance. France, he argued, had either to abdicate its security interests in Eastern Europe, or collaborate with all those countries threatened by Nazi Germany. One of the last Clemencists, he was convinced that war with Nazi Germany was inevitable, and he preferred to get on with it sooner rather than later. In 1938 Mandel opposed the **Munich agreement**. Some thought Mandel might be a second Clemenceau, but his religion got in the way. The **Right** accused him of being a warmonger, advocating **resistance** to Nazism because he was a Jew. In September 1939 he stood for an immediate offensive against the German army; instead, France waged the **Phoney War**. After the collapse of the French front in 1940, Mandel remained defiant. The **British** tried unsuccessfully to rescue Mandel from Morocco, where he had gone in June 1940. Local authorities blocked the attempt. He was "the first resister," according to Winston Churchill, and willing to fight on alone. His arrest by **Pétain's** government in June 1940 was a great loss to **Free France**.

*J.-N. Jeanneney, *Georges Mandel: l'homme qu'on attendait* (Paris, 1991); J. M. Sherwood, *Georges Mandel and the Third Republic* (Stanford, CA, 1970).

M. J. Carley

MAQUIS, a word originally designating thick underbrush on the island of **Corsica**, where anybody fleeing from justice could hide safely, used also in World War II to designate places where **Resistance** fighters could hide and also to designate the fighters themselves.

The geographic configuration of France did not lend itself in most areas to the creation of clandestine military operations against the German forces. There were some attempts at sabotage, early on, quickly punished by execution. In the unoccupied **zone**, large, wooded regions offered an ideal site for military re- sisters, although it took time after the shock of the 1940 defeat to get sufficient recruits. In June 1941, after the German invasion of **Soviet Russia**, the situation changed dramatically. Since all **Communist** and **Socialist** Party members were hunted, many of them went into hiding. The thinly populated existing *maquis* grew, and new networks were created, often close to German garrisons. When forced labor for all young Frenchmen, the **Service du Travail Obligatoire**, was initiated, many joined the various *maquis* as *réfractaires* (objectors). Still, arms were scarce. Increasing, but still insufficient, air drops by the Allies helped. The occupation of all of France in November 1942 eased communication between the two formerly separated zones. While the north afforded few opportunities for clandestine military operations, the southern zone saw many surprise attacks on German forces, harassing them, inhibiting their movements, and inflicting casualties. The Germans retaliated brutally.

As coordination progressed, and the various politically different segments of the Resistance became unified, *maquis* operations gradually grew more effective. These political differences went from the extreme **Right** and from military career officers to moderate, **socialist**, and communist units. The communists frequently tried to ensure the predominance of their party after the **liberation**. In London, however, the French counterintelligence under Colonel **Passy** often overstated communist influence, leading, in one case, to the failure to air-drop arms to the *maquis* prior to its decimation at the Battle of **Vercors**.

The military command of the unified Resistance tried to avoid casualties wherever possible, as the main goal of all armed Resistance was to coordinate their efforts with an eventual Allied landing. Nonetheless, assisted by the rail- road workers' sabotage of both track and rolling stock, still underarmed but determined, the *maquis* of the Massif Central inflicted heavy losses on superior German forces supported by tanks and planes. After D-Day, the *maquis* of **Nor- mandy** and Brittany supported the Allied landing operations. Their assistance was acknowledged by General Eisenhower as invaluable in producing the suc- cess of Operation Overlord. *Maquis* units also delayed reinforcements the Ger- mans tried to bring from southwest France to the Normandy front.

The psychological impact of the *maquis* on the German soldiers cannot be overestimated. Military and police, including the Gestapo, saw the *maquis* as a constant threat throughout early 1944. The liberation of France was due pri- marily to the Allied forces, but their action was powerfully seconded by the French Forces of the Interior (FFI), which suffered heavy losses throughout the campaign. The bloodiest battles were the ones at **Glières** and the Vercors.

R. Aron, *France Reborn, the History of the Liberation,* trans. H. Hare (New York, 1964 [original French ed., 1959]); M.-M. Fourcade, *L'Arche de Noé* (Paris, 1968); H. -

R. Kedward, *In Search of the Maquis, Rural Resistance in Southern France* (Oxford, 1993); H. Michel, *Histoire de la Résistance* (Paris, 1950).

K. Bieber

MARCHANDEAU LAW, named after justice minister Paul Marchandeau and promulgated in the form of a decree by the **Daladier** government on 21 April 1939, forbade attacks of a racial or religious nature in the press by modifying Articles 32, 33, and 60 of the freedom of the press law of 25 July 1881.

The Marchandeau Law was indicative of widespread xenophobia and **anti-Semitism**, which authorities regarded as a threat to public order and national unity. In the context of mounting international tensions, rising unemployment, and increased immigration, **Jews** were repeatedly portrayed as job stealers, economic parasites, destabilizing radicals, rapacious capitalists, and cultural invaders and were subject to virulent, scurrilous attacks, mainly from extreme **right-wing** newspapers. The Marchandeau Law was abrogated by **Pétain's justice minister**, Raphaël Alibert, on 27 August 1940. Presented in **press** releases as the abolition of a privilege, the nullification of the Marchandeau Law, in fact, opened the door to unbridled anti-Semitic attacks, which immediately reappeared with renewed vigor.

M. Marrus and R. O. Paxton, *Vichy France and the Jews* (New York, 1881); D. Rémy, *Les lois de Vichy* (Paris, 1992); S. Zucotti, *The Holocaust, the French, and the Jews* (New York, 1993).

N. Bracher

MARION, PAUL (1899–1954), head of propaganda services under the **Vichy** government from 1941 until early 1944. Marion's interwar itinerary took him from the French **Communist** Party in the 1920s, through the neosocialist and the *non-conformiste* milieux in the early 1930s, to Jacques **Doriot's Parti Populaire Français (PPF)**, where he remained from 1936 until the eve of the war. Throughout the 1930s, he worked to create a *"rassemblement national,"* a mass movement led by an elite of dissidents recruited from across the political spectrum, with the objective of forging a "third way" between parliamentary democracy and communism. In the most successful of these attempts, Doriot's PPF, Marion played a leading role as party propagandist and ideologist. As with so many others in the French forces in 1940, Marion was taken prisoner by the Germans.

Shortly after his release from a German prison camp, Marion joined the Vichy government, where, in August 1941, he became secretary-general for information in the **Darlan** ministry. Associated with the technocratic and **collaborationist** faction at Vichy, he launched a formidable, though finally unsuccessful, effort to build a totalitarian-style propaganda machine that would oversee the regimentation of French society. He also pushed—once again, without final success—for the creation of a *parti unique* and a *jeunesse unique* (single party and single **youth** organization). This activity aroused the hostility of traditionalists, who managed to block Marion from achieving his larger ambitions. Upon Pierre **Laval's** return to power in April 1942, Marion became secretary of state for information, though his effective power was more limited than under Darlan. He fled to Germany in 1944. Having returned to France after the defeat of Germany, Marion was condemned to 10 years in prison.

*D. Peschanski, "Vichy au singulier, Vichy au pluriel," *Annales* 3 (May–June 1988); G. M. Thomas, "The Political Career and Ideas of Paul Marion" (Diss., Oxford University, 1970).

P. Mazgaj

MARITAIN, JACQUES (1882–1973), religious and philosophical thinker. As a student, Maritain came under the influence of the philosopher Henri Bergson, the poet Charles Péguy, and the Catholic writer Léon Bloy—ties that led him to reject his family's Protestantism and the Sorbonne's scientism. In 1906, Maritain and his wife, Raïssa Oumansoff, the daughter of Russian-**Jewish** parents, converted to **Roman Catholicism**. Four years later, he began the systematic study of Saint Thomas Aquinas, the thinker who most deeply shaped his religious writings.

An early and regretted flirtation with Charles **Maurras'** writings came to an end in 1926 with the papal condemnation of **Action Française**. During the 1930s, Maritain committed himself to democratic and liberal causes; *Humanisme intégrale*, published in 1936, placed these values in a Thomistic context. Maritain inspired a number of Catholic intellectual manifestos, ranging from the defense of pluralist and humanist societies to the condemnation of the bombing of Guernica. He also spoke out against the rise of **anti-Semitism**.

Maritain was lecturing in North America when France fell in 1940. The Maritains remained in Canada and the **United States**, devoting themselves to political activity on behalf of a free France. In 1941, Maritain published *À travers le désastre*, which denounced the policy of **collaboration** and emphasized that hope resided in the French people, not any single individual—not only a dismissal of **Pétain's** pretensions but also a warning aimed at Charles **de Gaulle**. Though maintaining his independence from the Gaullist movement, Maritain served as French ambassador to the Vatican from 1945 to 1948.

*B. Doering, *Jacques Maritain and the French Catholic Intellectuals* (Notre Dame, IN, 1983); J. M. Dunaway, *Jacques Maritain* (Boston, 1978); J. Maritain, *Oeuvres Complètes* (Fribourg, 1987).

R. D. Zaretsky

MARQUET, ADRIEN (1884–1955), Bordeaux's astute, ambitious, and opportunistic political boss from 1925 through 1944, was the third **Republic's** last **interior** minister and the first of the **État Français**.

This dentist of uncertain parentage led the "neosocialists" out of the **Socialist** Party in 1933. Soon, his supporters, echoing Bordeaux's Boulangist past, were marching around in blue-gray shirts, condemning Republican institutions. The **right-wing** journal *Je Suis Partout* pinpointed him as a potential dictator.

Marquet supported the **Munich agreement** and denounced Léon **Blum** as a warmonger for the **Soviet Union** and world **Jewry**. When the government moved to Bordeaux on 14 June 1940, he threw the weight of the Gironde's political machine behind Pierre **Laval**. On 28 June, the day after becoming Marshal **Pétain's** interior minister, he formally welcomed the Germans to Bordeaux.

Until leaving office in September 1940, Marquet replaced Republican officials and put under surveillance groups whose loyalty was suspect (foreigners, Frenchmen who had been out of France in May and June, **Freemasons, communists**, and Jews). He also opened lines of communication with the SS and the German ambassador, Otto **Abetz**, in **Paris**. He established the Center for French Propaganda for European Reconstruction and participated in various **collaborationist** activities, traveling frequently to Paris, where he worked to advance his own political fortunes and to ameliorate German regulations and reprisals. Once German victory seemed less likely, however, Marquet's collaborationism cooled.

Arrested in August 1944, Marquet was sentenced to death in January 1948. The verdict was commuted. As much a product of the decline and fall of Third Republic democracy as a child of Eurofascism, Marquet loved power but never used it for personal enrichment.

*R. Dufourg, *Adrien Marquet devant la Haute Cour* (Paris, 1948); S. Mazey and V. Wright, ''Les préfets,'' in J.-P. Azéma and F. Bédarida, eds., *Le régime de Vichy et les Français* (Paris, 1992), 267–86; R. Terrisse, *Bordeaux, 1940–1944* (Paris, 1993).

H. H. Hunt

MARTY, ANDRÉ (1886–1956) was a French **communist** leader active in Moscow and Algiers. As a naval engineer, Marty, opposed to French intervention against the Bolshevik revolution in 1917, led a mutiny in France's Black Sea fleet. Tried and imprisoned, he was released in 1923 as a result of popular protests. He immediately joined the **Communist Party (PCF)**, rapidly becoming a member of its Central Committee and a parliamentary deputy. Appointed to the Comintern executive in 1932, he played a leading role in the International Brigades during the Spanish civil war.

In 1939 he became the French delegate to the Comintern secretariat in Moscow and was, accordingly, among the communist deputies stripped of their nationality. In the **USSR** during the early Occupation years, he attempted to establish a political headquarters for the PCF and campaigned for a clandestine, military-style party organization, castigating what he viewed as the naive parliamentarianism of the leadership in France. He later made broadcasts on Radio-Moscow aimed at France.

In November 1943, after the dissolution of the Comintern, Marty became leader of the communist group of representatives in the Assemblée consultative in Algiers. In the spring of 1944, the communists entered the *Comité Française de Libération Nationale*, later the **Provisional Government**, but Marty was overshadowed by the more politically astute Fernand Grenier and François Billoux, who became ministers. Fiery and acerbic, Marty made enemies easily and did not disguise his contempt for PCF leader Maurice **Thorez**.

Marty was a determined advocate of using the **Resistance** movements and their **liberation** committees as a launching pad for a **socialist** revolution in France. This aspiration found widespread support among rank-and-file communists but was firmly rejected by the majority of the leadership, who accepted Thorez's report that Stalin had decided otherwise. At the liberation, Marty was nominated to the PCF secretariat but was expelled from it, along with Charles **Tillon**, in 1952 in a row that rekindled wartime controversies.

*Y. Le Braz, *Les Rejetés du P.C.F.: l'affaire Marty-Tillon* (Paris, 1974).

M. Kelly

MASSILIA was the steamship that took 27 French political leaders from France to North Africa (21–24 June 1940).

With Marshal **Pétain's** consent and in the expectation that they might become the advance party of a French government move to North Africa, 26 deputies and one senator sailed from Bordeaux on 21 June for Casablanca. The most prominent among them were former premier Édouard **Daladier**, former minister of foreign affairs Yvon Delbos, and former minister of the **interior** Georges **Mandel**. By the time the *Massilia* reached Morocco, things had changed in the metropole. An **armistice** with German had been signed and the government was enroute to **Vichy**. Casablanca and Algiers were forgotten. The 27 political refugees were now seen as an embarrassment, potential troublemakers beyond the reach of metropolitan authority.

Only Mandel, who was on record as a die-hard opponent of any accommodation with Germany, posed any real problem for the new regime in France. Most of the other passengers on the *Massilia* wanted nothing more than to return home as quickly as possible. Mandel, however, spoke with both French and **British** representatives in Morocco about setting up a **Resistance** government. Even a top-level mission from London (which included a cabinet minister) was sent to Rabat to try to make contact with him. It was prevented from doing so by French authorities in Morocco.

The French **press** of the day described the voyage of the *Massilia* as a flight from France by deserters and traitors. It was nothing of the sort. Above all, it was a patriotic mission that failed.

R. Champoux, "The Massilia Affair," *JCH* 10: 2 (April 1975): 283–300; J. M. Sherwood, *Georges Mandel and the Third Republic* (Stanford, CA, 1970).

W. A. Hoisington, Jr.

MATISSE, HENRI (1869–1954), artist, born in Le Cateau-Cambrésis in the Nord department, was first known for his abstract use of color and as the leader of a group of painters called the *"fauves"* (wild beasts). Four of his works, labeled ''degenerate'' by the Nazis, were among those confiscated from German museums and sold at auction on 30 June 1939 in Lucerne.

Writer Louis Aragon said that Matisse personified France and the continuity of its great cultural traditions during its darkest hours. At the time of the 1940 defeat, Matisse was on his way to Genoa, intending to depart for Rio de Janeiro, but decided instead to remain in France. Returning to his home in Nice, he joined the local affiliate of the **Emergency Rescue Committee** and helped other artists who were without scarce materials by sending them some of his own supplies. In late 1940 he declined two invitations to emigrate to America. After a lengthy hospital stay in Lyons, where he underwent cancer surgery early in 1941, he returned to Nice. Despite the prior labeling of his paintings as ''degenerate'' art, the German Propaganda Ministry, in concert with **Vichy**, invited Matisse to visit Germany in November 1941, but he declined. He gave two interviews, discussing art and critiquing the French academic Beaux-Arts system on Vichy radio early in 1942, but in general lived quietly, producing many paintings, drawings, painted-paper cutouts, and illustrations for several books. Matisse moved from Nice to the more remote and safer hill town of Vence in June 1943. His ex-wife and his daughter Marguerite (Madame Duthuit), who were active in the **Resistance**—as was his son Jean—were arrested by the Gestapo in the spring of 1944. Madame Matisse was imprisoned for six months; Marguerite was freed after the Allies **liberated Paris**.

At the Salon d'Automne of 1945, Matisse was honored with a retrospective exhibition of his work, primarily paintings created during the war. Respected for having stayed in France while maintaining a sense of *joie-de-vivre* in his painting during the Occupation, Matisse was named commander of the Legion of Honor by the French government in 1947. Though a semi-invalid after 1941, he continued his artistic work until his death at Cimiez, near Nice.

*A. H. Barr, Jr., *Matisse, His Art and His Public* (New York, 1966 [original ed., 1951]); L. Bertrand Dorléac, *L'Art de la défaite, 1940–1944* (Paris, 1993); P. Schneider, *Matisse* (London, 1984).

S. Perkins

MAURIAC, FRANÇOIS (1885–1970), Nobel laureate, novelist, essayist, and critic, was born on 11 October 1885 into a religious, bourgeois family in Bordeaux, a background that was to dominate much of his life's work. His early work was characterized by a concern with the conflict between Catholic morality and the modern world, and he became a leader of the Catholic literary revival of the 1920s and 1930s. His 1927 novel, *Thérèse Desqueyneux*, remains one of the most influential novels of modern France, and Mauriac was elected to the French Academy in 1933. The years that followed saw him shift away from specifically Catholic themes toward more broadly defined spiritual and political ones. He became, along with Jacques **Maritain**, Emmanuel **Mounier**, and, later,

Georges Bernanos, a fixture of the Catholic **Left** and joined with them in supporting the Spanish Republic.

Although his wartime legacy is usually remembered for his **Resistance** activity, Mauriac had been somewhat slow to take this side. With the defeat in 1940, he had unambiguously supported Marshal **Pétain**, exemplifying what Robert Paxton has called the "self-flagellation" wing of French Catholicism that blamed the defeat on French "decadence." However, anti-German, he was horrified in particular by the anti-**Jewish** laws. Rejecting the ideology of the **National Revolution**, Mauriac made contact with Resistance circles by late 1941 and found his way into the Comité national des écrivains, becoming the only member of the academy to be an active resister. His political commitment grew throughout 1942, and, under the pseudonym "Forez," he wrote the famous *Cahier noir*, an attack on **Vichy** hypocrisy. As editor of the underground *Lettres Françaises*, Mauriac was increasingly of the opinion that the proletariat, whom he regarded as more inclined to resistance, were the only hope for France. This political stance was to characterize his postwar work as well, where he was a consistently left-of-center columnist for *L'Express* and a dedicated anti-imperialist. He was awarded the Nobel Prize in literature in 1952.

W. D. Halls, *Politics, Society, and Christianity in Vichy France* (Oxford, 1995); J. Lacouture, *François Mauriac* (Paris, 1980); R. O. Paxton, *Vichy France: Old Guard and New Order, 1940–1944* (New York, 1972); M. Scott, *Mauriac, the Politics of a Novelist* (Edinburgh, 1980).

S. D. Armus

MAURRAS, CHARLES (1868–1952), leader of the nationalist and royalist **Action Française**, which became a pillar of support for Philippe **Pétain** and the **Vichy** regime. During the first four decades of the twentieth century, Maurras stood as the most influential thinker of the nationalist **Right**. His daily editorials in the *Action Française* newspaper mixed sophisticated political analysis with vituperative, often vicious attacks on the enemies of "true" France—which included liberals, **socialists, communists, Freemasons**, foreigners, **Protestants**, and most especially by the late 1930s, **Jews**. Maurras also personified the growing disenchantment with the Third **Republic**, which he vilified on a daily basis, attacking not only its personnel but its democratic and representative principles.

With the defeat of 1940, Maurras rallied behind **Pétain**, despite the latter's early decision to collaborate with the Germans. The promise of the **National Revolution**—with the notable exception of the institution of monarchy—came close to fulfilling Maurras restorationist-exclusivist vision for France: a state that was authoritarian and a society informed by the principles of order, hierarchy, and corporate organization; and finally, a discrimination, written into law, that separated "alien" groups, particularly Jews, from the national community. Though Maurras refused all personal contact with the **Paris** collaborators, many of whom had passed through Action Française ranks, his daily editorials reflected his growing obsession for "unity" and against those who would disturb it—unrepentant Republicans, **Anglo-American** sympathizers, and, especially, Gaullist "terrorists" and their "Judeo-Bolshevik" allies. His support of Pétain remained unshaken until the end. Arrested in September 1944, Maurras was tried and found guilty of "intelligence with the enemy" in January 1945. Sentenced to life imprisonment, he was released on medical grounds in March 1952 and died eight months later.

*F.Ogé, *Le journal l'Action Française et la politique intérieure du gouvernement de Vichy* (Toulouse, 1984); E. R. Tannenbaum, *The Action Française: Die-hard Reactionaries in Twentieth Century France* (New York, 1962); E. Weber, *Action Française: Royalism and Reaction in Twentieth Century France* (Stanford, CA, 1962).

P. Mazgaj

MAXIM'S RESTAURANT was a famous *belle-époque* (pre-World War I) restaurant that became the favorite meeting place of the Parisian high society of the **collaboration** and the German High Command. Entering **Paris** in June 1940 amid the **exodus** of virtually three-quarters of the city's population, German officers quickly made Maxim's their own. When owner Louis Vaudable returned two months later, he found his establishment crowded with this new clientele and managed by a German officer, Otto Horcher. In truth, Vaudable was lucky, because Horcher was one of a distinguished family of Berlin restaurateurs.

During the Occupation the Germans treated Maxim's and its owner with favoritism and did not requisition the restaurant for their own exclusive use. Indeed, uniformed Germans were not allowed in the main dining room but were relegated to the second-floor dining rooms. In May 1941, when the Germans divided restaurants into four categories, Maxim's was placed among the "exceptional" ones that did not suffer food restrictions. Moreover, under Horcher's protection its employees were not deported to German labor camps. Ironically, Maxim's enjoyed one of its most prosperous eras.

Maxim's list of collaborationist and German celebrities is long and impressive, including the German ambassador and Francophile Otto **Abetz** and the writer Ernst **Jünger**, as well as Hermann **Göring** and other Nazi leaders officially visiting Paris. Joining them at table were aristocrats such as the marquis de Castellane, the marquise de Polignac, Countess Palffy, and Louise de Vilorin. **Industrialist** Louis Renault was a frequent diner, as was **press** corporation head Jean **Luchaire** and entertainers and writers Arletty, Sacha **Guitry**, Raimu, and Jean **Cocteau**.

The great boulevardier journalist Simon Arbellot claimed that as soon as the last Wehrmacht general left his reserved table, he was replaced immediately by an **American** counterpart. The **Resistance** soon forced Maxim's to close, but it was allowed to reopen in September 1946.

B. M. Gordon, "Fascism, the Neo-Right, and Gastronomy," in *Oxford Symposium on Food and Cookery, Taste, 1987* (London, 1987), 82–97; H. le Boterf, *La Vie parisienne sous l'occupation*, vol. 2 (Paris, 1975); G. and J.-R. Ragache, *La Vie quotidienne des écrivains et des artistes sous l'occupation, 1940–1944* (Paris, 1988).

W. S. Haine

MAYER, DANIEL (1909–1996) was general secretary of the clandestine **Socialist** Party in France. A Parisian, Mayer joined the Socialist Party (SFIO) in 1927 and was active in the socialist **youth** movement before becoming a journalist with the socialist daily *Le Populaire,* reporting on social affairs. He was close to Léon **Blum**, who advised him to remain in France after the defeat of 1940. With great energy Mayer gathered demoralized socialists and in March 1941 founded and led the clandestine Comité d'action Socialiste. Based in the unoccupied **zone**, it focused on ''spiritual **resistance**'' rather than **industrial** or military action.

In early 1943, Mayer was sent to London with Félix Gouin to make contact with General **de Gaulle**. Shortly afterward, the SFIO was formally reconstituted, with a policy of support for de Gaulle and with Mayer as general secretary. Nominated by **de Gaulle** as *Commissaire* for communications and transport, Mayer was also a member of the Comité Française de Libération Nationale and represented his party on the Conseil National de la Resistance, where he helped define the political aspirations of the **liberation**. He sought to preserve the unity of the **Resistance** and explored prospects for a political merger between **communists** and socialists, possibly in a single Labor Party. The plan made limited progress but was decisively rejected by Blum on his return from **deportation**.

Mayer played a central role in defining the socialists' policies in government. He was consequently a victim of the party's failure to live up to postwar expectations. In August 1946 the party congress voted to replace him as general secretary with Guy Mollet. Mayer went on to a long and distinguished public career, serving as cabinet minister from 1946 through 1949, as president of the *Ligue des droits de l'homme* (League of the Rights of Man), 1958–1975, and as president of the Conseil constitutionnel (Constitutional Council), 1983–1986.

†C. Juin, *Liberté . . . Justice . . . Le combat de Daniel Mayer* (Paris, 1982).

M. Kelly

MENTHON, FRANÇOIS DE (1900–1984), founded the **Resistance** movement Liberté, was the inspiration behind the creation of the **Comité Général d'Études**, and was later justice minister under General **de Gaulle**. Born into an old aristocratic family, Menthon became a professor of political economy, a Christian Democratic militant, and the father of six sons.

A captain in the reserves, he was wounded in June 1940 and taken **prisoner**. After escaping, he returned to his *château de Menthon* on the shore of Lake Annecy. There he organized the Resistance movement Liberté (Christian Democratic), which in November 1941 joined with Vérités, giving rise to **Combat**, the movement led by the French officer Henri **Frenay**.

Menthon was named professor of political economy in the Lyons Law Faculty in November 1940. Beginning in 1941, he created the Resistance **Comité Général d'Études (CGÉ)**, officially created on 1 July 1942 by Jean **Moulin**. Comprising nine respected members, including Alexandre **Parodi** and Michel **Debré**, the CGÉ was commissioned to plan the juridical and administrative measures that would follow the **liberation**. It published an article, "Pourquoi je suis Républicain" (Why I Am a Republican), in the first issue of the CGÉ's high-level review, *Cahiers Politiques*. In August 1942, Menthon was dismissed from his **university** post for his Resistance activities.

On 15 July 1943, he joined General de Gaulle in Algiers and became *Commissaire de la justice* in the Comité Français de Libération Nationale (CFLN), later the **Provisional Government** under de Gaulle in Algiers, from June through September 1944, and, in liberated France, from September 1944 through 1945. Menthon was the French prosecutor at the November 1945 Nuremberg trials.

D. de Bellescize, *Les Neuf Sages de la Résistance, Le Comité Général d'Études dans la clandestinité* (Paris, 1979).

D. de Bellescize

MERS-EL-KÉBIR was the site of a French naval base, attacked by the English, near Oran, Algeria, on 3 July 1940. A Royal Navy task force attacked a French naval squadron at anchor at Mers-el-Kébir. The unexpected action against an erstwhile ally showed that Britain was determined to ensure that the balance of naval power in the Mediterranean would never tip against it, despite Admiral Jean-François **Darlan's** repeated assurances that no French ship would ever fall into German hands.

The French squadron under Vice-Admiral Marcel Gensoul, which included the modern battle cruisers *Dunkerque* and *Strasbourg*, was caught by surprise. Gensoul was asked by the British to choose among four options or witness the destruction of his ships at point-blank range. He could sail with the British and continue the fight against the Germans and Italians, sail to a British port from which he and his crews would be repatriated, sail to a French port in the West Indies, or scuttle his fleet on the spot. Gensoul rejected the ultimatum as counter to French honor—it was made under the threat of force, and accepting any of its terms would have violated the Franco–German **armistice**—and said he was prepared to defend himself.

Given Gensoul's stance and knowing that **Vichy** had ordered reinforcements to Mers-el-Kébir, the Royal Navy opened fire. In less than 15 minutes the *Dunkerque*, the battleships *Bretagne* and *Provence*, and the destroyer *Mogador* were destroyed. More than 1,600 French sailors died or were wounded. Only the *Strasbourg* managed to escape.

What might be called a "melancholy action"—for the British commanders obeyed their order from the Admiralty with reluctance and anguish—caused a lasting resentment in the French navy and widened the breach between London and Vichy. To many in France it cast Britain once again in the historic and unhappy role of "perfidious Albion." In Britain, however, it was greeted with cheers, making plain, in the words of Winston Churchill, that "the British War Cabinet feared nothing and would stop at nothing."

C. Barnett, *Engage the Enemy More Closely: The Royal Navy in the Second World*

War (New York, 1991); E. Gates, *End of the Affair: The Collapse of the Anglo–French Alliance, 1939–40* (Berkeley, 1981); J. Roy, *Une affaire d'honneur: Mers-el-Kébir, 3 juillet 1940* (Paris, 1983).

W. A. Hoisington, Jr.

MILICE FRANÇAISE, the militia, **Vichy's** political **police** and counterinsurgency unit. On 5 January 1943 Marshal **Pétain** transformed the Service d'Ordre Légionnaire into the Milice Nationale, an elite organization built upon veterans of the 1930s **right-wing** conspiratorial *cagoule*, who, disappointed by the Vichy's Legion Française des Combattants, wanted a single, committed **National Revolution** party. Nominally headed by Pierre **Laval**, it was directed by Joseph **Darnand**.

At the founding meeting Darnand envisioned *miliciens* effecting general "intellectual, social and political renewal" in the civil service and in agricultural, business, legal, and medical associations. A civilian elite, trained in the milice's *École des cadres*, was envisioned as a new elite, co-opting all others, in Vichy France. In reality, however, this new civilian elite was stillborn, eclipsed by the milice's military branch, the Franc-Garde.

The Franc-Garde's senior officers received six-months of training at **Uriage**, while the higher officials nationwide had two-to three-week sessions. The Uriage *milice* school was headed by Acadian American Catholic royalist Pierre-Louis de La Ney du Vair, with ex-*cagoulard* counterinsurgency expert Jacques Duge de Bernonville as study director. Mystic La Ney du Vair was replaced by brutal Jean de Vaugelas—who, with de Bernonville, later commanded the attack of 1,000 *miliciens* and gendarmes on the **Glières** plateau **Resistance** fighters. Anticommunist counterinsurgency and hunting down **Jews** and Masons promoted contacts with the Germans. (Paul **Touvier** was in the first Uriage cohort.) By June 1943 there were about 35,000 *miliciens*, including 15,000 Francs-Gardes, many of them monarchist, **Maurrasian**, ultra-Catholic and **Action Française**, but with the youngest often proudly "**fascist**." The Germans distrusted them, allowing them to be armed only in extremis in November 1943.

In July 1943, Laval authorized French membership in the Waffen SS; in August Darnand vowed fidelity to **Hitler** and was named SS *Obersturmführer*. By early autumn as many as 300 *miliciens* joined the Waffen SS, many to fight on the eastern front. From January 1944 up to 4,000 Francs-Gardes were working with the Germans in the northern **zone**. During the French civil war of 1944, the État milicien made the Vichy government fascist in all but name. The *milice* controlled several prefectures, all French police, the media (with Philippe **Henriot** on the **radio**), and the **prison**, and the justice systems (*milice* judges holding court). As late as 5 June 1944—the eve of the **Normandy** landings—Pétain still addressed the *milice* as the most "faithful" of his soldiers.

As the *milice* "mopped up" after the Germans, they were hated and attacked. In return, the miliciens used torture on their countrymen. At the **liberation**, about 1,500 *miliciens* were shot. Others went into hiding in monasteries and convents in France and Quebec.

J. Delperrie de Bayac, *Histoire de la Milice* (Paris, 1969); B. M. Gordon, *Collaborationism in France during the Second World War* (Ithaca, NY, 1980); B. M. Gordon, "Un Soldat du fascisme," RDHDGM, 27:108 (October 1977), 43–70; R. Rémond, et al., *Paul Touvier et l'Église, Rapport de la Commission historique instituée par le cardinal Decourtray* (Paris, 1992); P. P. Lambert and G. Le Marec, *Organisations, mouvements et unités de l'État Français, Vichy, 1940–1944* (Paris, 1993).

J. Hellman

MITTERRAND, FRANÇOIS (1916–1996), was active in French political life from the 1930s until his death and president of the **Republic** from 1981 through 1995, the longest serving French head of state since Napoleon III. In 1994, Mitterrand's activity during World War II became a lightning rod for recriminations over how to remember the war in France.

Born into an affluent family in Jarnac in the Charente, Mitterrand received a Catholic education, came to Paris in 1934 to study political science and law, and supported the nationalist Croix-de-feu. Photographs of the era show him participating in **right-wing** demonstrations. Wounded during the **Battle of France**, Mitterrand was taken **prisoner**. In December 1941 he escaped and in January 1942 made his way to **Vichy**, where he was given a post in the documentation service of the **Légion Française des Combattants**, which he held until April 1942. He next joined the Board of Rehabilitation of Prisoners of War, where he remained until January 1943, when he, along with several others on the board, resigned after refusing to support Pierre **Laval's Relève**. Mitterrand, however, kept a position within the board's mutual aid bureaucracy and, in December 1943, was awarded the *francisque*, a high decoration by the Vichy government.

By 1943, however, Mitterrand had shifted his allegiance toward the **Resistance**. Supporting General Henri **Giraud**, Mitterrand in the spring began to infiltrate the Board of Prisoners and to receive funds from the Organization of Armed Resistance (ORA). Following the eclipse of Giraud by General **de Gaulle**, Mitterrand in November traveled to London, and the next month in Algiers he met de Gaulle, who put him in charge of unifying the Resistance factions of war prisoners. He returned to France in February 1944. Instrumental in creating the unified Mouvement national des prisonniers de guerre, Mitterrand became its head on 12 March 1944. During the spring of 1944, Mitterrand's activities in Paris brought him into contact with another resister, Danielle Gouze, whom he married in October, shortly after the **liberation**. Under the **Provisional Government** Mitterrand became president of the Mouvement national des prisonniers de guerre et déportés, involved with the return of hundreds of thousands of prisoners and deportees at the end of the war. In 1946, he was elected to the French parliament. He held cabinet posts in the Fourth Republic, reorganized the **Socialist** Party in the early 1970s, and was elected the first socialist president of the Fifth Republic in 1981.

As president, Mitterrand refused to accept blame on behalf of the Republic for the misdeeds of Vichy, arguing that Vichy and the Republic were different entities. He continued to socialize with former Vichy **police** minister René **Bousquet** at least until 1986 and had wreaths laid at Marshal **Pétain's** grave every Armistice Day (11 November) from 1986 through 1992. Suggestions were made that the president used his influence to protect friends from his 1930s right-wing days, such as those who were later in high places in L'Oréal cosmetics company, whose founder, Eugène Schueller, had supported Eugène **Deloncle** and the **collaborationist Mouvement Social Révolutionnaire** during the Occupation. One of France's most prestigious companies, L'Oréal was involved in the postwar Arab boycott of Israel.

The publication of a history of Mitterrand's early career by Pierre Péan in 1994, for which the president had allowed himself to be interviewed, together with an appearance on French television and other statements by Mitterrand toward the end of his presidency, gave wide publicity to his wartime record, which had been only vaguely known in France. When Mitterrand died in 1996, he was still seeking to "manage" his place in history.

†C. Andrieu, "Managing Memory: National and Personal Identity at Stake in the Mitterrand Affair," *FPS* 14:2 (Spring 1996): 17–32; M. Bar-Zohar, *Bitter Scent, the Case of L'Oréal, Nazis, and the Arab Boycott* (New York, 1996); G.-M. Benamou, *Le Dernier Mitterrand* (Paris, 1996); É. Conan and H. Rousso, *Vichy un passé qui ne passe pas* (Paris, 1994); R. J. Golsan, "Reflections on Mitterrand's *Années noires*," in N. Bracher, ed., *A Time to Remember, CFC*, 19:2 (Summer/Fall 1995), 292–311; S. Hoffmann et al., "Symposium on Mitterrand's Past," *FPS* 13:1 (Winter 1995): 4–35; F. Mitterrand, *Memoires interrompues* (Paris, 1996); P. Péan, *Une jeunesse française: François Mitterrand 1934–1947* (Paris, 1994).

B. M. Gordon

MODE RÉTRO is a term for what has been argued was a reawakening of popular fascination with, and reevaluation of, the Occupation period beginning in the early 1970s and extending to the present. The vogue touched many aspects of cultural life, including **fashion** and increased attendance at historical movies and visits to archives and historical museums.

The *mode rétro* is attributed to the questioning of dominant Gaullist representations of the Occupation. A series of public events challenged established accounts of the Occupation and fueled the retrospective mood. Youth of May 1968 were asking their parents new questions about the Occupation years. The death of General **de Gaulle** in 1970 and the appearance of Marcel Ophuls' film *The* **Sorrow and the Pity** in 1971, followed by Louis Malle's *Lacombe Lucien* and Lilianna Cavanni's *The Night Porter*, among others, undermined the Gaullist version of a heroic and resisting nation (*résistantialisme*). The banning of Ophuls' film from television only intensified the debate.

The *mode rétro*, some have argued, continued into the 1980s and 1990s. After the election of François **Mitterrand** to the presidency in 1981, *The Sorrow and* *the Pity* was finally released for television. The 1983 extradition of Klaus **Barbie** from Bolivia and his trial and conviction in 1987, reindictments of René **Bousquet**, Paul **Touvier**, and **Maurice Papon**, and the 50th anniversaries of de Gaulle's call to **resistance** and of the war's end have kept discussion of the period alive. Long-postponed films, memoirs, and novels written by participants or their children have both provoked and been inspired by the fashion of interest in the period.

"Forum: The Vichy Syndrome," *FHS* 19:2 (Fall 1995); A. Morris, *Collaboration and Resistance Reviewed: Writers and the Mode Rétro in Post-Gaullist France* (New York, 1992); P. Ory, *L'Entre-deux-mai: Histoire culturelle de la France, Mai 1968–Mai 1981* (Paris, 1983); H. Rousso, *The Vichy Syndrome: History and Memory in France since 1944*, trans. A. Goldhammer (Cambridge, MA, 1991).

L. A. Higgins

MONNET, JEAN (1888–1979), architect of France's postwar reconstruction and European unification. Experienced in negotiations on international cooperation during World War I and later as deputy secretary-general of the League of Nations, after a period in the family cognac business and in merchant banking, Monnet was recalled to public service in 1938 by Premier Édouard **Daladier** to purchase **American** aircraft to bolster French defenses. At the outbreak of war he became chairman of the **Anglo**-French Coordinating Committee.

When France fell, Monnet was sent under **British** aegis to join the British Purchasing Commission in Washington (August 1940). Through personal charisma and a network of powerful friends, he played a central role in the elaboration of Roosevelt's "Victory Program" and in the U.S. policy-making process generally. Following the Allied landings in Algeria, Monnet was sent there as an American emissary (February–October 1943) to oversee the rearming of the French forces and to prepare postwar government. He worked initially for General Henri **Giraud** but understood that French unity could not be achieved without **de Gaulle**. He negotiated the creation of the Comité Français de Libération Nationale (CFLN), foundation of the **Provisional Government**.

Returning to Washington as a member of the CFLN, he was able through his connections to promote French interests during the difficult transition to peace. Notoriously self-effacing, Monnet was driven by ideals of the common good rather than by personal ambition. Despite deep differences with de Gaulle (in personality, vision for Europe, and attitudes toward the **United States**), it was to Monnet that the general turned for the rebuilding of the national **economy**, and the "Monnet Plan" became the basis of the French recovery from 1945.

†D. Brinkley and C. Hackett, eds., *Jean Monnet: The Path to European Unity* (New York, 1991); F. Duchêne, *Jean Monnet: The First Statesman of Interdependence* (New York and London, 1994); J. Monnet, *Mémoires* (Paris, 1976).

C. W. Nettelbeck

MONTANDON, GEORGE (1879–1944), **Vichy** specialist on the "**Jewish** race." Born and educated as a medical doctor in **Switzerland**, Montandon emigrated to France, where he turned to anthropology. In 1928 he was named member of the Institut français d'anthropologie, in 1933 professor at the École d'anthropologie, and in 1936, the year he was naturalized as a French citizen, curator of the Broca museum. He also occupied the chair of anthropology at the Musée d'histoire naturelle. During the 1930s, Montandon gained a reputation as an extreme **anti-Semite**, writing a number of pseudoscientific works on Jews. The best known, *l'Ethnie française*, was published in 1935.

During the Occupation, Montandon was recognized by the Germans as an expert on **Jews** and at their demand was attached to Vichy's **Commissariat Général aux Questions Juives (CGQJ)**. He had a lucrative career conducting racial examinations and, for a price, declaring people non-Jewish. In 1941 he helped prepare a German-financed **exposition,** *La France et le Juif.* From March 1941 to February 1943 he was editor in chief of an anti-Semitic magazine with the same title as his 1935 book, *l'Ethnie française*. In February 1943 Montandon was named head of the *Institut d'étude des questions juives et ethnoraciales*, successor to the German-sponsored **Institut d'étude des questions juives**, re-organized and incorporated into the CGQJ. He taught courses on "Jewish ethnoraciology" and "racial hygiene." Montandon was executed by the **Resistance** in 1944.

J. Billig, *Le Commissariat général au questions juives* (Paris, 1955–1960); P. Birnbaum, *La France aux Français* (Paris, 1993); M. R. Marrus and R. O. Paxton, *Vichy France and the Jews* (New York, 1981).

D. Evleth

MONTHERLANT, HENRY DE (1895–1972), was a **collaborationist** writer noted for pro-German and frequently anti-French essays published in Pierre **Drieu la Rochelle's** *Nouvelle Revue Française* (NRF), Alphonse **de Châteaubriant's** *La Gerbe*, and the German publication *Deutschland Frankreich*. Many of the essays published in the *NRF* and *La Gerbe* were also published in book form in *Le Solstice de juin* (1941). Montherlant also launched a highly successful career as a dramatist during the Occupation with the staging of *La Reine morte* at the *Comédie Française* in December 1942.

Renowned in the interwar years as a gifted novelist and essayist whose fiction was noted for its celebration of virility, misogyny, and the "manly" pursuits of bullfighting, **sports**, and warfare, Montherlant was a decorated veteran of World War I. In collections of essays including *Service inutile* (1935) and *L'Equinoxe de septembre* (1938), his writing took a more overtly political turn. Although he criticized Mussolini's invasion of Ethiopia and the **Munich agreement**, his favorite target was French "decadence." His attacks on what he considered the French national character became so offensive during the Occupation that a bookstore displaying copies of *Le Solstice de juin* in its window was bombed in November 1941. Thereafter, Montherlant became somewhat less visible and outspoken in his collaborationism.

Following the **liberation**, Montherlant was tried by the Commission d'Épuration des Arts et Lettres and forbidden to publish for one year. He went on to resume a successful career as a writer and was inducted into the Académie Française in 1955.

*R. J. Golsan, "Henry de Montherlant: Itinerary of an Ambivalent Fascist," in R. J. Golsan, ed., *Fascism, Aesthetics, and Culture* (Hanover, NH, 1992); P. Sipriot, *Montherlant sans masque*, 2 vols. (Paris, 1982–1990).

R. J. Golsan

MONTOIRE-SUR-LE-LOIR MEETINGS (1940), meetings of Pierre **Laval** and Marshal Philippe **Pétain** with Adolf **Hitler** in Montoire-sur-le-Loir on 22 and 24 October 1940.

These meetings, requested by the **Vichy** government but also desired by Hitler, came about because the **armistice** situation for France and the fight against **Britain** for Germany had continued longer than expected. The French wanted relief from the economic strangulation of the **armistice** clauses: a rigid **Demarcation Line** splitting the country, exorbitant occupation fees charged by Germany, and an unfair mark-franc exchange rate. Hitler wanted French logistic support against the British, notably in Africa. Yet little was said on these subjects at the meetings themselves, which produced nothing concrete. **Pétain** accepted the principle of a **collaboration** with Germany whose terms would be defined later. This policy of collaboration heralded a new climate of hope on both sides.

The hopes were soon dashed. Although Vichy made concessions to Germany, it did not join the war against Britain. On economic issues crucial to France, Germany made no concessions at all. Collaboration became more and more unpopular. The most enduring legacy of the Montoire meetings was psychological. At their meeting, Pétain shook hands with Hitler, and the event was photographed. This photograph would become the **symbol** of the abject failure of the Vichy government and its collaboration policy.

P. Burrin, *Living with Defeat: France under the German Occupation, 1940–1944*, trans. J. Lloyd (New York, 1997) [original ed.: *La France à l'heure allemande, 1940–1944* (Paris, 1995)]; F. Delpla, *Montoire, Les premiers jours de la collaboration* (Paris, 1996); E. Jäckel, *Frankreich in Hitlers Europa: Die deutsche Frankreichpolitik im zweiten Weltkrieg* (Stuttgart, 1966); R. O. Paxton, *Vichy France: Old Guard and New Order 1940–1944* (New York, 1972).

D. Evleth

MONZIE, ANATOLE DE (1876–1947), French politician and frequent cabinet member under the Third **Republic**, supported an alliance with **Italy** and supported, then turned away from, **Vichy**.

De Monzie, the son of a middle-level government official, became an attorney. His first elective office was at the county level in his native southwest France, and he was elected mayor of Cahors. In 1910 he became a member of the National Assembly. Avoiding identification with any major political party, de Monzie was, nonetheless, appointed to many cabinet posts between 1917 and 1940. He introduced new methods into the merchant marine and helped reform national **education**.

Known for his stubbornness on matters of principle, de Monzie quixotically supported an alliance with Fascist Italy, despite Mussolini's increasing dependence on **Hitler** in the late 1930s. After the fall of France, he endorsed Marshal **Pétain**, only to realize very soon the disastrous orientation of the Vichy regime. De Monzie's frank and unabashed criticism did not endear him to the Vichy government, while at the same time he was mistrusted by the **Resistance**.

After the **liberation**, De Monzie for years was kept under investigation of treason without charges being formally raised against him. Embittered by what he called the "new inquisition," de Monzie kept more and more to himself. He died in 1947. Historians tend to recognize his lofty motives, granting him a respectable status.

E. Beau de Lomenie, *La Mort de la IIIe République* (Paris, 1951); A. de Monzie, *Ci-devant* (Paris, 1941); A. de Monzie, *La saison des juges* (Paris, 1943); L. Plante, *Un Grand Seigneur de la Politique, Anatole de Monzie* (Paris, 1955).

K. Bieber

MORAND, PAUL (1888–1976), was a poet and novelist whose literary fame as a modernist and cosmopolitan in the interwar years was eclipsed by his later support of **Vichy**. A keen observer of modernism and the changes in social mores in the interwar years, Morand was also fascinated by the **United States** and by the French colonies and wrote innovative travel chronicles, focusing on future global demographic and economic challenges rather than exoticism. In the mid-1930s, his cultivated image of elegant insolence seemed to give way in his writings to a condemnation of "decadence" and a return to tradition.

After 1940, Morand's career followed that of Pierre **Laval**, a personal friend. Leaving a post in France's economic war mission in London shortly after the 1940 **armistice**, Morand arrived hopeful for a post in Vichy, but he had left London without authorization, and Laval either could not or would not help him. When Laval was dismissed in December 1940, Morand followed him to **Paris**. There Morand socialized with longtime friends such as Jean **Cocteau** and Gaston Gallimard and German cultural figures such as Ernst **Jünger**, while contributing occasionally to such **collaborationist** publications as *La Gerbe* or *Combats* (not to be confused with the **Resistance** organization and newspaper *Combat*).

An ostensibly neutral observer of the Parisian scene, Morand promoted in his *Chroniques de l'homme maigre* (1941) the model of an invigorated, self-disciplined, lean as opposed to flabby Frenchman in opposition to demagogues, pessimists, or quitters. With Laval's return to power in April 1942, Morand was named director of the film-censoring commission. Appointed Vichy's ambassador to Bucharest in July 1943, then to Bern in July 1944, he was removed following the **liberation** in September 1944 as part of a general administrative **purge**.

Exiled for 10 years, Morand returned to Paris in 1954 and, though disgraced, continued writing. He sought election to the Académie française in 1959 but was opposed by General **de Gaulle**, among others. In 1968, however, he was elected to the Académie. By the time he died, in 1976, Morand had regained a literary following.

M. Burrus, *Paul Morand, voyageur du XXe siècle* (Paris, 1987); G. Guitard-Auviste, *Morand (1888–1976): légendes et vérités* (Paris, 1981); B. Thibault, *L'Allure de Morand: du modernisme au Pétainisme* (Birmingham, AL, 1992).

C. Keith

MOULIN, JEAN (1899–1943), main coordinator of the various French **Resistance** movements, indefatigable, and passionately **Republican** administrator, was tortured and assassinated by the Germans; his ashes were transferred to the Panthéon on 19 December 1964, where André **Malraux** honored him as "the martyrized king of the shadows."

Born in Béziers, 20 June 1899, Moulin became the youngest *Préfet* of France, while demonstrating an early talent for drawing and painting. During the German invasion, he was prefect in Eure-et-Loir, after having worked in the cabinet of air minister Jean Cot. Refusing to cooperate with the German invaders, who reached Chartres 17 June 1940, Moulin was beaten, imprisoned, and then released. Marshal **Pétain** dismissed him from his post on 2 November 1940. Leaving Chartres under the name of Joseph Mercier, Moulin went to Saint-Andiol in southern France, where he began collecting information about the nascent Resistance movements, meeting Henri **Frenay** in Marseilles and François **de Menthon** in Lyons.

On 19 October 1941 he left for London. There, on 25 October 1941, he met General **de Gaulle**, to whom he gave a *"Rapport sur l'activité, les projets et les besoins des groupements constitués en France en vue de la libération du territoire national"* (Report on the Activity, Projects, and Needs of the Groups Constituted in France in View of the Liberation of the National Territory), the most extensive document about the Resistance in metropolitan France. It covered the groups Liberté led by François de Menthon in Lyons; Libération Nationale, led by Henri Frenay in Lyons; and Libération, led by Emmanuel **d'Astier** de la Vigerie in Marseilles, Clermont-Ferrand, and Lyons. There seems to have been an immediate and reciprocal understanding between Moulin and de Gaulle, the general sending him back to the continent to collect documents about the internal Resistance, to represent him in the metropole, and to forward orders and messages from London to France.

Known as Rex, Max, and Régis, Moulin set up the Bureau d'Information et de Propagande, with Georges **Bidault** as its head; the Comité Général d'Études, to prepare for the postwar French political regime; the Noyautage des Administrations Publiques (Subversion of Public Administration), with Claude Bourdet as leader; and the Armée Secrète, headed by Charles **Delestraint**. Delegating responsibilities, Moulin also distributed funds and weapons. His interests in drawing and painting provided him with a professional cover during his Resistance years. In Nice, he owned an art gallery under his artist's name of Romanin. After a second visit to London, from February to March 1943, he unified most of the Resistance movements in metropolitan France, creating the Mouvements Unis de Résistance, and convened the first **Conseil National de la Résistance** on 27 May 1943.

Moulin's success exacerbated rivalries within the French Resistance with Frenay, d'Astier de la Vigerie, and Pierre **Brossolette**. A renewed campaign by the Gestapo against resisters, carelessness on the part of his associates, and perhaps treason (René **Hardy** being the foremost suspect) led to his capture at Caluire on 21 June 1943. Moulin officially died near Metz on 8 July 1943. Posthumous attacks by Frenay, Klaus **Barbie**, Charles Benfredj, and Thierry Wolton, all claiming without supporting documentation that Moulin was a secret agent of communism, attest to the **symbolic**, as well as the historic, importance of Jean Moulin.

J.-P. Azéma, F. Bédarida, and R. Frank, *Jean Moulin et la résistance en 1943* (Paris, 1994); D. Cordier, *Jean Moulin, L'inconnu du Panthéon*, 3 vols. (Paris, 1989–1993); J. Etènevaux, *Jean Moulin (1899–1943) et l'organisation de la résistance* (Lyons, 1994); P. Vidal-Naquet, *Le Trait empoisonné: réflexions sur l'affaire Jean Moulin* (Paris, 1993).

C. Lamiot

MOUNIER, EMMANUEL (1905–1950), was editor of the review *Esprit* and personalist philosopher. With a few well-known elders such as Jacques **Maritain**, Nicholas Berdyaev, and Gabriel Marcel, he founded the review *Esprit* in 1932. At the outbreak of the war Mounier was the acknowledged leader of the personalist movement, one of the most influential antiliberal communitarian philosophies of interwar Europe; his relatively small-circulation review "defending the human person against the communalism of the **Left** and the individualism of the **Right**," although erudite and difficult to read, had become one of the most influential of the 1930s.

After the **Munich crisis**, Mounier—with like-minded young critics of liberal democratic institutions such as anti-**Munich agreement** journalist Hubert Beuve-Méry (later founder of the newspaper *Le Monde*)—declared that France could survive the **fascist** challenge only by undergoing its own total revolution. With the advent of the **Vichy** regime Mounier and "Beuve" helped establish communitarian personalism at the **youth** movements' preeminent École Nationale Supérieure des Cadres d'*Uriage*, as well as in Uriage's myriad satellite schools and in other organizations charged with training new leaders.

Mounier's enemies in *Action Française*, as well as among traditionalist Catholics and the crypto-Nazis, engineered his elimination from Uriage and the silencing of *Esprit* by the fall of 1941. He was even imprisoned in 1942 for alleged ties to the **Combat Resistance** group and engaged in a hunger strike that, celebrated by Resistance propaganda, permanently damaged his health. After his release he refrained from political activity but turned to refashioning personalism as a left-wing/progressive/communitarian ideology for postwar France. At the **liberation of Paris**—thanks to the Uriage/progressive Catholic/ *Le Monde* network—Mounier was able to get the materials and permissions to relaunch *Esprit* months before other reviews and establish his reputation as an early resister, a consistent progressive Catholic, and a pioneer in a Resistance-nurtured Christian–**communist** cooperation.

*J.-M. Domenach, *Emmanuel Mounier* (Paris, 1972); J. Hellman, *Emmanuel Mounier and the New Catholic Left, 1930–1950* (Toronto, 1981); D. Lindenberg, *Les Années souterraines, 1937–1947* (Paris, 1990); M. Winock, *Histoire politique de la revue "Esprit"* (Paris, 1975).

J. Hellman

MOUVEMENT DE LIBÉRATION NATIONALE (MLN) was a title adopted by two **Resistance** movements.

The first movement was founded in the unoccupied **zone** in 1940 by Henri **Frenay**. His long-term aim was to establish a secret **army** and, like General **de Gaulle**, to prepare an army-in-waiting that would be mobilized when the military campaign for **liberation** was launched. Meanwhile, the MLN's practical work focused on intelligence and propaganda.

It published a small clandestine newspaper, *Les Petites Ailes*, which became *Vérités,* reflecting the aim of countering **Vichy** propaganda by publicizing the damage caused by the German occupation and official **collaboration**. The newspaper provided information and comment about the course of the war, especially on matters subject to censorship. Beginning in the southeast, the MLN spread throughout the south and even developed a small presence in the north. In November 1941, it merged with a similar organization, led by François **de Menthon** and Pierre-Henri **Teitgen**, to form the *Mouvement de libération française,* which was better known by the title of its newspaper, *Combat*.

The second MLN was created in January 1944 by a merger of the Mouvements unis de la Resistance (MUR) of the southern zone with the northern zone groups that were not represented in the **Conseil National de la Résistance (CNR)**, notably **Défense de la France, Lorraine**, and Resistance. The purpose of the movement was to form the basis for a broad political party of the **Left** and center that could become a **Republican** party of government after the war. Undercut by the formation of separate **Communist, Socialist**, and Christian democratic parties, this MLN divided and dispersed. In June 1945, surviving members attempted to create a new party, the *Union démocratique et Socialiste de la Résistance*, whose members included François **Mitterrand**. This small, weak grouping was eventually absorbed into the Socialist Party.

J.-F. Muracciole, *Histoire de la Résistance en France* (Paris, 1993).

M. Kelly

MOUVEMENT SOCIAL RÉVOLUTIONNAIRE (MSR), a small, conspiratorial, and especially violence-prone **collaborationist** political party established in September 1940 in **Paris** by Eugène **Deloncle**. Members came from the Cagoule and other prewar **right-wing** groups. Sources of financial support included cosmetics giant L'Oréal founder Eugène Schueller, who played a significant role in the movement from 1940 until early 1942, and possibly the Germans.

After his December 1940 ouster from power, Pierre **Laval** supported the formation of a larger **Rassemblement National Populaire (RNP)** by Deloncle and Marcel **Déat**, though the MSR maintained its separate identity and controlled the new party's paramilitary wing, which was rumored to be planning a "March on **Vichy**." Conflict emerged between Deloncle and **Déat**, who was suspicious of the still independent MSR. When **Laval** and **Déat** were wounded in an assassination attempt in August 1941, suspicion fell on the MSR. Finally, **Déat** broke with the MSR, which in October 1941 turned to the destruction of synagogues in **Paris** with explosives provided by the SS.

Deloncle's tactics failed to gain much French or German support and two party factions, one led by Jean Filiol and Henry Charbonneau, the other by Georges Soulès (Raymond **Abellio**) and André Mahé, expelled him from the MSR in May 1942. Filiol was arrested by the Vichy government, again under **Laval**. The Soulès-Mahé wing, more doctrinally oriented, attempted to generate a French-style ideology of race, land, and action but eventually moved toward Laval as the MSR declined.

Echoes of the Cagoule and of the MSR resounded again in 1991, with public disclosures that Schueller welcomed ex-Cagoulards and their relatives into L'Oréal after World War II. In particular, Jacques Corrèze, a high ranking MSR figure, eventually headed Cosmair, L'Oréal's affiliate in the **United States**.

M. Bar-Zohar, *Bitter Scent, the Case of L'Oréal, Nazis, and the Arab Boycott* (New York, 1996); P. Bourdrel, *La Cagoule* (Paris, 1992 [first ed. 1970)]; B. M. Gordon, *Collaboration in France during the Second World War* (Ithaca, NY, 1980); B. M. Gordon, "The Condottieri of the Collaboration: *Mouvement Social Révolutionnaire*," *JCH* 10:2 (April 1975): 261–82; George Soulès and André Mahé, *La fin du nihilisme* (Paris, 1986 [original ed., 1943]).

J. Blatt

MOUVEMENTS UNIS DE LA RÉSISTANCE (MUR) was a **Resistance** movement in the unoccupied **zone**.

The MUR was one of the achievements of Jean **Moulin** in his attempts to bring the disparate Resistance movements together into a coherent force. Formed in the spring of 1943, it brought together the three main movements of the southern zone: **Combat** (the largest), **Franc-Tireur**, and **Libération-sud**. The union was prepared by coordinating the different technical services and forging links between leaderships, including visits to London by Combat's Henri **Frenay** and **Libération-sud's** Emmanuel **d'Astier**.

The military wings of the three movements were merged into an Armée secrète, and the main technical services were merged, with groups established for landings and parachutings, **radio** and communications, a **press** and information bureau, and a study group to prepare policy proposals for the postwar reconstruction. A coordinating committee was established under the presidency of Moulin, with major responsibilities allocated to the constituent movements' leaders: Frenay initially had charge of military operations, d'Astier handled political matters, and Jean-Pierre Lévy dealt with security and intelligence. Each of the three movements retained its own propaganda and **publishing** activities.

The MUR was based on a separation of functions between military and political affairs and between national and regional operations. For security reasons, liaison was mainly confined to vertical lines of communication within functions, and the limited attempts at horizontal liaison tended to produce a high administrative burden. However, the functional distinctions were frequently contested, not least because the activists saw themselves, in Frenay's terms, as both soldiers and citizens.

The MUR had three seats on the **Conseil National de la Résistance** and in early 1944 merged with a group of northern movements to form the **Mouvement de Libération Nationale**.

J.-F. Muracciole, *Histoire de la Résistance en France* (Paris, 1993).

M. Kelly

MUNICH AGREEMENT (September–October 1938) was the culmination of **Anglo**–French appeasement policy and permitted Nazi Germany to achieve, through military intimidation, the dismemberment and occupation (March 1939) of Czechoslovakia. Ostensibly, the Munich agreement focused on self-determination for the Sudeten Germans, but it really concerned European security and the German quest for hegemony.

Soviet, Czech, and Anglo–French diplomats recognized the German threat to Czechoslovakia, which the Franco–**Soviet** and Czech–Soviet mutual assistance pacts of 1935 were intended to counter. After the German remilitarization of the Rhineland in March 1936, the French **army** lost its capability to attack in the west to relieve Czechoslovakia should it be attacked. In addition, the French High Command had no offensive plans against Nazi Germany. The French failure to react was symptomatic of a loss of confidence in their power. These divisions were exacerbated by the electoral victory of the **Popular Front** and the outbreak of the Spanish civil war. The French government became dependent on **Britain**, which did not want important continental commitments and did not have, nor wish to build up, an army to support them.

The German annexation of Austria in March 1938 made Czechoslovakia the next logical target and set in motion the process leading to the Munich crisis. At the same time the French and British governments determined that they could not defend Czechoslovakia and that the Czech government must make concessions. Poland, in theory a French ally but hostile to Czechoslovakia, refused support. All these factors led to heavy Anglo–French pressure on Czechoslovakia to yield to German demands. The **USSR** offered staff talks, but the French did not want them, and the Czechs would not fight with the Soviet Union as its only ally. At the same time Poland threatened war to seize the Teschen region. All these factors led to Anglo–French capitulation in spite of efforts by *bellicistes* to avert it. In May 1937 French foreign minister Yvon Delbos had observed that France could not abandon Czechoslovakia "without disappearing as a great power from the map of Europe." Delbos' observation proved to be correct.

*J.-B. Duroselle, *La décadence, 1932–1939* (Paris, 1979); R. A. C. Parker, *Chamberlain and Appeasement* (London, 1993); T. Taylor, *Munich: The Price of Peace* (New York, 1979); R. Young, *France and the Origins of the Second World War* (New York, 1996).

M. J. Carley

MUSÉE DE L'HOMME (MUSEUM OF MAN) NETWORK was created at the end of the summer of 1940 by a group of researchers and writers affiliated with the **Paris** anthropological museum. Specializing in anti-German propaganda and arranging secret passages to **Britain**, it was destroyed by the Abwehr (German military intelligence) during the winter of 1940–1941.

In the summer of 1940, Boris Vildé, Yvonne Oddon, and Anatole Lewitsky (linguist, head librarian, and anthropologist, respectively) set up a **Resistance** network, which extended into the unoccupied **zone**. They developed anti-Nazi propaganda, transmitted political and military information to **Britain** (notably in regard to the Saint-Nazaire submarine base and other port installations), and facilitated the transfer, via **Spain** and the Breton coast, of volunteers and escaped French and British **prisoners** of war who wished to continue the war. At the same time, Claude Aveline, a writer; Jean Cassou, the museum of modern art conservator; and Marcel Abraham, the inspector of national **education**, established an anti-**Vichy** propaganda group. By the end of the summer they were joined by art historian Agnès Humbert and by George Ithier, an airline administrator, and Pierre Walter, a photographer, both of whom were already working for the British Intelligence Service.

Wishing to create a newspaper for all the anti-German groups of the occupied zone, these nine people joined with Jules Andrieu, Leon-Maurice Nordmann, Alice Simmonet, Sylvette Leleu, René Sénéchal, Pierre **Brossolette**, and, later, Germaine **Tillion** and Jean **Paulhan** to form the National Committee of Public Safety. From 15 December 1940 through 25 March 1941, the committee's bulletin, "*Resistance*," appeared five times, each issue offering an editorial, local and international war news, and a verse of the "Marseillaise" at its end.

Between 13 January and 18 April 1941, the main leaders of the network were arrested. Vildé, Lewitsky, Walter, Andrieu, Nordmann, Ithier, and Sénéchal were executed at Mont Valérien on 23 February 1942. Yvonne Oddon, Agnès Humbert, Alice Simmonet, Sylvette Leleu, and Germaine Tillion, all arrested later during the war, survived Nazi **concentration camps**. Brossolette, Aveline, Cassou, and Abraham escaped from the German police and continued to pursue their Resistance activities.

M. Blumenson, *Le réseau du Musée de l'Homme. Les débuts de la Résistance en France* (Paris, 1979); A. Humbert, *Notre Guerre* (Paris, 1946); S. Martin-Chauffier, *A bientôt quand même . . .* (Paris, 1975); ''Musée de l'Homme,'' unpublished material, file in Bibliothèque de Documentation Internationale et Contemporaine, Nanterre, France; B. Vildé, *Journal et lettres de prison, 1941–1942* (Paris, 1997).

G. Piketty

N

NATIONAL REVOLUTION (la Révolution Nationale) was the name given to the **Vichy** government's (**État Français**) program of French renewal during the 1940–1944 Occupation. It was described by Raymond Postal in a pro-Vichy compendium in 1941 as the revival of a mystique of France centered around Marshal **Pétain**, who would lead France to the recovery of its spiritual values and political standing in Europe, lost by a so-called decadent Third **Republic** that had brought on the disaster of 1940.

The National Revolution was domestic, produced by the French, who turned in large numbers against the Republic, deemed responsible for the 1940 debacle. For many it was an opportunity to remake France in what appeared to be a revolutionary situation, a chance to gain revenge for real and imagined grievances against the Republican governing elites, and the hope that the protective persona of Marshal Pétain would somehow enable France to avoid a draconian German peace. The National Revolution, however, unfolded under a German occupation whose confines became more constricting as the war progressed. In its four-year history it never experienced peacetime conditions. With the German occupation of the previously unoccupied southern **zone**, the scuttling of the French fleet, and the loss of the **empire** in 1942, Vichy lost even the independence it had previously had. The National Revolution became linked increasingly with a **collaboration** that meant German exploitation of France, including the **deportation** of **Jews** and other enemies of the Reich to extermination camps. It and the Vichy government disappeared with the 1944 **liberation**.

The term "national revolution" preceded the 1940 defeat, appearing in 1924 as the title of a book by Georges Valois, leader of the pro-**fascist** Faisceau, and also in the political discourse of the interwar Jeunesses Patriotes, led by Pierre Taittinger. Although it came to designate Vichy's agenda, the term was not favored by Pétain, who used it infrequently, preferring "*Redressement national*" (national recovery) and "*Rénovation française*" (French renewal) instead of the word "revolution."

Given the many possibilities inherent in "mystique" and Pétain's disinclination to enunciate specific doctrine, the National Revolution incorporated contradictions. Its framework, however, was clear. In addition to supporting the rule of the would-be providential leader, Pétain, it stood for a Catholic, if not clerical, moral and corporate order, based on ''natural'' hierarchical elites and opposed the parliamentary democracy and egalitarianism of the Third Republic. It promoted a strong state, yet at the same time a ''revival'' of provincial authority against the dominance of Paris. Comprising a retrospective nostalgia that idealized village artisans and rural **peasants** over the cosmopolitanism of **Paris** and the other large cities, it also, however, embraced the technocratic elites and administrative reformers—the Paris *métro* was reorganized in 1942—whose role was highlighted under Admiral **Darlan** and whose legacy carried into the Fifth Republic.

Under the National Revolution, **communists** and **Freemasons** were hunted down, and Jews were deported to the extermination camps. Although it attracted trade unionists, **pacifists**, and others from the interwar **Left**, the National Revolution was rooted in the history of the French **Right**, looking to the pre-1789 French Old Regime, authoritarian Bonapartism, the hierarchical quality of the ''natural'' bourgeois elites of the Orléanist period, the ''moral order'' of the government of Adolphe Thiers, which had crushed the Paris Commune of 1871, a variety of Catholic social corporatist theorists, the **Action Française** of Charles **Maurras**, and contemporary fascism.

The National Revolution made changes in **symbols**, replacing the trilogy ''liberty, equality, fraternity'' with ''work, **family**, fatherland,'' borrowed from Colonel François **de La Rocque's Parti Social Français**, and de-emphasizing the 14 July Bastille Day holiday in favor of May Day, Mother's Day, and festivals associated with Joan of Arc. Although shifting its center of gravity over time from the idealism of the ''all things were possible'' mood of July 1940 to the **police** repression of Joseph **Darnand** and the **Milice Française** in 1944, the National Revolution was characterized throughout its era by **purges**, for example, of the local administration during the fall of 1940, and repression of those groups seen as outside the national community.

Historians still debate the degree to which the National Revolution represented a French form of fascism.

R. Aron, *The Vichy Regime 1940–44*, trans. H. Hare (Boston, 1969 [original French ed., 1955]); J.-P. Cointet, *Histoire de Vichy* (Paris, 1996); J.-M. Guillon, ''La philosophie politique de la Révolution nationale,'' in J.-P. Azéma and F. Bédarida, eds., *Vichy et les Français* (Paris, 1992), 167–83; R. O. Paxton, *Vichy France: Old Guard and New Order* (New York, 1972); R. Postal, ed., *France 1941, La Révolution Nationale Constructive, Un Bilan et un Programme* (Paris, 1941); O. Wurmser, *Les Origines doctrinales de la Révolution nationale* (Paris, 1971).

B. M. Gordon

NEW ORDER (NEW EUROPE, EUROPEAN UNITY), an umbrella term for Nazi Germany's policy of economic and political reorganization of the entire

European continent, based on military force, conquest, and belief in German racial superiority. In respect to France, without being a coherent doctrine, it resulted in the annexation of **Alsace-Lorraine** and in the fragmentation of the French **economy** and its subordination to German needs. The Reich leaders did not anticipate positive French participation in the construction of a New Order.

However, **Vichy** state **collaborationism**, predicated on a belief in German victory, had the goal of securing a place for France in the New Order, deliberately confusing this policy with its own **National Revolution**. Intimately associated with anticommunist ideology, the New Order was also the paradigm underlying Marcel **Déat's Rassemblement National Populaire**, Jacques **Doriot's Parti Populaire Français**, and the **Légion des Volontaires Français contre le Bolchevisme**. For intellectuals, such as Robert **Brasillach**, Pierre **Drieu la Rochelle**, and Lucien **Rebatet**, the sense of France's decadence rendered the ideal of a new Europe attractive, even if it meant collaboration with Nazi Germany.

Discrepancies between German perceptions and French illusions were evident as Vichy became more overtly a puppet regime. The Nazi New Order needs to be contrasted with more democratic ideals of European unity generated between the wars and developed within the **Resistance**. Controversy remains about whether Vichy ideas of European cooperation served the development of today's European Union or whether the latter grew out of an explicit rejection of the wartime New Order.

Y. Durand, *Le nouvel ordre nazi: la collaboration dans l'Europe allemande 1938– 1945* (Brussels, 1991); B. Gordon, "Frontiers in the Vichy Mind and Contemporary French Views of France in the European Union," in C. Baecheler and C. Fink, eds., *L'Établissement des frontières en Europe après les deux guerres mondiales* (Berne, 1996), 281–299; G. Loiseaux, *La Littérature de la défaite et de la collaboration* (Paris, 1984); A. Milward, *The New Order and the French Economy* (Oxford, 1970); R. O. Paxton, *Vichy France: Old Guard and New Order 1940–1944* (New York, 1972).

C. W. Nettelbeck

NIGHT AND FOG (NUIT ET BROUILLARD, 1956) was Alain Resnais' 31-minute documentary film devoted to the Nazi death camps. The title refers to **Hitler's** 1941 decree (Nacht und Nebel Erlass) mandating that civilians in occupied areas accused of offenses against the Reich and its military should appear to vanish into thin air and thereby cease to exist.

Resnais was approached in 1955 by the Comité d'Histoire de la Deuxième Guerre Mondiale to make a documentary on the **deportation**, but he accepted only after enlisting the help of Mauthausen survivor Jean Cayrol. Accompanied to Poland by a film crew and historical advisers Olga Wormser and Henri Michel, Resnais filmed color sequences on site at Auschwitz. Awarded the 1956 Jean Vigo Prize in recognition of Resnais' independence of spirit and quality of direction, the film was screened at Cannes over protests by West German officials. Two months later, it was shown at the Berlin Film Festival.

Black and white photographs of the camps taken in 1945 alternating with sequences from Nazi documentaries and color footage filmed a decade later helped Resnais extrapolate backward in time to bear witness to deeds of unimaginable cruelty. Images of barbed-wire fences, crematory ovens, and mountains of discarded boots conveyed grim evidence of the **Holocaust**, whose reality many preferred to deny. The film's visual impact was enhanced by Michel Bouquet's haunting voice-over and by the "terrifying sweetness" (François Truffaut) of Hanns Eisler's musical score. Shown around the world, *Night and Fog* became the vehicle of testimony through which countless nonvictims first saw what survivors of the deportation had experienced but were often unable to express.

A. Insdorf, *Indelible Shadows* (New York, 1983); J. Monaco, *Alain Resnais* (New York, 1979); R. Raskin, *Nuit et brouillard* (Aarhus, 1987); F. Truffaut, "Rencontre avec Alain Resnais," *Arts et spectacles* (22 February 1956):5.

S. Ungar

NIMIER, ROGER (1925–1962), a writer who came to prominence as the leader of the anti-*résistantialiste* literary "**Hussards**" (Hussars) during the immediate postwar years, was raised the son of an engineer in Paris' 17th *arrondissement* (district). Oriented by family background and education toward the aristocratic **Right**, the young Nimier, however, during the Occupation looked more to General **de Gaulle** than to the **Maurrasians** of **Vichy** for political inspiration.

The **purge** that followed the **Liberation**, especially de Gaulle's refusal to reprieve the **collaborationist** writer Robert **Brasillach**, who was executed in February 1945, turned Nimier toward the oppositional Right. In March 1945, he joined the army's Second Hussars (Hussards), but the war ended while he was still training in France, and he was demobilized in August. By late 1945, he had become active in right-wing monarchist politics and anti-*résistantialiste* literary circles. Disillusioned in his hope that de Gaulle would prevent what he saw as the reemergence of mediocrity in the early days of the Fourth **Republic**, Nimier turned his literary attention to the ex-*Résistant* writer Georges Bernanos, whom he perceived as a model of refusal to compromise with the pettiness of the new regime and who had just died in 1948. Nimier's *Le Grand d'Espagne* (1950) was an apotheosis of Bernanos as a noble Spanish grandee representing the opposite of *résistantialiste* hypocrisy.

Two novels, *Les Épées* (1948) and *Le Hussard bleu* (1950), made Nimier's reputation as one of France's premier Second World War novelists. In both novels, Nimier evoked the sincerity of ardent collaborators and resisters as preferable to those who had hypocritically evaded choices or remained in the middle. By relativizing the collaboration/resistance dichotomy, Nimier represented the choices of right-wing, bourgeois young Frenchmen of the immediate postwar era against the dominant directions of Sartrian existentialism. Nimier was killed in an automobile accident in September 1962.

N. Hewitt, *Literature and the Right in Postwar France: The Story of the "Hussards"*

(Oxford and New York, 1996); R. Nimier, *Le Grand d'Espagne* (Paris, 1950); R. Nimier, *The Blue Hussar*, trans. J. Russell and A. Rhodes (London, 1952) [original French ed.: *Le Hussard bleu* (Paris, 1950)]; R. Nimier, *Les Épées* (Paris, 1948).

B. M. Gordon

NOGUÈS, AUGUSTE (1876–1971), resident-general of France in Morocco, 1936–1943, resisted the Allied landings in **North Africa** in November 1942 (Operation Torch).

A student of Marshal Louis-Hubert Lyautey, France's celebrated practitioner of colonial conquest and rule, Noguès was named resident-general of Morocco by the **Blum** government in 1936. With the coming of war in September 1939 General Noguès commanded the North African Theater of Operations, headquartered at Algiers. After French reverses in Europe in May 1940, he counseled the government to continue the fight against Germany from North Africa. His telegrams still make stirring reading. Ultimately, however, he obeyed the orders to lay down his arms and accept the **armistice** with Germany; Noguès was given the assurance that no portion of France's territory in North Africa (Morocco, Algeria, and Tunisia) would be ceded to Germany, **Italy**, or **Spain**.

During his tenure under **Vichy**, Noguès followed the lead of General Maxime **Weygand, Pétain's** delegate in French Africa, who was convinced that the **armistice** had saved France from destruction and preserved the unity of its **army** and **empire**. Like Weygand, Noguès was determined to keep Morocco out of the war and securely in **Vichy** hands. An unenthusiastic supporter of Vichy's collaboration policy, he secretly stockpiled weapons and trained Moroccan troops in the Atlas mountains for the day when Germany "would break its promises."

When the **Americans** landed in Morocco in November 1942, Noguès met them with all the firepower he possessed, persuaded that only resistance to all comers would preserve France's increasingly fragile hold over Morocco. Overwhelmed by superior force, he managed to convince the Americans of his usefulness to the Allied cause and remained resident-general of Morocco until June 1943. Convicted by the postwar High Court (**Haute Cour de Justice**) of "offenses against the security of the state," Noguès was excused from all punishment for his wartime "acts of Resistance."

*W. A. Hoisington, Jr., *The Casablanca Connection: French Colonial Policy, 1936–1943* (Chapel Hill, NC, 1984); R. O. Paxton, *Parades and Politics at Vichy: The French Officer Corps under Marshal Pétain* (Princeton, 1966).

W. A. Hoisington, Jr.

NORMANDY, ALLIED INVASION (OPERATION OVERLORD OR D-DAY), the amphibious landing of **American, British**, and Canadian military forces along the beaches of Lower Normandy on 6 June 1944.

The Normandy invasion brought Allied armies to France for the first time since the British evacuation from the port of Dunkirk four years earlier. The D-

Day landing established the second front that **Soviet** leader Joseph Stalin had been demanding since early 1942 in order to relieve the Red Army, which had been single-handedly fighting **Hitler's** forces in Europe since the German invasion of the Soviet Union on 22 June 1941.

After assembling a formidable arsenal of manpower, weaponry, and supplies along the southern coast of England, supreme Allied commander Dwight D. Eisenhower launched an invasion armada across the English Channel in the early morning of 6 June. By the end of that day Allied soldiers had secured beachheads that were eventually expanded to form a supply line for the Anglo-American forces that poured into France during the summer of 1944 to launch a massive offensive against the retreating German armies. General **de Gaulle**, head of the **Free French** government in exile, had been excluded from the planning and execution of the Normandy invasion. Appearing in Bayeux, the first French city to be liberated, he promptly established liaison with the French **Resistance** and prepared the way for his accession to the leadership of the first postwar French government.

The spectacular success of the Normandy invasion represented a major turning point in the European theater of the Second World War, leading to the collapse of the **Vichy** regime, the **liberation** of France, and (in conjunction with the **Russian** army advancing from the east) the defeat of Nazi Germany.

C. D'Este, *Decision in Normandy* (New York, 1994); M. Hastings, *Overlord* (New York, 1984); J. Keegan, *Six Armies in Normandy* (New York, 1982).

W. R. Keylor

NORTH AFRICA, ALLIED INVASION (OPERATION TORCH). On 8 November 1942, 108,000 **Anglo-American** troops invaded French North Africa at three sites along the Atlantic coast of Morocco (Casablanca, Rabat, and Safi) and two points along the Mediterranean coast of Algeria (Algiers and Oran). Operation Torch was planned as the first step toward the **liberation** of the European mainland.

The American hope was to persuade French commanders not to resist the landings but to greet the invaders as allies and join them in a crusade to liberate France. American agents did recruit key French soldiers to aid their cause (notably, Generals Henri **Giraud**, Émile Béthouart, and Charles Mast), but ultimately they were unable to break the **Vichy** chain of command that linked North Africa to Marshal **Pétain**. The unexpected appearance in Algiers of Admiral Jean-François **Darlan**, Vichy's number two man, on the eve of the landings made things more, not less, complicated.

As a result, French troops opposed the Allied invasion, even though nowhere (except perhaps Morocco) with real enthusiasm. Still, in three days of fighting the French inflicted 1,500 casualties on the Anglo-American forces. In addition, the delay in Morocco and Algeria prevented a quick move into Tunisia, where the Germans—with Vichy approval—had rushed troops to block any Allied advance. In the end, U.S. General Mark W. Clark negotiated an agreement with

Darlan that provided for an immediate end to all French opposition to the landings and for French cooperation in the fight against the Axis. In return, the Allies agreed to leave the entire Vichy command in place with Darlan at the top as "high commissioner in French Africa."

Darlan's assassination in Algiers in December 1942 significantly altered the political situation in North Africa. Giraud succeeded him for a time, but after the establishment of the French Committee of National Liberation in June 1943 (with Giraud and Charles **de Gaulle** as cochairs), Giraud was quickly pushed aside.

A. Funk, *The Politics of Torch: The Allied Landings and the Algiers Putsch, 1942* (Lawrence, KS, 1974); W. A. Hoisington, Jr., *The Casablanca Connection: French Colonial Policy, 1936–1943* (Chapel Hill, NC, 1984); G. Howe, *Northwest Africa: Seizing the Initiative in the West* (Washington, DC, 1957, 1991).

W. A. Hoisington, Jr.

NOUVELLE REVUE FRANÇAISE (*NRF*, 1908–) was a literary monthly started by writers and intellectuals around André **Gide** that evolved between the wars under editors Jacques Rivière and Jean **Paulhan** into the exponent of a largely apolitical *moeurs littéraires* (literary ethos).

Because the German ambassador in occupied France, Otto **Abetz**, saw the *NRF* as a key to intellectual **collaboration**, he enlisted Pierre **Drieu la Rochelle**, onetime head of the French section of the Hitler Youth Movement, to keep the monthly in print after Paulhan shut it down in September 1940. When **Drieu** informed the *NRF's* **publisher**, Gaston Gallimard, that naming him editor would keep the Éditions Gallimard in business because of his contacts with Abetz and Gerhard Heller of the German propaganda staff in **Paris**, Gallimard relented. Drieu's *NRF* appeared in December 1940, bearing the same title and red colophon as its predecessor. The inclusion of pro-**fascist**, **anti-Semitic** texts by Abel **Bonnard**, Jacques Chardonne, and others, however, soon set a tone that isolated Drieu from his former colleagues. By the spring of 1942, he was ready to step down. In March 1945, a month after the editor of the fascist *Je suis partout* weekly, Robert **Brasillach**, was executed following his trial as a collaborator, Drieu committed suicide.

Because the *NRF* under Drieu had upheld German policy by banning **Jews** and others perceived as anti-Nazi, Gallimard was investigated during the postwar **purge** of suspected collaborators. In Gallimard's defense, Albert **Camus**, André **Malraux**, and Jean-Paul **Sartre** maintained that his office had been a meeting place for underground activities. Gallimard had to drop the *Éditions de la NRF* designation; the monthly reappeared only in 1954.

P. Assouline, *Gaston Gallimard: A Half-Century of French Publishing*, trans. H. J. Salemson (New York, 1984); P. Hebey, *La Nouvelle revue française des années sombres* (Paris, 1992); A. Kaplan, "Literature and Collaboration," in D. Hollier, ed., *A New History of French Literature* (Cambridge, 1989).

S. Ungar

O

OBERG, CARL (OR KARL) ALBRECHT (1897–1965), SS-Brigadeführer and Police Major General, head of the German police in occupied France. Supreme SS and police chief from May 1942 until the German withdrawal, he attempted to maintain internal security in France by **collaboration** with the French **police** and following relatively moderate policies toward the French.

Carl Oberg, a former lieutenant and a repeated failure in civilian life, in 1931 joined the National Socialist (Nazi) Party and its Security Service (Sicherheitsdienst, SD), led by Reinhard Heydrich. Working closely with Heydrich, Oberg rose rapidly in the German police after the Nazi accession to power in 1933, eventually serving as president of the police (*Polizeipräsident*) in Zwickau and SS and police chief in Radom. Supported after 1940 in France by Heydrich, then head of the Reich's high-security office (Reichssicherheitshauptamt), Oberg ended the policy of shooting hostages in reprisal for attacks on German soldiers and negotiated an agreement with French police chief René **Bousquet** whereby the French police took over, in most cases and with great success, hunting down **communist** assailants. Oberg maintained good relations with the Wehrmacht and supreme military commander Heinrich von Stülpnagel, a former regiment comrade. For this connection, in addition to his predilection for "the habits of a bureaucrat," at the time of the destruction of the old port of Marseilles in January 1943 Oberg was reproached by Heinrich Himmler, head of the German police. Because of the numerical weakness of his own forces, Oberg tried continually to energize the French police. He rejected as useless and counterproductive the mass reprisals for **Resistance** attacks repeatedly called for by the German leadership.

After 1945 he was brought to trial in France, sentenced to death in 1954, pardoned in 1962, and released to the Federal Republic of Germany.

R. B. Birn, *Die Höheren SS-und Polizeiführer* (Düsseldorf, 1986); J. Delarue, *Geschichte der Gestapo* (Düsseldorf, 1964), English ed., *The Gestapo: A History of Terror*, trans. M. Savill (New York, 1964, 1987), original French ed., *Histoire de la Gestapo*

(Paris, 1962); B. Kasten, *"Gute Franzözen:" die französische Polizei und die deutsche Besatzsungsmacht im besetzten Frankreich* (Sigmaringen, 1993).

B. Kasten

OFFICE OF STRATEGIC SERVICES (OSS) was the **American** intelligence service formed in July 1942 and staffed, for the most part, by the wealthy and well-connected graduates of the nation's most prestigious colleges. French **North Africa** was the organization's first major assignment. The OSS developed useful information for Operation Torch, but its efforts at sabotage and other infiltration operations proved disappointing. Consistent with American policy, it formed contacts with **Giraudist** elements in the French military and with anti-fascist groups, but these connections were compromised by the Allies' deal with Admiral **Darlan**.

Significant OSS operations in metropolitan France were delayed until early 1944 by jurisdictional agreements with the **British Special Operations Executive (SOE)**, infighting within the American government, and doubts about the reliability of the **Resistance**. As the time for an invasion of France grew nearer, the OSS overcame these obstacles. Thereafter it rapidly stepped up arms shipments to Resistance groups and developed contacts with their spy networks. During the **Normandy** invasion the OSS was in a position to help coordinate sabotage and intelligence gathering in support of the advancing Allied armies.

OSS operations existed throughout the French **empire**, and, as the war closed, its agents sometimes raised the ire of the newly restored French government. This was particularly true in Indochina, where American officers used Vietminh networks for intelligence gathering, made its leader **Ho** Chi Minh an officer, and, albeit unsuccessfully, attempted to convince their government not to support a return of French rule.

F. Calvi and O. Schmidt. *OSS, la guerre secrète en France, 1942–1945, les services spéciaux américains, la Résistance et la Gestapo* (Paris, 1990); B. F. Smith, *The Shadow Warriors, O.S.S. and the Origins of the C.I.A.* (New York, 1983).

A. A. Workman

ONE TWO TWO was a brothel in **Paris** in the 1930s and 1940s. During the Occupation, One Two Two was a marketplace of contacts between German authorities and the French underworld.

Managed by Marcel Jamet (1890–1964), alias "Fraisette," and his wife, Fabienne, One Two Two was the most famous Paris brothel, visited by artists and high society during the Occupation. Its name derived from its address at 122, rue de Provence. Frequent guests included members of the Carlingue or Bonny-Lafont gang of criminals, officially called the Lauristondienst (Lauriston Service), a French auxiliary group of the Abwehr. Henri Lafont, alias Henri Louis Chamberlin (1902–1944), head of the Carlingue, introduced Jamet to Captain Wilhelm Radecke and his superior, Colonel Hermann Brandl, alias Doktor Otto, head of the German purchasing bureau. Radecke, who enjoyed frequenting One

Two Two, helped to provide the brothel with **rationed** luxury goods. One Two Two was also visited by German middlemen, as well as Paris underworld personalities who made fortunes by doing business with the Reich. Such underworld figures included Joseph Joanovici (1902–1965), who satisfied German demands for scrap metal, and Mandel Szkolnikoff (1895–1945), who provided clothes for the Germans.

His relations with the Germans and the Carlingue almost proved Marcel Jamet's undoing. On 18 September 1944 he was arrested by the French criminal investigation department but released after nine days. The Carlingue group was tried, with most of its leaders sentenced to death and executed in December. One Two Two was closed by law in 1946.

F. Jamet, *One Two Two* (Paris, 1975); G. Ragache and J.-R. Ragache, *La vie quotidienne des écrivains et des artistes sous l'Occupation, 1940–1944* (Paris, 1988); H. Sergg, *Paris—Gestapo* (Paris, 1989).

W. Freund

ORADOUR-SUR-GLANE, MASSACRE is one of the worst atrocities the Germans committed in France. Elements of the Second SS Panzer Division (**"Das Reich"**) shot or burned to death nearly all of the inhabitants of Oradour-sur-Glane, a village in the Haute Vienne. The crime's brutality and the unsatisfactory postwar trial have been permanently implanted in the minds of many French citizens.

On 7 June 1944, Das Reich deployed northward from southern France to engage the Allies in **Normandy. Resistance** activities frustrated its progress, and on 8 June, the **liberation** of nearby Tulle by the *maquis* led to severe German reprisals. On 10 June, after an officer of the division had been captured by Resistance forces, the commander of the first battalion, a friend of the missing man, arrived in Oradour with the elite "Der Führer" regiment's third company. Acting on a tip that the missing officer had been in Oradour, SS troops assembled the inhabitants in the town square. The **women**, children, and elderly were then forced into the town's church, while the men were taken into other buildings. On command, the soldiers began shooting their captives. Afterward, they set fire to the church and buildings, killing nearly everyone. The massacre continued late into the night, as the Germans finished burning the town. In all, 643 men, women, and children were killed.

In 1953, 21 ex-members of the division stood trial. Conspicuously absent were any officers. Thirteen defendants were forcibly drafted **Alsatians**. Legal ambiguities frustrated attempts at effective convictions. Despite two death sentences, all of the Germans were shortly thereafter released. The Alsatians received amnesty. Emotions concerning the Oradour and Tulle massacres were intensified in the 1990s by denials that they had occurred, transmitted on the internet, and by a re-writing of the events by a German tourist guide book to make it appear that the massacres had been legitimate responses to French provocation.

S. B. Farmer, *Oradour: Arrêt sur mémoire* (Paris, 1994); S. B. Farmer, "Oradour-sur-Glane: Memory in a Preserved Landscape," *FHS* 19:1 (Spring 1995): 27–47; E. Grau and M. Kilian, *DuMont Kunst-Reiseführer, Das Limousin* (Cologne, 1992); M. Hastings, *Das Reich: Resistance and the March of the 2nd SS Panzer Division through France, June 1944* (New York, 1981); G. Guichetau, *La Das Reich et le cœur de la France* (Paris, 1974).

R. W. White

ORDRE NOUVEAU (ON) was a "nonconformist" intellectual movement whose personalist philosophy, related to **Esprit's**, and federalist politics influenced both **Vichy** and **Resistance** discourse. Its review, *L'Ordre Nouveau*, was published from 1933 to 1938. ON was an early supporter of Charles **de Gaulle's** military ideas, published in 1935 as a result of the efforts of Henri Daniel-Rops, the movement's best-known spokesman.

Some ON members went on to high-profile positions as civil servants under Vichy. These included Jean **Jardin** and two drawn from the technocratic X-crise group: Robert Gibrat, secretary of communications in 1942, and Robert Loustau, who helped draft the new regime's social policies. Albert Ollivier was director of Radio-Jeunesse for Jeune France, but like some other ON militants, he later joined the Gaullist Resistance movement **Combat**.

Another ON leader, Robert Aron, supported General Henri **Giraud's** Resistance faction and later wrote an important history of Vichy, published in 1954. ON's founder, Alexandre Marc, was an early member of the **Catholic** Resistance with the **Témoignage chrétien** group, together with many other personalists. Marc initiated Franco–German **youth** group dialogue before 1933, in contact with Otto **Abetz** at first and then, over a longer period, with Harro Schulze-Boysen, executed in Germany in late 1942 when his Rote Kapelle anti-Nazi Resistance network was dismantled. Around the same time, Marc had to flee to **Switzerland**, and Aron to Algeria. When the war ended, they and other former ON activists went on to promote their personalist ideas at the forefront of a distinctive current within the European federalist movement.

J. Hellman and C. Roy, "Personnalisme et contacts entre non-conformistes de France et d'Allemagne," in H. M. Bock, ed., *Entre Locarno et Vichy: les relations culturelles franco-allemandes dans les années 30* (Paris, 1993); J.-L. Loubet del Bayle, *Les non-conformistes des années 30* (Paris, 1969); P. Sigoda, "Charles de Gaulle, la 'Révolution conservatrice' et le personnalisme du mouvement 'l'Ordre Nouveau,'" Espoir, 46 (March 1984): 43–49.

C. Roy

ORGANISATION CIVILE ET MILITAIRE (OCM), founded in 1940, was one of the main northern **zone Resistance** movements and a member of the **Conseil National de la Résistance (CNR)**.

Early on, the OCM's military element was composed of officers, some of whom had not broken with **Vichy**, such as Colonel Alfred Heurtaux, who was an agent of the **Armistice Army**'s intelligence service, its "Deuxième Bureau," and the vice president of the **Légion Française des Combattants**. Colonel Alfred Touny succeeded Heurtaux, who was arrested in November 1941. Touny was president of the movement's steering committee from April 1943 until his arrest in February 1944. Maxime Blocq-Mascart replaced him.

Blocq-Mascart, who created the civilian component of the movement, had been an economic consultant and vice president of the interwar Confédération des Travailleurs Intellectuels. A representative of OCM in the CNR and a member of its steering committee, Blocq-Mascart played a role in defending the rights of the interior Resistance in discussions relating to the future of France. From 1942 on, he edited the *Cahiers de l'OCM*. The first *Cahier* created a scandal among the Resistance because of cultural **anti-Semitism** in one of its articles. The OCM looked to a future postwar France with economic planning, the reinforcement of the executive power, and the election of the president by universal suffrage.

An original aspect of the OCM was the creation of a **youth** affiliate, the OCMJ (OCM-Jeunesse) in July 1943. By the autumn of 1943, the OCM numbered more than 60,000 persons, but in the winter of 1944, the Germans destroyed the military structure of OCM, leaving only the local groups. After the war, the movement participated in the creation of a center-**left** political party, the *Union démocratique et Socialiste de la Résistance (UDSR)*, which it left in 1946.

A. Calmette, *L'OCM* (Paris, 1961); G. Groussard, *Service secret 1940–1945* (Paris, 1964); H. Noguères, *Histoire de la Résistance en France,* 5 vols. (Paris, 1967–1981); Passy (A. Dewavrin), *Souvenirs*, 3 vols. (Monte Carlo, 1947–1948, and Paris, 1951).

C. Andrieu

OTTO LISTS were a series of listings of books banned by the German occupying authorities. The suppression of unacceptable books, characteristic of the Nazi approach to literature, was applied vigorously in occupied France. Within a few days of the 1940 defeat a preliminary list, the *"liste Bernhard"* proscribed 13 titles. Over the next three months, the German Propaganda Abteilung (Propaganda Department) worked to establish a more comprehensive listing, which it drew up in consultation with the French **publishers'** association, the Syndicat des éditeurs français et des maisons d'édition. The resulting list of 1,060 titles was published in September 1940 and became known as the *"liste Otto."* This was the authoritative listing of banned books to which a set of additional titles was added in July 1941, with further amendments in July 1942 and May 1943.

The lists aimed to ban anti-German, antifascist, and oppositional writings, works by **Jewish** authors, and all Marxist or **communist** material. Many translations of **British** and **American** books, other than recognized literary classics, were banned. Later versions of the list banned **Russian** and Polish books and biographies of Jews. A substantial number of schoolbooks were also included. The publishers most affected were Gallimard (140 titles banned), Fayard (110),

Presses Universitaires de France (101), and Tallandier (51). Gallimard's partly Jewish ownership also led to its closure for three weeks in November 1940.

The immediate consequence of the lists was the seizure and destruction of more than 700,000 books in bookshops on 3 September 1940, followed a week later by an agreement on censorship with the publishers, who were obliged to destroy a further 8,000 books and to pulp several tons of paper. Despite their incompleteness and their incoherence, the Otto lists were symbolically the iron fist of the Propaganda Abteilung, which generally preferred to manage French opinion with a velvet glove.

J.-P. Azéma, *1940, l'année terrible* (Paris, 1990); P. Fouché, *L'Édition française sous l'occupation* (Paris, 1987); G. Loiseaux, *La littérature de la défaite et de la collaboration* (Paris, 1984).

M. Kelly

P

PACIFISTS grew in number throughout Europe after World War I, when so many men lost their lives in what appeared a futile attempt at resolving political differences among nations. Romain Rolland was awarded the Nobel Prize in literature for his *Jean-Christophe* in the middle of the war, when he accused both French and German military authorities of being barbarian. His book, *Au-dessus de la Mêlée* (Above the Battle) (1915), called on all men to stand up against war.

Political opportunists sometimes used pacifist arguments selectively for other ends. During the 1939 crisis that precipitated World War II, Marcel **Déat**, a former **socialist**, wrote an editorial opposing those who wished *"Mourir pour Dantzig"* (to die for Danzig). Articulating a defeatist current within France, Déat's words became a rallying cry for all those who wished to avoid confrontation with Nazi Germany over Poland, although some who agreed with Déat were willing to support Finland against the **Soviet Union** later in 1939.

Those more consistent than Déat in their pacifism who refused to fight Nazi Germany included Jean **Giono**, a World War I veteran who had written *Le Grand Troupeau* (The Great Flock) in 1931, a lyrical antiwar book. Refusing to serve again in the **army**, he was sentenced to prison in World War II. The paradox that led honest pacifists to unwittingly facilitate the defeat of their country was highlighted by Jean-Paul **Sartre**, who wrote of "the alliance of the most fervent pacifists with the very soldiers of a warrior society."

R. Cheval, *Romain Rolland, l'Allemagne et la Guerre* (Paris, 1963); N. Ingram, *The Politics of Dissent: Pacifism in France, 1919–1939* (Oxford, 1991); H. Michel, *The Second World War*, trans. D. Parmee (New York and Washington, DC, 1968); R. Young, *France and the Origins of the Second World War* (New York, 1996).

K. Bieber

PAPON, MAURICE (1910–), secretary-general of **Vichy's** regional administration in the Bordeaux region, the Gironde Prefecture, from 1 June 1942 until 22 August 1944, has been charged with crimes against humanity for his role in the arrest and **deportation** of more than 1,600 **Jews**. Prepared for an exceptional administrative career by the prestigious *lycée* Louis-le-Grand in Paris and by **university** degrees in law and political science, Papon began by holding several positions under the direction of Radical Socialist officials of the Third **Republic** from July 1935 to the end of August 1939. Called back into the military in August 1939, he served as lieutenant in the colonial infantry until his discharge in October 1940, when he resumed his career as a functionary in the **Interior** Ministry under the direction of Maurice Sabatier. Named prefect of the Aquitaine region by **Laval** in May 1942, Sabatier appointed Maurice Papon as his secretary-general for the department of the Gironde. In this capacity, given both the power to sign for the regional prefect Sabatier as well as the primary responsibility for relations with the Nazi occupants, Papon, according to Gérard Boulanger, functioned as the real technician of the deportations from the Bordeaux region, keeping records of Jews, supplying lists of those to be deported, planning and carrying out **police** raids, and organizing transfers to Drancy, from where almost all were to be deported to Auschwitz. Following the **liberation**, Papon was promoted prefect for the Landes department in September 1944. He also served as police prefect for Paris under **de Gaulle** from 1958 to 1967 and later as budget minister for President Valéry Giscard d'Estaing. Papon was indicted for crimes against humanity in January 1983. After years of legal maneuverings, he was convicted and sentenced to a ten year prison term in April 1998.

G. Boulanger, *Maurice Papon: un technocrate français dans la collaboration* (Paris, 1994); B. M. Gordon, "Afterward: Who Are the Guilty and Should They Be Tried?" in R. J. Golsan, ed., *Memory, the Holocaust, and French Justice* (Hanover, NH, 1996), 179–98; B. M. Gordon, "Collaboration, Retribution, and Crimes against Humanity: The Touvier, Bousquet, and Papon Affairs," *CFC* 19:2 (Summer/Fall 1995): 250–74; M. Slitinsky, *L'Affaire Papon* (Paris, 1983).

N. Bracher

PARIS, the political, economic, and cultural center of modern France, was occupied by German forces in June 1940 and replaced as political capital by **Vichy**. Nonetheless, although Marshal **Pétain** remained in Vichy, many of the government services eventually returned to Paris even during the Occupation.

With the outbreak of war in September 1939, Paris began to take on a wartime aspect, blacked out at night, with many of its official and historic buildings protected by sandbags. Tens of thousands of Parisians fled the German advance in June 1940. Upon entering Paris, the Germans found it a ghost town. With the June 1940 **armistice**, however, the Germans and many of the French wanted to give Paris the appearance of peacetime normalcy. Encouraged by the Germans, **refugees** returned, nightclubs reopened, and the city resumed much of its cultural activity of prewar days. **Cinema** and **theater** flourished—plays by Jean-Paul **Sartre**, among others, were performed. Nightclubs featured stars such as Maurice **Chevalier**. Pro-Axis literary and journalistic circles, exemplified by Lucien **Rebatet** and Jean **Luchaire**, respectively, flourished, more so in occupied Paris than in provincial Vichy, even though Vichy remained unoccupied by the Germans until 1942. The **collaborationist Parti Populaire Français** and **Rassemblement National Populaire** also had their bases in Paris.

Despite—or, in a way, because of—a Nazi view of Paris as a corrupt "Babylon," the Germans used occupied Paris as a rest and rehabilitation center for their troops, and postings there were highly prized. **Hitler** visited the city as a tourist shortly after it was occupied, and German troops paraded regularly down the Champs Élysées to the tunes of military marches. Germans were allowed to ride free on the *métro,* and designated cinemas, nightclubs, and restaurants were reserved exclusively for them. A biweekly tourist guide, published in German, was made available to the occupation forces, thousands of whom were given tours of the city by a unit of the Wehrmacht created for that purpose. Parisian museums were looted to enrich the private art collections of Hermann **Göring** and other German officials.

While life for the Germans and their allies in occupied Paris was good, most of the French civilians suffered under drastically reduced **rations**. Many had to seek food from friends and relatives in the countryside. Civilians were sometimes killed accidentally in Allied bombing runs, especially during the latter stages of the Occupation. Parisian **Jews** often suffered the loss of their homes and businesses, many were eventually deported to extermination camps, while others went into hiding. An anti-German student demonstration on Armistice Day, 11 November 1940, led to dozens of arrests and was not repeated.

Paris was spared destruction twice, in June 1940, when it was declared an open city by the French and occupied without resistance, and in August 1944, when the German garrison commander Dietrich von Choltitz disobeyed Hitler's order to destroy the city rather than abandon it to the French. With the liberation of Paris, General **de Gaulle** headed a victory parade down the Champs Élysées, then consecrated the victory at Notre Dame Cathedral. Once again, Paris resumed its flourishing cultural activities and night life—English-language guidebooks replaced the German ones—but with France now mobilizing to participate in the final defeat of the Axis, it took several more years for most Parisians to recover from the privations of war and Occupation.

*†L. Collins and D. Lapierre, *Is Paris Burning?* (New York, 1965); B. M. Gordon, "*Ist Gott Französisch?* Germans, Tourism, and Occupied France, 1940–1944," MCF, n.s. 4:3 (1996): 287–98; H. Michel, *Paris Allemand* (Paris, 1982); G. Perrault and J.-P. Azéma, *Paris under the Occupation,* trans. A. Carter and M. Vos (New York, 1989 [original ed., 1987]); D. Pryce-Jones, *Paris in the Third Reich* (New York, 1981).

B. M. Gordon

PARIS, HENRI COMTE DE (1908–), pretender to the French throne who became the fifth French king in exile upon the death of his father, Jean III, duc de Guise, on 25 August 1940. An accomplished aviator and a tireless activist for the restoration of the monarchy, the comte de Paris embraced the conservative and corporatist doctrines of Charles **Maurras** but publicly disavowed

Action Française in 1937 in an effort to gain greater freedom of action and a wider following through a policy of moderation.

The Third **Republic** enlisted the diplomatic services of the comte de Paris during the **Phoney War** but refused to abrogate the Law of Exile and permit the pretender to serve in the French armed forces until May 1940, when he was allowed to join the Foreign Legion as a private, under an assumed name and nationality. Never in actual combat, he retreated with French forces before departing for Morocco, where he instructed his followers to oppose the Germans in the occupied **zone** while supporting the **Vichy** government in unoccupied France. Although he never formally backed General **de Gaulle**, the pretender turned against Vichy after the Germans invaded the south in November 1942. He became involved in an ill-fated effort to gain appointment as either high commissioner for French **North Africa** or head of a **Provisional Government** in Algiers after the assassination of Admiral **Darlan** on 24 December but faced **American** opposition and was forced to leave Algiers in January 1943. He spent the rest of the war in isolation in **Belgium** and **Spain**, where he tried to resume his campaign in favor of restoration. The repeal of the Law of Exile in June 1950 allowed him to supervise the publication of a monthly information bulletin from his headquarters on the Rue de Constantine in Paris.

J. Bourdier, *Le Comte de Paris* (Paris, 1965); F. Laot, *La Comtesse de Paris* (Paris, 1992); S. Osgood, *French Royalism since 1870* (The Hague, 1970); Comte de Paris, *Mémoires d'Exil et de Combats* (Paris, 1979).

S. Kale

PARIS, LIBERATION OF (August 1944) was the process by which **Paris** was freed from German occupation. On 14 August 1944, as Allied troops approached, representatives of the Parisian **Resistance** within the **police** force issued a declaration calling for a general strike. The next day some 20,000 of the police struck and were joined by thousands of others, thus beginning the Paris uprising.

On 18 August **communist Resistance** leaders called for total revolt. Although noncommunist Resistance leaders were dubious about the call, they realized that all factions had to act together, and they joined forces. On 19 August armed Resistance members took control of the Préfecture de Police and repulsed German counterattacks. The next day they captured the Hôtel de Ville. That day Raoul Nordling, the head of the Swedish mission, negotiated a truce with the Germans that essentially amounted to a cease-fire. Although it was accepted by the **Conseil National de la Résistance**, it was not accepted by all German defenders or by the Paris communists, who viewed it as a **right-wing** sellout to the Germans. Barricades soon went up throughout Paris.

The breakdown of the truce emphasized the split between the Gaullists and the **communists**. General **de Gaulle** feared that without Allied intervention **communists** would take control of the city and, eventually, France itself. He wanted Paris to be liberated by his **Free French** forces and persuaded Generals

Dwight D. Eisenhower and Omar Bradley to occupy the city instead of bypassing it, as had been previously planned. On 22 August Eisenhower ordered the French Second Armored Division, commanded by General Philippe **Leclerc**, to advance to Paris. The first units of this division entered the city on 24 August, followed the next day by the **U.S.** Fourth Infantry Division. De Gaulle led a victory parade down the Champs Élysées on 25 August and on 28 August declared an end to the battle for Paris.

J.-P. Azéma, *From Munich to the Liberation 1938–1944*, trans. J. Lloyd (Cambridge, U.K., and Paris, 1984 [original French ed., Paris, 1979]); L. Collins and D. Lapierre, *Is Paris Burning?* (New York, 1965); P. Taittinger, *Et Paris ne fût pas détruit* (Paris, 1948); W. Thornton, *The Liberation of Paris* (New York, 1962).

C. J. Haug

PARODI, ALEXANDRE (1901–1979), successor of Jean **Moulin** as general delegate in March 1944, then minister in the **Provisional Government (GPRF)**.

Maître des requêtes (literally, in charge of requests, a French bureaucratic title) in the State Council (Conseil d'État), in 1938 Parodi became a technical counselor in the Labor Ministry. In 1939, as director of manpower, he had to face the needs brought on by the war. Dismissed in the fall of 1940, he rejoined the State Council, which had withdrawn to Royat.

In the southern **zone**, Parodi contacted Emmanuel **d'Astier** de La Vigerie of **Libération-sud** and Pierre Tissier, a juridical counselor for **Free France**. In May–June 1942 **Jean Moulin** launched the idea of a committee of experts to help prepare for the **liberation**. A study committee (**Comité Général d'Études**) was created in Lyons in which Paul Bastid was given the *nom-de-guerre* "Primus," Robert Lacoste "Secondus," François **de Menthon** "Tertius," and Alexandre Parodi "Quartus." Parodi specialized in questions relating to the **press**, administration staffing, in collaboration with Michel **Debré**, and finances for which a **Resistance** loan was floated.

In charge of a growing Resistance structure in Paris in 1943, Parodi accepted, rather than sparked, the insurrection that broke out there on 19 August 1944. Arrested, then freed during a truce, he returned to the **police** prefecture offices. He rejoined the insurrection when it flared up again on the twenty-second and continued fighting until the arrival of General **Leclerc's** tanks. On the twenty-sixth, Parodi joined General **de Gaulle** in the march down the Champs Élysées that celebrated the **liberation of Paris**.

As minister of labor after the **liberation**, Parodi wrote laws on social security, trade organizations (*comités d'entreprise*), the placement of workers, and the management of the job marketplace. In 1946 he was named ambassador to Rome and, shortly after, France's permanent representative to the United Nations Security Council.

L. Joxe, *Notice sur la vie et les travaux d'Alexandre Parodi (1901–1979), lue dans la séance de mardi 20 avril 1982* (Paris, 1982); H. Noguères, *Histoire de la Résistance en France,* 5 vols. (Paris, 1967–1981); F.-M. Samuelson, *Il était une fois Libération, reportage historique* (Paris, 1979).

O. Rudelle

PARTI FRANÇAIS NATIONAL COLLECTIVISTE (PFNC) was a small movement founded in 1934 by Pierre Clémenti whose political activity continued into the Occupation years.

Born in 1910, Clémenti became first a metalworker, and then a sportswriter. He believed that the **right-wing** leagues had not truly attempted to overthrow the **Republic** during their march on the Chamber of Deputies in February 1934. The following April, he created the Parti Français National Communiste. Staunchly **anti-Semitic**, Clémenti spent 92 days in prison for anti-Semitic and racial defamation in 1939. Competing with former **communist** Jacques **Doriot** and the **Parti Populaire Français (PPF)** for a similar proletarian clientele after 1936, the PFNC depicted Doriot as ''sold out to the **Jews** and manipulated by the capitalists.''

Demobilized in **Paris**, while most of his rivals were in **Vichy** immediately after the 1940 **armistice**, Clémenti refloated his party, with headquarters on the Champs Élysées. The name ''Communist'' in his group, however, was supplanted by ''Collectiviste'' at the insistence of the Germans. Attacks against **youth** hostel quarters and rampages along the Champs Élysées in August 1940 in which windows of Jewish-owned shops were smashed by the Gardes Françaises, affiliated with the PFNC, got the movement into trouble with the German police.

The PFNC never made much headway in its competition with the larger and better-organized PPF, and internecine quarrels drove most of its supporters away. Clémenti, however, was one of the few **collaborationist** leaders who actually served in the anti-Bolshevik **Légion des Volontaires Français**. He was the only collaborationist spokesman to demand the French annexation of the Francophone territories of **Belgium**, placing him in direct conflict with Belgian Rexist leader Léon Degrelle. Condemned in 1954 for his wartime political activity, Clémenti continued to be active in small parties, such as Ordre Nouveau (not to be confused with the pre–World War II movement of the same name; see **Ordre Nouveau**), until his death in 1982.

B. M. Gordon, *Collaborationism in France during the Second World War* (Ithaca, NY, 1980); P.-P. Lambert and G. Le Marec, *Partis et Mouvements de la Collaboration, Paris 1940–1944* (Paris, 1993).

G. Le Marec

PARTI POPULAIRE FRANÇAIS (PPF, 1936–1944), a **collaborationist** party based in **Paris** during the Occupation.

Founded in Paris by the former **communist** Jacques **Doriot** in the summer of 1936, the party's key platform was anticommunism. PPF leaders described the Communist Party as the ''party of the foreigner'' behind the **Popular Front**, promoting social disintegration and war. Membership before the war may have peaked at 100,000 in the anti-Popular Front hysteria of 1936, but it appears to have fallen to less than half that two years later. The evidence suggests a socially heterogeneous base, including a large working-class ex-communist contingent, as well as **right-wing** employers, **industrialists** such as Pierre **Pucheu**, and disenchanted writers and intellectuals such as Pierre **Drieu la Rochelle**. Both French financiers and the Italian government helped fund the party.

After the 1940 defeat, the party, resurrected in the unoccupied **zone** as the Mouvement Populaire Français, adopted an **anti-Semitic** and collaborationist line. Its members, who appear to have been increasingly marginal, idle, or criminal, favored uniforms, raised arm salutes, street violence, and the cult of their *chef*, (leader) Doriot, who along with other members of the party joined the French volunteers who served in German uniforms on the **Russian** front.

Vichy helped fund the party, but Doriot's rapport with **Pétain** was distant, and the PPF never had a strong presence at Vichy. It quickly became one of the main "ultra," or extremist, parties in **Paris**. At the **liberation** some of the party's surviving leaders and members fled to Germany, where, in February 1945, Doriot was killed during an Allied air raid. With him died the chief and, according to some, the only **fascist** movement in French history.

J.-P. Brunet, *Jacques Doriot* (Paris, 1986); P. Burrin, *La dérive fasciste, Doriot, Déat, Bergery, 1933–1945* (Paris, 1986); R. Soucy, *French Fascism: The Second Wave* (New Haven, CT, and London, 1995); D. Wolf, *Die Doriot Bewegung* (Stuttgart, 1967).

P. F. Jankowski

PARTI SOCIAL FRANÇAIS (PSF, 1936–1944), a **right-wing** party founded in the summer of 1936 and disbanded at the **liberation**.

When the Croix-de-Feu, the prewar veterans' parapolitical league, was dissolved in 1936, its leader, Colonel François **de La Rocque**, transformed it into an electoral party, the PSF. The PSF shared the anticommunism of the **Parti Populaire Français**, founded at the same time, but it eschewed the latter's **fascist** trappings and took pains to distance itself from the extreme Right as well as from the extreme **Left**, often drawing the ire of both. The PSF preached traditional conservative values, including the defense of the **family**, property, the middle classes, and the nation. La Rocque and the party's publications repudiated the label of fascism. PSF bases included **Paris**, Lyons, **Normandy**, and **North Africa**. In 1938 police put its membership in the Paris region alone at 172,120. At its peak, its national membership may have approached 1 million, making it by far the largest party in France. The evidence suggests a multiclass party, with the middle and lower-middle classes predominating.

After 1940 the party was resurrected in the southern **zone** as the Progrès Social Français. La Rocque supported **Vichy**, and a vice president of the prewar party, Jean Ybarnegaray, served in **Pétain's** cabinet. La Rocque, however, kept his distance from the regime, and members of the PSF joined different **Resistance** networks. One of its prewar leaders, Charles Vallin, joined the **Free**

French in London in 1942. La Rocque himself, who was deported to Buchenwald in 1944, appears to have had divided loyalties between Pétain and **de Gaulle**.

The party did not survive the war. Historians continue to debate its true nature; for some, it was an early mass conservative party, and for others, an essentially facist movement.

P. Machefer, "Sur quelques aspects de l'activité du Colonel de La Rocque et du 'Progrès Social Français' pendant la seconde guerre mondiale," *RDHDGM* 58 (April 1965); J. Nobecourt, *Le Colonel de La Rocque: Biographie d'un personnage clé de la IIIème République, à la croisée de la droite conservatrice et du fascisme* (Paris, 1996); R. Soucy, *French Fascism: The Second Wave* (New Haven, CT, and London, 1995).

P. F. Jankowski

PASSY, COLONEL (André Dewavrin; 1911–), head of General Charles **de Gaulle's** intelligence service 1940–1944.

Son of a Paris businessman and a graduate of the École Polytechnique, Passy was assistant professor of fortification at the St. Cyr military academy when war began. After service as a captain in the Norwegian campaign he left for **Britain**, where he joined de Gaulle on 1 July 1940. De Gaulle posed a few gruff questions on Passy's **army** status, his past, and his command of English, then selected him to head the **Free French** *deuxième bureau*, the intelligence service, whose eventual name was to be the Bureau Central de Renseignements et d'Action (BCRA). Like his chief, Passy both cooperated and clashed with the British, competing with British intelligence in recruitment of agents in France.

As BCRA chief, Passy was severely criticized for the interrogation tactics practiced by his office in London against presumed double agents—measures he claimed were exaggerated by both the British and **Americans**. He was also attacked by the French **communists** as a Cagoulard, or member of a prewar **right-wing** group, which he convincingly denied.

Passy landed in France in the winter of 1943 on a political mission, together with Pierre **Brossolette**. In 1944 the BCRA was reorganized, and Passy became chief of staff for General Pierre **Koenig**. A year later, Passy founded the postwar French foreign intelligence service, the Service de renseignement extérieure et de contre-espionnage. Accused by the **communists** in 1946 of malfeasance in using **Resistance** money, Passy was arrested and jailed for four months before the charges were dropped. After writing his memoirs, he retired from government service and entered private business.

R. Faligot and R. Kauffer, *Les résistants* (Paris, 1989); J. Lacouture, *De Gaulle*, 2 vols., vol. 1: *The Rebel, 1890–1944*, trans. P. O'Brian (New York, 1991); Passy (A. Dewavrin), *Souvenirs*, 3 vols. (Monte Carlo, 1947; vol. 3, Paris, 1953).

J. W. Friend

PAULHAN, JEAN (1884–1968), a well-known writer and editor considered one of the main figures of the literary **Resistance**.

Paulhan was the editor of the **Nouvelle Revue Française** but was replaced in 1940 by **Drieu la Rochelle**. However, he carried on with his activities as the editor of the Pléiade series for Gallimard, a position that allowed him to gather information for the Resistance. In January 1941, he became one of the editors of *Résistance*, a clandestine journal published by the group **Musée de l'homme**. When the network was infiltrated and destroyed in May 1941, printing materials were found in Paulhan's apartment, and he was arrested but later released, thanks to Drieu la Rochelle. Paulhan continued his Resistance work and helped Jacques Decour to found the *Lettres Françaises*, as well as being instrumental in the creation of the clandestine **publishing** house the **Éditions de minuit**.

Throughout the Occupation, Paulhan published in legally produced journals in the provinces and abroad that supported the Resistance, and his prose appeared in *Commœdia, Confluences*, and Pierre Seghers' *Poésie* series. He also wrote articles for clandestine publications, including his "Éloge du Jacques Decour," which appeared in *Chroniques interdites* (Éditions de minuit, 1943), and a short prose poem, "L'Abeille," published in *Cahiers de la libération* in February 1944.

Paulhan's perceived lack of commitment to a set political agenda and his opposition to *résistantialisme* led to an angry exchange with members of the Resistance, most notably, Vercors (Jean Bruller), at the end of the war, when he expressed his disapproval of the postwar trials in *Lettre aux membres du Comité national des écrivains* (1947) and *Lettre aux directeurs de la Résistance* (1952).

F. Badré, *Paulhan le juste* (Paris, 1996); P. Mercier, "Les écrits de Jean Paulhan dans la presse clandestine: une résistance appliquée, dégagée?" in *La Littérature française sous l'occupation, Actes du colloque de Reims, 30 septembre–1er et 2 octobre 1981* (Reims, 1989).

C. Gorrara

PEASANTRY UNDER VICHY constituted the largest socioeconomic group in France, with about a third of the working population. Consisting of nearly half the French population, the rural people were simultaneously envied and extolled but were miserable during the Occupation.

They were envied, as food was scarce, and urban dwellers saw that people in the countryside ate better. Farmers were courted and asked to give a few kilos of potatoes, some milk, or a bit of meat. An old farmer later remembered, "At the time we were considered good folk."

They were extolled by the regime, which made the agrarian image a key piece in the **National Revolution**. Marshal **Pétain** himself, on 25 June 1940, spoke of the "soil that does not lie. . . . A field that falls fallow is a part of France that dies. A fallow field that is again re-sown is a part of France reborn." His exaltation of the soil and the peasant **family** was echoed often by the regime.

Peasants were in a pitiable condition because of shortages of men and material necessary for agricultural production. One million three hundred thousand farmers had been mobilized, 55,000 killed, and 500,000 taken **prisoner** in 1940. Some returned, but in 1944 approximately 400,000 of the best men were still unavailable for agriculture. Means of production were lacking. For example, there were 1,321 tractors in 1938 and only 348 in 1944, in extremely bad condition. Fuel, manure, and the straw twine so well known in the countryside were also lacking. In addition, the Germans took large quantities, estimated at least at 10 percent, of available resources, especially significant coming from a production already reduced by 22 percent. In short, a damaged peasantry hid its wounds under the praises of the regime.

*†P. Barral, *Les Agrariens français de Méline à Pisani* (Paris, 1968); M. Cépède, *Agriculture et alimentation durant la IIème guerre mondiale* (Paris, 1961); P. Pétain, *La France nouvelle, Appels et messages*, 2 vols. (Vanves, 1941, and Montrouge, 1943); G. Wright, *Rural Revolution in France: The Peasantry in the Twentieth Century* (Stanford, CA, 1964).

I. Boussard

PÉTAIN, HENRI-PHILIPPE (1856–1951), marshal, head of the French State that governed the unoccupied and, nominally, the occupied portion of France following the French military defeat in the Second World War. Praised by his defenders as the savior and protector of his country in its time of troubles, Pétain has been portrayed in most recent historical scholarship as the leader of a **collaborationist**, authoritarian regime that oppressed its own population while facilitating the German war effort.

After distinguishing himself in the Battle of Verdun and in handling French **army** mutinies during the First World War, Pétain became in the 1920s his country's staunchest proponent of the defensive military strategy that prompted the construction of the **Maginot Line** at the end of the decade. Amid the turbulence of the 1930s, elements of the reactionary **Right** hailed Pétain, who had retired from active service in 1932, as a providential "man on horseback" who would restore social order and overthrow the hated **Republic**.

As German mechanized divisions drove deep into northern France in May 1940, French premier Paul **Reynaud**, seeking to broaden the appeal of his government, appointed the popular Pétain vice-premier. On 16 June, two days after German military forces occupied **Paris**, Pétain replaced Reynaud as prime minister with the mandate to open truce negotiations with Germany. The Franco–German **armistice** signed on 22 June partitioned the country into a northern **zone** occupied by the German army and a southern zone to be administered by Pétain's government, which reassembled in the spa town of **Vichy**. On 9–10 July the French parliament voted full powers to Pétain, who proceeded to replace the parliamentary system of the Third Republic with an authoritarian regime dominated by reactionaries committed to the restoration of religious, patriotic, and **family** values. A cult of hero worship developed around the octogenarian military leader, who promised to protect France from the ravages of war, salvage something of the country's honor, and preserve for it a privileged position in a Nazi-dominated Europe.

Pétain was under constant pressure from Pierre **Laval** and French **fascist** ideologues in Paris to collaborate more closely with Germany. He attempted to preserve a modicum of French independence by denying the Germans access to the French fleet based at the Mediterranean port of Toulon and then ordering its destruction when German military forces, following the Allied landings in **North Africa**, had invaded the unoccupied zone, preparing to seize the fleet in November 1942. On the other hand, his regime furnished raw materials, manufactured goods, and labor to the German war machine and fully complied with Nazi requests for the delivery of **Jews** for transfer to the **concentration camps** of the Third Reich. The German military occupation of the southern zone and Pétain's naming of Laval as his successor with the power to issue decrees in November 1942 removed the last vestige of the marshal's independent authority. In August 1944, as the Allied armies advanced south and east after their landings in **Normandy**, the Germans forcibly transferred the 88-year-old figurehead leader from Vichy to the old Hohenzollern castle of **Sigmaringen**. After the war, Pétain was tried, convicted of treason, and sentenced to death by a French tribunal. In deference to his advanced age the postwar French government commuted the sentence to life imprisonment on the Île d'Yeu off France's Atlantic coast, where he died at 95 in 1951.

*M. Ferro, *Pétain* (Paris, 1987); R. Griffiths, *Marshal Pétain* (London, 1970); H. R. Lottman, *Pétain, Hero or Traitor?* (New York, 1985); R. O. Paxton, *Vichy France; Old Guard, New Order* (New York, 1972); J. -R. Tournoux, *Pétain et de Gaulle* (Paris, 1968).

W. R. Keylor

PEYROUTON, MARCEL (1887–1983), **Vichy's interior** minister and ambassador to Argentina; governor-general of Algeria for **Free France**.

Bernard Marcel Peyrouton, who embarked on a career in colonial service in 1910, stood on the political **Right** before World War II. In 1936, the **Popular Front** government dismissed him as secretary-general in Tunisia and Morocco. He then became ambassador to Argentina but in May 1940 returned to Tunisia as resident-general. Prior to the signing of the **armistice** in June 1940, Peyrouton advocated continuing the war from the colonies.

Under Vichy, Peyrouton served as secretary-general to interior minister Adrien **Marquet** in July 1940, whom he succeeded as interior minister in September of that year. Interior minister until February 1941, Peyrouton implemented Vichy's **anti-Semitic**, anti-Masonic, and anti-**Republican** laws. He also created the **Groupes de Protection**, an elite guard in Vichy, and used them when he ordered **Laval's** arrest in December 1940.

Again ambassador to Argentina, from February 1941 to April 1942, Peyrouton resigned upon Laval's return to power. When Admiral **Darlan** changed sides in November 1942, Peyrouton left for Algiers. Arriving in January 1943, he supported General Henri **Giraud**, who appointed him governor-general of Algeria.

Upon **de Gaulle's** arrival in Algiers, Peyrouton resigned and joined the Free French army.

Peyrouton was arrested in December 1943, over protests from Eisenhower, Roosevelt, and Churchill, but his trial was postponed until after the **liberation**. Tried by the **Haute Cour de Justice** in 1948, Peyrouton was acquitted because of his opposition to Laval, service for the Free French in North Africa, and long postwar detention. In 1950 he became director of the daily *Maroc-Presse* in Casablanca. He died in 1983.

R. O. Paxton, *Vichy France: Old Guard, New Order* (New York, 1972); M. Peyrouton, *Du service public à la prison commune, souvenirs: Tunis, Rabat, Buenos Aires, Vichy, Alger, Fresnes* (Paris, 1950).

C. S. Bisson

PHALANGE AFRICAINE were volunteers from metropolitan France and **French North Africa** who fought in Tunisia for the Axis forces following the Allied landings of November 1942. Hopes were high among those who wanted Tunisia held for **Vichy** and those Germans who wished to see a major commitment from France to the Axis cause. Recruiting took place among the troops of the Légion Tricolor, in process of dissolution at the time, and within the European community in Tunisia. Without warning, however, the Germans blocked the sailing of a contingent of volunteers from the metropole.

On 28 December, a German airplane brought over six officers, quickly promoted for the occasion: Lieutenant Colonel Pierre Cristofini and Captains Daniel Peltier and Roger Euzière, active officers; and, from the reserves, the aviator Lieutenant Colonel Christian Sarton du Jonchay, Battalion Chief Henri Curnier, and Sublieutenant Henri Charbonneau. German opposition, however, prevented the departure of any additional volunteers from continental France.

On 8 March 1943, a local revolutionary committee in Tunis, supported by **Vichy's** resident-general Admiral Jean-Pierre **Esteva**, was able to enlist a company of some 210 local men, to be trained by German officers. Ten days later, this group, the Phalange, took oaths to **Hitler**, and on 9 April the company was sent into battle against **British** forces at Klioua, some 50 kilometers from Tunis. By 20 April, following a British offensive, the Phalange was relieved, only 64 of its volunteers still combat-ready. With the Allied victory in North Africa, the Phalange was dissolved on 6 May, its members given three months' pay to see them through to better times. Some of its officers were evacuated to continental France, but many of the Phalangists were heavily punished by military courts in Algiers and, later, the metropole.

H. Charbonneau, *Les Mémoires de Porthos*, 2 vols. (Paris, 1967); B. M. Gordon, *Collaborationism in France during the Second World War* (Ithaca, NY, 1980); R. Pellegrin, *La Phalange africain, la L.V.F. en Tunisie 1942–1943* (Paris, 1973).

G. Le Marec

PHONEY WAR (*DRÔLE DE GUERRE, SITZKRIEG*) saw the French **army** awaiting the German offensive in the west from 3 September 1939 until 10 May

1940. French strategy prepared for a protracted conflict, a "defensive-offensive," two-stage war, first repulsing a German offensive, followed by an Allied counteroffensive and breakthrough. The **Maginot Line** fortifications, designed to force a German offensive through **Belgium**, were to be supported with mechanized **Anglo**–French units designed to thwart the German assault. French plans envisaged a protracted conflict, while Germany sought a quick, decisive victory to avoid such a stalemate.

The fall of Poland to a combined German–**Soviet** attack, the German invasion of Norway, and the Soviet invasion of Finland frustrated Allied strategists. Goebbels' propaganda offensive against France developed **Hitler's** plan to "destroy the enemy from within." Some French journalists, called the "traitors of Stuttgart," harped insistently on the "unnecessary war" fomented by "warmongers," including **interior** minister Georges **Mandel**, Premiers Édouard **Daladier** and Paul **Reynaud**, and **Britain's** prime minister Neville Chamberlain.

In France, counterpropaganda slogans of liberty and democracy inspired indifference, while Radio-Stuttgart's broadcasts became "forbidden fruit," claiming that the "Tommies" (the British) would fight to the last Frenchman. The waiting war fostered skepticism and cynicism among both civilians and soldiers; propaganda accentuated divisions, undermining faith in France's military and political leadership. German propaganda had outthought, and German Blitzkrieg outfought, the French political and military leadership.

D. Alexander, "Repercussions of the Breda Variant," *FHS* 8:3 (Spring 1974): 459–88; J. -P. Azéma, "Munich," in J.-P. Azéma and F. Bédarida, eds., *1938–1948 Les Années de tourmente, de Munich à Prague, Dictionnaire Critique* (Paris, 1995), 855–64; J. Gunsberg, *Divided and Conquered: The French High Command and the Defeat of the West* (Westport, CT, 1979); J. Hughes, *To the Maginot Line* (Cambridge, MA, 1971); R. Young, *In Command of France: French Foreign Policy and Military Planning, 1933–40* (Cambridge, MA, 1978).

P. J. M. Coggins

PICASSO, PABLO RUIZ (1881–1973), acclaimed as the most prolific and versatile artist of the twentieth century, was born in Malaga, Andalusia. Remaining in France during the German occupation, Picasso was prohibited from exhibiting his work publicly due to Franco's influence on **Vichy**, but he sold and exchanged some paintings privately.

Picasso moved to Paris permanently in 1904 and became a major figure in the development of cubism. A supporter of the Republic during the civil war in **Spain**, he made a statement against "brutality and darkness" in his mural depicting the German destruction of the town of Guernica in 1937. The next year, his work was declared "decadent" by the Nazi government.

At the beginning of the war, Picasso divided his time between **Paris** and Royan, with companion Dora Maar and friend and secretary Jaime Sabartès, declining offers to emigrate to America or Mexico. In August 1940, he left Royan and remained in Paris for the duration of the war. He was denounced by

Nazi as well as Vichy sympathizers, for example, by former friend Maurice **de Vlaminck**, in *Comoedia*, 6 June 1942. Several of his paintings, together with others judged by the Nazis as not even worth selling, were burned on 27 July 1943 in the Tuileries garden. In constant danger during the Occupation, Picasso was harassed by visits of Gestapo officers, witnessed on some occasions by Françoise Gilot, Picasso's future companion, whom he had met in May 1943. During one visit, German officers slashed several paintings and called Picasso "degenerate." Those who protected him include German sculptor Arno **Breker**, poet Jean **Cocteau**, and former French government official André-Louis Dubois. In September 1943, Maurice Toesca, a prefect of the French **police**, illegally made Picasso a new foreign resident identification card, extending his stay in France. Picasso's output during the Occupation included several hundred paintings, as well as sculpture and graphic works. While he joined no **Resistance** movements, he assisted Spanish Republican **refugees**. He helped friends, such as Henri **Matisse**, whose private bank vault he administered, thereby protecting valuable artworks from German seizure.

Shortly after the **liberation**, Picasso was named chairman of a committee of the **Front National des Arts** that identified artist and critic collaborators for the **purge**. He also claimed to have joined the French **Communist** Party, which led to a violent anti-Picasso demonstration at the Salon de la Libération, where he was the only artist given a gallery of his own, exhibiting about 80 of his works. Picasso moved from Paris in 1946 to the Riviera, where he continued to create a prodigious and diverse body of work until his death at Mas Notre-Dame-De-Vie.

*†L. Bertrand Dorléac, *L'Art de la défaite, 1940–1944* (Paris, 1993); M. C. Cone, *Artists under Vichy: A Case of Prejudice and Persecution* (Princeton, 1992); F. Gilot and C. Lake, *Life with Picasso* (New York, 1964); L. H. Nicholas, *The Rape of Europa: The Fate of Europe's Treasures in the Third Reich and the Second World War* (New York, 1994); G. Ragache and J.-R. Ragache, *Des Écrivains et des Artistes Sous L'Occupation 1940–1944* (Paris, 1988).

S. Perkins

PINEAU, CHRISTIAN (1904–1995), was a **Resistance** leader, the founder of the **Libération-nord** movement. The son of an officer, he studied at the **Alsatian** school in Paris from 1914 to 1923 and received baccalaureates in philosophy and mathematics, a degree in law, and another from the École des Sciences Politiques. With a successful banking career, Pineau became an active **syndicalist** during the 1930s, organized the newspaper *Banque et Bourse*, and became secretary of the economics council of the **Confédération Générale du Travail (CGT)** in 1938 and 1939.

In November 1940 Pineau edited the Manifeste du **Syndicalisme** Français and created committees of economics and syndicalist studies, attracting CGT and Confédération française des travailleurs chrétiens militants into what would become the Resistance movement Libération-nord, of which he was the main founder. Beginning December 1940, he edited the clandestine newspaper *Libération* (north **zone** edition). Armed with a letter from General **de Gaulle** in 1942, Pineau rallied the **socialists** and syndicalists for **Free France**. De Gaulle also charged him with the creation of two military intelligence networks: Phalanx, which Pineau directed, in the southern zone; and Cohors, whose direction he entrusted to Jean Cavaillès, in the northern zone. Pineau was arrested for the first time in the fall of 1942, with Cavaillès, as they were trying to leave for **Britain**. After escaping, he returned to London in January 1943, where he requested a redefinition of his role now that Jean **Moulin** had arrived. In May, he was arrested by the Gestapo and deported to Buchenwald and was freed only in April 1945.

After the war, Pineau had a political career as socialist deputy from the Sarthe until 1958, as minister of provisions in de Gaulle's government in 1945, as president of the Commission of Finances of the National Assembly in 1946 and 1947, as minister of public works from December 1947 to February 1950, and finally as minister of foreign affairs from February 1956 until April 1958.

†C. Pineau, *La simple vérité 1940–1945* (Paris, 1983).

A. Aglan

PLEVEN, RENÉ (1901–1993), was a political figure who in 1939 was delegated by the air minister to negotiate the purchase of airplanes from the **Americans** and was named adjunct to a Franco–**British** coordinating committee for arms purchases. On 8 July 1940, he responded to General **de Gaulle's** appeal and joined the **Free French** in London. "From day one, Pleven was the companion, friend, and witness in a great work," said de Gaulle.

In association with General **Leclerc**, Claude Hettier de Boislambert, and Félix **Éboué**, Pleven worked to rally black Africa to the Free French: Chad in 1940 and French Equatorial Africa in 1941, becoming secretary-general for the latter. Having served prior to the war as the Automatic Telephone Company's director for Europe, he had an extensive knowledge of the **Anglo-American** business world which led to his appointment as director of foreign and economic affairs for the Free French delegation to the United States from May through October 1941. Returning to London, he headed the economics, finances, colonies, merchant marine, and then foreign affairs departments for the Comité National Français in London through 3 June 1943. Pleven masterminded the war effort of the **empire**. In July 1943 he became the **Provisional Government's** minister for overseas France, serving first in Algiers, then in **Paris**. The tasks of daily organization of the war effort, however, did not prevent him from planning for the postwar era.

In early 1944, he initiated and presided over the French African conference at Brazzaville (**Brazzaville Conference**), which was to redefine the relations between France and its colonies. In 1945 he became a parliamentary deputy from the Côtes d'Armor in Brittany and was regularly reelected until 1973. Under the Fourth **Republic**, he occupied various ministerial posts, serving twice as president of the council (premier, July 1950–February 1951 and August 1951–January 1952). Lastly, he was President Georges Pompidou's justice minister from 1969 through 1973.

†C.-A. Ageron, *L'Entourage de de Gaulle* (Paris, 1980); C. Bougeard, *René Pleven. Un Français en politique* (Rennes, 1995); E. Duhamel, "René Pleven (1901–1993)," in J. -F. Sirinelli, ed., *Dictionnaire historique de la vie politique française au XXe siècle* (Paris, 1995).

A. Rinckenbach

POLICE IN VICHY FRANCE, the domestic French forces of order, consisting of city police, Gendarmerie, Sûreté nationale, as well as the paramilitary forces of the old Garde mobile and the newly created Groupes mobiles de réserve (GMR).

Corresponding to its basic authoritarian structure, the French State attempted to increase the effectiveness of the police by nationalizing the commune police, establishing regional command structures for the regional prefects, and creating the GMR. The police generally welcomed the changes, eagerly hunted **communists**, and carried out orders for **deportation** of **Jews**. Gaullists, however, were secretly protected, and **collaborators** harassed. The German military authorities called the local police "good Frenchmen."

Only a few units, such as the Brigades spéciales in **Paris** or the Sections d'affaires politiques (SAP) in provincial cities such as Bordeaux and Poitiers, collaborated closely with the Gestapo. Apart from these exceptions, most of the French police, their leaders included, kept a correct distance from the Germans. With the occupation of southern France, the introduction of the **Service du Travail Obligatoire (STO)**, and the development of a wide-scale **Resistance** movement, the activity of the French police declined sharply in 1943. They were uninterested in hunting down evaders of the STO or in fighting the **maquis**. German brutality in the southern and Breton **Resistance** centers pushed the police increasingly into the opposition. The rest of France, especially **Paris** and Burgundy, saw occasional police strikes against the Resistance. A large majority of the police, however, waited with increasing passivity for the German withdrawal.

B. Kasten, *"Gute Franzosen": die französische Polizei und die deutsche Besatzungsmacht im besetzten Frankreich* (Sigmaringen, 1993); M. Rajsfus, *La police de Vichy: Les Forces de l'ordre françaises au service de la Gestapo 1940–1944* (Paris, 1995); J. F. Sweets, "La police et la population dans la France de Vichy," RDHDGM 39: 155 (July 1989).

B. Kasten

POPULAR FRONT, 1935–1938, was the center-**left** political coalition of the Radical, **Socialist**, and **Communist** Parties, headed by **socialist** Léon **Blum**, that won the legislative elections in 1936 but proved unable to maintain its cohesion afterward.

The Popular Front rose out of many origins: the rise of Nazism and the increase in strength of the French **right-wing** paramilitary leagues, the financial scandals of the early 1930s, and the depression. The immediate cause was the antiparliamentary riots of 6 February 1934, which the Left viewed as an abortive **fascist** attack on the **Republic**. Negotiations beginning in 1934 led to a common program in January 1936.

The coalition was unstable, but the Popular Front won the elections in April–May 1936. Blum formed a government in June, which immediately faced a wave of strikes asking for higher wages and the 40-hour week. Finance capital took fright, and the **British** Embassy in Paris reported that events were reminiscent of the early stages of the **Russian** revolution. In the autumn of 1936, the tumult quieted after the government approved major social legislation. Already, however, the coalition was weakened, with most Radicals fearing that France had turned too far left. Foreign policy issues, such as the Spanish civil war, and the Franco–**Soviet** mutual assistance pact also put stress on the coalition.

Amid financial and foreign policy crises in June 1937, the government fell. A new Popular Front cabinet was formed under Radical leadership, which marked the beginning of the end. Blum returned to power briefly in 1938, to be succeeded by Édouard **Daladier**, who soon broke with the communists and undid the Popular Front program. The *Anschluss*, **Munich agreement**, and an abortive general strike, crushed by the government (November 1938), marked the collapse of the Popular Front. France was politically divided as it entered the war in September 1939.

*J. Colton, *Léon Blum* (New York, 1966); N. Greene, *Crisis and Decline: The French Socialist Party in the Popular Front Era* (Ithaca, NY, 1966); J. Jackson, *The Popular Front in France Defending Democracy, 1934–38* (Cambridge, U.K., 1988); G. Lefranc, *Histoire du front populaire* (Paris, 1965); R. Young, *France and the Origins of the Second World War* (New York, 1996).

M. J. Carley

PRESS, CLANDESTINE, comprised more than 1,000 different newspapers and journals produced in France, forming one of the main activities of the **Resistance** during the Occupation.

The underground press ranged from short, often hand-produced documents of limited local circulation in the summer of 1940, such as Jean Texcier's pithy *Conseils à l'Occupé* (Advice to the Occupied), to widely distributed papers such as *L'Humanité* or **Combat,** which reached a national audience with circulation up to 300,000 or 400,000 copies by 1944.

The earliest papers were the result of scattered local initiatives, but their development closely mirrored that of the Resistance in general, with the emergence of more widespread and better-organized movements able to sustain more ambitious activities. Many newspapers came to be the organ of an eponymous movement, as with *Franc-Tireur, Libération,* or *Défense de la France,* providing both a channel of communication and an identity. The **Communist** and

Socialist Parties each published a series of papers: the Communist *L'Humanité* appeared clandestinely from October 1939 and therefore had well-organized systems in place before the defeat, while the Socialist *Le Populaire* reappeared in mid-1942. Both papers had numerous regional editions and offshoots.

The intellectual Resistance also produced a range of underground journals. The most influential of these was the ***Lettres Françaises,*** a broad literary and artistic review, but there were important magazines on film, **theater**, music, philosophy, painting, poetry, and other specialty areas. Several professional groupings produced clandestine papers, many of them sponsored by wider movements, notably the **Front National**. In this way teachers, farmers, academics, doctors, lawyers, students, the **police**, and other groups eventually had their own Resistance forum. Trade unions published clandestine papers, including 230 issues of the **Confédération Générale du Travail's La Vie ouvrière**. Religious groups also participated, despite the **Catholic** Church's generally pro-**Vichy** stance, which the **Témoignage chrétien** group was particularly prominent in opposing.

The aims of the clandestine press were to circulate opinions and information not available in the officially permitted media, which were heavily controlled and censored. Based initially on the call to resist and the criticism of **collaboration**, they called on patriotic pride and a national tradition of fierce independence. As their organization improved, the clandestine papers offered a broader and more sophisticated content, approaching the status of an alternative press, with a mission to provide unfettered reporting and comment. In the later stages of the war, they turned increasingly to consideration of the policies and structures that would be required after **liberation**, an aspiration expressed in the later subtitle of *Combat*: "From **Resistance** to Revolution."

News reporting drew on radio broadcasts from London, Moscow, **Switzerland**, and elsewhere, as well as networks of correspondents. Press bureau facilities were established, some vigorously supported by the **Free French** in London and Algiers, though others avoided too close a political dependency on General **de Gaulle**.

Production and distribution posed significant material problems. Early publications were achieved through artisanal methods, but the larger-scale operations depended on access to commercial printing facilities and large quantities of paper and ink, which were closely **rationed**. These were secured by an astonishing variety of solutions, combining ingenuity and heroism, for which many people gave their lives. Distribution posed comparable problems. Workers on road and rail networks secured the transport of large quantities of clandestine papers, which were circulated surreptitiously by teams of delivery workers, all at great risk to their lives.

Many clandestine papers and magazines continued publication openly after the liberation, though few survived the political collapse of the Resistance structures and the inhospitable economic conditions of the late 1940s.

C. Bellanger, *Presse clandestine 1940–1944* (Paris, 1961); C. Bellanger, H. Michel, and Cl. Lévy, *Histoire générale de la presse française de 1940–1958*, vol. 4 (Paris, 1975).

M. Kelly

PRESS IN OCCUPIED PARIS was dominated by **collaborationists** such as Jean **Luchaire** and Alphonse **de Châteaubriant** and generously supported with German money. It distinguished itself from the interwar **right-wing** press as well as from the Pétainist **Vichy press** of the occupied **zone** in its support for **Hitler's New Order** and its impatience with Vichy traditionalism.

The defeat of May–June 1940 brought significant and immediate changes to the Parisian press. Major interwar **left-wing** reviews such as *Marianne* simply disappeared, while many of the conservative right-wing Maurasian reviews, including *Candide* and *Gringoire*, moved to the unoccupied zone and adopted a Pétainist line. Relations between this pro-Vichy press and the pro-German press in **Paris** were unfriendly from the outset and remained that way throughout the Occupation.

Of some 40 daily and weekly newspapers and magazines published in occupied Paris, only six were holdovers from the interwar period. These included four dailies, *Le Matin, Paris-Soir, L'Œuvre*, and *Le Petit Parisien*, and two weeklies, *L'Illustration* and *Je Suis Partout*. Among the dailies, all took a strongly collaborationist and, indeed, pro-Nazi and pro-**fascist** line. The editor of *Le Matin*, Jacques Ménard, signed his letters ''*Heil Hitler!*'' while the editor of *Le Petit Parisien*, Claude Jeantet, transformed his paper into the mouthpiece for the French fascist Jacques **Doriot** and his **Parti Populaire Français.** *L'Œuvre*, on the other hand, supported the erstwhile **socialist** and now fascist leader Marcel **Déat** and his **Rassemblement National Populaire** following its creation in 1941. Of the holdover weeklies, *Je Suis Partout* would achieve the greatest notoriety both because of the star status of its editors and writers, including Robert **Brasillach** and Lucien **Rebatet**, and because of the virulence of its pro-Nazi and **anti-Semitic** views.

Among the newly created dailies, the best known was Jean **Luchaire's** *Les Nouveaux Temps*, launched with German money. Luchaire, a close personal friend of the German ambassador, Otto **Abetz**, also became head of the Paris Press Corporation and, like Brasillach, would be tried and executed during the **purge** following the **liberation**.

Another high-profile periodical created with German money was Alphonse de Châteaubriant's weekly literary and cultural review, *La Gerbe*. Attracting well-known writers, including Jean **Giono**, Henry **de Montherlant**, Marcel Aymé, and Colette, *La Gerbe* sought to convey the impression that French culture was continuing as usual even under Nazi rule. Pro-German (Châteaubriant had been a fervent admirer of Hitler before the war) in its politics, *La Gerbe* also backed Vichy, the result being a bizarre ideological mix that one of its editors, Lucien Combelle, referred to as ''*Hitlero-Pétainisme*.'' Political contributors to its pages included the likes of Fernand **de Brinon**, Vichy's "ambassador" to the occupied zone who was also executed after the liberation.

Other, smaller, and more ephemeral dailies and weeklies included the "left-wing" *Le Rouge et le Bleu*, edited by the former socialist Charles **Spinasse**, a minister under Léon **Blum**, and the virulently anti-Semitic *Au Pilori*, modeled after Germany's *Der Stürmer*. A German-language newspaper, the *Pariser Zeitung*, provided largely tourist information for the occupying forces.

P. Assouline, *Le Fleuve Combelle* (Paris, 1997); P.-M. Dioudonnat, *"Je Suis Partout," 1930–1944: Les maurassiens devant la tentation fasciste* (Paris, 1973); P.-M. Dioudonnat, *Les 700 rédacteurs de Je suis partout* (Paris, 1993); R. J. Golsan, "Ideology, Cultural Politics, and Literary Collaboration at *La Gerbe*," *Journal of European Studies* 23 (parts 1 and 2) 89, 90 (March–June 1993): 27–47; Cl. Lévy, *"Les Nouveaux Temps" et l'idéologie de la collaboration* (Paris, 1974); D. Pryce-Jones, *Paris in the Third Reich* (New York, 1981).

R. J. Golsan

PRESS UNDER VICHY. From June 1940 until August 1944, the French press lost its independence and was subordinated to two different regimes; in accordance with the 1940 **armistice** agreement, it responded directly to the German military government in the northern (occupied) **zone** and to the **Vichy** government in the southern (unoccupied) zone, at least until the Germans overran the unoccupied zone in November 1942. German control was stronger in the occupied zone, where 60 percent of the prewar press disappeared after the invasion. Only 32 percent disappeared in the unoccupied zone, where several **Paris** publications took refuge, though their relationship with the **Vichy** government was difficult as they tried to preserve their autonomy. Because of paper restrictions, most publications consisted of only a few pages. Transportation problems also made their diffusion difficult. In addition, Vichy kept newspapers criticizing Marshal **Pétain** in the occupied zone out of the unoccupied zone.

The press under Vichy was organized by the Office français d'information, which scrutinized articles and photographs submitted from local, regional, and foreign correspondents. It supported Vichy in pressuring newspapers to publish favorable commentaries on the government, especially in the first months of the Occupation. Censorship tightened when the Germans took over the previously unoccupied zone in November 1942.

In appearances the press did not change much from what it had been before the war. Many newspapers kept the same name and format, and their directors remained French. Yet, only those clearly sympathetic to the Germans and Vichy maintained their positions. Only publications that complied with both Vichy and the Germans remained active. New publications were created in order to reach the entire population, especially groups seen as necessary for national reconstruction, such as farmers, **youth, prisoners** of war, and **women**, who had to work in the absence of men.

Vichy used the press to propagate its idea of a **National Revolution**. It glorified Petain's idea of a new moral order based on clerical, national, and familial values and strongly criticized the indignity and material consequences of the defeat, which it attributed to an alleged prewar economic and social chaos. The press also supported Franco–German **collaboration**. Additional political themes after 1941 included the Bolshevik peril and hostility to the **United States**. The general rule was to create apparent unanimity among the newspapers, to avoid both alarming the French population and provoking reactions from the Germans. Food and other material restrictions were portrayed as temporary and necessary for reconstruction. References to the occupying forces were kept to a minimum in order to suggest Vichy's autonomy. Because the political goals and rhetorical devices of the press were so obvious, it had only a minor effect on the bulk of the population. It mostly served to reinforce the beliefs of the collaborationists.

*†P. Albert, *Histoire de la presse* (Paris, 1990); C. Bellanger et al., eds., *Histoire générale de la presse française, IV (de 1940 à 1958)* (Paris, 1975).

M. Guyot-Bender

PRISONERS OF WAR (POWs) were the 1.8 million French soldiers Germany captured during the 1940 **Battle of France**. The prisoners represented 4 percent of France's population, or one in seven men between ages 20 and 40. Over half were married, many with children. Nearly half the prisoners were taken between **Pétain's** 17 June statement that "the fighting must cease" and the **armistice**, effective 25 June. The Germans transferred 1.58 million of the prisoners from France to Germany, where they were put to work to mitigate labor shortages in agriculture and **industry**. Among them, 71,000 escaped, and 24,600 died in captivity. Of the 940,000 French prisoners remaining in Germany in 1945, most were repatriated between April and June.

The prisoners were a constant issue in Franco–German negotiations, a justification for **Vichy's** existence. The 1929 Geneva Convention governed their treatment, yet in November 1940 Vichy accepted Germany's proposal and replaced the **United States**, which had been appointed neutral "protecting power," with a Service diplomatique des prisonniers de guerre, led by Georges Scapini, a blinded war veteran, which inspected **prison** camps for compliance with the convention and disseminated Vichy propaganda.

Vichy obtained the release of groups such as World War I veterans and the 90,747 repatriated under the *Relève*. In France, the repatriated prisoner Maurice Pinot created the Commissariat général des prisonniers de guerre répatriés (CGPGR) in 1941, a public agency to assist repatriated prisoners and their families. Initially many were pro-Pétain but they became increasingly disillusioned as time went on. **Resistance** networks started in the camps and continued in the repatriated POW community in France. Eventually, the Mouvement National des Prisonniers de Guerre et Déportés united a **communist** group, a Gaullist group, and a group led by Pinot and François **Mitterrand**, both of whom left the CGPGR when the **collaborationist** André Masson took over. After the war, former prisoners often felt that they carried the stigma of the 1940 defeat and that French society dismissed their service and hardships.

Y. Durand, *La captivité* (Paris, 1980); S. Fishman, "Grand Delusions," *JCH* 26 (April 1991); C. Lewin, *Le retour des prisonniers de guerre français* (Paris, 1986).

S. Fishman

PRISONERS OF WAR, WIVES OF, were the nearly 800,000 **women** married to French **prisoners** of war (POWs) captured in the May–June 1940 campaign. Prisoners' wives represented a significant cross-section of the female population, and about 40 percent had children. **Vichy** considered itself responsible for them and paid military allowances to soldiers' wives who demonstrated need. The state also attempted to prevent adultery, passing a law 23 December 1942 punishing adultery with the spouse of a person "absent from his country because of circumstances of war." The Commissariat général des prisonniers de guerre rapatriés, initially created by and for repatriated prisoners, extended its concern to their families, where it collided with Madame Charles-Léon Huntziger's agency, La famille du prisonnier, which wanted to be protector of POW families. Prisoners' wives faced the difficulties of shortages, inflation, taking over family farms or businesses, working for wages, and raising children alone. Their politics spanned the range from Pétainism to **Resistance**. Many **Jewish** prisoners' wives were deported to **concentration camps**, suffering the same fate as their coreligionists and a fate worse than their husbands'.

Prisoners' wives created support groups, of which the largest, the Fédération des associations de femmes de prisonniers, or FAFP, was built on local grassroots activism usually initiated by women, such as FAFP president Andrée Aulas. In addition to mutual support, social events, and lobbying, the FAFP published a monthly, *Femmes de Prisonniers* (Wives of Prisoners), and commissioned a novel, *La Guerre des Captives* (Captives' War) and a survey, *Femmes d'Absents . . . Témoignages* (Wives of the Missing . . . Testimonies). Reunion went smoothly for many couples. Although some couples faced problems, only about 10 percent divorced. The experience might have led to long-term social changes, but most families attempted to return to prewar ways of life. Many couples had children after 1945, nicknamed "*les enfants du retour*" (children of the return).

G. Dermenjian, ed., *Femmes, famille et action ouvrière* (Villeneuve d'Ascq, 1991); J. Deroy, *Celles qui attendaient . . . témoignent aujourd'hui* (Melun, 1985). S. Fishman, *We Will Wait* (New Haven, CT, 1991).

S. Fishman

PRISONS under **Vichy** were administered from 1941 through 1943 by justice minister Joseph Barthélemy. Prisons in both occupied and unoccupied **zones** were overcrowded and understaffed. The number of individuals incarcerated increased from 18,000 in 1939 to 59,000 at the **liberation**. In addition to starvation, **prisoners** faced epidemics of dysentery and tuberculosis.

Escapes by prominent political prisoners and increased **Resistance** activity prompted the Vichy government to increase the repressive role of the prison. Arbitrary arrests increased, and torture was common. Riots at Cherche-Midi and other prisons resulted in the massacre of scores of prisoners. Joseph Barthélemy was replaced in 1943 by Maurice Gabolde. Under Gabolde's direction, the administration of Vichy prisons was transferred to the Ministry of the **Interior**. This move was mirrored by Germans, who transferred control of their prisons in both zones from their Wehrmacht to the Waffen-SS. Gabolde shared much of his power with Joseph **Darnand**, head of the Vichy police beginning in December of 1943 and leader of Vichy's militia (**Milice Française**).

After the liberation, French prisons were quickly filled again this time with Vichy personnel. Fresnes housed many prominent collaborators awaiting trial, Pierre **Laval** and Robert **Brasillach** among them.

*P. Pédron, *La prison sous Vichy* (Paris, 1993).

B. A. McKenzie

PROTESTANTS in **Vichy** France numbered approximately 800,000. The community had been divided since the late nineteenth century between evangelicals and liberals, Lutherans and Calvinists, and, during the interwar years, the politically progressive Social Christians and apolitical followers of Karl Barth. A fragile reunification was achieved in 1938 with the creation of the Reformed Church of France. Though most Protestants were liberal and **Republican**, extremes on the **Left** included pacifist groups, while on the **Right** the Sully Association grouped royalist and **anti-Semitic** Protestants.

With the advent of Vichy, most French Protestants supported Marshal **Pétain**. Though there was some fear concerning the clerical appearance of the regime, Protestants were quickly reassured. The government included Protestants René Gillouin (speechwriter and adviser to Pétain), General Charles Brécard (grand chancellor of the Légion d'honneur), Gaston Bruneton (commissioner of French manpower in Germany), and Admiral Charles Platon (colonial secretary of state). Marc **Boegner**, the leader of the French Protestant community, served on Vichy's Conseil national.

Protestants, however, were increasingly troubled by the oath of loyalty to Pétain and the anti-Masonic and anti-Semitic legislation (especially the second "*Statut des Juifs*" in June 1941). In the Midi and particularly the Cévennes, mistrust grew between Protestants and Catholics, while in **Paris**, André-Numa Bertrand, vice president of the Fédération protestante de France, openly criticized the regime. Protestant **Resistance** was rooted in their historical experience of persecution in France, the theological emphasis upon the individual conscience, the primacy of the Hebrew Testament, and the translated articles of the German Protestant thinker Karl Barth, who called for resistance to the Nazis.

In September 1941, 16 Protestant pastors, theologians, and laypersons meeting in Pomeyrol issued the "Eight Theses of Pomeyrol," a clandestine text that underscored the limits of obedience to the state and the inviolability of individual liberties and condemned Vichy's anti-Semitic legislation and **collaboration** with

Nazi Germany. Following the roundup of foreign-born **Jews** in mid-1942, many Protestants, according to a **police** report from Nîmes, assumed "a veritable fighting position." Official letters of protest from the Protestant Federation to Pétain and Pierre **Laval** heralded, in September 1942, the annual Protestant gathering at the Musée du Désert in southern France. There, Boegner instructed his pastors to save the lives of Jewish **refugees**—a move already anticipated by numerous Protestant groups and individuals—and to read from their pulpits an official message exhorting their parishioners "to show the compassion of the Good Samaritan for the distress of those who suffer." The calls to Christian conscience were reflected in the activity of largely Protestant refugee and rescue groups such as Cimade and instances of mass civil disobedience, as in Chambon-sur-Lignon and many Cévenol villages.

*P. Bolle and J. Godel, eds., *Spiritualité, théologie et résistance* (Grenoble, 1987); *Les Protestants français pendant la seconde guerre mondial: Actes du colloque de Paris* (Paris, 1994); R. D. Zaretsky, *Nîmes at War: Religion, Politics, and Public Opinion in the Department of the Gard, 1938–1944* (University Park, PA, 1995).

R. D. Zaretsky

PROTOCOLS DE PARIS (1941), the agreement between **Vichy** and Berlin granting German armed forces access to French facilities in the Middle East and Africa.

Throughout the spring of 1941, Vichy officials intimated that German naval and air units might make limited use of ports and airfields located in France's overseas possessions if Berlin recognized the Vichy regime as an equal partner and abolished the **Demarcation Line** dividing unoccupied from occupied France. German officials rebuffed such hints until mid-May, when the conjunction of a major anti-**British** revolt in Iraq, General Erwin Rommel's advances in North Africa, and successive Wehrmacht victories in Yugoslavia, mainland Greece, and Crete heightened German interest in installations around the Mediterranean littoral. On 20 May General Walther Warlimont of the German General Staff traveled to **Paris** to discuss terms under which the Luftwaffe could transfer matériel to Iraq through the airfields at Aleppo and Palmyra in Syria, and the Kriegsmarine could supply the Afrika Korps through the Tunisian port of Bizerte.

Vichy officials hastily granted permission to use these facilities, offered French warships as escorts for German convoys in the Mediterranean, and suggested that a submarine base be built at **Dakar** in Senegal. In return, Berlin promised to release French **prisoners** of war who were veterans of the First World War, facilitate movement across the Demarcation Line, and lower exactions levied to offset the costs of the Occupation. Vichy envisaged the protocols, signed on 28 May 1941, as the prelude to a comprehensive peace treaty that might enable France to take what Admiral **Darlan** called "her honorable place" in a German-dominated **New Order**. Berlin took a dimmer view of Franco–German strategic partnership, particularly after British troops crushed the revolt in Iraq and occupied Syria. Nevertheless, Darlan demanded that the 1940 **armistice** be overturned before German transports be allowed to dock at Bizerte. Even those in Berlin most sympathetic to Vichy considered such demands ''extortion,'' and by August 1941 the protocols lapsed.

W. L. Langer, *Our Vichy Gamble* (New York, 1947); R. O. Paxton, *Vichy France, Old Guard and New Order, 1940–1944* (New York, 1972); A. Roshwald, *Estranged Bedfellows* (New York, 1990).

F. H. Lawson

PROVENCE, ALLIED INVASION (August 1944), was the southern counterpart to Operation Overlord in **Normandy**.

Code-named Anvil (later renamed Dragoon), the invasion of southern France initially was to be launched at the same time as the northern invasion, called Hammer (later renamed Overlord). As the time for invasion came closer, however, the Allies abandoned the dual invasion for strategic, political, and practical reasons. The first Allied bombing attacks began on 28 April 1944 and intensified throughout the summer until the actual invasion in August. Bombers dropped 12,500 tons of ordnance between April and 10 August and another 7,000 tons between 10 and 15 August, the day of the invasion. Altogether some 200,000 Germans defended southern France, although their military quality was inferior to that of the Allies.

Three divisions of the **American** Seventh Army led by General Alexander M. Patch, Jr., and the French First **Army** led by General Jean **de Lattre de Tassigny** landed on the beaches east of Toulon. The first landing on the mainland took place at Cap-Nègre, and Allied forces secured the islands of Levant and Port-Cros. These successes were followed by landings farther to the east on the beaches of Cavalaire-sur-Mer, Pampelonne, Saint-Raphael, Cap du Dramont, and Anthéor. After the successful invasion de Lattre de Tassigny's forces moved toward Toulon and Marseilles. American units moved west toward Aix-en-Provence, north to Grenoble, and east toward Nice. Aix-en-Provence fell on 21 August, Cannes on 24 August, Toulon and Marseilles on 28 August, and Nice on 30 August.

The Allies then proceeded north through the Rhône valley. Lyons fell on 3 September, and during the night of 10 September a forward unit of **Free French** fighters met units from General Philippe **Leclerc's** Second Armored Division at Sombernon, a town slightly west of Dijon. The northern and southern invasion forces were finally linked.

J. J. Clarke and R. R. Smith, *Riviera to the Rhine* (Washington, DC, 1993); A. F. Wilt, *The French Riviera Campaign of August 1944* (Carbondale, IL, 1981).

C. J. Haug

PROVISIONAL GOVERNMENT (GOUVERNEMENT PROVISOIRE DE LA RÉPUBLIQUE FRANÇAISE, GPRF), formed in Algiers in June 1944 as successor to the Comité français de libération nationale (CFLN), headed until

January 1946 by General **de Gaulle**. At the **liberation**, the GPRF established itself as the sole legitimate government in France. It enjoyed virtually unlimited power until the first postwar general elections of October 1945 and the subsequent establishment of a Constituent Assembly. Thereafter, its authority was placed on a more regular democratic footing, although it continued to operate as the executive until the inauguration of the first government of the Fourth **Republic** in January 1947.

The GPRF's origins lay in the formative stages of de Gaulle's **Free France** movement. As early as 1940–1941 Free France took on certain aspects of a provisional government, with a cabinet (initially termed the Conseil de défense de l'empire and later the Comité national français) and a number of embryonic ministries (termed *commissariats*). In 1943, after the Allied liberation of French **North Africa**, de Gaulle transferred this skeletal government to Algiers, integrated it with the organization of General Henri **Giraud**, and thereby created the CFLN, which was widely recognized to represent all **Resistance** forces inside and outside France (although the United States and **Britain** refused to recognize it as the French government). Three days before D-Day, to advance its claim to governmental status, the CFLN transformed itself into the GPRF.

Over the course of the next two and a half years, this government, which brought together representatives from a wide range of political groupings, including the **Communist** Party, saw the country through a transitional period of great turmoil and complexity. In the aftermath of the liberation, it fended off **Anglo-American** plans for an **Allied Military Government** and thwarted both last-minute **Vichyite** plots and revolutionary impulses from the grassroots Resistance. Then, with its own authority consolidated—and finally recognized by the other Allied governments—the GPRF had to deal with the difficult legacies of the Occupation: punishing those who had collaborated with Germany, rebuilding a devastated **economy**, repatriating **prisoners** of war and deportees, restoring democratic institutions, and reasserting French influence and interests abroad. Such immediate concerns claimed most of the GPRF's attention in late 1944 and early 1945, and the government's responses prompted much public criticism (perhaps inevitably so).

After mid-1945 the GPRF increasingly switched its attention to the issue of postwar reconstruction. There, it capitalized on the relative absence of institutional or constitutional constraints to carry through an ambitious reform agenda. By the end of 1946 it had established a system of national economic planning; nationalized coal, electricity, gas, the largest clearing banks and insurance companies; renovated and expanded social welfare provisions; and created the École nationale d'administration. Even though the parallel movement for constitutional renewal ended in a disappointing failure (the Fourth Republic resembling in most respects the Third), the reformist achievements of the Provisional Government were substantial and contributed to the successful reconstruction of France in the postwar decades.

J. Lacouture, *De Gaulle*, 2 vols., vol. 1: *The Rebel, 1890–1944*, trans. P. O'Brian, vol.

2: *The Ruler, 1944–1970*, trans. A. Sheridan (New York, 1991–1992); J.-P. Rioux, *La France de la Quatrième République*, vol. 1 (Paris, 1980); A. W. H. Shennan, *Rethinking France: Plans for Renewal 1940–1946* (Oxford, 1989).

A. W. H. Shennan

PUBLISHERS AND PUBLISHING comprised a French world over which the German authorities exercised a degree of centralized control, although some publishers managed to escape the censor legally in the southern **zone** and abroad, as well as illegally with clandestine publications.

Publishing in France was overseen mainly by the literary service of the Propaganda Abteilung Frankreich in **Paris**. The **Otto lists** were introduced in October 1940 and continually updated, banning books that could prejudice or aggrieve the German forces. The lists were accompanied by a censorship agreement for French publishers to sign. The Germans did not attempt to appropriate all French publishing houses but relied instead on the **industry**'s policing itself and centralized control over paper distribution to keep the French publishers in line.

A program of **Aryanization** of **Jewish**-owned publishing houses, such as Nathan, Calmann Lévy, and Ferenczi, was set up, and these establishments were placed in the hands of ''French'' managers, some of whom were sympathetic toward the former Jewish owners. In some rare cases, such as those of Sorlot and Cluny the German authorities seized the financial holdings of publishers for a period. Hachette is an example of the difficulties the Germans faced when wishing to take more direct control. After taking control, the Germans were forced to negotiate who should be in charge with Hachette's managing director, René Schoeller, when he returned to Paris from the 1940 **exodus**. Ultimately, a German-sponsored management ran Hachette for the duration of the Occupation. In general, however, the Germans preferred to maintain a more discrete presence rather than assume control of publishing houses.

Most publishers who returned to Paris after 1940 accepted the ambiguities of the period and accommodated German demands in order to receive their paper allowance. Bernard Grasset worked with a German associate and socialized with the occupation army officers; Robert Denoël, after reestablishing control over his company, worked with a German accountant and published writers as diverse as Louis-Ferdinand **Céline** and Elsa Triolet. He also headed Les nouvelles éditions françaises, publishing anti-Semitic material, which made him a target for reprisals after the **liberation**.

Publishers in the provinces continued their activities, with new players entering the game, such as Robert Laffont, based in Marseilles until 1944. German control and censorship were less oppressive in the southern zone, giving publishing houses based there more freedom, especially early in the war. So-called contraband literature entered circulation, for example, some texts produced legally that passed the censor but had an ambiguous **Resistance** message. Although some writers refused to publish at all, such as Joseph Kessel, others, such as Jean-Paul **Sartre** and Robert Desnos, used the wide margin for ambiguity to continue writing for publication. In terms of clandestine publishing, the **Éditions de minuit**, set up by Vercors (Jean Bruller) and others in 1942, stands out as a venture considered by many to have embodied the spirit of the Resistance. French publishing developed abroad as well, particularly in **Switzerland**, where Les trois collines and Les cahiers du Rhine published work by French writers. New York was also a haven for writers and publishers in exile with the creation of Les éditions de la maison française.

At the liberation, various publishers and publishing houses were targeted for their wartime record. Trials were held from 1944 to 1955, such as that of Robert Denoël, who was ultimately acquitted. As the years went by, attitudes softened, and most publishing houses were able to make a good case for their wartime activities.

*"Des écrivains et de leurs éditeurs," in P. Fouché, *L'édition française sous l'occupation 1940–1944* (Paris, 1987), Chapter 8; G. Ragache and J.-R. Ragache, *La Vie quotidienne des écrivains et des artistes sous l'occupation* (Paris, 1988).

C. Gorrara

PUCHEU, PIERRE (1898–1944), minister of the **interior** in the **Vichy** government, was born in Algeria of working-class origins and won scholarships to the École Normale Supérieure. He then embarked on a career in **industry**, becoming managing director of Japy Frères and Pont à Mousson, a steel-marketing syndicate. In the 1930s, Pucheu joined Colonel François **de La Rocque's** Croix de Feu and then Jacques **Doriot's Parti Populaire Français (PPF)** but resigned in 1939 over Doriot's stand in support of the **Munich** appeasement policy.

Under Vichy, Pucheu first became president of a government-sponsored committee to regulate the engineering industry, and then minister of **industrial production** from February to June 1941. He advocated technocracy as the way to regenerate France. Pucheu next served as interior minister in Admiral **Darlan's** government from July 1941 until April 1942. As interior minister, he helped create the **Special Sections** in **Paris**, which primarily condemned **communists** to death. Pucheu placed the French **police** at Germany's disposal and harassed Doriot's PPF, making its efforts to recruit in Vichy difficult. He resigned as interior minister when **Laval** returned to power.

Disillusioned with Vichy, Pucheu left France in early 1943 but was arrested on his arrival in Casablanca in May 1943. The Comité français pour la libération nationale, which planned to try former Vichy officials after the **liberation**, acceded to the demands of the **Conseil Nationale de la résistance**, especially its communist members, to try Pucheu immediately. At his trial, Pucheu claimed to have actually reduced the number of hostages shot by the Germans. He was, however, condemned to death. On 20 March 1944 he was executed.

F. Kupferman, *Le procés de Vichy: Pucheu, Pétain, Laval* (Brussels, 1980); R. O. Paxton, *Vichy France: Old Guard, New Order* (New York, 1972); P. Pucheu, *Ma vie* (Paris, 1948).

C. S. Bisson

PURGE, POST-LIBERATION, a "purification" of France or "victors' justice," depending on one's viewpoint, was part of a pattern of defeat, **collaboration**, and subsequent retribution that has been played out in French history since the days of Caesar and Vercingétorix. Some 8,000 to 9,000 people were executed for collaboration with the Occupation authorities, many by vigilante justice in what has been called the "*épuration sauvage*" (wild, in the sense of nonlegal, purge) prior to the **liberation**. An additional 320,000 cases were heard after the liberation by judicial authorities of the **Provisional Government** and the Fourth **Republic**, resulting in some 44,000 prison terms and 1,500 death sentences.

The legal bases for the trials were taken from previously existing French jurisprudence, with additions such as the 8 August 1944 law that stipulated "*dégradation national*," the loss of civic rights, as a punishment for collaboration. A special **Haute Cour de Justice** (High Court of Justice) tried 108 **Vichy** dignitaries, of whom eight were sentenced to death. Three were actually executed. Thirty-one convictions carried varying penalties, and three cases resulted in acquittal.

In addition to criticisms of ex post facto proceedings, inequitable treatment resulted from the fact that those caught immediately after the liberation often received punishment harsher than those who managed to escape hiding and were caught later, after passions had cooled. Indeed, the fury unleashed at the time of the liberation on **women** accused of "**horizontal collaboration**," who were paraded publicly with heads shorn, may inadvertently, by releasing pent-up popular anger, have saved others from an even worse fate. Journalists and others who had taken public stands in favor of the Axis received penalties more severe than those, business leaders, for example, whose collaboration may have been more harmful to French interests but had also been more discreet. In addition, many of those who served on local purge tribunals were appointed by the **Resistance** committees, effectively combining the roles of prosecutor and judge. Interested in maintaining order and rebuilding the French **economy**, the Provisional Government also looked the other way with regard to the wartime activities of many among the French political and economic elites.

By 1947 and 1948, passions had cooled, and the pace of the purges slowed. Limited amnesty laws were passed in 1947, followed by more encompassing ones in 1951 and 1953. By 1964, there was no one left in prison as a result of wartime activity. That year, however, the French parliament passed a law removing the statute of limitations from crimes against humanity. As attention focused more closely in the 1970s and thereafter on official French complicity in the **Holocaust**, a few surviving participants were brought up for trial on charges of crimes against humanity. These included Klaus **Barbie**, head of the Gestapo in Lyons, convicted in 1983, and the *milice* officer Paul **Touvier**, the first Frenchman to be so convicted, in 1994. Maurice **Papon**, involved in the **deportation** of **Jews** as secretary-general of Vichy's regional administration in the Bordeaux region, was scheduled for an October 1997 trial for crimes against humanity.

R. Aron, *Histoire de L'Épuration*, 3 vols. (Paris, 1967–1975); P. Bourdrel, *L'Épuration sauvage 1994–1945* (Paris, 1988); B. M. Gordon, "Afterword: Who Were the Guilty and Should They Be Tried?" in R. J. Golsan, ed., *Memory, the Holocaust, and French Justice: The Bousquet and Touvier Affairs* (Hanover, NH, 1996), 179–98; B. M. Gordon, "Collaboration, Retribution, and Crimes against Humanity: The Touvier, Bousquet, and Papon Affairs," *CFC* 19:2 (Summer/Fall 1995): 250–74; H. R. Lottman, *The Purge: The Purification of French Collaborators after World War II* (New York, 1986); P. Novick, *The Resistance versus Vichy: The Purge of Collaborators in Liberated France* (New York, 1968); F. Rouquet, *L'Épuration dans l'administration française: Agents de l'état et collaboration ordinaire* (Paris, 1993); O. Wieviorka, "Épuration," in J.-P. Azéma and F. Bédarida, eds., *1938–1948 Les Années de Tourmente, de Munich à Prague, Dictionnaire Critique* (Paris, 1995), 933–43.

B. M. Gordon

R

RACIAL LAWS, VICHY, were decrees issued by the Vichy government that targeted mainly Jews by enacting increasingly specific definitions and by restricting their freedoms. Because Marshal Pétain wielded what amounted to dictatorial power, and the laws of the Vichy government were not democratically formed, the legal status of the decrees has been challenged.

From June 1940 to September 1944, all decrees were published in the *Journal Officiel*. At first, the decrees targeted recently naturalized citizens (revoking their French citizenship), but increasingly they applied to all Jews. On 27 September 1940, for example, Jews in the unoccupied zone were forbidden to return to the occupied zone, special identity cards were issued, and businesses owned by Jews were required to post a sign to this effect; it was followed by the *"Statut des Juifs"* of 3 October 1940, requiring all Jews to register with the police. Whereas the Nazi definition of a Jew required three Jewish grandparents, Vichy included persons with two Jewish grandparents and a Jewish spouse. On 28 September, the first of the "Otto lists" appeared, banning the works of Jewish authors, among others. By such small increments, Jews were gradually marginalized, until by the time of the Vélodrome d'hiver roundup, on 16 July 1942, the mechanisms—both "legal" and logistical—to identify, round up, and deport large numbers of French Jews existed, due to the Vichy government. Vichy law also created French agencies to handle Jewish issues, including the Comissariat Générale aux Questions Juives, the Contrôle des Administrations Provisoires, and the Police aux Questions Juives.

Centre de documentation juive contemporaine, *Les Juifs sous l'Occupation: Recueil des textes français et allemands, 1940–1944* (Paris, 1945); S. Klarsfeld, *Vichy-Auschwitz: Le rôle de Vichy dans la solution finale de la question juive en France*, 2 vols. (Paris, 1983, 1985); M. R. Marrus and R. O. Paxton, *Vichy France and the Jews* (New York, 1981); D. Rémy, ed., *Les Lois de Vichy* (Paris, 1992); R. H. Weisberg, *Vichy Law and the Holocaust in France* (New York, 1996).

M. Hawthorne

RADIO. The radio war for France was a three-way battle among **Paris, Vichy**, and London. Paris spoke for the 1940 victor; London, for the resister; and Vichy, for *la France seule* (France alone).

Vichy was compelled by the events of the war to adopt the propaganda of its conqueror. Radio-Paris, created by Goebbels' Propaganda Department in the autumn of 1940, was directed by Dr. Alfred Bofinger, of Radio-Stuttgart, with musical varieties and classical concerts featuring the best orchestras and virtuosi. Radio-Paris voices included those of Georges Oltramare, "Dr. Friedrich," in reality, Friedrich Dambmann, another veteran of Radio-Stuttgart, and pro-German French journalists who reproached Vichy policy for being insufficient in its ardor for the **New Order**. Addresses by Jacques **Doriot**, Colonel Roger-Henri Labonne, commander of the **Légion des Voluntaires Français**, and Jean **Hérold-Paquis** crusaded for the New Order, calling for "a pure France in a united Europe."

In August 1941, Radiodiffusion Nationale, having ceased operations with the 1940 defeat, resumed broadcasts to French colonies still loyal to Marshal **Pétain**. Radio-Vichy featured a monotonous program of **youth** and **peasant** projects, the changing of the guard, and the marshal's Sunday walkabouts. Gaullist broadcasts from London obliged Vichy to abandon its "neutrality," responding with repression, jamming, and counterpropaganda. Fines and imprisonment fell short of German demands for the death penalty for listening to the **BBC**. Jamming London's broadcasts forced Radio-Vichy to rely on German technical assistance to defend its radio sovereignty. Counterpropaganda featured Paul Creyssel and Philippe **Henriot. De Gaulle** was described as the "Kerensky of the Kremlin" and Churchill's mercenary. Loyalty to the marshal and obedience to Pierre **Laval's** compulsory labor draft were dominant themes. By 1943 Radio-Vichy had become a fief of the Germans. Attacking the Comintern, the Atlantic Charter, Allied "terror" bombing, and the promised invasion, Paris and Vichy attempted to swing the psychological balance with uncertainty and fear. Despite jamming, listeners preferred the broadcasts of London; Sottens, a Swiss radio station; and the Voice of America.

H. Eck, *La guerre des ondes: Histoire des radios de langue française pendant la Deuxième Guerre mondiale* (Paris, 1985).

P. J. Coggins

RASSEMBLEMENT NATIONAL POPULAIRE (RNP) was one of the major **collaborationist** parties during the Occupation. Founded at the beginning of February 1941, in the wake of Marshal **Pétain's** firing of Pierre **Laval** (13 December 1940), the RNP supported Laval and opposed the **Vichy** "reactionaries" in Pétain's entourage, as well as Jacques **Doriot's Parti Populaire Français (PPF)**, seen as too Stalinist in its methods and personnel.

Supported by Laval and Otto **Abetz**, the new party was headed by former **socialist** Marcel **Déat**, together with two leaders of the **Mouvement Social Révolutionnaire (MSR)**, Eugène **Deloncle** and Jean van Ormelingen, also known as Vanor; Jean **Fontenoy**, a journalist, formerly with the **communists**, then the PPF; and Jean Goy, president of the Union National des Combattants, a **right-wing** veterans' group. Although the party claimed half a million members, it never attracted more than 30,000 throughout France, although it did create subsidiary organizations for labor, **education, peasants**, and **North Africa**.

On 27 August 1941, during a rally for the newly created anti-Bolshevik **Légion des Volontaires Français**, Laval and Déat were wounded in an assassination attempt for which Déat blamed Deloncle, the former head of the interwar conspiratorial Cagoule. While convalescing, Déat organized the expulsion of the MSR faction from the RNP. In an operation that had comic opera qualities, Déat's supporters expelled the MSR faction from the RNP headquarters with the obvious connivance of French and German police.

The purged RNP looked to the interwar noncommunist **Left** for recruits. Déat, who emerged as the unquestioned leader, introduced former **socialists, syndicalists**, and teachers, such as Georges **Albertini**, who reorganized the party, giving it a more **Republican** image than its collaborationist rivals, chiefly the PPF. The party also attracted a relatively larger number of **women**, some undoubtedly hoping thereby to win the release of **prisoners** of war in Germany. With the changing tide of the war, the RNP was weakened, decisively after March 1944, when Déat became minister of labor and national solidarity and devoted his attention to other matters.

M. Déat, *Mémoires politiques* (Paris, 1989); Y. Durand and D. Bohbot, ''La Collaboration politique dans les pays de la Loire moyenne: étude historique et socio-politique du R.N.P. en Indre-et-Loire et dans le Loiret,'' *RDHDGM* 23 (July 1973): 57–76; B. M. Gordon, *Collaborationism in France during the Second World War* (Ithaca, NY, 1980).

G. Le Marec

RASSEMBLEMENT POUR LA RÉVOLUTION NATIONALE was a short-lived organization initially proposed by Gaston **Bergery** as a single mass party to embody the link between **Pétain** and the French people. It was created in July 1940 by Jacques **Doriot**, whose **Parti Populaire Français' (PPF)** activities were severely curtailed under the German law banning French political parties. Ostensibly swearing allegiance to Marshal Pétain, Doriot meant to rally anti-**Republican**, anticommunist, and Anglophobic elements in the hope of creating a single party he would lead. Shortly after the **British** attack on French naval vessels at **Mers-el-Kébir**, he announced in **Paris** the creation of the new movement (Rassemblement).

Its leadership included **communists** who had switched over to the PPF after the signing of the Nazi–**Soviet** Pact (former party secretary Marcel Gitton, Jean-Marie Clamamus, Marcel Capron, André Parsal, Marcel Bront, Fernand Soupé, Albert Clément, Émile Nédelec, and Joseph Barthélémy). The presence of ex-communists in the organization's ranks aroused **Vichy's** suspicions, while the Germans, judging Doriot too unpredictable, favored more traditional politicians such as Pierre **Laval** and Marcel **Déat**. Although mentioned in **Pétain's** 11 October 1940 message outlining the doctrine of the **National Revolution**, the Rassemblement never became the single mass party that its supporters had envisioned. Doriot's military engagement in the **Légion des Volontaires Français** and the subsequent reappearance of the official PPF in December 1941 rendered the Rassemblement politically irrelevant.

P. Burrin, *La Dérive Fasciste: Doriot, Déat, Bergery, 1933–1945* (Paris, 1986); B. M. Gordon, *Collaborationism in France during the Second World War* (Ithaca, NY, 1980); J.-M. Guillon, ''La philosophie politique de la Révolution nationale,'' in J.-P. Azéma and F. Bédarida, eds., *Le Régime de Vichy et les Français* (Paris, 1992); P.-P. Lambert and G. Le Marec, *Partis et mouvements de la collaboration: Paris, 1940–1944* (Paris, 1993).

L. Ditmann

RATIONING and the BLACK MARKET, born of shortages, affected food before being extended to other domains. Theoretically, rationing was put in place to help the most unfortunate and reduce inequalities, assuring the distribution to all segments of the population the quantities of foodstuffs to which they were entitled at moderate prices. This enabled the state to exercise control over prices and the distribution of merchandise.

Beginning September 1940, the **Vichy** government administered a system of ration cards allotting specific quantities of food according to one's needs, based on age and profession. The population was divided into six categories of consumers by age: category E for children from birth to 3 years of age, J1 and J2 for children up to 12 years old, J3 for adolescents, 13 to 21 years old, A for adults, and V for the elderly, above age 70. Heavy laborers such as miners were given extra supplements, as were pregnant **women**, adding two more categories for a total of eight. To obtain bread, meat, or sugar, each person had to have a certain number of tickets valid for a given week or month. Following the calculations of the nutritionists of the era, the base ration for urban dwellers barely exceeded 1,300 calories, which was lowered to 1,100 in 1943.

Problems quickly arose. Insufficient rations pushed families to resort to all sorts of means, legal (*colis familiaux*, or packages sent by family members, often from the countryside) and illegal (the black market). Resourcefulness became systematized, while the black market was essential for a proportion of households that sought food through direct and illegal purchases in the countryside. There was, nonetheless, a large difference, on one hand, between those who bought a kilo of butter or meat on the farm above the official price—which was tolerated after March 1942—and, on the other, the large-scale dealers who worked for the Germans or the luxury restaurants.

H. Amouroux, *La vie des Français sous l'Occupation*, 2 vols. (Paris, 1961); B. M. Gordon, ''Fascism, the Neo-Right, and Gastronomy: A Case in the Theory of the Social Engineering of Taste,'' *Oxford Symposium on Food and Cookery 1987, Taste, Proceedings* (London, 1988), 82–97; D. Veillon, *Vivre et Survivre en France 1939–1947* (Paris,

1995); D. Veillon and J.-M. Flonneau, eds., *Le temps des restrictions en France (1939–1949)* (Paris, 1996).

D. Veillon

REBATET, LUCIEN (1903–1972), was a **collaborationist** and avowedly **fascist** journalist and major contributor to *Je suis partout (JSP)*. Rebatet joined the *JSP* in 1932 and remained there until the journal ceased publication at the end of the Occupation. He wrote regular columns on the **cinema** and the arts, usually under the pseudonym of François Vinneuil, and contributed political articles under his own name throughout the 1930s and the Occupation years.

Educated in Lyons and Paris, where he received a degree in philosophy, Rebatet worked initially for an insurance company before launching his career as a journalist with *Action Française* in 1929. During the 1930s, he also wrote for *Candide, La Revue universelle*, and *Le jour*. At *JSP*, Rebatet established himself as a virulent **anti-Semite**, editing two special anti-Semitic issues for *JSP*, ''Les Juifs'' (April 1938) and ''Les Juifs en France'' (February 1939).

In July 1942, Rebatet became a celebrity with the publication of his best-selling memoirs, *Les Décombres* (The Ruins), a rabid **denunciation** of Third **Republican** ''decadence.'' In 1944, he joined the *milice* and contributed to *Devenir*, the organ of the French Waffen SS. In August 1944, he fled **Paris** and joined other collaborationist luminaries at **Sigmaringen**. He was arrested by the Allies in Austria in May 1945, condemned to death in November 1946, pardoned, and then freed in 1952. The same year, he published a lengthy novel often described as a masterpiece, *Les Deux Étendards*, with Gallimard. An unrepentant fascist, Rebatet continued to publish polemical articles in **right-wing** reviews, including *Rivarol* and *Écrits de Paris*, as well as another novel, *Les Épis murs* (1954), and a history of music.

R. Belot, *Lucien Rebatet: Itinéraire d'un fasciste* (Paris, 1994); D. Carroll, *French Literary Fascism: Nationalism, Anti-Semitism, and the Ideology of Culture* (Princeton, 1995); ''Cry Havoc,'' in G. Steiner, *Extraterritorial: Papers on Literature and the Language Revolution* (New York, 1971); L. Rebatet, *Les Décombres* (Paris, 1942).

R. J. Golsan

REFERENDUM (1945–1946) was a constitutional procedure proposed by General **de Gaulle** to give foundations to the French **Republic** that it had never before had.

On 10 July 1940, the National Assembly, meeting in **Vichy**, voted to revise the constitution under the authority of Marshal **Pétain**, president of the council (premier) of a Republican government. An amendment added that the institutions would be ratified by the nation or by assemblies created for that purpose. On 11 July, the first constitutional acts of the **État Français** appeared with no such ratification ever occurring.

The Republic, however, remained in the war in the form of **Free France** and the **Resistance**. President of the **Provisional Government** of the French Republic, General de Gaulle, having exercised republican authority in London and Algiers, arrived in Paris in August 1944. On 9 September he became head of a "national unity government." Victory on 8 May 1945 allowed for the end of the provisional status of the Republic. The country was to express itself, and, on 29 July 1945, the French learned that they would be consulted in a referendum, a new word used to exorcise the bad memory of the Bonapartist plebiscites of the years 1851 through 1870.

On 21 October 1945 two referenda took place: one to decline a return to the Third Republic (96 percent voting yes); the other to accept a procedure of ratification of the next constitution by referendum (66 percent voting yes). On 5 May 1946, one constitutional proposal was rejected. The following 13 October, despite heavy abstention, a second constitutional proposal was accepted: it was the birth of the Fourth Republic, the first to have been ratified by universal suffrage of men and **women**.

Opposed to both of the 1946 proposals, General de Gaulle resigned on 20 January 1946. He returned in June 1958 to propose a constitution, ratified in the referendum of 28 September 1958 (79 percent voting yes). The constitutional referendum had become commonplace.

†F. Goguel and A. Grosser, *La Politique en France* (Paris, 1984); Institut Charles de Gaulle, ed., *De Gaulle en son siècle*, vol. 2: *La République* (Paris, 1992); O. Rudelle, *De Gaulle pour mémoire* (Paris, 1990).

O. Rudelle

REFUGEES moved into and within France in several groups during the World War II era. Following **Hitler's** rise to power, German refugees began trickling into France, as did in the mid-1930s, a few Poles. The first major wave of foreign refugees resulted from the Spanish civil war, when many departments in southern France opened camps to house the fleeing Spanish Republicans in the mid-1930s. Many of these camps in the Pyrenees and the Cevannes and as far north as the Cher-et-Loire functioned until World War II and were subsequently converted to accommodate new refugee populations. The French government welcomed these political refugees and extended to some a minimal amount of financial support in the form of refugee allocations. Many of the refugees enlisted in the French **army** and fought in the **Battle of France**.

Following the June 1940 defeat, the overwhelming number of refugees were Belgians, **Alsatians, Lorrainers**, and **Jews**—foreign and French. On 5 July 1940, the prefect Pierre Marlier, director of the Service of Refugees for the **Vichy** government, met in **Paris** with General Alfred Streccius, the official representative of the German army, to discuss the status of French and foreign refugees in the unoccupied **zone**. The two parties agreed on conditions for repatriating refugees to the occupied zone and to Alsace and Lorraine, the latter two having been annexed by Germany. Foreign refugees, particularly Belgian and Dutch, were scheduled for return home in July and August.

During these discussions the two teams defined categories of refugees who qualified for repatriation to the occupied zone in France. Those denied access to the occupied zone included French and foreign Jews, **communists**, refugees of ''mixed blood'' (*sang mélangé*), and some categories of foreigners. During the following months of repatriation, German officials randomly turned back trains packed with more than 900 refugees due to the presence of one or two refugees of the excluded categories.

In the unoccupied zone, refugees received a daily stipend of 10 francs per adult and 8 per child. The Red Cross and other local charities organized the distribution of clothing and household utensils for refugees, many of whom lived in vacant hotels or public buildings such as schools. Vichy officials suspended relief on 30 September 1940 to all refugees eligible to return to the occupied zone. Only Alsatians and Lorrainers refusing to return to their now German-annexed regions, French and foreign Jews, and a small number of miscellaneous refugees continued to benefit from Vichy government aid. By May 1942 the protected status of Jewish refugees in the unoccupied zone had expired. Round-ups began in the summer of 1942, with state officials often using the same lists of refugee addresses previously used to administer aid. At least 150,000 Alsatians and Lorrainers remained in the unoccupied zone throughout the Occupation years and received preferential treatment with regard to lodging, schooling, and job placement, through programs organized by the Service of Refugees.

N. Dombrowski, ''Beyond the Battlefield: The French Civilian Exodus of May–June 1940'' (Diss., New York University, 1995); E. A. Lindquist, ''The Experience of the Spanish Republicans in the Auvergne, 1936–1946'' (Diss., University of Kansas, 1984); M. R. Marrus, *The Unwanted: European Refugees in the Twentieth Century* (New York, 1985); M. J. Proudfoot, *European Refugees 1939–42: A Study in Forced Population Movement* (London, 1956).

N. Dombrowski

RELÈVE, LA, was the 16 June 1942 agreement between Pierre **Laval** and Fritz **Sauckel** under which one French **prisoner** of war (POW) in Germany was returned to France for every three skilled French workers who volunteered to work in Germany. As Germany's need for manpower grew, and Sauckel intensified pressure for French labor, Laval proposed the Relève to avoid compulsory labor service. Announced on 22 June 1942, the Relève was supported by a massive propaganda campaign, with newspapers required to carry favorable reports of it. Laval hoped workers would volunteer, if not to help Germany defeat the **Soviet Union**, then out of sympathy for the **prisoners**. The three-to-one ratio was announced only in August, however, and newspapers were instructed to bury the information.

Although the Relève repatriated 90,747 POWs, it proved divisive, and the optimism it raised among the prisoners and their families quickly gave way to jealousy and suspicion. Many mistakenly believed that the Relève would liberate a prisoner whose family members volunteered to work in Germany. Because the results were unsatisfactory, French and German authorities quickly became coercive. On 4 September 1942 a **Vichy** law decreed a **Service du Travail Obligatoire** for men ages 18 to 50 and **women** ages 21 to 35 and initiated a census of workers. In certain factories Vichy imposed "voluntary" contracts on entire groups of workers. Public opinion considered the Relève thinly veiled forced labor, and disenchantment with Vichy deepened. With the 17 February 1943 mobilization of labor, Vichy abandoned the voluntary ruse.

Y. Durand, *La captivité* (Paris, 1980); S. Fishman, "Grand Delusions," *JCH* 26 (April 1991); G. Scapini, *Mission sans gloire* (Paris, 1960).

S. Fishman

RELIEF AND RESCUE ORGANIZATIONS varied greatly in their origins, affiliations, structure, and life spans. Yet they all shared the imperative to maintain and protect the lives of **refugees**, overwhelmingly **Jewish**, on French soil. The best-known organization was the Comité inter-mouvements auprès des évacués (Cimade). Founded in 1939 by Madeleine Barot, Cimade was a largely Protestant organization originally meant to aid inhabitants of **Alsace** and **Lorraine** evacuated by the French government. This narrow mandate, under the pressure of the defeat of France and the **exodus** of refugees to the south, broadened in the summer of 1940. Cimade established a presence in several internment camps, providing food and medical care, as well as placing children with foster families or the *centres d'acceuil* (supervised residences) that it ran. By mid-1942, Cimade was fully engaged in hiding Jewish refugees and helping them escape into **Switzerland**.

Several organizations worked alongside Cimade, including the Young Men's Christian Association (YMCA), the American Friends Service Committee, the Unitarian Service Committee, and Amitiés chrétiennes. In late 1940, these organizations, along with Jewish welfare agencies, branches of the Red Cross, and Secours suisse, created the Comité de coordination pour l'assistance dans les camps (Comité de Nîmes). Presided over by Donald Lowrie, the American YMCA representative, the Comité de Nîmes helped establish the *centres d'acceuil* and secure the subsequent release of the children from the internment camps.

This move saved the lives of numerous children who otherwise would have been eventually deported from the camps. This prescient policy was advocated by the Oeuvre de secours aux enfants (OSE), a Jewish agency led by Andrée Salomon and Dr. Joseph Weill. Incorporated in 1942 into the **Union générale des israélites de France (UGIF)** the OSE played a critical role not only in emptying the camps of most of their adolescent internees but also in providing health care and food. The group also ran several clandestine child rescue networks and fabricated false papers—identification cards, working permits, and **ration** cards—for its Jewish charges. Anticipating Gestapo raids in the southern **zone** in 1944, the OSE closed down its 15 centers and placed the children with Christian religious institutions and Gentile families. In the northern zone, the fate of the UGIF centers was grimmer: in July 1944, they were raided by the

Gestapo, and more than 250 children, along with their guardians, were deported to Auschwitz. None survived.

The ranks of the Éclaireurs israélites de France (ÉIF), or Jewish Boy Scouts, founded in 1923 by Robert Gamzon, overflowed with adolescent refugees who had either lost their families (through **deportation** or internment) or whose parents, fearful of imminent arrest, had placed them with the group. The ÉIF created several farms in the unoccupied zone, where Scouts were taught manual trades and Jewish history and culture. By late 1942, the leaders of the ÉIF began placing threatened foreign-born Scouts, armed with false documents, with non-Jewish organizations and individuals—an activity supported by the OSE and the Mouvement des Jeunesse Sioniste, or Zionist **Youth** Movement.

There were dozens of smaller and local operations, such as the Comité rue Amelot in **Paris**, the Service André in Marseilles, and the Maurice Cachoud Group in Nice. Members ran enormous risks in their clandestine activity; dozens of men and **women** were captured, shot, or deported. Yet, along with the courage of these relative few, the complicity of countless Frenchmen and French women was essential. Some 20,000–30,000 Jewish children are estimated to have been saved. Were it not for the help of a largely sympathetic population, the number saved would have been far lower.

P. Joutard et al., *Cévennes: Terre de Refuge 1940–1944* (Montpellier, 1987); S. Zeitoun, *L'Œuvre de secours aux enfants (O.S.E.) sous l'occupation en France* (Paris, 1990); S. Zuccotti, *The Holocaust, the French, and the Jews* (New York, 1993).

R. D. Zaretsky

RÉMY (GILBERT RENAULT, 1904–1984), was born in Vannes (Morbihan). A banker and film producer before the war, Renault in July 1940 joined **Free France**'s secret service, taking first the name "Raymond," then, beginning in 1941, "Rémy." He subsequently created the Réseau Confrérie Notre-Dame (Notre Dame Confraternity Network), which in 1943 helped link the Gaullists with the Francs Tireurs et Partisans.

Emerging a **Resistance** hero, Rémy wrote prolifically after the war. His 1946 *Mémoires d'un agent secret de la France libre* (translated into English as *Memoirs of a Secret Agent of Free France*) became a best-seller, with 650,000 copies sold. In 1947, he joined General **de Gaulle's** Rassemblement du Peuple Français, whose rallies he helped to stage.

Most important, Rémy sought to rehabilitate the reputation of Marshal **Pétain**. His article "La Justice et l'opprobe" (Justice and the Disgraced) in the 11 April 1950 issue of *Carrefour* raised a storm in French public opinion, by arguing not only that France had needed "two strings in her bow"—Pétain as well as de Gaulle—in 1940 but also that de Gaulle had confided as much to him in 1946. The two-strings claim was striking less for its originality in the late 1940s than because of Rémy's Resistance credentials and his closeness to de Gaulle.

In association with the *Abbé* Jean-Marie Desgranges' Fraternité de Notre-Dame de la Merci (Order of Our Lady of Mercy), Rémy sought to rehabilitate the memory of Charles **Maurras** and others **purged** in what they considered the "excesses" of the post-**liberation** period. Rémy continued to write histories of the war, arguing, as did de Gaulle, that the Resistance had really begun on 3 September 1939, the day of the declaration of the war. He died in 1984, a *Compagnon de la Libération*.

Rémy, *Memoirs of a Secret Agent of Free France*, trans. L. C. Sheppard (London and New York, 1948 [original French ed., 1946]); H. Rousso, *The Vichy Syndrome, History and Memory in France since 1944*, trans. A. Goldhammer (Cambridge, MA, 1991).

G. Le Marec

REPUBLIC (1940, 1944–1946, 1946) refers to the Third Republic, **Provisional Government** of the French Republic, and the Fourth Republic, respectively. As a concept in France "Republic" transcends specific governments or regimes.

Abolished on 11 July 1940, the Republic returned to continental France with the **liberation** and the arrival of the Provisional Government, which, headed by General **de Gaulle**, had still not been recognized by the Allies. Refusing to "proclaim the Republic" at the **Paris** Hôtel de Ville at the time of the liberation, on 25 August 1944, de Gaulle declared that the Republic already existed and had never ceased to exist.

This long-disputed theory of legality underlay the entire juridical construction of the **Free France** of 1940, which had become **Fighting France** in 1942 with the support of the **Resistance** organized by Jean **Moulin**. It is inherent in the proclamation of the need to "reestablish Republican legality," which was at the heart of the conflict between General Henri **Giraud**, who did not wish to go beyond the respect for "human liberties," and General de Gaulle, together with the Resistance, which proclaimed the legitimacy of the government of the Republic alone, the hope of a new Republic, the Fourth, announced in Algiers on 14 July 1943.

The Republic acceded with the instant disappearance of the **Vichy** regime and the triumphal welcome given by the French to the man of 18 June (1940) who had "reestablished" (or reincarnated) the Republic, "its name, its arms, and its laws." Faithful to its principles, the Republic sought, however, to transform itself into the "regime" so as to guarantee the "separation of powers." This resulted in a major conflict with the political forces, traditional and new; General de Gaulle resigned in January 1946. He returned to power in June 1958. His regime would be the Fifth Republic.

M. Agulhon, *La République. De Jules Ferry à François Mitterrand, 1880 à nos jours* (Paris, 1990); Fondation Charles de Gaulle, ed., *Le Rétablissement de la légalité Républicaine* (Brussels, 1996); C. de Gaulle, *The Complete War Memoirs, 1940–46*, 3 vols., trans. J. Griffin (vol. 1) and R. Howard (vols. 2 and 3) (New York, 1964); O. Rudelle, *De Gaulle et la République, Mai 1958* (Paris, 1988); M. Vovelle, *Révolution et République* (Paris, 1994).

O. Rudelle

RESISTANCE, a broad term referring to those who fought against, or in other ways attempted to subvert, German, Italian, and Japanese rule in the countries their forces occupied during World War II. After the defeat of France in 1940, few French sought to continue the fight. Aside from some members of parliament who took to the sea, trying to continue the war from Africa, hardly anyone had the heart to stand up to the Germans. General **de Gaulle** fled to London and proclaimed in his now famous speech of 18 June 1940 that the war had not been decided by the **Battle of France**, that as Germany had been victorious in 1940 by force of mechanized arms, it, in turn, would some day be defeated by even superior arms, and that "whatever happens, the flame of French Resistance must not and will not be extinguished." Few, however, heard him at the time. The 80 members of parliament who voted on 10 July 1940 against giving plenipotentiary powers to Marshal **Pétain** to create a new government have also been classified among the "first resisters." Gradually, the Resistance organized and intensified, helping the Allies in intelligence gathering and, eventually, on the battlefield as well.

Scattered acts of sabotage of phone lines began early. Isolated men and **women** who had endeavored to oppose military might often paid with their lives. In the northernmost region of France, closed off and made into a "forbidden" **zone** by Germany, some French citizens formed small groups of resisters, reminiscent of their elders in the northeastern area of France occupied by German forces during the 1914–1918 war. They kept their numbers small to avoid infiltration and arrest.

The earliest acts of Resistance, of necessity, were individual and unpublicized, and most of these will never be known. One of the earliest public gestures was a **symbolic** demonstration of secondary school students (*lycéens*), who celebrated the armistice of 1918 at the Arc de Triomphe on 11 November 1940. At the **Musée de l'homme**, also in **Paris**, a first nucleus of systematic Resistance was formed by ethnologists and other scientists who produced a clandestine paper calling on French people to fight the Occupation. Boris Vildé, an Estonian who had come recently to France, led this group, which included lawyers, mathematicians, and physicists. Their ranks, however, were infiltrated by Nazi informers, and almost all were arrested and executed by firing squads at Mont Valérien near Paris, even though the German military prosecutor spoke admiringly of their patriotism. One of them, Valentin Feldman, shouted at the moment of execution: "Imbeciles, it's for you, too that I die!"

The German invasion of the **Soviet Union** on 22 June 1941 freed the French **communists** from the ban decreed by the **Daladier** government following the 1939 Nazi–Soviet pact. The German attack on the Soviet Union brought the **communists**, whose semisecret organization suited them well for clandestine activities, into the Resistance. German executions brought more and more of the French into the Resistance. In the occupied zone of France, some of the most devoted patriots worked for clandestine newspapers and Resistance movements such as **Libération-nord**. Another group was the **Organisation Civile et Mil-**

itaire. By distributing illegal tracts and doing messenger service and by a few armed attacks, people sought to weaken the seemingly invincible power of the Germans.

In the unoccupied zone by early 1942, several Resistance organizations had formed, although none had more than a few thousand members. The three major ones were Henri **Frenay's Combat**, conservative, although it attracted some former **socialists**; **Libération-sud**, created by Emmanuel **d'Astier** de la Vigerie, more moderate in political viewpoint; and **Franc-Tireur**, a name meant to recall the 1870 war. Lyons, then the third largest city in France, became the principal center of the Resistance, though by the time of the **liberation**, as illegal action became easier, **Paris** once again became the focal point.

Despite deep political differences among the various Resistance movements and tensions between the external Resistance, headed by de Gaulle in London and, later, Algiers, and the underground in France, they never fought one another, as happened in other countries such as Yugoslavia. Eager to unite the Resistance groups under his own leadership, General de Gaulle dispatched a former prefect, Jean **Moulin**, to bring the groups together in France. In January 1943, after months of diligent and patient negotiations, Moulin was able to bring together the **Mouvements Unis de la Résistance**, which grouped together the noncommunist Resistance groups. In May 1943, Moulin organized the **Conseil National de la Résistance**, which included representatives from all the Resistance movements, together with the **Left** and center political parties and the trade unions. Shortly after his successes, Moulin fell into a trap, was taken prisoner, and was tortured to death. Moulin was succeeded by Georges **Bidault**. The institution in 1943 of the compulsory labor service (**Service du Travail Obligatoire**), which drafted young workers for service in Germany, drove many of them into hiding as outlaws in the *maquis*, from whence they often joined the Resistance. With the Allied landings in **Normandy**, many French Resistance groups, notably in Paris, emerged to help in the liberation of their country.

In retrospect, though the people who actually resisted were few in numbers, the Resistance contributed significantly to the Allied sweep through France in 1944. Equally memorable is the clandestine publication of books of real literary merit, such as Vercors' *Silence de la mer*, which have taken their place in the French literary canon. Clandestine literature was **published** in secret by presses such as **Éditions de minuit**, staffed by devoted, unafraid printers, risking their lives, and distributed at great risk, reaching the outside world to demonstrate that French culture had not been extinguished by the Occupation. The Cahiers du **Témoignage chrétien** preached a Resistance according to Christian and ecumenical principles. Despite the brutality of the occupation authorities, especially in the latter stages of the war, the Resistance writers, by and large, avoided the chauvinistic excesses of World War I, when virtually everything German had been debunked. Resistance ideals of a France "*pur et dur*" (pure and strong) may have receded after the war, but the image of Resistance heroism lived on, notably in the formal transfer of Jean Moulin's ashes to the Pantheon, the temple of French patriotic glory, in 1964.

M. Atack, *Literature and the French Resistance: Cultural Politics and Narrative Forms, 1940–1950* (Manchester, U.K., and New York, 1989); L. Aubrac, *Outwitting the Gestapo*, trans. K. Bieber (Lincoln, NE, 1993 [originally published in France as *Ils partiront dans l'ivresse: Lyon, mai 1943-Londres, février 1944*, 1984]); K. Bieber (with preface by A. Camus), *L'Allemagne vue par les Écrivains de la Résistance Française* (Geneva, 1954); D. Cordier, *Jean Moulin, l'inconnu du Panthéon*, 3 vols. (Paris, 1989–1993); L. Douzou, *La Désobéissance, Histoire du Mouvement Libération-sud* (Paris, 1995); F.-G. Dreyfus, *Histoire de la Résistance* (Paris, 1995); P. Miquel, *Les Quatre-vingts* (Paris, 1995); H. Noguères, *Histoire de la Résistance en France*, 5 vols. (Paris, 1967–1981); D. Rondeau and R. Stéphane, *Des Hommes Libres: Histoire de la France libre par ceux qui l'ont faite* (Paris, 1997); A. Rougeyron, *Agents For Escape: Inside the French Resistance, 1939–1945*, trans. M.-A. McConnell (Baton Rouge, LA, 1996).

K. Bieber

RESISTANCE, FOREIGNERS IN THE, were drawn from the 2.5 million immigrants in France, the main groups of whom were 800,000 Italians, 500,000 Poles, 400,000 Spaniards, and 120,000 foreign **Jews**.

Immigrants usually resisted in language groups. Italians joined the **Communist** Party with its paper, *La Parola degli Italiani*, the **Socialist** Party, union movements, and groups such as the Trotskyist Libérer et Fédérer in Toulouse. Antifascist Italians in the south formed Le Comité d'action pour l'union du peuple italien. The Polish community was strongly represented in the **left-wing** parties and trade union **Resistance** groups of the northern coal fields and formed the spying networks of "F2." Those who supported the London Polish government-in-exile gathered under the banner of Organisation polonaise de lutte pour l'indépendance. Spaniards joined underground Communist, Socialist, and anarchist (Alianza Democratica Española) Parties early in the war. In 1942 Spanish communists formed the Union Nacional Española and its armed wing, the Organisación Militar Española (later, the Agrupacion Guerrillera Española). Even small communities, such as the Armenians, resisted. Youngsters established La Jeunesse Armenienne de France, and prewar groups such as the conservative Dashnaks and the left-wing Comité de secours à l'Arménie formed clandestine groups.

Germans, virtually all of whom were political **refugees**, formed clandestine Communist and Socialist Parties in France and broader movements, including Travail Allemand (German Labor) and the Comité "Allemagne Libre" pour l'ouest. Particularly adept at anti-Nazi propaganda among German troops, most of these movements came together in the National Komitee Freies Deutschland. Foreign **Jews** intermingled with denaturalized French Jews in organizations such as the Éclaireurs Israelites de France (the Jewish Scouts), the Union de la jeunesse juive, and the Union des juifs pour la résistance et l'Entraide. Some founded the Organisation Juive de Combat **maquis**, succeeded by the Armée Juive.

Many immigrants worked within groups such as **Combat, Franc-Tireur** and Libération, but the only organizations that set out to promote immigrant Resistance across national boundaries were the communist-inspired Mouvement des Immigrés Ouvriers (MOI), its fighting wing, the FTP-MOI, and the anti**deportation** committees.

D. Bartosek et al., *De l'exile à la Résistance. Réfugiés et immigrés d'Europe Centrale en France 1933–1945* (Paris, 1989); D. Joutard and F. Marcot, eds., *Les étrangers dans la Résistance en France* (Besançon, 1992); G. Laroche, *On les nommait des étrangers: les immigrés dans la Résistance* (Paris, 1965).

J. C. Simmonds

RÉSISTANTIALISME is a term used to describe a **right-wing** reinterpretation of the Occupation and **Resistance** that focuses on the excesses of the **purge** that followed the **liberation**.

In the late 1940s, with the hardening of attitudes during the cold war, a section of the extreme right wing in France used the Occupation as a **symbolic** reference point in their struggle against communism. Their review of the war years condemned the purge and produced a radically different image of wartime France from what was widely accepted at the time. In this rereading of the Occupation, the defeat and the **armistice** were inevitable; **Vichy** resisted alongside a **left-wing** Resistance led by **communists**. At the same time, a right-wing, often anti-Gaullist, Resistance evolved that remained faithful to the French military tradition. Such right-wing ''resisters'' considered that, since the liberation, the officially accepted Resistance had drawn them into a Franco-French civil war.

This battle against the perceived injustices of the purge was waged by the writers of the **Hussards** and in journals such as *Écrits de Paris*, as well as in pamphlets like the Abbé Jean-Marie Desgranges' *Les Crimes masqués du résistantialisme* (1948), which defended the actions of Vichy ministers, as well as condemning false resisters. For many, in the late 1940s and 1950s, it seemed like the world turned upside down as **collaborators** were amnestied while former resisters were being tried.

The term *résistancialisme* is sometimes used for the generally heroic images of a united, resisting France that grew out of a Gaullist interpretation of the war years. This remained one of the official images of the Occupation, despite the Hussards' critiques, until challenged by the writers and filmmakers of the *mode rétro* in the 1970s. In this case, *résistantialisme* with a ''t'' refers more specifically to the right-wing reading of the Occupation. Often, however, the Gaullist view and the right-wing critique of it are grouped together under the rubric *résistantialisme*.

N. Hewitt, *Literature and the Right in Postwar France: The Story of the ''Hussards''* (Oxford and New York, 1996); A. Morris, *Collaboration and Resistance Reviewed: Writers and the Mode Rétro in Post-Gaullist France* (Oxford, 1992); H. Rousso, *The Vichy*

Syndrome, History and Memory in France since 1944, trans. A. Goldhammer (Cambridge, MA, 1991).

C. Gorrara

REYNAUD, PAUL (1878–1966), held cabinet office several times in the early 1930s, was finance minister in 1938, and was a *belliciste* and premier during the French military debacle in 1940. He supported resistance to Nazi aggression before the war and a vigorous pursuit of hostilities after he became premier in March 1940. Reynaud could not overcome the defeatism that struck his government after the German offensive in May 1940.

Reynaud, who first became finance minister in 1930, was a conservative politician and a member of the Democratic Alliance. In the mid-1930s, he did not hold cabinet office but supported Charles **de Gaulle's** ideas in favor of a professional **army** and the use of concentrated armor. Reynaud was a maverick and loner without a strong parliamentary base and could not win support for de Gaulle's ideas. In 1937 Reynaud urged a buildup of French air defenses, and in 1938 he became a member of Édouard **Daladier's** cabinet, first as justice, then as finance minister. During the **Munich crisis**, along with Georges **Mandel** and Jean Champetier de Ribes, he considered resignation to protest against French capitulation but ultimately remained in the cabinet. As finance minister, he restored confidence and developed a more productive **economy** at the expense of labor.

Reynaud gave the impression of a statesman of talent and energy who could be, in the view of a **British** contemporary, the French Churchill. After Reynaud became premier, he did not have time to establish his authority and he lacked Churchill's tenacity. He was at daggers drawn with **Daladier**, who remained as war minister, and he could not buck the system of political maneuvering and dishonest finesse that characterized the ''**Republic** of Pals.'' When crisis struck in May 1940, he made the fatal mistake of bringing defeatists Marshal **Pétain** and General Maxime **Weygand** into the government. They, along with **Laval**, blocked Reynaud's efforts to carry on the fight against Nazi Germany from **North Africa**.

*†M. Alexander, *The Republic in Danger: General Maurice Gamelin and the Politics of French Defence, 1933–1940* (Cambridge, U.K., 1992); P. Reynaud, *In the Thick of the Fight* (New York, 1955 [original French ed., 1951]); W. L. Shirer, *The Collapse of the Third Republic* (New York, 1969); R. Young, *France and the Origins of the Second World War* (New York, 1996).

M. J. Carley

RIGHT AND LEFT are a set of oppositional terms that relate to questions of social justice. Because relatively few political groups actually name themselves ''right'' or ''left''—the French Jeune Droite of the 1930s being something of an exception—these terms have been often used rhetorically, especially since the mid-1960s, to designate one's political opponents. Often qualifiers, such as "moderate" or "extreme," are used.

By common agreement, during the 1789 revolution the terms "right" and "left" were first used to denote opposing political factions, with the more revolutionary National Assembly deputies sitting to the left of the speaker's chair, and the more conservative to the chair's right. In general, right and left are differentiated by claims to privilege, accorded increasingly narrowly as one goes further right, from gender, race, caste, class, party, to the single privileged individual of despotic and some anarchist theories. Right-left dialogue, however, shifts continually as a consequence of changing historical circumstances.

Metaphorical usages parallel to "right" and "left" are evident long before 1789. They include "patrician versus plebeian," "Guelf versus Ghibelline," "Jesuit versus Jansenist," and "Cavaliers versus Roundheads." The eighteenth century produced Tories and Whigs in England, aristocratic "Hats" and liberal "Caps" in Sweden, governmental "*Négatifs*" and more democratic "*Représentants*" in Switzerland, and Loyalists and Patriots in America. Even after the appearance of "right" and "left," dualistic sets of terms continued to shift, giving rise to "Anglophiles" and "Patriots," "Girondins" and "Montagnards," "Jacobins" and "Enragés," and, after 1814, "Liberals" and "Conservatives," to name a few. "Right" and "left" gained greater currency with the spread of parliamentary government in Western and Central Europe during the last third of the nineteenth century. By the late-1930s, French right-left divisions were compounded by splits between *Munichois*, in favor of the 1938 **Munich** agreement, and *anti-Munichois*, the two factions also called *pacifistes* and *bellicistes*, respectively, a division that continued in the **collaboration–resistance** cleavage of the Occupation years.

During the Occupation, **collaborators, resisters,** and *attentistes* all came from various parts of the political spectrum. Although **Vichy** and the nongovernmental collaboration had largely right-wing origins, these groups were not monolithic, and they drew prominent supporters from the interwar Left, as in the examples of René **Belin**, Gaston **Bergery**, Hubert **Lagardelle**, and Marcel **Déat**. The Resistance attracted support from the interwar Left but also from the Right, as in the cases of Emmanuel **d'Astier de la Vigerie**, Henri **Frenay**, and Colonels **Passy** and **Rémy**. The complex role of the French **communists** from the signing of the August 1939 Nazi–Soviet pact to the German invasion of the **USSR** is still debated. After the **liberation**, the Right, tarnished by association with **Vichy** and the collaboration, found a voice with the "**Hussards**," who argued that "leftists" had often collaborated, and "rightists" had often resisted.

P. Burrin, *La dérive fasciste: Doriot, Déat, et Bergery* (Paris, 1986); A. Griotteray, *1940: La Droite était au rendez-vous, Qui furent les premiers résistants?* (Paris, 1985); R. Handourtzel and C. Buffet, *La Collaboration . . . à gauche aussi* (Paris, 1989); R. Rémond, *The Right Wing in France from 1815 to de Gaulle*, trans. J. M. Laux (Philadelphia, 1969 [from the French ed. of 1962; originally published as *La Droite française de 1815 à nos jours*, Paris, 1954]); J.-F. Sirinelli, ed., *Histoire des Droites en France*, 3 vols. (Paris, 1992).

B. M. *Gordon*

RIGHTEOUS AMONG THE NATIONS is a title awarded to non-Jews who risked their lives to rescue **Jews** during the *Shoah* (**Holocaust**). The Martyrs' and Heroes' Remembrance (*Yad Vashem*) Law, passed by the Israeli Kneset (parliament) in 1953, charged *Yad Vashem* with authenticating their deeds and perpetuating their memory. Since 1962 a public commission has been empowered to recognize the Righteous, based on contemporary documentation and the testimony of those rescued. The main criteria for recognition are (1) a concrete rescue action, (2) the rescue carried out at personal risk, and (3) remuneration neither requested nor received by the rescuer. By the end of 1995, 13,618 such cases were authenticated, including 1,366 from France, most of them involving couples or entire families.

The list of French Righteous includes eight bishops, such as Cardinal Pierre-Marie **Gerlier**, Jules Gérard **Saliège**, and Cardinal Pierre-Marie Théas, all of whom openly condemned the **deportation** of the Jews and, even if their lives were not in peril, contributed greatly to many rescues. More than 60 Catholic clergymen, such as Father Pierre Chaillet and Father Marie-**Benoît** (Pierre Péteul), who worked tirelessly to rescue Jews, are recognized. Forty-three Protestant clergymen are recognized, in most cases accompanied by their spouses. Such were André and Magda Trocmé of **Le Chambon-sur-Lignon**, who enrolled their entire communities into rescue actions. Some, such as André Trocmé, paid for their generosity with their lives.

Most of the Righteous, however, were ordinary people—social workers such as Renaudin Aline or Suzanne Boulat, who worked with the Jewish underground, and educators such as Juliette Vidal and Marinette Guy of Saint-Étienne, who saved many children. Lucien and Agnés Bertrand were bakers who hid and saved two persons unknown to them before the Occupation; Juliette Domenq, a worker, saved a family, unacquainted with her before. Josephine and Charles Baud, peasants, saved two young boys, one of them the son of an industrialist from **Luxemburg** who spent a vacation in their village before the war and another brought to them by the Jewish communist organization. Joseph and Ernestine Ducret were also peasants, who hid Jewish families on their farm by giving them their own identity papers. Valentin and Marie Daubas, from a small village in Gers, concealed a young woman and her family when Jews were being deported. The farm of Albert and Germain Guilmin in the village of Peloisières (Sarthe) served as a temporary haven for more than 100 Jews. Charles Gombert, a railway worker, saved two escapees from a **deportation** train in the Vosges. Gérard and Louise Bouquey saved Perla Waver, a Jewish woman and her three children, ages two through six, in Barenton, a small village in Normandy. Even a guard of the notorious Drancy camp Camille Mathieu, with the assistance of his wife, Denise, rescued three Jewish families.

A. Cohen, *Persécutions et sauvetages, Juifs et Français sous l'Occupation et sous Vichy* (Paris, 1993); M. Paldiel, *The Path of the Righteous: Gentile Rescuers of Jews during the Holocaust* (Hoboken, NJ, 1993).

A. Cohen

RIOM TRIALS (19 February 1942–11 April 1942) were convened to confirm a predetermined verdict in which the **Vichy** government accused the former **Republic's** ministers as responsible for the defeat.

Marshal **Pétain's** explanation for the catastrophe of 1940 was that France had too few weapons and too few children. Léon **Blum**, the former premier, was accused of having supported Republican **Spain** in 1936, threatening to embroil France in a war against its own interests; former premiers Édouard **Daladier** and Paul **Reynaud** and **interior** minister Georges **Mandel** were charged with declaring and pursuing war in 1939 against Pétain's and General Maxime **Weygand's** counsel. Air ministers Pierre Cot and Guy La Chambre were blamed for France's aerial inferiority. Maurice-Gustave **Gamelin**, former commander in chief, was also put on trial.

The indictments accused the defendants of leading an ill-prepared France, on **British** orders, to declare war on Germany. While the Germans expected the defendants to be found guilty of declaring war, Vichy wanted them found guilty of losing it. The trial opened to a war situation different in 1942 from that of 1940. Britain, undefeated and allied with the **Soviet Union** and the **United States**, cast doubts on Axis victory and French **collaboration** in the **New Order**. Maurice Schumann's **BBC** broadcasts noted that Pétain, as war minister in 1934, had neglected the Ardennes' sector, the very place where the Germans broke through in 1940.

Blum and **Daladier** defended the **Popular Front's** military rearmament, which had poured billions of francs into tanks and planes, rather than the concrete fortifications of the **Maginot Line**. The trial was a propaganda defeat for Vichy and was suspended indefinitely in April 1942 by Admiral Jean-François **Darlan**. The defendants were held as hostages until the end of the war.

H. Michel, *Le Procès de Riom* (Paris, 1979).

P. J. M. Coggins

ROMAN CATHOLIC CHURCH IN FRANCE was divided into various camps during the war years, representing the full range of options, from pro-German **collaboration**, to active armed **resistance**. The church had suffered from the separation of church and state in 1905 and had watched religious practice decline at an alarming rate, especially among the lower classes. It feared the expansion of the political **Left** and was virtually unanimous in its opposition to communism.

The church thus welcomed the advent of the **Vichy** regime, its self-styled **National Revolution**, and its rhetoric of **family** and social solidarity. Vichy's **anti-Semitic** legislation was not cause for outcry from the bishops. Even noted

Catholic progressives expressed hopes that the National Revolution would embody the radical transformation that they believed France needed. The **Jeunesse Ouvrière Chrétienne (JOC)** applauded Vichy's dissolution of **communist youth** groups, and it took Emmanuel **Mounier** roughly two years to move toward resistance. The École Nationale des Cadres, founded in 1940 at **Uriage**, was a veritable "macho" Catholic "think-tank" and training school for men committed to the Vichy vision. Initially, at least, the vast majority of vocal Catholics were collaborators in the Pétainiste mode.

However, some active Catholics were implicated deeply in more directly **fascist** and pro-Nazi activities. Xavier **Vallat** was the architect of Vichy's anti-Semitic legislation, Philippe **Henriot** was a leader of the *milice*, numerous Catholics joined Charles **Maurras** in his **Jew**-denouncing **Action Française**, and Cardinal Alfred **Baudrillart** was a militant advocate for the Nazi-led anti-Bolshevik crusade in the east. Fascist French Catholics were a small minority, but their prominence and the refusal of Catholic prelates to repudiate them helped tarnish the church.

Some devout Catholics joined the Resistance immediately after the fall of France. Most of these had been part of interwar Christian democratic organizations, progressive Catholic newspapers (such as *L'Aube*), and the confessional trade union movement. Henri **Frenay**, of the **Combat** movement, was a Catholic, as was General **de Gaulle** himself. Temoignage Chrétien and its well-organized team had impeccable Resistance credentials from the early years of Vichy, and by the latter years many members had taken up arms against the occupier. Catholicism gave many martyrs to the cause of **liberation**, not least of whom were the worker-priests Camille Folliet and Gilbert Dru, Catholic visionaries for a united Left.

After the 1943 forced labor requisition (**Service du Travail Obligatoire**), Catholic Resistance became a serious force in occupied France. The JOC had entered the Resistance in an organized way; the **Témoignage chrétien** team was in full flower; Gilbert Dru was trying to organize a Christian democratic movement; clandestine Catholic experiments were set in motion behind the backs of the Germans; and Georges **Bidault**, a devout Catholic, had been appointed by de Gaulle to lead the **Conseil National de la Resistance**. No longer the choice of only a few, Catholic Resistance had joined the national Resistance networks and had launched some of its own.

Both communists and Catholics, outsiders in the Third **Republic**, entered the postwar years with Resistance laurels. In the case of French Catholics it was overwhelmingly the work of the laity and a few "grassroots" clergy. The hierarchy's reputation had been seriously tarnished. This unusual situation allowed progressive Catholics to set a new tone for their church and nation that was instrumental in forming the character of the Second Vatican Council. In late September 1997, Archbishop Oliver de Berranger of Saint-Denis formally apologized on behalf of the Church for the "silence" of the majority of the hierarchy in the face of French collaboration with anti-Jewish persecution during the Occupation.

*L. Allen, "Resistance and the Catholic Church in France," *Resistance in Europe*

(Baltimore, 1976); J. Duquesne, *Les Catholiques français sous l'occupation* (Paris, 1966); J. Hellman, *The Knight-Monks of Vichy France* (Montreal and Kingston, 1993); N. Ravitch, *The Catholic Church and the French Nation* (London, 1990).

O. L. Cole-Arnal

ROMIER, LUCIEN (1885–1944), historian, journalist, and economist who served as a minister of state in the **Vichy** regime. Born into a bourgeois Catholic family from the Beaujolais, he entered the École des Chartes in 1905. Romier emerged a trained historian specializing in sixteenth-century French history. Because frail health kept him out of World War I, he was attached to the National Association for Economic Expansion, where he studied production problems. After the war he turned to journalism and became first editor in chief of *La Journée industrielle*, and then an editorial writer for *Le Figaro*.

A member of Redressement français, an economic study group founded by Ernest Mercier, Romier met Marshal **Pétain** at its meetings. The two men discovered their common affinity for a traditional rural and Catholic France. After the defeat of 1940, Romier joined the marshal's entourage at Vichy. In 1941 he was named to the Conseil national and presided over sessions of the commission charged with the administrative reorganization of the French state. That same year he became a minister of state. Romier was given responsibility for convening a national assembly that would reinforce **Pétain's** authority as well as presiding over the drafting of a constitution for the Vichy regime. Neither project ever materialized, however. German authorities having placed him on a list of "undesirable elements" to be eliminated, Romier resigned as minister of state at the end of 1943. His health, always precarious, gave way, and he died suddenly on 5 January 1944. Pétain attended the elaborate state funeral held for the man who was neither a **fascist** nor a **collaborator** but a technocrat completely loyal to the elderly marshal.

M. François, "Lucien Romier," *Bibliothèque de l'École des Chartes* 105 (1944): 338–44; C. Roussel, *Lucien Romier (1885–1944)* (Paris, 1979).

J. Friguglietti

RUNDSTEDT, GERD VON (1875–1953), German supreme military commander in the west, responsible for the defense against an Allied landing, an archetypical, experienced, nonpolitical Prussian staff officer.

Born into an old Prussian, aristocratic family, Rundstedt became an officer in 1892 and with a good service record was repeatedly promoted until being named general field marshal in 1940. Because he never challenged **Hitler's** authority, he was invariably given the highest command posts. Accordingly, during the 1940 western campaign, he commanded the Heeresgruppe A (Army Group A), which led in the main offensive against France. From October 1940 until June 1941 and from 14 March 1942 until 3 July 1944, Rundstedt was supreme commander of German forces stationed in France, **Belgium**, and the Netherlands. As opposed to his subordinate, Field Marshal Erwin Rommel, Rundstedt planned to defeat Allied landing forces not immediately on the coast but subsequently by means of a flexible introduction of larger armored reserves. Hitler opted for a compromise, so that neither Rommel's nor Rundstedt's strategies were followed. Deceived by the Allied intelligence agencies in 1944, Rundstedt anticipated a second landing at Calais and waited too long to send larger forces to the **Normandy** front. With heavy Allied air and matériel superiority, he urged a partial retreat and a switch to a flexible defensive strategy. Hitler rejected this and ordered the defense of every inch of territory. He relieved Rundstedt of his command on 3 July 1944.

C. Messenger, *The Last Prussian* (London, 1991); D. Ose, *Entscheidung im Westen* (Stuttgart, 1982).

B. Kasten

S

SABIANI, SIMON PIERRE (1887–1956), leader of the **Parti Populaire Français (PPF)** in Marseilles and wartime **collaborationist** leader.

Born in a **Corsican** village, Sabiani emigrated to Marseilles as a young man and led an unsettled life there until the First World War, in which three of his brothers were killed, and he himself lost an eye. In 1918, he entered Marseilles politics as a much decorated veteran and revolutionary **socialist**, and in 1920 he helped found the local branch of the new **Communist** Party. He soon left the party but continued to hold local office as an idiosyncratic **left-winger**. Tactical alliances with the **Right** won him election to the Chamber of Deputies in 1928 and 1932 and kept him in office as deputy-mayor of Marseilles during a turbulent and scandal-ridden period. In 1936 he joined the new PPF and began a lasting friendship with its national leader, Jacques **Doriot**. Sabiani devoted the rest of his career to an obsessive anticommunism that led him to support publicly the German occupiers after 1940. In 1942 his son was killed fighting alongside the Germans on the **Russian** front. Sabiani joined the exodus of French collaborators to Germany in 1944 and lived on in exile in South America and **Spain**, where he died in 1956.

Sabiani rendered many services to friends and followers, and many to this day recall his generosity as well as his courage. He appears to have had little regular contact with the Germans, restricting his support to vocal propaganda. But the PPF in his area degenerated into a rabble of criminals, bounty hunters, and German agents over whom he had little control but with whom his name is indissolubly associated.

P. F. Jankowski, *Communism and Collaboration. Simon Sabiani and Politics in Marseille, 1919–1944* (New Haven, CT, and London, 1987).

P. F. Jankowski

SAINT-EXUPÉRY, ANTOINE DE (1900–1944), writer and aviator with an established reputation before the war as a prizewinning novelist (*Vol de nuit*, 1931), essayist (*Terre des hommes*, 1939), journalist, and civil aviation pioneer in Africa and South America. During the "**Phoney War**" and until the fall of France, he served as a reconnaissance pilot.

From 1940 to 1942 he was in exile in the **United States**. Feted by the **Americans**, he continued his writing career with *Pilote de guerre, Lettre à un otage*, and *Le petit prince*. Despite closeness to high-placed figures in the American military establishment, he was unable to speak English, thereby limiting his efforts to encourage American participation in the war. In the French community his position was tenuous. Distrustful of **de Gaulle** and hostile toward **Vichy** (while harboring vestigial loyalty to **Pétain**), he claimed an "apolitical" patriotism that appeared misguided and naive to the sharply polarized expatriates. His "Open Letter to Frenchmen Everywhere" in the *New York Times*, 29 November 1942, urging reconciliation between Vichy and Gaullist factions in the interest of France's rejoining the war against Germany, earned him almost universal condemnation, best symbolized in an attack by Jacques **Maritain**, "Pour la Victoire," 19 December 1942.

In April 1943, Saint-Exupéry joined the reconstituted French forces in **North Africa**, while working on his monumental *Citadelle*. Humiliated by uncompromising Gaullists, marginalized by American authorities doubting his competency, and plagued by despondency, he remained determined to fly for his country. He prevailed, flying several reconnaissance missions over France and Italy in the spring of 1944. On 31 July, he failed to return. His disappearance has remained an enigma.

*C. W. Nettelbeck, *Forever French: Exile in the United States 1939–1945* (Oxford and New York, 1991); A. de Saint-Exupéry, *Écrits de guerre* (Paris, 1982); S. Schiff, *Saint-Exupéry: A Biography* (New York, 1994).

C. W. Nettelbeck

SALIÈGE, JULES-GÉRARD (1870–1956), archbishop of Toulouse from 1929 to 1956, was born in the Auvergne. Though paralyzed after 1932 in his legs and, increasingly, his speech, Saliège was among the most forceful moral spokesman for French Catholicism during World War II. A former member of Sillon, the liberal Catholic movement founded by Marc Sangnier, Saliège supported a rapprochement between the church and the **Republic**. This spirit of reconciliation was encouraged by Saliège's immediate circle—most notably, Monsignor Bruno de Solages, rector of the city's Catholic Institute—which had long been engaged in a dialogue with progressive political elements in Toulouse.

Though Saliège supported **Pétain**, he was skeptical about the **Vichy** regime. In his diocese's *La Semaine religieuse*, the archbishop repeatedly warned his readers that force must not be confounded with right. These warnings gained immediacy in the summer of 1942, with Vichy's roundup and **deportation** of foreign-born **Jews**. Informed of events unfolding at Noé and Récébédou, two nearby **concentration camps**, Saliège wrote a blistering condemnation. Ignoring the local prefect's intervention, Saliège ordered the sermon read in all the diocese's churches, and it quickly became one of the great texts of spiritual **resistance**.

Though Saliège emphasized that his criticism was limited to Vichy's Jewish policies, his ties to the regime increasingly frayed. In 1943, he refused to support the forced labor draft (**Service du Travail Obligatoire**) and, that same year, welcomed Francis-Louis Closon, a representative of General **de Gaulle**. On 9 June 1944, the Gestapo arrested a number of Toulouse's prominent Catholics; Saliège was spared due to his physical infirmity. After the **liberation**, he remained a critic of the established powers, preaching on behalf of the working class and denouncing "capitalist slavery."

P. Bolle and J. Godel, eds., *Spiritualité, théologie, et résistance* (Grenoble, 1987); J.-L. Clément, *Monseigneur Saliège archévêque de Toulouse 1929–1956* (Paris, 1994); J. Guitton, *Le cardinal Saliège* (Paris, 1957).

R. D. Zaretsky

SARTRE, JEAN-PAUL (1905–1980), philosopher, writer, and leading figure of Parisian existentialism whose postwar program of *littérature engagé* was inspired by solidarity among those opposed to Nazi occupation forces and the **Vichy** regime.

Mobilized for **army** duty as a meteorologist in September 1939, Sartre was already a rising literary figure who wrote for the prestigious *Nouvelle Revue Française* (NRF) and whose **fiction** appeared under imprint of the *NRF*'s **publisher**, Gallimard. Captured by the Germans in June 1940, Sartre was transferred two months later to Trier, where he remained in detention for seven months before escaping by posing as a civilian. *Bariona ou le fils du tonnerre*, a Christmas play he composed while in Trier, provided Sartre with a sense of literature's potential to convey the primacy of human freedom.

Unable to contact the French **Communist** Party underground after returning to **Paris** in March 1941 and trying without success to form a **Resistance** group, Socialisme et liberté, with Maurice Merleau-Ponty, Sartre devoted the next three years to teaching and writing. Two plays, *Les Mouches* (The Flies) and *Huis clos* (No Exit), and a major essay of philosophy, "L'être et le néant" (Being and Nothingness) were among texts that appeared alongside newspaper articles and reviews during the Occupation.

In 1943, Sartre joined the clandestine Comité national des écrivains and wrote for the *Lettres Françaises*. Following the **liberation**, in September 1944 he headed the editorial board of *Les Temps modernes*, a new monthly whose first issue appeared a year later. Four months thereafter, he traveled to the **United States** as a reporter for *Le Figaro* and *Combat*, the former underground newspaper on which he had worked with Albert **Camus**. By the end of 1945, Sartre was back in the United States visiting New York jazz clubs and lecturing at Columbia, Harvard, Yale, and even Carnegie Hall on topics ranging from Camus' *La Peste* to new tendencies in French **theater**.

*†A. Cohen-Solal, *Sartre, a Life*, trans. A. Cancogni (New York, 1987 [original French

ed., 1985]); M. Contat and M. Rybalka, *The Writings of Sartre*, trans. R. C. McCleary (Evanston, IL, 1973 [original French ed., 1970]).

S. Ungar

SAUCKEL, FRITZ (1894–1946), was the Reich's plenipotentiary for labor who ordered the conscription of hundreds of thousands of French laborers for work in Germany between 1942 and 1944. A Nazi from the early days of the party, Sauckel was serving as *Gauleiter* of Thuringia when he was put in charge of labor allocation at the war's outbreak in 1939. In March 1942, he was appointed head of the newly initiated foreign labor conscription program by minister of armaments Albert Speer. Dissatisfied with the results of Pierre **Laval's** policy of recruiting laborers for work in Germany, Sauckel decreed a labor draft in France's occupied **zone** on 20 August 1942. With the rest of France occupied after November 1942, the drafting of whole age groups began in February 1943, enforced by the *Service du Travail Obligatoire*. By the end of 1943, French labor conscripts recruited by French and German services to work in Germany numbered 1.4 million, and France was Germany's largest source of skilled labor in all of occupied Europe. Simultaneously, the detested policy served to swell the ranks of the armed **Resistance** groups in France.

Early in 1944, Sauckel announced plans to move another million French workers to Germany by the end of the year. He condoned increasingly violent methods in order to secure this goal in the last eight months of the Occupation but succeeded in conscripting only about 40,000 additional French workers in the face of growing Resistance. Upon being sentenced to death at Nuremberg after the war, he protested: "I have never been cruel myself. I always wanted the best for the workers." He was hanged on 16 October 1946.

J. Gillingham, *Industry and Politics in the Third Reich* (New York, 1985); E. L. Homze, *Foreign Labor in Nazi Germany* (Princeton, 1967); A. S. Milward, "French Labour and the German Economy, 1942–1945," *Economic History Review* 23 (1970): 336–51.

R. MacKinnon

SERVICE D'ORDRE LÉGIONNAIRE (SOL) was created 12 December 1941 under Joseph **Darnand**, a hero of both the 1914–1918 and the 1940 wars. Darnand was a **right-wing** activist who had been a member of **Action Française** until 1928 and was fanatically loyal to Marshal **Pétain**. However, he did not quite fit in with the military elites who obtained power at **Vichy**; he came from a humble background, and he resented the fact that he had not been allowed to become an officer in 1919.

From a unit of the **Légion Française des Combattants** in his native Alpes-Maritimes, Darnand created the SOL, which he envisioned as a paramilitary elite that would carry through Pétain's National Revolution. The SOL was provided with a doctrine, summarized in its "Twenty-One Points," that endorsed "racial purity" as well as "Christian civilization" and condemned Gaullism, communism, Freemasonry, and Judaism. Although not initially armed or linked to **collaboration**, the SOL was seen as a dangerously radical group by many legionnaires. When Darnand handed over the colors of the new SOL, thereby initiating it, in Haute Savoie, for example, only one-quarter of the original legionnaires turned up. In January 1943 Darnand was entrusted with the creation of another body, the *Milice*.

B. M. Gordon, *Collaborationism in France during the Second World War* (Ithaca, NY, 1980).

R. C. Vinen

SERVICE DU TRAVAIL OBLIGATOIRE (STO), the program under which all Frenchmen aged between 18 and 50 and **women** between 21 and 35 could be mobilized for work in Germany or in German factories in France. The legislation (passed on 4 September 1942) was instigated by Pierre **Laval**, whose ''**Relève**'' scheme had failed to deliver the numbers of French workers demanded by Fritz **Sauckel** for Nazi labor needs.

Officially operative from 15 February 1943, the STO was a major example of French state **collaborationism**. However, evasion attained massive proportions. When the program ended in July 1944, some three-quarters of a million French workers had been sent to Germany (half the figure demanded by Sauckel), with another half million engaged in German factories in France. Conditions were generally harsh, and French workers killed in Allied bombings probably numbered in the tens of thousands.

The STO aided the **Resistance** by contributing substantially to the population's disaffection toward **Vichy** and the Occupation. The armed underground movements were strengthened by their involvement in large-scale creation of refuges and networks for STO rebels. Further, the statement by Cardinal Achille **Liénart** (15 March 1943), permitting Catholic noncompliance with STO laws, marked a critical break in church support for Vichy.

At the **liberation**, repatriated STO workers often faced ostracism and have remained a discomfort in the national conscience, because the question that they raised—did nondisobedience to a collaborationist French law constitute collaboration?—had national implications.

J. Duquesne, *Les Catholiques français sous l'Occupation* (Paris, 1988 [original ed., 1966]; Y. Durand, *La France dans la deuxième guerre mondiale 1939–45* (Paris, 1989); J. Evrard, *La déportation des travailleurs français dans le IIIe Reich* (Paris, 1972); C. W. Nettelbeck, ''Robbe-Grillet and Friends at Nuremberg: Exorcising the STO,'' *French Cultural Studies* 3:9 (October 1992).

C. W. Nettelbeck

SÉTIF MASSACRE (1945) occurred when French **police** fired upon demonstrators on VE Day in the northeastern Algerian city of Sétif.

After **Vichy** authorities balked at demands for constitutional guarantees for all Algerians and a limited degree of self-determination contained in the March 1943 Manifesto of the Algerian People, the liberal nationalist Ferhat Abbas drafted a supplement to the manifesto advocating "the political autonomy of Algeria as a sovereign nation." **Free French** officials, who took charge of Algeria on 1 June, refused to discuss autonomy, but in March 1944 General **de Gaulle** personally launched a program designed to open the country's electoral system and judiciary to greater indigenous participation. Conservative Algerian notables joined **communist** and **socialist** leaders in welcoming the reforms, although Abbas and the radical Algerian People's Party (PPA), headed by Messali Hadj, denounced them. The latter formed a loose coalition, the Friends of the Manifesto and of Liberty (AML), to agitate against the **New Order**.

By the spring of 1945, PPA cadres stood poised to win control of the AML, precipitating clashes between Abbas' moderates and militant trade unionists loyal to Messali Hadj. Jockeying between the two factions accompanied escalating unemployment and decreasing food stocks in local markets. May Day demonstrations in Algiers and Oran turned violent, as **police** assaulted marchers carrying the banner of the nineteenth-century anti-French leader al-Amir Abd al-Qadir. AML representatives in Sétif—which had a history of both anti-French and anti-**Jewish** violence—and in the nearby town of Guelma were granted permission to organize rallies celebrating VE Day on condition that no Algerian flags or inflammatory placards be displayed. Demonstrators ignored the prohibition; gendarmes in the two towns first attempted to seize nationalist emblems and then shot into the crowd, sparking a wave of attacks against government installations and *colon* farms scattered across the northeastern highlands. French commanders called in some 10,000 troops to quash the insurrection, used aircraft transferred second-hand from the **U.S.** Army Air Force to destroy villages suspected of harboring rebels, and deployed warships to interdict traffic moving along the coast. At Guelma, authorities permitted *colons* to form a vigilante group, which indiscriminately slaughtered inhabitants of surrounding villages. Meanwhile, the Algerian Communist Party publicly dissociated itself from the insurrection, which it considered "**fascist**-inspired," and collaborated with the government to suppress it.

French officials abruptly terminated two separate boards of inquiry into the events of May 1945, so casualty figures remain in dispute. At least 100 Europeans died during the rebellion, along with 6,000 to 35,000 indigenous Algerians. The ruthlessness with which the authorities crushed the revolt propelled Radicals into the vanguard of the Algerian national movement, thoroughly discredited local communists, and convinced the country's *colons* that the drive for independence could be stopped by brute force.

J.-P. Azéma, "Sétif," in J.-P. Azéma and F. Bédarida, eds., *1938–1948 Les Années de tourmente, de Munich à Prague, Dictionnaire Critique* (Paris, 1995), 891–97; A. Clayton, "The Sétif Uprising of May 1945," *Small Wars and Insurgencies* 3 (Spring 1992); A. Clayton, *The Wars of French Decolonization* (London, 1994); M. Halpern, "The Algerian Uprising of 1945," *World Politics* 2 (April 1948); J. Ruedy, *Modern Algeria* (Bloomington, IN, 1992).

F. H. Lawson

SIEBURG, FRIEDRICH (1893–1964), a German writer considered somewhat sympathetic to France. In 1940 Otto **Abetz** recruited him to help with the German Embassy in **Paris**, where he supported French–German cooperation.

During the 1920s and 1930s Sieburg was a foreign correspondent for the *Frankfurter Zeitung* in Copenhagen, Paris, and London. He developed a fascination with French culture and in 1929 published *Gott in Frankreich*, translated into French in 1930 as *Dieu est-il Français*, in which he portrayed France as a likable country, but too much attached to its past.

After the collapse of France, Sieburg, at the German Embassy in Paris, actively promoted **collaboration** between France and Germany. His book *Dieu est-il français* was brought out in a new edition in 1942, with a new preface in which Sieburg wrote that the victory of 1940 had proven the superiority of the German over the French civilization. He also contributed to Alphonse **de Châteaubriant's** *La Gerbe* and was associated with the Deutsches Institut in Paris, which encouraged cultural exchanges and interaction between French and Germans. It became a meeting place for many French artists and writers who either supported or did not object to associating with the German authorities. In 1945 the French government banned his professional work until 1948.

C. Bellanger, *Histoire générale de la presse française*, vols. 3, 4 (Paris, 1975); F. Bondy, "Einführung," in F. Sieburg, *Gott in Frankreich?* (Frankfurt/Main, 1995 [original ed., 1927]); B. M. Gordon, "*Ist Gott Französisch?* Germans, Tourism, and Occupied France, 1940–1944," *MCF* n.s. 4:3 (1996): 287–98; F. Sieburg, *Dieu est-il Français?* trans. Maurice Betz (Paris, 1942).

D. D. Buffton

SIEGFRIED LINE, German fortifications stretching from the Swiss border near Basel to just south of Nijmegen in the north. It secured the western border of Germany and deterred French offensives during the invasions of Czechoslovakia and Poland (1939). The Allied advance into Germany was greatly slowed by the Siegfried Line, which was breached at the cost of more than 150,000 Allied casualties from September 1944 to March 1945.

Construction was begun in 1938 under the direction of Dr. Fritz Todt. From May 1938 to August 1939 close to a half million workers in the Organization Todt worked on the three-mile-deep line of tank traps and bunkers. Although incomplete and lightly manned in 1939–1940, the Siegfried Line intimidated French politicians and generals, in part due to a vigorous propaganda campaign by the German army. In September 1939, General Maurice-Gustave **Gamelin**, in command of French forces, launched a minor offensive in the Saar region in an attempt to relieve Poland. Its effect was minimal, however, as Gamelin prohibited French forces from approaching the Siegfried Line.

Hastily finished in 1944, the Siegfried Line proved to be a valuable defensive formation. In December 1944 it was the starting point for the Germans' last offensive, the Battle of the Bulge. After the offensive's failure and the Germans' subsequent withdrawal the Siegfried Line was abandoned.

D. R. Bettinger, *Der Westwall: die Geschichte der deutschen Westbefestigungen im Dritten Reich* (Osnabrück, 1990); E. Christoffel, *Krieg am Westwall 1944–45: Das Grenzland im Western zwischen Aachen und Saarbrucken in den letzten Kriegsmonaten* (Trier, 1989); C. Whiting, *Siegfried: The Nazis' Last Stand* (New York, 1982).

B. A. McKenzie

SIGMARINGEN GOVERNMENTAL DELEGATION (DELEGATION GOUVERNEMENTALE POUR LA DÉFENSE DES INTÉRÊTS FRANÇAIS EN ALLEMAGNE, 1944–45) was the French government in exile constituted by the **collaborationist** Ultras after the **liberation** of France. Created after meetings of **Hitler**, his foreign minister Joachim von Ribbentrop, and the French Ultra leaders, from 28 August through 1 September 1944 at the German General Staff Headquarters in the Steinort castle, the delegation was the last chance for the extreme collaborationists to hold power, however **symbolically**.

On 6 September 1944, the delegation was proclaimed in Belfort (eastern France), then, retreating before the Allied advance, moved to Sigmaringen in Baden-Württemberg, where it was housed in the Hohenzollern castle overlooking the Danube. Renamed the ''French Governmental Commission for the Defense of National Interests'' in October, it was headed by Fernand **de Brinon**. Also active in it were Joseph **Darnand** as head of the **police** and security services; Marcel **Déat** in charge of ''national solidarity'' and the protection of French workers in Germany; General Eugène-Marie Bridoux, overseeing the protection of French **prisoners** of war; and Jean **Luchaire** as commissioner for information and propaganda.

The delegation claimed to act under the authority of Marshal **Pétain**, who never officially recognized it, even though he too followed it into exile in Germany, though he had been brought there as a prisoner by the Germans. Well-known persons fleeing the **purge** in liberated France also found their way to Sigmaringen. These included Pierre **Laval**, Paul **Marion**, Jean Bichelonne, Louis-Ferdinand **Céline**, Lucien **Rebatet**, and Alphonse **de Châteaubriant**, among others. Absent from Sigmaringen was Jacques **Doriot**, who continued the internecine quarrels among the collaborators, now on the other side of the Rhine, by gathering his supporters in Mainau, where he created, on 6 January 1945, a Comité de la Libération de France, which de Brinon, acting for the delegation, finally joined. The sudden death of Doriot, killed in his automobile by aircraft fire on 22 February, ended the activities of both the committee and the delegation and sounded the death knell to collaborationism as a historical reality.

L.-F. Céline, *Castle to Castle*, trans. R. Mannheim (New York, 1968 [first published as *D'un château l'autre*, 1957]); B. M. Gordon, *Collaborationism in France during the Second World War* (Ithaca, NY, 1980); H. Rousso, *Pétain et la Fin de la Collaboration Sigmaringen 1944–1945* (Brussels, 1984).

M. Lacroix

SILENCE DE LA MER, LE (1942), was a short novel by Jean Bruller (1902–1991) under the pseudonym Vercors, about an idealistic German officer, Werner Von Ebrennac, housed from November 1940 to June or July 1941 in the village home of a Frenchman and his niece whose resolute silence the German accepts as a challenge to be overcome.

While the narrator and his niece seem hardly to acknowledge his presence, Von Ebrennac bares his soul in nightly soliloquies that border on declarations of love addressed to the niece, whom he sees as embodying a French soul that he admires. After returning from a leave in **Paris** that has opened his eyes to **Hitler's** plans to liquidate France and French culture, he announces that he has volunteered for the eastern front. On the eve of his departure, the niece returns the German's nightly "Je vous souhaite une bonne nuit" (I wish you good night) with a barely audible "Adieu," which expresses the inner emotion and turmoil she had previously suppressed.

The clandestine **Éditions de minuit** printed some 250 to 350 copies of the novel in February 1942 but waited six months for security reasons before distributing it. Parachuted back into France in 1943 after being serialized in the London-based **Free French** publication, *La Marseillaise*, and honored with an English translation by Cyril Connolly printed in London and New York, the story soon became a worldwide object of curiosity about which many spoke but few read.

A feature film based on the novel and directed by Jean-Pierre Melville appeared in 1949. The same year, Jean Mercure produced a stage version at the Théâtre Édouard VII.

J. W. Brown and L. D. Stokes, eds., *The Silence of the Sea* (New York, 1991); W. Kidd, *Le Silence de la mer* (Glasgow, 1991); Vercors, *The Battle of Silence* (New York, 1968).

S. Ungar

SOCIALIST PARTY, the Section Française de l'Internationale Ouvrière (SFIO), furnished many members to the **Resistance** but did not itself appear clearly as a resister party.

The **Munich agreement** saw two camps within the SFIO, one led by Secretary-General Paul **Faure**, pacifist and strongly anti**communist**, the other by Léon **Blum**, director of the party newspaper *Le Populaire*, who advocated alliance with the **Soviet Union** and was opposed to concessions on Czechoslovakia. Party unity was only partially patched during 1939, although the Nazi–Soviet agreement removed one cause of dissent.

In the 10 July 1940 vote to grant full powers to Marshal **Pétain**, 89 socialist senators and deputies (of 168) voted for Pétain; only 36 were against, with six abstentions; the others were absent. Though never given a political office by **Vichy**, Paul Faure was on good terms with Pierre **Laval**. Another SFIO minister in Blum's 1936 government became editor of a **collaborationist** newspaper in **Paris**.

In the occupied **zone**, a Comité d'Action Socialiste (CAS) was formed by a small group of Parisian militants as early as January 1941. Party activist Daniel **Mayer** began in early 1941 to reorganize the party in the unoccupied zone, as a CAS. The CAS emphasized reestablishing the Socialist Party, at a time when many current or potential *résistants* rejected the old political parties in favor of activism in Resistance.

While many socialists and unionists worked in the Resistance group Libération-nord, others were active in a variety of movements in France and London. The SFIO itself did not figure as a major force in Resistance. In postwar elections the socialists lost their previous predominance on the **Left** to the Communist Party and did not recover it for 40 years.

*†B. D. Graham, *Choice and Democratic Order* (New York, 1994); D. Mayer, *Les socialistes dans la Résistance* (Paris, 1967); M. Sadoun, *Les socialistes sous l'occupation* (Paris, 1982).

J. W. Friend

THE SORROW AND THE PITY: CHRONICLE OF A FRENCH CITY UNDER THE GERMAN OCCUPATION (1971), a four-hour documentary film by Marcel Ophuls with André Harris and Alain de Sédouy.

The German **Jewish** Ophuls family fled to France in 1933, then to California, where father Max became a successful Hollywood director. Marcel worked for French television news before turning to documentary filmmaking.

Relying exclusively on interviews and newsreel footage, Ophuls constructs a complex portrait of the Occupation in Clermont-Ferrand near **Vichy**. Interviewees include shopkeepers, schoolteachers, journalists, farmers, soldiers, and other ordinary French citizens as well as German personnel stationed in the town, **British** volunteers parachuted into France, political activists of all stripes, and major figures such as Pierre Mendès-France, Jacques **Duclos**, and Anthony Eden. **Resistance** heroes, collaborators, and the indifferent are represented, as are Catholic and **communist**, military and civilian, bitter and philosophical perspectives. The filmmaker highlights discrepancies and contradictions through aggressive questioning.

Interviews were conducted shortly after the revolts of 1968, when a new generation began challenging official accounts of the Occupation. Made for French television but banned until 1981, the film is nevertheless credited with inaugurating the *mode rétro*, or what Henry Rousso calls the "broken mirror" phase of postwar memory, when "obsession" with **collaboration** and guilt began to dispel a Gaullist history of a country united in Resistance (*résistantialisme*).

With this film, Ophuls launched a new approach to documentary filmmaking. His subsequent documentaries include *The Memory of Justice* (1976) about the Nuremberg trials and *Hotel Terminus: The Life and Times of Klaus* **Barbie** (1987).

A. Morris, *Collaboration and Resistance Reviewed: Writers and the Mode Rétro in*

Post-Gaullist France (New York, 1993); M. Ophuls, *Le Chagrin et la pitié* (Paris, 1980); H. Rousso, *The Vichy Syndrome: History and Memory in France since 1944*, trans. A. Goldhammer (Cambridge, MA, 1991).

L. A. Higgins

SOUSTELLE, JACQUES (1912–1990), was a political figure and ethnologist, national commissioner of information, then head of the Direction générale des Services Spéciaux (DGSS) during the war. Subsequently, he was a minister for General **de Gaulle** and then governor of Algeria.

A student at the École Normale Supérieure who passed the *agrégation* in philosophy, Soustelle became professor of sociology at the École des Hautes Études, specializing in pre-Columbian Mexican ethnology, then subdirector of the **Musée de l'homme**. He was a member of the League of Anti-Fascist Intellectuals prior to the Second World War.

Arriving in London from Mexico at the end of 1940, Soustelle began to work in **Free France's** external affairs and information services. In 1941 he made a propaganda tour in Central America and the **United States** for the Gaullist movement and in August 1942 became *Commissaire National* for information. Adjunct director of General de Gaulle's cabinet in July 1943, he was named general director of the DGSS in Algiers on 27 November. *Commissaire de la République* at Bordeaux at the end of the summer of 1944, he held the portfolios of information, then of colonies in de Gaulle's government.

In April 1947 with de Gaulle out of office, Soustelle was one of the founders of the Gaullist Rassemblement du Peuple Français. He sat in the Chamber of Deputies from 1951 through 1958. Governor of Algeria in 1955–1956, Soustelle defended French Algeria and the political integration of the Muslim community. Minister of information in July 1958 and then minister delegate for the departments of the Sahara until 1960, still a partisan of French Algeria, he was forced into exile in 1962. Returning to France in 1968, again a deputy, from 1973 until 1978, he was elected to the Académie Française in 1983.

†J. Soustelle, *Aimée et souffrante Algérie* (Paris, 1956); J. Soustelle, *Envers et contre tout*, vol. 1: *De Londres à Alger (1940–1942)* (Paris, 1947), vol. 2: *D'Alger à Paris (1942–1944)* (Paris, 1950); J. Soustelle, *L'espérance trahie 1958–1961* (Paris, 1962); J. Soustelle, *Vingt-huit ans de gaullisme* (Paris, 1968); B. Ullman, *Jacques Soustelle* (Paris, 1995).

G. Piketty

SPAIN, RELATIONS WITH FRANCE (1938–1946), ran from chilly, through an uneasy entente, and back to open hostility. In June and July 1940, the German victory in France opened a number of possibilities for Spain but its ambitions were held in check by a healthy fear of German intentions plus a realistic, and **British**-financed, understanding of its own weaknesses.

With the Second World War approaching, France wanted to secure its border on the Pyrenees. Consequently, Marshal Philippe **Pétain** was sent as ambassador to Francisco Franco's capital of Burgos, during the Spanish civil war, in early 1938. Pétain pressed the French government to restore Spanish government property (gold, merchant and naval fleets, and works of art) that had been spirited out of the country. Once the process was begun, Franco sent Felix de Lequerica to Paris as ambassador in March 1939.

As the French **army** collapsed in June 1940, Ambassador Lequerica was asked to help arrange an **armistice** with Germany (whereupon all French communications with Spain were immediately handed to the Germans). The Franco government considered expanding Spanish Morocco south to the Spanish enclave of Ifni and east to Oran. Having first proclaimed Spain neutral, Franco on 12 June declared Spain a "nonbelligerent" power and two days later seized full control of the international zone of Tangiers. This turned out to be the extent of Spanish gains during the war, since the Germans did not demand the demilitarization of French forces in North Africa, and General Auguste **Noguès**, the French commander in Morocco, made it clear he would resist any further Spanish expansion.

Although German Admiral Erich Raeder favored a strategy to engage Spain, seize Gibraltar, and establish a German presence in the Mediterranean and **North Africa, Hitler** ignored his advice. Thus Franco's offer of 19 June to enter the war on Germany's side, if compensated at French expense, was not taken seriously until August when the Germans finally became receptive to the idea, but by then their failure to invade Britain and generous British bribes, paid between May and July to leading Spanish Falangists such as General Antonio Aranda Mata, had produced second thoughts in Spain about the advisability of an alliance with Hitler.

By 23 October, when Hitler met Franco at Hendaye, the German army was already deployed to occupy France rather than move south, while British resistance had stiffened. These factors, combined with Spain's need for **American** grain, following the debilitating civil war, all went far to temper Franco's initial enthusiasm for joining the Axis. The German failure to act more quickly, it could be argued, cost them the chance to block the British from the Mediterranean during a brief window of opportunity in June-July, when Britain was highly vulnerable. Hitler was left without a secure western front and saw the World War I nightmare of a two-front war come about again when the Germans did attack the **Soviet Union** in June 1941.

Until November 1942, the Falangist press continued to demand Spain's "place in the sun" at French expense, but Spanish diplomats never seriously pressed the matter. Instead, efforts were made to develop closer Franco-Spanish relations, emphasizing economics, religion, and their shared "Latin" heritage. Thus, visits between Spain and France were exchanged, but little else. The head of the French Catholic Church visited Spain, and Franco made a quick stop in Montpellier to see Pétain in February 1942. By then, both countries wanted to keep the Germans out of the western Mediterranean and, consequently, did their best to discourage German interest in the area. With the Allied invasion of **North**

Africa in November 1942 the three cards that **Vichy** had held (the southern two-fifths of unoccupied France, the French fleet, and French North Africa) were trumped. Franco, for his part, had given up any dreams of expansion and thought only of survival.

Although Spain continued to recognize the Pétain government, it began hedging its bets by establishing contacts with **de Gaulle's** Comité français de la libération nationale (CFLN). Thousands of young Frenchmen (30,000 by the spring of 1944) were crossing into Spain to join the **Free French** forces. In August 1944, Lequerica was recalled from Vichy to become foreign minister (and never replaced), and on 1 September 1944 Vichy ambassador François Piétri handed over the French Embassy to Jacques Truelle, the representative of the CFLN, now the **Provisional Government**. One final item handed over, on 31 July 1945, was Vichy's former head of government, Pierre **Laval**. Relations, however, remained troubled as the French allowed Spanish Republicans to start guerrilla operations in Catalonia and closed the border from 1946 to 1948.

Spain was never in a position, by itself, either to help or threaten France in any serious way between 1938 and 1946. Spain's unrealistic imperial dreams, which might have had some potential had Hitler been more forthcoming in June 1940, were soon replaced by a more practical desire for self-preservation, as Germany's chances for victory became increasingly problematic. Thereafter, the governments of Pétain and Franco could attempt only to survive in a hostile world.

*†J.-M. Delaunay, ''L'Espagne et la France, 1940–1945,'' *Guerres mondiales et conflits contemporains* 162 (April 1991): 99–103; J. A. Farré, ''L'ambassade de Lequerica et les relations Hispano-Françaises, 1939–1944,'' *Guerres mondiales et conflits contemporains* 158 (April 1990): 65–78; Militärgeshichtliches Forschungsamt (Research Institute for Military History), Freiburg im Breisgau, Germany, ed., *Germany and the Second World War*, vol. 2: *Germany's Initial Conquests in Europe*, trans. D. S. McMurry and E. Osers (Oxford, 1991); M. Séguéla, *Pétain-Franco* (Paris, 1992); D. Stafford, *Churchill and Secret Service* (London, 1997); G. Warner, *Pierre Laval and the Eclipse of France: 1931–1945, a Political Biography* (New York, 1968).

H. H. Hunt

SPECIAL OPERATIONS EXECUTIVE (SOE, 1940–1946) was an independent **British** secret service whose purpose was to conduct subversive warfare in France and other occupied countries during World War II.

The SOE was formed in July 1940, after the fall of France. It encouraged **Resistance** in Axis-occupied countries and trained those in the occupied countries who would serve as a **fifth column** at the time of a future British invasion. The SOE was willing to work with all anti-Nazi elements, no matter what their stripe. However, SOE leaders learned that some strong anti-Nazi people in **Vichy** were also opposed to General **de Gaulle**, who, in turn, refused to work with anyone who had dealings with the Vichy regime.

The SOE's contribution to the Resistance in France was great, more than that of the **Americans** or the **Russians**. All the arms and explosives funneled to the French resisters were sent through the SOE. Former SOE agent Michael Foot stated that "without them [the SOE], Resistance could not have exerted a tenth of its actual effort." Also, without the SOE, the unified Resistance under de Gaulle would never have been formed. By 1944 de Gaulle and the unified Resistance worked closely with the SOE.

The Resistance groups that the SOE had helped were able to effect over 1,000 interruptions of rail traffic in a single week in June 1944. Although in the end the Gaullists and the SOE were successful, the Germans, before they succumbed, put thousands of Resistance workers, including some 200 agents trained by the SOE, into **concentration camps**. Only about 40 of the SOE veterans survived the war.

M.R.D. Foot, *SOE in France, an Account of the Work of the British Special Operations Executive in France, 1940–1944* (London, 1966); R. Kramer, *Flames in the Field, the Story of Four SOE Agents in Occupied France* (London, 1995); D. Stafford, "Britain Looks at Europe," *Canadian Journal of History* 10:2 (1975): 231–48.

E. H. Murphrey

SPECIAL SECTIONS were courts set up by **Darlan** government legislation on 14 August 1941 to combat a growing **Resistance** to the **Vichy** regime and to judge those suspected of politically motivated Resistance, especially **communists** and anarchists. They formed part of a general repression of "terrorists" and were generally attached to military or naval tribunals (courts-martial). In areas lacking such tribunals, their powers devolved to the courts of appeals, as in the case of **Paris**, which was empowered to pronounce verdicts on both guilt and punishment.

Alleged offenders caught in the act were brought directly before these courts for immediate sentencing. There was no appeal. Sentences, including imprisonment, hard labor, and death, were carried out without delay. With increased cooperation between German authorities and the French forces of order, these courts reflected an emerging **police** state and the end of the **National Revolution**. Justice minister Joseph Barthélemy prevailed upon the courts of appeals to appoint judges who would act firmly against those, particularly communists, with whom opposition to the regime was identified. The hastily created Paris Special Section condemned three communists to death in August 1941 for breaking the 1939 decree banning the existence of their party.

The deterrent effect of the Special Sections was restricted, as their executions served only to bolster communist resolve and enhance their martyr reputation as "*le Parti des Fusillés*" (the party of the executed). Declaring his passion for defending hopeless cases, Jacques Isorni, the lawyer who later defended Marshal **Pétain** against treason charges, figured prominently in the defense of communists and other resisters brought before these courts. The creation of the Special Sections marked an important turning point in Vichy's attitude and ideology and evidence of increased **collaboration** with the Germans.

R. O. Paxton, *Vichy France, Old Guard and New Order 1940–1944* (New York, 1972); D. Veillon, *La collaboration* (Paris, 1984); H. Villéré, *L'Affaire de la Section spéciale* (Paris, 1973).

J. Wright

SPINASSE, CHARLES(1893–1979), **socialist** deputy from the Corrèze between 1924 and 1940 and twice minister in a Léon **Blum** cabinet, became leader of a socialist faction in favor of **collaborationism** during the Occupation years.

Spinasse, a former philosophy student at the Sorbonne, ran the *Populaire du Centre* newspaper in the 1920s and taught at the Conservatoire National des Arts et Métiers, specializing in the history of the workplace. He participated in X-crise, one of several informal groups of technocrats who met in the 1930s to plan new interventionist solutions for the economic woes of France. Spinasse was named economics minister by Blum in 1936, and then finance minister during Blum's second and brief mandate in 1938. Nevertheless, Spinasse, a much decorated veteran of World War I, remained loyal to Blum's rival, the pacifist Paul **Faure**, general secretary of the Socialist Party.

Spinasse was among the 89 socialist parliamentarians who supported giving full powers to Marshal **Pétain**, on 10 July 1940. Spinasse edited two pro-**Vichy** newspapers with a neosocialist agenda, *L'Effort* and the more culturally oriented *Le Rouge et le Bleu*, in which he sought to convince French socialists that dignified collaboration with Nazi Germany was the only option for a defeated people. "The conquerors," he wrote, "need France as much as the old Roman Empire once needed Gaul." By August 1942, he was made aware that his relatively moderate views in favor of collaborationism were neither welcome to the Nazis nor the pro-Nazi **Rassemblement National Populaire (RNP)** of Marcel **Déat**. Spinasse retired to his hometown, Egletons (Corrèze), and *Le Rouge et le Bleu* stopped publication. Condemned to ineligibility for life as a deputy by a **liberation** tribunal and excluded from the Socialist Party, he became a bookseller but remained active in Corrèze politics. There he helped to launch the political career of Jacques Chirac, elected president of France in 1995.

P. Burrin, *Living with Defeat: France under the German Occupation, 1940–1944*, trans. J. Lloyd (New York, 1997) [original ed.: *La France à l'heure allemande, 1940–1944* (Paris, 1995)]; M. C. Cone, *Artists under Vichy: A Case of Prejudice and Persecution* (Princeton, 1992); B. M. Gordon, *Collaborationism in France during the Second World War* (Ithaca, NY, 1980); M. Sadoun, *Les Socialistes sous l'Occupation* (Paris, 1982).

M. C. Cone

SPORTS occupied a large place in the **Vichy** plan to regenerate the French nation. Within three days of assuming power, Marshal **Pétain** appointed the former international tennis star Jean **Borotra** as head of the Commissariat Général à l'Éducation générale et sportive in the Ministry of **Family** and **Youth**. Although the Germans and their **collaborationist** allies distrusted Borotra because of his **Jewish** wife and his connections to General **de Gaulle** and **Britain,** **Borotra** managed to retain his post until **Laval** returned to power in April 1942.

Vichy sports policies, under Borotra, were a fertile hybrid. They retained many of Léo Lagrange's **Popular Front** programs and anticipated much of the dynamism of sports organizations in post-1945 era. For example, Vichy's national sporting license (Brevet Sportif National) was merely a change in adjective from that of the Popular Front. Due to Borotra's energy and to the increase in the number of hours devoted to sports in **education**, athletic participation by both boys and girls rose dramatically. The number of **university** and school competitors rose from 17,000 in 1938 to 47,000 in 1942. Over the same period, marked increases were noted in other sports: from 188,000 to 294,000 in the Football Federation and from 26,000 to 46,000 in track and field. To handle the heavy demand, Borotra initiated a massive training program for athletic coaches, but by the eve of his dismissal (April 1942) only 2,000 had been graduated. Nevertheless, 2 national and 15 regional athletic training centers had been established. Borotra was also successful in obtaining large capital expenditures for sports facilities.

Colonel Joseph Pascot, who had served under Borotra, was his successor. Under Pascot sports were drawn heavily into collaborationist politics by helping to round up Jews, including the world champion swimmer Alfred Nakache, by providing athletic training for the National **Police**, and by sending French labor to work in German factories through the Service du Travail Obligatoire.

*†J.-L. Gay-Lescot, *Sport et éducation sous Vichy (1940–1944)* (Lyons, 1991); P. Giolitto, *Histoire de la jeunesse sous Vichy* (Paris, 1991).

W. S. Haine

STRIKES OF 1941 in the Nord and Pas-de-Calais coal mines, metalworks, and textile factories culminated in the actions of 27 May–6 June 1941. The Germans incorporated the Nord and Pas-de-Calais departments under their **Belgium** and North France military command to maximize the transfer of war materials to the German army. As a result, French workers had to work longer hours, with less food, clothing, soap, and other necessities.

The strike began as a call for better work conditions, salaries, and food distribution. Workers at first directed their anger at the bosses, who they believed exploited German demands to renege on the 1936 collective labor agreements. French **police** attempted to control the situation by making arrests on 28 May.

Quickly the strike took on an anti-German tone and spread to all mines in the area, with 80 percent of the miners (nearly 100,000) on strike by 4 June. **Women** played a major role in the strike, walking out of several factories, standing at the shafts to deter miners from entering, and trying to prevent the authorities from arresting the men. General Heinrich Niehoff, the German commander in Lille, crushed the strike with troops and courts-martial. About 400 workers were arrested; 235 were deported to work in Germany; 130 never returned. The strike cost the German war effort about 500,000 tons of coal, one-quarter of the normal regional monthly output. It was a limited, if costly, success, for the Germans ordered better rations for the workers once they ended the strike. These actions constitute the first French mass movement to confront the German occupiers.

E. Dejonghe, ''Chronique de la grève des mineurs du Nord/Pas-de-Calais,'' *Revue du Nord* 273 (April–June 1987): 323–46; D. Tartakowsky, ''Manifester pour le pain, novembre 1940–octobre 1947,'' in D. Veillon and J.-M. Flonneau, eds., *Le temps des restrictions en France (1939–1949)* (Paris, 1996), 465–78; C. Wallart and M. Dumont-Reniez, eds., *Le Nord Occupé* (Lille, 1990).

D. F. Ryan

SUHARD, CARDINAL EMMANUEL (1874–1949), archbishop of **Paris** during the German occupation, a collaborator yet one of French Catholicism's most creative innovators.

Monseigneur Suhard had served two sees prior to being called to the archdiocese of Paris on 8 May 1940, just days before the fall of France. Though a seminary professor early in his career, Suhard was essentially a pastor deeply imbued in the piety of St. Thérèse de Lisieux. Suhard joined his colleagues in their support of **Vichy**, lauded the values of the **National Revolution**, and appeared publicly with **Pétain** well into 1944. He also joined in the ceremonies at the funeral of Philippe **Henriot**, a noted leader of the **milice**. So repugnant was he to the **Resistance** that, when Paris was liberated in August 1944, General **de Gaulle** refused to enter Notre Dame Cathedral for celebrations until Suhard left the nave of his own church.

Nonetheless, the cardinal protested to Vichy against the **deportation** of **Jews** to Germany and joined other prelates in protesting the **Vélodrome d'hiver** roundup. He defended working-class Catholic Action members against deportation to German factories, and when this failed, he organized a program of clandestine chaplains to go to Germany with these **youth**. He convinced his colleagues to create a seminary, the Mission de France, designed to reach **peasants** and workers alienated from the church. Finally, in 1943–1944 he became the patron of the fledgling Mission de Paris, the forerunner of the postwar ''worker-priest'' experiment.

Since his death in 1949, the image of the Suhard who welcomed Vichy has given way to that of the cardinal who created, promoted, and defended his church's radical **left-wing** and thus paved the road to the Second Vatican Council.

O. L. Arnal, *Priests in Working-Class Blue* (New York, 1986); J. Duquesne, *Les Catholiques français sous l'occupation* (Paris, 1966); J. Vinatier, *Le cardinal Suhard* (Paris, 1983); J. Wright, ed., *The Collected Writings of Emmanuel Cardinal Suhard* (Chicago, 1953).

O. L. Cole-Arnal

SWING, LES, also called *les zazous*, urban **youth** counterculture. ''Swing'' refers to the **American** jazz movement, widely imitated by French popular musicians like Johnny *"Je suis swing"* [I am swing] Hess. The Swings, men and **women**, ages 17 or 18, defied **Vichy's** moral order. They expressed their animosity visually, with the young men growing thin mustaches. Flaunting the stipulation that clothing should use as little fabric as possible, they wore long jackets and short pants with big, baggy knees and narrow ankles over white socks. Young women thumbed their noses at the conservative, fresh-scrubbed feminine look Vichy promoted by dying their hair blond, piling on makeup, and wearing short, pleated skirts, jackets with large, padded shoulders, and heavy, flat shoes. For both sexes, dark sunglasses and an umbrella functioned as the ultimate trademark.

Les swings listened to jazz, music associated with so-called degenerate American culture. They spent time in cafés, while Vichy called on French youth to work hard and avoid idleness, and developed their own ironic language, such as calling the **Paris** *Metropolitain* (subway) the *"Pétain mollit trop"* (Pétain is getting too soft). The *zazous* shocked the pro-Vichy **press**. Their rejection of Vichy moralism and austerity and refusal of hard work and clean living led the collaborationist newspaper *La Gerbe* to recommend a "public spanking." The official press, **Vichy**, and even the Germans interpreted swing culture as a political statement in favor of the **British**, Americans, and **de Gaulle**. Some *zazous* carried their defiant lifestyle into **Resistance**. Several were arrested and deported for wearing yellow stars inscribed "swing." The swings disappeared from public view in response to the threat of forced labor in 1943.

J.-C. Loiseau, *Les Zazous* (Paris, 1977); J.-P. Rioux, "Survivre," *L'histoire* 80 (1985); D. Veillon, *La mode sous Vichy* (Paris, 1990).

S. Fishman

SWITZERLAND was neutral and provided an important escape route and communication link with the outside world for occupied France.

Swiss neutrality sought to preserve national independence, within the constraints of heavy economic dependence on Germany, and was conditioned by Switzerland's role as headquarters for the Red Cross, whose humanitarian activities were recognized by all the belligerent countries in Europe. In late 1996, however, Switzerland was accused of accepting and failing to return gold looted from occupied Europe by the Germans.

During the defeat of 1940, some 30,000 French soldiers fled to Switzerland, where they were interned and repatriated a year later. Under agreements with the **Vichy** government, the Swiss authorities returned most illegal entrants from France, though, in some cases, entrants were allowed to remain or to travel to a third country, as happened with a small number of **Jews** who were passed on, mostly to the **United States**.

The number of French citizens recorded as attempting to enter Switzerland was negligible until 1942, when it rose sharply, reaching a peak of 11,700 in 1944. The Franco–Swiss border became a frequent destination for **Resistance** escape routes, with networks of *"passeurs"* (guides who led clandestine travelers across the mountains). A growing number of refugees were allowed to stay or pass through, though in all more than 10,000 were returned to the French authorities. Swiss officials played a significant role in arranging humanitarian aid and in facilitating exchanges of **prisoners** and a more limited role as diplomatic intermediaries. They appear to have made discreet interventions on behalf of particular individuals in French prisons, as in the case of Emmanuel **Mounier** in 1942.

Swiss radio stations Radio-Sottens and Suisse-romande, though careful about German sensitivities, were listened to in eastern France as independent sources of news and comment. Literary and intellectual publications in French from Geneva, Neuchatel, or Lausanne were much sought after in France despite the circumspect terms in which they were often framed.

Under international pressure in 1997, Swiss banks released a list, published in several newspapers around the world, of the holders of unclaimed accounts from the wartime years in a belated attempt to make restitution to survivors and their heirs. Published by *Le Monde* in France, the list included French citizens, some of whom had not even been aware of the existence of the accounts.

*T. Bower, *Nazi Gold: The Full Story of the Fifty Year Swiss-Nazi Conspiracy to Steal Billions from Europe's Jews and Holocaust Survivors* (New York, 1997); "La Suisse," a special issue of *RDHDGM* 121 (January 1981).

M. Kelly

SYMBOLS IN WARTIME FRANCE proliferated in daily life, which partially explains why World War II France produced so many novels, plays, poems, films, and memoirs. Because of the restrictions and politicization of the war and Occupation, objects of everyday life, such as the radio, often acquired enhanced symbolic value.

In 1940, for the first time in French history, a major national decision became known through broadcasting: Marshal **Pétain's** call for an **armistice**. Pro-German **Radio-Paris** and the English **BBC** vied for listeners' attention. Like bicycles, **ration** tickets, curfews, and the *Système D* (a term for surviving by one's wits—somehow making do), the **radio** itself became a symbol in everyday life in wartime France. Verbal symbols broadcast on the radio included Pétain's call for an armistice, represented in the "gift of his person" to spare the French in their defeat, and **de Gaulle's** radio addresses from London, which symbolized him as "the man of 18 June" (his first broadcast having been 18 June 1940). As a symbol of social cohesion "Pétain" appeared in *La Semaine réligieuse* (The Religious Week), in coloring books for children, and on posters and post cards, as well as in **l'Art maréchal** generally. His emphasis on a return to tradition and regionalism highlighted symbols of village and rural life. Symbols of collaboration included widely disseminated photographs of the **Montoire** handshake between Pétain and **Hitler**. Joan of Arc acquired symbolic value on both sides of the **resistance/collaboration** divide. Songs such as the **"Chant**

des Partisans" and "Maréchal, nous voilà" evoked Pétainist and Resistance symbols respectively.

Resisters' poems and anti-German propaganda, often using symbols such as the Cross of **Lorraine**, were dropped from Royal Air Force planes. The battle of **Bir Hakeim** became a Resistance symbol of successful military action against the Axis. A little publicized governmental service at **Vichy**, the Contrôles techniques, implicitly recognized the widespread presence of political symbols by violating the privacy of the mail, opening 320,000 to 370,000 letters every week, and tapping phone conversations to report opposition to the **police**.

In a larger sense "France" itself was a symbol as were "**Vichy**" and "**Free France**" each with ramifications usually associated with literary texts. The importance of symbols and their diffusion in the years from 1940 through 1944 did not escape the French at the **liberation**, whose celebrations, including shaving the heads of **women** accused of "**horizontal collaboration**" with the enemy, were organized as symbolic rituals.

A. Brossat, *Libération, fête folle* (Paris, 1994); N. Dompnier, *Vichy à travers chants* (Paris, 1996); C. Faure, *Le Projet culturel de Vichy* (Paris, 1989); P. Laborie, *L'Opinion française sous Vichy* (Paris, 1990); G. Miller, *Les pousse-au-jouir du maréchal Pétain* (Paris, 1975).

C. Lamiot

SYNARCHY was the spurious object of a conspiracy theory, feeding on a widely publicized fear that France was about to be taken over by modernizing technocratic elites, which rocked the **Darlan** government after the suicide of the plot's alleged leader, Jean Coutrot, on 19 May 1941. The Coutrot affair provided an opportunity for elements within **Vichy's** intelligence network to construct and spread rumors of a "synarchist plot" by connecting disparate pieces of evidence relating to the rise of managers and technicians, perceived as pro-**British** and **American**, in key positions in the new regime.

Vichy traditionalists, **Paris collaborationists**, and others fearful of technocracy and resentful of a new sociopolitical elite seized upon the widely diffused plot rumors. These rumors were based on an actual document, entitled the *Pacte synarchique*, that had circulated before the war. A ponderous manifesto by a small, politicized, occultist, Masonic sect, the *Pacte synarchique* called for a revolution from above to form a technocratic imperial state. A copy found in Coutrot's possession had been given to the authorities by his brother-in-law and partner in the family paper firm.

Coutrot, a small-time industrialist, had joined X-crise (X-c) soon after this forum on public affairs was launched in 1931 by young alumni of the École Polytechnique (nicknamed "L'X"), who looked to economic planning for solutions to the depression of the early 1930s. In 1933 this group began publishing a review, *X-Crise*, which lasted until 1939, and, early on, started referring to itself as the Centre polytechnicien d'études économiques (CPÉÉ). Coutrot played a leading role.

By the early 1930s, an X-crise network of persons later prominent during the Occupation was taking shape. Georges Soulès (Raymond **Abellio**), a member of the CPÉÉ, was also heading the more **left**-leaning Centre polytechnicien d'études collectivistes (CPÉC). The tandem of Robert Gibrat and Robert Loustau joined the **Ordre Nouveau** (ON) personalist movement to head its technical cell; there, they vainly tried to become the social think tank for Colonel François **de La Rocque's** Croix de Feu and instead led a splinter group away from it. Gibrat became a director of the **Parti Populaire Français** in 1937–1938 and then **Laval's** secretary of communications in 1942, inviting Loustau to work with him. By the late 1930s, X-crise, along with Coutrot's parent initiatives, such as a Centre d'étude des problèmes humains, with Alexis **Carrel** supporting a planned rationalization of French society and with connections to the Banque Worms, had acquired great prestige.

The political vacuum left by the fallen regime in 1940 did, in fact, open new possibilities for the technocratic elites, which had grown restive under it, lending an appearance of truth to the rumors of a plot in 1941. Many high Vichy officials, especially under Admiral Darlan (including Paul **Baudouin**, René **Belin**, Jean **Berthelot**, Jean Bichelonne, Jean **Borotra**, Yves Bouthillier, Jacques Le Roy Ladurie, Jacques Rueff, and Alfred Sauvy), came from this milieu of technocrats, eager to modernize France's economic infrastructure. Due to its continental scale, this vision led some of them (Jacques Barnaud, Pierre **Pucheu**, Jacques **Benoist-Méchin**, François **Lehideux**, and Paul **Marion**) to submit to **Hitler** through Otto **Abetz** in April 1941 a "Plan pour un Ordre Nouveau en France," calling for full integration in a German-dominated Europe. It marked the apex of the modernist strand of state collaboration.

Suspicion of modernizing technocratic elites ran so deep in France that long after the war, both Left and **Right** continued to spread rumors of conspiracies. Paradoxically, whereas Vichy technocrats who looked to Germany were sometimes accused by rumormongers of Anglo-American orientation, the postwar innuendos were often directed against too pro-German a stance on the part of the technocratic modernizers.

P. Bauchard, *Les technocrates et le Pouvoir* (Paris, 1966); G. Brun, *Techniciens et technocratie en France, 1918–1945* (Paris, 1985); R. Kuisel, "The Legend of the Vichy Synarchy," *FHS* 6:3 (Spring 1970): 365–98; R. Mennevée, unpublished papers, University of California–Los Angeles library.

C. Roy

SYNDICALISM, a revolutionary doctrine of workers' control for **industry**, suffered greatly under the **Vichy** government, which adopted a **corporatist** model for labor.

After the formation of the Vichy government, the new minister of production and labor, Réne **Belin**, a leader of the **Confédération Générale du Travail's** (**CGT's**) **right wing**, signed a decree (9 November 1940) dissolving all unions, accusing them of not adequately protecting themselves against **communist** infiltration. On 4 October 1941 the **Pétain** government issued the **Labor Charter**, based on a vague combination of Italian corporatism and Catholic socialism, which made both workers and employers members of the same unions and outlawed strikes and lockouts. Later in November a group of Christian unionists opposed to the Labor Charter issued a competing document, the *Manifeste du 15 novembre 1940*, which declared that French syndicalism was unalterably anticapitalist and independent from the state. It declared that French syndicalists could never accept **anti-Semitism**, religious persecutions, or privileges based on wealth. Throughout the Occupation, most workers gravitated toward one of these two positions. Some, led by **Belin**, accepted the Occupation and the Labor Charter. Others, led by Léon Jouhaux, a moderate arrested in 1942 and deported in 1943, urged a return to traditional syndicalism.

The **liberation** brought a transformation of labor policy. On 27 July 1944 the **Provisional Government** abolished the Labor Charter and reestablished the old unions as they had been in 1939. The Communist Party was welcomed back to the labor movement and given a position of honor within it. By 1946, largely because of its prominent role in the **Resistance**, the Communist Party had come to dominate the French labor movement.

*A. Kriegel, *Aux origines du communisme français* (Paris, 1964); J.-P. Le Crom, *Syndicats nous voilà! Vichy et le corporatisme* (Paris, 1995); G. Lefranc, *Les expériences syndicales en France de 1939 à 1950* (Paris, 1950); G. Ross, *Workers and Communists in France: From Popular Front to Eurocommunism* (Berkeley, 1982).

C. J. Haug

T

TEITGEN, PIERRE-HENRI (1908–1997), a Christian democratic politician who played a leading role in the **Resistance** and the **Provisional Government**. From a middle-class Catholic background with a strong social commitment, Teitgen studied at Nancy, leading to the *agrégation* in public law. He was appointed to a chair in law at Montpellier in 1940 and edited the journal *Droit social*.

Teitgen launched Resistance activity in 1940 and joined François **de Menthon** and other Christian democratic academics in the nonoccupied **zone** to found a movement and paper, entitled *Liberté*, to counter the defeatist propaganda of the **Vichy**. His **university** lectures boldly reflected his opposition to Vichy's policies and laws, and he was suspended without salary for six months. In the autumn of 1941, Liberté merged with Henri **Frenay's Mouvement de Libération Nationale** to form the major southern Resistance movement, **Combat**, in which Teitgen was a member of the executive committee and an energetic organizer.

When Combat merged with the other main southern movements to form the **Mouvement Unis de la Résistance** (MUR), Teitgen became one of the MUR's leading figures. He was a friend and adviser of Jean **Moulin**, who appointed him general secretary of the committee of experts, the **Comité Générale d'Études**, which had responsibility for preparing proposals for the post-**liberation** legislative program and which published the clandestine *Cahiers politiques*. In 1943, Teitgen was appointed *Commissaire Général* for information by General **de Gaulle**. Arrested by the Gestapo in June 1944, Teitgen made a daring escape from a train.

With the liberation, Teitgen became a founding member and parliamentary deputy for the centrist Mouvement Républicain Populaire and later its president. He held a number of ministerial positions, including information and justice, where he was regarded as a proponent of rigorous punishment for collaborators. Teitgen played a major political role throughout the Fourth **Republic**, returning to an academic post after 1958.

P.-H. Teitgen, *Faites entrer le témoin suivant* (Paris, 1988).

M. Kelly

TÉMOIGNAGE CHRÉTIEN, CAHIERS DU, the most important Christian **Resistance** publication in occupied France, was a series of tracts, first published in Lyons in November 1941. It warned that "pagan" Nazi occupiers were out to destroy "spiritual liberties" and condemned **anti-Semitism**, castigated **Vichy's collaboration**, and called all of France to resist.

The *Cahiers'* first issue, *France prends garde de perdre ton âme* (France, Beware of Losing Your Soul), was disseminated to about 5,000 people. Some issues reached 60,000 people, and when it emerged as a full-fledged newspaper at the **liberation**, the original *Cahiers* had been passed to well over half a million people. Though inspired and led by the Jesuit Pierre Chaillet, the *Témoignage Chrétien* team comprised about one-third clerical and two-thirds lay resisters. The learned professions predominated. Most had been militants in Catholic Action, the Christian democratic parties, or Catholic trade unions. Fidelity to the Catholic faith underscored all 14 of the *Cahiers*, from *France, prends garde*, to *Espoir de la France* (Hope of France) in July 1944.

Témoignage Chrétien survived the war to become the leading press voice of the postwar Catholic **Left**. It supported collaboration with **socialists** and **communists**, upheld the radical Catholic experiments of the postwar years, and denounced French colonialism. *Témoignage Chrétien* maintains its progressive reputation to this day.

R. Bédarida, *Témoignage Chrétien* (Paris, 1977); J. Duquesne, *Les Catholiques français sous l'occupation* (Paris, 1966); *Témoignage Chrétien: Cahiers et Courriers*, vols. 1, 2 (Paris, 1980).

O. L. Cole-Arnal

THEATER IN OCCUPIED FRANCE thrived because of subsidies from **Vichy**, because theaters were relatively safe and warm, and because theater remained prominent in French culture even in the midst of defeat.

While *Les Pirates de Paris (L'Affaire Stavisky)* by Michel Daxiat (alias Alain **Laubreaux**) marks the low point of French theater as a site of **collaboration**, candidates for a high point include Paul **Claudel's** *Le Soulier de Satin* (1943), Claude Vermorel's *Jeanne Avec Nous* (1942), Jean-Paul **Sartre's** *Les Mouches* (1943) and *Huis Clos* (1944), and Jean Anouilh's *Antigone* (1944). Although postwar critics viewed these latter not only as important literarily but as in some way embodying what was best about France, more recent commentators have questioned how, under the scrutiny of censors (German for plays produced in private theaters, Vichy for state theaters), any work performed in occupied **Paris** could project a positive national image or communicate subversive, pro-**Resistance** messages.

The theatrical output during the Occupation years was an extension of what came immediately before. Yet a number of changes make Occupation plays and productions significantly different from those of the Third **Republic**. Plays were subject to censorship, **Jews** and other minorities were purged from the stage, as well as from backstage and auditorium; some talented theater personnel fled Paris and France; and much of the **press** criticism of the stage was now in the hands of **collaborationists**.

After the 1940 **armistice**, theaters reopened slowly during the summer. Autumn brought the Occupation's first season (1940–1941), comprising largely revivals and frivolous comedies, which, because they ignored realities such as **ration** coupons, Robert **Brasillach** dubbed *"comédies sans tickets."* Starting with *Pasteur* (July 1940), Sacha **Guitry** produced a four-year marathon of his own scripts at the Madeleine. In the first season, Jean Anouilh became popular through productions of plays written before the defeat: *Léocadia, Rendez-vous à Senlis, Bal des Voleurs*, and, later, *Eurydice* (produced 1941–1942) and *Antigone* (1944) brought still greater acclaim. **Fascist** mobs closed Jean **Cocteau's** *La Machine à écrire* in April 1941. In addition to his work at the *Comédie Française*, Jean-Louis Barrault produced and starred in André Obey's *Huit cents mètres* (July 1941) about the front-runner's defeat in a footrace, performed at Roland-Garros Stadium.

As the Occupation wore on, Parisian audiences continued to patronize theaters in spite of curfews, Gestapo raids, and electrical shortages. Henry **de Montherlant** followed his successful *La Reine Morte* (1942–1943 at the *Comédie Française*) with *Fils de Personne* (1943–1944), one of the few Occupation dramas set during the Occupation. **Sartre**, who began writing plays while a **prisoner** of war (his *Bariona* was a stalag pageant performed Christmas 1940), wrote *Les Mouches* (produced in 1943 at the Sarah-Bernhardt Theater, renamed at the time because of the actress' **Jewish** ancestry) and *Huis Clos* (1944). Albert **Camus** launched his playwriting career with *Le Malentendu* in 1944. Jean **Giraudoux**, who died before D-Day, wrote *Sodome et Gomorrhe* (1943–1944) as well as *L'Apollon de Bellac* and *La Folle de Chaillot*, both of which premiered after the war, and Claudel allowed Barrault to stage *Le Soulier de Satin* (1943–1944).

Shortly before Paris was liberated, theaters closed, but soon afterward they reopened. *Huis Clos, Antigone*, and *Le Malentendu* resumed their runs. While critics tend to regard postwar theater as breaking with the past, many playwrights and plays from the Occupation went on to greater successes in France and abroad. Trying to depict the wartime Parisian theater world in *Le Dernier métro* (1980), François Truffaut emphasized its contradictions and ambiguities, perhaps best expressing the difficulties of later generations in coming to terms with this problematic era.

*S. Added, *Le Théâtre dans les années Vichy, 1940–44* (Paris, 1992); H. Le Boterf, *La Vie Parisienne sous l'occupation, 1940–1944*, vol. 1 (Paris, 1974); P. Marsh, "Le Théâtre à Paris sous l'occupation allemande," *Revue de la Société d'histoire de Théâtre* 33:3 (1981).

K. Krauss

THOREZ, MAURICE (1900–1964), was secretary-general of the **Communist** Party (**PCF**) during the war. From a poor family, he worked in mining and other laboring jobs, but in 1923, when appointed a local Communist Party official, he turned professional politician. By 1936 he had become the national party's secretary-general. His aim, he declared, was the creation of "a **Soviet** France." His loyalty to Stalin was always absolute. In 1935, when the **USSR** reversed its policy and advocated a united front against **fascism**, he supported French rearmament. In 1939, after the Nazi–Soviet pact, he opposed the war, branding it as a struggle between "imperialist" powers. He demanded immediate peace.

Drafted in 1939, after Premier Édouard **Daladier** had outlawed the Communist Party on 26 September, Thorez deserted his regiment and fled to Brussels, where the exiled party had established temporary headquarters. In November he flew to Moscow, where he remained. His exile years are shrouded in mystery, although he appears occasionally as the author of articles published in the clandestine PCF **press**. In August 1941, when the Soviet Union first contacted the **Free French** in London, it was proposed he go to **Britain**, but this was vetoed by General **de Gaulle**. In January 1944 he assured de Gaulle's Moscow representative that his party had no intention of seizing power when France was liberated or in the reconstruction period. Thus, in November 1944, after the **liberation**, Thorez returned home, where he exhorted his fellow countrymen to "work, fight for victory, for the greatness of France."

In January 1946, when the Communist Party briefly joined forces with the **socialists** and the Mouvement Républicain Populaire to form a government, he became a deputy prime minister under Félix Gouin. By 1950 he was already suffering from a paralytic illness, thus limiting his political activities. In 1964 he resigned as party chairman and died shortly afterward.

*†J.-P. Azéma, A. Prost, and J.-P. Rioux, *Le Parti Communiste dans les années sombres* (Paris, 1986); J. Fauvet, *Histoire du Parti Communiste français, 1920–1976* (Paris, 1977); M. Thorez, *Fils du Peuple* (Paris, 1960).

W. D. Halls

TILLION, GERMAINE (1907–), ethnologist, specialist in Algeria, one of the founders of the underground network created in the summer 1940, the **Musée de l'homme** network. After the war, as an official executor of the group, she gave this network its current name, Musée de l'homme, the name of the main **Paris** museum of ethnology, the site of clandestine meetings in 1940. Tillion was arrested and deported to the Ravensbrück **concentration camp**, where captured **women** resisters from throughout Europe were imprisoned.

The motivations that made a resister of the young Tillion as early as June 1940 were patriotic and political. She could accept neither the occupation of France nor the **Vichy** regime. As a former student of the sociologist Marcel Mauss and as an ethnologist, she rejected racial theories. As a woman who had gone on four field trips alone among the Berber nomads, she was also a pioneer and a nonconformist. In the **Resistance** she helped **British** and French **prisoners** of war escape and transmitted military information to London. She also helped several **Jewish** families. At Ravensbrück she was assigned the status of NN

(Nacht und Nebel), earmarked for death in the "**Night and Fog**" extermination program, but managed to survive the war.

Tillion wrote the first scientific monograph about Ravensbrück, showing that the camp existed within a profitable economic system and with its own gas chamber from January 1945. Her militant activities did not end with the war. A Resistance veteran and a specialist in Berber ethnology, she also played a role in the Algerian war, fighting, notably, against torture.

M. Blumenson, *Le Réseau du Musée de l'Homme* (Paris, 1979); G. Tillion, *Le Harem et les cousins* (Paris, 1966); G. Tillion, "Première résistance en zone occupée," *RDHDGM* 30 (April 1958); G. Tillion, *Ravensbrück* (Paris, 1988 [original ed., Neuchâtel, 1946); G. Tillion, *La Traversée du mal, Entretien avec Jean Lacouture* (Paris, 1997).

C. Andrieu

TILLON, CHARLES (1897–1993) took part in the Black Sea mutiny of the French fleet in 1919 and was a member of the French **Communist** Party (**PCF**) from its inception, a union leader in the chemical industry, a member of the **PCF** Politburo, deputy for the Paris working-class suburb of Aubervilliers from 1936, resister "of the first hour," and leader of the communist-dominated, armed **Resistance** group Francs tireurs et partisans (français) (FTP(F)).

After the dissolution of the PCF in September 1939, Tillon was sent by the party's clandestine leadership to regroup the organization in Bordeaux, where his underground party publications, including the *Manifeste de Bordeaux* of 18 July 1940, went far beyond the confines of the PCF's "imperialist war" line. Called back to **Paris** in December 1940, he began organizing what became the Organisation spéciale. By October 1941, this had been expanded into the FTP with a newspaper, *France d'abord* (France First), its own *maquis*, immigrant Main d'Œuvre Immigrée (MOI) group, and **women's** sections.

Tillon developed the FTP along military lines into a **Resistance** pseudo**army** on the **Left**, with local, regional, and national command structures for all its sections. He also fought to prevent its inclusion in the **Forces françaises de l'intérieur** under General Pierre **Koenig** and disputed the control of armed forces at the time of the **liberation**, when Tillon's conception of the "national insurrection" as a popular revolutionary uprising put him at odds with the Gaullist representatives of the **Provisional Government** and his own party leadership, whom he later accused of betraying the working classes. A minister in the tripartite governments of the period 1945–1947, he fell out with the leadership of the PCF in 1952 and was stripped of all his party posts.

C. Tillon, *Les FTP* (Paris, 1962); C. Tillon, *On chantait rouge* (Paris, 1977).

J. C. Simmonds

TOUVIER, PAUL (1915–1996), was head of the Second Section (intelligence) of **Vichy's** militia (**Milice Française**) for the Savoy region. Named to the post in April 1943, Touvier participated in the arrest and murder of **Jews** until the **liberation** of Lyons in September 1944. For these crimes, he was first charged with crimes against humanity in November 1973 and finally tried and convicted on the same charge in 1994.

Raised in an extremely **right-wing** Catholic family, Touvier received his education in Catholic schools, performed his military service in 1935–1936, and thereafter began an undistinguished career working as a railway clerk. After brief service in the **army** in 1940, he joined the **Légion Française des Combattants** the same year and climbed rapidly through its ranks and those of its successor organization, the **milice**. With the help of Catholic clergymen and high-ranking church officers, Touvier and his family hid out and avoided arrest during the immediate postwar period. In September 1971 he secured a pardon from President Georges Pompidou for crimes committed during the Occupation. Public outcry forced Touvier to go into hiding again. He was finally arrested at an *intégriste* (fundamentalist) monastery in Nice in May 1989. After a number of controversial legal decisions, he was tried and convicted in March–April 1994 for ordering the 1944 murder of seven Jews at Rillieux-la-Pape near Lyons. Touvier was sentenced to life in prison.

F. Bédarida, *Touvier, Vichy et le crime contre l'humanité* (Paris, 1996); J. Delperrie de Bayac, *Histoire de la Milice* (Paris, 1969); R. J. Golsan, ed., *Memory, the Holocaust, and French Justice* (Hanover, NH, 1995); L. Greilsamer and D. Schneidermann, *Un certain Monsieur Paul* (Paris, 1994); A. Jakubowicz and R. Raffin, *Touvier, Histoire du Procès* (Paris, 1995); R. Rémond et al., *Paul Touvier et l'Église* (Paris, 1992).

R. J. Golsan

TULARD FILES were a record system set up at the **Paris** Prefecture of **Police** in October 1940, used to identify and arrest **Jews**. The files were named for André Tulard, assistant director of the Bureau of Aliens and Jewish Affairs, who organized and took care of these records.

The files described 149,734 **Jews** living in the department of the Seine who had reported for a Nazi-ordered census. French authorities transferred data by hand from each census declaration to at least four color-and size-coded cards, which classified Jews according to surname, nationality, gender, profession, and address. Files also provided details about date and place of birth, marital status, national identity card number, employment history, and any personal property declared. Domicile files proved especially useful in locating Jews to deport, because of color coding—white for foreigners, colors for French citizens—and detailed addresses, specifying floor and stairwell and location on the street or courtyard. With such detail French police and the Gestapo could make arrests with greater accuracy and less disturbance of neighbors. According to *Sicherheitspolizei* (security service) records, French police delivered duplicate files to the anti-Jewish section (Abteilung IVB4), providing a critical tool for German **deportations**.

The card drawers disappeared after the war. In 1991 a scandal erupted when Serge **Klarsfeld**, a lawyer and noted war criminal hunter, accidentally found the files in the Archives du Sécretariat d'État aux Anciens Combattants (Veterans

Affairs Office). Accusing officials of purposely hiding the files, Klarsfeld raised questions about French reluctance to acknowledge bureaucratic complicity in the **Holocaust**.

J. Adler, *The Jews of Paris and the Final Solution* (New York, 1987); A. Kahn, *Le Fichier* (Paris, 1993).

D. F. Ryan

U

UNION GÉNÉRALE DES ISRAÉLITES DE FRANCE (UGIF) was the National **Jewish** Council created by the 29 November 1941 law to coordinate Jewish social and philanthropic organizations in the occupied and unoccupied **zones**. Although the Nazi specialist in Jewish affairs, Theodor **Dannecker**, demanded the establishment of the UGIF, it was actually the creation of Xavier **Vallat**, first head of the **Commissariat Général aux Questions Juives**, who wanted to maintain control of Jewish property. All Jews had to join the UGIF.

Headed by André Baur in the occupied zone and Albert Lévy and, later, R. R. Lambert in the unoccupied zone, the UGIF subsumed all Jewish organizations, except those that were purely religious. The Germans closely monitored the UGIF in the occupied zone and undermined its efforts to render assistance to needy Jews. For example, relief packages sent to the Drancy concentration camp were confiscated for German use. In the southern zone, the UGIF preserved greater autonomy, kept material assistance flowing to indigent Jews, and eventually became a cover for limited **Resistance** activities.

Both branches of the UGIF have been the focus of controversy among historians of the **Holocaust**. Critics charge that its very existence provided a false sense of security for endangered Jews. Most damaging is the fact that records kept by the UGIF were available to authorities hunting Jews. In some cases UGIF facilities served to concentrate Jews and assist German **deportations**, as in the case of children's homes around **Paris** and in Marseilles. Defenders argue the UGIF allowed important Jewish agencies to continue to aid Jews impoverished by **Vichy anti-Semitic** laws and provided cover for Resistance activities.

J. Adler, *The Jews of Paris and the Final Solution* (New York, 1987): R. Cohen, *The Burden of Conscience: French Jewry's Response to the Holocaust* (Bloomington, IN, 1987); S. Zuccotti, *The Holocaust, the French and the Jews* (New York, 1993).

D. F. Ryan

UNION OF SOVIET SOCIALIST REPUBLICS [USSR], RELATIONS WITH FRANCE. During the interwar years, Franco–Soviet relations were almost always difficult, having been poisoned by the Bolshevik revolution in 1917. There were occasional efforts to improve relations, but these produced no lasting results. Franco–Soviet relations could not be extricated from French domestic politics and the deepening split between **Right** and **Left**. The Right exploited fear of the French **Communist** Party and communist revolution in France to overturn the Cartel des gauches in the 1920s and the **Popular Front** in the 1930s.

Advocates of improved relations with the Soviets, for example, Édouard Herriot, Georges **Mandel**, and Paul **Reynaud**, were motivated primarily by the desire to re-create an eastern counterweight to Germany. They argued that judgments about Soviet communism should not affect matters of French security. If France could ally with the ''white tsar'' before 1914, it could ally with the ''red tsar,'' Stalin, against Nazi Germany.

Most of the French Right rejected the Soviet alliance. Pierre **Laval**, who became French foreign minister in 1934, fearing offense to Germany and the spread of communist revolution in Europe, slowed a promising movement toward closer relations with the USSR. He signed the Franco–Soviet mutual assistance pact in 1935, but before he did, his officials reduced it to a meaningless scrap of paper. Parliamentary ratification did not occur until after the German reoccupation of the Rhineland in March 1936. In 1936–1938 the Soviet government pressed the French for military staff talks, but the government was divided, and the French general staff was opposed to closer relations. General Maurice-Gustave **Gamelin's** instructions were clear: do not offend the Soviets but stall, stall, stall!

During the **Munich crisis**, the French government snubbed the USSR. Foreign minister Georges **Bonnet** distorted or concealed Soviet statements on willingness to support Czechoslovakia. Afterward, the Soviet government accused France of having failed even to secure its honor at **Munich**. In spite of French rebuffs and Soviet cynicism, there was a last chance before the war to conclude an **Anglo**–Franco–Soviet alliance. It occurred after the Nazi occupation of the remnant of Czechoslovakia (March 1939), but Bonnet and Édouard **Daladier**, while more favorable than before to a Soviet agreement, still hesitated and fell in behind the **British**, who wanted to go ''very slowly.'' The Soviet government matched Munich with perfidy of its own, signing the Nazi–Soviet nonaggression pact on August 1939.

Franco–Soviet relations went icy cold and came near to belligerency after the outbreak of the Soviet–Finnish war in November 1939. The French government seemed keener on fighting the USSR than on fighting Nazi Germany and planned to send troops to Finland and to bomb Soviet oil installations in the Caucasus. These imprudent ideas were cut short by the end of the Soviet–Finnish war in March 1940 and the French military debacle in May–June 1940.

The **Free French** government in exile, after the German invasion of 1941, saw the virtue of improved relations with the USSR as a counterbalance to Britain and the **United States**. The Soviet government was supportive, though not to the point of offending its British and **American** allies. However, in 1943 the USSR recognized the Algiers government, and in December 1944 a Franco–Soviet mutual assistance pact was concluded. General **de Gaulle** had no illusions about Soviet political objectives in Europe and was concerned about the strength of the French Communist Party arising out of its important role in the **Resistance** movement. The resumption of Soviet-Western tensions in 1945 returned Franco–Soviet relations to the hostility of the interwar years.

*†M. J. Carley, "Down a Blind-Alley: Anglo-Franco-Soviet Relations, 1920–39," *Canadian Journal of History* 29: 1 (1994): 147–72; M. J. Carley, "Prelude to Defeat: Franco-Soviet Relations, 1919–1939," *Historical Reflections* 22: 1 (1996); M. J. Carley, "End of the 'Low, Dishonest Decade': Failure of the Anglo–Franco–Soviet Alliance in 1939," *Europe-Asia Studies* 45: 2 (1993): 303–41; Ministerstvo inostrannykh del SSSR, *Sovetsko-frantsuzskie otnosheniia vo vremia velikoi otechestvennoi voiny, 1941–1945*, 2 vols. (Moscow, 1983).

M. J. Carley

UNITED STATES, RELATIONS WITH FRANCE (1939–1945), were characterized by neutrality after France and **Britain** declared war on Germany in September 1939. Although the Francophile American ambassador William C. Bullitt attempted to use his influence to get aid for France, President Franklin D. Roosevelt did little to help for fear of antagonizing his nation's isolationists. Roosevelt believed that the 1940 defeat had made apparent the weakness of French society and ended its role as a major power. The American president hoped to limit the extent of French **collaboration** with the Germans, to undermine the influence of the **communists**, and to dismantle the French **empire**. Although the U.S. State Department argued for a restoration of French power, the president worked against it.

The United States initially chose to work with **Vichy** in the hope that it would be able to prevent German acquisition of France's fleet and colonies. The Roosevelt administration continued this policy up to the November 1942 invasion of **North Africa**, when Vichy troops fired on the Americans. In order to end resistance, the Americans allowed Admiral **Darlan**, then in Algiers, to administer North Africa. Following Darlan's assassination in December 1942, the United States helped place the ineffectual General Henri **Giraud** in power in North Africa and backed him in his competition with Charles **de Gaulle** for control of French colonial forces.

In early 1943 Roosevelt joined with British prime minister Winston Churchill, whose government backed de Gaulle, in arranging a rapprochement between the **Free French** leader and Giraud. Their organizations were merged in June with the creation of the Comité français de libération nationale (CFLN). De Gaulle's increasing control over French forces disturbed American officials, who saw him as too unpredictable and too independent to be an appropriate instrument for their policies. Roosevelt, wishing to limit the influence of both de Gaulle and the communists, who comprised much of the **Resistance**, ordered General

Dwight D. Eisenhower to exclude both from planning the **Normandy** invasion and from subsequent civil administration. Roosevelt favored instead a military government with the possible collaboration of the **Pétain** regime.

Administration of France proved more than Eisenhower's army could handle, and the Gaullists increasingly took charge over civil matters. Forced to choose between antipathy for de Gaulle and the possibility of a **left-wing** France, Roosevelt granted the CFLN, now transformed into a **Provisional Government**, de facto recognition in July 1944 and fully embraced it in October. The United States rearmed the French and allowed them to participate in the defeat of Germany.

After the war, fear of the **Soviet Union** and economic self-interest led the Americans to help rebuild France's **economy** and international stature. The United States allowed the French to take part in the occupation of Germany and to return to Indochina and most other parts of its old **empire** and backed its bid for a permanent seat on the United Nations' Security Council.

*†H. Blumenthal, *Illusion and Reality in Franco–American Diplomacy, 1914–1945* (Baton Rouge, 1986); J. G. Hurstfield, *America and the French Nation 1939–1945* (Chapel Hill, NC, 1986); G. E. Maguire, *Anglo-American Policy towards the Free French* (London, 1995); M. Rossi, *Roosevelt and the French* (Westport, CT, 1993).

A. A. Workman

UNIVERSITIES were hostile to the clericalism and anti-intellectualism of **Vichy** and jealous of their own independence. They were broadly opposed to **collaboration** and supportive of **resistance**.

Marshal **Pétain's** first ministers of **education** were academics who defended the universities in general, even though they intervened, as did Georges Ripert, to ban **communists**; Jacques **Chevalier**, to increase Catholic influence; or Jérôme Carcopino, to dismiss **Freemasons**. Their successor, Abel **Bonnard**, endorsed Pétain's attacks on individualism and "bookish pseudoculture" and undertook further-reaching action to purge trade unionists, **Jews**, and known critics of the regime. Bonnard increased direct ministerial powers over university governance, and in 1942 a new chair of the history of Judaism was created to promote **anti-Semitism**.

There was little support for Vichy policies, let alone Nazism, among students or academics, and if most reacted passively, many took a more active stance. On 11 November 1940 thousands of Parisian students defied a ban to lay flowers on the grave of the Unknown Soldier at the Arc de Triomphe. Several were shot dead when the march was broken up, and the universities were closed temporarily, signaling the beginning of public Resistance.

Demonstrations were staged against Nazism, against the few academic collaborators, and against anti-Semitic lectures. Scientists manufactured explosives in their laboratories, and many students joined the *maquis*. One of the first organized Resistance movements was based in the **Musée de l'Homme** (Museum of Man) and was an early victim of German repression. Professors such as Pierre-Henri **Teitgen** and François **de Menthon** were among the earliest resisters in the south. Communist academics Georges Politzer and Jacques Decour published one of the first clandestine journals, *L'Université libre*, in late 1940 and subsequently died by firing squad. Several eminent scholars were killed for their Resistance activities, including Jean Cavaillès, Victor **Basch**, and Marc **Bloch**, and many others were imprisoned and deported.

When the **liberation** arrived, there were relatively few scores to be settled within the universities, and many acts of bravery were honored.

*A. Rosier, "L'Université et la Révolution nationale," in P. Arnoult et al., *La France sous l'occupation* (Paris, 1959).

M. Kelly

URIAGE, ÉCOLE DES CADRES, was the **Vichy** government national leadership school. In October 1940 Marshal **Pétain** helped "baptize" the first cohort of the École Nationale Supérieure des Cadres. The next month it moved to the Alpine Château d'Uriage above Grenoble to train young elites to pioneer national renewal. Although headed by the royalist Pierre **Dunoyer de Segonzac**, the "communitarian personalism," taught by *Esprit* intellectuals such as Emmanuel **Mounier** and Hubert Beuve-Méry, made the school a unique laboratory and think tank, with 11 regional schools in the southern **zone** alone.

From November 1940 to late 1942 Uriage publications inspired many in Vichy and in the regional affiliates who remained particularly loyal to the "mother school." Uriage was much admired by the Scouts, the **Chantiers de la Jeunesse**, the **Compagnons de France**, and Jeunesse et montagne for its "knight-monk," the "new man." Uriage protested German excesses, fought off rivals, protected some **Jews**, and trained elites (4,000 at Uriage alone) for the political culture that was to succeed liberal democracy: authoritarian, hierarchical, Scoutish, personalist, communitarian, and spiritual, with a significantly downsized role for **communists**, Jews, and **Freemasons**. Pierre **Laval's** return to office, the occupation of the southern zone, and a power struggle over directing French **youth**, however, led to its closing at the end of 1942.

The **milice** then established its own *école des cadres* in the château under a mystical royalist who wanted holy war on communists and restoration of the king. The milice Uriage trained *cadres* and taught counterinsurgency tactics, until it was attacked by the **Resistance** on 5 July 1944. Meanwhile Segonzac's original Uriage network, united in a secret order, tried to influence the *maquis*. With the **liberation** Beuve-Méry and company founded Le Monde, revived Éditions du Seuil and *Esprit*, helped found the École Nationale d'Administration, François **Mitterrand's Socialist** Party, the Federalist movement, Christian-Marxist dialogue, the Second Vatican Council, *tier-mondisme*, and the cause of a united Europe.

P. Bitoun, *Les hommes d'Uriage* (Paris, 1988); B. Comte, *Une Utopie combattante,*

L'École des cadres d'Uriage, 1940–1942 (Paris, 1991); A. Delestre, *Uriage, une communauté et une école dans la tourmente, 1939–1945* (Nancy, 1989); J. Hellman, *The Knight-Monks of Vichy France, Uriage, 1940–45* (Montreal and Kingston, 1993).

J. Hellman

V

VALLAT, XAVIER (1891–1972), **right-wing** politician, coordinator of **Vichy's** anti-**Jewish** program 1941–1942. Vallat's political career was shaped in the mold of Charles **Maurras'** movement, **Action Française**—militantly nationalist, Catholic, and authoritarian. A badly wounded war veteran in 1918, he was a right-wing parliamentarian before 1940. In March 1941 **Pétain** appointed Vallat head of the General Office for Jewish Affairs or **Commissariat Général aux Questions Juives**, charged with administering anti-Jewish policy and legislation. Committed to the elimination of Jews from French public life and to reducing their role in French society, Vallat stood for what he called "*antisémitisme d'état.*" This meant that **anti-Semitic** policy was to serve the interests of the French state, not the dictates of the Nazis. Implicit in his approach was the hope that the Germans would gradually withdraw from this field, leaving the task to the French alone. Vallat operated in a highly legalistic manner and in rare instances made exceptions favoring distinguished, French-born Jews. Anti-German as well as anti-Jewish, Vallat resisted an anti-Semitic policy that would materially aid the Reich. By the end of 1941 Vallat was losing credibility, both with his French colleagues and with the Germans. Notably, Vallat failed to replace German regulations in the occupied **zone** with French law; at the same time, Vallat appeared to the Germans as an irksome rival in the anti-Semitic field, prone to making legalistic distinctions and opposing extreme measures. The occupation authorities forced him out of office in March 1942, when their plans turned to the **deportation** and murder of the Jews. Sentenced to 10 years in prison in 1947, Vallat was released 2 years later.

*S. Klarsfeld, *Vichy-Auschwitz: Le rôle de Vichy dans la solution finale de la question juive en France,* 2 vols. (Paris, 1983, 1985); M. R. Marrus and R. O. Paxton, *Vichy France and the Jews* (New York, 1981); X. Vallat, *Le Nez de Cléopâtre* (Paris, 1957).

M. R. Marrus

VÉLODROME D'HIVER, an indoor sporting arena located in the 15th *arrondissement* in **Paris**, was the scene of a roundup on 16 and 17 July 1942 of

13,152 **Jews**, foreign-born or of foreign extraction, among them 4,115 children, by the French **police**. The arrests resulted in the **deportation** of 12,884 individuals, most of whom never returned. Single persons and couples without children were sent to the Drancy internment camp immediately, while families with children were detained under deplorable conditions in the Vélodrome d'Hiver before being sent first to various internment camps in France and then to Auschwitz.

The result of an agreement between René **Bousquet**, secretary-general of the **Vichy** police, and Carl **Oberg**, chief of the German police in Occupied France, the roundup of the "Vel d'Hiv" has become an important **symbol** of the complicity of the Vichy government in carrying out the Nazis' Final Solution. The Germans would never have succeeded in rounding up so many individuals without the active assistance of the French police.

On the occasion of the 50th anniversary of the roundup in 1992, the Committee of the Vélodrome d'Hiver asked President François **Mitterrand** to make a formal statement denouncing the crimes of the French State against the Jews. The French president refused, claiming that to do so would imply that France and not Vichy, which he viewed as an illegitimate regime, was guilty. The following year, **Mitterrand** announced a national day of mourning, designated as 16 July, for the victims of the racist and anti-Semitic persecutions committed "under the so-called government of the French State." Mitterrand's successor, Jacques Chirac, in a statement made during the ceremonies marking the 53d anniversary of the roundup in 1995, acknowledged the responsibility of the French and of the French state in deporting Jews to the Nazi death camps.

É. Conan and H. Rousso, *Un passé qui ne passe pas* (Paris, 1994); S. Klarsfeld, *Vichy-Auschwitz; Le rôle de Vichy dans la solution finale de la question juive en France*, vol. 1 (Paris, 1983); Cl. Lévy and P. Tillard, *La grande rafle du Vel d'Hiv* (Paris, 1992 [original ed., 1967]); M. R. Marrus and R. O. Paxton, *Vichy France and the Jews* (New York, 1981); M. Simons, "Chirac Affirms France's Guilt in Fate of Jews," *New York Times*, 17 July 1995.

V. Datta

VERCORS BATTLE was fought by one of the largest *maquis* groups in southeastern France. The Vercors mountain near Grenoble is a natural bastion. In 1942, this site became a **Resistance** stronghold. Officers of the **Armistice Army** were often reluctant to form cadres for the *maquis*, but civilians, such as Clément (Eugène Chavant), from all walks of life filled their ranks.

The Vercors *maquis* fighters were decidedly on the political **Left**, but there were few **communists** among them. Pierre Dalloz, a military leader, was realistic about the limits of any protracted action outside the Vercors. High-ranking representatives of the London **Free French** planned massive air drops in support of the Vercors, but they never came.

The domestic Resistance leadership enthusiastically supported the formation of the mountain redoubt, destined to go into action only when Allied landings on the Mediterranean coast would pin down important German forces that were then to be attacked from behind by sorties from the Vercors. The *milice*, however, attacked the Vercors with heavy armament from the south, which was difficult to protect, while German bombers intervened. On 19 July 1944, the *maquis* force was surrounded by 20,000 German soldiers. The battle raged for five days. The Germans suffered heavy losses, but the Vercors was conquered. Those *maquisards* not killed in battle were handed over by the milice to the Germans, who executed them.

To the end, the combatants and their leaders still expected Allied support. Among the leaders shot by the Germans was the brilliant young writer Jean Prévost. Some scattered survivors joined other *maquis* units. The withholding of air support promised by leaders sent from London bolstered the claims of betrayal later voiced by survivors and families of those slain.

R. Aron, *France Reborn: The History of the Liberation,* trans. H. Hare (New York, 1964); H. Michel, *Histoire de la Résistance* (Paris, 1950).

K. Bieber

VICHY, a resort town in the Auvergne, known for its spas and its mineral water, became the provisional capital of France under the government of Marshal **Pétain** shortly after the 1940 **armistice**. Despite occasional talk of moving to **Paris**, the Pétain government remained in Vichy until its demise with the 1944 **liberation**. General **de Gaulle's Provisional Government** thereupon established itself in Paris.

With the June 1940 German advance threatening Paris, the government fled, first to Tours, then to Bordeaux, from where it concluded the armistice with Germany. Bordeaux, however, had been occupied by the Germans, and the government chose Vichy, a town that, unlike the larger of the then-unoccupied cities, was not in the political domain of any of the major leaders of the time. As a resort, Vichy also possessed a large number of hotels that could be requisitioned for government use. The population of the Vichy metropolitan area expanded from 30,000 to over 130,000 during the war, as politicians and bureaucrats streamed to the provisional capital. Government requisition of most of the large hotels, in addition to wartime travel restrictions, severely curtailed the spa trade and hurt the town's tourism industry.

Because of its association with the government of Marshal Pétain and the policy of **collaboration** with Nazi Germany, the town of Vichy has been unable to fully restore its image, and its name evokes emotional responses unlike those of other French towns. As a **symbol** of betrayal, Vichy was denounced even during the war not only by the **Free French** but also by those for whom the Pétain government was insufficiently zealous in pursuing the **National Revolution** and collaboration with the **New Order**. Opprobrium for the name was such even outside France that a cookbook published in English in 1941 renamed the soup ''Vichyssoise'' ''Crême Gauloise,'' and in 1943 a New York restaurant listed it as ''de Gaullesoise.'' In September 1944, just after the **liberation**, the

Municipal Council of Vichy requested that any allusion to the Vichy regime be stricken from the French language. Two months later, the council protested against what it called the undeserved opprobrium linking the town with the term "Vichy government."

Since the war, the "Vichyssois," nongovernment residents of the town who themselves suffered as much as others in France during the Occupation, have sometimes been identified with "Vichyistes," who had either served in Pétain's government or had ideological affinities with it. In 1959, General **de Gaulle**, newly installed as president of the Fifth Republic, in an attempt to restore the town's good name, gave a speech there that ended with the cry of *"Vive Vichy."* Periodic attempts by Pétainists to commemorate the marshal's activities there during the Occupation, which in 1978 led to police intervention, however, kept the symbolic linkage fresh in public opinion. Meanwhile, Vichy suffered from a decline in spa visitors from a high of 129,600 in 1931, many of whom were military and colonial officials on leave, to as few as 19,009 in 1983.

By the late 1980s, however, increasing numbers of tourists were becoming interested in specific locations in the town of the various Occupation-era ministries and state functions. Yielding to a curiosity, which came largely from visiting Germans and **Americans**, the Tourism Office in 1987 created a *"sites vichyssois du régime de Pétain"* (Pétain regime Vichy sites) circuit, after winning the assent of police and **Resistance** veterans' organizations. In 1988, the historian Marc Ferro, by no means pro-Pétain, who was invited to speak in Vichy about his then-new biography of the marshal, was obliged to give his lecture across the Allier River because of suggestions that even to speak of Pétain in Vichy was a step toward his rehabilitation. On 26 August 1992, a temporary plaque was erected on the former Hôtel du Parc, which had housed the offices of Pétain and many of his key associates, commemorating the roundup of foreign **Jews** in the then-unoccupied **zone** exactly 50 years earlier. This plaque was made permanent in 1993.

In the 1990s, Vichy town leaders were still trying to restore the good name of their town. Its citizens were still coping with the opprobrium for a history that, as a local historian emphasized, had not been their fault.

S. Barcellini and A. Wiewiorka, *Passant, souviens-toi, Les lieux du souvenir de la Seconde Guerre mondiale en France* (Paris, 1995); É. Conan, "Vichy malade de Vichy," *L'Express*, 26 June 1992, 36–37; J. Débordes, *A Vichy, La vie de toutes les jours sous Pétain* (Paris, 1994); H. Rousso, *The Vichy Syndrome, History and Memory in France since 1944*, trans. A. Goldhammer (Cambridge, MA, 1991).

B. M. Gordon

VILLON, PIERRE, né Roger Ginsburger (1901–1981), architect, **communist** leader, head of the **Front National** in the northern **zone** from February 1942, delegate of this movement to the National Council of the **Resistance (CNR)**, and president of the **Comité d'action militaire (COMAC)** from May 1944. A man of action and an organizer, Pierre Villon (one of his pseudonyms in the **Resistance**) was also a persuasive speaker.

Roger Ginsburger joined the Communist Party (PCF) in 1932. In October 1939, after the banning of the PCF, he went underground, in charge of editing the clandestine newspaper *L'Humanité*. Arrested by the French **police** in October 1940, he was condemned to prison. The letters he then wrote constitute an anthology of the communist spirit. In winter 1941, he expressed his faith in the **USSR** and in the imminence of Bolshevik revolution in Germany and France.

As a member of the CNR's steering committee, Villon had more influence than the PCF's official delegate to the CNR. With Jacques **Duclos**, he proposed a charter for the CNR. The **socialists**, for their part, had their own proposal. These texts led to the Action Program of the Resistance, which was adopted unanimously on 15 March 1944. In COMAC, the military commission of the CNR, Villon defended the autonomy of the interior Resistance in France, in contrast to headquarters in London, and endeavored to organize a general insurrection.

In 1945, Villon was appointed to the PCF's Central Committee and elected deputy in the Allier department. He left the Central Committee in 1970 and remained a deputy until 1978.

C. Andrieu, "Le Conseil national de la Résistance, juin 1944–janvier 1945," in Fondation Charles de Gaulle, ed., *Le Rétablissement de la légalité républicaine, 1944* (Brussels, 1996); C. Andrieu, *Le programme commun de la Résistance* (Paris, 1984); P. Villon, *Pierre Villon, résistant de la première heure* (Paris, 1983); C. Willard, "Pierre Villon," in *Dictionnaire biographique du Mouvement ouvrier français* (Paris, 1983).

C. Andrieu

VLAMINCK, MAURICE DE, (1876–1958), was the "enfant terrible" of the *fauve* movement (1905–1907) who combined a dramatic, emotional, and provocative use of color in his paintings with predilections for anarchist political and social views and a nonconformist way of life. The First World War shattered Vlaminck's "confidence in civilization, in science, progress, socialism," and he withdrew to the countryside, where he created somber views of nature in paintings that depicted the harsh, simple values of rural life and represented a decisive turn away from the exuberant colors of the *fauve* period.

Overshadowed by surrealism and other avant-garde movements during the interwar years, Vlaminck was part of a conservative "return to order" that became the pursuit of a middle-of-the-road style in the arts under **Vichy**. During the Occupation Vlaminck enjoyed great popularity and received warm praise from Lucien **Rebatet**, art critic for *Je suis partout*. His paintings were widely shown in Parisian galleries and commanded top prices.

In the fall of 1941 Vlaminck joined 12 other artists on a sponsored cultural and propaganda tour of major German cities to promote Franco–German understanding and demonstrate Nazi support for the arts. After his return to France, he published a bitter **denunciation** of Pablo **Picasso**, whom he accused of decadence and of corrupting French culture. With the **liberation** a **purge** committee, of which Picasso was the nominal chairman, found Vlaminck guilty of **collaboration** and forbade him to exhibit and sell his work for a year. Vlaminck represented a mix of emotional expressionism and rejection of cosmopolitan ''decadence'' that reflected Vichy's cultural preferences.

*L. Bertrand Dorléac, *L'art de la défaite, 1940–1944* (Paris, 1993); M. C. Cone, *Artists under Vichy: A Case of Prejudice and Persecution* (Princeton, 1992); J. Selz, *Vlaminck* (Milan, 1963); S. Wilson, ''Collaboration in the Fine arts,'' in G. Hirschfeld and P. Marsh, eds., *Collaboration in France: Politics and Culture during the Nazi Occupation, 1940–1944* (Oxford, 1989), 103–25.

K. Munholland

W

WAFFEN-SS, FRENCH UNITS were composed of French volunteers for service in the elite German fighting force during the Second World War. Although the Germans began accepting Frenchmen as individuals into the Waffen-SS in 1942, only in July 1943 did Pierre **Laval** and Heinrich Himmler authorize a uniquely French contingent. For the remainder of the war, this unit fought holding actions against the continuous **Soviet** offensive.

The German military's manpower shortages acted as the impetus for the first French Waffen-SS volunteer formation: the Sturmbrigade-SS Frankreich. This unit fought in the Carpathian mountains alongside a German Waffen-SS division until the Soviet summer offensive of 1944. The assault brigade suffered heavy casualties and returned to Germany, where it was reconstituted together with some 6,500 Frenchmen: volunteers from the German navy, the **Légion des Volontaires Français contre le Bolchevisme (LVF)**, the National Socialist Motorcorps, and the **Milice Française**. Under a German officer's supervision, an ex-Foreign Legionnaire and member of the LVF commanded this "Charlemagne Division." Despite its divisional status, it never reached more than brigade strength. The soldiers were a curious mix of anti-Bolshevik crusaders, Nazi idealists, students, and ardent collaborators. Until February 1945, Charlemagne underwent intensive training to prepare for battle, purge its weaker elements, and create a cohesive fighting force free of political and ideological rivalries.

From February to March 1945, the unit engaged the advancing Red Army in Pomerania. After its encirclement, Charlemagne was all but destroyed, the German commander salvaging only part of one regiment. While some of its soldiers escaped through Narvik, others fell into **Russian** hands. Around 100 survivors defended the Reich Chancellery until the end during the Battle of Berlin. Of those who reached France, many were tried for treason and imprisoned or shot.

B. M. Gordon, *Collaborationism in France during the Second World War* (Ithaca, NY,

1980); A. Merglen, "Soldats français sous uniforms allemands," *RDHDGM* 27:108 (October 1977); P. Rusco, *Stoi! Quarante mois de combattant sur le front russe* (Paris, 1988).

R. W. White

WEIL, SIMONE, (1909–1943), was a **left-wing Jewish** intellectual and philosopher, educated at the École Normale Supérieure, after which she followed an ascetic, even eccentric, career. First she worked as a schoolteacher, requesting assignments to working-class areas, but she also sought work as a manual laborer (first in factories, later in agriculture) in order to understand the working-class condition and to develop her philosophy linking spirituality and labor. She visited Nazi Germany and Fascist Italy and participated briefly in the Spanish civil war.

When **Paris** was declared an open city in 1940, Weil and her parents left immediately for the south. They lived for two years in Marseilles, then joined Simone's brother André Weil, a mathematician in Pennsylvania. In June 1942, they arrived in New York, where Simone studied nursing in Harlem. She remained in New York until November 1942, when she went to London to join the **Free French**. Poor health precluded the dangerous missions she sought, and she was assigned the role of a bureaucrat preparing for the postwar social reconstruction of France. After a breakdown in July 1943, she was hospitalized and subsequently died of a combination of tuberculosis and anorexia on 24 August 1943.

Despite her Jewish background, Weil was strongly drawn to Catholicism, and her mysticism influenced her left-wing political thinking, but she never officially joined either the Catholic Church or the **Communist** Party. Her writings include *La Pesenteur et la Grace* (1948, translated as *Gravity and Grace*, 1952) and *L'Enracinement* (1949, translated as *The Need for Roots*, 1952).

*J. Cabaud, *L'expérience vécue de Simone Weil* (Paris, 1957); G. Fiori, *Simone Weil* (Athens, GA, 1989); N. Oxenhandler, *Looking for Heroes in Postwar France* (Hanover, NH, 1995); S. Petrement, *La Vie de Simone Weil* (Paris, 1973).

M. Hawthorne

WEYGAND, MAXIME (1867–1965), a general, commander of the French **army** from 1931 to 1935, was sidetracked to Beirut as chief of the French forces in the Levant on the outbreak of hostilities in September 1939 by his rival, General Maurice-Gustave **Gamelin**, and his enemy, Premier Édouard **Daladier**.

Summoned on 19 May 1940 by Daladier's successor as premier, Paul **Reynaud**, to replace a discredited Gamelin, Weygand found himself in the middle of a French defeat that was mushrooming into a *crise de régime*. His second order, 26 May, established the *Götterdämmerung* of the remaining French forces along the river lines between **Paris** and the front. It thus confined the battle to continental France, excluding its overseas **empire**.

As the military crisis degenerated into a chaotic **exodus** toward the Spanish frontier, Weygand applied military pressure that demoralized the Reynaud cabinet and led to its fall on 16 June. Refusing to leave France to continue the war from North Africa, Weygand also refused to surrender the army if allowed to remain behind, and he refused to resign. Reynaud was succeeded by Marshal **Pétain**, who immediately sent out a message for "peace negotiations" to the Germans. In imposing on the civilians his particularist military interpretation of honor and national security, Weygand was, in **de Gaulle's** words, "*le grand coupable de 1940*" (the great guilty one of 1940).

Weygand's acerbic anti-Germanism soon got him banished to North Africa as high commissioner. In Algiers until his dismissal on 18 November 1941, Weygand exercised an anti-Axis, anti-Gaullist, and pro-**American** policy, creating the nucleus of what emerged as a resurrected French **army** in the Tunisian campaign of early 1943. By that time, Weygand had been kidnapped by the Gestapo in France and imprisoned in the Tyrol. On his liberation on 4 May 1945, he was placed under arrest by General de Gaulle's government. With **Pétain** imprisoned and **Laval** executed, Weygand became the **symbol** of the **armistice** and **Vichy** that liberated France rejected. Charged with treason, Weygand was exonerated in 1948. He later headed the **Association pour Défendre la Mémoire du Maréchal Pétain**.

*P. C. F. Bankwitz, *Maxime Weygand and Civil–Military Relations in Modern France* (Cambridge, MA, 1967); B. Destremau, *Weygand* (Paris, 1989); J. Weygand, *Weygand, mon père* (Paris, 1970); M. Weygand, *Mémoires*, vol. 1: *Rappelé au service* (Paris, 1950).

P. C. F. Bankwitz

WOMEN, ROLES IN OCCUPIED FRANCE were characterized by the difficult material conditions of everyday life, which most directly affected women. **Vichy's National Revolution** was not only political and social but also, and above all, moral. First and foremost, women were assigned the role of wife and "mother of the family." Women's work was denounced that interfered with their role in the **education** of children. In contradiction of the fact that since the spring of 1940 more than a million Frenchmen were being held **prisoner** in Germany, Vichy launched a vigorous campaign for a high birthrate. The "ideal" Frenchwoman was to renounce affectation (*coquetterie*) "to assume a simple life," described as indispensable for the reconstruction of the country. In reality, many women had to shoulder new responsibilities, often as heads of families, managing farms and businesses in place of their imprisoned husbands.

Because of shortages caused by the Occupation, the state, in the autumn of 1940, began imposing restrictions that impacted the lifestyles of everyone. As household managers, however, women were directly impacted by these measures. Formerly routine activities such as buying a coat or a pair of shoes for the children became extremely difficult. Each day, women had to spend time and energy managing **ration** cards, now necessary to obtain provisions, and wait in long lines. These lines became the places where news circulated, and a new space for social interaction among the generations, as all age groups were represented there. The hardships of daily life for women, especially those in the cities, led to increasing frustration and eventually opposition to the occupation and Vichy authorities. Tracts denouncing their conditions of life circulated within the lines.

As had occurred under the Old Regime (prior to the 1789 revolution), women began to agitate for change. Beginning in the summer of 1940, spontaneous demonstrations of housewives took place in front of town halls and local prefecture offices. Accompanied by their children, women demanded more bread and milk for their families. Riots erupted in the Paris suburbs and in southern France in reaction to the deplorable conditions. In the Var, for example, some 40 spontaneous protests against the lack of provisions occurred in front of empty store windows between January and May 1942.

Clearly, the government's inability to solve the problems of daily life placed women in the forefront of an anti-Vichy turn in public opinion and brought them into the political field.

*†C. Bertin, *Les Femmes sous l'occupation* (Paris, 1993); L. Douzou, "La Résistance, une affaire des hommes?" in D. Voldman, ed., "Identités féminines et violences politiques (1936–1946)," *Les Cahiers de l'IHTP* 31 (October 1995); H. Eck, "Les Françaises sous Vichy," in F. Thébaud, ed., *Histoire des femmes en Occident*, vol. 5: *Le Vingtième siècle* (Paris, 1992); D. Veillon, *Vivre et survivre en France, 1939–1947* (Paris, 1995).

D. Veillon

WOMEN, ROLES IN RESISTANCE have historically been overlooked. Of 1,065 "**Compagnons de la Libération,**" only six were women. Much of the work of **Resistance**—providing food and shelter for members of the underground and escapees, acting as letter drops, observing troop movements—was routine and easily done by women. Therefore, although such tasks carried risk (and numerous women were indeed deported, tortured, imprisoned, and executed for their efforts), the women's activities were not always viewed as important. Because Resistance work was perceived as an extension of women's "natural" role, their activities in the Resistance have been underestimated both by historians who have focused on organizations and armed military actions and sometimes by the women themselves. The contrasting image of André versus Clara **Malraux** is a case in point.

A conference on women in the Resistance organized by the Union des Femmes Françaises in 1975 marked a major turning point in such perceptions. In fact, sex stereotypes could be an advantage, instead of a handicap: the social invisibility of a female secretary, for example, made her clandestine activities equally invisible. Thus, Jeanne Berthomier was able to gather intelligence just by going to work at the Ministry of Public Works in **Paris**, while Paule Letty-Mouroux worked as a secretary in the Toulon naval offices in order to be able to report on Axis ships. One Allied intelligence victory, consisting of vital information about the German warship *Scharnhorst*, came from details let slip at a tea party attended by Yvonne Le Roux, an agent of the Johnny network.

Although much of what women did was commonplace, some women also took leadership roles: Lucie **Aubrac** participated in daring raids to free her husband, Raymond. Berthie Albrecht was a leader of the **Combat** movement; Marie-Louise Dissart was a leader of the Françoise network; Claude Gérard organized Combat's Secret **Army** in the Dordogne; and Marie-Madeleine Fourcade (née Méric), headed the **Alliance** intelligence network, to name but a few.

Women worked in all areas of Resistance. They helped repatriate downed pilots and other escapees; wrote for, printed, and distributed clandestine newspapers that boosted morale; gathered intelligence and smuggled it out of France (often involving **radio** operations and cryptography); and trained, organized, and led armed Resistance. Women participated in the Resistance for different reasons. Many were not motivated by political commitments such as communism or by ethnic affiliation with **Jews** but saw their actions as an extension of family roles or as part of the defense of country and home. Others did have political affiliations or were motivated by religious belief, as in the case of the "*jocistes*" (Jeunesse Ouvrière Catholique, or JOC), which included a branch for women (JOCF). Noor Inayat Khan, shot at Dachau after being deported for Resistance activities as a **radio** operator, became the first woman Sufi saint.

Women resisters came from every social class, from the aristocratic (Mary Lindell, the comtesse de Milleville, who organized the Marie Claire escape line), to the humble, such as sexagenarian Marie Louise Dissard, and from every walk of life, including the families of notable artists (both the ex-wife and the daughter of the painter Francis Picabia) and politicians (Charles **de Gaulle's** sister-in-law Madeleine and his niece Geneviève).

*C. Bertin, *Femmes sous l'Occupation* (Paris, 1993); A. Francos, *Il était des femmes dans la résistance* (Paris, 1978); M. L. Rossiter, *Women in the Resistance* (New York, 1986); Union des Femmes Françaises, *Les femmes dans la Résistance* (Paris, 1977); M. C. Weitz, *Sisters in the Resistance: How Women Fought to Free France* (New York, 1995).

                                                                    M. Hawthorne

WOMEN, VICHY POLICIES REGARDING were determined by rigid definitions of masculinity and femininity that underlay its search for national renovation. **Vichy** sought to remedy what it saw as the disorder and promiscuous spirit of *laisser aller* (everything goes) of the 1930s, which, it held, Frenchwomen had helped create. Women's vanity, material concerns, and neglect of patriotic duty (bearing children) had contributed, according to Vichy, to France's defeat. The government initiated a campaign to strengthen the **family** and promote births.

Married women working outside the home were urged to return to their homes. A law of October 1940 required married women employed by the public sector to quit their jobs. As the war progressed, the manpower shortage forced Vichy to reverse its policies and urge women to work outside the home. With so many Frenchmen abroad, Vichy was obliged to change the Napoleonic Code, which placed married women under their husband's authority and considered them legally "incapacitated." A September 1942 law eliminated married Frenchwomen's legal incapacity (although the husband remained the legal head of the household until 1970). The Famille du Prisonnier agency, formed to help families, exercised paternalistic surveillance over **prisoners' wives**, largely women of working-class background.

While Vichy made no effort to change the policy of equal schooling for the sexes, the absence of male teachers necessitated the introduction of mixed elementary classes. In March 1942 Vichy instituted compulsory home management instruction for girls; while male students received physical **education**. Girls could voluntarily attend one of 380 **youth** centers set up for them, in lieu of the obligatory work camps for young men of draft age. They received "professional" training, largely limited to sewing and similar activities. There were no women at **Uriage**, the best known of the 60 centers Vichy set up to train the future leaders of the nation; only 2 were designated for women interns. In most of its endeavors the Vichy government had difficulty reconciling ideology and policies regarding women with the realities of the Occupation.

C. Bertin, *Femmes sous l'Occupation* (Paris, 1993); W. D. Halls, *The Youth of Vichy France* (New York, 1981); F. Muel-Dreyfus, *Vichy et l'éternel féminin* (Paris, 1996); M. Pollard, "Women and the National Revolution," in H. R. Kedward and R. Austin, eds., *Vichy France and the Resistance: Culture and Ideology* (London, 1985); P. Smith, *Feminism and the Third Republic: Women's Political and Civil Rights in France, 1918–1945* (Oxford, 1996); M. C. Weitz, *Sisters in the Resistance: How Women Fought to Free France* (New York, 1995).

M. C. Weitz

Y

YOUTH, VICHY POLICY, a major part of **Vichy's** effort to capture the imagination of, and discipline, French youth, concerned their activities beyond the classroom. The creation on 12 July 1940 of a Ministry of **Family** and Youth marked the first time that a French government devoted a cabinet post to this age group and provided ample funding. On 6 September 1940 the youth section of this ministry was transferred to the Secretariat général à la jeunesse (SGJ) in the Ministry of **Education**. On 25 September the fervent Catholic Georges Lamirand assumed leadership. He held this post until April 1942, when the incoming **collaborationist** minister of **education** Abel **Bonnard** replaced him with Georges Pelorson, whose failure to mobilize French youth for German victory resulted in the suppression of the SGJ on 31 December 1943. For the remaining Vichy period, youth affairs were assigned to a commission in the Ministry of **Education**.

Non-**left-wing** youth movements—Catholic, Scouting, and youth hostel—remained influential under Vichy. Many of Vichy's most prominent youth leaders—for example, General Joseph **de La Porte du Theil** (head of the **Chantiers de la Jeunesse**) and Pierre Schaeffer (head of the **Compagnons de France**)—had earlier been in Scouting. Vichy supplied large subsidies, and Scout membership jumped from 42,000 in 1940 to 160,000 in 1944. Lamirand protected **Jewish** Scouting until he was removed from office; Bonnard, however, expelled Jews from all youth movements. Vichy strictly regulated the youth hostels (*auberges de jeunesse*) and then outlawed them in August 1943.

A telling measure of Vichy's failure to politicize the youth in its favor is that French Scouting remained the largest youth group between 1940 and 1944. The second biggest, the Chantiers de la Jeunesse, established in July 1940 to replace conscription, claimed a membership of 100,000. The Compagnons de France, set up in 1940 to help youth under 20 uprooted by war and unemployment, numbered only 25,000 to 30,000. Other groups included Jeunesses nationales populaires, Jeunesse populaire française, Jeunesses francistes, Jeunes de l'Europe Nouvelle, **Jeunes du Maréchal**, Jeunesse de France et d'Outremer,

Équipes et Cadres de la France Nouvelle, Jeune Legion, Camarades de la Route, Maisons de jeunes, Équipes nationales, Les Campeurs Français, and Jeune France. These groups were largely either youth affiliates of the **Paris**-based **collaborationist** parties or independent proto**fascist** organizations and had memberships ranging between 3,000 and 6,000. In addition, the Vichy government set up 60 schools to train leaders, the school at **Uriage** being the most famous.

This labyrinthine set of organizations, however, is but one indication of Vichy's failure to develop a coherent youth policy. **Pétain**, for example, dissolved the organization created in his honor—the *Jeunes du Maréchal*—when its members displayed Nazi leanings. Within the Vichy inner circle, factions battled constantly. Catholics asserted the autonomy of their own organizations, grouped under the Association Catholique de la Jeunesse Française, fearing that a single, state-controlled youth movement (such as proposed by Parisian collaborationists Marcel **Déat** and Jacques **Doriot**) would swallow their own. The Germans, in keeping with their divide-and-rule policy, opposed a single, all-powerful French youth movement, while at the same time imposing the Hitler Youth movement in **Alsace**.

Between 1940 and 1942, Vichy organizations enlisted one-third of the youth in the unoccupied **zone**. The remaining two-thirds were never organized. By the time of the **liberation**, Vichy's youth legions had either shifted to the **Resistance** or dissolved into apathy. Nevertheless, the spirit of the leadership school at Uriage, exemplified by such figures as Hubert Beuve-Méry, later founder of Le Monde, had much influence in the postwar era.

B. Comte, *Une utopie combattante. L'école des cadres d'Uriage (1940–1942)* (Paris, 1991); P. Giolitto, *Histoire de la jeunesse sous Vichy* (Paris, 1991); R. Hervet, *Les Chantiers de la jeunesse* (Paris, 1962); W. D. Halls, *The Youth of Vichy France* (Oxford, 1981), R. Hervet, *Les Compagnons de France* (Paris, 1965); A.-R. Michel, *La JEC, Jeunesse étudiante chrétienne face au nazisme et à Vichy (1938–1944)* (Lille, 1988).

W. S. Haine

Z

ZONES. With the signing of the June 1940 **armistices** with Germany and Italy, France was partitioned into several administrative zones, while **Alsace** and **Lorraine** were annexed outright by Germany. A **Demarcation Line** established the most basic fracture in France, into a northern zone, occupied by Germany, and an unoccupied southern, sometimes called the "free" zone. The line stretched across France from the Atlantic coast south of Bordeaux, up to Vierzon, southeast to Moulins, north to Chalon-sur-Saône, east through Dole, and south to Geneva. Moulins was established as the main station for crossing the line, allowed only for those bearing an officially issued *laissez-passer*. Some 24 million inhabitants lived in the occupied zone; 16 million in the unoccupied zone. The rich coal regions of the north and France's major **industrial** sectors in **Paris** fell under German control in the occupied zone, as did also the industrial wealth of Alsace and Lorraine. Italy occupied several southeastern departments near the Franco–Italian border.

France's capital was relocated in **Vichy**, in the unoccupied zone, due south of Moulins. Although Vichy was theoretically the capital of all of France, the German occupation authorities severely limited its authority outside the unoccupied zone. In November 1942, following the Allied landings in French **North Africa**, the Germans broke the armistice agreement and overran the "free" zone, applying a more direct hand in Vichy affairs. Italy's occupation zone was extended to the Rhône River. The overturning of Mussolini's government in the summer of 1943 brought German occupation to the former Italian zone.

The Germans subdivided the occupied zone into "forbidden" and "reserved" zones. Most of the Atlantic seaboard and the coastline of the channel as well as the Ardennes forest fell under the "forbidden" category. In the northeast near the Ardennes, the Germans expelled most French civilians in order to use the area as a rocket-testing location but also to settle some of the farm areas with Germans under a project titled "Ostland." In addition, the German command defined beach zones stretching from Brittany to **Normandy** as off-limits.

The **liberation** of France in 1944 reunited the various zones under the jurisdiction of the **Provisional Government** in **Paris**.

H. Michel, *Paris allemand* (Paris, 1964); J. F. Sweets, *Choices in Vichy France: The French under Nazi Occupation* (New York, 1944 [original ed., 1986]).

N. Dombrowski

Chronology

1938

Raymond **Aron,** *Introduction à la philosophie de l'histoire*

Jean **Cocteau,** *Les Parents terribles*

Jean-Paul **Sartre,** *La Nausée*

Charles **de Gaulle,** *La France et son Armée*

29–30 September: **Munich agreement**

1939

André **Gide,** *Journal*

Jean **Giraudoux,** *Ondine*

Antoine de **Saint-Exupéry,** *Terre des hommes*

Jean Renoir, *La Règle du jeu*

14 February: France officially recognizes Franco government in **Spain; Pétain** sent as ambassador (March)

15 March: Germany occupies remnant of Czecho–Slovak state

28 March: Franco takes Madrid; end of Spanish civil war

23 August: Nazi–**Soviet** Pact signed

1 September: German forces invade Poland

3 September: France and **Britain** declare war on Germany

17 September: **Soviet Union** attacks Poland

26 September: Dissolution of the French **Communist Party (PCF)**

30 November: **Soviet Union** attacks Finland

1940

22 March: Paul **Reynaud** named premier

9 April: Germans attack Denmark and Norway

10 May: German attack on the West; invasion of Netherlands, **Belgium**, and **Luxemburg**

15 May: Dutch army surrenders

18 May: Marshal **Pétain** named vice president of the council (vice-premier)

19 May: **Weygand** replaces **Gamelin** as head of the French military forces

27 May: King Leopold III orders Belgian forces to surrender

28 May: Evacuation of French and **British** forces from Dunkirk

5 June: General **de Gaulle** named undersecretary of state for defense and war

10 June: French government leaves **Paris**; Italy enters the war against France

14 June: French government moves to Bordeaux; German forces enter **Paris**

16 June: **Reynaud** is replaced as premier by Marshal **Pétain**

17 June: **Pétain** asks for **armistice; de Gaulle** leaves for London

18 June: **De Gaulle's** first **BBC** broadcast calling for **Resistance**

22 June: French and German representatives sign an **armistice** at Rethondes near **Compiègne**, going into effect 25 June

23 June: Entry of **Laval** into the government

28 June: **De Gaulle** is recognized as head of **Free France** by the **British**

3 July: **British** attack French fleet at **Mers-el-Kébir**, near Oran

4 July: National Assembly meets in **Vichy**

10 July: National Assembly votes full constituent powers to Marshal **Pétain**

11 July: **Pétain** promulgates three constitutional acts establishing the French State (**État Français**)

12 July: **Laval** is named "dauphin," or successor to **Pétain**

3 August: Otto **Abetz** named German ambassador to **Paris**

7 August: Germans absorb three eastern departments

September: Liberté founded

23–25 September: Failure of **Free French** to take **Dakar**

24 September: Marcel **Déat** takes over *L'Œuvre* in **Paris**

25 September: **Musée de l'Homme** network publishes its first pamphlet calling for **Resistance**

26 September: **Japanese** forces enter Indochina

27 September: **Jews** in unoccupied **zone** forbidden to return to occupied **zone**

October: First manifesto of **Ceux de la Libération**

3 October: **Vichy** orders first "**Jewish** Statute" (Statut des Juifs)

23 October: Hitler meets Franco at Hendaye, fails to gain Spain's entry into the war

24 October: **Pétain** meets **Hitler** at **Montoire**; endorses **collaboration**

27 October: General **de Gaulle's** Brazzaville Manifesto

October–November: **Défense de la France** formed

November: Manifesto of the **Mouvement de Libération Nationale**

11 November: Anti-German demonstration of students in **Paris**

15 November: Manifesto of **Syndicalisme** Français

16 November: General **de Gaulle's** "Organic Declaration," completing the **Brazzaville** Manifesto

13 December: **Pétain** dismisses **Laval**

14 December: **Flandin** named foreign minister; **Déat** arrested in **Paris**

15 December: Remains of "l'Aiglon" (Napoleon's son) returned from Vienna to Invalides in **Paris**

25 December: **Darlan** meets **Hitler** near Beauvais

1941

1 February: **Déat** and **Deloncle** establish **Rassemblement National Populaire**

9 February: **Flandin** resigns; **Darlan** named vice president of the council and **Pétain's** heir apparent

March: Departure from Marseilles of a small contingent of surrealists for America

April: Liberté publishes its first newspaper

10 May: Jeune France sponsors show *Young Painters in the French Tradition* in **Paris**

13 May: **Hitler–Darlan** meeting at the Berghof

27–28 May: Protocols of Paris

22 June: Germany attacks **Soviet Union**

25 June: **De Gaulle**–Lyttelton accords on the Middle East

7 July: Creation of the **LVF**

August: first issue of underground newspaper, *Défense de la France*, published

12 August: **Pétain's** speech in which he detects a "bad wind" blowing

21 August: **Fabien** kills a German soldier in the **Paris** *métro*

27 August: Attempted assassination of **Laval** and **Déat**

4 September: **Doriot** leaves for **Russian** front with **LVF**

5 September: Opening of **exposition** The **Jew** and France in **Paris**

24 September: Creation of Comité National Français

3 October: **Vichy** adopts anti-**Jewish** statutes

4 October: Government issues a **Labor Charter**

1 November: **Mouvement de Libération Nationale** and Liberté merge to form **Combat**

20 November: **Weygand** retires

5 December: Sacha **Guitry**, "Le Destin fabuleux de Desirée Clary"

7 December: **Japanese** attack Pearl Harbor

1942

Albert **Camus**, *Le Mythe de Sisyphe*

Vercors, *Silence de la Mer*

January: Jean **Moulin** parachuted into France from London

15 February: **Japanese** take Singapore

19 February: Opening of **Riom trials**

1 March: Opening of **exposition** *Bolshevism against Europe*

27 March: First "racial" **deportations**

28 March: **Sauckel** ordered to recruit French workers for German war effort

15 April: **Riom trials** suspended

17 April: General **Giraud** escapes from German prison; **Darlan** resigns

18 April: **Laval** returns to power, with increased authority in new post as "head of Government"

27 April: M. Carné, *Les Visiteurs du soir*

15 May: Arno **Breker** retrospective in **Paris**

18 May: Germans demand the transfer of skilled workers to the Reich

29 May: **Jews** required to wear the yellow star in the occupied **zone**

22 June: **Laval** announces the **Relève** and publicly supports German victory

14 July: **Free France** becomes **Fighting France**

16–17 July: Roundup in **Paris** of some 13,000 **Jews** in the **Vélodrome d'hiver**

18 July: **Vichy** establishes Légion Tricolor

24 August: Roundup of internment camp **refugees** and first **deportations** to extermination camps from the unoccupied **zone**

3 November: Germans defeated at El Alamein

8 November: **Anglo-American** landings in French **North Africa**

11 November: Germans occupy the previously unoccupied **zone**

14 November: In **North Africa, Darlan** goes over to the Allied side

17 November: **Laval** is authorized to sign laws and decrees

27 November: Germans dissolve the **Armistice Army**; French scuttle their fleet at Toulon

24 December: **Darlan** assassinated in Algiers

1943

Simone **de Beauvoir**, *L'Invitée*

Jean-Paul **Sartre**, *Les Mouches*

Jean Anouilh, *Antigone*

Antoine de **Saint-Exupéry**, *Le Petit Prince*

22 January: Anfa Conference in Morocco: Roosevelt, Churchill, **Giraud, de Gaulle**

24 January: Destruction of the Old Port of Marseilles

26 January: Creation of MUR

30 January: Creation of the *milice*; Jean **Bazaine**, "La Peinture bleu-blanc-rouge," in NRF

2 February: German forces surrender at Stalingrad

5 April: **Vichy** turns **Blum, Daladier, Mandel, Reynaud**, and **Gamelin** over to the Germans

17 April: Perreux accords: underground **Confédération Générale du Travail (CGT)** reunified

10 May: H.-G. Clouzot, *Le Corbeau*

27 May: First meeting of **CNR**

31 May: General **de Gaulle** in Algiers

3 June: Creation of Comité Français de Libération Nationale (CFLN), **Giraud** and **de Gaulle** copresidents

25 June: Publication of Jean-Paul **Sartre's** *L'Être et le néant*

8 July: Probable date of the death of Jean **Moulin**

10 July: Allied landings in Sicily

17 July: Congress of **Groupe Collaboration**

22 July: Creation of French unit of the **Waffen-SS**

26 July: Resignation of Mussolini

August: Landing of French shock troops in **Corsica**

17 August: M. Carné, ***Les Enfants du paradis***

8 September: Germans occupy the formerly Italian **zone** in France

17 September: Speer–Bichelonne agreement

2 October: **De Gaulle** emerges as clear leader of the **Resistance; Giraud** loses influence

6 October: **Liberation** of **Corsica; de Gaulle** in Ajaccio

29 November: Opening of Teheran Conference

1 December: **Doriot** receives the Iron Cross for action on the **Russian** front

1944

Jean-Paul **Sartre**, *Huis clos*

Artists Otto **Freundlich**, Robert Desnos, Max Jacob disappear in **Holocaust**

1 January: **Darnand** put in charge of all security forces

6 January: Philippe **Henriot** becomes secretary of state for information and propaganda

20 January: **Vichy** creates **Special Sections** for secret courts-martial

30 January–8 February: **Brazzaville Conference** calls for more autonomy for French colonies in the postwar world

26 March: Germans and **Miliciens** lay siege to the *maquis* on the **Glières** plateau

21 April: CFLN orders the right to vote for **women**; provisional organization of public authority

26 April: **Pétain** acclaimed in visit to **Paris** after Allied bombardment

3 June: CFLN becomes **Provisional Government** (Gouvernement Provisoire de la République Française, GPRF)

6 June: Allied landings in **Normandy**

9 June: German hangings of citizens at Tulle after **Resistance** forces had occupied the town

10 June: German massacre at **Oradour-sur-Glane**

14 June: **De Gaulle** at Bayeux

20 June: Jean Zay assassinated

28 June: Philippe **Henriot** assassinated

7 July: Georges **Mandel** assassinated

12 July: Last meeting of **Vichy** Council of Ministers

9 August: Ordinance for the reestablishment of **Republican** legality in France

15 August: Last convoys of deportees from Drancy to extermination camps; **Paris police** strike; Allied landings in **Provence**; attempt to name Édouard Herriot as head of French government

17 August: Last appearance of **collaborationist press** in **Paris**

18 August: **De Gaulle** at Cherbourg

19 August: Beginning of **Paris** insurrection

20 August: Germans move **Pétain** and **Laval** to Belfort

25 August: German surrender in **Paris**

26 August: Triumphal parade of General **de Gaulle** in **Paris**

8 September: **Pétain** arrives at **Sigmaringen**

15 September: Creation of special courts to try collaborators

23 November: **Liberation** of Strasbourg

10 December: Franco–**Soviet** pact

1945

Les Temps modernes, directed by Jean-Paul **Sartre**, Raymond **Aron**, and Maurice Merleau-Ponty

Liberation of Auschwitz and other extermination camps

16 January: Renault plant nationalized

12 February: Yalta agreements

27 February: René Clément, *La Bataille du rail*

29 April (and 13 May): Municipal elections, first elections in which **women** vote

8 May: German surrender; end of war in Europe

10 May: Beginning of large-scale return of deportees and **prisoners**

5 June: France is given an occupation zone in Germany

31 July: **Laval** returned to France from **Spain**

15 August: **Japanese** surrender

2 September: **Ho** Chi Minh declares independence of Vietnam

21 October: **Referendum** and election of Constituent Assembly

1946

20 January: **De Gaulle** resigns as head of the **Provisional Government**

13 October: **Referendum** approves constitution for the Fourth **Republic**

November: French forces bomb Haiphong in Indochina; war intensifies

1949

April:Creation of NATO (North Atlantic Treaty Organization) with France and West Germany members

1950

Publication of Roger **Nimier's** novel *Le Hussard bleu* gives name to "**Hussard**" group

1951

5 January: First amnesty granted for crimes committed during Occupation

23 July: Death of Marshal **Pétain**

December: French Parliament ratifies ESCS (European Steel and Coal Community), a step toward the integration of the French and German economies

1957

March: Signature in Rome of treaty creating European Economic Community (Common Market; later, European Union)

1958

1 June: General **de Gaulle** returns to power as premier during Algerian war; constitution for Fifth **Republic** approved, 28 September

1964

18–19 December: Jean **Moulin's** ashes moved to Panthéon

26 December: Unanimous vote of parliament establishes law regarding crimes against humanity with no statue of limitations

1970

9 November: Death of General **de Gaulle**

1971

April: *The Sorrow and the Pity* released

1978

28 October: Louis **Darquier de Pellepoix** gives interview, arguing that only lice were gassed at Auschwitz, in *L'Express* magazine

1987

4 July: Klaus **Barbie** sentenced in Lyons to life in prison for commission of crimes against humanity

1993

8 June: Murder of René **Bousquet**, former **Vichy** chief of **police**, awaiting trial on charges of crimes against humanity

1994

20 April: Paul **Touvier** sentenced to life imprisonment for crimes against humanity committed during the Occupation

12 September: President François **Mitterrand** in television interview discusses his **Vichy** activity and his continued friendship with René **Bousquet** through 1986

1995

16 July: President Jacques Chirac formally recognizes responsibility of the French state for crimes committed by the **Vichy** government

1997

23 January: Appeals Court rules that former Vichy official Maurice **Papon** stand trial on charges of crimes against humanity

8 October: **Papon** trial began

1998

2 April: **Papon** convicted of crimes against humanity, sentenced to ten years in prison

General Bibliography

There are many bibliographical sources for World War II France. One of the best is Donna Evleth, ed., *France under the German Occupation, 1940–1944, An Annotated Bibliography* (Westport, CT, 1991). To keep up with the growing literature in this field, the reader should consult the *Bibliographie Annuelle de l'Histoire de France*, which lists both books and articles in English and other languages as well as French. The *BAHF* issue for 1994 shows 761 titles. The list below is selected, oriented to more recent literature and works in English. It is based mainly on the bibliographical notices of the articles in this *Historical Dictionary*. Some of the items listed relate to more than one category below, so the reader is advised to cross-check. Finally, at the end of this bibliography, several web sites offering material on World War II France are listed. Two sites are listed under the relevant headings below.

COLLECTIONS AND ANTHOLOGIES COVERING A RANGE OF SUBJECTS

Arnoult, Pierre, et al. *La France sous l'occupation*. Paris, 1959.
Azéma, Jean-Pierre, and François Bédarida, eds. *1938–1948 Les Années de tourmente, de Munich à Prague, Dictionnaire Critique*. Paris, 1995.
———. *La France des années noires*. 2 vols. Paris, 1993.
———. *Le régime de Vichy et les français, Actes du colloque de l'IHTP*. Paris, 1992.
Carlier, Claude, and Stefan Martens, eds. *La France et l'Allemagne en guerre, septembre 1939–novembre 1942*. Paris, 1990.

GENERAL HISTORIES, COLLABORATION, AND RESISTANCE

Amouroux, Henri. *La Grande histoire des Français sous l'occupation, 1939–1946*. 8 vols. Paris, 1976–88.
Azéma, Jean-Pierre. *From Munich to the Liberation*. Trans. Janet Lloyd. New York, 1984 [original French edition, 1979].
Dank, Milton. *The French against the French: Collaboration and Resistance*. Philadelphia, 1974.

Durand, Yves. *La France dans la deuxième guerre mondiale 1939–1945*. Paris, 1989.

Kedward, Harry Roderick. *Occupied France. Collaboration and Resistance 1940–1944*. Oxford, 1985.

Kedward, Harry Roderick, and Roger Austin, eds. *Vichy France and the Resistance: Culture and Ideology*. London and Totowa, New Jersey, 1985.

Sadoun, Marc. *Les socialistes sous l'occupation: résistance et collaboration*. Paris, 1982.

Shennan, Andrew. *Rethinking France: Plans for Renewal 1940–1946*. Oxford, 1989.

Sweets, John F. *Choices in Vichy France: The French under Nazi Occupation*. Oxford, 1986.

THE INTERWAR YEARS AND THE COMING OF THE WAR

Alexander, Martin. *The Republic in Danger: General Maurice Gamelin and the Politics of French Defense, 1933–1940*. Cambridge, U.K., 1992.

Bankwitz, Philip C. F. *Maxime Weygand and Civil-Military Relations in Modern France*. Cambridge, Massachusetts, 1967.

Carley, Michael Jabara. "End of the 'Low, Dishonest Decade': Failure of the Anglo-Franco-Soviet Alliance in 1939." *Europe-Asia Studies* 45:2 (1993); 303–41.

———. "Prelude to Defeat: Franco-Soviet Relations, 1919–1939," *Historical Reflections* 22:1 (1996); 159–88.

Gates, Eleanor M. *End of the Affair: The Collapse of the Anglo-French Alliance, 1939–40*. Berkeley, 1981.

Hughes, Judith. *To the Maginot Line: the Politics of French Military Preparedness in the 1920s*. Cambridge, Massachusetts, 1970.

Jackson, Julian. *The Popular Front in France Defending Democracy, 1934–38*. Cambridge, U.K., 1988.

Jeanneney, Jean-Noël. *Georges Mandel: l'homme qu'on attendait*. Paris, 1991.

Jordan, Nicole. *The Popular Front and Central Europe*. Cambridge, U.K., 1992.

Micaud, Charles A. *The French Right and Nazi Germany, 1933–1939*. New York, 1943, 1964.

Réau, Elisabeth du. *Édouard Daladier, 1884–1970*. Paris, 1993.

Reynaud, Paul. *In the Thick of the Fight*. New York, 1955 [original French edition, 1951].

Sherwood, John M. *Georges Mandel and the Third Republic*. Stanford, 1970.

Shirer, William L. *The Collapse of the Third Republic*. New York, 1969.

Weber, Eugen. *Action Française: Royalism and Reaction in Twentieth-Century France*. Stanford, 1962.

———. *The Hollow Years: France in the 1930s*. New York, 1994.

Young, Robert. *France and the Origins of the Second World War*. New York, 1996.

———. *In Command of France: French Foreign Policy and Military Planning, 1933–40*. Cambridge, Massachusetts, 1978.

THE 1940 DEFEAT

Azéma, Jean-Pierre. *1940, l'année terrible*. Paris, 1990.

Bell, Philip Michael Hett. *A Certain Eventuality: Britain and the Fall of France*. London, 1974.

Bloch, Marc. *Strange Defeat: A Statement of Evidence Written in 1940*. Trans. Gerard Hopkins. New York, 1949, 1968 [original French edition, 1946].

Crémieux-Brilhac, Jean-Louis. *Les Français de l'an 40*. 2 vols. Paris, 1990.

Gunsburg, Jeffrey A. *Divided and Conquered: The French High Command and the Defeat of the West, 1940*. Westport, Connecticut, 1979.

Horne, Alistair. *To Lose a Battle: France 1940*. Boston, 1969.

Jordan, Nicole. "Strategy and Scapegoatism: Reflections on the French National Catastrophe, 1940." *Historical Reflections* 22:1 (Winter 1996); 10–32.

Lottman, Herbert R. *The Fall of Paris: June 1940*. New York, 1992.

Militärgeshichtliches Forschungsamt [Research Institute for Military History], Freiburg im Breisgau, Germany, ed., *Germany and the Second World War*, vol. 2: *Germany's Initial Conquests in Europe*. Trans. Dean S. McMurry and Ewald Osers. Oxford, 1991.

Rowe, Vivian. *The Great Wall of France, The Triumph of the Maginot Line*. London, 1959.

Vidalenc, Jean. *L'exode de mai-juin 1940*. Paris, 1957.

Web Site: MacDonald, Charles B. "Fall of the Low Countries and France." Grolier Online. http://www.grolier.com/wwii/wwii__4.html

THE 1940 ARMISTICE, GERMAN POLICY, AND THE GERMANS IN FRANCE

Böhme, Hermann. *Der deutsch-französische Waffenstillstand im Zweiten Weltkrieg*, in *Entstehung und Grundlagen des Waffenstillstandes von 1940. Quellen und Darstellungen zur Zeitgeschichte*, 12. Stuttgart, 1966.

Jäckel, Eberhard. *Frankreich in Hitlers Europa: Die deutsche Frankreichpolitik im zweiten Weltkrieg*. Stuttgart, 1966 [French edition: *La France dans l'Europe de Hitler*. Paris, 1968].

Jünger, Ernst. *Journal de guerre et d'occupation 1939–1948*. Trans. H. Plard. Paris, 1965.

Neugebauer, Karl Volker. *Die deutsche Militärkontrolle im unbesetzten Frankreich und in Französisch-Nordafrika 1940–1942*. Boppard am Rhein, 1980.

Sergg, Henri. *Paris—Gestapo*. Paris, 1989.

Steinberg, Lucien, and Jean-Marie Fitère. *Les Allemands en France, 1940–1944*. Paris, 1980.

Umbreit, Hans. *Der Militärbefehlshaber in Frankreich 1940–1944*. Boppard am Rhein, 1968.

FRANCE AND THE REST OF THE WORLD

Blumenthal, Henry. *Illusion and Reality in Franco-American Diplomacy, 1914–1945*. Baton Rouge, 1986.

Couture, Paul. "Politics of Diplomacy: The Crisis of Canada-France Relations, 1940–1942." Unpublished thesis: York University, 1981.

Dreifort, John E. *Myopic Grandeur: The Ambivalence of French Foreign Policy toward the Far East, 1919–1945*. Kent, Ohio, 1991.

Duroselle, Jean-Baptiste. *La décadence, 1932–1939*. Paris, 1979, and *L'Abime 1939–1944*. Paris, 1982 (in series, *Politique étrangère de la France, 1871–1969*).

Hurstfield, Julian G. *America and the French Nation 1939–1945*. Chapel Hill, North Carolina, 1986.

Langer, William L. *Our Vichy Gamble*. New York, 1947.

Maguire, G. E. *Anglo-American Policy towards the Free French*. London, 1995.

Nettelbeck, Colin W. *Forever French: Exile in the United States 1939–1945*. Oxford, 1991.

Prevost, Philippe. *La France et le Canada, d'un après-guerre à l'autre 1918–1944*. Saint-Boniface, 1994.

Rossi, Mario. *Roosevelt and the French*. Westport, Connecticut, 1993.

THE VICHY GOVERNMENT AND ITS LEADERS

Alméras, Philippe. *Un Francais nommé Pétain*. Paris, 1995.

Aron, Robert. *The Vichy Regime 1940–44*. Trans. Humphrey Hare. Boston, 1969 [original French edition 1955].

Bloch-Lainé, François. *Hauts fonctionnaires sous l'Occupation*. Paris, 1996.

Bourderon, Roger. "Le régime de Vichy était-il fasciste? Essai d'approche de la question." *RDHDGM* 23 (July 1973); 23–45.

Boussard, Isabel. *Vichy et la Corporation paysanne*. Paris, 1980.

Burrin, Philippe. "Le fascisme." In Jean-François Sirinelli, ed., *Histoire des Droites en France*. Vol. 1. Paris, 1992, 603–52.

Cointet, Jean-Paul. *Histoire de Vichy*. Paris, 1996.

———. *La Légion Française des Combattants*. Paris, 1995.

Cointet-Labrousse, Michèle. *Vichy et le fascisme: Les hommes, les structures et les pouvoirs*. Brussels, 1987.

Couteau-Bégarie, Hervé, and Claude Huan. *Darlan*. Paris, 1989.

Dreyfus, François-Georges. *Histoire de Vichy*. Paris, 1990.

Durand, Yves. *Vichy 1940–1944*. Paris, 1972.

Farmer, Paul. *Vichy, Political Dilemma*. New York, 1955.

Ferro, Marc. *Pétain*. Paris, 1987.

Fondation Nationale des Sciences Politiques, ed. (Janine Bourdin and René Rémond). *Le Gouvernement de Vichy, 1940–1942. Institutions et politiques*. Paris, 1972.

Gervereau, Laurent, and Denis Peschanski, eds. *La propagande sous Vichy, 1940–1944*. Nanterre, 1990.

Griffiths, Richard. *Marshal Pétain*. London, 1970.

Hellman, John. *The Knight-Monks of Vichy France. Uriage, 1940–45*. Montreal and Kingston, 1993.

Jaffré, Yves-Frédéric. *Il y a 50 ans Pierre Laval: le procès qui n'a pas eu lieu*. Paris, 1995.

Kasten, Bernd. *"Gute Französen:" die französische Polizei und die deutsche Besatzungsmacht im besetzten Frankreich, Kieler Historische Studien 37*. Sigmaringen, 1993.

Kupferman, Fred. *Laval, 1883–1945*. Paris, 1988.

———. *Le procès de Vichy: Pucheu, Pétain, Laval*. Brussels, 1980.

Laborie, Pierre. *L'Opinion française sous Vichy*. Paris, 1990.

Lambert, Pierre Philippe, and Gérard Le Marec. *Organisations, mouvements et unités de l'état français. Vichy, 1940–1944*. Paris, 1993.

Le Crom, Jean-Pierre. *Syndicats nous voilà! Vichy et le corporatisme*. Paris, 1995.

Lottman, Herbert R. *Pétain. Hero or Traitor?* New York, 1985.

Michel, Henri. *François Darlan*. Paris, 1993.

———. *Pétain et le régime de Vichy*. Paris, 1978.

———. *Vichy. Année 40*. Paris, 1966.

Milza, Pierre. *Fascisme Français. Passé et présent*. Paris, 1987.

Paxton, Robert O. *Parades and Politics at Vichy: The French Officer Corps under Marshal Pétain*. Princeton, New Jersey, 1966.

———. *Vichy France: Old Guard and New Order, 1940–1944*. New York, 1972, 1982.

Rajsfus, Maurice. *La police de Vichy: Les Forces de l'ordre françaises au service de la Gestapo 1940–1944*. Paris, 1995.

Rémy, Dominique. *Les lois de Vichy*. Paris, 1992.

Rossignol, Dominique. *Histoire de la propagande en France de 1940 à 1944: L'Utopie Pétain*. Paris, 1991.

Thalmann, Rita. *La Mise au pas: Idéologie et stratégie sécuritaire dans la France occupée*. Paris, 1991.

Villéré, Hervé. *L'Affaire de la Section spéciale*. Paris, 1973.

Warner, Geoffrey. *Pierre Laval and the Eclipse of France*. London, 1965.

Webster, Paul. *Pétain's Crime: The Full Story of French Collaboration in the Holocaust*. Chicago, 1991.

Wormser, Olivier. *Les Origines doctrinales de la Révolution nationale*. Paris, 1971.

COLLABORATION (SEE ALSO GENERAL HISTORIES, COLLABORATION, AND RESISTANCE)

Andreu, Pierre, and Frederick J. Grover. *Drieu la Rochelle*. Paris, 1979.

Assouline, Pierre. *Le Fleuve Combelle*. Paris, 1997.

Boulanger, Gérard. *Maurice Papon: un technocrate français dans la collaboration*. Paris, 1994.

Brunet, Jean-Paul. *Jacques Doriot. Du communisme au fascisme*. Paris, 1986.

Burrin, Philippe. *La Dérive fasciste: Doriot, Déat, Bergery, 1933–1945*. Paris, 1986.

Chadwick, Kay. "Alphonse de Châteaubriant, Collaborator on Retrial: Un Non-lieu individuel d'une portée nationale." *FHS* 18 (Fall 1994); 1057–82.

Déat, Marcel. *Mémoires politiques*. Paris, 1989.

Delarue, Jacques. *Trafics et crimes sous l'occupation*. Paris, 1968, 1976, 1993.

Delperrie de Bayac, Jacques. *Histoire de la Milice*. Paris, 1969.

Delpla, François. *Montoire. Les premiers jours de la collaboration*. Paris, 1996.

Dieudonnat, Pierre-Marie. *Je Suis Partout 1930–1944*. Paris, 1987.

———. *Les 700 Rédacteurs de "Je Suis Partout," 1930–1944*. Paris, 1993.

Godard, Henri. *Céline scandale*. Paris, 1994.

Gordon, Bertram M. *Collaborationism in France during the Second World War*. Ithaca, New York, 1980.

———. "The Condottieri of the Collaboration: *Mouvement Social Révolutionnaire*," *JCH* 10:2 (April 1975).

———. "The Morphology of the Collaborator: The French Case." *Journal of European Studies* 23 (parts 1 and 2): 89 and 90 (March–June 1993); 1–25.

Handourtzel, Rémy, and Cyril Buffet. *La Collaboration . . . à gauche aussi*. Paris, 1989.

Hirschfeld, Gerhard, and Patrick Marsh, eds. *Collaboration in France. Politics and Culture during the Nazi Occupation 1940–1944*. Oxford, 1989.

Hoffmann, Stanley. "Collaborationism in France during World War II." *JMH* 40:3 (September 1968); 375–95.

Jankowski, Paul F. *Communism and Collaboration. Simon Sabiani and Politics in Marseille, 1919–1944*. New Haven and London, 1987.

Lambert, Pierre Philippe, and Gérard Le Marec. *Partis et monuments de la collaboration. Paris 1940–1944*. Paris, 1994.

Ory, Pascal. *Les Collaborateurs 1940–1945*. Paris, 1976.

Rousso, Henry. *La collaboration, Les noms, les thèmes, les lieux*. Paris, 1987.

———. *Pétain et la Fin de la Collaboration Sigmaringen 1944–1945*. Brussels, 1984.

Soucy, Robert. *Fascist Intellectual: Drieu la Rochelle*. Berkeley, 1979.

Thiher, Allen. *Céline: The Novel as Delirium*. New Brunswick, New Jersey, 1972.

Tucker, William R. *The Fascist Ego: A Political Biography of Robert Brasillach*. Berkeley, 1975.

Veillon, Dominique. *La collaboration*. Paris, 1984.

Vitoux, Frédéric. *Céline, A Biography*. Trans. Jesse Browner. New York, 1992.

Wolf, Dieter. *Die Doriot-Bewegung: Ein Beitrag zur Geschichte des französischen Faschismus*. Stuttgart, 1967 [French edition: *Doriot, du Communisme à la Collaboration*. Paris, 1969].

RESISTANCE (SEE ALSO GENERAL HISTORIES, COLLABORATION, AND RESISTANCE)

Aglan, Alya. *Mémoires résistantes, le réseau Jade-Fitzroy (1940–44)*. Paris, 1994.

Andrieu, Claire. "Le Conseil national de la Résistance, juin 1944–janvier 1945: les logiques de l'insurrection." In Fondation Charles de Gaulle, ed., *Le rétablissement de la légalité républicaine, 1944*. Brussels, 1995.

———. *Le programme commun de la Résistance: Des idées dans la guerre*. Paris, 1984.

Aubrac, Lucie. *Outwitting the Gestapo*. Trans. Konrad Bieber. Lincoln, 1993 [original French edition, *Ils partiront dans l'ivresse*, 1984].

Aubrac, Raymond. *Où la mémoire s'attarde*. Paris, 1997.

Azéma, Jean-Pierre, François Bédarida, and Robert Frank, eds. *Jean Moulin et la Résistance en 1943. Cahiers de l'IHTP*. Paris, June 1994.

Bellescize, Diane de. *Les neuf sages de la Résistance: Le Comité Général d'études dans la clandestinité*. Paris, 1979.

Blumenson, Martin. *Le réseau du Musée de l'Homme. Les débuts de la Résistance en France*. Paris, 1979.

Calvi, Fabrio, and Olivier Schmidt. *OSS, la guerre secrète en France, 1942–1945, les services spéciaux américains, la Résistance et la Gestapo*. Paris, 1990.

Chauvy, Gérard. *Aubrac Lyon 1943*. Paris, 1997.

Cordier, Daniel. *Jean Moulin, l'inconnu du Panthéon*. 3 vols. Paris, 1989–93.

Crémieux-Brilhac, Jean-Louis. *La France Libre: De l'appel du 18 juin à la libération*. Paris, 1996.

Debû-Bridel, Jacques. *La Résistance intellectuelle, Textes et Témoignages*. Paris, 1970.

Douzou, Laurent. *La Désobéissance: L'Histoire d'un mouvement et d'un journal clandestin: Libération-sud, 1940–1944*. Paris, 1995.

Dreyfus, François-Georges. *Histoire de la Resistance*. Paris, 1995.

Ferrières, Gabrielle, ed. *Jean Cavaillès: un philosophe dans la guerre*. Quimper, 1997.

Fink, Carole. *Marc Bloch: A Life in History*. Cambridge, U.K., 1989.

Fittko, Lisa. *Escape Through the Pyrenees*. Evanston, 1991.

Foot, Michael Richard Daniel. *SOE in France, An Account of the Work of the British Special Operations Executive in France, 1940–1944*. London, 1966.

Frenay, Henri. *La Nuit finera*. Paris, 1973.

Gaulle, Charles de. *The Complete War Memoirs, 1940–46*. 3 vols. Trans. Jonathan Griffin and Richard Howard. New York, 1964 [original French edition, 1954–59].

Granet, Marie. *Ceux de la Résistance (1940–1944)*. Paris, 1964.

Guillon, Jean-Marie, and Pierre Laborie, eds. *Mémoire et Histoire: La Résistance*. Toulouse, 1995.

Hostache, René. *Le Conseil national de la Résistance*. Paris, 1958.

Institut d'Histoire des Conflits Contemporains, *Colloque sur les maquis*. Paris, 1986.

Kedward, Harry Roderick. *In Search of the Maquis: Rural Resistance in Southern France, 1942–1944*. Oxford, 1993.

———. *Resistance in Vichy France*. Oxford, 1978.

Kramer, Rita. *Flames in the Field: The Story of Four SOE Agents in Occupied France*. London, 1995.

Lacouture, Jean. *De Gaulle*. 2 vols. [Vol. 1: *The Rebel, 1890–1944*. Trans. Patrick O'Brian, Vol. 2: *The Ruler, 1944–1970*. Trans. Alan Sheridan]. New York, 1991–92 [original French edition, 3 vols., Paris, 1984–86].

Michel, Henri. *Histoire de la France libre*. Paris, 1980.

———. *Histoire de la Résistance*. Paris, 1950.

Miquel, Pierre. *Les Quatre-vingts*. Paris, 1995.

Muracciole, Jean-François. *Histoire de la Resistance en France*. Paris, 1993.

Noguères, Henri, M. Degliame-Fouché, and J.-L. Vigier. *Histoire de la Resistance en France de 1940–1945*. 5 vols. Paris, 1967–81.

Passy [Dewavrin, André]. *Souvenirs*. 3 vols. Monte Carlo, 1947–48, Paris, 1951.

Rondeau, Daniel, and Roger Stéphane. *Des Hommes Libres: Histoire de la France libre par ceux qui l'ont faite*. Paris, 1997.

Rougeyron, André. *Agents for Escape: Inside the French Resistance, 1939–1945*. Trans. Marie-Antoinette McConnell. Baton Rouge, 1996.

Sainclivier, Jacqueline, and Christian Bougeard, eds. *La Résistance et les Français, Enjeux stratégiques et environnement social*. Rennes, 1995.

Schoenbrun, David. *Soldiers of the Night: The Story of the French Resistance*. New York, 1980.

Seghers, Pierre. *La Résistance et ses poètes, France 1940–1945*. Paris, 1974.

Simonin, Anne. *Les Éditions de minuit 1942–1955: le devoir d'insoumission*. Paris, 1994.

Sweets, John F. *The Politics of Resistance in France, 1940–1944: A History of the Mouvements Unis de la Résistance*. DeKalb, Illinois, 1976.

Tillion, Germaine. *La Traversée du mal, Entretien avec Jean Lacouture*. Paris, 1997.

Veillon, Dominique. *Le Franc-Tireur: Un journal clandestin, un mouvement de Résistance*. Paris, 1977.

Vidal-Naquet, Pierre. *Le Trait empoisonné: réflexions sur l'affaire Jean Moulin*. Paris, 1993.

Vildé, Boris. *Journal et lettres de prison, 1941–1942*. Paris, 1997.

Wieviorka, Olivier. *Nous entrerons dans la carrière*. Paris, 1994.

COMMUNISTS

Azéma, Jean-Pierre, Antoine Prost, and Jean-Pierre Rioux, eds. *Les Communistes Français de Munich à Chateaubriant, 1938–1941*. Paris, 1987.

———. *Le Parti Communiste dans les années sombres*. Paris, 1986.

Buton, Philippe. *Les lendemains qui déchantent. Le Parti communiste français à la Libération*. Paris, 1993.

Courtois, Stéphane. *Le PCF dans la guerre. De Gaulle, la Résistance, Staline*. Paris, 1980.

Robrieux, Philippe. *Histoire intérieure du parti communiste*. Vols. 2 and 4. Paris, 1984.

FREEMASONS

Rossignol, Dominique. *Vichy et les franc-maçons: la liquidation des sociétés secrètes 1940–1944*. Paris, 1981.

THE EMPIRE

Ageron, Charles Robert. ''La deuxième guerre mondiale et ses conséquences pour l'empire.'' In Jacques Thobie et al., *Histoire de la France coloniale 1914–1990*. Paris, 1990.

———, ed. *Les chemins de la décolonisation de l'empire colonial français (1936–1956)*. Institut d'Histoire du Temps Présent. Paris, 1986.

Funk, Arthur L. *The Politics of TORCH: The Allied Landings and the Algiers Putsch, 1942*. Lawrence, Kansas, 1974.

La Gorce, Paul-Marie de. *L'Empire Écartelé 1936–1946*. Paris, 1988.

Hammer, E. *The Struggle for Indochina 1940–1955: Vietnam and the French Experience*. Stanford, 1966.

Hoisington, William A., Jr. *The Casablanca Connection: French Colonial Policy, 1936–1943*. Chapel Hill, North Carolina, 1984.

Howe, George F. *Northwest Africa: Seizing the Initiative in the West*. Washington, D.C., 1957, 1991.

Isoart, Paul, et al. *L'Indochine française (1940–1945)*. Paris, 1982.

Shipway, Martin. *The Road to War: France and Vietnam, 1944–1947*. Providence and Oxford, 1996.

Suret-Canale, Jean. *L'Afrique noire, occidentale et centrale*. Vol. 2. Paris, 1964.

THE ECONOMY

Andrieu, Claire. *La Banque sous l'Occupation: Paradoxes de l'histoire d'une profession (1936–1946)*. Paris, 1990.

Beltran, Alain, Robert Frank, and Henry Rousso, eds. *La vie des entreprises sous l'Occupation*. Paris, 1994.

Brun, Gérard. *Technocrates et Technocratie en France 1918–1945*. Paris, 1985.

Cépède, Michel. *Agriculture et alimentation durant la IIème guerre mondiale*. Paris, 1961.

Hazéra, Jean-Claude, and Renaud de Rochebrune, eds. *Les patrons sous l'occupation*. Paris, 1995.

Kuisel, Richard F. "The Legend of the Vichy Synarchy." *FHS* 6:3 (Spring 1970); 365–98.

———. "Technocrats and Public Economic Policy: From the Third to the Fourth Republic." *Journal of European Economic History* 4 (1973); 53–99.

Margairaz, Michel. *L'État, les finances et l'économie. Histoire d'une conversion 1932–1952*. 2 vols. Paris, 1991.

Milward, Alan S. *The New Order and the French Economy*. Oxford, 1970.

Sauvy, Alfred. *La vie èconomique des Français de 1939 à 1945*. Paris, 1978.

Vinen, Richard. "The French Coal Industry during the Occupation." *The Historical Journal* 33; 1 (1990); 105–30.

———. *The Politics of French Business, 1936–1945*. Cambridge, U.K., 1991.

LITERATURE

Atack, Margaret. *Literature and the French Resistance: Cultural Politics and Narrative Forms, 1940–1950*. Manchester and New York, 1989.

Bieber, Konrad. "André Gide and the German Occupation." *Modern Language Quarterly* 15 (1954); 246–51.

Carroll, David. *French Literary Fascism: Nationalism, Anti-Semitism, and the Ideology of Culture*. Princeton, New Jersey, 1995.

Fourny, Jean-François, and Richard J. Golsan, eds. *The Occupation in French Literature and Film, 1940–1992, L'Esprit Créateur* 33:1 (Spring 1993).

Hebey, Pierre. *La Nouvelle revue française des années sombres*. Paris, 1992.

Joseph, Gilbert. *Une si douce Occupation: Simone de Beauvoir, Jean-Paul Sartre, 1940–1944*. Paris, 1991.

Loiseaux, Gérard. *La littérature de la défaite et de la collaboration: que lisaient les Français sous l'occupation*. Paris, 1984.

Lottman, Herbert R. *The Left Bank: Writers, Artists and Politics from the Popular Front to the Cold War*. Boston, 1982.

Sapiro, Gisèle. "La raison littéraire. Le champ littéraire français sous l'Occupation, 1940–1944." *Actes de la recherche en sciences sociales* 111–112 (March 1996); 3–35.

THE PRESS AND RADIO

Bellanger, Claude. *Presse clandestine 1940–1944*. Paris, 1961.

Bellanger, Claude, Henri Michel, and Claude Lévy. *Histoire générale de la presse française de 1940–1958*. Vol. 4. Paris, 1975.

Eck, Hélène. *La guerre des ondes: Histoire des radios de langue française pendant la Deuxième Guerre mondiale*. Paris, 1985.

Fouché, Pascal. *L'édition française sous l'occupation 1940–1944*. Paris, 1987.

La Presse clandestine, 1940–1944, Actes du colloque d'Avignon 20–27 juin 1985. Avignon, 1987.

EDUCATION, YOUTH, AND SPORT

Gay-Lescot, Jean-Louis. *Sport et Éducation sous Vichy 1940–1944*. Lyons, 1991.
Giolitto, Pierre. *Histoire de la jeunesse sous Vichy*. Paris, 1991.
Halls, Wilfrid D. *The Youth of Vichy France*. Oxford, 1988.

FINE ARTS, PERFORMING ARTS, AND POPULAR CULTURE (SEE ALSO LITERATURE)

Added, Serge. *Le Théâtre dans les années Vichy, 1940–44*. Paris, 1992.
Barron, Stephanie. *Exiles and Emigrés: The Flight of European Artists from Hitler*. New York, 1997.
Bazin, André. *Le Cinéma de l'Occupation et de la Résistance*. Paris, 1975.
Bertin-Maghit, Jean-Pierre. *Le Cinéma français sous l'Occupation*. Paris, 1994.
———. *Le Cinéma sous l'Occupation*. Paris, 1989.
Bertrand Dorléac, Laurence. *L'Art de la défaite, 1940–1944*. Paris, 1993.
———. *Histoire de l'Art: Paris 1940–1944, Ordre national, traditions, et modernités*. Paris, 1986.
Chateau, René. *Le Cinèma Francais sous l'Occupation, 1940–1944*. Paris, 1995.
Cone, Michèle C. *Artists Under Vichy: A Case of Prejudice and Persecution*. Princeton, New Jersey, 1992.
Darman, Pierre. *Le Monde du Cinéma sous l'Occupation*. Paris, 1997.
Dompnier, Nathalie. *Vichy à travers chants*. Paris, 1996.
Faure, Christian. *Le Projet Culturel de Vichy*. Lyons, 1989.
Feliciano, Hector. *The Lost Museum*. New York, 1997 [original edition: *Le Musée Disparu*, Paris, 1995].
Fry, Varian. *Surrender on Demand*. New York, 1945, 1965.
Gordon, Bertram M. "Fascism, the Neo-Right, and Gastronomy: A Case in the Theory of the Social Engineering of Taste." *Oxford Symposium on Food and Cookery 1987, Taste, Proceedings*. London, 1988, 82–97.
———. "*Ist Gott Französisch?* Germans, Tourism, and Occupied France, 1940-1944." *M&CF*, NS 4:3 (1996); 287–98.
Nicholas, Lynn. *The Rape of Europa: The Fate of Europe's Treasures in the Third Reich and the Second World War*. New York, 1994.
Prevert, Jacques. *Children of Paradise: A Film by Marcel Carne*. Trans Dinah Brooke. New York, 1968.
Ragache, Gilles, and Jean-Robert Ragache. *La vie quotidienne des écrivains et des artistes sous l'occupation, 1940–1944*. Paris, 1988.
Raymond, Agnes. *Jean Giraudoux: The Theater of Victory and Defeat*. Amherst, Massachusetts, 1966.
Rearick, Charles. *The French in Love and War: Popular Culture in the Eras of the World Wars*. New Haven, 1997.
Rioux, Jean-Pierre, ed. *La Vie culturelle sous Vichy*. Paris, 1990.
Siclier, Jacques. *La France de Pétain et son cinéma*. Paris, 1981.
Taylor, Lou. "The Work and Function of the Paris Couture Industry During the German Occupation of 1940–44." *Dress* 22 (1995); 34–44.
Turk, Edward Baron. *Child of Paradise: Marcel Carne and the Golden Age of French Cinema*. Cambridge, Massachusetts, 1989.

Veillon, Dominique. *La Mode sous l'occupation: Débrouillardise et coquetterie dans la France en guerre 1939–1945*. Paris, 1990.
Web site: Varian Fry Foundation Project. http://www.almondseed.com/vfry/fryfoun.htm

DAILY LIFE, PARIS

Amouroux, Henri. *La vie des Français sous l'Occupation*. 2 vols. Paris, 1961.
Burrin, Philippe. *Living with Defeat: France under the German Occupation, 1940–1944*. Trans. Janet Lloyd. New York, 1997 [original edition: *La France à l'heure allemande, 1940–1944*. Paris, 1995].
Dutourd, Jean. *The Best Butter*. Trans Robin Chancellor. New York, 1955 [original French edition, *Au bon beurre*. Paris, 1952. (novel)].
Guéhenno, Jean. *Journal des années noires*. Paris, 1947, 1973.
Le Boterf, Hervé. *La Vie Parisienne sous l'occupation. 1940–1944*. 2 vols. Paris, 1974–75.
Michel, Henri. *Paris Allemand*. Paris, 1982.
Perrault, Gilles, and Azéma, Jean-Pierre. *Paris under the Occupation*. Trans. Allison Carter and Maximilian Vos. New York, 1989 [original French edition, 1987].
Pryce-Jones, David. *Paris in the Third Reich: A History of the German Occupation, 1940–1944*. New York, 1981.
Veillon, Dominique. *Vivre et Survivre en France 1939–1947*. Paris, 1995.
Veillon, Dominique, and Jean-Marie Flonneau, eds. *Le temps des restrictions en France 1939–1949*. Paris, 1996.

CATHOLICS AND PROTESTANTS, CHURCHES

Atkin, Nicholas. *Church and Schools in Vichy France, 1940–1944*. New York, 1991.
Doering, Bernard. *Jacques Maritain and the French Catholic Intellectuals*. Notre Dame, Indiana, 1983.
Duquesne, Jacques. *Les Catholiques français sous l'Occupation*. Paris, 1966, 1988.
Fouilloux, Étienne. *Les Chrétiens entre crise et libération 1937–1947*. Paris, 1997.
Halls, Wilfrid D. *Politics, Society, and Christianity in Vichy France*. Oxford, 1995.
Hellman, John. *Emmanuel Mounier and the New Catholic Left, 1930–1950*. Toronto, Buffalo, London, 1981.
Maritain, Jacques. *A Christian Looks at the Jewish Question*. New York, 1973.
Redpath, Peter A., ed. *From Twilight to Dawn: The Cultural Vision of Jacques Maritain*. Notre Dame, Indiana, 1990.
Rémond, René, et al. *Paul Touvier et l'Église, Rapport de la Commission historique instituée par le cardinal Decourtray*. Paris, 1992.
Société de l'Histoire du Protestantisme Français, ed. *Les Protestants français pendant la seconde guerre mondiale*. Paris, 1994.

JEWS

Adler, Jacques. *The Jews of Paris and the Final Solution: Communal Response and Internal Conflicts, 1940–1944*. New York, 1987.

Badinter, Robert. *Un Antisémitisme Ordinaire: Vichy et les avocats juifs (1940–1944)*. Paris, 1997.

Cohen, Asher. *Persécutions et sauvetages: Juifs et Français sous l'Occupation et sous Vichy*. Paris, 1994.

Cohen, Richard. *The Burden of Conscience: French Jewish Leadership during the Holocaust*. Bloomington, Indiana, 1987.

Hallie, Philip P. *Lest Innocent Blood Be Shed*. New York, 1979.

Kahn, Annette. *Le Fichier*. Paris, 1993.

Kaspi, André. *Les Juifs pendant l'Occupation*. Paris, 1991.

Klarsfeld, Serge. *Vichy-Auschwitz: le rôle de Vichy dans la solution finale de la question juive en France*. 2 vols. Paris, 1983, 1985.

Lagrange, Simone. *Coupable d'Être Née: Adolescente à Auschwitz*. Paris, 1997.

Latour, Anny. *The Jewish Resistance in France*. Trans. Irene R. Ilton. New York, 1981.

Lazare, Lucien. *Rescue as Resistance: How Jewish Organizations fought the Holocaust in France*. Trans. J. M. Green. New York, 1996.

Malaquais, Jean. *Journal de guerre suivi de Journal du métèque*. Paris, 1997.

Marrus, Michael R. "Jewish Resistance to the Holocaust." *JCH* 30 (1995); 83–110.

Marrus, Michael R., and Robert O. Paxton. *Vichy France and the Jews*. New York, 1981, 1983.

Modiano, Patrick. *Dora Bruder*. Paris, 1997.

Poliakov, Léon. *The Jews under the Italian Occupation*. New York, 1955, 1983 [original French edition, *La Condition des Juifs sous l'occupation italienne*. Paris, 1946].

Poznanski, Renée. *Être juif en France pendant la seconde guerre mondiale*. Paris, 1994.

Ryan, Donna F. *The Holocaust and the Jews of Marseille: The Enforcement of Anti-Semitic Policies in Vichy France*. Champaign, Illinois, 1996.

Weisberg, Richard H. *Vichy Law and the Holocaust in France*. New York, 1996.

Zuccotti, Susan. *The Holocaust, the French, and the Jews*. New York, 1993.

GYPSIES

Peschanski, Denis. *Les Tsiganes en France 1939–1946*. Paris, 1994.

LOCAL AND REGIONAL

Gold, Mary Jayne. *Crossroads, Marseilles*. New York, 1980.

Rigoulot, Pierre. *L'Alsace-Lorraine pendant la guerre, 1939–1945*. Paris, 1997.

Terrisse, René. *Bordeaux, 1940–1944*. Paris, 1993.

Wallart, Claudine, and M. Dumont-Reniez, eds. *Le Nord Occupé*. Lille, 1990.

Zaretsky, Robert. *Nîmes at War: Religion, Politics, and Public Opinion in the Department of the Gard, 1938–1944*. University Park, Pennsylvania, 1995.

D-DAY, THE LIBERATION, AND THE PROVISIONAL GOVERNMENT

Aron, Robert. *France Reborn, The History of the Liberation*. Trans. Humphrey Hare. New York, 1964 [original French edition, 1959].

Bendjebbar, André. *Libérations rêvées, Libérations vécues, 1940–1945*. Paris, 1994.

Brossat, Alain. *Libération, fête folle. Autrement, Série Mémoires*, no. 30. Paris, 1994.

Clarke, Jeffrey J., and Robert Ross Smith. *Riviera to the Rhine.* Washington, D.C., 1993.

Collins, Larry, and Dominique Lapierre. *Is Paris Burning?* New York, 1965.

Este, Carlo D'. *Decision in Normandy.* New York, 1994.

Footitt, Hilary, and John Simmonds. *France 1943–1945.* Leicester, U.K., 1988.

Foulon, Charles-Louis. *Le pouvoir en province à la libération: Les commissaires de la république, 1943–1946.* Paris, 1975.

Hastings, Max. *Das Reich: Resistance and the March of the 2nd SS Panzer Division Through France, June 1944.* London, 1981.

Hastings, Max. *Overlord.* New York, 1984.

Kedward, Harry Roderick, and Nancy Wood, eds. *The Liberation of France, Image and Event.* Oxford, 1995.

Keegan, John. *Six Armies in Normandy.* New York, 1982.

Kershaw, Robert J. *D-Day: Piercing the Atlantic Wall.* Annapolis, 1994.

Koreman, Megan. ''A Hero's Homecoming: The Return of the Deportees to France, 1945.'' *JCH* 32:1 (January 1997); 9–22.

Kruuse, Jens. *Madness at Oradour, 10 June 1944—and After.* London, 1969.

Todorov, Tzvetan. *A French Tragedy: Scenes of Civil War, Summer 1944.* Trans. M. B. Kelly. Hanover, New Hampshire, 1996 [original French edition, 1994].

Wilson, Theodore A., ed. *D-Day 1944.* Abilene, Kansas, 1994.

Wilt, Alan F. *The French Riviera Campaign of August 1944.* Carbondale, Illinois, 1981.

THE POST-LIBERATION PURGE

Aron, Robert. *Histoire de l'épuration.* 4 vols. Paris, 1967–1975.

Assouline, Pierre. *L'Épuration des intellectuels.* Paris, 1985.

Bourdrel, Philippe. *L'Épuration sauvage 1944–1945.* Paris, 1988.

Lottman, Herbert R. *The Purge: The Purification of French Collaborators after World War II.* New York, 1986.

Noguères, Louis. *La Haute Cour de la Libération, 1944–1949.* Paris, 1965.

Novick, Peter. *The Resistance versus Vichy, The Purge of Collaborators in Liberated France.* New York, 1968.

Rouquet, François. *L'épuration dans l'administration française. Agents de l'État et collaboration ordinaire.* Paris, 1993.

Werth, Léon. *Déposition Journal 1940–1944. 33 Jours. Le Procès Pétain.* Paris, 1997.

WOMEN

Bair, Deirdre. *Simone de Beauvoir: A Biography.* New York, 1990.

Beauvoir, Simone de. *Journal de Guerre: Septembre 1939–Janvier 1941.* Paris, 1990.

Bertin, Célia. *Femmes sous l'Occupation.* Paris, 1993.

Duras, Marguerite. *Hiroshima mon amour.* Trans. Richard Seaver. New York, 1961 [original French edition, 1960].

———. *The War: A Memoir.* Trans. Barbara Bray. New York, 1986 [original French edition: *La Douleur*, 1985].

Eck, Hélène. ''Les Françaises sous Vichy.'' In Georges Duby and Michelle Perrot, eds.,

Histoire des femmes en Occident. vol. 5: Françoise Thébaud, ed., *Le Vingtième siècle*. Paris, 1992.

Fiori, Gabriella. *Simone Weil: An Intellectual Biography*. Athens, Georgia, 1989.

Fishman, Sarah. *We Will Wait: Wives of French Prisoners of War, 1940–1945*. New Haven, 1991.

Muel-Dreyfus, Francine. *Vichy et l'éternel féminin*. Paris, 1996.

Rossiter, Margaret L. *Women in the Resistance*. New York, 1986.

Rouquet, François, and Daniele Voldman, eds. *Identités féminines et violences politiques 1936–1946. Cahiers de l'IHTP* 31 (October 1995).

Tillion, Germaine. *Ravensbrück*. Trans. Gerald Satterwhite. Garden City, New York, 1973.

Union des Femmes Françaises. *Les Femmes dans la Résistance*. Paris, 1977.

Vircondelet, Alain. *Duras: A Biography*. Trans. Thomas Buckley. Normal, Illinois, 1994 [original French edition: *Duras: Biographie*. Paris, 1991].

Weitz, Margaret Collins. *Sisters in the Resistance: How Women Fought to Free France*. New York, 1995.

THE WAR REMEMBERED

Andrieu, Claire. ''Managing Memory: National and Personal Identity at Stake in the Mitterrand Affair.'' *FPS* 14:2 (Spring 1996); 17–32.

Barcellini, Serge, and Annette Wieviorka. *Passant, souviens-toi! Les lieux du souvenir de la Seconde Guerre mondiale en France*. Paris, 1995.

Bar-Zohar, Michael. *Bitter Scent, the Case of L'Oréal, Nazis, and the Arab Boycott*. New York, 1996.

Bédarida, François. *Touvier, Vichy et le crime contre l'humanité*. Paris, 1996.

Bracher, Nathan, ed. *A Time to Remember. CFC* 19:2 (Summer/Fall 1995).

Conan, Éric, and Henry Rousso. *Vichy, Un passé qui ne passe pas*. Paris, 1994.

Farmer, Sarah Bennett. ''Oradour-sur-Glane: Memory in a Preserved Landscape.'' *FHS* 19:1 (Spring 1995); 27–47.

Finkielkraut, Alain. *Remembering in Vain: The Klaus Barbie Trial and Crimes against Humanity*. Trans. Roxanne Lapidus and Sima Godfrey. New York, 1992 [original French edition: *La Mémoire vaine: Du Crime contre l'humanité*. Paris, 1989].

''Forum: The Vichy Syndrome.'' *FHS* 19:2 (Fall 1995); 461–526.

Golsan, Richard J., ed. *Memory, the Holocaust, and French Justice*. Hanover, New Hampshire, 1996.

Greilsamer, Laurent, and Daniel Schneidermann. *Un certain Monsieur Paul*. Paris, 1994.

Hewitt, Nicholas. *Literature and the Right in Postwar France: the Story of the ''Hussards.''* Oxford and New York, 1996.

Higgins, Lynn A. *New Novel, New Wave, New Politics: Fiction and the Representation of History in Postwar France*. Lincoln, Nebraska, 1996.

Hoffmann, Stanley, et al. ''Symposium on Mitterrand's Past.'' *FPS* 13:1 (Winter 1995): 4–35.

Hoyos, Ladislas de. *Klaus Barbie: The Untold Story*. Trans Nicholas Courtin. London, 1985.

Klarsfeld, Arno. *Touvier, un crime français*. Paris, 1994.

Morgan, Ted. *An Uncertain Hour: The French, The Germans, the Jews, the Klaus Barbie Trial, and the City of Lyon, 1940–45*. New York, 1990.

Morris, Alan. *Collaboration and Resistance Reviewed: Writers and the Mode Rétro in Post-Gaullist France.* New York, 1993.

Ophuls, Marcel. *The Sorrow and the Pity; a film.* New York, 1972.

Paris, Erna. *Unhealed Wounds: France and the Klaus Barbie Affair.* New York, 1985.

Péan, Pierre. *Une jeunesse française: François Mitterrand 1934–1947.* Paris, 1994.

Rousso, Henry. "La Seconde Guerre mondiale dans la mémoire des droites françaises." In Jean-François Sirinelli, ed., *Histoire des Droites en France.* Vol. 2. Paris 1992, 549–620.

———. *The Vichy Syndrome: History and Memory in France Since 1944.* Trans. Arthur Goldhammer. Cambridge, 1991 [original French edition: *Le Syndrome de Vichy de 1944 à nos jours.* Paris, 1987, 1990].

WORLD WAR II FRANCE RELATED WEB SITES

The worldwide web is changing rapidly but, as of the publication of this book, the following sites offered information of World War II France.

Grolier Online. "World War II Commemoration." In English, includes articles from the *Encyclopedia Americana* on General de Gaulle, Marshal Pétain, and the Maginot Line. Web site: http://www.grolier.com/wwii/wwii_mainpage.html

Of special interest at this site, see MacDonald, Charles B., Chief, World War II Branch, Office of the Chief of Military History, Department of the Army. "Fall of the Low Countries and France." Web site: http://www.grolier.com/wwii/wwii_4.html

H-France Book Reviews. Reviews of books on various aspects of French history, including World War II. Web site: http://www.h-net.msu.edu/~france/reviews/

Institut National de l'Audiovisuel, France. Weekly newsreels "Archives de guerre 1940–1944." Web site: www.ina.fr (VivoPlayer—Netscape Plug-in—software required to view this material may be obtained at www.vivo.com)

Organisation Amgot, France. Material about France in World War II, in English, contains book reviews and is especially helpful in linking to additional sites of related interest. Web site: http://www.amgot.org/fr-hist.htm

Paris Pages (France Telecom). "Liberation of Paris, Chronology of the events of August 1944." Illustrated with French and English text. Web site: http://www.paris.org/Expos/Liberation/

University of San Diego, Department of History. "World War II Timeline." In English, linked to additional World War II sites. Web site: http://ac.acusd.edu/History/WW2Timeline/start.html

For a published guide to the rapidly changing world of internet sites for historians, see Dennis Trinkle et al., *The History Highway: A Guide to Internet Resources* (Armonk, N.Y., 1997).

Index

About the Author

BERTRAM M. GORDON is the Frederick A. Rice Professor of European History at Mills College. He is the author of *Collaborationism in France during the Second World War* (1980). His field of specialization is modern France, specifically the French Right and World War II. He serves on the Editorial Board of *French Historical Studies*, the International Editorial Advisory Board of *French Historical Studies*, the International Editorial Advisory Board of *Modern and Contemporary France*, and is coeditor of the H-France electronic history network.

ISBN 0-313-29421-6

9 780313 294211   90000>

EAN

HARDCOVER BAR CODE